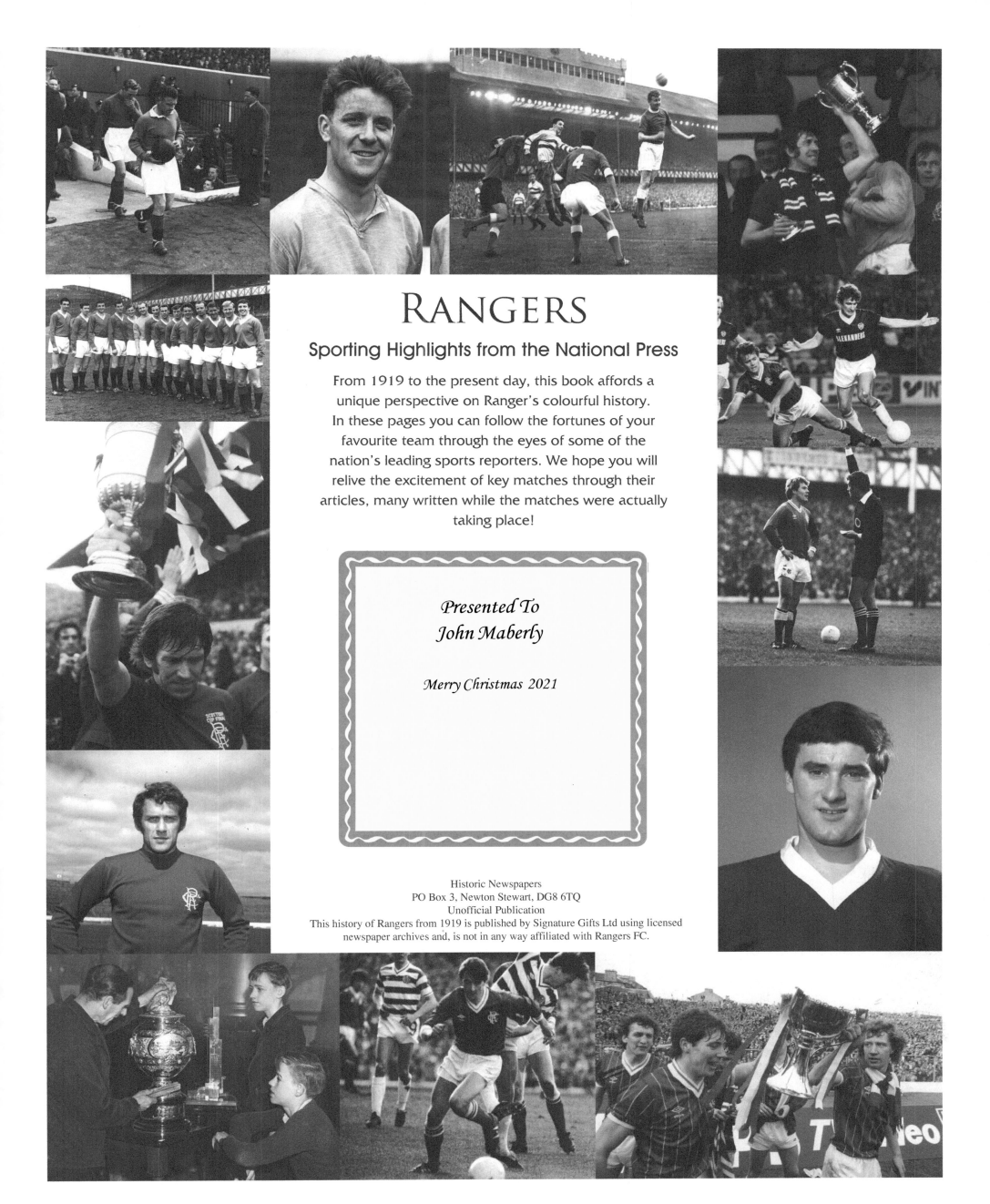

RANGERS

Sporting Highlights from the National Press

From 1919 to the present day, this book affords a unique perspective on Ranger's colourful history. In these pages you can follow the fortunes of your favourite team through the eyes of some of the nation's leading sports reporters. We hope you will relive the excitement of key matches through their articles, many written while the matches were actually taking place!

Presented To
John Maberly

Merry Christmas 2021

Historic Newspapers
PO Box 3, Newton Stewart, DG8 6TQ
Unofficial Publication
This history of Rangers from 1919 is published by Signature Gifts Ltd using licensed newspaper archives and, is not in any way affiliated with Rangers FC.

Published by Historic Newspapers
PO Box 453
Harpenden
AL5 9AL

ISBN-13:   978-1-905966-28-8

EXPERIMENTAL IBROX ELEVEN SUCCEEDS AGAINST THE CELTS.

Dr. J. Paterson, Rangers F.C.

RANGERS RISE AND SMITE THEIR CELTIC RIVALS.

POWER CARRIES THE "LIGHT BLUES" THROUGH.—PUNCH LACKING IN THE SWEETER MOVING PARKHEAD ATTACK.

PUSHFUL CAIRNS.—CLEVER PATERSON.—ANDREW CUNNINGHAM'S TWO GOALS.

By "Waverley."

RANGERS (H)..............3 CELTIC..............0

Those who are agitating against the shilling gate, or "bob football," as it has been called, would extract few crumbs of comfort from Saturday's spectacle at Ibrox Park, where a record crowd turned out to see Celtic and Rangers in their first League encounter of the season. Long ere the hour fixed for the kick-off, the already well-filled and spacious enclosure presented a pretty appearance, and before three o'clock money was being refused for admission to the grand stand. Truly King Football rules more subjects now than ever he did. It was not a great match. There were few thrills, but their absence was compensated for by the strenuous nature of the contest. Every man-jack went into his work as if the fate of a nation depended upon his individual efforts. As often happens when Scotland's two greatest rivals meet, the "glorious uncertainty" of the game was demonstrated. Celtic, who have been playing pretty, combined, and effective football since the season started, were expected to win, but the boot was on "the other leg." An enthusiastic, whole-hearted Ibrox eleven, which contained two experimental placings, won handsomely by three goals to nothing, and thus atoned in a measure for their Glasgow Cup defeat at Parkhead on September 6.

As I prepared you for on Saturday morning, the "form club" went down at Ibrox Park. The Celts were beaten, and beaten well, in the race for the League Flag by a team that was ever so much their inferior in the Glasgow Cup semi-final six or seven weeks ago. Of such are those meetings of the "old firm." One never knows what will happen.

In the end the "Light Blues" were well worthy their 3 to 0 victory, but although they led by a Cunningham goal at the interval, up till then they were not the better side. Indeed, it was only after the big fair-haired Ayrshire forward—in the centre for the day—put them further ahead that they took thorough command.

After that the Celts struggled on in a kind of way to put a better complexion on affairs, but their first-half confidence had deserted them. Their more methodical and prettier game of the opening stage was knocked on the head by another of a more robust description featured by their opponents. The play of the Parkhead crowd had not the punch of that of their Ibrox rivals, hence the result.

R. Manderson, Rangers F.C.

When Mr. Wilton told me that Archie Ritchie was unable to strip; and that Gordon would take up the left back position, I could not help thinking that this was not at all a bad arrangement for the Rangers. In my mind's eye I saw a picture of M'Atee and Gallagher toying with the Dumbarton back in the cup game at Parkhead.

"Andy" and "Patsy" did not toy with Gordon at Ibrox. "J. E." rattled in on both like a miniature avalanche, Walls followed suit, and Manderson, Bowie and Dixon were always there or thereabout. The strong, stick-at-nothing work of this Rangers rear quintette began the breaking up of the Celts which Andrew Cunningham's second goal virtually completed.

To Doctor Paterson belongs most of the credit of the first point which came along eight minutes after the start. "The Doc.," who was moving, oh so sweetly on the left, getting the ball from Cairns slipped it in just as he should, and a series of misses followed before Cunningham came on to send it home. I heard some folks say that Cunningham was offside. There was not the slightest suggestion of Andrew being out of play.

While this early Ibrox success did not put the Celts out, it "bucked" the Rangers wonderfully. It was just the tonic they required. It spurred them on to go in and win. All the same, I feel that had the League champions counted first my tale would have been different this morning.

Before and after the scoring of this early goal much of the Celtic play was delightful. M'Menemy, the master mind of the attack, and Gallagher in a lesser degree, kept the ball going nicely, M'Atee and Adam M'Lean centred very well, but none of the lot shot hard enough or often enough. Occasionally they hesitated, too; and to do so in this hard-fought-out and strenuous rather than pretty contest was fatal. It was truly a case of no waiting, no delay.

If not the, by comparison, well-oiled machine the Celtic attack were, the Rangers five were quite as often dangerous; indeed, but for Cairns getting in the way they might have got another goal. Shaw and Lock both dealt smartly with a few good balls, but neither was tested as often as he should.

RANGERS.
Lock.
Manderson, Gordon.
Bowie, Dixon, Walls.
Muirhead, Cairns,
Archibald, Cunningham, Paterson.
O
M'Lean, M'Inally, M'Atee.
M'Menemy, Gallagher,
Cassidy, Cringan, Gilchrist.
M'Stay, M'Nair.
Shaw.
CELTIC.

Referee—W. Bell, Hamilton.

A goal down only at the interval, the Celts were not out of the hunt by any means. Lock was called on right away, first Cassidy and then Cringan shot over; then the second goal and a Rangers' victory! The half was only four minutes old, when Archibald, from the corner flag almost, slashed a ball across; Cunningham jumped up for it, but Shaw got there first. Charley's clearance was not decisive enough, however, and Cunningham, up again, got his cranium on this time.

There is little use dwelling on what happened during the next half-hour. The Celts stuck in right manfully, but to all intents and purposes the points were safe in the Rangers' pockets. It did not require Paterson's lovely goal to decide the issue. The doctor's grand oblique shot beat Shaw all the way. It was a thing of beauty.

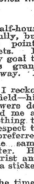

A. Cunningham, Rangers F.C.

His spectacular goal apart, I reckon Paterson the best forward afield—his elusive footwork and centring were delightful. Jamie M'Menemy told me at the close that he could see nothing to beat Cairns, but with all due respect to the great Celt, I repeat that I preferred the doctor on the day. At the same time, "Tommy" never did better. He kept boring in, and gave Gilchrist and Alec M'Nair no rest. Cairns is a sticker if ever there was one.

Muirhead was a worker all the time; if Andrew Cunningham was not a great centre-forward he was a worrying one, and—he got two goals. Archibald, only fair in the first half, improved later on. The physically well-endowed "Fifer" does not yet get the ball across as smartly as he should. Take a tip from the doctor, Alec.

A. M'Nair, Celtic F.C.

Immediately behind the line stood as resolute a trio as ever did duty for the Rangers, with Gordon out of the three this may seem strange reading, but it is a fact just the same. And Bowie was the pick of the bunch. By the way, Jamie's summing up of the game is a trifle different from mine. His verdict is—"The Celts were beaten before we were midway through the opening half."

Further back, nothing was given away; indeed, to my way of thinking, Manderson and Gordon were more convincing than M'Nair and M'Stay. Alec was as crafty and safe as Manderson was impetuous and successful. The breezy and speedy Irishman is playing better than ever. Gordon was not an orthodox back. "J. E." had a way of his own of doing things, and very much oftener than not he "got there."

Lock did nothing wrong, and the only charge that can be laid against Shaw is that he didn't get away more decisively that Archibald cross, which brought about the middle goal. Cringan was the best of the Celtic half-back line, which lacked power on the wings. What a lot of work Willie put in!

As I have already indicated, M'Menemy and Gallagher were the best of the forwards, even if "Patsy" seemed a bit more subdued than usual. M'Inally did some really smart things in the first half, but he was too well watched to get doing any damage, and he enjoyed little luck. M'Lean, who, I thought, should have scored once, was not particularly happy with his centres. M'Atee, who started fairly bright, was well held by Walls after the interval.

W. Cringan, Celtic F.C.

A BETTER LEAGUE.

ONLY A POINT BETWEEN THE LEADERS.

RECORD CROWD AT IBROX PARK.

73,000 PEOPLE PAID.

By "Waverley."

Yes, my masters, we have a very much better Scottish League this morning. For the sake of the competition it was a good job the Rangers won, and I feel certain that the Celtic directors, after they got over their first disappointment, were not very much put out by the Ibrox triumph. A three goals to nothing defeat takes a bit of swallowing, but even that is better—and eke more profitable—than a League with too many points separating the leaders. And it isn't a far cry to New Year's day—what a crowd we will have at Parkhead then! I shouldn't wonder much if Saturday's record figures will get a shake. Seventy-three thousand people paid to get in on Saturday, which means that there would be between 75,000 and 76,000 enthusiasts accommodated within the spic-and-span Ibrox enclosure—it was a pretty sight. Great game football!

Celtic were without Hugh Brown, for whom Joe Cassidy deputised, while the Rangers fielded an experimental side, and as has hapened before in the matches, it "came off." James Gordon figured in yet another role. "J. E." was at left back, and Andrew Cunningham led the attack. The unexpected placings were justified by their success. No goals were lost, and Cunningham collected two.

We were regaled with a few other surprises. Queen's Park, who fielded J. Thom, a new back from Coatbridge, and J. V. Russell, a centre forward from the Strollers, not only prevented Ayr United from bagging their first brace of points at Hampden, but they whacked them soundly. J. B. Bell gathered in three of the Amateurs' half-dozen goals. It is only fair to Ayr to mention that Gordon Kerr was off for alterations and repairs when two of the goals were scored.

PAISLEY'S DOUBLE.

On Saturday evening I ran against Willie Cook, a present day St. Mirren director, and Bob Smith, who before his migration to Russia, was honorary secretary to the Paisley club. Both beamed! And little wonder! The League team had handed out Aberdeen their first defeat at Pittodrie, and the Reserves had knocked Partick Thistle out of the Scottish Second Eleven Cup competition at Firhill. A fine "double," gentlemen.

A sparkling display gave the Hearts the points at Celtic Park, where an excellent Clyde defence was beaten once; and Partick Thistle came a bad cropper at Easter Road. Four of the Hibernian's six goals were clapped on what time Alec Stewart was having a damaged leg attended to.

Airdrieonians went down by the odd goal at Kirkcaldy; Third Lanark brought back a point from Clydebank; and plucky Albion Rovers held Motherwell in Airdrie. Duncan and Jack Bell saw to it that Hugh Ferguson was given precious few chances.

Kilmarnock pulled themselves out of the rut by sending Falkirk empty away from Rugby Park; Dumbarton went further down at Greenock; and Dundee followed their fine appearance in Dumbarton by dumping the Academicals at Hamilton. Davie Brown got the goal that made the Dens Park people happy.

My good friend Tom M'Intosh, the Middlesbrough manager, was at Douglas Park, and so too were a few Everton people. Thomson and Nicol of Dundee were the men most closely watched. Hutchison, the Dens Park left half-back was also "mentioned in despatches." There's no change in the position regarding Andrew Wilson. Mr. M'Intosh tells me. "We don't require money, what we want is the player."

WHAT'S ON.

SCOTTISH LEAGUE.—Airdrieonians v. Hamilton Academicals, Ayr United v. Hibernian, Celtic v. Queen's Park, Dumbarton v. Raith Rovers, Dundee v. Rangers, Falkirk v. Albion Rovers, Hearts v. Aberdeen, Motherwell v. Kilmarnock, Partick Thistle v. Clydebank, St. Mirren v. Morton, Third Lanark v. Clyde

INTERNATIONAL.—Ireland v. England.

ENGLISH LEAGUE (FIRST DIVISION).—Arsenal v. Bradford City, Bradford v. Chelsea, Burnley v. Liverpool, Derby County v. Oldham Athletic, Everton v. Blackburn Rovers, Manchester City v. Sheffield Wednesday, Middlesbrough v. Aston Villa, Preston North-End v. Newcastle United, Sheffield United v. Manchester United, Sunderland v. Bolton Wanderers, West Bromwich v. Notts County.

HEARTS COME BACK.

FORWARDS TOUCH OLD-TIME STANDARD.

CLYDE'S FAILINGS.

By "Brigadier."

HEARTS..............1 CLYDE (H)..........0

Cut that incident of the goal out of the game at Parkhead and you have two teams with practically nothing between them. But, of course, you can't get away from the goal; it was too well managed to be pushed aside as a mere accidental success in a match where cool heads and a modicum of precision at other times would have brought more successes.

It was some six minutes after the start, and when the play had been running slightly in Clyde's favour, that Miller carried on with a pass from Sinclair. After beating a couple of opponents in his own inimitable style, George seemed as if he would spoil everything by overdoing it, but at the right moment he lofted the ball over to Murphy.

Cowan and Frame were caught in two minds, and before they coud get to business Murphy let go a beautiful shot from well outside the penalty area and Shingleton was helpless.

It was a swaying game from that point on to the interval. True, both Shingleton and Kane got some stiff shots to deal with, but for consistency of good marksmanship neither lot of forwards was winning any medals.

Still, some of the combination among the Hearts inside men was as good as anything a Tynecastle attack has shown since 1914. Low joined in with his short, speedy runs and nice centres.

About the Clyde forwards there was any amount of bustle. They got ahead quickly, but they never varied their game an iota, and as time went on the Hearts defence knew exactly what was going to happen and, of course, were the more easily able to provide counter measures.

A TEARING SHOT.

It was the same throughout the second half—with a few exceptions. The first of these was a tearing shot by Marshall, who having come out of the half-back line for the day, evidently thought it time he showed his forwards how to do it. The ball was almost under the bar when Kane got his hands to it.

Clyde's effort at this juncture was admirable in everything but brain work, and Crossan and Wilson got excellent opportunity tt exercise their colossal punting power.

Then the Hearts' forwards came into the game again, and after Low and Graham had puzzled Rae and Cowan, the winger was on the point of scoring when he stumbled.

Marshall, in the course of another rally by the Clyde forwards, got away another glorious shot only to hit the bar—at least, so thought the referee, although I thought Kane touched the ball first. The Hearts were making all the running at the finish.

Both Shingleton and Kane were splendidly safe. Crossan and Wilson had a reserve of physical strength that was inexhaustible and, whether in tackling or clearing, they made few mistakes. Cowan and Frame were also sound, although the latter went off a bit in the second half.

Nellies, at centre half-back, was a good enough stopgap, but it required the forceful help of Preston and Birrell to counterbalance the advantage Clyde enjoyed in the person of M'Andrew. At the same time, I saw precious little ground passing done by the Hearts' wing halfs.

I fancy the Hearts have now got something like a forward line. Graham showed all his old elegance of style, and his faultless passes brought out the very best of the clever lad, Low. Murphy needed a lot of watching, thanks, largely, to the coaching he got from Miller.

I must give a pat on the back to Marshall for his big-hearted attempt to pull the game round for Clyde, and he had an erratic partner in Morris. M'Gowan had not the battering power to go through. The left wing was good up to twenty yards from goal. Then more often than not the machinery broke down.

CLYDE—Shingleton; Cowan and Frame; Rae, M'Andrew, and Forrest; Morris, Marshall, M'Gowan, Boyton, and Aitken.

HEARTS—Kane; Crossan and J. Wilson; Preston, Nellies and Birrell; Sinclair, Miller, Murphy, Graham, and Low.

FALKIRK'S BAD DAY.

A NEW EXPERIENCE FOR THE KILMARNOCK BOYS.

By "Netherton."

KILMARNOCK (H)....3 FALKIRK..........0

It was only occasionally that we saw any concerted action at Rugby Park, where far too much careless kicking was indulged in. There was a tendency to sky the ball, the result being that the defences were very much in evidence.

Shortt nearly caught Ferguson unprepared with a good shot, and M'Phail warmed the goalkeeper's fingers. Add to these M'Naught's effort which struck the bar, and you have summed up the scoring chances of the first half.

Shortly after the interval, M'Lean made things more lively by getting the better of Ferguson. A little later another was sent home by Smith, but was disallowed. Further success was, however, only delayed.

Ferguson was forced to retire as the result of an injury, and another goal by Culley ten minutes from the finish gave Kilmarnock the victory.

Kilmarnock, the team that altered their first-half tactics and contrived to keep the ball on the floor, deserved to succeed. They were quite a different company in the closing portion. Smith was the master mind in their attack,

KILMARNOCK—Blair; Hamilton and Gibson; Bagan, Shortt and Maitland; M'Naught, Smith, Culley, M'Lean, and M'Phail.

FALKIRK—Ferguson; Scott and Maxwell; Townsley, Reilly, and Harvie; M'Dougall, Waugh, Rutherford, Wood and Glancy.

FECKLESS FORWARDS.

HALF-BACKS AND BACKS PREVAIL AT CLYDEBANK.

By "Craigpark."

CLYDEBANK (H) ..0 THIRD LANARK ..0

At Clydeholm the play was scrappy and disjointed. There was little or no intelligent collaboration between the middle-men and those in front, and for this the half-backs were most to blame. I am not forgetting that the middle-men were highly successful in a destructive sense.

Their task was rendered comparatively easy by the poverty of the wing forwards. The passing of the wing supports was extremely faulty, the ball oftener finding a billet at the foot of an opponent than that of a colleague.

M'Lavin and Flannagan obliged with clever touch-line runs and crosses, and Anderson and Orr occasionally went off on individual runs, but the goal scoring efforts were few and far between. Brownlie disposed of an express drive from Trueman in the opening half, and M'Turk got rid of a teaser from Orr, while in the closing portion the International custodian had some difficulty in clearing a corner well placed by Fulton. Clydebank were a shade the better side after the interval, and had they possessed a decent shot they might have gained the points

CLYDEBANK—M'Turk; Stevenson and Ferguson; Neish, Gilhooley, and Trueman; M'Lavin, Fulton, Anderson, Croot, and M'Adam.

THIRD LANARK—Brownlie; Lennon and M'Gowan; I. Walker, Hendry, and J. Walker; Allan, Bennie, Orr, Donaldson, and Flannaghan.

A SHOCK TO AIRDRIE.

RAITH ROVERS WEAR DOWN THE BROOMFIELD DEFENCE.

By "Culdean."

RAITH ROVERS (H)..3 AIRDRIE..........2

Airdrieonians' somewhat unique goal record underwent a bit of a transformation at Kirkcaldy, where Raith Rovers added 50 per cent. to their total of "six against." A good game it was, punctuated with thrills.

Immediately after the kick-off we had a sensation. Snape, getting clear away, parted to Duff, who had the ball in the net in a flash. This early reverse upset the Rovers somewhat. For a bit they were at "sixes and sevens," but they settled down, and ultimately emerged good winners of as keen a game as has been witnessed at Stark's Park for many a day.

Raith's half-backs won them the points. All three were good, but Porter was really great. Inglis and Robson were a bit rocky, but young Macdonald in goal covered up many of their mistakes.

In a better-balanced Airdrie side, Snape gave Inglis a troublesome time, and the Reid's did well throughout, Duff was dangerous when near goal, and Willie Neil completed a capital line. Hart was outstanding in a strong middle division, and the backs were magnificent for three-fourths of the game.

RAITH ROVERS—Macdonald; Inglis and Robson; Rattray, Porter, and Anderson; Birrell, M'Lean, Welsh, Duncan, and Dunn.

AIRDRIEONIANS—Fotheringham; Macdonald and Watson; Knox, Summers, and Hart; J. Reid, Neil, A. Reid, Duff, and Snape.

RANGERS CREEPING UP ON CELTS—ONLY 4 LEAGUE WINS BEHIND.

34,000 BRAVE THE STORM.

AYR UNITED IN A VERY BAD WAY NOW.

By "Waverley."

Talk about Rudyard Kipling's "muddied oafs"! There was lots of the sticky stuff at Ibrox yesterday, and most other places where Ne'erday football was played or attempts made to play it.

I cannot recall ever before seeing a Rangers-Celtic match played on such a field. It was a case of splash and splutter and the ball stopping dead or spinning in the churned mud. Ugh! it was awful.

As nobody changed clothes at the interval—Mr. Small kept his men on the field all the time—you who were not among the 34,000 present can hardly imagine in what a bedraggled state some of the players were at the finish. It rained persistently nearly all the time.

PREVIOUS "WORSTS."

I can recall a Ne'erday "old firm" battle played at Parkhead in a snowstorm in the long ago; then there was the "fog match" of a couple of years back, but the conditions yesterday overhead and underfoot were even worse. Ibrox was not quite so bad as Sheffield Wednesday's field was on the day of that memorable, muddy England-Scotland 'National of 1920, but it was a good—or should I say bad?—second.

Despite the depressing conditions 34,000 were present. Which is surely a tribute to the pulling power of football, and to Rangers and Celtic particularly. And I make bold to say that had I been able to state definitely in yesterday's "Record" that Gallagher would play, a goodly few thousands more would have been present. But as I have told you, Patsy is down with influenza.

Bailie Duncan Graham, Rangers.

Rangers won with a bit to spare, but I would not care to say they were three goals the better side. There was something in the winning of the toss. And the fact that the "Light Blues" scored four goals reminds me that not since season 1913-1914 has either side scored four goals against the other in a League match.

LAST TIME 4 GOALS.

And then the Celts won by 4-0. But it should also be mentioned that the Rangers were badly handicapped that afternoon. Jamie Gordon and Bobby Brown were injured and the Ibrox side finished with nine men. Rangers are creeping up on their old-time rivals. In the 70 "old firm" League matches played Celtic have won 24, Rangers 20, and 26 have been drawn. And only 4 goals separate them now—Celtic have scored 110, Rangers 106

I had a word with Messrs. T. White and J. Kelly, of the Celtic Board, at the finish. Both took the defeat in sporting spirit. Mention of this talk upstairs reminds me that Bailie Duncan Graham, of the Ibrox Board, told me that he leaves for South Africa on Tuesday. The City Treasurer, who is recovering from an illness, hopes, of course, to benefit by the trip. Bon voyage, Treasurer Graham.

At Firhill 10,000 people braved the storm, at Easter Road there were 4000 more. The Hearts, beaten 2-1 by the Hibernian, were without both their usual backs. Paddy Crossan is nursing an injury and Jock Wilson is down with "'flu."

Of course Third Lanark are delighted with their 3-0 victory at Firhill; therefore it is not surprising that the same eleven have been chosen to face St. Johnstone at Cathkin to-morrow. A few of the boys are suffering from injuries, Mr. Galt tells me, but he expects they will all be fit.

HOW THEY STAND.

I didn't expect any shuffling at either end of the points' table and none took place. The three leaders, Rangers, Airdrieonians and Hibernian succeeded, so that the "Light Blues" are still three points in front of their Broomfield challengers, and seven ahead of the Easter Road confederacy.

Third Lanark's success at Firhill raised them into fifth place along with Morton, who got through against St. Mirren. They are only a point behind Celtic who, however, have a match in hand.

St. Mirren dropped into fourth bottom place. They have 18 points one fewer than the totals of St. Johnstone and Aberdeen, both of whom have fulfilled 23 matches against the Love Street fellows 21.

Queen's Park and Motherwell, both unengaged in the League tourney, are still third and second from the basement respectively. Overwhelmed at Kilmarnock, Ayr United are now in a very precarious position at the foot.

Off yesterday by reason of the condition of Douglas Park, the Hamilton Academicals—Motherwell match has been fixed provisionally for Wednesday. Those who have tickets for booked seats can either have their money returned on application to Mr Scott Duncan or use the tickets on Wednesday.

"OLD FIRM" NE'ERDAY BATTLE IN THE MUCK.

IBROX SIDE THE STRONGER AND CLEVERER—PARKHEAD BOYS MAKE A GRAND RALLY—WILLIE M'STAY A GIANT.

GEORGE HENDERSON GETS TWO GOALS—ALEC ARCHIBALD AT HIS BEST.

By "WAVERLEY."

Rangers (h).......................4 Celtic.......................1

WHILE the "old firm" battle at Ibrox yesterday ended, as most folks expected, in Rangers pocketing the points, the score was more than a trifle severe on the plucky young fellows who sported "green and white." Although losing a couple of goals in 8½ minutes and a third before half an hour had gone, the Parkhead confederacy faced their task with hearts of steel.

And their second half showing, when they had the gale and the rain behind them, merited more than a solitary goal. The beaten Celts possessed cleverness, determination, and stamina; the vital factors missing were subtlety and craft.

Young Corrigan, who faced the huge task of trying to fill Patsy Gallagher's shoes, is a promising boy, who has not yet developed the artistry or cunning of Parkhead's "mighty atom." "Patsy's" influence and driving power would have gone a long way to steady the Eastern attack.

FLEMING'S WORTH.

I was having my first peep at Fleming, and he surprised me. I had been told things about this lad, but on the day I liked him. His ball control surprised me particularly. Time and again after the turn Fleming carried the ball Robb-wards very cleverly, and when the chance came from Connelly to pierce the Ibrox defence he was "on it like a bird." No veteran could have bettered his goal.

But first place in the Celtic forward quintette I award to Thomson. He was not so spectacular as Fleming or Connelly, but like Cairns on the other side he was a plodder all the time, a plodder who made the best use of the ball. "The Fifer" did not get from M'Lean the response he should—well, Adam was never comfortable. Another thing—Davie Meiklejohn and Bert Manderson gave him little room.

"GALLOPING GEORDIE."

While there were heaps of individual cleverness in the Celtic movements forward, it was left pretty much to the "Light Blue" quintette to provide the solid machine-like sweeps. Archibald I have seldom seen do better. He lagged once or twice, yet I might say that he kept forging ahead all the time. Sometimes before the interval his progress was made easier through M'Farlane being out of his place; but "Archie's" crossing was delightfully accurate.

Two of the goals—the first and last—both galloping Geordie Henderson counters, accrued from Archibald's capital work. Alan Morton, if he took things easily latterly, scintillated before the cross-over, even if his direction was faulty on occasion. Yes, "Wee Alan" gave young Beith Wilson a worrying time

George Henderson, Andy Cunningham, and Tommy Cairns—and Captain Tom particularly—were grand grafters. When I recall the awful overhead conditions and the sloppy, churning ground, the movements of the Ibrox forwards in the first half-hour were wonderfully bright.

Unquestionably it was a stroke of fortune for the League champions when Cairns "found the lady." The spin of the coin gave them the wind; it meant the tide running with them to begin with. And they made the most of Dame Fortune's lavish gift. They went off full steam ahead; every man-jack was a worker—and within five minutes Shevlin was beaten.

As I have mentioned, Archibald's fine wing work gave Henderson the opening, but it was a masterly-taken goal. When the ball was swung over George burst after it, got it on the drop and in his stride. He timed his shot perfectly, and poor Shevlin was helpless. It was a glorious goal. Less than five minutes after this Cunningham crashed on a second—a left foot smasher from six yards range, and again Shevlin was beaten through no fault of his.

IBROX "ARCHIE."

ALEC ARCHIBALD, RANGERS.

Rangers were in one of their brightest moods now. The other fellows battled hard to change the run of things, but with little or no success. M'Lean and Connelly gave Robb balls to return, and M'Farlane smashed one in just bar high, but these were but interludes in the fight which raged about continually in Shevlin's vicinity.

Rangers—Robb; Manderson and M'Candless; Meiklejohn, Dixon and Muirhead; Archibald, Cunningham, Henderson, Cairns and Morton.

Celtic—Shevlin; W. M'Stay and Hilley; Wilson, J. M'Stay and Macfarlane; Connelly, Corrigan, Fleming, Thomson and M'Lean.

Jamie and Willie M'Stay, with Hugh Hilley, were giants in defence, yet Hilley made a glaring blunder. He upended Archibald within the box, and M'Candless made no mistake with his kick from the spot. Twenty-five minutes had gone now—right on to the interval the Rangers dominated matters.

Turned round without the usual adjournment the Celts quickly got in touch with Willie Robb. A curling ball from Fleming gave Willie some trouble; then an unexpected cold douche for the luckless Parkhead party. Twice Archibald lobbed over a ball, and the second one was caught up by Henderson and sent home just as George can send them.

Only four minutes had gone, and before many more seconds had been clocked the Ibrox goal had undergone a great escape. Thomson fired in a ball which had Robb "beaten to the world," but M'Candless came from somewhere. The little Irishman got up and "headed" out on the goal-line—or where the goal-line had been.

A FIGHTING CELTIC.

That bit of play which led up to this "near thing" fairly cheered up the hitherto despondent Celtic faithful who had not long to wait till Fleming gave them something worth shouting about. Muirhead missed, or rather failed to trap a ball which Connelly smartly snapped up, and quickly dropped it into the middle. Fleming dashed in and scored a brilliant goal—one almost as brilliant as Henderson's first one.

This finished the scoring, but in the remaining half-hour, the younger Celts strove hard for another goal. Fleming made several attempts to break through on his own, but he was invariably crowded out.

I have already told you how the forwards comported themselves—individually and collectively. In the rear none did quite so well as Willie M'Stay, whose work was reminiscent of the Celtic we used to admire and laud so much.

BUIRDLY WILLIE.

Buirdly Willie's power, determination, craft and resource placed him on a pedestal of his own. He brought us back to the days when giant Celts—by comparison—figured in the fiercest and most exhilarating of the old-time epic "old-firm" Ne'erday battles. Even if a trifle fitful, Hilley did much good work. Manderson and M'Candless formed a stonewall bodyguard for Robb. "Big Bert," I thought, was particularly lively.

Rangers had a big pull in the middle division. Arthur Dixon fairly revelled in the mud. Towards the close "Lil" Arthur, like Tommy Cairns, might easily have passed for an "All-Black" instead of a "Light Blue." Jamie M'Stay was also a tireless worker, but the Ibrox wing halfs were ahead of the Celtic pair. Tommy Muirhead was quieter than was his wont, I thought. Yet his ground passes to Morton and Cairns were as accurate and effective as ever.

LOST IN FIRST "TWENTY."

TYNECASTLE ATTACK FAILS.

By "Donovan."

HIBERNIAN (h) .... 2 HEARTS 1

Looking back upon the game at Easter Road, the Hearts' players will admit that they lost the points because of the failure of the forwards to "make good" in the first twenty minutes. Wind and sleet blew towards the Hibs' end—phew, what a day! All the play was with the Hearts, but—nary a goal.

After the turn the Hibs had their innings. The storm had moderated by that time and the Tynecastle defence never was "put through it" in the same way as the Easter Road rear had beeen. Still, the Hibs were betteer at their chances. There you have the secret of their success.

Dunn carried his side through with as fine a goal as I have seen for many a day. Working nicely into position when M'Coll found his way blocked, the little fellow waved for a forward pass, got it, and drove home a lovely shot just as Jamieson made to tackle..

EXHILARATING!

Considering the awful conditions, it was a wonderfully exhilarating contest. First the Hearts worried, but never broke down the Easter Road defence. Four "corners" came in quick succession. Harper made fine saves from Edgar and Smith, and Dornan was just in time to nip in when Murphy was going to drive home.

Things looked bad for the Hibs when Dunn had to spend 15 minutes in the pavilion. Yet it was just hereabout that they began to get their heads above water—or, shall I say, above mud. Halligan let away Ritchie, who got over a fine ball which Willie White picked almost off M'Coll's head.

Murphy, Hearts.

Then a close call for the Hibs. Harper came out to get his fingers on a ball sent across from a "corner." M'Millan seeing a chance, let drive, and his shot knocked out Dornan just under the bar, but the back had the satisfaction of having saved a goal. Dunn back again, he tried a shot that might have come off had M'Coll not got right in the way.

FROM JOHN WHITE.

All the best of the Hearts' efforts were coming from John White. Twice he landed in a troublesome shot to Harper. Then—after 40 minutes — he slipped out the ball to Smith, who lobbed it nicely into the centre. Murphy and Harper went for it together, the Hearts' man won the race by inches, and Hibs were one down.

Murphy did well there, but it can hardly be said that he was a successful centre-forward. More first-time work was needed. "Spud" missed a grand chance of putting his side further ahead just on the interval. M'Millan rushed in and tried to mend matters, but the ball caught an upright.

Seven minutes after the men had got into dry "togs" we saw the equaliser.

Dand brought down Halligan outside the penalty-line, and Walker's shot from the "free" curled right into the net. Dunn put on the winning goal seven minutes later.

But we were by no means finished yet. Hearts fought hard, and more than once they came very near to getting level, and Murphy really ought to have done it. Harper made a great save on the line from Smith; White did an equally brilliant bit of work in stopping a M'Coll "header."

HEART'S HANDICAP.

Hearts were a bit unfortunate in that they had to get along without their regular backs. Still, Ramage and Jamieson made quite a fair pair. Jamieson had a lot of difficulty with Ritchie, but Ramage played a strong, confident game.

Harper and White both made some fine saves. Dornan was the sounder of the Hibs' pair, yet Templeton gave nothing away.

In the middle the Easter Road trio were the more consistent, with Shaw the pick of the bunch. Still Miller was continually doing good work in his own quiet way. Dand stood out most prominently in the Tynecastle company; Wright was sometimes good, and sometimes not so good.

Forward, the Hibs were a level, well-balanced lot with Dunn and Halligan, who led out nicely, the pick. John White came more into prominence than any of the other men in the Hearts' attack. The Tynecastle quintette were clever, but a bit of "punch" was needed. Murphy couldn't supply it.

HIBERNIAN—Harper; Templeton and Dornan; Kerr, Miller and Shaw; Ritchie, Dunn, M'Coll, Halligan and Walker.

HEART OF MIDLOTHIAN—W. White; Ramage and Jamieson; Dand, Wright and A. Johnstone; Smith, J. White, Murphy, M'Millan and Edgar.

December has proved a disastrous month for St. Mirren in a playing sense. From the last five games they have taken only one point, whereas from the previous five they took eight.

WINNERS AND LOSERS—THE POSITION.

SCOTTISH LEAGUE.

FIRST DIVISION.

MORTON	2	ST. MIRREN	1
HIBERNIAN	2	HEART OF MID.	1
DUNDEE	2	ABERDEEN	0
RANGERS	4	CELTIC	1
KILMARNOCK	4	AYR UNITED	1
PARTICK THISTLE	0	THIRD LANARK	3
FALKIRK	0	AIRDRIEONIANS	2
COWDENBEATH	1	RAITH ROVERS	1
HAMILTON AC.	X	MOTHERWELL	X

	Matches.				Goals.		
	Pld	Won.	Lost.	Drn.	For.	Agst.	Pts.
Rangers	22	17	1	4	52	14	38
Airdrieonians	22	16	3	3	47	16	35
Hibernian	22	14	5	3	48	25	31
Celtic	22	9	7	6	40	26	24
Third Lanark	23	8	8	7	33	33	23
Morton	23	9	9	5	26	39	23
Partick Thistle	22	7	7	8	38	37	22
Hamilton Acad.	21	10	10	1	33	32	21
Dundee	22	7	8	7	31	32	21
Cowdenbeath	23	7	9	7	46	49	21
Heart of Mid.	24	8	11	5	41	45	21
Kilmarnock	22	7	9	6	33	42	20
Falkirk	22	8	11	3	32	30	19
Raith Rovers	21	7	9	5	28	33	19
St. Johnstone	23	7	11	5	36	50	19
Aberdeen	23	6	10	7	30	38	19
St. Mirren	21	8	11	2	35	42	18
Queen's Park	22	6	11	5	25	44	17
Motherwell	20	5	9	6	29	36	16
Ayr United	22	5	12	5	24	45	15

SECOND DIVISION.

ALBION ROVERS	1	ARBROATH	1
CLYDEBANK	1	DUMBARTON	0
BATHGATE	0	ARMADALE	1
BROXBURN UN.	3	BO'NESS	1
ALLOA	1	D'FERMLINE ATH.	0
EAST FIFE	5	STENHOUSEMUIR	1
FORFAR ATH.	0	DUNDEE UN.	0
JOHNSTONE	1	ARTHURLIE	1

(Game abandoned.)

CLYDE	X	ST. BERNARD	X
KING'S PARK	X	EAST STIRLING	X

	Matches.				Goals.		
	Pld.	Won.	Lost.	Drn.	For.	Agst.	Pts.
Dundee United	21	12	3	6	38	26	30
Clyde	20	12	4	4	41	17	28
Clydebank	21	12	5	4	39	26	28
Dumbarton	22	9	6	7	30	23	25
Bo'ness	22	10	8	4	45	29	24
Albion Rovers	21	10	8	4	45	29	24
Alloa	20	8	6	6	29	22	22
Arthurlie	21	10	9	2	36	35	22
Arbroath	21	9	8	4	25	27	22
Bathgate	22	8	8	6	41	38	22
King's Park	21	8	8	5	33	23	21
Broxburn Un.	21	8	9	4	21	32	20
Armadale	21	8	10	3	31	40	19
East Fife	20	8	10	2	30	34	18
Dunfermline A	22	7	11	4	29	33	18
Stenhousemuir	21	6	10	5	21	35	17
Johnstone	21	7	11	3	30	48	17
St. Bernard	22	7	12	3	30	46	17
Forfar Athletic	21	5	11	5	19	29	15
E. Stirlingshire	21	4	11	6	32	46	14

SCOTTISH LEAGUE.

THIRD DIVISION.

NITHSDALE WAN.	3	CLACKMANNAN	1
PEEBLES ROVERS	1	ROYAL ALBERT	1
BEITH	4	GALSTON	2
HELENSBURGH	2	MID-ANNANDALE	1
MONTROSE	3	BRECHIN CITY	1
SOLWAY STAR	1	LOCHGELLY UN.	1

(Game abandoned.)

QUEEN OF SOUTH	2	LEITH ATHLETIC	0

(Game abandoned.)

SCOTTISH ALLIANCE.

ABERDEEN A	1	HEARTS A	2

ORDINARY.

QUEEN'S PARK	2	CORINTHIANS	0
ST. JOHNSTONE	1	GLAS. JR. LEAGUE	2

ELGIN CITY, 2; FORRES MECHANICS, 1.

Wigan Borough 6, Glasgow Junior F.A. Select 4.

ENGLISH LEAGUE.

THIRD DIVISION—NORTHERN.

CHESTERFIELD	3	WREXHAM	0
DURHAM CITY	5	LINCOLN CITY	0
ASHINGTON	3	ROTHERHAM C.	1
HARTLEPOOL UN.	3	WALSALL	1
ACCRINGTON S.	2	DARLINGTON	0
TRANMERE R.	1	NEW BRIGHTON	3
BRADFORD	1	BARROW	1
GRIMSBY	1	DONCASTER R.	1

AIRDRIE'S IDOL.

Jamie Reid, of Broomfield.

ENGLISH LEAGUE.

FIRST DIVISION.

SUNDERLAND	1	CARDIFF CITY	0
NEWCASTLE UN.	0	SHEFFIELD UN.	0
BOLTON WAND.	3	BIRMINGHAM	0
BURY	5	TOTTENHAM H.	2
EVERTON	3	BURNLEY	2
BLACKBURN ROV.	X	NOTTS FOREST	X

	Matches.				Goals.		
	Pld.	Won.	Lost.	Drn.	For.	Agst.	Pts.
W.B. Albion	23	14	5	4	36	17	32
Huddersfield	23	11	4	8	36	15	30
Bolton Wand.	23	11	4	8	43	24	30
Birmingham	24	11	7	6	26	29	28
Sunderland	24	12	8	4	35	30	28
Newcastle Un.	25	7	5	13	33	24	27
Liverpool	22	10	6	6	31	23	26
Bury	22	8	5	9	31	32	25
Aston Villa	22	7	5	10	36	33	24
Notts County	23	9	8	6	19	16	24
The Arsenal	23	10	9	4	30	25	24
Manchester C.	23	8	8	7	47	41	23
Blackburn R.	24	7	9	8	31	35	22
Sheffield Un.	24	6	9	9	27	36	21
Tottenham H.	24	6	9	9	30	30	21
West Ham Un.	23	7	10	6	27	34	20
Cardiff City	23	7	10	6	32	34	20
Everton	24	6	10	8	24	34	20
Leeds United	23	6	10	7	28	33	19
Burnley	22	4	10	8	22	35	16
Notts Forest	23	5	12	6	18	37	16
Preston N.E.	23	6	15	2	22	48	14

SECOND DIVISION.

MANCHESTER UN.	1	CHELSEA	0
STOCKPORT C.	1	WOLV'HAMPTON W.	1
THE WEDNESDAY	1	OLDHAM ATH	0
SOUTH SHIELDS	4	COVENTRY CITY	1
MIDDLESBROUGH	1	FULHAM	3
STOKE	0	BRADFORD CITY	0

	Matches.				Goals.		
	Pld.	Won.	Lost.	Drn.	For.	Agst.	Pts.
Manchester Un.	23	14	3	6	34	13	34
Derby Co.	23	14	3	6	48	21	34
Chelsea	24	10	3	11	32	16	31
Leicester City	23	12	6	5	43	23	29
Portsmouth	22	7	4	11	25	24	25
Crystal Palace	23	10	8	5	30	27	25
W'hampton W.	23	10	8	5	32	29	25
Clapton Orient	23	9	8	6	26	21	24
Fulham	22	7	6	9	22	25	23
The Wednesday	24	10	11	3	32	35	23
Southampton	23	6	7	10	20	24	22
Stoke	23	8	9	6	20	23	22
Blackpool	22	8	9	5	40	29	21
Hull City	22	8	9	5	29	29	21
Bradford City	23	5	8	10	21	28	20
Middlesbro'	23	5	8	10	18	24	20
Oldham Ath.	24	7	11	6	18	36	20
Port Vale	21	7	10	4	24	33	18
South Shields	22	4	9	9	21	25	17
Stockport Co.	22	6	11	5	16	33	17
Barnsley	22	5	11	6	24	34	16
Coventry C.	21	4	14	3	26	53	11

THIRD DIVISION—SOUTHERN.

ABERDARE	X	CHARLTON ATH.	X

HOLIDAY MATCH.

Millport v. R. S. M'Coll's Past International XI., at Mill Park, Millport.

FIERY FIRHILL FIGHT—JACKY ROBERTSON DISCUSSES DUMBARTON.

RANGERS' BRILLIANT CLIMAX

KILMARNOCK DEFENCE CAUGHT IN THE STORM.

By "BRIGADIER."

Rangers (h)..................5 Kilmarnock..................1

A HISTORIC day for Rangers!

In their 55 years' story of ups and downs, triumphs, and disappointments, this day was unique.

It was a day of which there was no replica, for to their week-old Scottish Cup success they were engaged in adding a Scottish League Championship.

Upon this first double achievement by the club, Chairman Joseph Buchanan and Manager William Struth warmly congratulated the team in the dressing-room. All the players were quietly delighted at the tribute thus spontaneously bestowed, but I doubt if there were a happier pair than the two old warriors, Andrew Cunningham and Alan Morton. They had been through many hard-fought battles together, and now the greatest ambition of their football lives had been realised.

POWERFUL CHAMPIONS.

It was just such a display as ought to be given by a team attempting to justify its title of champions. I doubt if I have seen Rangers more compact, more self-assured, or more suggestive of power in defence and attack than in this match.

In conditions that were favourable to fast, correct football, the champions seemed capable of doing pretty nearly anything they aimed at. The wings worked out some ornate designs, which were executed with a crispness that was delightful to see.

But before the game began before 27,000 enthusiasts, the Cup was carried round the track by Archie Swan, now in "civies," with the band swigging behind playing a rousing march. The trophy was bedecked with red, white, and blue ribbons and a natty silk Union Jack brought from Denmark by Manager Struth, who had kept it for such an occasion—the optimist.

Before Rangers opened the scoring they enjoyed a "life," for, with Harry Cunningham stealing a march, and going between Gray and Robert Hamilton, he struck the bar with a clipper shot.

That was the last we saw of real menace from Kilmarnock until late in the second half. Morton was running and dribbling and swerving like a professor, and it was from a dazzling little circular movement of his, after he had taken a straight pass from Cunningham, that Fleming rolled home the opening goal after eleven minutes.

Five minutes more, and Morton went off with a M'Phail pass, lobbed the ball across for Clemie to punch out, whereupon Cunningham got his right foot to it and into the net it went swishing.

Cunningham, prancing about like a youngster, and working the ball freely and precisely, shot the third goal with a long shot which Clemie might have saved but for the swerve which seemed to put him in two minds and cause him to slip when he went for it.

THE PRETTIEST OF ALL.

Fleming had the fourth goal to himself 16 minutes after the turn round, and, 14 minutes later, Harry Cunningham caught Gray napping and made no mistake with his shot. Kilmarnock never played so well as now. They nearly scored again, but this simply made the Rangers' forwards open the throttle again, after having eased off.

As pretty a movement as has been seen on a football field was crowned by a fifth goal. M'Phail and Morton started a close interchange of passes, altered positions in the process, and when the exact moment arrived Morton dodged round Robertson to take the final pass from M'Phail and slip to Fleming, who gave Clemie no chance.

And so the end. Rangers were the perfect machine, with all the parts working in unison. If Fleming may have seemed to be in position to score oftener, it should be said of him that he was playing under the disadvantage of bruises and aches resulting from the gruelling game at Dundee.

Tom Hamilton had little to do, but he was always safe behind two fine backs—Gray polished and sure and Robert Hamilton a strong tackler with a powerful punt that seldom went over the touchline.

The half-backs were auxiliary forwards, and so we had the game that wins championships and cups.

Kilmarnock were thrown out of gear by the early reverses. They lost confidence for a long time. But the forwards gave glimpses of real cleverness.

I fancy Connell would shine under more favourable circumstances. Smith tried hard to keep the line going, but the marking by the Rangers' half-backs was too good to allow him to work out his schemes.

A forcing half-back of Hugh Morton's type would have been invaluable. Robertson and Nibloe were plucky but overwrought.

RANGERS—T. Hamilton; Gray and R. Hamilton; Buchanan, Meiklejohn, and Craig; Archibald, Cunningham, Fleming, M'Phail, and Morton.

KILMARNOCK—Clemie; Robertson and Nibloe; Hogg, M'Leod, and M'Ewan; Connelly, Smith, Cunningham, Ramsay, and Millar.

Referee—A. H. Leishman, Falkirk.

Rangers—Fleming 3, Cunningham 2. Kilmarnock—Cunningham.

SMART DUMBARTON LADS.

CENTRE WITH A SURE SHOT.

By JACKY ROBERTSON,
Scottish International Half-Back.

DUMBARTON (h) 4 STENH'SEM'R 1

FATAL Boghead, they used to call it. Bonnie Boghead, I would say, is as good. I have travelled a bit, but a prettier sight I have never seen than Boghead Park bathed in Saturday's sunshine.

And Dumbarton had a team in keeping with the scenery. They won well against a Stenhousemuir side in which were several clever lads.

I had heard a lot about Miller, the Dumbarton left half, and I am bound to say that the praise bestowed on him is not misplaced. He is a strongly-built boy, has two good feet, and can head as he wants to.

All he needs is a speeding-up, and this can be secured by application to the spikes during the close season.

CARRIES A SHOT.

Crawford, the inside left, also justified the good things said of him. He, also, has two good feet, he opens up the game intelligently, and carries a fine shot. A little more weight and he would be fit for any company. He is a footballer.

Urquhart, a big strong fellow, likes the ball to be placed in front of him. That done, he can hit it with either foot, and hit it hard. He reminded me of Willie Devlin, of the Hearts, in the way he drives the ball.

Muir, the right back, is a player in the making, something after Jock Hutton's style. A little prone to dribbling the ball, he can easily get rid of that fault.

John Bradford shows all the old cleverness. He had three beautiful saves, such as only a man of coolness and judgment could make.

Both Hamil and Kirk are raiders who get over the ground quickly, and should be shaping for promotion before long.

As a team, Dumbarton played better than Stenhousemuir. With a little more vigour, Copland, the Larbert centre-half, would take some beating. I fancy White, the left half, has a future. He is always trying to work for position, which is a valuable feature in a half-back.

URQUHART'S BULL'S-EYES.

I was impressed by L. Robertson, the outside left, who can use either foot well and centres a good ball. He has splendid build, and is full of determination.

It was a capital game to watch, even if the goals went mostly the one way. Urquhart scored twice in the first half with driving shots, and twelve minutes after the interval he registered a third.

Kirk got a fourth, and L. Robertson notched one for Stenhousemuir.

Dumbarton—Urquhart 3, Kirk. Stenhousemuir—L. Robertson.

DUMBARTON — Bradford; Muir and Shaw; M'Lardie, Harvie, and Miller; Hamil, Gillies, Urquhart, Crawford, and Kirk.

STENHOUSEMUIR—Shortt; Wilkie and Murdoch; Jack, Copland, and Whyte; Howie, J. Robertson, Scoullar, Junior, and L. Robertson.

Referee—J. Leggat, Coatbridge.

FIERY FINISH AT FIRHILL.

CELTIC LOSE THEIR LEAD IN THE LAST SECOND—M'GRORY'S TWO.

By "GRAMPIAN."

Partick Thistle (h)..............3 Celtic..............3

I WENT to Firhill hopeful of seeing something unusual. Nothing to make one sit up and take notice occurred for quite a while, and I began to think the game was going to fall far short of its many thrilling predecessors.

To be frank, the first half, while not actually drab, was disappointing. And turned round, little improvement showed itself until about the twentieth minute, at which point Thistle swung into an odd goal in three lead. Then we had excitement enough up to the very closing second.

Celtic galvanised properly into action now, by losing the lead for the first time, straightaway bore down on Jackson's charge, and three minutes saw them equalise. A penalty award was the means of placing Parkhead level, a fact which did not help to relieve any the newly created tension.

THE REVERSE.

It was anybody's game after this, but both Firhill and Paradise rear lines held out, and with only about three minutes remaining, I thought the scoring at an end. The reverse proved the case, however, for the afternoon's main tit-bits were still to come.

M'Grory got through to place Celtic on the lead once more, which late "counter" infused fresh energy into Thistle.

Away they came with one last desperate rush, and Wilkie out on the right got round M'Farlane by sheer doggedness. Firhill's deputy winger carried well down ere finishing with a high ball into the middle, and Harry Gibson, beating the final whistle by not more than a second, headed smartly past Thomson into the net.

Partick had if anything the better of the early exchanges, and Gibson on one occasion narrowly missed with his head a Salisbury cross. Following this "Sally" had the misfortune to see a splendid shot of his hit the near upright and bounce behind.

Not until the twelfth minute did the Celts trouble Jackson seriously. Then the Queen's Cross last line smartly put over a treacherous free-kick from Willie M'Stay.

A Celtic "counter" was not long in materialising. Ere the first "quarter" had elapsed Connolly, profiting by a Wilson-Thomson-M'Grory move, got round Paton, and his resultant lob middlewards, placing Firhill's defence in a tangle, was tipped home by M'Grory.

Partick Thistle's equaliser, with five minutes to go, provided the only other real thrill this half. From Gibson, Salisbury situated well out got possession to drive in a low ball that touched a defending boot en route to Thomson's left-hand post.

THISTLE RALLY.

There was a touch of luck about the point which placed the "Jags" ahead twenty minutes after the restart, and incidentally put the necessary "ginger" into the subsequent exchanges. More than forty yards away young Elliott directed a "grounder" towards goal. Donoghue stationed close in made to clear, but clean missed, and the ball was over before Thomson could cover up his back's mistake.

At the same time Celts' penalty award three minutes later, which equalised matters, was also of the fortunate order. Denis O'Hare handled true enough, but I thought his offence more accidental than anything else. From the "spot" Willie M'Stay made no mistake.

Parkhead's third goal near time, placing them ahead again, was in a measure due to an error of judgment on Lambie's part.

Followed that do-or-die Thistle rally, inaugurated by Wilkie and finished by Gibson's scoring "header."

The thing that strikes me is that Partick Thistle performed so well, carrying as they did so many doubtful links. Rarely have I seen a Firhill middle-line so weak.

PARTICK THISTLE—Jackson; O'Hare and Paton; Elliott, Lambie and Boardman; Wilkie, Grove, Gibson, M'Dougall and Salisbury.

CELTIC—J. Thomson; W. M'Stay and Donoghue; Wilson, J. M'Stay and M'Farlane; Connolly, A. Thomson, M'Grory, M'Inally and M'Lean.

Referee—W. G. Holborn, Glasgow.

Partick Thistle—Salisbury, Elliot, Gibson. Celtic—M'Grory (2), W. M'Stay (penalty).

PERTH PLEASE.

BUT AIRDRIE DO THE SCORING.

By "Malvern."

AIRDRIEONIANS (h) 2 ST. JOHNSTONE 0

No one could have grudged the Saints a point. Their forward play in the outfield was far ahead of Airdrie's, but they could do nothing right with the lively, bouncing ball in the scoring zone.

Black and Stevenson kept their colleagues ever on the move during the first half, and the wing play was delightful to watch, but it led nowhere. Either M'Dougall or the men behind broke up the Perth raiders, who showed little craft and even less marksmanship.

Airdrie's attacking party did not move with accustomed understanding and daintiness, but there was a directness in their work, and Muir's dash was a constant source of worry to the defenders. The little centre had a share in both goals. It was while he was bustling Steel in the fourteenth minute that the ball went to Bertram, whose low cross shot spun out of M'Laren's hands over the line.

Airdrie were the dominating force in the second half, but the power was supplied mainly by the intermediate trio, and especially by M'Dougall, who was the outstanding player afield. A. Wood and Bertram got along better than the right wing pair.

Murdoch did not give his usual response to Neil, but nevertheless the line gave the Perth defenders no end of trouble, and a deserved goal came along in half-an-hour, Muir heading through a Bertram cross.

Despite the fact that there was nothing at stake, the play was always interesting, and a liveliness developed after the interval which had a tonic effect on the crowd.

All the backs kicked with power, Crapnell the best of the lot. Swallow was not far behind M'Dougall in effectiveness among the middlemen. Lafferty also played a strong game.

Stevenson was the star forward, closely followed by Black, Neil and Muir. Webb filled Gavigan's place with credit.

Airdrieonians—Bertram, Muir.

AIRDRIEONIANS—Currie; Crapnell and M'Queen; Preston, M'Dougall and J. Wood; Murdoch, Neil, Muir, A. Wood and Bertram.

ST. JOHNSTONE—M'Laren; Steel and Jamieson; Imrie, Swallow, and Lafferty; Webb, Black, Main, Stevenson and Nicholson.

Referee—G. Ritchie, Leith.

DUNDEE ON THE DOT

QUEEN'S PARK DON'T HIT THE HIGH SPOTS.

By "Allwill."

DUNDEE ...... 2 QUEEN'S PARK (h) 1

Spring was in the air at Hampden, and if I may be excused my effort at being witty, I would say that there wasn't much "spring" about the players.

When defeat stared them in the face, Queen's Park certainly strove hard enough to retrieve themselves, but even then the game did not reach hectic heights. There could be no doubt that victory went to the side deserving of it.

Smarter and more enterprising, the Dens Park forwards, particularly Cook and Lawley, gave the Amateur defenders a warm time, and that they did not score oftener was a tribute to Harkness, M'Leod, and Wiseman. This trio infused plenty of determination into their work—they were compelled to do so!

Gillespie, skilful and forceful, also showed some eagerness when the tide of fortune was running swiftly against them, but apart from M'Alpine, the elusive, and Nicholson, he received poor response. Dundee's first goal was registered just on the interval, and a delightfully taken point it was.

Smith cut out to the right, and, sensing his scheme, Cook ran into the centre. Smith swept the ball across to Lawley, whose oblique, close-in shot looked a certain scorer. Harkness, however, threw himself at the ball, and managed to stop it, but before he could recover, Cook, standing almost under the bar, flashed it into the net.

Midway through the second half Dundee's second came along. Lawley made it possible. He went through alone before sending the ball over to the unmarked Smith, who carried it over the line. Harkness was again powerless.

In a desperate rally, M'Alpine knocked one off the deficitit with a tremendous left-foot drive—a glorious effort. Our Amateurs seldom afterwards looked like saving a point; indeed, they all but found themselves further behind before the final whistle went.

Dundee—Cook, Smith; Queen's Park—M'Alpine.

QUEEN'S PARK—J. D. Harkness; H. R. M'Leod and W. Wiseman; J. M'Donald, R. Gillespie and W. S. King; E. R. Scott, W. S. Chalmers, D. M'Lelland, J. B. M'Alpine and W. G. Nicholson.

DUNDEE—Marsh; Brown and Gilmour; M'Nab, Ross and Thomson; Lawly, Craddock, Smith, Townrow and Cook.

Referee—A. Allan, Glasgow.

FIRHILL'S FLIERS.

TRACKLESS HARE AND HOUNDS START THIS EVENING.

By "Waverley."

At Carntyne on Saturday, where the electric hare fused and was torn to shreds by the dogs, which caused a race to be re-run, I ran against Dick Cumberledge, the man behind the "trackless hare" affair which starts business at Firhill Park this evening. Mr. Cumberledge, who had just arrived from Queen's Cross, told me that immediately after the Thistle-Celtic match his plant was laid down and three very successful trials were engaged in.

All will be ready for this evening's opening show, to which (for this night only) admission will be by programme—sixpence each. I'll be surprised if "Puss" does not have a big gallery at "her" introduction to North-West Glasgow—we Scots dearly love a bargain.

For the nimble sixpence we are to have eight races, and—the chance of these unsatisfactory "re-runs" will be reduced to the minimum. In every instance the dog first past the post will be the winner. Only should a "race" become something approaching to a farce will the "buzzer" announce that it is no race.

THE CARD.

The programme of eight races is as follows:—

PARTICK THISTLE STAKES — Marchbloom, Blue Lass, Fly Fanny, The Constant Nymph, My Man James, and Heatherbrae.

RANGERS STAKES — Leonti, Campile Lase, Strange Daisy, Eulaghmore, Borris Belle, and Fearful Weapon.

CELTIC STAKES—Orange Boy, Oliver Twist, Coming Knight, and Whitbla.

QUEEN'S PARK STAKES (HURDLES) Bonny Charlie, Black Pencil, Dan's Delight, and Juggling Posh.

CLYDE STAKES (HURDLES)—Glenoren Lad, Funny Jim, Royal Delivery, and Little Bertie's Boy.

MOTHERWELL STAKES—Banana Girl, Strange Ranger, Little Keating, Mikky, Call Steward, and Jamais.

AIRDRIE STAKES—Mayo's Pride, Princess Boy, Milcraft, First Scout, The Wiggar, and Flying Debris.

CLYDEBANK STAKES—Against You, Aerated, Willow Glean, Well Beloved, Brown Pom, and Shanafonaman.

BUOYANT HEARTS.

COWDEN CONQUERED AT CENTRAL PARK.

By "Gunner."

HEART OF MIDLOTHIAN 1 COWDENBEATH (h) 0

Only one goal separated Cowdenbeath and Heart of Midlothian at Central Park. Murray was the actual scorer ten minutes prior to the interval, but it was really M'Millan who brought it about.

"Lachie" fired in a powerful drive, which Falconer brilliantly saved. The Tynecastle extreme left winger fastened on to the rebound and placed the ball out of the Fife 'keeper's reach.

Although the game was not too strenuous, knocks were frequent. In the opening portion Dixon was laid low and later Morgan and Miller had to go off for repairs. An outstanding feature was the display of Johnston. Unobtrusive, he was always in position, and rarely has Lindsay been so firmly held.

Cowdenbeath did the major share of attacking in the first half, and Leonard had a lovely left-foot volley neatly turned over by White. Later, the Tynecastle 'keeper had to look lively to keep out a pile-driver from Lindsay. At the other end Falconer held and cleared a good Morgan try; then came Murray's goal, which gave the Tynecastle side more confidence.

After the cross-over neither side claimed any advantage, although Rankin came near with one which flashed past White's right-hand upright. Both Forrest and Murray got the ball over cleverly, but Dixon and his backs saw to it that Falconer wasn't troubled.

A SPURT.

Near the finish the Fifers put in a spurt. Pratt and King were so vigilant and able, however, that the Fifers were baulked.

Behind, Heart of Midlothian were sound. They had a formidable intermediate line, in which Johnston excelled.

In front M'Millan was active and enthusiastic throughout. Morgan was a dashing and virile leader.

While Cowdenbeath had no luck so far as goals were concerned, their forwards did not reveal the craft or steadiness in front of goal that usually feature their play. Dixon and Chambers were the most consistent half-backs, and the rear defenders made no vital mistakes.

Heart of Midlothian—Murray.

COWDENBEATH — Falconer; M'Donald and Moyes; Glancy, Dixon, and Chambers; Pullar, Rankin, Lindsay, Leonard, and Wilson.

HEART OF MIDLOTHIAN—White; Pratt and King; Cowie, Johnston and Shaw; Forrest, Miller, Morgan, M'Millan, and Murray.

Referee—A. B. Williamson, Glasgow.

RITCHIE'S RAKER.

DUNFERMLINE MEN'S DYING KICK.

By "Donovan."

HIBERNIAN (h), 3; DUNFERMLINE ATHLETIC, 3.

For a club "down and out," Dunfermline Athletic showed a wonderful amount of vitality at Easter Road. They sprang a mild surprise by snatching the lead early in the first half. They did even better in the second period, wiping out a two-goal deficit and then grimly defying all the Hibernian efforts to get the winning goal.

In the end Hibs. had their defenders to blame for the loss of a point. Robb did nothing amiss, but a mistake by Stark led to one of the Dunfermline goals, and a blunder on the part of Dick paved the way for another.

A weak clearance by Stark let Carruthers away to put across the centre, from which Tallis scored the opening goal. Ten minutes later Hibs. were on the lead. Harris having been enticed out, Finlay put the ball quietly into a tenantless goal. On top of that Halligan "nodded" through a cross from Ritchie. A few minutes later Preston was brought down after a delightfully clever bit of work. Ritchie's shot from the penalty-spot was the sort no goalkeeper could save—a cannon-ball drive that burst a hole in the net.

TWICE-TAKEN "PENALTY."

Hibs. seemed "on velvet" now. But Dick put the Easter Road goal in danger by an awkward pass-back to Robb, and, in trying to better things, made them worse by bringing down Tallis. Wilson sunk the "penalty" all right, but as the ball entered the net the whistle went for an infringement by one of Hibs.' defenders, and John had to do the job all over again. Fortunately, he has a sure foot. Within a couple of minutes the Fife side were on level terms, T. W. Dickson putting on the equaliser following a "corner."

The Dunfermline defenders kept their end up during a trying last half-hour. Ritchie had another chance of scoring from the penalty-spot—the result of "hands" by Young—but his shot this time did no damage to the net. The ball went straight to Harris, who made a good clearance.

Hibs.' forwards were the superior company. Preston did lots of clever things, and Finlay played tolerably well in Dunn's position.

Dunfermline got best service from their defenders

Hibernian—Finlay, Halligan, Ritchie (p.). Dunfermline Athletic—Tallis, T. W. Dickson, Wilson (p.).

HIBERNIAN — Robb; Wilkinson and Stark; Murray, Dick, and Gilfeather; Ritchie, Finlay, M'Coll, Halligan, and Preston.

DUNFERMLINE ATHLETIC — Harris; Young and Wilson; Paterson Cameron, and Dand; Carruthers, Penman, Tallis, J. Dickson and T. W. Dickson.

Referee—A. Scott, Mossend.

RANGERS' SIXTH SCOTTISH CUP.

BREAKS THE ICE.

J. MARSHALL, Rangers.

HAIL! AGAIN, RANGERS.

MUCH PRAISE IS DUE TO PLUCKY PARTICK.

OUR CITY OF SOCCER.

By "Waverley."

IT'S all over. The 1930 Scottish Cup final is a thing of the past and that blessed pot goes where I thought it would since the third stage of the competition—since Motherwell went out. Partick Thistle's Firhill band, who fought a plucky fight, have reason to congratulate themselves and be congratulated by many more than their own directors.

IBROX'S TEAM OF THE YEAR.

While dubbing Rangers the team of the year, I raise my hat to the clever Queen's Cross combine, nine of whom were juniors when they arrived at Firhill.

As I have told you before, only Jamie Rae and Davie Ness had any previous senior experience. Rae was four years with King's Park at Stirling, and Ness has only a month or two with Sanquhar's senior club.

FROM THE JUNIORS DIRECT.

Playing in last night's successful Rangers side were Tom Hamilton, Dougie Gray, Davie Meiklejohn and Jamie Marshall, who came direct from the juniors. Their calf clubs—Kirkintilloch Rob Roy, Aberdeen Mugiemoss, Maryhill and Shettleston respectively.

When we remember the Thistle's team worries round about semi-final time the merit of their performance is considerably enhanced. They were forced ultimately to go on without Dennis O'Hare and Johnny Simpson.

ALAN MORTON CROCKED.

Rangers, too, have had their team worrries. Jock Buchanan was unable to strip last night, and Alan Morton, after standing down suffering from a leg muscle pulled at Wembley, was crocked midway through the first half last night.

I said yesterday that if the weather kept fine I would look for the hundred thousand being topped. It was. Hampden Park presented a pretty picture, and as on Saturday everything passed off without a hitch—surely a tribute to this dark sea-born city—our great city of football.

ORDERLY GLASGOW.

Mr. A. D Smith, Glasgow's Chief Constable, has a good word to say of our football crowds. The other day "A. D." told me with a touch of pride in his voice that Saturday's match at Hampden finished at four forty-five, and that by six o'clock the traffic in the city was normal. More—not a single accident was reported. Wonderful.

PROUD MEIKLEJOHN.

It was difficult to get a word with Davie Meiklejohn, so busy was he receiving congratulations, a considerable number of which were from ladies.

"Considering we finished with ten men, our victory was splendid. Proud I am to be captain of the winning team. the Thistle put up a magnificent fight, and were worthy opponents."

CRAIG'S SHOT A LOB.

Alec Lambie considered Partick were a bit unlucky in losing the second goal. Craig's counter, I am certain, was meant for a lob into the middle of the goal, and would have been saved had the sun not been blinding Jackson. Had we done extra time I think we would have won.

"But we have no regrets. One of the teams had to win, and I congratulate the Rangers wholeheartedly. We undoubtedly were beginning to get a real grip towards the end. The sun and wind were disturbing factors, and it was late on before our boys really settled. But here's a hand to the winners."

THE FIRHILL MANAGER.

Mr. Donald Turner, the Firhill manager, was disappointed that extra time had not been played. "Our boys were just beginning to get into their stride in the later stages of the game, and I feel certain they would have given something like their usual form had that goal of Craig's not come along in the last four minutes.

"But, after all, we were beaten by a better side. I congratulate Rangers, not only on their victory, but on their magnificent achievements during the season."

104,000 SEE THEM CONQUER PARTICK THISTLE.

MERITED WIN UNDER HANDICAP.

By JACKY ROBERTSON, Scottish International Half-Back.

Rangers..................2 Partick Thistle..................1

At Hampden Park.

FOR the sixth time, Rangers are winners of the Scottish Cup, the most coveted prize in football. They beat worthy opponents in Partick Thistle, last night, at Hampden Park, where 104,000 people witnessed the replay after a goalless draw on Saturday, when the crowd numbered 108,000. Great is football! Rangers won despite the handicap of a muscle injury sustained by Alan Morton, who was lame for a three-quarters part of the match. Marshall scored for Rangers the only goal of the first half four minutes from the interval, while playing against a strong wind. Torbet equalised 26 minutes after the restart, and Craig registered the winning goal five minutes from time.

YOU will remember, perhaps, what I told you about the effects of Wembley on the Rangers players as seen on Saturday. Well, here at Hampden last night, the effects had worn off. It was a different Rangers team altogether.

Rangers, facing the stiff wind in the first half, were the only team who played the game as we expected both to play it, and more especially the Thistle, who, as on Saturday, had the great good fortune to win the toss.

But the Thistle sadly disappointed in the first half. Nobody seemed able to pull the team together. Passes were short or into the feet of an opponent. And Rangers were not slow to take full advantage of what was offered them. Though their goal was delayed until four-and-a-half minutes from the interval, they had, long before that, proved themselves the superior side, both in team work, positional play, and individually.

EVEN a mishap to Alan Morton, about 15 minutes after the start, which rendered him of little use afterwards, could not be turned to advantage by the Thistle. In centring from the touchline with his right foot, he jarred his thigh muscles. It is, as I know only too well, a most painful injury, and it gets worse the longer you remain on the field.

Rangers more than merited their narrow half-time lead. From the way they had played, I looked for an even better second-half display, when they had the wind, but, for some curious reason, the standard of play all round went back. Rangers came back somewhat to the Thistle's level, although still

Cup Crowd—Cash.
Saturday—
107,475 ... ... £4424 12s 6d.

having the best of it. Morton's incapacity had begun to tell; and, under the circumstances, I think the ball was played too much to him.

THISTLE'S LOST CHANCE.

WHEN Torbet equalised, 26 minutes after the second half had started, the Thistle had a great chance to pull themselves together. They missed the chance completely, faded back, and were deservedly beaten by Craig's goal scored five minutes from the end.

Many finals have been won by curious goals. This was another. I think the sun in Jackson's eyes may have been troubling him, but, in any case, Craig's quickly-taken lob, beautifully timed, did not seem so difficult to save as many of the shots the Thistle custodian had previously saved.

But, on the game, as a whole, Rangers right well deserved to win the Cup for the sixth time. As for the Thistle, they must have some regrets, for they were not half the team they were in the first game. I could not fathom them at all. Still, they have done well to get to the final.

WELL DONE!

I CONGRATULATE the winners, and condole with the losers. I know what it is to be in a Scottish Cup winning team, and in a defeated one, as well.

All the players were agreed that the wind was worse than in the first game, and there is nothing worse than a wind when you are trying to play real football. Beating into it, the Rangers half-backs sent the ball well through to the forwards. Marshall and Archibald were strong on the run, and from their driving movements the Thistle defence was hard put to it.

Once Fleming went in with a lovely pass from Marshall, and there was instant danger for Thistle when Rae, anticipating Fleming's run-in, got his foot to the ball just as the Ibrox centre shot.

THE longer the game went, the more surprising was the grip the Rangers took. Half-backs and forwards worked the ball skilfully and seemed able to judge the breeze to a fraction. But the Thistle half-backs could not get the weight of it at all, and the forwards quite failed to get together.

It was no surprise when Rangers went ahead. M'Donald, who had been playing with rare judgment, swung the ball across. Marshall fastened on, and without hesitation, shot hard. Lambie was in the way, and the ball rebounded to Marshall, who, this time, shot hard into the net low down at Jackson's left hand. There was a telling click in the shot, and Jackson, with a crowd of men in front of him, had no chance to make a desperate save.

JACKSON'S SAVES.

THIS happened, as I have told you, four-and-a-half minutes from the interval. It was good going for Rangers to score against such a breeze, and I looked for something special from them after the turn-round. Here we were disappointed.

Morton, of course, was practically a passenger, and Meiklejohn came by an injury which caused him to go behind the goal for repairs. But in the first few minutes of the second half, Fleming got away a great shot which Jackson saved grandly.

Rangers were still playing the better game, although nothing like so good as in the first half. Jackson saved again brilliantly from Marshall, and then Archibald swept the ball just over the bar.

But the danger was not all at the one end. From a miskick by Newry Hamilton, Grove got through, and just as he was boring in on goal, Craig dashed round and nipped the ball away from Grove's toe.

TORBET'S EQUALISER.

THEN came the equaliser with 27 minutes of the second half gone. Ness got well away, and centred right across to the other wing. Torbet met

RANGERS CUPS.

1893-4	Celtic	3-1
1896-7	Dumbarton	5-1
1897-8	Kilmarnock	2-0
1902-3	Hearts	2-0
1927-8	Celtic	4-0
1929-30	Partick Thistle	2-1

the ball first time, and his right foot shot, from close in, left Hamilton helpless.

Right on the top of this the Rangers' forwards went through and Jackson drew loud cheers for another grand save from M'Phail. When M'Leod sent Torbet away a fine chance was opened up for the Thistle. Torbet transferred to Ness, who had a clear run in, but Hamilton recovered quickly and dispossessed him.

By this time the play had fallen off, and there was some rash passing. There were visions of another draw, but it was not to be. Less than five minutes from the end Marshall was tearing through with a pass from Meiklejohn when his heels were clicked.

CRAIG'S MASTERPIECE.

MEIKLEJOHN placed the free-kick into the goalmouth. Lambie headed out, and Craig, catching the falling ball on the instep of the left foot, sent it, from about 25 yards out, high towards goal.

It was a splendidly-judged effort by Craig, and I rather fancy the alertness and the accuracy with which he took his chance surprised Jackson. The sun, too, may have been in the Thistle goalkeeper's eyes. He never got his hands to the ball, and—the Cup was won.

In the last minute Morton hobbled in to accept a certain chance when the ball came over from the right, but his injury beat him.

BOTH Hamilton and Jackson did their parts well, although I thought the Thistle man was not so cool and confident as he usually is; still, there is no doubt he saved Thistle from a heavier defeat. Hamilton had very little to do by comparison.

Gray was a splendid back all through. I liked particularly his heading in the first half, when he had to make some desperate interventions. Newry Hamilton was best in the second half. His recovery to beat Ness was one of the best things he did in the tie.

Rae played another fine defensive game. He had something to grapple with in Marshall, and he stood to his guns with magnificent courage. Calderwood seemed upset a bit by Elliot's uncertainty, and though he did well his game was not so finished as in Saturday's match.

HALF-BACKS ON TOP.

AT half-back Rangers were greatly superior, especially in the first half, when M'Donald and Craig played beautifully to their forwards, with nice variations in their passing. Meiklejohn was a grand tactician. I hope any young players present were taking note of his heading back which, as I have often said, is one of the most valuable assets a man can have against a breeze. Forward heading against the breeze is

Cup Crowd—Cash.
Last Night—
103,688 ... ... £4269 19s 2d.

always dangerous. Such great centre half-backs as James Cowan, Johnny Holt, and Bobby Neil were adepts at the head-back.

What went wrong with the Thistle half-backs? In the first half Elliott and M'Leod made many mistakes, and even Lambie seemed unable to make the ball answer. M'Leod came better on to his game in the second half, but he could not get his forwards to galvanise themselves into life.

Marshall was the most paying forward on the ground. He was a tremendous worker—going back, coming on, shoving the ball to the right and through the centre, and—well, didn't he begin the scoring? In the first half, Archibald forged ahead in dashing style, and got the ball across well. Fleming was getting a lot of balls too high, but he was always in the busy places.

M'PHAIL AND CRAIG.

M'PHAIL and Craig showed some of the prettiest combination in the match, and, until he was injured, Morton joined in to make a triangle of it.

Thistle's forwards disappointed me. They can play very much better—I have seen them do it. They did it on Saturday. Ballantyne tried hard, but he could not get the machinery to work. Torbet, I thought the best of the line, but even he was not the thrustive raider I have seen him.

Ness seemed to lack confidence in himself, and Grove's passes too often lacked precision. The sense of touch was lost. Boardman, between two wings playing below their best, could not get scope to fit in.

But, here's to both teams. It may be Thistle's turn next time.

RANGERS CUP-WINNING TEAMS.

1893-4.	1896-7.	1897-8.	1902-3.	1927-8.	1929-30.
D. Haddow.	M. Dickie.	M. Dickie.	M. Dickie.	T. Hamilton.	T. Hamilton.
N. Smith.	N. Smith.	N. Smith.	A. Fraser.	D. Gray.	D. Gray.
J. Drummond.	J. Drummond.	J. Drummond.	J. Drummond.	R. Hamilton	R. Hamilton
R. Marshall.	N. Gibson.	N. Gibson.	G. Henderson.	J. Buchanan.	R. Macdonald.
A. M'Creadie.	A M'Creadie.	R. G. Neil.	J. Stark.	D. Meiklejohn.	D. Meiklejohn.
D. Mitchell.	D. Mitchell.	D. Mitchell.	J. T. Robertson.	T. Craig.	T. Craig
J. Steel	T. Low.	J. Miller.	A. Macdonald.	A. Archibald.	A. Archibald.
H. M'Creadie.	J. M'Pherson.	J. M'Pherson.	A. Mackie.	A. Cunningham.	J. Marshall.
J. Gray	J. Miller.	R. C. Hamilton.	R. C. Hamilton.	J. Fleming.	J. Fleming.
J. M'Pherson.	T. Hyslop.	T. Hyslop.	F. Speedie.	R. M'Phail.	R. M'Phail.
J. Barker.	A. Smith.	A. Smith.	A. Smith.	A. Morton.	A. Morton.

RANGERS.

T. HAMILTON.
D. GRAY.
R. HAMILTON.
R. M'DONALD.
D. MEIKLEJOHN, CAPT.
T. CRAIG
A. ARCHIBALD.
J. MARSHALL.
J. FLEMING.
R. M'PHAIL.
A. MORTON.

Referee—W. Bell, Motherwell.

PARTICK.

J. JACKSON.
S. CALDERWOOD.
J. RAE.
A. ELLIOTT.
A. LAMBIE.
E. M'LEOD.
D. NESS.
R. GROVE.
G. BOARDMAN.
J. BALLANTYNE.
J. TORBET.

THE WINNER.

T. Craig, Rangers.

AFTER THE BATTLE.

NICE THINGS SAID OF BOTH TEAMS.

RANGERS' ½-MILLION.

By "Waverley."

IN the Hampden Recreation Room "after the battle," Mr. R. Campbell, the S.F.A. president, opened the proceedings by saying that the crowd had broken all records for mid-week games. Mr. Campbell was introduced by his vice-president, Mr. James Fleming, of Paisley.

"To the thousands who, like myself," continued Mr. Campbell, "belong to the unattached, sympathy must be felt for the losers and congratulations for the winners. The tie contained much of the most stern, strenuous football I have seen for years. Partick Thistle have fought their way through the ties, and they have fallen very gallantly indeed." (Cheers.)

A VALIANT FIGHT.

"Rangers, too, have fought a valiant fight. They have won through only after a very long struggle. I liked the fine sporting spirit in which the tie was fought. There were never any untoward incidents.

Mr. Campbell went on to speak of the growing appeal of the Scottish Cup competition. He pointed out that this year the ties all over the country have been witnessed by more people than ever before.

RANGERS' RECORD.

Rangers had set up a record that is unique all over Britain. In their ties this season they had attracted something like half-a-million people. Rangers are undoubtedly the team of the year, concluded Mr. Campbell. "This we acknowledge with pride."

After the Trophy had been handed over, Bailie J. Buchanan replied. He thanked the chairman for his complimentary reference to the Rangers' team. He complimented his players on their grand endurance in a long and testing fight.

SUPERIORITY AND PUNCH.

He referred to the game as a typical Cup-tie—hard, fast and without quarter. "Victory," he declared, "went to the team that had that little bit extra superiority and punch.

"Partick Thistle have a good team and it may be their turn next. If they win 'the Scottish' next year, no one will be more sincere in their congratulations than the Rangers F.C."

ONE CONSOLATION.

Mr. Tom Rei, the Firhill chairman, was short, and very much to the point. He was a disappointed man, but he thought, nevertheless, that his boys had played a very good game. "There is one consolation for us at any rate, we have played a Scottish team (laughter) to a goal. I am only sorry both teams could not win."

Q.P. POLICE—THANKS.

Mr. W. M'Intosh, the S.F.A. treasurer, thanked the chairman for the dignified manner in which he had passed over the trophy. In reply Mr. Robert Campbell said a few closing words.

He thanked Queen's Park F.C. and the police for their perfect arrangements in and out of the ground. After the recent experience they had gone through at Wembley, he thought that the London Police and officials would do well to come North to learn how to conduct a huge crowd.

MR. W. STRUTH.

Mr. William Struth, the Rangers' manager, happy with the result, said that while both games had been strenuously contested, they had been fought out in a manly and sportsmanlike spirit. "I think we were just the better side and deserved to win, but I must congratulate the losers on their gallant fight. They died gamely."

PRAISE FOR M'DONALD.

Johnny Ballantyne was disappointed, and said so. "We were sort of unlucky in respect that Jackson was blinded by the sun when Craig sent in the shot that won the Cup. The wind put us off our usual game, the conditions for playing being even worse than Saturday. And —I want to compliment M'Donald; the Rangers' right half-back played a splendid game."

Daily Record
and Mail
THURSDAY, APRIL 17, 1930

RANGERS WIN SCOTTISH CUP AFTER THRILLING REPLAY.

Meiklejohn, the captain (centre) with Craig and Marshall, the goal-scorers, wearing the smile of victory as they pose beside the coveted Cup.—"Daily Record" photograph.

Jackson, the Thistle custodian, punching clear during a brisk bit of work.—"Daily Record" photograph.

Lambie (Thistle) heads clear from Fleming (Rangers) in the Thistle goal-mouth.—"Daily Record" photograph.

An incident in the Partick Thistle goal area during last night's thrilling Scottish Cup Final replay at Hampden before 103,688 spectators. Rangers won 2-1. Left to right:—Jackson, M'Leod, Rae, Elliot, Lambie, and Calderwood (Thistle) and Fleming (Rangers).—"Daily Record" photograph.

BRINGING UP FATHER : : : : : BY GEORGE McMANUS.

RANGERS RECORD THEIR 7th SCOTTISH CUP TRIUMPH

105,000 OUT AT HAMPDEN.

GLASGOW GREAT CITY OF FOOTBALL.

WONDERFUL!

By "Waverley."

AGAIN Glasgow's great city of football has given itself over to our wonderful game. Last night at Hampden Park 105,000 assembled to see the finish up of the Rangers-Kilmarnock final tie, which was drawn at one all on the same field on Saturday.

WONDERFUL ALMOST.

This assemblage—wonderful for a week evening—fell only some two thousand short of the week-end attendance. A slight rainfall had rendered the pitch just sufficiently holding, and as there was no wind to speak of the conditions were really ideal.

"KILLIE" NOT QUITE SO KEEN.

While Kilmarnock fought a good stuffy fight it early became evident that their tackling and forcing work was not quite so keen as on Saturday. And—Rangers, who had brought in Jamie Fleming for the injured Alan Morton, were a stronger force forward.

A BETTER RANGERS.

All over, too, they were a better, a more powerful, a more business-like company. To Jamie Fleming fell the credit and satisfaction of registering the first goal—this in the eleventh minute. In the middle of the field at the moment he let go first time from a good twenty-five yards out, and Willie Bell was beaten.

SECOND HALF GOALS.

Round about the middle of the second half—and one goal came two minutes after the other—Archibald and English consolidated the Ibrox position. Rangers were easy winners now.

GRAY AND M'AULAY—GREAT.

I liked the Ibrox defenders. Dougie Gray and Bob M'Aulay—beautiful backs—lived up to the high estimate I have formed of their ability. They were again surely the best club pair in Scotland.

TOM SMITH OF KILLIE.

Forward Alec Archibald, Jamie Fleming and Sam English were best. Of the Kilmarnock forces young Tom Smith delighted me most. A coming Scotland centre half-back is this young man, I feel. He goes to France with the S.F.A., you will notice.

YOUNG BUD MAXWELL.

Hugh Morton, knocked in contact with Davie Meiklejohn, was a sticker throughout. Forward I was delighted with young Maxwell. The pity is that he had to fend so much for himself. "Bud" didn't get the ball as he should.

A GOLDEN CUP.

I congratulate "Auld Killie" on their grand final fight, and also on the pot of money they take out of this (for them and Rangers) golden cup. But—Jacky Robertson deals with the match in the adjoining columns.

WILLIE MALEY "SHAKES."

At the close of the Cup final, Willie Maley, the Celtic secretary-manager, looked into the Rangers dressing-room. He heartily congratulated the Ibrox players, with whom he shook hands all round, and told them they were the better team.

JAMIE KERR'S THIRD.

Jamie Kerr, the Rangers trainer, will collect his third Scottish Cup medal—come the time. The Ibrox trainer has now looked after three Scottish Cup-winning teams.

TOM HAMILTON'S "FAGS"—WON.

Tom Hamilton landed a little bet over the final. The Ibrox custodian had a wager of a box of cigarettes that he wouldn't lose a goal in the replay. And let me add that big Tam has a tremendously high opinion of young Tom Smith, the "Killie" centre half-back.

MONTROSE'S MEN.

Montrose make for the Capital on Saturday. The Links Park club will field the appended eleven against Edinburgh City:—

Gerrand; M'Intosh and J. M'Donald; Burns, G. White, and Robertson; Paterson, M'Meekin, R. M'Donald, T. White, and Garland.

WHAT'S ON TO-NIGHT.

ABERDEENSHIRE CUP—Final. (Second Game.)

Huntly v. Aberdeen, at Christie Park.

INVERNESS CUP—Semi-Final.

Caledonian v. Citadel.

ON TOUR.

Ross County v. Dundee, at Dingwall.

EDINBURGH DISTRICT LEAGUE.

Murrayfield Amateurs v. Bathgate, at Pinkhill.

SCOTTISH LEAGUE (EASTERN SECTION).

Camelon v. Denny Hibernian.

DUNDEE LEAGUE.

Violet v. Arnot.

ABERDEEN COUNTY CUP—First Round.

Hawthorn v. Banks o' Dee.
Richmond v. Parkvale.
Woodside v. Muglemoss.

FIFE ADVERTISER CUP—Semi-Final Replay.

Novar Athletic v. Burntisland United, at Dunnikier Park, Sinclairtown.

Dundee (Campbell 2, Robertson, Troup), 4; Highland Select (Scott), 1. At Station Park, Nairn.

SCOTTISH CUP FINAL REPLAY.

Rangers' Seventh Cup Triumph.

J. Fleming, Rangers.

STRENGTH AND PACE TELLS—FLEMING'S SNAPPY GOAL IN 11th MINUTE—KILLIE FIGHT PLUCKILY—M'PHAIL AND ENGLISH SETTLE IT.

T. Smith, Kilmarnock.

WINNERS FINISH THE STRONGER SIDE.

By JACKY ROBERTSON.

Rangers............3 Kilmarnock............0 (At Hampden Park)

RANGERS are winners of the Scottish Cup for the seventh time. That is not as often as they might have won it, but they should be satisfied.

When the players got back to their dressing-room at Hampden last night, they were all very happy, quietly happy, for men who have been through the mill get used to ups and downs, and don't make a fuss whether they win or lose.

I want to say right away that Rangers were good, out-and-out winners. Even if they did not touch the game all the time which I have seen them produce more than once this season, they were too strong and too clever for plucky Kilmarnock.

The real turning point was at the period of the second half when Rangers, within a couple of minutes, scored their second and third goals.

THE RIGHT STUFF.

They were playing then as I would expect them always to play. The game they pursued was open and fast, and the ball was finding the man every time. It showed what real football is worth.

Kilmarnock fought it gallantly until the issue was beyond them. Rangers' second goal practically put their hopes to rest, and the third goal sealed their doom. But old Killie need have no regrets. They have fought a good fight, and can look back on the 1932 twice-played final with a good deal of pride.

The conditions were almost perfect. Rain had given a grip to the ground, and there was practically no wind, so that the players had a chance to judge the pass.

And 105,000 spectators let themselves be heard. That great Rangers roar when the team came out, and when the goals were scored, showed that Ibrox was out to a man; but Kilmarnock also had good support, and they deserved all they had.

RANGERS TAKE THE LEAD.

There was really no advantage in Rangers winning the toss. They opened with a flourish, and in the first minute Archibald raced clear of Nibloe and swished the ball across in front of goal. M'Phail tried to connect, but the ball was travelling too fast.

Maxwell eased the Rangers pressure with a dash through the middle, but Rangers' forwards came on again. The Kilmarnock defence was hard pressed, and it was no surprise when Rangers went ahead in the eleventh minute.

In an attempt to clear an overhead kick by English, Bell put the ball out to his right. Fleming, who was well in, fastened on, and, getting the ball to his right foot, shot hard. It was going away from Bell all the time, and though he got his hands to it he could not prevent it going into the net.

KILMARNOCK COME ON.

This set the Rangers going in style, and Bell, with his left hand, punched away a shot by Archibald, who was going great guns.

Then on came the Kilmarnock forwards. Maxwell cleverly trapped the ball, wheeled and transferred to Aitken, who went ahead and shot for Hamilton, safe as a house, to save.

In a collision, M'Aulay and Connell were injured, and, following the throw down, Smith twice drove the ball towards the Rangers goal, and Hamilton had to be on his mettle to get it away.

Then more Rangers. Archibald raced in to take a pass from Marshall, who was keeping the game open hereabout, but Nibloe tore across and managed to spoil the shot.

Kilmarnock changed the scene. With Brown lying crippled, Morton came through with the ball, but Meiklejohn ran across and conceded a free kick to stop the "Killie" right half.

HAMILTON THERE.

Smith took the free kick, and Hamilton had to save quickly with Maxwell in on him. Then English was hurt, and his nose was bleeding, but he carried on.

Kilmarnock had strengthened all over by this time, and were holding their own well. They even forced the game with all the appearance of getting through the Rangers defence, but their inside forwards failed at the vital moment. So far the play had not run well for Connell and Aitken, and this made all the difference to Kilmarnock. Maxwell was the real danger, and with head and feet he showed some very clever moves.

COLLISIONS.

Rangers were making the running when the interval arrived, and they opened the second half in the same breezy style. But a halt had to be called when English and Leslie collided, and the Ibrox centre had to go to the touchline for attention. Hard on top of this, M'Phail and Morton collided, and were in the trainers' hands.

Following a bit of strong Kilmarnock attack, which looked good, Rangers forced them on to the defensive, and M'Phail had a great chance from English, but headed wide with only Bell to beat.

In the next minute, a centre by Archibald was taken by English, who looked a scorer when Leslie came to the rescue. We were seeing some real Rangers pressure now, and Fleming, after cleverly eluding Morton and Leslie, shot across goal, with no takers.

BELL THE BOY.

From another Fleming centre, Marshall, two yards out, got the ball to his feet, but he failed to get in the shot properly, and it went behind. Bell was doing grand work here, and I feel I must give him a hearty pat on the back before I go any farther.

The pace set by the Rangers forwards could be seen to be telling on the Kilmarnock wing half-backs and backs, and after 24 minutes of the second half the second goal came.

Leslie conceded a corner to Fleming, and when the ball was cleared it travelled to Archibald, who centred beautifully. English, clearly with purpose, avoided the ball, as he was covered by Smith. It was a wise move, for when M'Phail met it with his right foot, he was clear to shoot into Bell's left-hand corner of the net.

AND ANOTHER.

If this was not enough to send the Cup to Ibrox, the third goal, scored two minutes later, did it. Kilmarnock conceded a free-kick in a dangerous position. Marshall took up position to take it, but Captain Meiklejohn said, "I'll take it"; and, approaching the ball as if going for a smashing shot, placed it, instead, over the heads of the Killie defenders.

Bell came out, but before he could reach the ball English got to it with his head, and cleverly steered it into the net over the goalkeeper's head.

It was all over now, but Kilmarnock fought to the end, and seemed determined to go down with colours flying. Muir got in a shot which Hamilton saved well, but the greater danger was at the other end, and Fleming might have headed another goal, after Marshall had placed the ball sweetly to him.

WORTHY WINNERS.

That Rangers deserved to win the old Cup no one will deny. They were superior in team play, and though not absolutely at their best all the time they showed what was in them when the match seemed won.

No one knows better than I do the strain that is on players in a final. We are not all built alike, and allowance has to be made for that.

One thing that stood well to the Rangers was their knowledge of one another's moves.

The younger forwards on the Kilmarnock side seemed upset by the bigness of the occasion, though I am bound to say that Maxwell revealed great ability, which he would have turned to account had Muir and Duncan been able to bring him more into action.

Hamilton was a grand goalkeeper for the winners. He never made a mistake, and his clutching of the ball and cleanness in his general work could not but give confidence to all his colleagues.

NUMBER ONE BACKS.

And what splendid backs were Gray and M'Aulay! They could not have been better. Gray's timing with head and feet was very nearly perfect, while M'Aulay took everything with a confidence and power that must have been a complete reversal of his Saturday's display, from all I heard.

Neither Aitken nor Connell ever had a chance to exploit their undoubted cleverness. Meiklejohn and Brown were usually in the way and would not leave an opening for Muir and Duncan to get the wingers free.

Simpson did his part well, and could always be depended upon.

In the Rangers front—well, now, here's something for you. Sandy Archibald, going since 1917, was the war horse—the best forward on the ground. Why, he was an inspiration to the entire team. He was strong, elusive, direct, and powerful in his centring. Well played, Sandy! On the other wing, Fleming was another strong raider, and his goal was a beauty.

SMITH A TOWER.

Rangers' inside forward game did not work well until the second goal came, but both Marshall and M'Phail then came on as I know they can do, and that made the real Rangers. English had a hard row to hoe against Smith, a strong, capable young centre-half, who has a future, or I am mistaken. I admired no one more than Smith. He comes out, and is enterprising. But Sam got his goal, and was happy.

I give great praise to Kilmarnock's defence. They had a hard fight, and if the pressure told on them they had no discredit in that. Bell kept a grand goal in every way, and Leslie and Nibloe stood firm as long as possible. Morton's knock tired him, and M'Ewan found Archibald too strong for him. But "Killie" died gamely.

Rangers—Fleming, M'Phail and English.

THE TEAMS.

RANGERS.	KILMARNOCK.
T. Hamilton.	W. Bell.
D. Gray.	J. Leslie.
R. M'Aulay.	J. Nibloe.
D. Meiklejohn.	H. Morton.
J. Simpson.	T. Smith.
G. Brown.	J. M'Ewan.
A. Archibald.	W. Connell.
J. Marshall.	J. Muir.
S. English.	J. Maxwell.
R. M'Phail.	J. Duncan.
J. Fleming.	J. Aitken.

Referee—P. Craigmyle, Aberdeen.

HOW J. FLEMING PUT THE RANGERS IN FRONT.

Rangers' first goal in the replayed Scottish Cup Final against Kilmarnock at Hampden Park, Glasgow, last night.—"Daily Record" photograph.

AFTER THE BATTLE.

CUP HANDED OVER TO THE RANGERS.

216,000 PEOPLE LOOK ON

By "Waverley."

IN the Queen's Park Boardroom after the match, in presence of all the football heads, the Cup was handed over to the Rangers. Mr. Robert Campbell, the S.F.A. Chairman, opened by saying that 216,000 people had watched this Scottish Cup final over the two matches. "This," continued Mr. Campbell, "was a wonderful tribute to our game, to the Scottish competition, and to the clubs who had contested the final so strenuously.

"RUBBER" FOR IBROX.

"Kilmarnock and Rangers were very old clubs with honoured careers, and it was not the first time they had met in the final. They had met three times. Each prior to this engagement had won a match, so that that day Rangers had carried off the 'rubber.' Two splendidly contested matches, and — although Rangers had won by what was regarded in football as a very definite score, the proceedings never lost the merit of a great contest."

CONGRATULATIONS.

Mr. Campbell thought that Kilmarnock deserved their congratulations and commendations for the great game they had put up. They had a very young team, and it was to their credit that that team was recruited largely from their own famous county of Ayrshire.

FOR SEVENTH TIME.

Rangers he heartily congratulated also. Mr. Campbell was sure that the football public of Scotland would congratulate them on winning the cup for the seventh time.

A WORD FOR THE CROWD.

Before handing over the cup to ex-Bailie Buchanan, the S.F.A. chairman paid a little tribute to the conduct of the crowd at these two matches. It was wonderful how they had behaved so orderly in assembling and in parting.

TO THE POLICE, TOO.

They had also to pay tribute to Captain Sillitoe, Glasgow's new Chief of Police, and to his staff, for the manner in which they dealt with the assemblages. The police deserved the very best thanks. He also congratulated the Queen's Park people, whose arrangements were always of the very highest value.

WHAT A HOPE.

It was now his duty and privilege, he said, to hand over this very coveted trophy to ex-Bailie J. Buchanan to take charge of for another year. "Might I hope," continued Mr. Campbell, "that the ex-Bailie will also hope that it would be handed to some other club next year." (Laughter and cheers.)

EX-BAILIE BUCHANAN.

Ex-Bailie Buchanan said that, on behalf of the Rangers Club, he had great pleasure in accepting the custody of this coveted trophy, the Scottish Cup. He thanked Mr. Campbell for the exceedingly kind and complimentary references which he had made regarding the Rangers, and which he assured him were appreciated very highly indeed.

THRICE IN FIVE YEARS.

That was the third time within the last five years that Rangers had won the Cup. It was a record of which his club were proud.

HONOUR AND PRESTIGE.

He knew what it had meant to their players—it was a most strenuous and testing time. But they would regard it as a source of great satisfaction that their efforts had brought to the club honour and added prestige.

HISTORY, AND A HOPE.

Bailie Buchanan then reviewed briefly the history of the clubs. This he followed by expressing the hope that all who were interested in the game would see that nothing was done to imperil the position it occupied as being their principal sport.

MR. DOUGLAS DICK.

Mr. Dick, replying, said that he would not camouflage the position so far as to say he was the happiest man in Glasgow that night. His little team was not taking home that little bit of silver, but he was not downhearted. (Hear, hear). He wanted to compliment the Rangers on the sporting way in which their men had played the game and wished them every success in the future.

AWAY WITH A RED FACE.

He then told a story to illustrate how strenuous an opposition Kilmarnock had put up. An English gentleman went to Aberdeen for the shooting. One day he had a shot at a pheasant, but missed it. The gamekeeper remarked that he hadn't brought that one down. "No," replied the Englishman, "I did not, but it is away with a red face." (Laughter.)

TO RANGERS THE PALM.

Mr. Dick did not think that Rangers would object to his saying that they sent them home with a red face. He must, however, give the palm to Rangers. They were just a little too good for Kilmarnock, and he might just as well say that the cheques Kilmarnock would receive for these games would be more welcome than the Cup. Mr. Wm. M'Intosh, the hon. treasurer of the S.F.A., moved a hearty vote of thanks to Mr. Campbell for the able way he had presided. That was all.

SCOTTISH CUP'S EIGHTH VISIT TO IBROX

HANDING CUP OVER

Rangers' Colts At The Ceremony

By "Waverley"

SIDE-LIGHTS from the Scottish Cup presentation ceremony are worth putting on record. In the Queen's Park library and billiards room, Mr. James Fleming, chairman of the S.F.A. and also a director of St. Mirren, caused a laugh when he "wondered" why Mr. Fred Linder, of Aston Villa, after seeing forty English Cup finals, had chosen this—his first Scottish final—for the visit! Sir John T. Cargill presented the Cup to Rangers' chairman, ex-Baillie Duncan Graham. Sir John added another touch of humour when he explained that he himself is not only honorary president of the S.F.A., but also of Rangers F.C.

TRIBUTE TO "CHIEF"

Mr. Fleming thanked quite a number of prominent people notably, the Glasgow Lord Provost and the Paisley Provost. He thanked also Captain Sillitoe, chief of the Glasgow Police, for the admirable arrangements. Sir John Cargill said that he had never played soccer. Rugby was his game till he was "crocked" at the age of twenty. But he recalled the days of Walter Arnott and the brothers Walters, of Corinthian full-back fame. These three, along with "that prince of goalkeepers, Macaulay," lived in his memory.

MAGIC NAME

At that stage in the speech I noticed right in front of me in the room a line of young capless fellows. One I identified when a comrade of his turned to him and saluted in a way that meant something. It meant a name. The name, "M'Aulay." This was the young fellow who is to be an inside-right star for Rangers in due course. Apparently all the Rangers' reserves had been sent in to the room to hear the presentation ceremony. Not a bad gesture on the part of Rangers' management! Just after the ceremony started, two prominent officials "gate-crashed." They were Chairman Tom Reid, of the Scottish League, and Manager Willie Struth, of Rangers.

MANAGER STRUTH STOPS

Mr. Reid penetrated the crowd and secured a place at the "top of the table." Mr. Struth stopped half-way to the dais. There he listened to the eulogism of the team. I'd like to have heard him speak about his eleven! But the Ibrox manager seldom says much. Manager Phil Bache, of Middlesbrough, was frankly disappointed with the game. But that doesn't mean that he was disappointed with certain players. Chairman Duncan Graham, of Rangers, struck a happy note when accepting the Cup. He said that Rangers had got into the habit now of taking the Cup every second year. "So you will see that we are not selfish."

SAINTS' CHAIRMAN

Chairman Tom Hart, of St. Mirren, was happy in his remarks. He couldn't go so far back as Sir John Cargill in his reminiscences, but he brought in a topical touch when he said that Rangers owed Saints something for clearing out Celtic and Motherwell—"teams that might have given Rangers a harder run than we did." All of which shows that St. Mirren accepted their defeat in the right way. The Saints' chairman added: "We live to fight another day." Of course, they do. But they'll have to fight with more skill and power.

* * * *

Sir Harry Lauder kicked off in the Morton Juniors and Yoker Athletic game at Cappielow. If Sir Harry remained through the game he saw Weir of Yoker and Wilson and Copland of Morton Juniors ordered off.

Rangers Outclass St. Mirren

Bobby Main, Rangers.

Brown Supreme Master: Saints' Heroic Defence: M'Cloy Quite Blameless: Nicholson's Fine Goals

Fulton Wilson, St. Mirren.

By "WAVERLEY"

Rangers.................5 St. Mirren..................0

At Hampden Park

RANGERS, by their smashing victory at Hampden, established themselves as one of the most brilliant combines in Scottish football since pre-war days. In every movement, in skill, in determination, in opportunism, they clearly outpointed St. Mirren. Their five goals victory eloquently indicates the measure of their superiority. St. Mirren failed to recapture even one minute of the flashing play that carried them through against Motherwell in the semi-final at Tynecastle. They themselves—and their representatives who spoke at the presentation of the Cup after the game—acknowledged the Light Blue might which staggered and shattered them.

Gone were all hopes of a St. Mirren victory, gone even the chance of a draw, when Davie Meiklejohn guessed correctly the fall of the coin. With that fast wind in their favour, and with a blinding sun to bemuse St. Mirren, Rangers had an advantage that was worth a "bundle" of goals. The luck that no one could anticipate fell to Rangers. It is idle to speculate what might have happened had St. Mirren won the toss. I simply must face the game as I saw it.

SAINTS' GALLANT MEN

For more than half-an-hour St. Mirren's gallant defenders held Rangers at bay. There was, however, one weak link in the Saints' defensive chain. Miller very seldom reproduced the live-wire tactics that earned him his Wembley cap. Slow in tackling and often out of position, he must have conveyed to the general of Light Blues side—Meiklejohn—the impression that he was off colour. Despite Ancell's early successful attention to Main, I anticipated that most danger would develop on that right wing.

DANGER ZONES

Yet after the half-hour the danger actually developed on the left, where Hay and Gebbie had courageously held M'Phail and Nicholson in check. Danger remained there till the interval. After that it switched over to the right, where Main took charge. Then it flitted about, prodding now Marshall, now Smith, now M'Phail, and never once alighting on a Paisley player—unless we consider that Miller received a touch when he hit the strongest shot of the match towards Tom Hamilton.

BETTER AGAINST WIND

At half-time my colleague "Brigadier" remarked to me, "Rangers will play better against the wind. You will see more control." And it was so. The Light Blues played the football that charms. With more convincing opposition we would probably have had a memorable second half. As it was, the impoverished play of the Saints' forwards robbed the match of any quality it may have possessed in the opening half-hour, and justified Chairman Fleming's remark at the Cup presentation: "Mr. Fred Linder, of Aston Villa, came North to see his first Scottish Cup final. I wonder why!"

THE GOALS

Nicholson's opening goal resulted from a fierce ball that might have found the net direct, but that was deflected by Ancell's shoulder. The second was secured by the ever-ready M'Phail, after Nicholson had shot in. M'Phail's deft flick into the net is the kind of thing that stamps a man as a master. All hopes of St. Mirren rejuvenation after the interval were dispelled when Miller blundered badly and let Main away to score brilliantly. This player in every move in the second half must have set Director Alan Morton jumping with joy, metaphorically. Here, on the right wing, we saw Alan himself again.

The fourth goal might not have been scored but for silly hesitation on the part of at least one St. Mirren defender. When Marshall, boring through, was grassed in the penalty area, a Saint sinned by turning to indicate to the referee that there had been no foul in the incident. Just then Jimmy Smith stepped in and very easily sped the ball well out of M'Cloy's reach. Nicholson capped an excellent day's work when he smartly added the fifth after an inviting cross from Main.

In a team which contained many stars, George Brown of Rangers stood out. On many occasions I have criticised Brown for his failure to assist his full-back thoroughly. This time he was the complete half-back, not merely checking an opponent, but also most times securing the ball in a tackle and then advancing with a definite purpose. Brown certainly earned the bouquet. His display, and that of others on the side, is a material argument in favour of fixing the big international game for a date after the Scottish and English finals.

THE TEAMS

ST. MIRREN—M'Cloy; Hay and Ancell; Gebbie, Wilson and Miller; Knox, Latimer, M'Gregor, M'Cabe and Phillips.

RANGERS — Hamilton; Gray and M'Donald; Meiklejohn, Simpson and Brown; Main, Marshall, Smith, M'Phail and Nicholson.

Referee—M. C. Hutton, Glasgow.

Rangers—Nicholson 2, M'Phail, Main, Smith.

FINAL BOUQUET

George Brown, a master of the football arts, took the honours in the Cup Final.

HAMILTON'S EASY DAY

Tom Hamilton accomplished all that was required—and that was mighty little—in Rangers' goal. Gray and M'Donald were not merely defending full-backs. They placed the ball brainily, particularly in the second half, when a hard-hit ball would have been blown back. Meiklejohn played the "veteran" part skilfully. His value is inestimable. Simpson seldom figured obtrusively. His was simply the watchman's part. Right well he acted! Brown I have mentioned.

MAIN A MORTON

Were not the bouquet to go to Brown, Main would get it. Here again we must regret that the international came before the Cup final. If the Scottish team were to be selected this afternoon, almost every man of Rangers would be favourite for a place—and Main would be one of the first to be selected. Marshall appeared in an entirely different light from that of Wembley. His understanding with Main provided a noteworthy feature. His pass for that third goal was as neat as Main's culminating shot.

WILSON'S BEST

Smith found a ready opponent in Wilson. The centre-half compelled the centre to wheel right or left, but usually Smith succeeded in applying an adroit touch that gave Marshall or M'Phail, or either winger, a chance to make progress. Smith was a big success. M'Phail recovered all his form. In harassing, in passing, in shooting, he showed that his rest has restored his energy. Nicholson I have seldom seen do better. He had a powerful adversary in Hay, but in the end he was master of that doughty defender.

M'CLOY EXCELLENT

M'Cloy I do not blame in any way. This lad had the hardest day's work of his career. On several occasions he saved brilliantly. Hay and Ancell clearly transcended the other sections of the Saints' team. Wilson I consider the best of the halfs. Ubiquitous and daring, he intervened as often on the wings as in the centre. I have never seen him do better. Gebbie topped Miller in both an attacking and a defending sense.

HELPLESS FORWARDS

What can I say about the Saints' forwards, save that I was extremely disappointed. I found no excuse for the useless Knox-Latimer switch (operated three times during the game) till I learned from a leading St. Mirren forward that Latimer was not up to par before the match. Even so, Knox would have been better on the wing all the time—if he was to be good at all. His free-kicks—one across and past, low, and the other over the bar, were far from his usual type. M'Gregor was much too light for the task at centre. The sturdier M'Cabe made a slightly better shape towards the end when he accepted the leading berth, and indeed he was the only Paisley forward with punch throughout the game. Phillips had far too much to do when facing Meiklejohn and the quick-stepping Gray. The light-haired winger could beat one man cleverly, but in a few yards he was confronted by a second, and had not the ability of Main to turn or to dart past.

COATBRIDGE SPECIAL TRAIN

Alloa's Newcomers To-Night

ALBION ROVERS are in such a promising position in the Second Division that they find themselves backed by supporters who a few weeks ago had given up hope of promotion. That's good. The Rovers will want all the support they can get when they start off on their journey to Dundee (Tannadice) on Saturday at one o'clock. The Rovers have organised a special excursion.

CHEAP TRIP

Those who intend to take advantage of the remarkably cheap fare—4s 6d—and a stop-over of three hours after the match—should apply at once to Mr. Webber Lees at the Cliftonhill ground or to the secretary of the Supporters' Club, Mr. Griffen, at 6a Finlayson Street, Coatbridge.

ALLOA'S TEAM

East Stirlingshire and Alloa must love each other; they are meeting three times in just a week. To-night the pair clash at Firs Park, Falkirk, where the 'Shire will welcome Alloa in the first of the Stirlingshire Cup final. The second game will be played on Saturday. Alloa have signed two new men for this game—Gerrand, the Montrose goalkeeper, and Cameron, the Cowdenbeath inside-left. The team—Gerrand; Young and Kerr; Bolling, M'Dougall and Polland; Hamilton, Curley, Bell, Cameron and Borland.

CELTS' CHANGES

Celtic play Hamilton at Parkhead to-night. Unfortunately for the green-and-white brigade Joe Kennaway and Peter Wilson will not be fit to play. The goalkeeper was rather badly injured in the game against Dundee, and Wilson has sprung a muscle. Wallace will take the goal position, and probably "Chic" Geatons will occupy Wilson's place. Young Divers will carry on at inside-left. This boy is a distinct attraction.

TREAT AT FIRHILL

Partick Thistle are apparently determined to give the public a chance to weigh up their young men in their Tuesday evening game against St. Mirren. Both M'Lennan and Bain are chosen, and Regan comes in in place of Ness. The half-back line is restored to normal by the return of M'Leod at left-half. The Firhill eleven:—Johnstone; Calderwood and Cumming; Elliot, Donnelly and M'Leod; Regan, Miller, M'Lennan, Ballantyne and Bain.

* * * *

Arsenal—leaders—beat Sunderland in the English League. Huddersfield, challengers for the flag, succumbed to Middlesbrough. Arsenal are "certs," just as Rangers are for the Scottish guerdon.

THE SCOTTISH CUP FINAL
20 PHOTOGRAPHERS DO SOME "SNAPPY" WORK —— M'CLOY KEEPS A BLACK AND WHITE WREATH IN THE BACK OF HIS GOAL.
BUT AFTER 15 MINUTES HE COULD HAVE DONE
WITH IT IN FRONT OF HIM.
AND WHEN 'NICKY' SCORED THE WHITE FLOWERS WILTED AND THINGS LOOKED VERY BLACK.
THEN M'PHAIL SCORED AND CREATED A COMMOTION IN THE CROWD — (SQUARE 18) AS THE WIRELESS ANNOUNCER SAYS.
18
PAISLEY FORWARD FINDS OUT THAT THE TON IN HAMILTON MEANS 20 HUNDRED WEIGHT
RANGERS GOT THE CUP AND
HIC!
A ST. MIRREN SUPPORTER GOT NO MORE THAN A HICCUP.
THERE WAS SUPPOSED TO BE 3000 PAISLEY MILL GIRLS THERE WHO COULD HAVE MADE A BETTER JOB OF PUTTING RANGERS "THROUGH THE MILL".

M'PHAIL PLAYS A CAPTAIN'S PART

AFTER THE FURORE

Tommy Craig Gets A Send-off

By "BRIGADIER"

WINNING cups has become such a habit with Rangers that even a "Scottish" victory does not ruffle them unduly. But in the Hampden dressing room at the finish of the final there was a feeling of satisfaction mingled with sincere sympathy for the Academicals.

This was no pretence. The Rangers players said frankly that though glad to win they would have been as glad to congratulate the Academicals on having got the Cup.

Coming off the field, the men of both teams spontaneously exchanged greetings. To the Rangers' room came Chairman James Lyon and Director Dodd to offer felicitations.

Players Dined

As is usual on these big occasions, the Rangers Board entertained the team to dinner in St. Enoch Hotel. Mr James Bowie, the chairman, and the other directors warmly congratulated the players on their fine victory.

Mr Bowie pointed out that the position of the players in the Rangers team was no sinecure. Every Saturday, they were called to produce something exceptional. All recognised the strain imposed on every man to live up to the consistency required at Ibrox.

Captain's Compliment

"Hamilton Academicals," said Mr. Bowie, "have proved worthy opponents, and no good Rangers would have grudged them a win."

Deputy Captain Bob M'Phail acknowledged the toast, and said that, while sorry Davie Meiklejohn had to stand down, he must compliment Jamie Kennedy, his substitute, on his very fine display.

Then came a note of sentiment and regret. Mr. Bowie said that, while everyone was only too pleased to congratulate their old colleague, Tommy Craig, on his appointment as manager of the Falkirk club, they felt deeply sorry that a severance should take place.

Tommy's contract had been renewed for another season, but when the directors were approached they readily agreed that he should have his chance to rise in his new sphere.

Good Luck To Tommy

"I am certain he will," added Mr. Bowie. "We all wish him the very best of luck—let's be certain of that."

As an old colleague, Mr. Alan Morton said he wished to associate himself with all that Mr. Bowie had said of Tommy. "If Tommy carries his Ibrox enthusiasm to Brockville—as he will do—he will be all right."

It was not without emotion that Tommy replied. He spoke of his happy times at Ibrox, and said, "Wherever I be, or wherever I go, I shall never forget the Rangers football club."

Addressing the younger players, he counselled them to pay strict attention to everything Manager Struth said to them. "Mr. Struth will be strict, but you will get a square deal from him always. He has got to be served, but he recognises service."

A Splendid Lot

The manager was not to get away without saying something. Mr. Bowie called upon him.

"I am fortunate," Mr. Struth said, "to have such a splendid lot of players with me. They love the blue jersey, and I know that nothing is too onerous for them to undertake. They have respect for the traditions of the club. Nothing matters so long as we carry on in the good old way."

And to finish, all hands went on deck to give Tommy Craig a great send-off.

MASTER OF STRATEGY IN RANGERS' CUP WIN

Harrison Live Wire Of Hamilton | Young Morgan Hero In Cup Baptism

By "WAVERLEY"

Rangers................2 Hamilton Academicals................1

THE MOMENT brings the man. How often have I observed it! Think back your Cup finals and you will find that in almost every one a player stands out in your memory. For me, Bob M'Phail will live in this narrowly-won 1935 final at Hampden.

To his genius, to his industrious fetching and carrying, to the inspiration he conveyed to his followers I attribute Rangers' success. After the game I heard him criticised for his first-half manœuvres. In my opinion, his first-half work laid the foundation of victory.

Where was M'Phail in that first half? Back with George Brown most of the time. M'Phail knew what Meiklejohn's absence meant. "Meek" is the man who usually weighs up the opponents, and compels his colleagues to adopt tactics to suit the circumstances. M'Phail early realised that Hamilton were very much on their toes. Harrison and M'Laren prompted Reid and King. The inside men, possibly deliberately, left Dave Wilson "in the cold." They appeared to know that towering Jimmy Simpson would guard their dangerous centre.

ON DEFENCE

M'Phail played a half-back game. Venters took his cue from Bob. He, too, came back. Main, Smith, and Gillick were left up-field, keeping Wallace and Bulloch and M'Stay in defensive position. Yet both Venters and M'Phail had the urge of attack at times; that's why Main and Gillick sparkled on the wings. At the same time, I consider that Hamilton were unlucky in being one goal down at the interval. The Academicals should have been awarded a penalty for an infringement more apparent to me than was Cox's infringement against Venters.

PENALTY—I THOUGHT

Simpson was the aggressor. On one of his all too few dashes, Wilson seemed set to get the ball when the Ibrox pivot nudged him aside. Wilson made no appeal. I cannot recall any occasion when I've seen the English lad make a claim or a protest. That doesn't alter the fact that he was pushed. Cox's upending of Venters must have been considered intentional by the referee. Cox, to my mind, went for the ball. He missed. Venters fell. A penalty. Ominous! Yet M'Phail drove straight at Morgan from the spot. The 'keeper stopped the ball; released it; and then, on his knees, fisted it clear as M'Phail was dashing in.

SMITH'S FOOT

From that moment, M'Phail ceased his half-back strategy. He became a forward, and once again Venters took his cue from the captain. I could see the goal coming. Rangers had the ascendancy. Inch-accurate passing by Brown and M'Phail kept Gillick on the move. From one of the left wing raids, Smith had a chance, difficult, put there for him. He thrust a foot. Connected. Morgan, over-anxious, had come out a step or two. The ball seemed destined to cross the line when Wallace made his great effort to clear. The ball sped into the net off the full-back's foot. In the remaining nine minutes of the first half I could discern the diminution of energy on the part of the Academicals. Harrison alone maintained the electric spirit that had animated the Douglas Park lads in the first half-hour.

HAMPDEN GATE

People	87,286
Pounds	£3,109

It was significant that Gray, and Kennedy, too, kicked into touch for safety when Harrison and Reid were on the move. Early in the second half Wilson got a chance. The heavy ground may be blamed for his length-of-a-second delay in shooting. As it was, his drive, deflected by a tackler, demanded all Dawson's agility to save the situation.

MAN IN CHARGE

Mr. Hugh Watson, Glasgow.

But the Rangers' 'keeper was well beaten a couple of minutes later, when, from the right, Wilson back-headed and Harrison brow-headed, into the net.

Smith at centre for Rangers played a queer kind of game about that period. On one occasion he could have charged Morgan, ball in hand, over the line. He refrained. Next minute, with a less easy chance, he dived, missed the 'keeper, and landed, head-on, in the back of the net.

RANGERS—Dawson; Gray and M'Donald; Kennedy, Simpson and Brown; Main, Venters, Smith, M'Phail and Gillick.

HAMILTON ACADEMICALS — Morgan; Wallace and Bulloch; Cox, M'Stay and Murray; King, M'Laren, Wilson, Harrison and Reid.

Referee—H. Watson, Glasgow.

Rangers—Smith (2). Hamilton Academicals—Harrison.

Rangers' winning goal came after another uncertain decision. I took it that Referee Watson was on the point of awarding a goal-kick to Hamilton when one of the linesmen signalled a corner. Gillick, wisely using his right foot, as he had done at all corners, lobbed the ball towards the far upright. M'Phail, at centre, jumped, Smith, at inside-right, jumped. Smith got it into the net. The Cup seemed clearly destined for Ibrox once again. But Hamilton were by no means dispirited. Can't you recall that occasion when King had a great chance and the referee whistled him offside?

Wrong decision. Dougie Gray was yards nearer Dawson than was King. And have you any thoughts about the occasion when Wilson, as we know him, should have got clean through, but tripped over himself, so to speak? Still, it was Rangers' game in that second half. They worthily won against gallant opponents.

THE STARS

In a weigh-up of the players I must, after M'Phail, mention Morgan, Harrison and Brown. Shevlin's deputy, cast into the team on the eve of the game, need have no personal regrets about the result. He was splendid. Harrison stood out in the Hamilton attack. Not his reddish hair alone made him conspicuous. He is a brilliant player. George Brown, like M'Phail, appeared to realise that a bit extra was demanded. He participated in defence to a greater extent than I've ever seen him do. But I must not forget M'Donald, staunch; nor Gray, nippy and cute. Then there's Dawson, a 'keeper well worthy of the delayed Scottish Cup honour. Simpson and Kennedy can be included in the list of successes.

THEY WILL DO

I cannot say anything better of the Light Blues' front five—Main, Venters, Smith, M'Phail and Gillick—than that they'll do perfectly well for next season's League and Cup competitions. Morgan I have mentioned. Wallace and Bulloch had not the craft of Gray and M'Donald, but they played a gallant part. Cox was best of the halfs. M'Stay didn't attempt to force play. I wish he had. He knows how to do it. But his duty, probably, was to guard M'Phail and Smith—a heavy task. Murray shone in the first half. King and Reid were dangerous wingers all the time. Wilson was too closely watched, but was unlucky. I expected a bit more from M'Laren. But Harrison—the laurels to him!

RANGERS IN HIS BLOOD

Mr. Lyon's Joke At Ceremony

By R. M. CONNELL
(Bedouin)

THE one touch of humour in the speeches at the Cup presentation in the Q.P. pavilion library, emanated from Mr. James Lyon, the Hamilton chairman.

The audience roared merriment when he blandly confessed that his father was a great Rangers supporter." His brother, another enthusiastic Light Blue, had written to him from America stating that for Jamie's sake, "I will forsake my club." Blood is thicker than water!

I was pleased to hear the Hamilton chief declare that the Academicals had won their way to the final by keeping their players, and that from the money made in the Scottish Cup this season, they would continue to resist the temptation of English gold.

MIGHT HAVE BEEN

County clubs are not so happily placed as the Rangers. Just consider what a grand team the Academicals would have had, if they had not been compelled, in recent years, to part with sterling players like Herd and M'Luckie to Manchester City, Frank Wilson to Preston North End; Dougall and Phil Watson to Blackpool; Allan to Motherwell, Gibson and M'Kay to Bolton Wanderers; and Sommerville, Hunt and Steel to Burnley!!

I thought of those accomplished players as I watched the valiant and courageous fight the Academicals put up in this latest struggle for the cup against a speedier and more accomplished defence than they had! Always fighting against the odds.

In their enthusiasm for the lads who sported the red and white hoops of Hamilton at Hampden Park, some good people, I know, in the town where famous Dukes of Hamilton once held court, rate the present Hamilton team the best ever.

NOT MY OPINION

I do not subscribe to that opinion. When the Academicals appeared at Ibrox Park in the 1911 final, against a famous Celtic side lead by Jamie Quinn, and almost impregnable at back with Alec M'Nair and Jamie Hay, their team comprised J. Watson; John Davie and Adam Miller; Phil Watson, W. M'Laughlin and Matt Eglinton; George H. M'Laughlin, J. Waugh, W. Hunter, J. Hastie and R. M'Neill, the present trainer.

If we take, for the sake of argument, that the modern Rangers are comparable with the Celts of 1911, Hamilton's first Cup final team was stronger at back and half-back than the men in those sections of the 1935 team. Wasn't Adam Miller a bonnie kicker!

BRILLIANT DAVID

An odd remark of my old friend, Mr. Robert Smellie, on Saturday, may confirm this view. Said this once brilliant international back. "The Hamilton forwards were capable of an even greater effort, had they been supported."

I saw both games in the 1911 final! The one outstanding member of the present Hamilton team who outrivalled the old lot is David Wilson, the ablest, of all; a brilliant leader of soccer men!

I wonder how many of the present Hamilton following are aware that Mr. Smellie, who resides in Hamilton, was the greatest full back the Academicals ever had. He joined Queen's Park from the Academicals to partner Walter Arnott, whose previous colleagues in defence were:—Andrew W. Holm, J. W. Holm, Andrew ("Black") Watson, and Wm. M'Leod!

AS WELL AS EXPECTED

I don't want to be hypercritical! The Academicals played as well as I expected against the Rangers. They fought to the last ditch with their backs to the wall. All credit to them. And a clap on the back to James Morgan, the substitute goalkeeper, who rose nobly to a big occasion.

Hamilton links the old and the new in football! The Hamilton Gymnasium F.C. gave Queen's Park one of their first matches in 1869. That was long before my time, but in later years I got to know Honorary Sheriff Cassells and ex-Bailie Small, two of the Gymnasium officials. Mr. Small was the intimate friend of Mr. James Kelly, of the Celtic

One of the most sporting towns in Scotland, is Hamilton. Long may the Academicals maintain its tradition The club was founded in 1875.

SATURDAY'S WINNERS AND LOSERS

SCOTTISH CUP FINAL

Rangers	2	Hamilton Acas.	1

SCOTTISH LEAGUE

First Division

Airdrieonians	2	Dunfermline	3
Falkirk	5	Hibernian	2
Hearts	2	Aberdeen	1
Motherwell	2	Ayr United	3
Queen of South	1	Albion Rovers	0
St. Mirren	2	Partick Thistle	1

Second Division

Brechin City	2	St. Bernards	3
Leith Athletic	4	Dundee United	0
East Fife	6	Stenhousemuir	1

FIFE CUP—Semi-Final

Cowdenbeath	3	Raith Rovers	0

SCOTTISH ALLIANCE

Aberdeen A	1	Q.P. Strollers	0

SECOND XI. CUP—Final

St. Johnstone A.	4	Celtic A	3

HIGHLAND GAMES

Wick Groats, 6; Wick Thistle, 3.
Brora Rangers, 5; Seaside Swifts, 4.

HIGHLAND LEAGUE

Buckie Thistle, 3; Nairn County, 1.
Peterhead, 5; Clachnacuddin, 1.

FRIENDLY GAMES

Kilmarnock, 7; Inverness Select, 0.
Elgin City, 1; Clyde, 1.

NAIRN DISTRICT CUP

Ross County, 3; H.L.I., 2.

ABERDEENSHIRE LEAGUE

Huntly, 2; Elgin City, 2.
Fraserburgh, 7; Aberdeen University, 3.

SOUTHERN LEAGUE

Wigtown, 2; St. Cuthbert Wands., 2.
Whithorn, 2; Newton Stewart 1.

KING CUP—Final

Peebles Rovers, 2; Duns, 2.

EAST OF SCOTLAND LEAGUE

Chirnside United, 5; Selkirk, 3.
Coldstream, 1; Berwick Rangers, 3.

F.A. AMATEUR CUP—Final—Replay

Bishop Auckland	2	Wimbledon	1

BELFAST CITY CUP

Ards	1	Glenavon	0
Coleraine	0	Ballymena	1
Glentoran	0	Derry City	3
Larne	3	Distillery	0
Newry Town	1	Cliftonville	2
Linfield	2	Belfast Celtic	2
Portadown	3	Bangor	1

ENGLISH LEAGUE

First Division

The Arsenal	1	Huddersfield	0
Blackburn R.	6	Everton	2
Birmingham	2	Sunderland	2
Manchester C.	1	Preston N.E.	2
Sheffield Wed.	1	Leicester City	1
W. Bromwich	4	Derby County	3
Middlesbro'	6	Grimsby Town	2
Liverpool	6	Chelsea	0
Portsmouth	0	Wolverhampton	1
Leeds United	1	Aston Villa	1
Stoke	4	Tottenham H.	1

Second Division

Blackpool	3	Notts County	1
Bury	2	Bradford City	1
Notts Forest	4	Barnsley	1
Newcastle	1	Bolton Wand.	3
Bradford	3	Swansea	1
Plymouth Argyle	2	Burnley	2
Hull City	0	Sheffield United	3
Brentford	8	Port Vale	0
Norwich City	0	Oldham	0
West Ham	2	Southampton	1
Fulham	3	Manchester United	1

Third Division—Northern

Wrexham	0	Hartlepools Utd.	2
Lincoln City	4	Southport	1
Rotherham	1	Stockport	0
Halifax Town	1	Crewe Alex.	0
Walsall	5	Gateshead	0
Barrow	0	York City	3
Carlisle United	4	New Brighton	1
Chesterfield	0	Accrington S.	0
Mansfield Town	2	Darlington	2
Rochdale	3	Chester	3
Tranmere	0	Doncaster Rovers	2

Third Division—Southern

Coventry City	3	Swindon Town	0
Gillingham	1	Cardiff City	0
Northampton	2	Luton Town	1
Reading	4	Brighton	4
Watford	3	Bristol Rovers	0
Bournemouth	2	Southend United	1
Bristol City	5	Q.P. Rangers	1
Clapton Orient	3	Aldershot	1
Crystal Palace	0	Exeter City	1
Millwall	4	Torquay United	2
Newport County	0	Charlton Athletic	2

DAWSON PROVIDES BIG THRILL

BRILLIANT SAVE THAT BAULKED THIRD

Warriors Threw Away Chance Of Achieving Glory

By "WAVERLEY"

Rangers............1 Third Lanark............0

THERE will be plenty of people to condemn this latest Scottish Cup final as one of the poorest ever. True, it was deficient in artistic skill, but it was plentifully endowed with eager effort, and the uncertainty of the result led to a maintenance of sustained interest right up to the final whistle. The crowd thoroughly enjoyed the unexpected spectacle of the Cathkin fellows hemming the Light Blues down to defence for the major portion of the second half, even though Hay and his colleagues seldom looked like scoring.

I am one of those who sympathise with Third. Their courage, if not their finishing power, deserved another chance at least, and, but for a miraculous save by Jerry Dawson half-a-dozen minutes from the end, we would all have been Hampden bound again on Wednesday.

Third were attacking when the ball was slung into the right, to the feet of Kennedy, who had changed places with Hay. The Warrior seemed to be bunched by friend and foe, but, swerving and tapping the ball to his right foot, he saw an opening and let go. The leather travelled at a really fast pace, never rising more than a few inches from the ground, to Dawson's left-hand post.

It looked a certainty, but Dawson threw himself and got his hands to the ball, and palmed it clear. One of the greatest saves I've seen. The ball only travelled about fifteen yards, and it's possible that the 'keeper never saw it until it was well on its journey.

The Big Thrill

That shot and save constituted the big thrill of the game, coming as it did when Rangers had lost the place and were definitely on the defensive. When it didn't find a billet, I made up my mind that the Cup, for another year, was the property of Rangers, for all other efforts by the Third to score had been weak-kneed stuff in comparison.

The goal that won the match was first cousin to a gift, and again it was a piece of ill-timing by Denmark that led to the score. In the second minute Meiklejohn slung a ball up the centre. Denmark made for it, to stop it with his breast, but M'Phail was on his top, and bustled off the centre-half to give himself a clear run in on Muir, who advanced vainly to narrow the width of the goal.

Denmark must accept the major responsibility, but at the same time I thought that his backs were positioned too square on. Either Carabine or Hamilton should have been handier for such an eventuality.

In the last two minutes Denmark made another bloomer, when he let a ball slip past him to give Smith a chance in a lifetime, but otherwise the pivot played a skipper's part. Smith was helpless against him, the centre-forward being made to look awkward, cumbersome, and never permitted to be venturesome.

Reduced To Impotency

In plain language, he reduced Smith to impotency, just as the others in the defence made Turnbull and Fiddes appear distinct second-raters. There was an excuse for the latter, though. He wasn't fit, and Rangers took a distinct risk in playing him. He was limping for most of the game.

Rangers, in effect, had only two forwards, Venters and M'Phail, worth their salt, and, when I say that, I don't wish to take the slightest credit away from the Third defenders, who, in point of fact, saw that the inside men didn't get a chance to develop whatever value their wingers or centre-forward might have had.

The feature of Carabine's play was his positioning and tackling, in which he was most impressive, but there were times when his kicking left a little to be desired. His partner hasn't played finer stuff for a long time, I wager. There was elegance in the play of Hamilton, and that left foot controlled the ball wonderfully despite the difficulties presented by the elements.

The recognised skill of George Cummings, Scotland's back, in keeping the ball in play from awkward angles, and when on the turn, had nothing in the ability of the man from Newry.

Blair was solid from first to last, and it was one determined run through the opposition early in the second half that led to Third's dominance. His manner of carrying the ball up on that occasion was an inspiration to his mates.

Of Classic Type

M'Innes was a schemer, and more than ever, as a result of his engaging display here, do I think that Third have in this junior of a year ago a player of the classic type. Delightfully played, young man.

Kennedy I noted down as Third's best forward. Unlike Gallacher, he could open up play, scheme for openings. The inside-right was far too close. He was under special survey by George Brown, who was on him like a bird the minute he got possession. Now and again Gallacher got away with it, but only to meander into trouble.

When he saw how closely the Rangers left-half was attending him he should have indulged more in swinging passes instead of giving the impression that the game was staged in order to show the crowd that he could diddle Brown or anyone else. Too often he carried on, and got muddled—and dispossessed.

Howe and Kinnaird were decidedly not the same pair as played so well in the League encounter, and the outside-left mulled several grand chances in the second half. A quicker thinker, one less hesitant, it is conceivable, would have scored a couple of goals in the second half. He wants to practise first-time shooting from the left-hand side of the penalty box. His hesitancy may have been due to lack of confidence.

Brown's Masterly Touch

Hay certainly was asked to do difficult things by bringing down high balls with Simpson on top of him, but there were times when he got the leather running nicely to his feet. However, like the others, he just couldn't put the finishing touch to things.

Gray was the better of two backs, but even he was not too impressive, and spooned the ball too much, in addition to finding, with abnormal frequency, safety in touch. Cheyne never inspired as dependable, and against the wind in the second half his kicking was ragged.

Brown was one of the few stars on the field, although now and again his parting was a bit out. But his bottling-up of Gallacher was masterly, while his timely interventions when danger threatened were invaluable.

Simpson's defensive qualities were pronounced, and his head was ever prominent. Those long legs, too, could make contact at the exact moment. He didn't worry much about construction. He hadn't much time to in the second forty-five.

Meiklejohn now and then appeared to be a bit out of it, but he rose to a great height when his best was necessary, and the mind of the old and confident campaigner was in evidence when twice he hypnotised the opposing attack by cheekily heading back to Dawson.

I have already given you my opinion of the attack. It was just about the poorest front rank, in regard to achievement, that I've seen Rangers field.

The goalkeepers. Muir had no chance with the goal, and otherwise gave a fine display, but he was overshadowed by the brilliance of Dawson, whose punching or clutching of crosses were features of the game. And that save from Kennedy. It was hard on Third.

If the two attacks had been on the level of the men in the rear divisions we would have seen a game to remember. As it was the forward play was poor, poor, indeed.

Rangers—M'Phail.

RANGERS — Dawson; Gray and Cheyne; Meiklejohn, Simpson and Brown; Fiddes, Venters, Smith, M'Phail and Kinnear.

THIRD LANARK—Muir; Carabine and Hamilton; Blair, Denmark and M'Innes; Howe, Gallacher, Hay, Kennedy and Kinnaird.

Referee—J. M. Martin, Ladybank.

CUP TREASURE

DRAWINGS (exclusive of stand and tax) £3304
Attendance... 88,859

That one went over. Muir comes out to baulk one of M'Phail's scoring efforts, but the Ranger's elevation was at fault. Blair is also seen in the picture.

THE HARVEST OF TEN

Third Lanark Had Skill But Not Cunning

By "BRIGADIER"

I HAVE seen the Rangers win the Scottish Cup ten times. To do it the first time, I paid sixpence, which was top price for the terracing. That was in 1894, and if you had been there you might have observed a wee fellow in short trousers wondering what all the excitement was about. Now I know.

Well, of these ten finals, Rangers never had a harder job to win than the latest. This may have surprised a lot of people, but not the Rangers. The fact is, there was more than one man in the team not a hundred per cent. fighting fit, but the best was made under the circumstances so far as selection was concerned. If the Cup had been won by Third Lanark they would have received all credit due.

* * * *

Third Lanark may never have a better chance. Taking them from goal to frontage, they were the better-balanced side, played the principal role as aggressors, and then contributed to their own defeat.

For one thing, Kennedy and Gallacher, clever in working the ball, were too slow in parting, and, with the wind behind them, too hesitant in shooting. But even a greater fault was the tardiness with which free kicks were taken. The referee was prompt to signal permission for the kick to be taken, but the Cathkin players ignored his generosity given equally to both teams.

One man would leisurely place the ball, another one would as leisurely walk up to take the kick, and by this time the Rangers' defenders were in a phalanx to guard their goal. Towards the end, there was a marked speeding up in the taking of the "frees," but how many golden chances had been lost by them!

* * * *

After M'Phail had struck that dramatic blow by scoring with only 61 seconds gone, it was left to the Rangers' defence to see the Cup won. Not many defences could have stood up to wind and pressure as they did.

In Rangers' dressing room at the finish, Bob M'Phail said, "Hadn't we a great defence?" He was giving the men behind him the credit. And Bob added, "That's seven medals for me, and if I can get just one more, that will be another record."

Dougie Gray told me the wind was much worse to grapple with than anyone off the field could believe. "It wasn't only extra strong in the second half," said Doug, "but it was cantankerous. The ball would be coming to you apparently on a straight course when it would dip like an aeroplane, and made you change your mind all at once."

* * * *

This Hampden wind, which has affected so many Cup-finals and Internationals, should, let us hope, get one in the eye when the extensions are made.

When I complimented Jerry Dawson on his wonderful full stretch, one-handed save in the second half, he just smiled. To him it was all in the day's work. The supreme confidence his colleagues reposed in him was indicated in the second half by the long passes back to him. With a less accomplished custodian, this manœuvre would have been absolutely perilous, but Dawson, at the present time, is the goalkeeper par excellence.

Almost as good as this save referred to was the one in the first half, when he had to dash out and handle the ball outside the penalty line. Visions of the 1922 final in which Morton defeated Rangers by scoring direct from a "free" conceded under similar circumstances must have flashed before the eyes of many. But history was not to be repeated.

* * * *

By the time the Rangers officials, manager and team reached St. Enoch Hotel to celebrate the victory at a private dinner, captain David Meiklejohn was as happy as a bird, but just at the finish of the match he was feeling the effects of the gruelling struggle. Three weeks off and very little training had taken the edge off his condition.

"Anyway," he said to me, "I hope I did my bit." He did.

At the dinner, Mr. James Bowie, chairman, complimented the players on finishing an arduous season with such a splendid result.

"You have made a record for modern times by winning the Cup three times in succession, something of which we are all very proud," added the chairman.

CHIEF INCIDENTS IN THE PLAY

By "RUFUS"

M'PHAIL, back in defence, initiated Rangers' first attack, and Meiklejohn, backing up on the right, tried a narrow-angle shot. This looked good for Rangers, but we hardly expected the shock which followed. Less than two minutes had passed when M'Phail, getting the ball a yard or two outside the penalty area, found Denmark in two minds and tore through with his long stride to beat Muir. The Third Lanark defenders were caught on the hop here.

With the wind and sun in their favour, Rangers kept up the pressure. Third Lanark had one or two breakaways, and in one Kennedy, catching an attempted clearing headed by M'Phail, lashed in a grand shot, which Dawson, covering the exposed gap, held safely.

Fiddes Goes Off

Gallacher produced a bit of his sleight-of-foot in mystifying M'Phail, then sent over a cross which Kinnaird headed in, Dawson coming out to catch and clear.

In fifteen minutes Fiddes went off, and was absent four minutes. Immediately after he left, Smith, who had previously netted after the whistle had gone for a handling offence, got away, but was recalled for offside.

Third Lanark had a bright spell, when the Rangers' defence went through some trouble. Gallacher's shot, however, did not trouble Dawson.

Howe's Mistake

A lob from Meiklejohn into the goalmouth saw M'Phail, trying to tip the ball over Muir's head, send it soaring over the bar. Back to the other end, and Dawson running out to gather a ball that was going to Hay, found himself outside the penalty area and compelled to knock the ball down with his hand.

The free kick came to nothing, but Rangers were getting more worry than they relished. Brown and Cheyne in turn fell when trying to get back after being beaten. Howe got the benefit, but Simpson and Cheyne arrived in time to block his shot. Getting a second chance, Howe had the ball driven from his toe by Simpson, when a pass to one of three waiting Cathkin comrades might well have produced a goal.

Meiklejohn tried to bring off a surprise coup just before half-time by taking a corner kick. He put just a little too much spin on the ball, however, and it carried over.

Soon after the restart Smith, just outside the penalty area, was impeded, but retained the ball. A free kick, however, was given, and when M'Phail pointed out to the referee that he should have let play go on, all he got for his pains was a severe dressing-down.

When Third Lanark got their turn, play ran mostly in Kinnaird's direction. He had one try which landed on the top of the net, but erred badly twice in trying to dribble past Gray.

M'Innes got a nasty smack on the face with the ball, but soon recovered. He was concerned later in a tussle with Smith, allowing the centre to rob him and cross a ball which M'Phail headed past. Then came a lecture for Gallacher, following a bit of ankle-tapping on M'Phail.

Trouble For Rangers

The scene changed once more to Dawson's end, where Simpson's height came in very useful. Kinnaird, after a clever touch in beating Gray, shot feebly. Dawson fielded, right under the bar, an awkwardly bouncing ball.

Rangers were going through it here, and for once in a way Gallacher got the better of Brown and crossed a ball which Kennedy headed just over the bar, with Dawson's fist handy if needed. Third Lanark now had Kennedy at centre, but the best scoring effort came from M'Innes.

Dawson's Great Save

A free kick from Hamilton gave Dawson a tricky problem. He thought at first the ball was going outside, but it didn't, and he bumped his elbow against the post in kicking out.

Smith got in a very clever backheeler which might have came off had Muir been less alert.

The big thrill of the game came six minutes from the end. Kennedy, at short-range, pushed in a shot at the foot of the post, and with a remarkable spring, Dawson flashed along the ground and pushed the ball out. How the Rangers' followers cheered!

Smith provided a bit of comedy to finish up. Denmark had failed to stop a clearance and the Rangers' centre dashed off into the Third Lanark penalty area, where he stopped the ball dead. Muir tried to pounce on it, but it was pulled away like a ball of wool from a kitten. Then Denmark arrived, and also failed to dispossess Smith, who lobbed the ball to the foot of the post. But by this time Blair was also on the scene, and kicked the ball away from almost under the bar.

Third Lanark pressing. Howe and Hay close in, while Dawson kicks clear, with Meiklejohn anxiously watching.

Garry Owen RACING

Cromwell Now 10-1 For 'National'

CROMWELL, 100-7 "National" favourite at the last call-over, was backed at tens on the course after his Runnymede 'Chase victory at Windsor on Saturday. He beat Happy Home by three-quarters of a length, with Roimond a bad third.

Roimond can hardly be fancied for Aintree now but though Cromwell was meeting Happy Home on 8lbs. worse terms than in the "National," Happy Home cannot be ruled out as he jumps the course.

Bryan Marshall, Happy Home's jockey, said: "The better horse over the distance, three miles, beat me."

Lord Mildmay was delighted with Cromwell and he added that they will not go so fast in the "National" as they did at Windsor.

FAIR JUDGEMENT

Jack Jarvis's Fair Judgement, second favourite for the "Lincoln," finished first in a gallop of seven and a half furlongs at Newmarket on Saturday.

E. Smith rode Fair Judgement, who beat Welsh Honey by a length and a half.

The third, well beaten, was Molecomb. Bakersgate and Flaming Tin-

man were further behind. The gallop was watched by Lord Rosebery.

Fair Judgement is to be preferred to Drakkar, who was impressive in a spin last week. He is the more dependable of the two.

Heathbird's Fancies

WOLVERHAMPTON. — 1.30—Hal o' the Wynd.** 2.0—Friar's Dream.* 2.30—Sailor II. 3.0—Caddie II 3.30—Twenty-Twenty. 4.0—Winco.

WYE.—1.30—The Solid Man. 2.0—Jack-a-Dandy. 2.30—Cyprien II. 3.0—Bamboozle 3.30 — Astroco. 4.0—Pretence.

F. Durr, who recently returned from South Africa, where he has been riding, will ride Tratveller in the "Lincoln."

W. Heavey broke three ribs when his mount, Henri Quatre, fell at Windsor on Saturday. He will not be able to ride for at least three weeks

WOLVERHAMPTON—Probables, Jockeys

1.30—NEWPORT NOVICES' HURDLE (Div I.) of 250 sovs Two miles

401 Port Light (Yates) 3-11-12	120 Mainstay III. (Lowe) 8-12-7 Ashurst
14 Hal o' the Wynd (Street) 5-11-9	120 Prince Tol (Doyle) 8-12-7.. D Doyle
	311 Black Moen (Rimell) 7-11-9 E Vinali
	J Morahan
040 Shivallee (Hollinshead) 6-11-3	14 War Bond (Owen) 6-11-8...McMorrow
Mr R Hollinshead	221 Liffey Valley (Roberts) 10-11-6
03 Torphelim (Beard) 10-11-3	120 Debra Dun (Hannon) 8-11-4 R Bates
004 Laches Bridge (Hammonds) 8-11-3	000 Belted Monarch (Wilson) 11-11-1
A Mullins	E Hannigan
Loyaute (Studd) 10-11-3	312 Sailor II. (Piggott) 6-11-1 R Turnell
00 Landing Light (Williams) 5-11-3	000 King Stephen (Walwyn) 5-10-13
Mr A Williams	B Marshall
0 Punchestown Star (Mercer) 5-11-0	102 Colleen Oge (Nicholson) 7-10-11
M Morris	R Nicholson
312 Wainwright (Mason) 4-11-0 J Smith	300 Fleur de Lys (Hawtin) 9-10-9 C Laver

DAILY SPECIAL
AFRICAN SCOUT (3.30, Wolv.)

2.0—STANTON SELL. B'CAP of 200 sovs. Two miles and 50 yards.

3.0—INGESTRE HANDICAP 'CHASE of 250 sovs. Three miles.

3.30—NEWPORT NOVICES' HURDLE (Div. 2) of 250 sovs. Two miles

Safe conduct

NO sensible man will dart into a stream of traffic, even on a crossing. He knows cars can't stop instantly, especially in wet weather. He will wait for a gap, so that the next driver can see him and stop.

And the sensible driver will gladly give way to pedestrians on a crossing. He knows that if people are encouraged to use the marked crossings, fewer will dodge across elsewhere.

People on foot can contribute just as much as drivers or cyclists to the safety of our roads. We can all see that more regular use of the crossings, and better observance of the rules, will help *everyone* to get about more easily, more *safely*.

Mind how you go

Issued by the Ministry of Transport

WOLVERHAMPTON
1.30—WAINWRIGHT
2. 0—BLAKESLEY
2.30—SAILOR II.
3. 0—LEAP MAN
3.30—AFRICAN SCOUT
4. 0—SWISS CHALET

WYE
1.30—THE SOLID MAN
2. 0—JACK-A-DANDY
2.30—CYPRIEN II.
3. 0—BAMBOOZLE
3.30—ASTROCO (Nap)
4. 0—PRETENCE
Double—
SAILOR II. and ASTROCO

Training Hints

WOLVERHAMPTON
BLEWBURY—Twenty-Twenty good.
UPAVON—Blakesley fancied.
WETHERBY—Sergeant Kelly fancied.
WROUGHTON — Caddie II well fancied.
WANTAGE—Paper Weight fancied.
MALTON—Hal o' the Wynd fancied.

WYE
BLEWBURY — Cyprien II. well fancied.
TILSHEAD—The Solid Man fancied.
UPAVON—The Solid Man fancied.
WANTAGE—The Editor and Ladies Beware fancied.

A. Wright, an apprentice attached to Persse's stable, is to ride Tetrashah for Nelson, the Lambourn trainer in the "Lincoln."

KLONDYKE'S THREE
***AFRICAN SCOUT (3.30 Wolv.)
**HAL O' THE WYND (1.30 Wolv.)
*CYPRIEN II. (2.30 Wye.)

WYE—Runners And Riders

1.30—DOVER SELLING 'CHASE of 150 sovs. Two miles.

2.0—NOVICES' HURDLE (Div 1.) of 150 sovs. Two miles.

2.30—SPRING GROVE HANDICAP 'CHASE of 200 sovs Two miles

3.0—HARVILLE HANDICAP 'CHASE of 150 sovs. Three miles.

3.30—CANTERBURY HANDICAP HURDLE of 200 sovs. Two miles.

4.0—NOVICES' HURDLE (Div. 2) of 150 sovs. Two miles.

" Handicap Book " Special Code—12 8 12 24 15 25 24 18 28 11 26 (Nap)—3 8 18 10 9 2 23 18 15 18. Saturday's code gave Montignac (won 9-4) For key, see "Sporting Chronicle Handicap Book," every Saturday, 6d.

Galliard ("Sunday Chronicle"): 8 17 25 6 28 5 27 5 7 (5 7 6 8). Next best—5 5 25 7 4 6 5 25 7 6 8.

Killie Gave Him 'Cap' Rehearsal

KILMARNOCK are feeling mighty proud of themselves this week-end and they deserve to be (writes Bob Ferrier). Their latest acquisition, 17-year-old amateur goalkeeper Andy Black, from Galston, guards Scotland's goal at Belfast on Wednesday evening. He's had little experience of big-time stuff so Killie made him 'keeper for the Boghead game.

He gave an excellent display and included a penalty kick save, proving that our last line of defence in the International is in capable hands.

Andy deputises at Belfast for Ronnie Simpson (Queen's Park and Army). Ronnie was told he could not be freed for the game but his C.O. later stated he could play. Amateur officialdom said, "No. it was too late."

McLaren Again

Liverpool manager, George Kay, with two directors, were at Dumbarton to see Hugh McLaren, the Kilmarnock inside-left. Although scoring a magnificent goal, McLaren did not completely satisfy and nothing definite was done.

Liverpool however, are not in urgent need of players before the transfer 'deadline" on Wednesday, and may be back.

Blackpool scout Donald Menzies was at Broomfield for the Airdrie-Stirling Albion game. Earlier in the season, Blackpool were interested in Albion's George Dick, and this may mean a resumption of their quest.

Ouch!—But The 'Keeper Held It

Raith Rovers' 'keeper, Westland, has just pulled down the ball after a high cross at Hampden. Willie Thornton, of Rangers, charges him while left-back Willie McNaught keeps a watchful eye. Bob Ferrier comments on this incident in his report alongside.

Rovers Upset 'A' Division Notions
By BOB FERRIER

RANGERS 2   RAITH ROVERS 0

RANGERS took the League Cup off the Hampden field on Saturday afternoon, but little in the way of credit from the game. It was scarcely credible that these were the players who had pulverised Partick the week before.

In one sense they were barely worthy of victory, since Raith played so very well, but two flashes of the football brain of Willie Thornton, and these alone, gave Rangers the League Cup.

To make Rangers' first goal, Thornton took a "pop through" from McColl, jiggled and dummied past Colville, and crossed the ball for Gillick's scoring header.

The second came when Thornton, with typical and immaculate headwork, took a cross-field Shaw clearance and headed it down and back against the trend of the defence, to Paton in the inside-left position. Paton was thus given clear possession at 18 yards range.

Thornton's Task

It was an attenuated Rangers attack, and the thought of it without Thornton becomes almost physically painful. His is a heavy responsibility.

Rutherford was timid and indecisive. Duncanson never

seen and Paton was not too successful. Gillick was Gillick.

In many ways Raith were unlucky. Penman and Joyner, two big fellows with a touch of awkward genius in their play, harassed the defence in the first half, and it was well that Brown was inspired.

Two Down, But—

In the second half, when two down, Rovers fought spiritedly. Brady, foot cocked to shoot, had his boot held; Maule whipped in a shot so quickly that it had rebounded off Brown's chest before he knew it was coming, and Woodburn "climbed" over Penman to head his clearance.

If nothing else, Raith Rovers upset some Division "A" notions and proved that such players as Willie McNaught, Andy Young and Johnny Maule are fit for the best of company.

Puzzling Decisions

The refereeing, which was mixed, puzzled me on one point—the controversial "charging the goalkeeper."

Brown, in the first half, pulled down magnificently a Maule corner kick, and was charged fair and square by Alan Collins. Result—foul.

Within minutes at the other end, Westland pulled down equally brilliantly a Cox free-kick, and was immediately charged, equally fairly by Thornton. Result play on.

'£10 Player'—£20,000 Bid

BILLY REES, who cost Cardiff City a £10 signing-on fee in 1942, is likely to be transferred to-day for Tottenham Hotspur to-day for a sum in the neighbourhood of £20,000. Rees played inside-right for Wales against Ireland at Belfast last Wednesday.

He made a wartime appearance for Wales against England as a centre-forward, in which position he normally plays for Cardiff.

Rivals For Junior

St. Mirren have entered into competition with Falkirk for Charlie Gardiner, Carnoustie Panmure left-half. Gardiner was approached by Mr. Williamson of St. Mirren on Saturday, but he was unable to give a decision, because he is to have a talk with Tully Craig of Falkirk on Wednesday. Charlie is a Dundee boy at present working in a Clydeside shipyard. He travels to Carnoustie for his game each week-end.

SUPPORTERS' CORNER

RANGERS.—General—Branch secretaries please note, no League International tickets issued by Association. Secretaries make own arrangements. Olympic—Meet Washington Street School, 7.30; uplift dance tickets; all must attend; new members enrolled.

Holland and Belgium drew their Soccer international at Amsterdam, yesterday, each side scoring three times. Belgium had led 2-0 at half-time.

"Lads today have better chances of getting on than I did"

—*says Colliery Manager, aged 32*

"If you really apply yourself you can get a good way in Mining," says Mr. L. M. Hart, Manager of Mains Colliery, Wigan—"I entered Mining at 18 and became Colliery Manager at 32. But lads today have far better chances than I had, even 14 years ago. There's plenty of scope if you've average ability, and a fine future for brains and skill."

Coalmining conditions are constantly improving

Better lighting and transport, as shown above, are two of many ways in which Mining is being improved. There's a variety of skilled jobs to learn; there's training with pay and, as to wages, lads of 15 get 39/6 a week above ground with half-yearly increases. Experienced face - workers earn from £7 to £9 a week.

★ JOIN THE MINERS

Ask any Colliery or Employment Exchange or Youth Employment Officer for free booklet.

COALMINING OFFERS GREATER SCOPE

Issued by the Ministry of Labour and National Service in conjunction with the National Coal Board.

THE CUP FINAL & OTHER IMPORTANT MATTERS!
IT SHOULD HAVE BEEN A "RAIN"GERS DAY HAD A' THE EXPERTS GOT THEIR WAY,
BUT THE WEATHER MAN TURNED OFF THE "JUICE" WHILE CLYDE TURNED ON THE HEAT,—NAE USE!
FOR EVERY SHOT AT GOAL THEY RUIN BY WONDERIN' JIST HOW MOTHERWELL'S DOIN',
AND MILLIGAN, WHILE UPSETTIN' RANGERS WAS REALLY THINKIN' O' THE DANGERS
— AND PENALTIES THAT WOULD ACCRUE IF MORTON MANAGED TAE WRIGGLE THROUGH.
YEH, YOU ARE IN A SPOT!
THE PENALTIES FOR THINKIN' THUS, BIG GEORGE CONVERTS WITHOOT A FUSS.
HALFTIME! CLYDE KNOW THAT MORTON'S DOWN SO GALLETLY SLIPS THE BALL PAST BROWN,
WHILE RANGERS HEAR THAT DUNDEE'S UP AND SCORE AGAIN TO WIN THE CUP.
WHICH LEAVES THEM FREE TAE CONCENTRATE, AN' EVEN THOUGH THE CLYDE GOT BATE—
IF WE BEAT MORTON AN' DUNDEE DON'T BEAT FALKIRK AN' MOTHERWELL YOU'LL BE SAFE AN' WE'LL GET THE FLAG!
STATUS QUO
IF RANGERS WIN THE FITBA' DOUBLE CLYDE WON'T HAVE RELEGATION TROUBLE.
LINDSAY

Aikman May Be The Third '16th Man' For U.S.

A YEAR ago, in Paris, when the Scots party stepped out of their hotel to enter the bus for conveyance to the Colombes Stadium for the match with France, it was revealed that Billy Campbell's boots were unplayable. The officials held a conference in the street, and there and then chose Sammy Cox to take the Morton man's place at right half.

Orr Off

That was recalled to my mind at Hampden on Saturday (writes Waverley), when Secretary George Graham, with Messrs. Robert Williamson, Robert McKinnon and George Brown, of the Selection Committee, left the boardroom to go into conference in an adjoining room

They had been informed that Tommy Orr, chosen to take the place of the unfortunate Jimmy Mason against France on Wednesday, was suffering from a damaged ankle that couldn't possibly be healed in time.

A few minutes later Mr. Graham intimated that it had been decided to play Willie Thornton at inside-right — a position, of course, to which he is no stranger.

The U.S. Trip

When asked to deputise for Mason, Orr was also invited to make the American trip. The S.F.A. have not yet had a reply from him, but I understand that Tommy intends regretfully to decline.

Apart from the fact that his injured ankle requires prolonged rest, the player's mother is ill, and he does not wish to leave her.

On receipt of Tommy's intimation of refusal the man to fill the breach will be chosen—probably to-day. From what I can gather, Aikman, of Falkirk, may be offered the vacancy.

At Hampden on Saturday almost every one to whom I spoke expressed sympathy for the luckless Jimmy Mason, and more than one club official expressed the view that the little Warrior should be taken in the hope that he may be able to play in New York towards the end of the tour.

A Year Ago . . .

A YEAR ago, just a few days before they thrashed the Scots XI in Paris, France played Holland, and were beaten.

On Saturday France played the Dutch at Rotterdam . . . and were beaten 4-1.

This Was Not Play Of "Doomed" Men

ALTHOUGH at the finish Rangers ran out good winners of the Scottish Cup final at Hampden, let us emphasise the fact that Clyde emerged from the game with high credit. They got none of the breaks, and hardly deserved to be two goals down at the interval. Their play, indeed, makes their lowly League position appear absolutely false.

That half time lead by the Light Blues no doubt caused most of the 120,000 present to believe that the second half would be a one-sided affair, the means to causing one big yawn. But within three minutes the Bully Wee had reduced the leeway, and there were high hopes among their supporters that the men from Shawfield would go on to cause the season's biggest upset. However, things just didn't happen that way, and form for once ran true.

Hadn't Power

It was a jittery sort of Rangers that opened the proceedings what time Clyde, apparently not in the least suffering from nerves, played confident football, a brand of play that made one wonder at the fact that relegation threatens them. Linwood, showing a mobility that had Woodburn trailing him up, down and across the pitch, succeeded in opening the Light Blues' defence. Unfortunately, his mates hadn't the power to finish off their outfield work.

Signal To Keeper

For half an hour or so it was anybody's game, but gradually Rangers began to settle down and with Waddell developing punch of the right one foresaw Ibrox dominance. Five minutes from the interval Williamson made to go through on his own,

By
WAVERLEY

only to be upended by Milligan. As the players lined up for the resultant penalty, I noticed one of the Clyde men waving frantically to his goalkeeper to concentrate on his left side. Maybe George Young, who took the kick also saw the signal. Anyway, he calmly placed the ball past Gullan's right.

Got On Top

Going all out to drive home this advantage, Rangers, for the first time, got really on top. McColl swung a beautiful ground pass out to the unmarked Waddell. Mennie dashed over for the tackle. Waddell beat him inside and crossed with his left foot for Williamson to throw himself at the leather and head home at express speed. All over bar the shouting was the general impression.

First-Timer

But three minutes after the restart Clyde were in again with a chance. Campbell, near the touchline, took a free kick awarded against Cox. It was accurately placed and held by the wind before it dropped for Galletly to nip in and first time it to the net.

Pushed Centre

Clyde's joy at the score was short lived, however — ten minutes, to be precise. Once again Milligan gave away a penalty by foolishly pushing Thornton

Penalty Claims

Young again took the kick, and it was a replica of the first one, a gentle placing of the ball just inside the keeper's right hand post. The heart was knocked out of Clyde, and no wonder. They had given of everything they had with a will and had lost two penalty goals. In addition, they felt they themselves were entitled to a couple of penalty awards, an opinion that was shared by thousands of neutral spectators.

Defence Overrun

It was now definitely Rangers' Cup, and Duncanson's counter, secured by an opportune run in to shove out a foot and make contact with a knee-high Rutherford cross, was almost unnecessary.

As long as Clyde were in with a chance their two wing half-backs, Campbell and Long, particularly the latter, played great stuff and their intelligent positioning and timely tackling led to Rangers attack in the first half-hour being ragged. In addition, Campbell and Long were skilful in the constructive sense.

Faded

In the first half, Linwood was the Clyde forward who looked most likely to beat Brown. After the turn-about he faded a bit, and Davis was the man who promised to do damage, and that despite the fact he was opposed to a great back in Shaw.

Missed Chances

But the line, as a whole, just couldn't take toll of the Ibrox defence when it was in a condition easily to be upset, and so the opportunities that presented themselves were dissipated. Rangers were allowed to settle down, and once they did the trophy was booked to be dressed in Royal Blue.

Most Vital Match Of The Season

ARE Clyde to escape the fall downstairs? Are Morton fated to accompany Albion Rovers to the Second Division? These are the queries prompted by the victory of Motherwell over the Greenock team on Saturday. This evening Morton play Rangers at Love Street, and it is indeed a strange circumstance that on this match depends both championship and relegation.

Rangers must win to have a chance of regaining the flag they lost to Hibernian a year ago; it is essential that Morton are successful to save their status. Never before has such a type of game been thrown up in Scotland.

More Bad Luck

The bad luck that has been Morton's in the way of injuries is dogging them right to the end of the chapter, and they will require to take the field without their star forward Tommy Orr, suffering, as I explain elsewhere, from a damaged ankle. Tommy is the saddest man in the game that he cannot be out with his mates in their last great effort to avoid disaster.

Clyde Will Watch

There will be a large contingent of Clyde officials at the match. Needless to say they just can't bear to wait in Glasgow for the result. They want to be present to see for themselves, to have first hand knowledge of their fate.

The general impression now is that Rangers will win, and that Morton will go down.

Special Effort

If it should happen that way, will we see the breaking up of a team that promised so well at the beginning of the season, and unquestionably contains talent of high degree.

Already the whisperers are at work with the story that more than one in the ranks don't relish the idea of playing in "B" Division football.

The reply to that allegation, if it is true, is obvious. The players should put forward a special effort this evening to keep their team upstairs. Anyway, there is every promise of a great contest and one of the biggest crowds of the Love Street season.

Benefits For Eight

Hearts' "Bonus" Will Cost £5000

HEARTS have had another good season financially, and the directors have decided that the players should reap a just reward.

The club have asked the League Management Committee for permission to give benefits to eight of their players—Brown, McKenzie, Currie, McFarlane, McSpadyen, Laing, McLure and Martin—and I understand (writes Waverley) that the total cost of this splendid gesture will come to over £5000.

All the players are still in their early twenties, and have years of soccer—and more benefits—ahead of them.

FIFERS, TOO

Another club who intend giving benefit gifts to players is East Fife, whose chairman, Mr. John McArthur, for so long has made the personnel happy and contented by generous treatment. It is because of this attitude that one seldom hears of a player wishing to leave Methil.

Both Hearts and East Fife have staffs of most promising youngsters, and the knowledge that there are benefits, more or less guaranteed, awaiting them in the future will encourage them to be loyal club men.

SUPPORTERS' CORNER

CELTIC.—Shettleston—No bus for International. Trial game, Shettlestonhill, to-morrow, 7. Townhead—To—night, St. Mungo's School, Glebe St., 7.30. Must show membership cards.

RANGERS.—Albert Drive—Coach for Paisley, usual place, 6.15. Names for Coatbridge to secretary. All members requested to pay fees at once and to return cards with monies. St. Rollox—Bus for Paisley Fountainwell Rd., 6.

This Might Have Made It 2-2

Rangers have turned round with a 2-0 lead; Galletly has scored for Clyde, and, with Rangers 'keeper Bobby Brown well beaten, a header from Clyde inside-right, Archie Wright, hits the bottom of the post and is cleared—one of the many occasions on which the woodwork saved a goal at Hampden on Saturday.

Scots Coached Pompey To Flag Win

PORTSMOUTH are sitting on top of the world in this, their Jubilee year. On Saturday they won the English League Championship for the first time in their career, and it is good to know that Scots played a leading part in this great achievement.

On the field they have three grand players in Ferrier, Scoular and Reid, while behind the scenes as trainers and coaches they have Jimmy Stewart, Jimmy Easson and David Thackery, each of whom played for Scottish clubs before migrating south. Then, of course, there are about half a dozen other Scots, teen-agers who are being brought to maturity in the second and third elevens.

The Third Gray

The younger school is likely to be added to by the signing of Stuart Gray, junior international centre-half of Blairgowrie. The Coupar Angus lad is likely to travel south to-morrow to talk things over with the Fratton Park folks.

One of the points involved is Stuart's civilian job with one of the Ministries. But even if a job transfer cannot be arranged, it is quite likely that, should other details be suitable, he will join brothers Davie (Preston) and Tommy (Dundee) as a senior.

Q.P. May Play In Sweden

QUEEN'S PARK have now almost completed their arrangements for a visit to Norway next month. There is a possibility, too, that they will play a game in Sweden, having received an invitation from the famous Norrkoepping club, which made a tour of England a couple of seasons back

Twenty-One Re-sign

Manager David McLean has been busy these past few days with pen and paper among the Hearts boys, and he reports that to date twenty-one players have been re-signed for next season. The signatures are:—

Goalkeepers — Brown and Watters; backs — Mathieson, Mackenzie, Darling and Adie; half-backs — Cox, Fordyce, Glidden and Laing; forwards—Bauld, Currie, Dixon, Durkin, Flavell, Prentice, Urquhart, Wardhaugh, Williams, Conn and Buchan.

The Belgian Stan

IRELAND .... 0 BELGIUM .. 2

BELGIUM have another Stan Matthews. In yesterday's Belgium v. Ireland match at Dublin, won by Belgium 2-0, outside-right Lemberechts gave a scintillating display of dribbling and, after Matthews, is the best winger seen in Dublin since the war.

Following a goalless first half, Belgium took the lead with a lucky goal. Mees, the left-half, lobbed the ball into the goalmouth. Centre-half. Martin and the Irish keeper both went for the ball, collided, fell and the ball bounced over their bodies into the empty net.

After this the Irish goal bore a charmed life and seven minutes from the end Belgian centre Mermans added a second goal

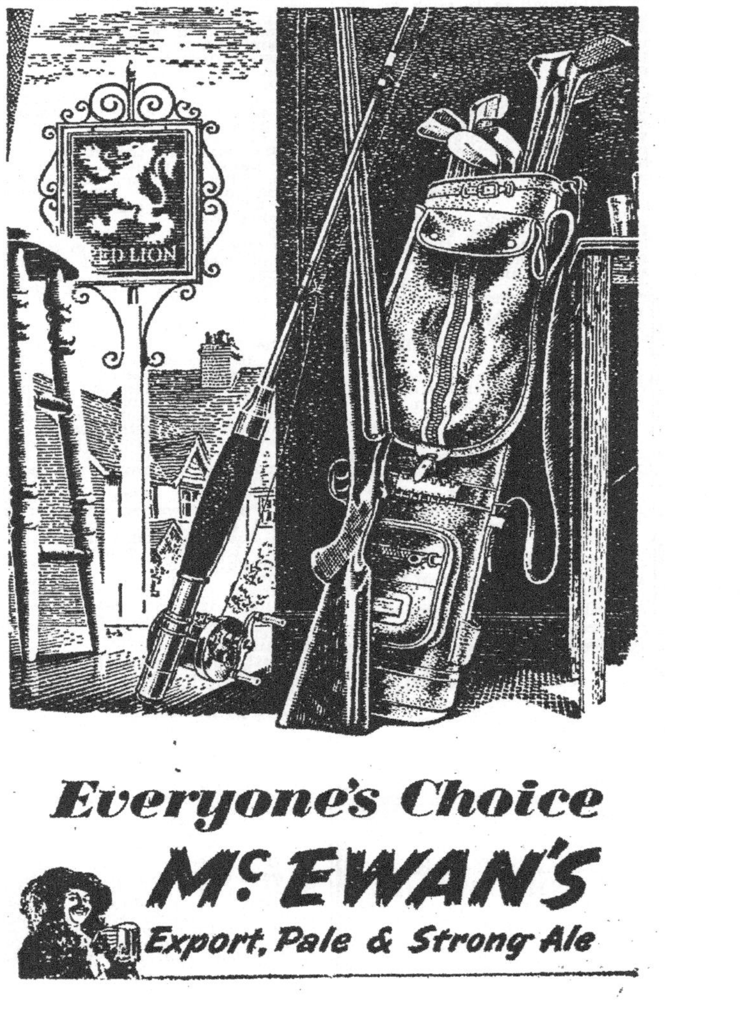
RED LION
Everyone's Choice
McEWAN'S
Export, Pale & Strong Ale

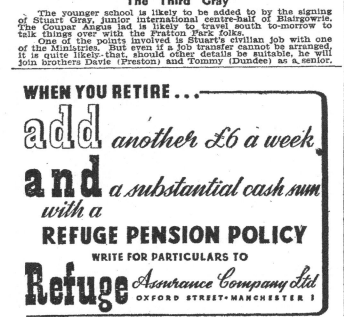

Bobby Collins "A Very Doubtful Starter"

"HE is a very doubtful starter." Thus S.F.A. Secretary George Graham to me last night in reference to Bobby Collins' chances of playing for Scotland against Switzerland at Hampden on Wednesday (writes Waverley). Bobby injured an ankle on Saturday, and, although he finished the game, it was obvious that he was more than mildly damaged.

Yesterday he turned up at Celtic Park for treatment from trainer Alec Dowdells, and after a try-out Bobby expressed a desire to wait twenty-four hours before coming to a decision in regard to a withdrawal from the team. We shall know the verdict some time to-day.

Campbell Deputy

It will be tough luck on "Midge" if he cannot avail himself of the big opportunity offered him, and he will be offered sympathy by more than the large and faithful army of Celtic supporters with whom he is such a favourite.

If he doesn't play the outside right berth will go to Bobby Campbell (Chelsea) once of Glasgow Perthshire and Falkirk, who can play on either touchline or inside.

Campbell was a candidate for honours against England but his form was a bit of mixture. He was a grand winger when I saw him against Manchester United in an English Cup-tie, but didn't impress greatly when he was watched a couple of weeks later.

If Campbell plays he will be up against a former Chelsea player, Willi Steffen who was with the Stamford Bridge club for some time.

Thornton Inspires A New Rangers

One-Pace Fifers Pack A Punch

THIS season East Fife's three inside-forwards, Fleming, Morris, and Brown, have, between them, scored 66 goals, and rightly have come to be recognised as the strongest finishing trio in Scottish football. On Saturday, at Hampden, in the Scottish Cup Final against Rangers, they gave the impression, in regard to punch at close quarters, that they couldn't burst a balloon. It was all very astonishing.

So much was justifiably expected of them and their two wingers, Black and Duncan, who also proved strangely inept, that their failure was thrown into bolder relief.

On the other hand, the much criticised Rangers' attack turned the tables on their detractors in no uncertain manner by produc-

By Waverley

ing a measure of spirited and intelligent play that had everyone at the end declaring it was the Ibrox attack's best display of the season.

The unexpected improvement in Rangers forward play indisputably was due to Thornton. From the very outset it was obvious he was high on his toes and, finding wholehearted response from his inside men, Findlay and Duncanson, he led a line that brought anxiety to the Bayview defence every time it got moving.

Held Ball

Apart altogether from their weak efforts to find the net, Fleming and Brown, particularly the latter, clung to the ball too much. Times without number the inside left hung on when he should have made the leather travel.

I expected him to open up play as the most likely way in which to find a chink in the Iron Curtain, but he persisted in individualism to such an extent that at the vital moment he and his mates were forced into close passing that was properly up the Ibrox defence's street.

Rangers got off to a great start, scoring in the first minute. Rutherford had two bites at a cross which ultimately went over chest high. Findlay running in, timed it beautifully to throw himself almost into a horizontal position to head home as he crashed to the ground.

Young Easson, playing his first game in the first eleven, had no chance with it, but even so he could easily have been upset and lost his nerve. He certainly did not and went about his work thereafter in confident manner. A pat on the back for so doing!

East Fife got over this early shock and went on to play some good football in the outfield, but when they got within shooting distance they faded out.

I have a vision yet of Woodburn standing solidly to head or kick clear, Cox going in with some great tackling, Jock Shaw, playing a real skipper's part, putting the hens on Black, Duncan finding Young's long legs an insurmountable obstacle.

The Rangers' forwards when they got going had more zip and the right and left passing of Thornton found his mates running into the open space in intelligent anticipation.

Aitken Excellent

For a time after the start of the second half East Fife suggested they might at least pull level. The Rangers' attack, temporarily as it was proved, lost some of its sparkle, and the balance of play lay with the Fifers.

This was due, slightly to the excellence of Aitken, who, like Cox, is a strong tackler, sent the ball forward in precise fashion to build up attack. But, alas! the finishing touch was never there, and Bobby Brown was never seriously troubled.

Then suddenly the Rangers forwards again sprang to life, and within a couple of minutes the trophy was definitely booked for Ibrox.

Thrilling Goal

McColl sent a lovely forward pass to Rutherford, who, all through, had been giving Stewart an uncomfortable time. The winger crossed hard on the run, and Thornton came into the picture free of all opposition to nod down and away from Easson. A thrilling goal.

Two minutes later, Rutherford again got away with Findlay taking up position in expectation of a pass. The transfer arrived all right close to Easson's left-hand post. The ball seemed to be blocked between the inside-right and the goalkeeper, and bounced high in front of goal. Thornton and East Fife's Finlay rose for it. The Ranger got there, and on went four number three.

As a contest the match was now over. East Fife never giving the slightest promise of staging a grand stand finish. Indeed, the near things were at their end of the field.

"Diddler" Young

The Light Blues played now with all the confidence in the world, and that quality was completely exemplified by Young when, near his own goal, he dispossessed an opponent, and proceeded to diddle two more before sending a hefty but well directed punt upfield. A magnificent example of cool craftsmanship.

I would not write this latest Cup Final down as one of the best I have seen. However, it had some splendid moments, with Rangers emerging as a thoroughly deserving victory. They were a most enthusiastic team, obviously imbued with the will to win, seen in the manner they could accelerate when the occasion demanded.

East Fife, on the other hand, appeared incapable of finding that necessary spirit, apparently being content to jog along at one pace.

However, they had in their ranks one of the finest players on the field in George Aitken. Scotland, indeed, are fortunate, on this showing, to have such grand left-halfs as Aitken and Sammy Cox.

At Shawfield

"C" Division (S.W.) match between Clyde and Queen of the South will not take place to-night as previously stated elsewhere. Game goes on at Shawfield to-morrow night. The Rangers v. Dumbarton "C" Division fixture will take place to-morrow night at Ibrox.

Didn't

Four years ago, this picture was taken at Hampden Park. It was Swiss full-back Willi Steffen limbering up the day before the international against Scotland. To-morrow, Willi, who played with Chelsea for some time, will be getting ready again to take his place at left back in Switzerland's team.

Manchester U. Bid For Brown Soon

IT is on the cards that within the next week or two English gold will cascade into Scotland in return for very much-wanted players.

Some days ago (writes Waverley) I told you that Dundee's Gerrie would probably go to Newcastle United. The Dens Parkers play a friendly at St. James's Park on Wednesday, and if Gerrie satisfies the United board, as he has already satisfied Manager George Martin and three of his directors, there will be a deal likely to involve an all-time record fee for a leather-chaser.

Directors Stanley Seymour and Walter Hurford of Newcastle were at Hampden on Saturday, and on their way by road to Glasgow met Dundee's Director-Manager George Anderson. Gerrie's name, needless to say, came into the conversation.

Competition For Brown, If . . .

Newcastle also fancy Allan Brown and George Aitken, East Fife, but if they make a bid for the former they undoubtedly will encounter strong competition from Manchester United.

Manager Matt Busby of the Lancashire club took a great notion to Brown early in the season, and he has never left the trail. In a fortnight or so the United cross the Atlantic for an American tour, and Matt would like to have Brown fixed prior to the departure.

Not Keen To Part

I understand that he will make contact with the Bayview club within the next few days in an effort to carry through a deal.

Both Brown and Aitken have intimated they are not averse from a change of jersey. Manager Scot Symon and his board are not the least bit keen on parting with these two and thus weakening their team, but it may happen, as it almost invariably does, that the players will have the last word.

Want Winger Also

The Old Trafford club are also searching for a successor to Jimmy Delaney. It is realised that the ex-Celt can't go on for ever, and to find his successor in the outside-right position United are prepared to put down the cash good and heavy. They have been watching several Scots wingers for some time past, but up to now have received nothing but polite rejection of their overtures.

Irish Changes v. 'Central'

IRISH Intermediate League team to meet the Central League at Firhill on Saturday shows two changes from the team that played the Western League.

At outside-right, Torrance (Crusaders) comes in for Minford (Bally Clare), and at outside-left, where Green (Brantwood) is preferred to Hudson (Glenavon 11). Team is:—

Neil (Lindfield Swifts); Stewart (Dundella), Barnes (Brantwood); McAuley (Dundella), Caruth (Larne), McLoy (Lindfield Swifts); Torrance (Crusaders), Lowry (Glentoran 11) Orr (Banbridge Town), Williamson (Banbridge Town), Green (Brantwood).

Charity Cup Referees

Glasgow Charity Cup tie referees are as follows:—
Celtic v. Clyde (April 28)—W. G. Livingstone, Glasgow; Partick Thistle v. Queen's Park (May 1)—P. Fitzpatrick, Glasgow; Rangers v. Partick Thistle or Queen's Park (May 3)—R. J. Smith, Cambuslang; Third Lanark v. Celtic or Clyde (May 3)—R. M. Main, Glasgow.

Trial Game Is Off

Glasgow Welfare League trial game arranged for Wednesday to select the team to play an Edinburgh Welfare Select has been cancelled owing to this week's cup-tie.

Lanarkshire Junior XI

THE Lanarkshire Junior F.A. yesterday selected the following team to oppose an East of Scotland Junior F.A. team at Broomfield Park, Airdrie, on May 3:—

Henderson (Forth Wanderers); Malloy (Blantyre Celtic), Liddell (Lanark United); Mair (Lesmahagow), Murray (Wishaw), Black (Larkhall Thistle); Stewart (Royal Albert), Telfer (Thorniewood Utd.), Todd (Stonehouse Violet), Campbell (Douglasdale), Morton (Bedlay Juniors).

Travelling reserves — Hunter (Cleland) and Dobson (Stonehouse Violet).

Wembley Centre Doubt

Liverpool centre - forward Stubbins who slightly pulled a leg muscle against Portsmouth is expected to be fit for the Wembley Cup final with Arsenal on Saturday. He reports for treatment to-day.

SUPPORTERS' CORNER

CLYDE. — Glasgow — To-night, Tenters' Rooms, 7-8. Travel returns. Names for Cardiff and Wembley. Dunoon. Closing date for names for children's outing, May 8. Re-enrolment.

CELTIC. — Shettleston — To-night, Hart Street Hall, after Celtic-Derry City match. Return concert money. Re-enrolment. Final date names for International at Hampden.

To-day's Football Fixtures

English League III (South)—Bristol Rovers v. Newport.
Division "B "—Queen's Park v. Stenhousemuir.
Division "C" (S.W.)—Airdrie v. Partick Thistle, Albion Rovers v. Stranraer, Falkirk v. Hamilton, Morton v. Celtic.
Division "C" (N.E.)—Leith Ath v. Dundee, Aberdeen v. Brechin City.
Friendlies—Celtic v. Derry City, Buckie Th. v. Stirling Albion.
Division "B" Supplementary Cup—Forfar Athletic v. Arbroath.
Glasgow Junior Cup—Semi-final—Maryhill v. Shawfield (Firhill).
Lanarkshire League Championship (Decider)—Carluke R. v. New Stevenston (Fir Park).
Lanarkshire League Cup (3rd Round)—Royal Albert v. Thorniewood Utd.

Citizen Cup—1st Round (2nd game)—Bedlay v. Stonehouse V. 1st Round (1st game)—Burnbank Ath. v. Newarthill Hearts, Douglas Water Th. v. Larkhall Th.
100 Guineas League—Forth Wand. v. Mount Ellen U., Douglasdale v. Coltness, Lanark U. v. Wishaw Jrs.
Secondary Schools Representative Match—Glasgow v. Rest of Scotland.
TOURNAMENTS
Dennistoun Waverley—St. Mary's v. Garscube Ath. Glenboig—Tradeston Holmlea v. Croy Juveniles. Bellshill—Clyde Alloy v. High Blantyre Thistle. Bellgrove — Cambuslang Strollers v. Barrowfield United (Golfhill Park). 6.50. 100 Guineas—Kilsyth St. Pat's v. Meechan's Welfare.

Swiss Send 6 Of Team Who Beat Scots In 1948

THE Swiss party arrive to-morrow for Wednesday's international at Hampden, and they will be the guests at lunch of Lord Provost Victor Warren. There will be 14 players (writes Waverley) and of them there will be three who are no strangers to the Hampden turf or roar. These are Gyger, Steffen and Bocquet, who played for their country against us in 1946 when Scotland won 3-1. In addition to Steffen and Bocquet, Corrodi, Fatton, Eggiman and Bickel were of the eleven that beat us by the odd goal in three at Berne a couple of years ago.

In achieving that success they didn't spare themselves in the physical sense and, as they say in boxing, they hit some of our fellows with everything but the pail. The Scots were warned by the officials in charge that they must not retaliate, and to their credit they took what was dished out to them without complaint.

Sensational Recovery

I don't suppose the Swiss will bring those 1948 tactics into being on Wednesday.

Only Antenen is new to International honours, and he is included in the fourteen because he can play in every position in the forward line.

Nine of his travelling mates took part in a sensational match in Vienna against Austria three weeks ago.

The Austrian national team is reckoned one of the best in Europe—as they were in pre-war days—and with twenty minutes to go they were leading the Swiss 3-0.

The game finished in a frenzy of excitement with the Austrians fighting to avoid defeat, and the final whistle blew with the teams square at three goals each.

Capped 50 Times

As a pointer to the experience of the Swiss players, I should tell you that Bickel has played in 50 Internationals, Gyger in 40, and Steffen, Eggiman and Fatton each in over 20.

One of the most interesting personalities among them is 33-year-old Armin Scheurer, who is rated Switzerland's perfect all-round athlete. Among other things he is his country's pole vault champion and is graded No. 5 in Europe.

14 Chosen

THE 14 players chosen by Switzerland to make the trip to Scotland are:—
GOALKEEPERS — Eugene Corrodi (age 28); George Stuber (25).
FULL BACKS — Willi Steffen (25), Rudolf Gyger (30) (captain); Armin Scheurer (33).
HALF BACKS — Andre Neury (25), Roger Bocquet (29), Olivier Eggiman (31).
FORWARDS — Charlie Antenen (20), Rene Bader (28) Alfred Bickel (32), Jacques Fatton (25), Walter Schneiter (32), Jean Tamini (31).

They Pin Hopes On Defence

SWITZERLAND'S team has been chosen mainly with an eye for defence (writes Hugo Kuranda from Berne).

"There have been no all-or-nothing experiments; it is simply the very strongest team Switzerland can muster at the moment," said Mr. L. Minelli, head of the Swiss soccer selection committee.

"The defence," said Mr. Minelli, "appears to be our greatest hope in the coming match which is going to be very very hard indeed for us."

Against the defence advantage has to be set Switzerland's major problem in the attacking line. Bickel and Tamini — the latter scored two goals in the Vienna game — seem to be the most reliable in a doubtful lot.

THE Eagle BY GOODYEAR

"Stamina, strength and appearance—all outstanding"
— say Motorists and Tyre Suppliers alike

* The tread rubber is tougher, more shock-resisting than ever before.

* Wider, flatter tread area grips more road for more traction, and wears more slowly.

* The improved All-Weather Tread—with its new Stop-Notches for quicker, safer stops—resists every direction of skid throughout the tyre's longer life.

* Handsome buttressed sidewalls provide protection from kerb damage, and make cornering steadier than you've ever known.

INSIST ON GOODYEAR TUBES

You can trust GOODYEAR
THE LONG-LIFE HARDEST-WEARING TYRE

Fastest Scots dog killed

SCOTLAND'S fastest greyhound, Congress Convoy, was killed in a solo trial yesterday.

The dog smashed against a staunchion at London's Walthamstow Stadium.

Congress Convoy—valued at £2000—was making a final trial before leading Shawfield against Walthamstow in a return National Track's Championship match on Saturday.

Oh joy, joy, joy, for Ibrox—and Baird

by JAMES SANDERSON

CELTIC .... 0 RANGERS 4

BIG Sam Baird walked off Parkhead in the gathering gloom last night with the cheers of Rangers' delighted thousands ringing in his ears and with a big smile on his face.

For Sam, who had the Ibrox faithful moaning after his two-game flop, was the hero last night.

Scoring the first two goals, he did a lot to wipe out that Rangers' whipping from Celts last Saturday.

But not only that. He showed he has the football that made him the toast of Shawfield not so long ago; the football that made Manager Scot Symon detetmined to sign him from Preston.

Pace, power

If you were at Saturday's game, you had to rub your eyes and take another long look before believing this was the same Rangers. Celtic began with an attack as frisky as a French can-can chorus—but it was the Light Blues who had the pace, power, punch AND the football.

The attack was right in form, the defence was *really* an Iron Curtain.

And Celtic? We must remember that Stein hirpled on the left wing all of the second half, that Fallon was hurt and that young McVittie was out of his depth. But this was still a Parkhead shadow of Saturday's bhoys.

Array of tricks

No. 1 goal showed the shape of things to come. Hubbard—what an array of tricks there are in his cupboard—baffled Haughney, slipped the ball to Simpson. He gave it to Baird—and in it went past Bonnar.

eltic chopped, changer, and panicked, but couldn't stem the Light Blue tide. And when Maird got No. 2 Celts were on the way out.

Goals 3 and 4 just had to come. Simpson sent in a special that buzzed past Bonnar, and Ibrox babe Murray took the next as if he's been wearing the Light Blue for two years instead of two months.

Celtic—Bonnar; Haughney, Fallon; Evans, Stein, Peacock; Collins, McVittie, Mochan, Smith, McPhail.

Rangers—Niven; Caldow, Little; McColl, Young, Rae; Scott, Simpson, Murray, Baird Hubbard.

Referee—W Brittle, Glasgow.

This was one time Rangers did not score

● *With a great kick, a hefty kick, Jock Stein clears almost on the Celtic line in the match against Rangers at Parkhead.*

It's a round 1 away for Bo'ness

by BITMARK

THE Scottish Junior Cup sets off to a colourless start this season. The first round draw, made in Glasgow last night, produced no outstanding ties.

The holders, Kilsyth Rangers, at home to Fifeshire's Markinch Victoria, should have no trouble going into the next round. Beaten finalists Duntocher Hibs also start with ground advantage against Douglas Water Thistle.

Only in three ties do Central League clubs clash—Vale of Leven v. Perthshire, Renfrew v. Yoker Ath. and Strathclyde v. Blantyre Celtic.

The last pair have a cup rehearsal on Saturday, when they meet in the first round of the League Cup at Blantyre.

'Hill travel

Irvine Meadow, usually an Ayrshire hope, will have a tough game at Bellshill Petershill travel to Kello and should win.

Bo'ness United, who dominated the Edinburgh and District League last season, start off with an away game with Preston Athletic. Armadale Thistle go to Fife, where they play Thornton Hibs.

A junior now

Last night's S.J.F.A. meeting reviewed the case of Willie McInnes, 24-year-old ex-Falkirk and Alloa goalkeeper, whose application for reinstatement was rejected at the beginning of the month.

Now McInnes has been given junior status to play for Lesmahagow.

J. Collins, outside-right of Hiram Walkers, has signed for Duntocher Hibs. Kilsyth Rangers have added a left back to their staff, 17-year-old Joe Gibson, of Banknock Juveniles.

The draw (ties to be played on or before October 1) is:—

Falkirk forwards shine

FALKIRK 4
QUEEN OF THE SOUTH .. 0

QUEEN OF THE SOUTH did not come into this game until Falkirk had scored their four goals. The Dumfries effort came only because of grand play by Jenkins, their only worthwhile forward.

Falkirk, capably led by Wright, were stronger and sharper on the ball and their forward play was good enough to suggest that Celtic will not have matters all their own way at Brockville on Saturday.

Hamilton was grand in goal and others who shone were Parker, McIntosh, Sinclair and O Hara.

Fast work

Falkirk were business-like right from the start and in six minutes took the lead, Wright, from a pass by Sinclair, sending an unsaveable shot into the net.

Eleven minutes later, McCrae made the most of good work by O'Hara and scored from close range.

Queen of the South hit back for a spell and Jenkins had two fine tries which were near the mark

Falkirk, however, capably led by Wright, were soon attacking again, and from another cross by O'Hara, Wright once more flashed the ball past Smith to put Falkirk three up 11 minutes from the interval.

O'Hara again

In just over a minute, O'Hara met a Sinclair cross and scored with a grand header.

Queen of the South had one grand forward in Jenkins and a try of his seemed to be destined for the net but Hamilton brought off a fine save.

Falkirk — Hamilton; Parker, Rae; Fletcher, Colville, McIntosh; Sinclair Morrison, Wright, McCrae, O'Hara.

Queen of the South—W. Smith; Sharp, Binning; King, Alex Smith Gibson; Black McGill, Patterson Jenkins, McGuire.

Referee—D. McTaggart, Glasgow.

7-GOAL WARNING TO 'OLD FIRM'

HAMILTON ACAS. 7
ARBROATH 0

ARBROATH were no match for Hamilton, who with the prospect of meeting Celtic or Rangers in the quarter-finals went all out from the start. Their forwards were far too good for a stuffy Arbroath defence.

Rutherford put Acas ahead in four minutes from a corner by Armit, but soon afterwards at the other end McPherson saved from Smith.

Barrett then went close with a good effort before Armit increased Acas' lead in the 16th minute. Acas kept up the pressure, and there were near things, one of them being a Clark header from the goal-line with Williamson beaten. Later, a header by Miller tipped the bar on its way over.

McGrory had a great try for Arbroath which just missed, but Shearer added No. 3 for Acas just on the interval.

Great save

Arbroath attacked on the restart and Smith hit the side netting with a good effort. Acas came back, and Williamson had a great save from Shearer before Armit headed home a Rutherford corner in the 58th minute.

Soon after Rutherford connected with a corner on the left but Gray cleared on the line.

Shearer added a fifth goal in the 73rd minute, following a perfect Rutherford cross and then Miller netted a sixth three minutes later . . . before he made the score 7-0.

Hamilton Acas. — McPherson; Richmond, Quinn; Barrett, Boyd, Holton; Rutherford, Shearer, Miller, Reid, Armit.

Arbroath—Williamson; Clark, Gray; D. McKenzie, McKinven, J. McKenzie; Lawrence, Smith, McGrory, Walker, Cruickshank.

Referee—Mr. H. Spence, Kilmarnock.

Devine comes back to score two

QUEEN'S PARK .... 2 AYR UNITED 0

QUEEN'S PARK should have won this return League Cup tie at Hampden last night by the proverbial barrow load. They were so vastly superior to Ayr in all departments that two goals was poor consolation for such concentrated effort. Seventeen-year-old Douglas Orr had a pleasing debut for Queen's, and Devine took his brace of goals in opportunist fashion.

Round was undoubtedly Ayr's hero. He put in a "double shift."

Queen's, with any break at all, should have been two up in the first 15 minutes alone. Only Round stood between them and the goals which their splendid outfield play warranted.

The Englishman was in grand form and well deserved the ovation he got as he leaped through the air to turn round the post a terrific Devine whizz-bang.

Fortune smiled on the 'keeper, too, as Devine, in a further Queen's foray, headed an Orr corner for the net, only to see Leckie clear on the line.

Concussion

How the "Honest Men" managed to keep their goal intact was astonishing, as Queen's applied the "screw," but all honour went to Gallagher, another Ayr stalwart.

Devine went off for the last 15 minutes of the half suffering from slight concussion, but even with 10 men Queen's were masters.

With Devine back in their attack on the restart, Queen's resumed where they left off, putting the Somerset Park defence through the mill.

In the 54th minute success crowned their effort. Devine took a slip from Dalziel to beat Round all ends up with a lovely daisy trimmer from 15 yards. Crampsey was lucky, however, when a 40 yards drive from McMillan struck the bar.

Twelve minutes from the end Devine got a second goal for Queen's.

Queen's Park—F. Crampsey; G Savage, G. Church; R. Cromar, J. Valentine, J Robb, R. McCann, J. H. Devine, J. Ward R. Dalziel, D Orr.

Ayr United — Round,; Leckie, Thomson; Traynor Gallacher, Birch; Tracy, McMillan, Price Stevenson, McKenna.

Referee—R. Morris Falkirk.

'Well late burst see 'em home

DUNDEE UNITED 0
MOTHERWELL 3

UNITED'S lively little attacks worried Motherwell. They lacked the craft of the visiting forwards, but until the last ten minutes there was only a goal in it.

In a quick late burst, 'Well scored two more for a well-merited win in their League Cup section.

United were lively, but more methodical Motherwell scored after 35 minutes. From an Aitken pass, Bain ran almost to the bye line, touched the ball past the advancing McLaren and netted from a difficult angle.

Penalty miss

Four minutes later, McGairy fouled Reid in the penalty box, but Aitkenhead shot past from the spot.

United had luck at the start of the second half. Unaware that McLaren was out of his goal, Cross passed back, but the ball hit the post and ran to safety.

Nine minutes from the end Bain capped a great wing-to-wing move with another goal for Motherwell, and three minutes later Aitkenhead scored in a scramble.

Dundee United—McLaren; Massie, Cross; Callaghan, Arnold, Stewart; Jim Coyle, Reid, John Coyle, McGairy, McBain.

Motherwell — Weir; Kilmarnock, Shaw; Aitken, Paton, Redpath, Sloan, Reid, Bain, Humphries, Aitkenhead.

Referee—G. Bowman, Clydebank.

JUNIOR CUP—ROUND 1

PERTHSHIRE — Auchterarder Primrose v Blairgowrie, Perth Celtic v Errol, Comrie Rovers v. Alyth United, Stanley v. Luncarty, Perth Craigie v Coupar Angus, Jeanfield Swifts v. Bankfoot, Kinnoul v Crieff Earngrove. Bye —St. Johnstone Y N

FORFARSHIRE — Forfar West End v. Arbroath Anchorage; Kirrie This. v. Bervie Utd.; Forfar East End v. Stobswell; Auchinblae v. Johnshaven; Dundee North End v. Downfield; Luthermuir v. Arbroath Victoria; Dundee St Joseph's v. Gourdon Selby; Dundee Violet v. Dundee Elmwood; Matrix v Brechin Vic; Carnoustie Panmuir v. Dundee Arnot; Broughty Athletic v. Forfar Celtic; Dundee East Craigie v Montrose Roselea; Arbroath Ashdale v Dundee Osborne. BYE—Lochee Harp.

EAST OF SCOTLAND, FIFE, STIRLING—Dalkeith This. v. Bathgate This., Dunipace v. West Calder Utd, Nairn This. v Bonnyrigg Rose Ath., Arniston Rangers v. Loanhead Mayflower, Blairhall Colliery v. Linlithgow Rose, Forth Rangers v. Haddington Ath., Dundonald Bluebell v. Rosyth Rec., Kilsyth Rangers v. Markinch Vic., St. Andrews Utd v. Rosewell Rosedale, Stoneyburn v Lochore Welfare Easthouses Lily v. Ormiston Primrose, Musselburgh Ath. v. Whitburn, Valleyfield Colliery v. Fauldhouse Utd. Rosslyn v. Pumpherston Alva Albion Rangers v Glencraig Colliery, Steelend Vic. v. Penicuik Ath., Thornton Hibs v. Armadale This., Tranent v. Lochgelly Albert, Broxburn Ath v. Camelon, Dunbar Utd v. Edinburgh Utd. Newtongrange Star v. Bonnybridge Auchtermuchty v. Newburgh, Preston Athletic v Bo'ness Utd. Crossgates Prim. v Grange Rovers

WEST OF SCOTLAND—Duntocher Hibs v Douglas Water Thistle Douglasdale v St. Anthony's, Hurlford United v. Maryhill, Ardeer This. v. Glencairn. Largs This. v. Cleland, Kilbirnie Ladeside v. Burnbank Ath., Vale of Clyde v. Saltcoats Vic. Cumnock v Maryhill Harp, Larkhall This. v. Kilmarnock Muirkirk v Port Glasgow, Annbank Utd. v. Glenafton Ath., Vale of Leven v. Perthshire, Renfrew v. Yoker Arthurlie v. Lesmahagow, Ardeer Rec v. Whitletts Vic., Royal Albert v. Maybole. Newarthill Hearts v. Pollok, Kello Rovers v. Petershill, Irvine Vic. v Carluke Rovers, Ayr Newton Rovers v Baillieston, Mount Ellon v Wishaw Benburb v Thorniewood Utd., Blantyre Vic. v Gourock Craigmark v Dennistoun Wav., Shawfield v Beith Ardrossan Winton Rovers v. St Roch's Lanark Utd. v. Rob Roy; Cambuslang Rangers v. Shotts Bon Accord, Neilston v Ashfield; Strathclyde v Blantyre Celtic; Stonehouse Violet v Auchinleck Talbot; New Stevenston Utd. v. Bridgeton Wav.; Troon v. Coltness Utd.; Dreghorn v. Lugar Boswell; Clydebank v Darvel; Parkhead v Nithsdale Wands.; Forth Wands. v Shettleston; Bellshill v. Irvine Meadow; Kilwinning Rangers v. Dunoon Athletic. BYE—Dalry This.

Supporters' corner

PARTICK THISTLE.—Thornwood—Bus 12 Sawmill Rd. North West—Meet to-morrow. 7.30-8.30; pay dues. Bus 12.15. Seats Morecambe, September week-end.

RANGERS. — Fallside — Bus, 1.45 Motherwell, Bellshill 1.55, Fallside 2. Gen meeting, Sept. 8 Tannochside Welfare, 7.15 Ruchazie East—Those interested in new branch contact Mr Millin, 81 Crofterolghn Rd.

CELTIC. — Newmains — Bus 1.30 Thornliebank and District—Bus 1.15. Meet Mon 8, School Hall Uplift fund cards. Names Falkirk Wishaw—Bus 1.30. Falkirk names soon as possible. Norman St.—Bus 1.30. Hartfield—Bus 1 Meet Sun 7.30. Clear all dues Tollcross—Bus 1.30. Camden—Bus 1.15. Meet Sun 7. Dance returns and money, social convener. Kilbirnie and Howwood—Bus 11.45 Kilbirnie Howwood 12.15. Comm. Sun. 2. Gen. 2.30 Co-op Hall, Howwood. Lanchar —Bus 1.30, Charlotte St; seats non-members. Meet Sun 6.30 Robroyston—Bus 1. Tickets on bus.

HAMILTON ACAS. — Larkhall—Bus 1 30, Hamilton 1.45.

HEARTS.—Glasgow—Bus 1.15 St. Enoch Sqr.

ALBION ROVERS.—Social Club—Monthly meeting to-night, 8, British Legion Hall.

West tennis team

West of Scotland men's tennis team to play Northumberland in the first round of the British inter-counties hardcourts championships on Saturday at Newcastle is:—

C. V. Baxter, Titwood; J. B. Wilson, Pollokshields; J. G. Rutherglen, Newlands; R. G Harris and M MacDonald, Pollokshields, and I. Louden, Titwood.

Allan's 72 keeps him ahead

HOLDER DAVID ALLAN, overnight leader with 70, topped the Craw's Nest Tassie qualifiers with a 142 aggregate at Carnoustie yesterday.

His Championship Course 72 was scored in a high wind.

LEADING QUALIFIERS
(Championship Course first)

142—D. G. Allan (Carnoustie), 72, 70.
145—V. Finlayson (Carnoustie), 73, 72; S. Saddler (Forfar), 74, 71
146—D. H. Blair (Carnoustie), 74, 72; D. Bell (Caledonian), 73, 73.
149—I MacNiven (Mortonhall), 75 74.
150—D M. Low (Carnoustie), 76, 74; J. S. Tasker (Panmure), 74, 76.
151—T G. Gass (Longniddrie), 76, 75; T. Tennant (Caledonia), 77, 74; W. C. Hunter (Kirriemuir), 73, 78; J. W. Montgomery (Eastwood) 75, 76; D. Hunter (Broughty), 78, 73.
152—H. B. Moncur (Downfield), 81, 71; A L. Paterson (Greenock), 78, 74, N. J Duncan (Downfield), 78, 74; R. A Bowie (Prestwick St. Nicholas), 76, 76; A M. Forbes (Craigmillar Park) 75, 77; G J. Mason (Blyth), 81, 71
153—K. Strachan (Ralston), 79, 74; A. Norrie (New Taymouth), 80, 73; D. L. Hayward (Musselburgh), 79, 74; S Douglas (Wishaw), 78, 75; J. R. Walkinshaw (Haggs Castle), 75, 78; J. K. Shepherd (Kirriemuir), 83, 70.
154—J. C. Gilchrist (Cathin Braes), 75, 79; T G McLeok (Douglas Park) 78 76; D. Fowlis (Kirriemuir), 77, 77; D. Adamson (Carnoustie), 81 73; A. S. Gall (Dundee), 76, 78
155—R. O Neaves (Uddingston), 79, 76; W. J. Mowatt (Milton Park), 78, 77; D. M Soutar (Downfield), 81 74; W L Howat (Caledonia), 83 72.
156—T R. Callen (Prestwick St. Nicholas) 78 78; A. L. Ramsay (Panmuir), 78, 78; J. M. Doig (Monifieth), 78, 78; K. W. Hutchison (Panmure), 76, 80; R. L. Duncan (Blairgowrie) 8-1, 75.
157—R. Smart (Newbattle) 84, 73; R. G. Manson (Dunbar) 79 78; L. Blyth (Downfield), 80, 77; J. Cattanach (South Beds) 81 76; Dr. A. J J Nimmo (Dulwich) 78 79; W. A. Graham (Blairgowrie), 81, 76, A Paterson (Monifieth) 78, 79.
158—A. Maxwell (Kirkcaldy) 80, 78; S. C. Watson (Kilspindie), 81, 77; G B Henderson (Dalmahoy), 79, 79 J McLagan (Swanston), 79 79; R. H. Assleck (Craigmillar Park), 78 80; T. Stevenston (Tillicoultry), 85, 73; J Scrimgeour (Downfield), 79 79; G M. Thomson (Pitreavie), 87 71.
159—E. Bisset (Downfield) 75, 84; A. Syme (Ingliston) 82, 77; J. W. Stephenson (Swanston) 83 76; P. B Scott (Davyhulme) 83 76.
160—D. B. Marshall (Carnoustie), 80 80; J. M. Watt (Lothianburn), 80 80; C. M Suttie (Broughty), 82, 78; R. Ronaldson (Torphin Hill), 78, 82; J. A Maxwell (Vale of Leven) 80 80; W. M. Crichton (Deeside), 80 80.

FIGHT REFEREE IS TOLD: YOU STEP DOWN

by HAROLD MAYES

LONDON boxing referee Charles Davidson is to appeal against yesterday's decision by the Stewards of the B.B.B. of C. to downgrade him from class "A star" to class "A". This means he is no longer able to control championship contests.

Davidson appeared before the meeting to answer a complaint by the Scottish Area Council that during the contest between Frankie Jones, of Plean, and Dick Currie, of Dalmarnock, for the Scottish flyweight title at Firhill Park, Glasgow, recently he addressed a remark between rounds to a ringside reporter.

● LASTED 2 HOURS

He was represented by Mr. Michael Eastham, Q.C., and evidence was given by members of the Scottish Area Council by Joe Aitcheson, manager of Currie, and two newspaper men. The inquiry lasted two hours.

Afterwards Davidson said he would prefer to make no comment, "*since a remark I apparently addressed to a newspaperman has been responsible for the decision.*"

A referee for 30 years, he has held a star for five years and has refereed many championship bouts.

These include one in Italy this year for a European championship, when he received an official commendation from the president of the Italian Boxing Federation for his handling.

Apparently no complaints were made against either his handling of the bout or regarding his decision in favour of Jones.

Class "A" referees can officiate at area championship bouts, but not eliminating fights for national titles or British, British Empire, European or world title contests.

● FIRST GREEN . . .

Earlier this year Ben Green, of Leeds, had his referee's licence withdrawn after complaints regarding his decision in the first contest between Peter Waterman, now British welter champion, and former world welter champion Kid Gavilan.

There are at present seven star officials—Jack Hart and Tommy Little (London), Frank Wilson (Glasgow), Eugene Henderson (Edinburgh), Ike Powell (Bargoed, S. Wales), Andrew Smythe (Belfast) and Fred Blakeborough (Bradford).

Rangers one up after a near Battle-of-Berne Europe tie

This was fantastic—now what will happen in Nice?

by WAVERLEY

RANGERS .... 2 NICE 1

CAN Rangers, renowned for maintaining the prestige of Scottish football abroad, keep their traditional superiority over Continental teams in the European Cup?

Before 55,000 spectators last night they defeated Nice, but it is questionable if their one-goal lead will carry them through in the return game in the South of France a week today.

In the second half with Rangers hammering at their goal, the Frenchmen were fortunate not to lose two more goals . . .

A SECOND HALF THAT SAW WORLD FAMOUS REFEREE ARTHUR ELLIS FROM HALIFAX OCCUPY A FEATURE ROLE IN SOME FANTASTIC HAPPENINGS. CONSIDER:

(1) Shortly after half-time when the match, because of the behaviour of some of the players threatened to become a free-for-all, Arthur Ellis called a conference of the two teams and threatened drastic action.

(2) The whistler stopped the game 5 minutes too soon, and, despite the fact that this was pointed out to him by the linesman, he determinedly led the players from the field.

(3) Two minutes later he led them back minus Caldow, for whom George Young had to dash to the dressing room to restore him to the field. He was in the act of stripping.

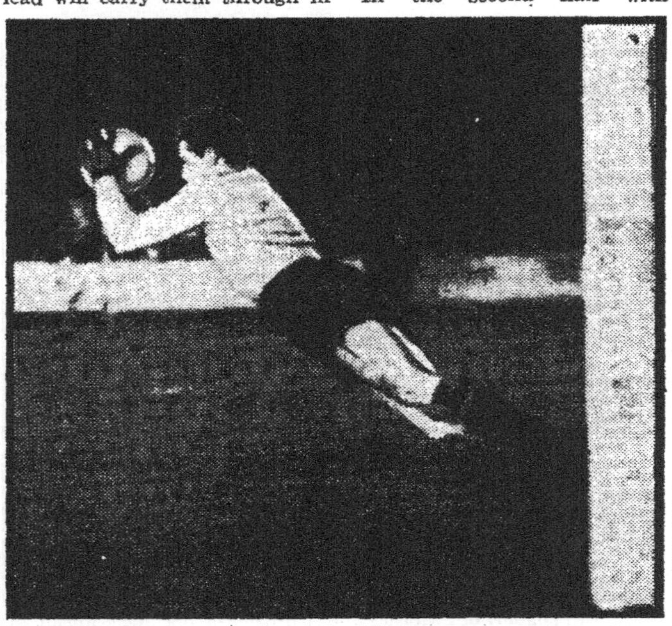

● With two eyes on the ball Colonna saves a header from Rangers' Simpson.

Exhausted

The Frenchmen were guilty of pushing, using the elbow, obstructing, and making gesticulating appeals to the referee when they were penalised.

Baird's retaliation showed that Rangers' patience, as well as the referee's, was exhausted.

IT IS SINCERELY HOPED THAT THE REFEREE NEXT THURSDAY WILL HAVE STRONG WILL-POWER AND UNQUESTIONABLE IMPARTIALITY.

If not, some of last night's happenings, fresh in the memory, will affect the return match.

Weak control

On occasions I have sampled weak control by referees across the Channel—and play hasn't been pretty to watch.

Nice have some good players, particularly in their forward line did I like Bravo at centre, and Faivre at outside-left.

But they are not a team depending on individualism. They work as a collective whole, and while many of their approach moves were delightful to the eye many, because of weakness at close quarters were wasted on the Govan air.

Rangers did not depend on the same rhythm of movement but on strong purposeful play that took them along the shortest route to a goal occupied by a brilliant custodian in Colonna.

In that second half barrage by Rangers Colonna was blessed with the luck that so often is a good 'keeper's right-hand man.

McColl undoubtedly was the great man of Rangers' team. While highly capable in a defence that faced with resource the quick-moving, quick-thinking French attack, Ian was masterly in giving the urge to the men in front.

Not effective.

For once in a while Rangers were not effective on the touchline, although it must be said for Scott and Hubbard, especially the latter, that they were frequently stopped by the illegal use of an arm.

If we can forget the shady stuff and bear in mind all the good play, and the earnestness of it, the match must be written down as hard, fast, and endowed with purple patches of skill.

But Rangers most assuredly have learned that progress in the European Cup, as Hibernian found last year, is not easy.

COME HERE, SAID ARTHUR

ARTHUR ELLIS for the dramatic. This famous English referee who officiated at the famous battle of Berne, World Cup-tie between Hungary and Brazil — stopped play at Ibrox last night.

Then he gathered both teams round him and called on an interpreter. He then in no uncertain fashion explained to the players that he would take drastic action if the shady stuff that had crept into the match continued.

His words had the desired effect.

In three minutes . . . a clash

Play was only three minutes old when Shearer and Nuremberg clashed.

This because the Frenchman, trying to make up too much ground to regain the ball, threw himself.

It was a case of hurling himself against a brick wall, and he went down in pain. A free-kick was awarded against him, and Shearer's lob into goal saw Simpson heading wide

The Frenchmen were playing accurate man-to-man passing but it didn't seem to get them very far.

McColl gave them a lesson on how to make progress, and was unlucky not to find an opening.

Baird, however, did, when, on the run, he shot a powerful 20-yarder that Colonna saved chest-high.

Rangers, in this first quarter of an hour, were having the best of it and most of the play was in the Frenchmen's half.

Narrow escape

The Light Blues, however, had one narrow escape.

The Nice left-wing produced a good-to-look-at movement.

Young crossed to cover a beaten Shearer, and, in turn, was passed inside by Faivre who cut in to position himself square on the goal.

But he made a hook of what conceivably could have been a scoring shot.

The much-boosted Bravo, with skilful delaying tactics, brought his line into perfect formation.

And, after making machine-like progress, Muro banged in an angular right-footer that on its way to the target was deflected over the bar.

The game was good to watch hard, interesting, and at times enthralling

THERE WAS, TOO, A TOUCH OF NEEDLE IN THE PROCEEDINGS. A TYPICAL CUP-TIE CONTRIBUTION.

Although much of their cleverness went for nothing, there was always a danger that one of the Frenchmen's cute touches would show a profit. And this it did in the 22nd minute.

Fernie-ism

A shot from Bravo, near the midfield line, to Faivre and the Rangers' defence was in a quandary.

The outside-left introduced Fernie-ism to the game—**CARDIFF FERNIE-ISM.**

He dribbled his way through on his own to end up by shooting past Niven for the opening goal.

Taking the lead on an opponent's ground, particularly in a strange country, is a booster to the confidence of any Continental team.

So it proved here. Nice produced their best football so far.

Technically, they were very good, and there was method in everything they did, either in attack or defence.

The aforementioned needle came into evidence a couple of times with Baird one of the central characters.

But Korzuk was no angel of innocence, although he would have referee Ellis think he had parked a harp and a set of wings in the dressing-room.

Just five minutes from the interval, when we were beginning to think that the Rangers' attack was not so good at close quarters—it had apparently got into the habit of depending on a Simpson header—the Light Blues got the equaliser.

Well placed

Baird set out on his own, travelled 10 yards, and when closed in by two opponents, pushed the ball forward to an expectant Murray.

Max had placed himself well to accept the judiciously-made pass and give Colonna no chance.

IMMEDIATELY AFTER, BONVIN RAISED THE IRE OF THE CROWD BY HIS SHABBY AND COMPLETELY UNCALLED FOR TREATMENT OF HUBBARD, AND THE FRENCHMAN WAS BOOED FROM THE FIELD AT THE INTERVAL.

Before that, however, Rangers' urgent prompting by a brilliant McColl put on the pressure, and only a splendid high-up save by Colonna from a Baird free-kick prevented Rangers from taking the lead.

Rangers, on resuming and playing into the wind, soon made us appreciate, as if we didn't already, that a goal lead was necessary to travel with to Nice.

In other words, they had set about making the manner of the going tough.

Nice gave the impression that they were content to concentrate on defence. But the coolness of the set-up was upset when Bonvin completely missed his kick and Hubbard just missed getting to the ball.

Hereabout there was a deal of shady stuff. Referee Ellis who had been generously lenient with some of the delinquents, called his conference

A comparative tenseness entered the match but this in no way helped to keep Rangers from their objective and within 16 minutes they deservedly took the lead.

Hubbard slickly took a throw-in, put the ball to Murray, who had run towards the touchline.

Tactics change

The centre turned and whipped the ball hard and high to the front of the goal, where Simpson timed it nicely to head home.

Nice now altered their tactics, deserting defence concentration and methodical approach play ended with Muro smacking the leather narrowly past.

Next, in the midst of French pressure, there was a hard shot McColl, a yard out, met with his head. But not as he intended, the ball hitting the crossbar. A couple of inches lower and it would have been in the net.

Then, once again, it was Rangers on the attack. Powerfully so, and Rangers should have gone further ahead from a Hubbard cross.

They dominated

Baird met it two yards from the goal line, but instead of nodding it forward headed it down in front of him to the ground, and Collona stepped in to clear.

Tremendous excitement as Rangers, dominating play, making all the going, surged in on Collona. A Simpson cross was headed by Hubbard, stretched on the ground, to be saved by a lucky foot from Gonzales

Scott fastened on to the rebound and had bad luck to hit the crossbar.

Back came the Light Blues with a surge again for Murray to beat Colonna only for Benvin to do a Dougie Gray act on the goal line and clear from under the bar.

It seemed impossible that the French goal should come through unscathed.

But escape it did and we had the sight of the Rangers defence, which for so long had the job principally of thumping the leather into the Nice defensive area, themselves having to skip lively to deal with a suddenly developed quick-fire move.

Then that early final whistle. After the players, 4½ minutes too early, had been in the pavilion they were brought out again in a short lasting hailstorm.

Rangers didn't require to be told they needed another goal. And they resumed their hammering of the Nice defence. Scott placed a corner and Simpson's head got there only for the brilliant Collona to save.

Rangers — Niven; Shearer, Caldow; McColl, Young, Logie; Scott, Simpson, Murray, Baird, Hubbard.

Nice—Colonna; Bonvin, Nani; Korzuk, Gonzales, Nuremberg; Foix, Muro, Bravo, Diratz, Faivre.

Referee—Arthur Ellis, Halifax.

TONIGHT'S DOG CARDS

LINLITHGOW—7.15

280—Bill's Lass (scr), Coal (3), My Lass (4), Dick (4), Linda (5), Chrome (3).

280—Bang (scr), Moon (1), Mario (1), Book (1), G.H.B. (1), Bus (2).

280—Blue Gillette (scr), Flag (2), Gow (4), Wee Midge (4), Teviot (5), Rusty (5).

280—Norrie (scr), Time (1), H.L.B. (2), Ramona (2), Pat (2), Gamp (2).

280—Nyoka, No Good, Decker, Eva, Pout's Gift, Hut.

280 — Beef, Sceptre, C.P., Gaiety, Millenium, Ella P.

280—Casey (scr), Hose (3), Chindit (4), Rossie (5), Vanboy (5), Lily (6½).

475—Meg's Boy (scr), Lanza (2), Fawny (4), Jaguar (8), Beat (8), Gundy (8).

Armadale, 7.30—Big Head, Belladon, Jenny's Cup, Ness, Drobny, Randolph, Lizzie.

Mount Vernon, 7.30—Good Hope, Iona, First Wall, Jimmy, Jean's Pet, Sun, Taigo, M.S

Blantyre, 7.30—King, Easter B., Tap, Rocky, Zip, Oak, Stewart, G.B.

DOG RESULTS

POWDERHALL — Starlight Heaven (1), 5-2 fav; Hot Spring (5); 8s, 37s 6d. **Safely Home** (4), 3-1; Barcloy Denis (6); 9s 6d, 48s. **Happy Seal** (5), 7-2; Barcloy Menace (1); 10s 3d, 37s 9d. **Solway Besom** (4), evens fav; Caddon Bolt (6); 3s 9d, 12s 9d. **Tillside Bobbie** (1) 8-1; Merlin Lad (6); 18s 3d, 99s 3d. **Barcloy Flier** (3), 5-1 Eden Dawn (5); 9s 6d, 41s. **Caledonian Mist** (3), 5-1; Bridge Score (6); 12s 9d, 81s 6d. **Supreme Harmony** (1), 3-1; Cheery Word (5); 8s, 39s 6d.

KIRKCALDY—True Silver (1), 4-1; n.r. Nipper. **Charity** (2), 4-6 fav; n.r. Rainless. **Sabrina** (2), 1-2 fav; n.r. Stone, Steel. **Newsboy** (1), 5-2. **Bull** (1) 5-1. **Tinkle** (1), 3-1; n.r. My Obb. **Brown Boy** (5), 5-4 fav. **Wee Murray** (3), 3-1; n.r. Christmas.

Late win for Students

TWO tries in the last five minutes of the game gave Glasgow University second XV. a 9-3 win over United College, St. Andrews, in their rugby match at St. Andrews yesterday.

The Glasgow men were the stronger team, though held until the closing minutes at one try each. Their forwards excelled in the loose and the line-outs, the backs ran well, but desperate defending by College kept them at bay until that late rush. Scorers were:—

United College—R. Parkinson. Glasgow University—W. J. Nelson, A. H. McDiarmid, R. B. McLeod.

Rugby results

Edinburgh University "A" 0, Royal (Dick) Veterinary College 14.

R.A.F. Turnhouse 15, Royal Scots 8.

Edinburgh City Police XV 0, Edinburgh University Vikings 12.

2 down—Gillon wins

AFTER losing the first two frames, Jack Gillon (Leith) fought back magnificently to defeat holder Bob McKendrick (Falkirk) by three frames to two in Edinburgh last night to enter the third round of the East of Scotland amateur snooker championship.

Scores (Gillon first) — 20-57, 35-63, 59-52, 70-44, 65-61.

FOOTBALL YESTERDAY

European Cup—First leg—Rangers 2 (Murray, Simpson), Nice 1 (Bravo).

Scottish Reserve League—Motherwell 2 (Bain, S. Brown), Partick Thistle 1 (Newman).

F. A. Charity Shield — Manchester City 0, Manchester United 1.

Representative games—Dutch Select 0, English Combination XI 6 (at Amsterdam); Irish F.A. 1 (Shields), Army 2 (Walker, Brand).

Perth Half-Holiday League — Half Holiday Un. 4, R.A.F. 2; Co-operative 0, Black Watch 10.

West of Scotland Police League — Stirling and Clackmannan 1 (Alexander), Motherwell and Wishaw 1 (Pender)

Glasgow Police League—Central 1 (Hurst), Marine 0.

Friendly—Luton v. C.C.A. Roumania (7.15).

Glasgow Police League—Northern v Headquarters (at Saracen Park, 2.45).

. . . and today

Youth 'National — England v. Hungary (at Sunderland, 7.15).

Saturday's teams

DUNFERMLINE—Mackin; Burns, Duthie; Samuel Colville, Mailer; Peebles, McWilliam, Dickson, Reilly, Anderson.

ST. MIRREN—Forsyth; Lapsley, McTurk; Neilson, Telfer, Dallas; Devine Flavell, Humphries, Holmes, McGill.

ST. JOHNSTONE—Bell; Woodcock, Montgomery; Robertson Follon, Palmer; Fraser, Russell, Rodger, Ewen, Whitelaw.

BRECHIN CITY—Nicol; Paterson, Hodge; Rennie Aitken, Christie; Warrender, Muir, Selway, Scott, Duncan.

LANG'S BANANA

GOLD MEDAL

JAMAICA RUM

With a tradition of over 80 years of quality

Football Specials

Saturday, 27th Oct.

Scottish League Cup Final

PARTICK THIS.

v.

CELTIC

A frequent service of trains will be run from Glasgow (Central) to Mount Florida between 1.10 and 2.0 p.m., returning from Mount Florida immediately after the match. Return fare 9d.

		p.m.	Fare
Coatbridge (Cent.)	lve	1.05	1/8
Whifflet (Lower) ...	"	1.07	1/8
Bellshill	"	1.18	1/8
Uddingston (Cent.) .	"	1.25	1/4
Newton	"	1.30	1/4
Kirkhill	"	1.42	10d
Burnside	"	1.46	6d
King's Park	arr	1.52	—

Return from King's Park at 4.20 p.m. (or in the event of extra time, at 4.50 p.m.)

BRITISH RAILWAYS

SELECTORS SHOULD PICK FIVE RANGERS

Here was one black moment for Rangers, five minutes after the start. Centre-forward Jimmy Millar goes down heavily after colliding with a Killie defender. He recovered quickly after treatment.

Waverley

THE NAME THAT MEANS FOOTBALL

I PREDICT that it won't be "Waverley's Team" who will line up against the Irishmen, at Hampden on Wednesday of next week.

When the S.F.A. Selection Committee sit down today to choose the team I don't suppose they will even consider my suggestion of a 16 players pool, with the ultimate selection of eleven, according to ground conditions. The idea is too advanced for the conservative thinking of Park Gardens.

Anyway there is still a school of thought that a good player can play under any conditions, despite what happened at Cardiff.

IF MY ASSUMPTION IS CORRECT, MY VIEWS ON WHO SHOULD BE PICKED WILL BE PROVED TO BE GREATLY AT VARIANCE WITH THE SELECTORS. NOT ONLY IN ONE POSITION, BUT IN SEVERAL.

PICK RANGERS' FULL-BACKS

Lawrie Leslie will be accepted without demur for goal. His excellent goalkeeping at Ninian Park demands that. Immediately in front of him I nominate Eric Caldow and Bobby Shearer of Rangers for the full-back division.

There is no finer partnership in all Scotland. Recently I have been comparing it with that grand club pair of not so many years ago, Male and Hapgood of Arsenal who were so often chosen for England.

The selectors, or some of them at least, have been making jaunts into England. They have been watching Jackie Plenderleith.

I cannot speak to how he is playing over the Border, but it cannot be said he proved himself of international rating when at Easter Road.

The best centre-half I have seen this season is Toner of Kilmarnock, and if Cardiff proved one thing it was that experience is a necessity in the pivotal berth.

It is too early to talk of Ian Ure, Dundee, for whom I have a great admiration. It might not be fair to him to place him thus early.

AFTER ALL, HE HAS HAD ONLY HALF-A-DOZEN GAMES IN THE POSITION.

TONER'S BID

I would say that if ever a player played himself into a Scotland team Toner did against Rangers on Saturday.

CONSIDER THE BRILLIANCE OF THE OPPOSITION IN ASSESSING HIM.

Ron Yeats, Dundee United, was reserve for the Welsh game, and it is on the cards that he will be promoted.

I think Bert McCann was unjustifiably dropped, and I advocate his return to left-half.

For right-half there are Dave Mackay and Harold Davis. While the former was no failure at Cardiff he was no five-star success.

In view of the splendid season which the Ranger is having, and believing a home Scot should get preference when it's a toss-up I go for Davis.

Regarding the forward line, one could spend hours discussing the pros and cons of the numerous claimants.

In fact, you could take seven or eight players and permutate them in such a manner that would make Hearts manager Tommy Walker's activities in that direction appear the work of an apprentice.

SKILL, POWER

Without any palaver, however, I offer an attack that carries skill and a sufficiency of power: George Herd, Alex Young, Jimmy Millar, Denis Law and Dave Wilson. My team, therefore, would be:—

Leslie (Airdrieonians); Shearer (Rangers), Caldow (Rangers); Davis (Rangers), Toner (Kilmarnock), McCann (Motherwell); Herd (Clyde), Young (Hearts), Millar (Rangers), Law (Manchester City), Wilson (Rangers).

FIVE RANGERS? I HEAR YOU ASK. AND WHY NOT? THE LIGHT BLUES HAVE BEEN CHOSEN IN SUCH NUMBERS BEFORE AND HAVE DONE US PROUD.

But those who might think there is too much Ibrox in my suggested line-up needn't be too alarmed. I've already told you the Selectors have different ideas from mine!

CUP OF JOY FOR FOUR

Mr. SYMON PATERSON BRAND SHEARER

IT was cheers all the way for Rangers on Saturday . . cheers that must have sounded extra sweet to four men (writes RODGER BAILLIE).

For all four have felt the cruel lash of criticism . . . the jeers as well as the cheers. They are Bill Paterson, Bobby Shearer, Ralph Brand and manager Scot Symon.

Each of the players has been dropped . . . but how magnificently they've fought their way back.

Brand is the leading scorer in the First Division with 17 goals. Shearer is being tipped for a Scotland cap. And Paterson, the quiet man of Ibrox, has finally been "accepted" by the fans.

Special welcome

They showed this on Saturday when they roared out a special welcome to big Bill, who had been doubtful because of an ankle injury.

And what about the man behind the scenes, the man who takes the criticism off the field . . . manager Scot Symon.

Rangers have lost only once in their last 17 games, yet at the start of the season the team was being torn to pieces by the fans. Now they are calling it Rangers best post-war team.

Take a bow, Mr. Symon. The football manager is the guy everybody guns for when things go wrong . . . and forget when things go right.

'I'M WILLING TO HELP THE S.F.A.' —MATT BUSBY

THE week-end has fairly buzzed with rumours about the Scotland team management.

Andy Beattie officially resigned from the job on Saturday when he made a statement to the effect that he now found it impossible to carry out two jobs.

We take leave of Andy in the hope that he succeeds in one— the saving of Notts Forest from relegation.

IAN McCOLL.

Who will succeed him? The Selection Committee will get into a huddle today and discuss the position — the first opportunity they've really had to get together since the chaos created at Cardiff by the non-appearance of Mr. Beattie.

If one were to accept the rumours that have been flying around each selector will go to the meeting with a different man in mind

THE MANAGERS OF ALL OUR BIG-TIME CLUBS HAVE BEEN MENTIONED, WHILE THE NAME OF IAN McCOLL, RANGERS AND SCOTLAND RIGHT-HALF, HAS BEEN INCLUDED IN THE LIST.

I know of one man who definitely will be considered— Matt Busby. Matt held the job before, but was forced to resign for health reasons following the Munich disaster in which he was so terribly injured.

Faith

Matt is prepared to take on the job again, feeling that he has now regained his health

"But, of course," he says, "it is entirely a matter for the S.F.A. Selection Committee to decided.

"I MUST CONFESS, HOWEVER, THAT I'M KEEN TO HELP THE ASSOCIATION TO THE BEST OF MY ABILITY."

While Matt is in full control at Old Trafford I think he is one manager who can spare the time for a second job, because of the great faith he has in his assistant, Jimmy Murphy.

Jimmy is the Welsh team manager—and proving himself a very successful one.

Ibrox Real idea kept out Killie

THERE were certain people closely associated with Rangers who went to Hampden on Saturday feeling a touch of anxiety.

They were afraid that Wednesday's tremendous effort at Tynecastle would have a reaction in the shape of listlessness which would be fully exploited by the strong Kilmarnock combine.

IT SEEMS TO ME THAT THESE PEOPLE DO NOT YET FULLY REALISE THE GREATNESS OF THIS RANGERS TEAM.

The Light Blues deserved this triumph, and Kilmarnock need not feel any sense of disgrace at their defeat.

SO SMOOTH

Indeed, the Rugby Parkers are to be highly complimented on a fighting performance.

They doggedly kept going to the final whistle in a game that I put down as being very near to the best League Cup final ever.

At the start those who feared for Rangers may have felt they had cause for anxiety. In the opening ten minutes Killie, with great spirit, went out for a quick goal.

BUT IN THAT OPENING STANZA KILLIE GAVE LITTLE INDICATION THAT THEY WOULD SUCCEED IN BREAKING THROUGH THE PLANNED IBROX DEFENCE.

Stretched right across the field, as though operating on a pivot, were six Ibrox men—the two full backs, three half-backs, and either McMillan or Brand, according to the flank on which Kilmarnock made headway.

To me, in this form of defence, there was great similarity to that practised by Real Madrid.

Gradually Rangers came into the game as an aggressive force.

And there was about them—as there continued to be throughout—a smoothness in their approach play that was never matched by their counterparts.

Rangers first goal came after 37 minutes' play, and it resulted from the fine understanding between Millar and Brand.

The centre delivered one of those short flicks to his inside man who caught the opposition defence on the turn to whip a low oblique shot well away from Brown.

After the turnover, while there was only this goal on the scoreboard, Kilmarnock came within inches of scoring the equaliser.

Andy Kerr got to the spot to meet a lovely cross from the right. He was perfectly poised to head it home, BUT THE BALL APPEARED TO BE CAUGHT BY THE WIND AND HE DIDN'T MAKE PROPER CONTACT.

IT WAS A BAD BREAK FOR KERR, AND FOR KILLIE.

But not long afterwards the tie was definitely won—WITH SIXTEEN MINUTES LEFT FOR PLAY.

Scott, who always had the beating of Watson for speed, from near the corner of the penalty box, lobbed a high one to the far post.

Brown, who had positioned himself at the other upright ran the breadth of the goal and with his eyes on the ball which he maybe thought was going over.

But it suddenly dropped and struck the inside of the woodwork to bound to the net.

DIFFERENCE

THE BIG DIFFERENCE BETWEEN THE TEAMS WAS UP FRONT, AS I FORECAST IT WOULD BE, AND SELDOM DID KERR GET THE FORM OF SERVICE THAT WAS GIVEN MILLAR.

Neither McInally nor Black had the ingenuity of McMillan and Brand, while Scott and Wilson were given opportunities —and did well with them—that seldom came the way of Brown and Muir.

The result was that Rangers' defence did not have so much thrown on them as Kilmarnock's in which Toner was really a splendid centre half.

A PIVOT OF LESSER CALIBRE MIGHT HAVE ALLOWED THE RANGERS' INSIDE TRIO TO CAUSE DEVASTATION.

Army keeps me fit, says Baxter

By *JIM RODGER*

JIM BAXTER hasn't done a day's training at Ibrox in the past ten weeks.

Yet he was probably one of the fittest men on the field at Hampden on Saturday.

Said Black Watch Jim: "The Army is the life for getting you fit, but I would have preferred to have got some training at Ibrox.

"Now that I am on seven days' leave I'll travel from my Cowdenbeath home to Ibrox every day."

Against old pals

Rangers' costliest buy, £17,500 Baxter has been a big hit since he was transferred from Raith Rovers in the summer.

Now he plays against his old Rovers pals on Wednesday, in the league match at Ibrox.

What had the Rangers scorers to say on this happy Monday morning?

RALPH BRAND: "My goal just came at the right time. I am playing well because the team is clicking. All I want is to keep a regular first team place."

ALEX SCOTT: "It was the first time I've scored in a cup final, and the goal clinched the result. My form is back and naturally I would like to win back a place in Scotland's team."

Quotes

Explaining how he lost the second goal, Kilmarnock 'keeper JIMMY BROWN said:—"I had to cover the near post, and I thought Scott was going to shoot there. But, instead, he tried a lob to the far post and the ball went in."

Secret of Rangers' come-back —they lost three games in one week at the start of the season —was summed up by skipper ERIC CALDOW: — "We are playing FOOTBALL. The man off the ball is doing as much work as the man on the ball."

It looks like Old Firm 1, 2

IBROX fans are already claiming the League Championship with only a quarter of the games played . . .

For Hearts let another point slip away, Dundee went down to slick-moving Dunfermline and Kilmarnock showed they are not just Rangers' standard.

Who'll be second, they ask. The answer to that one might be **CELTIC.** The return of Willie Fernie has put the Parkhead fellows on the rails, and four wins in a row have hoisted them to the top half of the table.

They are relatively six points behind Rangers but only one point behind the teams who separate them on the chart.

Astonishing

And one of them is astonishing **DUNDEE UNITED.** When they were promoted the gloomy ones were saying that after one season upstairs they would find themselves again in the lower flight Everything at the moment points the other way.

At long last **HIBS** have found the winning touch, and they did so at the expense of **ST. MIRREN** who might find themselves forced into an uphill fight

But I'm not forecasting that when the vital period of the season arrives the Buddies will be seriously threatened with demotion. Rather do I think there will be several teams in the danger zone with St. Mirren having the best prospects of escape.

Good judges tell me that the **MOTHERWELL - HEARTS** encounter at Fir Park was a soccer treat. The pair, in opposition, invariably serve up a delightful dish.

And here's a spot of good news for the 'Well supporters. Ian St. John is now well on the road to recovery and there are high hopes that he will turn out against St Mirren on Saturday.

BE IN THE MONEY WITH 'POOLMAN'

THE football results were just right on Saturday—if you followed POOLMAN'S selections—for he gave another display of brilliant forecasting. Look at this list of his successes:—

FOUR AWAYS on Littlewood's, Vernon's, Cope's and Sherman's . . .

THE EASY SIX on Sherman's and Cope's . . .

CORRECT SCORES—a 144-1 double on Hill's and McLean's (Accrington 2-0 with Middlesbro' 3-1), and an 120-1 double on Littlewood's, Vernon's and Hill's (Birmingham v. Wolves 1-2 with Middlesbro' v. Sheffield United 3-1).

So if it's lolly you're after (and who isn't?) you can't do better than follow Poolman, in the 'Record' every week.

Pin-pointing eight draws in the 12 returned on the major coupons on Saturday could be ticklish, and first dividends are likely to be good.

Other pools:—10 Results and Three Draws, good; Points Pools and Easy Six, moderate; Four Aways, low.

Record soccer quiz

This week's 'Record' soccer quiz and film show will be at Beith Juniors Football Club, Boys' Brigade Hall, New Street, Beith, TOMORROW, and at Routenburn Golf Club, Red Road, Largs, on THURSDAY.

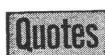

'GERS DATE MUDDLE

From
TOM NICHOLSON
Florence, Sunday

FIORENTINA have asked the Mitropa Committee to fix the dates of the games between themselves and Rangers in the Final of the European Cup winners' tournament.

The committee decision will end the deadlock between the two clubs over mutually suitable dates.

RANGERS WANT MAY 24 AT IBROX, AND THE RETURN IN FLORENCE ON MAY 31.

Fiorentina suggested May 17 in Glasgow and May 27 for the second leg. The Mitropa Committee which runs the tournament holds its meetings in Prague.

"I wrote to the committee three days ago, asking them to arrange the dates," Fiorentina secretary Luciano Giachietti told me on Saturday.

"THEY WILL BE WRITING DIRECT TO RANGERS AND TO US."

I caught the Fiorentina party just before they set off on Saturday on a four-hours' train journey for their league match with Lanerossi today.

From there they were going straight to Rome, where on Thursday in the Olympic Stadium they play Roma in the quarter-finals of the Italian Cup.

SINCE WE KNOW SOMETHING OF THE STRENGTH OF ROMA, THIS GAME SHOULD PROVIDE A FAIRLY GOOD INDICATION OF WHAT RANGERS ARE UP AGAINST.

Another thing that is in Rangers' favour, is that Fiorentina are in the midst of the kind of crisis that cost the Barcelona president his job after Hibs beat them in the Inter-Cities Fairs Cup.

THEY HAVE BEEN DOING BADLY RECENTLY AND THE FANS, IN THE BEST LATIN TRADITION, HAVE BEEN KICKING UP BLAZES ABOUT IT.

So much so that Signor Enrico Befani, president of the club for ten years, was this week-end forced to resign.

Fiorentina drew 0-0 with Lanerossi today, and remain in sixth place in the league.

Rangers manager Scot Symon said last night: "We are not keen to play at Ibrox on May 17, because six of our players are in the World Cup and they do not return from Czechoslovakia till May 16.

"We wanted to keep that week clear to let them recover from the travelling and also any injuries they may receive.

"We would have played on Saturday, May 20, but the Junior Cup is being played that day which rules that date out."

Everyone counts in the Rangers set-up

By JIM RODGER

WHAT makes champions? Tradition, skill, spirit, resilience, determination all play a part. And certainly Rangers, mighty Rangers, who have won the league flag for the 32nd time, have ALL these qualities.

But these are the obvious things. There must be something else in the mystique of Rangers that makes them our most notable football champions.

After the celebrations on Saturday were over, I tried to find out: WHAT MAKES RANGERS TICK?

There were all kinds of answers from the players and officials of the league champions, who are also finalists in the European Cup-winners competition and who next season take part again in the glamorous European Cup.

"The enthusiasm of the players," says chairman John Wilson

"THE WORK OF MANAGER SCOT SYMON," SAYS VICE-CHAIRMAN JOHN LAWRENCE.

"The club spirit of our players, who didn't mind switching positions when injuries hit us," says manager Symon.

"Everyone playing not for himself but FOR the team," says Ian McMillan, brilliant general of the Ibrox attack.

AGAIN . . . THESE ARE THE OBVIOUS THINGS.

Perhaps the man who got nearest the real heart of Rangers was director George Brown, who said simply that perhaps a moving tribute to the little old lady of Ibrox before Saturday's match was really their success secret.

"You see," remarked Mr. Brown, "everybody counts at Ibrox. It was only fitting that we should pay tribute to Mrs. Jane Paterson, who died on Friday."

For more than half a century 78-year-old Mrs. Paterson worked loyally behind the Ibrox scenes, washing shirts, darning socks, "mothering" the players.

"She was as much a Ranger as any of us," said Mr. Brown.

But only a club as great as Rangers would have paid the tribute.

Mr. Brown is right. The spirit of "togetherness" is probably the most vital Rangers' secret.

On Saturday, Rangers beat Ayr like real champions.

But United went down gallantly —and no-one tried harder than centre-forward Jim Christie, the new rage of Somerset Park.

CAN AYR KEEP JIM? ALREADY THREE ENGLISH CLUBS, MANCHESTER CITY, STOKE CITY AND BLACKBURN ROVERS, HAVE APPROACHED AYR FOR HIS TRANSFER.

Well, I know Jim won't mind playing for Manchester City. His idol is Denis Law

SUPERIORITY

But the team of teams for him is . . . that's right . . RANGERS. "I'm Rangers-daft," he told me.

He enjoyed scoring against his favourites. "Wish I'd got more," he said. But the 7-3 score merely proved Rangers' superiority.

● Teenage Allan Gray, Queen's Park centre-half, may be with Rangers soon

The Ibrox scouts have been watching Gray for some time. And Allan hasn't yet re-signed for Queen's Park.

Wolves and Partick Thistle are also interested.

But Allan, who has six Scottish youth and one amateur international cap, won't decide on his soccer future until he finds out how he has fared in his higher leaving certificate exams.

There's no word yet of Johnny Little, Rangers back re-signing. "I'm dissatisfied with the terms," he told me. "I have been offered less than the others"

● Just three of the men who make Rangers tick. On the right team captain ERIC CALDOW and below chairman JOHN F. WILSON (left) and manager SCOT SYMON.

THEY MAKE LIGHT BLUES TICK . . .

JUNIOR GAMES

TOMORROW — *Pompey Cup fourth round*—St. Rochs v. Parkhead. **Central League** — Duntocher v. Renfrew; Dennistoun v. Strathclyde. **Erskine Hospital Cup**—Gourock v. Port Glasgow. **Benefit**—Western League v. West of Scotland Association (at Muirkirk).

THURSDAY — **Glasgow Junior Cup semi-final** — Maryhill v. St. Rochs (Firhill)

FRIDAY — **Pompey Cup** — **Fourth round**—Baillieston v. Johnstone Burgh.

SATURDAY — **Renfrewshire Cup Final** — Greenock v. Renfrew (Love Street). **Stirlingshire Cup final**—Grangemouth v Kilsyth Rangers (Falkirk). **Maryhill Charity Cup final** —Maryhill v. Petershill or Ashfield (Firhill). **West of Scotland Cup—Fifth round** — Cambuslang Rangers v. St. Rochs. **Central League**—Blantyre Vic. v. Rob Roy, Duntocher v. Glencairn; Yoker v. Vale of Clyde. **Erskine Hospital Cup**—Benburb v. Pollok.

HARLEY WANTS IBROX MOVE

By RODGER BAILLIE

ALEX HARLEY, the highest scorer in Scotland, who has refused to re-sign for Third Lanark . . . would like to play for Rangers.

Last night 24-year-old Alex told me: "I have turned down the re-signing terms offered by Third. If they don't offer improved terms I definitely want a transfer.

"If it means moving to England I don't mind, but my football ambition is to play for Rangers. That would make a dream come true."

Alex has been at Cathkin for four seasons, and this year, his best-ever, he has scored 42 of his side's 100 goals.

Yesterday Alex joined Matt Gray and Davie Hilley to play golf at a coast club.

STAR INSIDE FORWARD DAVIE HILLEY IS ANOTHER WHO HAS REFUSED TO RE-SIGN FOR THIRD LANARK.

"My position is exactly the same as Alex's," he told me last night.

"I want to stay in Scotland, but, if I have to move South, I am prepared to do so."

Last summer Davie spent his summer holidays in Spain . . . and since then he has wanted to play there.

Manager's hint

"I think there are too many snags for a British player to move there. But certainly I would move to a foreign club, say the Italians, if I got the chance."

Third Lanark manager George Young hinted at the week-end that unsigned players would not be taken on the club's American tour which starts this month.

But last night both Alex and Davie said: "We would be very sorry to miss the American tour, but if the club take that attitude we won't re-sign simply to go on the tour."

No Morton move yet for Cowie

By KEN GALLACHER

MORTON have made no move yet for Dundee's ex - internationalist wing half, Doug Cowie, who was placed on the transfer list last week.

Dundee manager, Bob Shankly, said yesterday: "No one has been in touch with me about the player."

TWO OF DUNDEE'S FREE TRANSFER YOUNGSTERS MAY BE FIXED UP THIS WEEK

Raith Rovers manager, Bert Herdman, on the look-out for young players after his mass free transfer clean out has approached centre-forward Bobby Adamson.

May step in

The bustling leader will go to Starks Park for an interview on Tuesday.

After the promise he showed in his first team games for Dundee, Adamson might be the man to replace Willie Wallace.

Left-winger Fred Jardine has been contacted by Oldham and Leeds. But the Edinburgh lad, due to be married to a Dundee girl in a couple of months, may not have to move south.

Partick Thistle manager, Willie Thornton, the man who took him to Dens Park from Edina Hearts, may step into the picture

* * *

EX-RANGERS inside man, Derek Grierson, has been placed on the transfer list by Forfar, who have retained eight players

Retained are — D. McKay, D. Sweenie, D Berrie W. Knox, A. Robertson, A. Wann, J Coburn.

Retained but not signed — E. Brodie.

Freed—J. Roger, J. Buchan, R. Hill, J. Markie, R. Ewen, E. Gray, G. Lowe, R. Aitken provisional, and N McKay, also provisional.

FOR SUPPORTERS

CELTIC — Wishaw — Bus tonight, Young Street, 50 mins before k.o.: Branchal Rd., 5 mins earlier

TOP LEAGUE GAMES . . . BY THE TOP EXPERTS

This was Black magic

By BILL WYLIE

KILMARNOCK, the champion runners-up, are right in the mood to go one better in the New York tournament.

The way they dissected Partick Thistle at Rugby Park to win 4-1 was a football work of art.

All the goals were scored in the first half with the one collected by inside-right Bertie Black in the sensational class.

41 goals

Right back Jim Richmond sent Black away with a perfect pass and after a 30-yard run in which he beat **THREE** defenders Bertie shot past 'keeper Jim Gray from the edge of the penalty box.

THERE ISN'T A BETTER CENTRE IN SCOTLAND THAN ANDY KERR ON THIS SHOWING.

He led the line with skill and intelligence and brought his goal tally to 41 for the season.

Never gave up

Killie's strength stemmed from their half-back line with wing halfs Frank Beattie and Bobby Kennedy ever ready to help the forwards.

Give Thistle credit for never giving up. Their top men were Frank Donlevy, Davie McParland and Neil Duffy, and their goal was scored by Joe McBride.

Hugh Brown got Kilmarnock's other two goals.

CLYDE CAN BLAME ARMY

SOME folks point to George Herd's long absence as the reason for Clyde going down (writes IAN THOMAS).

Others mention injuries to Joe Walters and Davie White . . . but the real culprit was the British Army! When the Army took Dan Currie away to Germany, Clyde lost a player who would have run himself into the turf to make his mates fight on.

He did that on Saturday. Wearing £40,000 George Herd's jersey, the inside-right pounded all over Shawfield, starting attack after attack, then helping out in defence.

He got Clyde's first goal, setting them off to an easy 3-1 win over Airdrie. Now if only Clyde had had Currie's drive earlier in the relegation battle. . . .

Currie, along with ex-Hamilton winger Jim McLean, who scored two goals, can be Shawfield's inspiration in attack for next season's promotion battle—a battle that shouldn't be too tough for this skilful Clyde team.

Airdrie's forwards were woeful. Only inside-left Jim Storrie showed any good touches. New right-winger McAllister got their goal. And in defence, it was disturbing to see the indecision of international 'keeper Lawrie Leslie.

For Scotland's sake, let's hope there are no similar mistakes from Lawrie against Eire at Hampden on Wednesday!

HI HI MEN HIT THE HUNDRED

NO honours yet for Third Lanark, but their form against Hibs promises the brightest future Cathkin has known for generations (writes HARRY MILLER).

Hibs scarcely knew what had hit them in losing two goals to Gray and Hilley in less than three minutes, and never quite recovered.

A hat-trick by Harley (two penalties) and goals by Gray, Reilly and Hilley, brought the goals century amid wild enthusiasm. McLeod's score for Hibs was incidental

Hibs had six positional changes from the mid-week team in Rome, but this does not lower Third's performance, which might have pulverised any opposition.

The Cathkin forwards were devastating, with McInnes and Harley the master-minds.

Hibs were comparatively sluggish, but the most interesting comparison was between the respective centre-forwards—Joe Baker and Alec Harley.

Baker got much less support than Harley, but the Cathkin star excelled in distribution and is clearly marked for the big time.

YOUNG BROGAN MAY GET CHANCE

LOOK out for Celtic ringing the changes for the match against Queen's Park in the Charity Cup tonight (writes JOHN McPHAIL.

Celtic have Pat Crerand, Billy McNeill and Duncan McKay in the party, from which Scotland's team will be picked to meet Eire at Hampden on Wednesday night

I say Celtic will bring in John Kurila at centre-half, John McNamee at right-back, and John Kelly at right-half.

Young Frank Brogan will probably get his first chance in the big team at outside-left

The ex-St. Roch's junior has been playing well in the reserves.

The Motherwell - Celtic 2-2 draw again stressed how well Celtic are for reserve defenders Willie O'Neill, who shone at left-back in the final, proved his display was no fluke. He had a good game against Motherwell.

Well, snappy in attack in the first half with Hunter and Quinn outstanding, deserved their first-half lead.

Celtic's defensive power told in the second half and Willie Fernie's late equaliser made the result just right.

MIGHTY 'GERS RETURN TO OLD GLORY

RANGERS 3   HEARTS 1

Scorers: Rangers—Millar, Brand, McMillan. Hearts—Davidson.

A MIGHTY chorus of "We will follow Rangers" was still splitting the smog over Hampden last night long after the League Cup Final replay teams had gone to their dressing rooms.

It was the wildly enthusiastic Ibrox fans' tribute to the RETURN TO GLORY of their team.

They just couldn't leave the scene of Rangers' latest triumph.

And what a great victory it was—a victory which deserved the most thrilling after-match spectacle I've seen at Hampden since the Real Madrid-Eintracht European Cup Final.

This was a Rangers back to their best—

WAVERLEY

Light Blues 1-2 shocks Maroons...

RANGERS set off at a terrific pace, obviously intent on a quick goal. With slick approach play, they worked their way deep into Hearts' half and twice McMillan had shots charged down.

But they were rewarded in the seventh minute. After an all-out effort Scott cleverly tricked two defenders to send over a cross that Millar headed home high up just inside Cruickshank's right-hand post from six yards.

Any notion that this early counter would lay the foundation of an Ibrox victory was dispelled in exactly 60 seconds. A free kick was awarded.

Hearts were awarded a free kick after a tackle by Davis on Hamilton.

Cumming crossed the ball and Davidson, unchallenged, raced in to head the ball away from Ritchie.

WHAT A FANTASTIC START TO THIS GAME. Rangers were at their near-best, determined to take the initiative. But Hearts were EQUALLY STUBBORN.

But it was Rangers who emerged on TOP. They almost had the tie settled when within five minutes—starting in the 15th—they knocked up two goals.

Wilson led up to the first. He crossed a ball. Brand, timing the ball's flight beautifully, nodded it to the net. It was spectacular. But it was NO MORE EXCITING to look at than the one that followed from McMillan.

Scott fired in a shot. It was blocked and the winger, turning round to meet the rebound, nodded it down for Shearer who had moved up to support attack.

The back swung the ball into the goal area. There was a scramble. The ball came loose and McMillan slammed a shot in.

The ball hit the crossbar and bounded out again. Again it went to McMillan who this time used his left foot to drive it into an empty net.

Hearts switched their formation after the interval.

FIERY

In the early stages at least it didn't appear as if it would seriously upset Rangers' hold on the game.

Indeed, the Light Blues were more than ever on the attack.

A couple of fiery Wilson crosses panicked the Hearts defence before we saw the first Tynecastle piece of aggression . . . and a pathetic-looking spectacle it was.

The lone Bauld shooting weakly from an angle, 30 yards out.

Doug Baillie was having a great game and the Maroons forwards found it almost impossible to get past him.

A great save by Cruickshank stopped Wilson from increasing the lead.

Rangers were still on top and seven minutes from the end Brand was injured in a clash with Holt but the inside-left soon recovered after attention

especially in the first-half, when play was about as one-sided as an earthquake.

Their soccer was slick and effective. Hearts hadn't an answer as Rangers turned on one of their most fascinating shows of the season.

FORGOTTEN was the defeat by Dunfermline on Saturday as Rangers set a cracking pace from the start—AND WENT ALL OUT FOR GOALS.

A TRIUMPH

This was a triumph for ATTACKING football. Those confident, aggressive Ibrox forwards had Hearts dazed by the interval. I could hardly believe I was watching the same team as I saw at Dunfermline. Actually, it wasn't!

For Rangers last night had Baxter and McMillan. Their skill on the ball had a devastating effect on Hearts. And how their colleagues responded!

Take the first goal. It came in the seventh minute when Millar headed a fine goal.

Hearts hit back gallantly—and equalised in exactly 60 seconds. Davidson was the scorer.

AND THEN WE SAW THE REAL MIGHTY RANGERS.

They staggered Hearts with crisp, skilful soccer and goals by Brand and McMillan put them on the way to their first trophy of the season before half-time.

What of Hearts? They had been toying at the start with their 4-2-4 plan. When they were two down they changed their tactics.

BUT IT WAS TOO LATE.

Despite a gallant fight-back in the second half when they changed their side, they could do little against a super-confident Rangers.

And Rangers were unlucky not to win by a bigger margin. FOUR TIMES they hit the Hearts' woodwork.

WONDERFUL

This was a wonderful return to glory by a team whose form recently has had their fans muttering. Last night they were back at their best.

Rangers were a grand team, richly endowed with all the skills, always operating as a team, every man playing his part.

The most Hearts can take out of the match is the consolation of knowing that they fought all they knew in the second half.

TRIBUTE

The attendance of 47,552 was surprisingly small.

This was due to the fog threat.

Certainly Rangers didn't lack encouragement!

What an ending there was! After the presentation of the League Cup in the stand, skipper Eric Caldow returned to the field with his players, trophy held aloft.

The noise was DEAFENING!

But, as I've said, it was a well-deserved tribute to the team who came back so impressively.

BAXTER A WORLD ACE: ITALIANS

JIM BAXTER, an almost unknown Fifer when he joined Rangers 18 months ago, yesterday shot into WORLD soccer ratings.

For the Italian magazine Illustrated Soccer named him as one of the world's TOP players . . . the ONLY Scot in the list

Seven other British players join Baxter in the ratings . . . 'keeper Ron Springett, right-back Jim Armfield, half-backs Danny Blanchflower and Ron Flowers, and forwards Johnny Haynes, Bobby Charlton and Phil Woosnam.

Football yesterday

Scottish League Cup Final Replay
RANGERS ..... 3 HEARTS 1
Millar, Brand.   Davidson
McMillan
H.T.—3-1   ATT.—47,522
English League Cup — First round (replay)—Leeds Utd. v. Rotherham Utd (Postponed.)
English League L.—West Ham 4 Wolves 2.

THE LINE-UP

RANGERS

RITCHIE

SHEARER   CALDOW

DAVIS   BAILLIE   BAXTER
McMILLAN   BRAND

SCOTT   MILLAR   WILSON

● Ref.—R. H. Davidson (Airdrie)

HAMILTON   BAULD   FERGUSON
BLACKWOOD   DAVIDSON
HIGGINS   POLLAND   CUMMING
HOLT   KIRK

CRUICKSHANK

HEARTS

TAKE A TIP!

WHAT is the policy that has taken provincial club Burnley to the top in English football?

How can our provincial clubs take a tip from Burnley, who never spend fabulous money on transfer fees?

A fascinating series by 'Record' Sport's Rodger Baillie on the secrets of Burnley starts tomorrow. Don't miss it!

PICTURE ★ ★ PARADE

CONNACHAN IS IN 'CAP' LUCK

DUNFERMLINE goalkeeper Eddie Connachan, whose exclusion from the "Pool" from which the recent Hampden wizards were picked was a big shock, is now favourite to be in again against Uruguay on May 2.

Another stroke of fantastic bad luck that has dogged Lawrie Leslie on the eve of International games makes Connachan the obvious No. 1 choice.

The West Ham 'keeper broke a finger against Arsenal on Saturday and played out the game ON THE LEFT WING.

Friends

With Spurs' Bill Brown unavailable because of the F.A. Cup Final on May 5, Leslie was regarded as a cert for the Uruguay match. His injury now makes him a cert TO MISS IT.

That's THREE times in just over a year that luckless Lawrie has been robbed of "caps" by eleventh-hour injuries.

Said Eddie Connachan yesterday: "Lawrie is a good friend of mine and a fine chap. It's real tough luck that this should happen to him again."

The selectors name their side against Uruguay on Thursday.

Champagne for the heroes . . .

● It's all over now, Rangers have won the Cup, and Hampden's goal-scoring heroes—Davie Wilson and Ralph Brand—pose proudly with the trophy at the after-match champagne celebration. Here's how Record Sport cameras caught the big game drama . . .

● Lured out of goal by the wily Davie Wilson, St. Mirren 'keeper Bobby Williamson is beaten by the winger's snap shot . . . and as Rab Stewart looks on, the ball crosses the line for Rangers' second and decisive goal.

If it's a point you're after . . .

By TOM NICHOLSON

YOU'RE in relegation trouble. You need points desperately. Then pop along to Tynecastle, the happy hunting ground for teams at the bottom of the league.

That's the way it's been this year. In February doomed Stirling took a point, in March, St. Johnstone took another and Raith Rovers grabbed two. In Saturday's April sunshine Falkirk deservedly lifted another two.

There's no consolation for worried St. Mirren. They were the only club involved in the present dog fight at the bottom who lost at Tynecastle away back in January.

Until Billy Higgins stepped forward in the second half to put some real body into the Hearts attack it was like so many Tynecastle sides of late . . . THEY WERE GOING NOWHERE FAST !

Dangerous

How different with Falkirk. The strain and effort of fighting for their First Division life was ever present . . .

BUT IT NEVER BLINDED THEM TO THE FACT THAT BRAINS BEAT BRAWN.

And they had the brainiest forward afield in ex-Hib Duchart who was well supported by Reid and Thomson.

Every single Brockville boy deserves to take a bow with 'keeper Whigham and Lowry tops in defence.

Falkirk were top of the world at half-time, with a two-goal lead from Reid and Duchart that could easily have been more.

But Hamilton and the ever-dangerous Higgins levelled the score, and things looked black until Oliver's golden goal five minutes from time.

Joining Falkirk in the golden goal stakes were Raith Rovers who smashed Celtic's unbeaten home league record with a Bobby Adamson goal (writes SANDY ADAMSON).

And while the other partner in the Old Firm double were doing a victory dance before 120,000 cheering fans, the Celtic players had to slink off the park to the jeers of 11,000 soccer sick supporters.

Fault

In the other league game Kilmarnock proved again they are Motherwell's bogy team . . . at Fir Park

The last time Motherwell won at home against Killie in the League was six seasons ago (writes BILL WYLIE).

Killie won 2-0 and 'Well can blame that old fault . . . too many frills, not enough punch.

For Kilmarnock D a v e Snedden was the big star with Andy Kerr and Bertie Black the goal grabbers.

The position at the bottom of the table is:—

	P.	W.	L.	D.	F.	A.	Pts
Raith Rov.	33	9	17	7	48	72	25
St. John	33	9	17	7	35	58	25
Falkirk	33	10	19	4	43	68	24
Airdrie	33	8	18	7	56	78	23
St. Mirren	32	9	18	5	48	77	23
Stirling	33	6	21	6	33	73	18

SPORT ROUND THE WORLD

Dope report is ridiculous
says GERRY HITCHENS

By 'RECORD' SPORTS REPORTER

GERRY HITCHENS of Inter-Milan, who has been chosen for England's World Cup squad, was last night linked with the Italian soccer drug scandal.

Hitchens was shocked into silence at his wife's Pontypridd, Glamorgan, home when I told him by telephone that he had been denounced by the Italian League's Medical Commission for allegedly taking stimulants.

Home less than 24 hours after a successful season as the blond bombshell of Inter-Milan's attack, Hitchens snapped:

"This is ridiculous. It's more than that, it's fantastic.

"THE STRONGEST DRUG I'VE EVER TAKEN IS A PILL TO CURE A TOOTHACHE.

"Somebody will have to answer for this when I get in touch with my club."

Hitchens, along with Omar Sivori of Juventus, was alleged by the Italians to have showed a "slightly positive" reaction following a spot test for pep drugs on March 4.

Five fined

Their names along with eight others, were submitted to the Disciplinary Commission of the Italian League.

Five players, including three of Hitchens team mates were fined the equivalent of £84 and suspended for two games yesterday after being found guilty of taking drugs.

DICK MEETS INGEMAR

DICK RICHARDSON will defend his European heavyweight title against Sweden's Ingemar Johansson at Ullevi Stadium, GOTHENBURG, on June 17.

Richardson will leave London on June 7 to complete the final stages of his training in Gothenburg.

Carlos Ortiz, the 25-year-old Puerto Rican, outpointed veteran holder Joe Brown to win the world lightweight title in LAS VEGAS.

The new champion said he would fight anybody "if the money is big enough"—which could mean another world fight for Britain's Dave Charnley.

● Their mascot shield and cup lie snugly in the corner of the net . . . but that's the nearest St. Mirren will come to the real silverware this season, for all the power of the "lucky" charms (and "Cockles" Wilson) can't stop Ralph Brand poking this Wilson pass into the empty net to give Rangers the lead. Looking on is Paisley skipper Jim Clunie (right).

WAVERLEY

★ Secrets of the Hampden Wizards ★

THEY restored Scotland's football prestige in breath-taking fashion. They'll go down in history as the Hampden wizards. They're being hailed as Scotland's greatest international team.

What are their secrets? A brilliant new series in 'Record' Sport tomorrow. THE SECRETS OF THE HAMPDEN WIZARDS. Don't miss it.

RANGERS TWO UP WITH ONE TO GO

NOW for the League Championship to round off the Big Treble. That was the champagne toast at Rangers Scottish Cup victory celebrations on Saturday night.

And if Aberdeen, whom they meet at Pittodrie on Wednesday, and Kilmarnock, who visit Ibrox on Saturday don't show a big improvement on the St. Mirren of Saturday . . . THEN THE LIGHT BLUES WILL CRUISE INTO THE EUROPEAN CUP TOURNAMENT NEXT SEASON.

Saints started off with great spirit, but as they gradually let Rangers get on top they sagged so much that the last twenty minutes of the game was of little or no interest.

ATTACK

Certainly there was nothing to excite the crowd, and even the fans who proudly waved their blue scarves couldn't muster up enough enthusiasm to sing their Follow Follow song in the usual fashion. They realised it was too easy for their team.

But there was a period when one began to doubt if Rangers could cap their outfield mastery with those all important goals.

That feeling lasted up to five minutes from the interval when Brand threw himself forward to squeeze a Wilson cross over the line.

Rangers previously had launched attack after attack on the Paisley goal.

But just as often they were foiled and frustrated by a courageous defence . . . and bad luck.

BURST

BIG JIM CLUNIE, FOR INSTANCE, APPEARED ABSOLUTELY UNBEATABLE.

The Buddies' centre-half was able to guess just where to be to charge down or get in the way of Rangers shots.

Although Ritchie had to deal with the odd shot there was only one brief period in the match when Rangers supremacy was threatened.

That was shortly after the interval when St. Mirren produced a sudden burst and hammered the Light Blues' goal.

Then right on top came the goal that decided the game. Davis and McMillan combined and the ball came over to the left to be met by an unmarked Wilson.

The winger cut in and with Williamson moving to the far post Dave smashing the ball into the narrow space between the 'keeper and his right hand post.

Williamson managed to touch the ball as it fiercely sped into the net, but he had no chance of holding it.

PLODDING

It was after this that St. Mirren gave the impression their task was a hopeless one. But they kept plodding away until Fernie, damaging a leg muscle, dropped out of business and the Buddies lost their architect-in-chief.

Every Ranger played his part with McMillan as the artist up front, while young Henderson had a splendid game.

St. Mirren's big men were Clunie, McLean and Fernie in that order of merit. The centre-half had a tremendous game, while McLean kept forcing on his forwards.

Every St. Mirren player did his best, gave of all they had. The simple explanation of their defeat was that they were not good enough.

Police helped Bobby

By JIM RODGER

BOBBY SHEARER has won every Scottish soccer prize. But he will always remember how he won his Scottish Cup medal with the help of HAMILTON POLICE.

Bobby's thoughts were on winning a Scottish Cup medal to complete his collection of international honours, League championship and League Cup medals with Rangers, when he left his Hamilton home on Saturday.

But after only a few miles his car broke down.

Remembered

He looked at his watch as he tried to repair the car . . . the minutes were passing by . . . his deadline was coming near . . and he remembered how Willie Henderson missed a European Cup-tie because of a car breaking down.

Then a police patrol car drew up, and the officer recognised Bobby.

When Bobby explained his problem, the policeman said: "Right, jump in and we'll go back to the headquarters and get you a Police car."

Thanks . . .

Bobby was given the keys of a Morris Oxford, and dashed into town to join the rest of his Ibrox team-mates.

After the banquet Bobby went back to the Police with the car . . . plus his medal . . . to say thanks.

Six other Rangers winning their first Scottish Cup medal on Saturday were Billy Ritchie, Harold Davis, Ronnie McKinnon, Jim Baxter, Willie Henderson and Ralph Brand.

Ralph has another target. It is to score two more goals in the two remaining games to beat Max Murray's Rangers record of 39 goals in a season.

WILLIE HENDERSON, Ron McKinnon, George McLean and Willie Fernie—three wonder soccer babes and a veteran—are my Hampden heroes of 1962.

Their sheer soccer ability make this a Scottish Cup Final to be remembered.

I watched the match with old rival Willie Woodburn, one of Scotland's greatest-ever centre-halfs.

The player who caught our eye and brought glowing comments from Willie was young Ron McKinnon, a lad in the Woodburn mould, and I can't possibly pay him a higher tribute.

Cash- in

The cool assurance . . . the command . . .. the sharp, quick head glance to veteran colleague Harold Davis, marks this boy as a soccer great.

A player with a mind of his own, and the ability and knowledge to back it up.

I PREDICT A FAMOUS FUTURE FOR THIS YOUNG RANGER.

Wee Willie Henderson, too,

MY FOUR CUP FINAL HEROES...

By JOHN McPHAIL

cocky, confident, looked a great Rangers player, and once Willie learns to cash in on the tactical advantage gained by his speed and positional sense —he could turn out to be a prolific goal-scorer.

RIGHT NOW WILLIE IS JUST TO SLAVISH IN HIS SERVICE TO HIS OTHER FRONT LINE MATES.

Paisley fans, critical after the match, and convinced that McLean should have been played in attack were wrong in my opinion.

Don't blame McLean for this defeat.

The power dribbles and the aggressive quality of his play put the Paisley boy in the Baxter class.

GEORGE McLEAN ON THIS FORM MAY ONE DAY CHALLENGE JIM FOR A NATIONAL PLACE.

Never better

And now the Wizard of Dribble, Willie Fernie. As a playing colleague and critic, I have known Willie since 1949.

I have seen him star for Scotland, help win cups for Celtic, but never ever have I seen him play a more noble part than he did on Saturday.

Perhaps this was Willie's last big-time Hampden appearance—if so it was well worth the admission money alone.

A bright final from the Rangers viewpoint.

The Ibrox boys played a fast, super-brand of football, looked fitter and sharper than Saints, and always had that skilful little match-winner Davie Wilson.

A big hand to Clunie, a splendid centre-half.

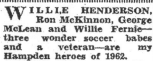

● Delighted Rangers fans swarm round to congratulate skipper Eric Caldow, who grins widely as, with the Cup held high, he leads team-mates Bobby Shearer, Billy Ritchie and Davie Wilson out for their victory lap after the presentation.

Ibrox held to ransom!

RANGERS reserves DEMANDING more than £20 a week to learn to play football. That's the fantastic situation at Ibrox.

They have been given an offer of £20 (an increase of £4), but with one exception outside-right Craig Watson, who is a part-timer, they have turned it down.

SOME OF THEM WANT £25.

It is not so long ago that one of those who have refused the 1962-63 terms told me that he would willingly play for Rangers for nothing.

"It's hard to believe," he said, "that I'm attached to the greatest club in the country."

And it's equally hard for me to believe that a bunch of youngsters who have yet to prove whether or no they can make the grade are holding the club—or trying to—to ransom.

Meeting

In the meantime two others have accepted first team terms, quiet man Ian McMillan, veteran of the side, and Willie Henderson.

Ron McKinnon has already agreed.

The directors, at their meeting this week, will consider the situation, but it's unlikely that they will make any move.

Anyway, the existing contracts, so far as the full-timers are concerned, have still three months to run, and by that time I have a notion that there will not be the same solidarity in the ranks as there seems to be just now.

CELTIC MAY PLAY JOHN

JOHN HUGHES, who missed the Raith Rovers league game on Saturday, may be back at centre-forward for Celtic at Motherwell this afternoon.

He is recovering from a knee injury but if big John doesn't make it, Bobby Carroll is expected to continue in the No. 9 position.

Celtic will not name their team until just before the kick-off, while the Fir Parkers likewise hold off for a late decision.

County derby

There should be a good sized holiday crowd at Firhill for the visit of Dundee United.

This will be Partick Thistle's last home league game of the season, and the fans have no desire that it should be a losing one.

At Douglas Park, Hamilton Academicals and Albion Rovers are engaged in a Lanarkshire County derby.

DON'T BOTHER TO CLAIM

WITH 14 draws on the major Treble Chance coupons on Saturday, no claims are needed and first dividend on tu'penny lists will be around £540.

On penny T.C. top price should be about £250, with farthing first yielding £60 and "eight for a penny £30.

Other pools news: Four Aways —520-1; Nine Results—200-1 and Three Draws—25-1.

Big chance for Celts

AT long last Celtic may get an opportunity to play the top continental clubs.

The Racing Club de Paris have put forward an idea for staging a new style tournament.

At a meeting in the French capital attended by Rangers director John F. Wilson, jnr., it was suggested that Manchester United, Arsenal, and Rangers should link up with top European clubs like Real Madrid, Barcelona, and Juventus to form a sixteen-club tourney.

Full list

The full list of clubs has not yet been compiled and that is why I ask if Celtic will get their chance.

If there are two clubs from England why not two from Scotland and Celtic would be the top draw.

They have the supporters and the playing facilities needed to compete against Europe's glamour boys.

HIBS AWAIT BAIRD OFFERS

SAM BAIRD is on Hibs' retained list, out over the week-end, though he has yet to re-sign.

The news will disappoint a few clubs anxious to use his long experience, for there was a feeling that he might be given a "free."

The Easter Road club, however, are willing to consider any reasonable offers for Baird and for his utility forward or half-back Bobby Kinloch.

WAVERLEY

Centre beat flu and Celts

JIMMY MILLAR IS THE HERO OF IBROX

RANGERS .... 4 CELTIC 0

Scorers—Davis, Millar, Greig, Wilson.

JIMMY MILLAR is the pride of Ibrox this morning, the toast of every happy Rangers supporter in the country after their great win over Celtic at Ibrox yesterday . . . for it was Millar who dragged himself out of his sickbed to play and score the goal that really finished Celtic.

Jimmy woke up shivering early yesterday morning and right away he knew the signs . . . FLU.

He had breakfast and travelled from his Edinburgh home to Glasgow three hours earlier in an effort to get himself fit to play.

When he arrived at Ibrox trainer Dave Kinnear joined the battle and after some pills the flu bug was beaten and Jimmy went on to the field . . . AND ON TO GLORY.

For it was his goal in the sixty-ninth minute which settled the game in Rangers favour and from then on Celtic were completely outclassed.

Let there be no mistake about it, Rangers, at the end of the day, were the easiest of winners.

Celtic had quite a lot of the play, but once either Crerand or Price, both good class wing-halfs doing all that was expected of them, parted with the ball all the fire went out of the Celtic team.

SINGING

The Parkhead forward line, as they have done for a long time now, lacked the killer touch, and although they occasionally got in a shot at Ritchie, they really never looked like a scoring line.

What a difference with the Rangers attack, every one of whom was goal-minded, and ready at every opportunity to have a go—sometimes too ready when a pass to a better-placed mate would have paid off.

Their first counter came along in the twelfth minute.

Acott, operating on the most treacherous part of the pitch, placed a short corner to Davis.

The wing-half neatly beat an opponent and shot.

THE BALL STRUCK CRERAND, ROSE HIGH IN THE AIR AND DROPPED TO THE NET INSIDE HAFFEY'S RIGHT HAND POST.

Celtic's supporters, by their singing did not seem very worried.

But they were silenced twenty-three minutes after the interval.

Brand, out on the left, crossed a hard vicious ball. Haffey pushed it out and Millar on the spot, hooked it into the empty net.

Rangers now took over completely and within two minutes they were three up.

Greig and Brand inter-passed for forty yards and completely upset the Celtic defence before Greig cracked in an angular 18-yarder that gave Haffey no chance.

Celtic were down and out, and their supporters started the retreat from Ibrox, and thousands of them failed to see the final goal. Shearer passed to Davis, who had run into the outside-right position.

The half-back cleverly beat Kennedy and cut the ball across goal. It reached Wilson, who slashed it home past Haffey.

LOYALTY

The great players in the Rangers team — apart from Jimmy Millar, whose club loyalty played such an important part in the victory— were Baxter and McKinnon.

The latter was a rock and mastered Hughes, who latterly went to outside-left.

Watching Baxter I wished more than ever that this truly great player would make his peace with Rangers and decide that he wants to stay at Ibrox.

Celtic's best were Haffey, Kennedy, Crerand and Price.

But Rangers had the team work, the pace and the punch.

On this showing they could very well stay at the top of the league for the rest of the season.

It was a sporting game, the only discordant note being in the first half when referee McKenzie, a highly capable official found it necessary to speak to McKinnon and Hughes, when the pair were needled at one another.

Rangers — Ritchie; Shearer, Caldow; Davis, McKinnon, Baxter; Scott, Greig, Millar, Brand, Wilson. Celtic—Haffey; McKay, Kennedy; Crerand, McNeil, Price; Chalmers, Murdoch, Hughes, Gallacher, Brogan. Referee—A. McKenzie. Attendance—55,000.

● It's Rangers' first. And no wonder Ralph Brand jumps for joy. Right-half Harold Davis (not in picture) has just beaten Celtic 'keeper Frank Haffey to open the scoring at Ibrox yesterday.

● Rangers left-winger Davie Wilson turns away delightedly after crashing in the fourth against Celtic at Ibrox yesterday.

● A wonderful drive by Ralph Brand screams across the Celtic goal. 'Keeper Frank Haffey gets to the ball but can't hold it and Jimmy Millar is on the spot to grab Rangers second.

● Rangers inside-right John Greig has just made it 3-0 against Celtic at Ibrox. Ralph Brand follows the ball into the net to make sure.

Celts' fortieth perm flops
LEFT HOOK GIVES 'GERS THE CUP

● BOBBY CRAIG . . . a perm flop.

By HUGH TAYLOR
'Record' Sports Editor

LONG before half-time the Hampden terracings told the story of the most EMBARRASSING Cup Final in the history of Scottish football.

AT THE RANGERS END the densely-packed fans in their light-blue scarves chuckled, chortled and chanted the new, derisive cha-cha : EASY . . . EASY . . . EASY.

AT THE CELTIC END, where gaps as wide as prairies were showing, the disconsolate men in green shuddered, shivered and sickened as their team, once famed as Scotland's most courageous cup-fighters, took their most humiliating defeat.

It was Rangers' easiest Cup Final victory. Their win last night equals Celtic's record of 17 successes, and gave them a League and Cup double for the eighth time.

But it was also the tamest final seen for years—and a great disappointment for the 120,000 crowd.

Indeed, all the excitement came just BEFORE the teams lined up.

The teams weren't announced before the game . . . which was perhaps just as well.

SHELL SHOCKED

For the Celtic fans were still SHOCKED by the formation of the attack named on the morning of the match by the Parkhead bosses—Murdoch, Craig, Hughes, Divers and Chalmers.

They're still arguing about the absence of the impish, dashing Jimmy Johnstone and the game had started before they realised the REAL line-up was: Craig, Murdoch, Divers, Chalmers and Hughes . . . Celtic's 40th forward perm of the season.

Why all the kidding? I don't know. The fans didn't know.

And, frankly, either did the Celtic players.

For at the start they didn't seem only shocked . . . they were SHELL SHOCKED.

I can only hope that Craig and Hughes were so baffled by the kidology that they were in a trance. For they never looked like wingers.

But then, Celtic never looked like the real Celtic. AND IT WAS NEVER REALLY A CONTEST.

Rangers, icy professionals, had made only one enforced change—Ian McMillan for the injured George McLean.

And before Celtic, who had permed FIVE from FIVE in their previously-announced attack, had time to realise just who was playing where, Rangers were a goal up.

Only six minutes had gone. Menacing Jimmy Millar, back to form, flashed a fine pass out to the right.

Wee Willie Henderson had anticipated it so well that Jim Kennedy was left standing like a traffic light.

He darted in, crossed, and Ralph Brand shot neatly past the helpless Frank Haffey.

IF WE HAD ONLY KNOWN, WE COULD ALL HAVE GONE HOME THEN.

GRAND GOAL

For Celtic never recovered . . . whether from that grand goal or from the effects of yet another permutation I don't know.

Anyhow, it was Rangers, Rangers, Rangers all the way. Casual Jim Baxter dictated play as he wanted. Ian McMillan gave Henderson a service that couldn't have been equalled by a butler in the stateliest of homes.

The lethal left hook of Wilson and Brand thudded against the Celtic defence with the zip of a Sonny Liston punch.

And all the time the Rangers defence looked on . . . as aloof and as unmolested as spaceman Gordon Cooper more than a hundred miles up in the air.

Only the persevering Billy Price, the resolute Billy McNeill and the sturdy Duncan MacKay were making any gestures of protest against this Rangers domination.

The Parkhead forward line might as well have been listening to the Spurs match on the radio.

CLASSY

Rangers were stamped with class, Celtic with desperation.

And a minute before half-time it was all over.

Again Millar dashed and passed. This time to Brand. Haffey could only parry the shot and Wilson ran in to score easily.

The "EASY EASY" cha cha began — and the Celtic end began to empty.

To be fair to Celtic, they fought with some of their old spirit in the second half.

But now they faced the slight breeze — and they didn't have a chance.

CONFIDENT

Rangers tried to turn on the style — but without great success. Not that they needed to for the game was finished.

And in the 73rd minute any slight hope Celtic might have had vanished.

Ralph Brand, from more than 20 yards, tried a happy-go-lucky shot, and no one was happy with Haffey, especially Frank himself, when the ball bounced into the net.

Rangers had the class—a confident, never-stretched defence, commanding half-backs and an attack which showed more than a few glimpses of top form.

NO DEVIL

Celtic . . . well, they lacked devil and cohesion up front.

But whether another permutation would have helped I don't know.

Frankly, I've never seen them so much out of a game and I can award pass marks only to MacKay, McNeill, Price and Chalmers, who tried so hard.

Celtic—Haffey; MacKay, Kennedy; McNamee, McNeill, Price; Craig, Murdoch, Divers, Chalmers, Hughes.

Rangers—Ritchie; Shearer, Provan; Greig, McKinnon, Baxter; Henderson, McMillan, Millar, Brand, Wilson.

Referee—T. Wharton, Clarkston.

IT'S MEDAL HAT-TRICK FOR IAN

Inside-right Ian McMillan was the 33-year-old comeback king of Hampden last night when he steered Rangers to their Cup win.

Sure, the wee Prime Minister faded. Sure, he lacked pace . . . especially in the second half (writes KEN GALLACHER).

BUT HE BROUGHT THE FLASHES OF GENIUS, THE DELICATE PROBING PASSES TO CELTIC'S WEAK SPOTS, THAT HAD BEEN LACKING IN THE FIRST GAME.

This was McMillan's THIRD Cup medal since joining Rangers from Airdrie five years ago.

Wonderful

After the champagne celebration in the Rangers' dressing room, Ian said: "It's a wonderful, wonderful feeling."

Comments from players and officials were:

Rangers' manager Scot Symon—"I'm really delighted and I thought the team played well."

Chairman John Lawrence—"A great sporting game. I am very happy that we won the Cup in my first term as chairman."

John Greig, injured in the first half after a clash with John McNamee—"My nose bled quite badly to start with . . . but nothing would have got me off the field."

"It was plugged at half-time and again at the end of the game."

Best team

And from the disappointed Celtic side:

Chairman Bob Kelly: "We are very, very disappointed !"

Skipper Billy McNeill: "The best team won . . . what more can I say ?"

To add to the Celtic troubles, McNeill took a leg knock 10 minutes from time . . . and he was still limping as he left Hampden. He will get treatment today.

Celtic lost it all up front

By WAVERLEY

THE Scottish Cup goes once more to the Ibrox Trophy Room . . . and no wonder !

From the seventh minute, when Brand swept the ball home from a Henderson cross, Rangers always looked emphatic winners, and if it had not been for the magnificent first half defensive play of Billy McNeill, the score would have been much greater at the interval.

The big difference between the teams was up front. The Celtic fans maybe found it hard to understand the permutation that had Craig at outside-right.

But the Rangers defence never found it hard to deal with.

And the fact that Ritchie had nothing to deal with but loose balls — until a Hughes 20-yarder five minutes before the interval—showed the poverty of the Celtic forward play.

THE DIVERS-LED LINE NEVER GOT GOING. HOW DIFFERENT WITH RANGERS !

Millar, playing his best game, led his men skilfully, and his distribution could hardly have been improved upon.

And remember, he faced a grand centre-half, which made his performance all the more creditable.

McMillan emphatically showed that he was the right man for inside-right, and his passes inside Kennedy to the on-running Henderson frequently had the left-back in a tizzy.

Celtic's worst

On the other side of the field, Brand and Wilson had stiffer opposition in McKay, but that they overcame it successfully is proved by the fact that they got their side's goals.

The fact that the Celtic forward line could never get going, threw extra work on McNamee and Price, who, in turn, were sorely harassed by the Rangers attack.

IT WAS NOT A HAPPY NIGHT FOR HAFFEY, WHO, IN GREAT CONTRAST TO THE FIRST MATCH, WAS NEVER REALLY AT EASE, AND COULD BE FAULTED FOR THE SECOND AND THIRD GOALS.

Ritchie generally had a long-distance view of the tie. His backs were never worried.

Baxter, indeed, had time on occasion to bring in the odd bit of kidology to further humiliate Celtic.

IT WAS NOT A GREAT CUP FINAL

Indeed, it was poor and Celtic must take full responsibility. They were no match for their great rivals.

I have seen Celtic in many finals, but this was their poorest showing of the lot, and those responsible for sending out such a weak forward line must accept their share of the blame.

The attendance was officially returned at 120,273, and those who came to cheer Celtic started to leave Hampden in disgust long before the final whistle.

The Celtic end, indeed, was almost deserted when referee Tom Wharton ended what was really a one-horse race.

McLEAN GETS A CHEER . . .

IT was the second Scottish Cup final in two years for Rangers' inside-right George McLean . . . and the SECOND DISAPPOINTMENT.

Last year he was in St. Mirren's team beaten by Rangers. This year he sat it out in the stand with an ankle injury, which will keep him out of soccer until next season.

However he forgot his disappointment as he joined the celebrations after the game. And he earned a special cheer when he left wearing a BOWLER HAT on the back of his head.

● The exuberance of victory . . . smiling Jim Baxter, mischievous as ever, grabs the ball after the Cup final replay and . . . er . . . you can see what he has done with it ! But Slim Jim had taken it to hand over to veteran Ian McMillan, appearing in his THIRD winning Rangers' Cup final team in five years.

THE BIG GAME

● No wonder they are smiling . . . no wonder even the Morton fans in the 105,000 crowd at Hampden cheered them at the end. They are Rangers' teenage terrors (left to right) Jim Forrest, Alec Willoughby and Willie Henderson . . . the terrible trio who carved up Morton's defence and gave Rangers a 5-0 win and another League Cup.

Teen Terrors

Jim's spying trip is a winner

By JIM RODGER

ONE of the first people to congratulate Jim Forrest on his four goals against Morton was the odd man out in Rangers' Cup team—Jimmy Millar.

As Forrest went into the dressing-room Millar went straight to him and said: "WELL DONE, JIM."

Forrest's four goals on Saturday brings his total to 27 this season—the top mark in Scottish football.

Young Jim is in his third season with Rangers. In the third team he netted 38 and when promoted to the second team his season's total was 52.

Now he has netted 27 in the first team and has every chance of adding many more before the end of the season.

To get to the top he had to displace three Rangers centre-forwards, Jimmy Millar, Max Murray and Jim Christie.

Advice

Jim, just turned 19, has a great future and the big question is—will he be able to take the success? Right away I say 'YES.'

I have studied young Jim since he played for Scotland Schools and Youth International teams. He is a quiet, modest young lad. After the game he summed it all up:

"I'm still serving my soccer apprenticeship. I have a lot to learn and I'm willing to listen to good advice."

Jim has dedicated himself to football and he watched every Morton move in the semi-final against Hibs so that he knew where to strike.

His cousin, Alec Willoughby, got the other Rangers goal and, like Jim, it was his first big-team medal.

Willie Henderson, too, was thrilled to get his first League Cup medal. "It's wonderful," he said. "Now I've won the lot with Rangers."

Famous

As kids Willie, Alec and Jim had offers to go to Manchester United.

But they all preferred to join Rangers, and they can look forward to a bright future with the famous club.

Craig Watson, who took a groin knock in the final tie, is doubtful for Wednesday's League game with Queen of the South at Ibrox. There was an attendance of 105,907 fans who paid a record admission total of £26,000.

Rangers will hold a victory banquet on Thursday.

Morton now face the big hurdle of getting more points to make sure of promotion and return to the First Division where they belong.

PLAYERS ASK FOR TV PAY

SCOTLAND'S soccer players last night launched a campaign to cash in on television. (writes JIM RODGER).

They want paid for appearing in TV excerpts shown after games. At present the players get nothing.

Said Secretary John Hughes after the annual meeting of the Players Union in Glasgow:

"We feel very strongly about this. The payment goes to the S.F.A. or the League, who in turn pay the clubs concerned.

"We will seek a meeting of the Football TV Sub-Committee, and also the two television companies to thrash it all out."

The players also decided that they were willing to co-operate in any plans to make the game more lively and entertaining.

They are willing to play their part in any coaching schemes if any of the top coaches are brought from abroad.

Contract question

On the vital question of players' contracts, the Union are determined to keep their members well informed.

Said Mr. Hughes: "Once a new draft contract is drawn up, we will discuss it and call an extraordinary meeting.

"The members will be informed in plenty of time before the new season.

"AND BEFORE ANYTHING IS FINALISED IN SCOTLAND OUR UNION WILL HAVE TO BE A PARTNER TO IT."

Scots M.P., Mr. James Dempsey of Airdrie and Coatbridge addressed the annual meeting.

Officials: Chairman—Willie Toner (Hibs), Committee—Roy Barry and Willie Hamilton (Hearts), Jim Hannah (Stenhousemuir), Davie Thomson (Arbroath), Bill Taylor (St. Johnstone), Ally McLeod (Third Lanark). Secretary — John Hughes.

TENNIS SCOTS HIT BACK TO DRAW

SCOTLAND and Ireland drew 6-6 in the invitation international lawn tennis series which ended at Largs, Ayrshire.

Ireland after holding a 6-3 overnight lead, lost all three of yesterday's matches.

CELTIC—IN EUROPE . . .

HOW will Celtic fare in the next tie of their European Cup-winners Cup? Just how good are their opponents, Dynamo Zagreb of Yugoslavia?

For the answers, don't miss an absorbing new series by JOHN McPHAIL starting only in the Daily Record tomorrow.

McPhail, former international player and one of soccer's most knowledgeable experts, watched Dynamo beat Linz in Austria last week.

NOW HE'LL TELL YOU WHAT CELTIC CAN EXPECT WHEN ZAGREB COME TO PARKHEAD

And he'll also start you talking with shrewd comments on European football

● Rangers are already two up when inside-right Alex Willoughby (right) gets into the act to score a third as Morton 'keeper Alex Brown looks on helplessly . . . also looking on is Willoughby's cousin Jim Forrest (left), who scored the first two and the last two.

● Poor Morton! It's that man Jim Forrest (right) again, flashing into deadly action to score Rangers' fourth and complete his hat-trick. 'Keeper Brown has no chance to stop the ball despite a desperate dive across goal.

Slater for Southend

THE mystery of the missing Montrose soccer star—Malcolm Slater—has been solved.

Last night at his home in Buckie, he said: "I HAVE SIGNED FOR SOUTHEND UNITED . . . the manager told me he would inform Montrose."

And that is why Malcolm FAILED TO TURN UP at Links Park on Saturday to play against Dumbarton.

Four years ago he was freed by Celtic at his own request, and had spells with Highland League clubs Buckie Thistle and Inverness Caley before joining Montrose. He has

signed for Southend as a full-timer, and the £6000 fee was FOUR TIMES what Montrose paid to Caley.

Said Slater: "I didn't know there was any bother at all. It was late Friday before the deal was settled and I thought no more about it. I expected Montrose to get word right away.

"I have spoken to the Montrose secretary, and he says everything is O.K." Slater flies south at the week-end to fix up for his new club, but returns to work out his notice as a Civil Servant with the National Assistance Board in Aberdeen.

Blackpool manager Ron Suart took in two Scots games at the week-end—St. Mirren v. Third Lanark and Motherwell v. Dundee United.

In Friday night's game at Love Street he was watching left-winger Jim Robertson of St.

Mirren. And on Saturday the man who caught his eye was Dundee United right-winger Walter Carlyle.

Tonight, Chelsea manager Tommy Docherty brings his team north to play East Stirling at Firs Park.

'NATIONAL TICKETS ON SALE

STAND tickets for Scotland's first two home internationals, against Norway and Wales, will go on sale today.

The prices are £1, 10s and 7s 6d for the Norway game and 15s tickets are also available for the Welsh match. They can be bought at Lumley's, Sauchiehall Street, Sportsman's Emporium, St. Vincent Street and the S.F.A. H.Q., Park Gardens. Postal applications will be accepted by the S.F.A.

The game against Norway is on November 6 and the one against Wales, November 20. Kick off in each game is 7.30 p.m.

CUP FINAL SPECIAL

Morton's inside men were weak link

REAL RANGERS

By Sports Editor HUGH TAYLOR

RANGERS, taking a lesson from Real Madrid, used their heads BEFORE the League Cup Final against Morton at Hampden—and that's one of the main reasons they won so convincingly.

Certainly the back-room planning, feature of the technique of all the top Continental sides, paid off. Rangers had closely studied Morton's play. That was obvious . . .

BECAUSE danger-man Alan McGraw was so tightly marked by John Greig—as Brand was against Real—that he didn't have a chance, until late in the game and it didn't matter, to make us gasp with that thundering shooting of his.

BECAUSE Rangers exploited unmercifully the lack of pace of centre-half Jim Kiernan, invariably floundering in the wake of speedboat Jim Forrest.

BECAUSE of the cute tactics of the Ibrox wingers—especially Willie Henderson — in cutting the ball BACK and into the path of an onrushing colleague.

Yet although Rangers ended up so tremendously on top this was a sparkling League Cup Final—packed with drama and tension for the whole of the first half.

STUDYING

And at the start Morton showed that they, too, had been studying Rangers' play.

Their mighty opening offensive upset the Ibrox defence

Ibrox boys are learning how to plan

and they were unlucky not to score at that stage.

Nevertheless, I feel that, even had they scored then, they wouldn't have won.

They are a fine team, a credit to the second division—but the longer the game continued the more you realised just how many weaknesses Morton had.

And the biggest were up front. McGraw and inside-right Bobby Campbell were disappointing, never equalling the pace or subtlety of Brand and Willoughby.

Mind you, they won't meet wing-halfs of the calibre of Baxter and Greig every week.

The Greenock heroes, I thought, were the backs, Jim Reilly, a clever, inspiring skipper, and Morris Stevenson, who would have caused more havoc if he'd had better support.

GREAT BLOW

Rangers had their shaky moments—but after that first goal went in there was never any doubt.

Rangers grew stronger and

stronger—and even the stout-hearted Morton men must have known their chance had gone.

Still, they were flattered to win by 5-0. Brave Morton didn't deserve to lose by such a humiliating margin.

They have struck a great blow for the wee Scottish clubs. They have brought colour and romance back to football.

And I'm sure their loyal fans will stand by them until they can cheer them, as they surely

will, into the first division next season.

Well, what of Rangers?

They won with power and skill. They proved again that they are practically unbeatable in Scotland.

YOUNG JIM FORREST IS A REMARKABLE CENTRE-FORWARD — LETHAL AS HUGHIE GALLACHER, SMART AS LAWRIE REILLY . . . AND HE'S ONLY 19.

If he keeps rattling the goals in as he's doing he'll end up with a record total.

SINGING

Alex Willoughby had his wonder moments, too. Baxter, after a surprisingly dreadful start, was superb.

Greig, too, was first-class—as was Henderson. And everyone else played a notable part in the win.

BUT — how would this Rangers have fared against the Continental cracks? Not so well, I fear.

Yet the hearts of the legions of Rangers fans must be singing in the knowledge that REAL PLANNING is now a No. 1 priority of the Ibrox management.

Forrest set the Rangers fans cheering early in the second second half when he cutely flicked a cross from Henderson into the net—with 'keeper Brown out of his goal.

GOAL RUSH

Then the goal rush really started.

Forrest got a second, then cousin Alex Willoughby made it a family affair with a third.

Alas, the Morton bubble had burst. Now they were facing football realism in the raw.

It's true McGraw, with Greig easing off, had two terrific shots.

But Forrest finished gallant Morton with two more goals—gems of opportunism, brilliantly snapped up.

Hal Stewart has the final say: " I would like to pay tribute to Queen's Park about their wonderful dressing rooms.

" Our boys thought they were in Buckingham Palace.

" They should open them to the public at two shillings a time.

FORREST MUST GET A CAP

By WAVERLEY

THE League Cup Final has certainly given Willie Terris, Ian McColl and Hal Stewart, plenty to think about.

After our defeat by Ireland I said Ian St. John was finished as our centre-forward and young Jim Forrest should take over the centre spot.

By his skill and prolific goal-scoring on Saturday Forrest must have impressed on Mr. Terris, the chairman of the S.F.A. Selection Committee that my recommendation was on the mark.

RECORD

I feel certain that on Thursday, when the selectors choose the eleven to meet Norway, Forrest must be at the top of the list.

Young Jim is my ideal of what an international player should be. Like his predecessor Willie Thornton he is great sportsman — without being big-headed.

When Rangers brought the cup on to the field he trailed modestly behind his mates, as though all the fuss was an embarrassment to him?

It may be argued that he is too young for the International team.

But I say look at his record this season, and think about the play that has brought him so many goals—27 in 20 games.

Scottish team manager Ian McColl would be quick to note how Rangers smashed Morton's efforts at a tight defence which has frequently baffled

the Light Blues on the continent.

Forrest's four goals were all the same pattern.

TWICE HENDERSON CUT A LOW BALL BACK FROM THE BY-LINE FOR THE CENTRE TO MAKE CONTACT. TWICE WATSON DID THE SAME AND THE MORTON REAR MEN WERE CAUGHT ON THE TURN.

It's an old move. I have discussed it time and again.

I first saw it practiced with tremendous effect by those great Huddersfield and England players, Willie Smith and Clem Stephenson 40 years ago.

For all I know the pair devised the move thinking the high cross was outmoded, old fashioned.

Since then I have seen it only on the odd occasion. Now manager McColl could insist on that cut-back to Scotland's profit.

Morton director manager Hal

Stewart is determined to give Greenock a team to match the best.

I believe it is a certainty that he will steer his club to the First Division if he knows what is needed if the Cappielow side is to match the best in Scotland.

MASTER

But knowing Hal when he was a keen student under his friend and "master," the late George Anderson of Dundee, he will take the inevitable set-backs in his stride.

It is being said that Hal is a bit of a showman. Of course he is, for he intelligently realises, as so many football bosses DON'T, that he is in show business.

So was the late Herbert Chapman and Matt Busby.

But these and a few others have knowledge and organisation capabilities behind them, and a psychological understanding of the men on whom they depend for success.

Stewart, by his undoubted success during his brief rule at Cappielow, has shown that he has the desired qualities.

● The game is over and it's Rangers cup. Left back Davie Provan and outside left Graig Watson shoulder skipper Bobby Shearer high as he proudly holds the trophy. Also in the victory parade are 'keeper Billy Ritchie and centre half Ron McKinnon.

● IAN McCOLL . . . the Scottish team boss must have been impressed by Rangers' young centre, Jim Forrest.

FOOTBALL TODAY

Challenge Match—East Stirling v. Chelsea.

English League Cup—Second round (second replay) — Huddersfield v. Plymouth (at Birmingham).

English League I.—Manchester Un. v. Blackburn.

English League III — Colchester v. Peterborough; Millwall v. Oldham; Port Vale v. Reading.

English League IV—Halifax v. Southport; Tranmere v. Exeter; York v. Doncaster.

Everton watch big Alan Gilzean

EVERTON'S all-embracing search for soccer talent took in the Dundee - Dunfermline game on Saturday.

Chief scout Harry Cook and a director were there and after the match spent 20 minutes in deep conversation with the Dundee chairman.

It could be the Everton representatives were just having a look-see — and it could be they were checking up on goal grabber Alan Gilzean who, although he plays with a No. 10 on his

back, is the Dundee team's spearhead.

Gilzean, who is 24, has been his club's leading scorer for the past three seasons, topping 30 goals each time.

Bonanza

Gilzean hit Dundee's winner against Dunfermline and has scored 19 this season already.

Dundee manager Bob Shankly does not want to part with his star forward and has no pressing cash problems, having recently

received over £60,000 from Arsenal for Ian Ure.

But Everton would like a goalscoring forward, Gilzean has proved he can do it and if the Merseyside club want him badly enough they can be very persuasive.

December could be a soccer bonanza month for Dundee football fans.

On Tuesday, director Jack Swaddell flies to Brussels with Alex Hamilton, where he hopes to arrange a flood-lit friendly with Anderlecht.

Right-back Hamilton will play for a European Select against Anderlecht on Wednesday night in a benefit

match for Anderlecht captain, Martin Lippens.

The Belgian side were one of Dundee's victims on the road to the semi-finals of the European Cup, and Hamilton was delighted yesterday at being given the honour of representing Dundee on the Continent.

Tremendous

" It's simply tremendous," he said yesterday. " I only hope I justify my selection."

Arsenal have already agreed to play a friendly at Dens Park, and if Dundee succeed in arranging a game with Anderlecht, both could go on in December.

● They told you so—and they were right! 'Record' experts Hugh Taylor and Waverley on Saturday forecast what would happen in the Scottish Cup Final—and correctly analysed the play and styles of Rangers and Dundee.
Read again what they said.

RANGERS, rich in breezy football adventurers, and Dundee, weavers of dream soccer, will present at Hampden today a Scottish Cup Final that will go down in history as an epic.
Of that I am convinced. How can it be otherwise?

● Hugh Taylor said it on Saturday.

Rangers, I feel, will win because they have the greatest individualists in Scotland today.

● Another Hugh Taylor prediction comes true.

...feel according to give the points to Rangers, particularly, as Millar and Brand appear to have rediscovered that deadly double spearhead act.
In Henderson they have a match-winner on his own.

● Waverley said it on Saturday.

WHY I HAVEN'T RE-SIGNED

I WANT TIME TO THINK IT OVER

By

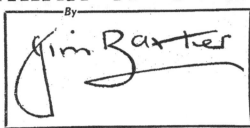
Jim Baxter

SO far I haven't re-signed for Rangers . . . but the way I see it there's plenty of time to do that.

The season is just finishing and this will be the first chance I've had to relax and think things over.

At the moment I haven't given an awful lot of thought to re-signing. Still, it's something I'll be discussing with manager Symon, as soon as I have thought it over.

Right now all I want to do is relax for a bit.

Saturday's final was the finest climax I could have asked for to four glorious years with Rangers.

Four years that have given me a fantastic treble hat-trick of soccer gold.

Three Scottish Cup medals, three League Cup medals and three League championship medals, that's what I've won.

And it's a record I couldn't have equalled with any other club in the world. Out of 12 possible medals in four seasons I have won nine.

It's almost unbelievable . . . but then playing for Rangers was unbelievable four years ago.

I never thought for one minute that this kind of thing was possible when I played with Raith Rovers.

WRONG

If anyone had told me that I would win every honour in Scottish football three times over in four years I would have laughed at them.

But there they are in my display cabinet now. And I reckon the game against Dundee was one of the finest I've played in while winning these medals.

And I don't think any of the

● Ralph Brand cools down his team mates with a bucket of water as they take a bow after winning the Cup . . . let's hope the Cup and medals, plus Davy Wilson's bowler, are rust-proof !

120,000 people who were there will argue about that.

I'm speaking from the football point of view, not for myself. Because I know that I didn't have a good game.

I don't know what was wrong. Things just weren't coming off for me.

But still the result couldn't have been better for the team.

What a season it's been for us. Despite the amazing run of injuries which had Eric Caldow, myself and Davy Wilson all off at one stage, we've pulled off the treble for the first time in 15 years.

Though I did think for a long time that Dundee were going to delay our celebrations.

After Dundee equalised I didn't think we could do it. We had so much bad luck in front of goal and Bert Slater had been so magnificent that I thought we were going to have a replay.

Then came that last minute burst which made everything right.

I told you on Friday that wee Willie Henderson would be the man of the match for us and I'm still saying it today.

What a wonderful player he was once again on Saturday

BAD LUCK

And John Greig and Ronnie McKinnon weren't far behind him. Ronnie played very well and John did exactly the job he went out to do.

Of course he's that kind of player. When John is told he must stop a certain player he does just that. The man he had to watch on Saturday was Alan Gilzean and Alan must have had his quietest game for weeks.

I also rated Jimmy Millar and Ralph Brand among our top players, though Ralph had some bad luck.

Dundee had three five-star men, 'keeper Bert Slater and wing-halfs Bobby Seith and Alex Stuart.

SLATER WAS MAGNIFICENT. THERE WERE TIMES WHEN I THOUGHT WE WOULD NEVER BEAT HIM.

TREMENDOUS

It was a really great performance and one that came close to breaking our forward line's hearts.

It's been a hard season and the strain has been tremendous . . . but nothing can spoil the memory of the final, or dim the glitter of these nine medals.

Nine medals that mean a miracle . . . ONE THAT COULD ONLY HAPPEN AT IBROX.

● *Jim Baxter's story was told to 'Record' Sports reporter KEN GALLACHER.*

● It's goal Number One for Jimmy Millar and Rangers as Davy Wilson and Ralph Brand watch the centre's header beat Bert Slater and pass between Hamilton and Cox on it's way to the net.

● That man Millar again . . . and it's goal No. 2. Looking on as his header goes into the top corner of the net are (left to right) Wilson, Ryden, Millar, Brand, Slater and Cox.

Wee clubs will stick together

THE five Second Division clubs —Albion Rovers, Berwick Rangers, Brechin City, Stenhousemuir and Stranraer—who will be axed if league reorganisation goes through WILL NOT ENTER BY THE BACK DOOR.

That was made clear yesterday when ten clubs met at the invitation of Berwick Rangers in a Glasgow hotel, 48 hours before the Rangers meet the 31 clubs who they hope will make up two leagues of 16 clubs in the new plan for Scottish football (writes JIM RODGER).

Stenhousemuir secretary Jim Weir acted as spokesman for the meeting.

He said: "The attendance was gratifying. Other clubs who were not present have promised support. Several First Division clubs are strongly against the methods being adopted to put the plan into operation.

"The Second Division clubs will be holding another meeting.

"It has been suggested that if one of the 32 clubs don't approve of the plan at the special meeting called by Rangers at Ibrox on Tuesday, then one of the five clubs to be axed will be asked to come in.

"However these five clubs have assured the others that they will NOT ACCEPT this type of invitation."

Clubs attending yesterday's meeting were: Albion Rovers, Berwick Rangers, Brechin City, Cowdenbeath, Forfar Athletic, Hamilton Acas, Montrose, Queen's Park, Stenhousemuir and Stranraer.

We're not worried say Celts

CELTIC fly off to Hungary this morning for the second leg of the European Cup Winners' Cup semi-final against M.T.K. Budapest . . . confident they can reach the final.

But they are cautious too, and both manager Jimmy McGrory and coach Sean Fallon know this will be a tough, tense battle writes JOHN McPHAIL.

Coach Fallon said: "The first 20 minutes can decide this tie, we will try to grab that early goal and if we do, I'm sure we'll win.

"A repeat of the Bratislava display should be enough to hold M.T.K."

I asked coach Fallon how he felt about the return to the Budapest side of Karoly Sandor, famous Hungarian international winger.

"We must respect him," he said, "but we aren't unduly worried about him. I am sure Young or Gemmell can take care of him."

Boss Jimmy McGrory also knows that this will be a really hard game.

Worry

"We have a first class defence, and I am quite sure our three-goal lead from the first game will clearly see us through to the final in Brussels"

One worry though the Celtic officials must have is just how strict the Austrian referee will be in his control of this semi-final second leg.

Two Budapest players were booked at the first match at Parkhead and there was a toughness about the Hungarians' play in the second-half that could really break into big trouble in Budapest.

Apart from the regular team, Madden; McKay, Willie O'Neil; Cushley, Lennox, Frank Brogan will be in the party. Johnny Divers failed a fitness test and won't travel.

KILMARNOCK FINISH SECOND AGAIN !

FOR the fourth time in five years, Kilmarnock are runners-up to Rangers in the League.

In their last league match of the season they required one point against Third Lanark at Rugby Park to collect second place talent money . . . they made sure by beating Thirds 2-0.

Teenage centre Ronnie Hamilton scored twice and he deserves full marks for the way he grabbed his goals, although the first looked suspiciously offside.

This now brings his goal tally to five in two games and should give this hustling, bustling youngster plenty of confidence for the Summer Cup games.

● Ralph Brand (left) falls backwards as he watches his shot cross the Dundee goalmouth, hit the post, then go into the net for Rangers third goal. Looking on are McLean, Slater and Ryden.

Henderson is best in Europe

WEE WILLIE

WONDERFUL!

Don't put blame on Bobby Cox

IF an inquest was set up to look into the cause of Dundee's defeat by Rangers only one verdict could be returned . . . suicide !

They came out on to Hampden Park fully aware that the little man on the Light Blues' right-wing was a soccer soccer (writes ALAN SAUNDERS).

From past experience they knew that jack-in-the-box Willie Henderson had enough deadly tricks to poison their chances of winning the Cup.

Everyone had seen him only a fortnight before hypnotise the English as he weaved wonderful patterns in their defence.

Yet Dundee made no pre-match preparations to prevent him casting his spell . . . or if they did they forgot them in the excitement of the big occasion.

Bobby Cox can hardly take the blame. I doubt if ANY full-back could stop Henderson single-handed without resorting to foul tactics, which I am glad to say skipper Cox did not use.

Second shadow

I am sure every Dundee fan expected to see left-winger Hugh Robertson pulled back as a second shadow for Henderson. Instead, Willie was allowed to move deep for the ball, getting the chance to turn and face Cox on the run. A sight that no left-back likes to see.

Unlike their opponents, Rangers did not ignore the threat of Alan Gilzean. John Greig shadowed him brilliantly and confidently tackled him out of the game until he caused little trouble.

In the Dundee team, Slater was a magnificent goal-keeper, with Hamilton, Seith, Stuart and Cousin tremendous in front of him.

● It's a victory hug for wee Willie Henderson, the hero of Hampden, from Rangers skipper Bobby Shearer—and no wonder . . . for wee Mr. Wonderful had just laid on the third goal in the Ibrox boys' great win over Dundee in one of the best cup finals ever seen at Hampden. What a moment for Rangers who won the Cup for the third year running.

C ALL him Wee Willie Wonderful. For there's not a better winger in Europe today than Willie Henderson, a mighty tot with the gaiety of Garrincha, the magic of Matthews and the whiplash of Waddell.

He's probably soccer's most wonderful entertainer of the moment. Every time he's on the ball the roar's deafening. And he was the hero of Rangers magnificent Cup Final victory over Dundee at Hampden.

I'll never forget the moment that brought Rangers a win when time was running out and gallant Dundee seemed certain of a draw.

Once again—for no reason I can think of—Henderson had been appealing in vain for the ball. Then, suddenly, like the principal trick of a master magician, the wee fellow appeared on the left wing.

HOW DID HE GET THERE? DON'T ASK ME. DON'T ASK THE DUNDEE DEFENDERS. THEY WERE EQUALLY MYSTIFIED.

And then that beautiful cross and the thud of Millar's brow on ball and a roar that almost split the grey Hampden sky—and time had run out for Dundee.

What a player is Willie! His sudden change of direction is startling, his ball control uncanny, his pace bafflingly fast, his crossing pin-pointed as accurately as Robin Hood's arrows.

WINNING MOVE

Certainly he was the player of the final—and that is high praise for this was a game that lived up to all the publicity—an epic, a feast, a credit to two fine teams.

And now you can call me Mr. Bighead if you like. For — as at the international — my predictions came true. I said Rangers would win. I said Henderson or Baxter would be the match-winner.

In fact, the slim one was quieter than usual

HUGH TAYLOR

— BUT HE STILL PLAYED A GREAT PART IN THE VICTORY.

For it was Baxter's cunningly-placed pass from a free-kick to Henderson, who had so cutely slipped to the left, that started the winning move

Dundee thought he meant to put the ball to the right. Instead, he cut it to the left.

And now, too, those who consider the high cross and glorious header out of date will have to think like me . . . IT'S STILL THE MOST EFFECTIVE WEAPON IN FOOTBALL.

Alan Gilzean, frustrated, out of touch, firmly in the grip of the stalwart John Greig, didn't this time play the hero's part. BUT JIMMY MILLAR DID

MARVELLOUS

And his perfect headers showed how right the Ibrox management were to field him.

No doubt that Rangers were the superior side. If it had not been for the marvellous goal-keeping of Bert Slater, they would have won much easier

Bert was tremendous — and yet he should have done better at the vital times when two goals were scored.

Rangers had the verve, the individualists of genius. More — they had the snap of Brand.

He deserved his goal — and with Millar grabbing two the old firm partnership of M and B was again the pride of Ibrox.

DUNDEE'S INSIDE FORWARDS WERE DISAPPOINTING.

Alan Cousin worked tremendously hard but his was, of necessity, a grafting role.

And with Gilzean and Cameron shadows because of the fine play of Greig and McKinnon Dundee never really were allowed to play the sweet soccer for which they are famous.

Still it was a memorable final, packed with tension, incident, and a finish only Hitchcock could have dreamed up.

GREAT REF.

It was in keeping with a great occasion that it was refereed admirably by the calm Hugh Phillips.

In a season in which referees have been severely criticised and not without reason — I applaud Mr. Phillips for his splendid control, his lack of fussiness and the brilliant way he showed he was boss.

Yes, it was a great climax to the season—and if only games like this were to be seen every Saturday there would be a new rush to the turnstiles.

This was one to remember

BY the wonder Cup final they produced at Hampden on Saturday, Rangers and Dundee have restored much of the lost prestige of Scottish club football.

It was a game plucked from the old time, and I personally got additional delight from it in the reflection that the play was traditionally Scottish, without a hint of Continental ideas.

It completely justified my assertion that our moderns, instead of trying to emulate the gimmicks of the foreigners, should concentrate on the methods of our old masters.

FOUR - TWO - FOUR BE DAMNED !

High drama

I have been watching Cup finals on both sides of the Border since Morton sensationally defeated Rangers in 1922, and, as I told you on Saturday, I have always looked upon the 1937 clash between Celtic and Aberdeen as the best of all.

Now I relegate that game to second place.

And I feel that the 120,982 tensed up fans who watched the Light Blues achieve their 18th Cup triumph, as long as they take an interest in soccer, will feel proud to have witnessed it.

This was a game that had everything, individual and collective skill that provided scores of intelligent and thrilling moves, and high drama

WAVERLEY

culminating in the winning goals being scored within a minute, the second with only seconds left for play.

The two great personalities of the match were Rangers' outside-right Willie Henderson, and Dundee's goalkeeper, Bert Slater.

The winger, as he has done with so many backs these past two years, had Cox in a maze with his swerving and dummying while travelling at speed.

But not once did Bobby stoop to foul tactics. He was the sportsman all through

Fantastic

Slater was fantastic. I cannot recall seeing a keeper get his hands to so many balls booted and headed at him from inside the six yards line.

Maybe he was lucky on occasion, but he must be credited with a fine sense of anticipation, which prevented at least three first-half goals.

He was a trifle unfortunate to lose the first goal 26 minutes after the restart.

As Millar headed the ball, Brand crossed in front of the keeper and unsighted him.

Slater was obviously upset, but seconds later he was happy

From the kick-off the ball was steered past Ritchie, the finishing touch being applied by Cameron who, taking a long one from Stuart, used his right

foot to steady the ball before smashing it to the net with his left.

IT WAS THE SPECTACULAR GOAL OF THE MATCH.

Then with only two minutes to go, when we were all preparing for a replay, Henderson got the ball in a place where he should never have been, out on the left.

He sent over a peach, right on to Millar's head, and Slater was beaten.

And while Dundee were still suffering from the shock Rangers struck again, an all-in attack ending with Brand shooting from an acute angle and the ball hit the far post before reaching the net.

There can be no denying that Rangers merited their success. They were faster, more subtle at their work.

Gilzean, on whom Dundee depended so much, was not his usual effective self, mainly because of the excellence of Greig, while on the other side of the bustling Cameron, Cousin was too busily engaged keeping Baxter from cutting through to help maintain continuity in attack.

1000-1 TREBLE FOR POOLMAN

WHAT a Final day it was for 'Record' fixed odds expert Poolman who ended the season with a 1000-1 treble.

On Ladbroke's coupon he correctly forecast Rangers 3-1 win over Dundee, Manchester United's 3-2 defeat of Notts Forest and Newport's 2-1 win over Hartlepools.

Poolman also correctly forecast five results for all Nothing Barred coupons.

Low dividends on all Treble Chance coupons are likely to follow 14 draws on the major lists.

Possible payouts: 1d—24 points, £55. ¼d—24 points, £15. ⅛d—24 points, £9.

Four Aways should yield about 3000-1; 9 Results, 35-1; and Three Draws, 5-1.

NO GOAL!

¶ No, it wasn't a goal.

That's the verdict of the Daily Record team of reporters and photographers who covered the League Cup Final at Hampden.

Celtic say the ball crossed the line after goalkeeper Ritchie dropped a Murdoch shot. Rangers say it didn't.

The arguments still rage. But concensus of opinion of the Record team is that Ritchie stopped the ball before it reached the goal-line.

'RECORD' SPORT SPOTLIGHTS

● This is the incident which sparked off the big goal row at Hampden on Saturday.

Rangers 'keeper Billy Ritchie scrambles round to stop the ball after failing to hold a shot from Bobby Murdoch.

Celtic say the ball crossed the line. Rangers say it didn't — and the 'Record' sports writers at the match agree.

DANE JORN IS THE NEW MORTON ACE

By TOM NICHOLSON

SCOTLAND'S team manager, Ian McColl, rightly keeps his views on what he sees in his travels for the conference room.

He was at Easter Road on Saturday to check, probably among other things, the reports that Hibs' Willie Hamilton is the most consistently successful inside-forward in the country this season.

I don't think Mr. McColl, on what he saw, would argue. Once again, the blond ball-player turned on one of his most bewildering displays in the 2-1 win over Morton.

He had the hardest of luck in not scoring. But he made the brilliant winner that Cormack scored in the final minutes and "teed" up several more that weren't taken.

I would be more interested to know what Scotland's team manager thought of 18-year-old Peter Cormack, once again a trump card for Hibs.

Wonderful home produce

He created the situation which brought them their penalty equaliser, and no-one in the business could have taken that points-winning goal any better than the youngster.

If Morton have been depending on their Danes a lot in recent times to bring home the bacon, Hibs are raising a wonderful line in home produce in the shape of Cormack.

The latest member of Morton's Danish quartette, Jorn Sorensen, shook Hibs in the first half with a fine goal from all of 25 yards, that proved he could shoot. All the rest of the time he was proving that he hasn't much to learn about any branch of the game. Jorn will bring a lot of joy to Greenock.

The glimpse of Morton was more than enough to convince Hibs fans in the 18,000 crowd that their high position in the league is no fluke.

Mix-up

I daresay both Johansen and Bertelsen have played better, but 'keeper Erik Sorensen was all anybody expected.

No blame on him to be outwitted by Scott's penalty kick, though he was clearly annoyed at his failure, and none at all for failing to get near Cormack's cracker.

Kiernan, Adamson and Stevenson were other Morton five-star men. The former Hibs reject certainly turned on the style against his old club.

● The dramatic first-half incident that brought the roar of " PENALTY " from the throats of thousands of Celtic fans. Jimmy Johnstone hits the deck as Eric Caldow clears and Stevie Chalmers joins in the appeal.

Airdrie fade again

FOR the second week in succession, Airdrie had victory within their grasp yet failed to snatch their first League win.

Three times at Broomfield they forged ahead but were pulled back by Dundee United. Indeed, in the closing stages Airdrie were lucky to salvage a point.

According to the official programme, Airdrie's defence is the weakness. The programme says: "Obviously there's something lacking in defence."

Since the beginning of this season supporters have been saying just that.

Out in front Reid and Murray were in sparkling form. McCall on the left couldn't get the better of right-back Millar and on the right Ferguson was a shade disappointing.

BUT HIS FINE OPENING GOAL IN THE 26TH MINUTE WAS AN INSPIRATION.

Great service

Prior to that Airdrie had thrown away at least three easy chances.

The equalising goal — a penalty by Briggs — came in the 31st minute and was tough luck on Marshall who seemed to handle accidentally.

THE MAN OF THE GAME FOR DUNDEE UNITED WAS WING-HALF STUART FRASER.

Always on the alert he provided great service.

Like Airdrie, Dundee's shooting was erratic.

Reid put Airdrie ahead in the 38th minute but just before half-time from a Millar free-kick Gillespie crashed home the equaliser.

Again Reid gave Airdrie the lead in the 47th minute but two minutes later Howieson cancelled it with a well-taken goal.

We can't give up Europe!

DISCUSSIONS are going on this week about the formation of a British championship — and the clubs hope it will start next season.

It's a mouth-watering prospect, for such a tournament would certainly bring back the missing millions to the terracings (writes HUGH TAYLOR).

Morton have written to the other Scottish First Division clubs asking them for action now, and I understand several of the top English clubs are in favour.

The enterprising Greenock club want the present championship to count for places, with the glamour tournament starting after the League Cup Final next season.

The proposal calls for the tourney to be played in two sections of eight clubs, four Scots, four English, with the top clubs then playing off in the semi-finals and final.

It sounds a grand idea and several Scottish clubs, with Celtic in the vanguard, have been advocating a British championship for some time.

BUT—there are difficulties. And the major problem will be to find dates.

As it is now, with so many competitions, the clubs are at their wits' end finding vacant nights, even in mid week, for the matches.

One solution would be for the First Division of the Scottish League to be streamlined.

That's coming. I'm sure of that. But when?

Half-a-dozen clubs have already shown interest in this first season junior.

We all know how difficult it is for the crusaders of brighter football to win their point — that the Scottish divisions must be shortened.

Anyhow, we are now probably coming to a major issue . . .

SHOULD WE FORGET ABOUT EUROPEAN COMPETITION AND RELY ON A BRITISH SET-UP TO PROVIDE THE THRILLS?

I know that already informal talks have taken place between leading Scottish and English clubs. Opinion is divided. Some want to avoid European football.

BUT OTHERS SAY IT IS ESSENTIAL TO PLAY ON THE CONTINENT SO THAT WE CAN KEEP UP TO DATE ON WORLD SOCCER.

And I agree with these officials. I feel it is essential for our clubs to play in the European Cup and European Cup-winners' competitions.

So the answer is an immediate conference of all the leading clubs to iron out the problems.

COAKLEY SET TO SIGN

ASHFIELD are set to sign inside-right John Coakley, brother of the Saracen Park wing half-back Eddie.

The other member of the Coakley family is Tommy, who plays with Motherwell.

John, earlier this season, was with Glenafton Athletic, but he bought his transfer from the Ayrshire club. On Saturday he played for Ashfield against Strathclyde.

That " friendly " game Rob Roy are playing against Stirling Albion under the Annfield lights tomorrow night could bring out the talent scouts who have been watching Rabs' winger Henry Hall.

BIG HAMPDEN 'GOAL' ROW

NO GOAL!

> From my seat in the lofty Press-box, looking down, I thought there was still a gap between ball and line when the Rangers' keeper saved at the second attempt.

BALL DID NOT CROSS THE LINE

By HUGH TAYLOR

ARGUMENTS are still raging bitterly about the dramatic incident in the 55th minute of the torrid League Cup Final between Rangers and Celtic at Hampden.

Was it a goal? Bobby Murdoch blasted a drive at goal. Billy Ritchie couldn't hold the ball. As it rolled agonisingly to the line, the keeper made a desperate clutch and stopped the ball.

Was the ball over the line? NO — say Rangers. YES — say Celtic.

MY VIEW is that Ritchie saved before the ball crossed the line.

From my seat in the lofty Press-box, looking down, I thought there was still a gap between ball and line when the Rangers' keeper saved at the second attempt

And, although this is not conclusive, it is significant at least that NOT ONE photograph of the scores I studied yesterday showed the ball OVER the line.

Here are the comments from my colleagues of the Record Sports Team at Hampden:

THEY'RE WRONG

WAVERLEY : I think Chairman Bob Kelly and Manager Jimmy McGrory are wrong in thinking Referee Phillips denied Celtic a goal.

The Laws of the Game say "a goal is scored when the whole of the ball has passed over the goal line."

If this particular ball had crossed the line before Ritchie grabbed it I would have seen, from my very excellent vantage point in the Press Box, the white marking.

In fact, I didn't see even a thousandth part of the five inch broad line concealed from my view.

It was not a goal.

JOHN McPHAIL : Celtic coach Sean Fallon was strong in his view that the ball was over the line, and so, too, were most of the Parkhead players and officials.

I feel the Ritchie incident was debatable.

From my seat in the Press Box I couldn't definitely say. Only the players present on the spot know.

JIM RODGER : It didn't look like a goal to me. But in incidents like this, where the referee is nearer I have always given the official the benefit of any doubt.

I watched Hugh Phillips carefully looking at the goal-line and also at the linesman up with the play to see if he had a different view. Apparently he hadn't either.

There you are. And, anyhow, that fine referee, Hugh Phillips, had no doubt.

Instead of blaming the referee, Celtic should be analysing the reasons for their defeat.

Sure, they were unlucky. Still, two great flashes brought the Rangers goals. Celtic, on the other hand, went all out all the time and their old failing was evident — lack of response, lack of a cool head at the right time.

Rangers won because of the steadiness of their seasoned warriors, because in the white heat of battle first Brand, then Baxter, did the right thing — and so, of course, did Jim Forrest, who snatched the goals so well.

Well, I wasn't so daft in tipping Rangers after all. But I must confess there was little in it and I congratulate the teams on a refreshing, exciting display.

SWITCH WAS MASTER STROKE...

By JIM RODGER

JIM BAXTER attained the stature of a real Rangers captain on Saturday — and what praise can be higher?

What a bold decision he made in the second half — and how it paid off!

Jim Forrest had scored two goals to put Rangers in the lead. Then Jimmy Johnstone got one back — and Celtic were storming in with a chance.

They switched their wingers, John Hughes crossing to outside right with Jimmy Johnstone going to the left.

That was when Slim Jim, captaining Rangers for the first time in a final made his decision like a veteran general.

HE ORDERED HIS FULL BACKS, ERIC CALDOW AND DAVE PROVAN TO SWITCH PLACES.

Shocking

Just in time. For it had seemed for a few hectic minutes that Hughes, racing past Caldow, would win the game for Celtic.

BUT WHEN THE BACKS CHANGED, THE FIRE AGAIN WENT OUT OF THE CELTIC ATTACK. BAXTER BACKED HIS JUDGMENT — AND WON.

Here's JOHN McPHAIL'S verdict.

Celtic were unhappy about Jimmy Johnstone's roving. Trainer Bob Rooney once rushed to the touchline to tell Jimmy to keep in his place.

CELTIC LOST BECAUSE OF SHOCKING MISSES.

You can look out for the return of Charlie Gallacher and Bobby Lennox to the League match against Kilmarnock on Wednesday.

● Rangers skipper Jim Baxter "crowns" wee Willie Johnstone with the League Cup as the players leave the field after taking a victory bow. This was only Willie's fifth first team game for Rangers and he was the youngest player on the field.

The walk-away fans let Celts down

By WAVERLEY

BECAUSE of Rangers' dominance in recent years it appeared as if the Old Firm contest was destined to lose its status as our greatest club game.

But on Saturday — and I was not forgetting their recent League win over the Light Blues — Celtic by their display materially helped to restore the clash to its one time eminence in the world of football.

It was hard, ever so hard going as in the days of Bob McPhail and Peter Wilson, with the players rightly using their physical attributes in legitimate and manful fashion. No Cissie stuff from the Continent here.

The game was marked by two of the greatest defence-splitting passes I have ever seen, the first from Ralph Brand, the second from Jim Baxter. And both were coolly, neatly, capped by young Jim Forrest steering the ball to the net.

Valuable

But these two goals alone did not give Rangers victory. Great credit must be given the defence, in which Ronnie McKinnon was a powerful stopper and to which Jimmy Millar made a most valuable contribution in the second half when Celtic launched attack after attack.

Jimmy became a fourth half-back, a third full back, as he brought the ball from the ruck of defence to counter-attack. No man in the Ibrox eleven did more for victory than the inside-right.

One of the most intelligent moves in the game was the switching of Dave Provan and Eric Caldow after John Hughes and Jimmy Johnstone had changed places in the 67th minute.

Up to then Caldow, delighting his admirers with an emphatic come-back, had been Mr. Frustration so far as the Celtic outside-right was concerned, while, after the first ten minutes, Provan had a grip of Hughes.

It was, therefore, a grand tactical move to have Hughes and Johnstone continue to be faced by the men who held them down in the earlier stages of the game.

The chief impression Celtic made on me was that they no longer suffer from the inferiority complex that cramped their style against Rangers last season.

They have recovered a confidence in themselves — even without Billy McNeill, who in my opinion, master-minds the team.

Despite his absence the defence was good and was caught out only by two touches of near genius — from Brand and Baxter.

Up front, however, there is still a vital weakness in finishing, chiefly because of an inclination to add an extra frill before applying the final touch.

In this respect Johnstone continues to be a sinner. He has speed and balance and is clever on the ball, but when is he to learn that he can overdo his trickery?

There is no profit in beating two opponents, only to lose possession to a third. Caldow demonstrated how to reduce the red-haired winger's effectiveness.

But my chief criticism of Celtic is directed towards their supporters. Just after Rangers' second goal thousands of them made for the exits, deserting a team of great fighting spirit.

Their job I suggest, if they are really supporters, was to stay and encourage their side. It is when a team are a goal or two down that they need support, not when they are on top.

GOURLAY BLASTS BACK TO TOP

IF Partick Thistle manager Willie Thornton, who is still looking for a winger, had seen Falkirk's Billy Gourlay on Saturday he would have been wishing he had never let Gourlay leave Firhill.

But against Dundee United last week and Third Lanark on Saturday the new Gourlay was the man who carried all the threat in the Falkirk front rank

Billy has stopped trying to beat the other team on his own and has run into the kind of form which could save manager Alex McCrae a lot of headaches.

Falkirk were just too good for Thirds. They never looked like being beaten and when Maxwell scored just before half-time the game was as good as over.

After the interval Falkirk emphasised their superiority. Gourlay dragged the ball to the corner, crossed and Wilson scored easily.

And before the finish Kenny Scott notched number three with a grand drive from 20 yards.

For Thirds' player-manager Bobby Evans there are problems. The only man to show up in his forward line was Jimmy McMorran.

POOL PROMOTERS ASSOCIATION
CERTIFIED DIVIDENDS
FOR 23rd APRIL 1966

LITTLEWOODS
WINNERS EVERYWHERE THIS WEEK

1d TREBLE CHANCE POOL
24 Pts ...... £283. 8.0 for 1d
23 Pts ...... £4. 0.0 for 1d
22½ Pts ...... £2. 6.0 for 1d
22 Pts ...... 8.0 for 1d
(4 Divs only—see Rule 9G)

12 MATCH POINTS POOL
(11 matches and 1 postponed Max Pts 22. No all correct forecast received)
21 Pts .... £169. 2.6 for 2d
20 Pts .... £22. 6.0 for 2d
19 Pts .... £4.14.0 for 2d

SELECT SIXTEEN POOL
(Max Draws 14—No client with 14, 13 or 12 Draws)
11 DRAWS ... £390. 8.0 for 6d
10 DRAWS ... £12. 6.0 for 6d
9 DRAWS ... 18.0 for 6d
5 DRAWS 40/-
9 RESULTS 248.552/-
4 AWAYS 140/-
EASIER SIX
(5 corr. and 1 post.) ... 212/-

Except where otherwise stated dividends are to units of 1/- and are subject to rescrutiny. Expenses and commission for 9th April—26.0%. Send today for Coupons
LITTLEWOODS POOLS LTD., GLASGOW, S.W.2

VERNONS
WORLD'S LARGEST £300.000
¼d TREBLE CHANCE

¼d TREBLE CHANCE
24 Pts. .... £80.11.0 for ¼d
23 Pts. .... £1. 3.0 for ¼d
22½ Pts. .... 13.0 for ¼d
3 dividends only—See Rule 9
GOALDEN FOUR 528/-
5 DRAWS 32/-
8 RESULTS 211,760/-
4 AWAYS 112/-

12 MATCH RESULTS POOL
1 postponed match
11 Correct .. £932.16.0 for 2d
10 Correct .. £8. 4.0 for 2d
9 Correct .. 16.0 for 2d

Dividends (which are subject to rescrutiny) are to units of 1/- except where otherwise stated. Expenses and commission for 9th April, 1966—32.9%.
Send now for Four Dividend ¼d Treble Chance Coupons, if over 21, to:
VERNONS POOLS LTD., LIVERPOOL

COPE'S
THOUSANDS OF EASY WINNERS SHARE THIS WEEK'S BIGGEST PAYOUT FOR ONLY EIGHTH OF 1d STAKES

14 draws on 50-match list
EIGHTH OF 1d TREBLE CHANCE
24 Pts. ......£46.18.0 FOR
23 Pts. ......£0.14.0 ⅛d
22½ Pts. £0.10.0
12 MATCH RESULTS POOL
Only 11 matches played
11 Correct .. £90.18.0 for 1d
10 Correct .. £1.12.0 for 1d
9 Correct .. £0. 4.0 for 1d
EASY SIX 196/-

7 MATCH JACKPOT
No client with 21 pts
20 Pts. ......£874.10.0 for 1d
19½ Pts .. £163. 8.0 for 1d
19 Pts ..... £34. 0.0 for 1d
18½ Pts. ...... £7.12.0 for 1d
18 Pts. ...... £2.12.0 for 1d
3 DRAWS (15 Draws—48 match list) 38/-
9 RESULTS (48 match list) 5840/-
4 AWAYS (13 aways 48 match list) 112/-

Except where otherwise stated dividends are to units of 1/- and subject to rescrutiny.
Expenses and commission for 9th April, 1966—31.7%. Send now, if over 21, for Cope's easy entry coupons and free book of winning methods.
COPE'S POOLS LTD., LONDON, E.C.4

ZETTERS
YOU WILL BE DELIGHTED WHEN YOU SEE OUR "NEW" SUMMER COUPON—IT'S THE BEST YET!

8 MATCH TREBLE CHANCE POOL
(14 Draws on Coupon)
24 Pts .... £37. 3.0 FOR
23 Pts .... £0.12.0 ⅛d
22 Pts £0. 6.6
7 MATCH TREBLE CHANCE POOL
21 Pts .... £66.10.0 FOR
20 Pts .... £1. 2.0 ½d
19½ Pts. £0.13.0
18 Pts. £0. 2.0
12 MATCH RESULTS POOL
(Only 11 matches played)
11 Correct .. £199. 6.0 FOR
10 Correct .. £2.18.0 1d
9 Correct .. £0. 4.0

5 DRAWS (14 draws on coupon) 42/-
8 RESULTS 17,792/-
4 AWAYS 192/-
12 Home Teams failing to win 11,604/-
12 MATCH POINTS POOL
(Only 11 matches played)
20 Pts. .... £140. 0.0 FOR
19 Pts £12. 8.0 1d
18 Pts. £1.12.0
Subject to rescrutiny. Dividends to 1/- unless otherwise shown. Expenses and Commission for 9th April, 1966—33.6%.

Send now for coupons if over 21 to:
ZETTERS POOLS LTD., LONDON, E.C.1.

EMPIRE
EMPIRE TOPS THE LOT YET AGAIN—HIGHEST ON ALL DIVIDENDS ON 8 LINES FOR A PENNY TREBLE CHANCE

8 MATCH TREBLE CHANCE
24 Pts .... £106.19.0 FOR
23 Pts. .... £1. 8.0 ⅛d
22½ Pts. £0.18.0
7 MATCH TREBLE CHANCE
21 Pts. ...... £41. 7.0 FOR
20 Pts. ...... £1. 3.0 ½d
19½ Pts. £0.18.0
19 Pts £0. 2.0
3 DRAWS 86/-
8 RESULTS 4448/-
4 AWAYS 120/-
3 RESULTS 324/-
4 from 4 RESULTS .. 21/-
(for only 3 corr. & 1 post.)

CORRECT SCORES
1st Dividend £148. 4.0
2nd Dividend £1.16.0
EASY SIX 112/-
(for only 5 corr. & 1 post.)
12 MATCH POINTS POOL
Only 11 matches played
Possible Points 19.
19 Pts. .... £175.12.0 for 1d
18 Pts. .... £10.18.0 for 1d
17 Pts. .... £1. 4.0 for 1d
Except where otherwise stated, dividends are to units of 1/- and subject to rescrutiny.
Expenses and Commission for 9th April, 1966—28.4%.

Send now for Britain's most "go-ahead" coupon and unique each way "bonanza" plans exclusive to Empire, if over 21.
EMPIRE POOLS LTD., BLACKPOOL

SOCCER
AWAYS TREBLE CHANCE AGAIN PAYS BIGGEST T.C. DIVIDEND OF THE WEEK

TREBLE CHANCE DRAWS
(14 Draws on list)
24 Pts. ..... £42.15.0 For an
23 Pts ..... £1. 0.0 ⅛d
23½ Pts £0. 7.0
TREBLE CHANCE AWAYS
24 Pts. ..... £1431. 9.0 For
23 Pts £8.14.0 3d
22½ Pts. £4. 4.0
22 Pts. £0. 9.0
21½ Pts. £0. 6.0
NINE RESULTS (Paid on 8 correct) 2274/-

THREE DRAWS (14 Draws on list) 40/-
FOUR AWAYS 164/-
BINGO £79.0.0
SIX RESULTS (Only 5 matches played) .. 70/-
TWELVE RESULTS
(Only 11 matches played)
11 Correct ... £232.16.0 For a
10 Correct ... £7.10.0 1d
9 Correct ... £0. 6.0
LO-SCORE COMPETITION
No client with 1 goal.
2 Goals ...... £51.18.0 for 1/-
3 Goals ...... £1.10.0 for 1/-

Expenses and Commission for week ending April 9, 1966—34.1%. Except where otherwise stated dividends are to units of 1/- and subject to rescrutiny. Send for Bingo Coupons and the fabulous Soccer Plan 38 to:
SOCCER POOLS LIMITED, LEICESTER

SEND YOUR COUPON TODAY

THE HERO OF HAMPDEN. Kaj Johansen (left) makes himself the golden boy of Scottish soccer as he lashes the ball past Ronnie Simpson for Rangers' Scottish Cup winner. Celtic's beaten defenders are Bobby Murdoch, Tommy Gemmell and Billy McNeill.

It's his first goal for Rangers—and what a goal. Kaj Johansen leaps high as team-mates Henderson and McLean congratulate him.

Quotes

GOAL-SCORER KAJ JOHANSEN, the first Dane to score a goal in a Scottish Cup final, said with tears in his eyes:

"I honestly cannot say much tonight. I am overwhelmed. I really did not think my shot was going to go into the net because the goalmouth was too crowded.

"This is my greatest moment ever in football."

● JOHN GREIG, Rangers' captain: "This is the greatest moment of my career. On the two previous occasions I played in a Cup final Rangers were favourites. But this time we were the underdogs and victory gave me tremendous satisfaction.

"Most of the credit must go to manager Scot Symon, who planned the blueprint for success."

● Celtic chairman BOB KELLY: "It was a good final. Celtic played well enough to win but Rangers scored the goal and it's goals that count."

● Rangers manager SCOT SYMON: "What more can I say than that I am delighted."

● S.F.A. president TOM REID: "A toughly-contested final but I thought Jimmy Millar wrote his name all over the match. And, of course, it was a glorious winning goal by Johansen."

● JIMMY MILLAR: "This is my fifth Cup-winners' medal but the one I will treasure most."

"FAB-FOUR"
EIGHT DIVIDENDS
MULTI-CHANCE POOL
WEEK ENDING 23rd APRIL, 1966
1st Div. 25 each win £621.18.6
2nd Div. 109 each win £25. 3.5
3rd Div. 314 each win £8.14.9
4th Div. 881 each win £3. 2.3
5th Div. 1426 each win £3.17.0
6th Div. 113 each win £5 .0.0
7th Div. 336 each win £2.14.5
8th Div. 243 each win £3.15.3
Pontoon—Aggregates £3093.11.11
Pontoon—Homes £1829. 3.10
Dividends Published Subject to Rescrutiny
Commission and Expenses—29.1%
P.O. Box No. 9
BRUNEL HOUSE, BRISTOL, 1.

SPASTIC LEAGUE CLUB
WEEK ENDING 23rd APRIL, 1966
MERIT PRIZES
1st 1 wins Vauxhall Viva Motor Car
2nd .... 9 each win £100. 0.0
3rd .... 453 each win £5. 0.0
4th .... 6010 each win £2.10.0
104 STOKES CROFT
BRISTOL, 1

HILL'S NATIONAL POOLS
TREBLE CHANCE POOL
Fifteen draws on coupon.
24 Pts. .... £123.17.0 for ¼d
23 Pts. .... £1. 2.6 for ¼d
22½ Pts. .... £0.13.6 for ¼d
3 DRAWS 28/-
8 RESULTS 34,980/-
10 RESULTS (paid on 8 correct) 822/-
5 RESULTS 142/-
4 AWAYS 90/-
3 SCORES (18 matches) ... 782/-
LUCKY SEVEN 1608/-
Minimum stake on all pools other than Treble Chance 2d.
Certified dividends for matches played April 23 (subject to re-scrutiny) declared in units of 1/- unless otherwise stated. Expenses and commission for April 9 34.3%. Send today for coupon if over 21.
WILLIAM HILL LTD., London, S.E.1, and Glasgow, C.1

CORALS CERTIFIED DIVIDENDS
MATCHES PLAYED 23rd APRIL, 1966
8 RESULTS (paid on 8) 8800/-
3 DRAWS 36/-
3 RESULTS 192/-
4 DRAWS 208/-
4 AWAYS 128
7 RESULTS FROM EACH RULED SECTION (paid on 8) 885/-
5 TEAMS SCORING ONE GOAL 14/-
3 CORRECT SCORES 862/-
£440 DIVIDEND 8 RESULTS
Dividends to units of 1/-. Expenses and Commission for 23rd April—24.8%.
Write for Corals Pools/Fixed Odds Coupon if over 21
DEPT D.R., JOE CORRAL (FOOTBALL) LTD., LONDON, W.8.

Glory goal—and Rangers win Cup

IT'S KING KAJ

CELTIC 0
RANGERS 1

Scorer: Johansen.

A VIKING goal gave Rangers a heroic victory over Celtic in a full-blooded Scottish Cup final at Hampden last night.

Danish right-back Kaj Johansen was the toast of every Rangers fan in the 96,862 crowd as he hammered a shot into the Celtic net with all the verve and ferocity of a longboat raid by his intrepid ancestors.

Seventy minutes had gone—seventy minutes of fire and fervour, clashes that made you wince. Desperate, all - out attack and he-man action.

Still the game was swinging like a Sinatra party. And if you felt that Celtic were the more composed, more methodical, more incisive team, you couldn't disregard Rangers' power on the break.

Nowhere . . .

And suddenly Willie Johnston swung over a low cross that became a blockbuster, bringing red-hot danger to Celtic's defence.

George McLean, who had been engaged all night in jousts with Billy McNeill that were as clanging as the clashes of armoured knights, just failed to get the ball.

Sailing in was wee Willie Henderson, a winger more like his old self. "Goal" screamed the Rangers supporters as his shot tore towards goal.

But, frantically, Bobby Murdoch was brilliantly in the way—and out came the ball, to a thundering sigh of disappointment from the men in blue behind Simpson's goal.

BUT NO-ONE HAD NOTICED KAJ JOHANSEN SPRINTING IN FROM NOWHERE.

He was still running when he met the ball inside the penalty area and, with Viking fury, he

Johansen shatters a great Celtic fight

By HUGH TAYLOR

swing his foot at it and, a speed-blobbed blur, it flew past the helplessly groping fingers of Simpson.

A gorgeous goal. A dramatic goal. Kaj's first in Scotland—and what a time to score.

Rangers players went berserk with joy, jumping into the air, turning somersaults.

NO WONDER THEY CHAIRED JOHANSEN—TEARS STREAMING DOWN HIS CHEEKS—OFF AT THE END.

For his goal was all there was between the teams, two teams who had given everything they had in a final which, if not an epic of artistry, was fought at blistering pace.

It was a night of the valiant. And Rangers' great Dane, Johansen, wrote his name in glaring letters in Scotland's football history. So did Jimmy Millar.

Old form

The old warhorse of Ibrox, I described him. He's all that—AND MORE.

He was a tremendous player last night, summoning energy from goodness knows where, always in the thick of battle—and holding the ball as only he can.

Davy Provan became unsure after his name was taken for a tackle on Jimmy Johnstone —but the little right-winger although tricky on the ball did little once he was in the open.

But Willie Henderson, on the right-wing last night, found some of his old form—and, indeed, after Rangers scored he helped to give them their best spell of the night . . .

. . . A spell in which they might have scored two more goals as Celtic left gaps in all-out efforts to equalise.

In the end, Celtic were beaten by one of their own favourite secret weapons — A MARAUDING BACK.

George McLean soon was moving well for Rangers, and from a slick pass from the centre-forward the Ibrox boys forced a corner.

Really thrilling stuff this and the next thing of note was a sparkling raid by Hughes which brought danger to Rangers.

Despite the wind Celtic looked more incisive, more in the mood than Rangers.

Yet Rangers had pace up front and in an exciting race between McLean and McNeil anything could have happened.

What did happen was—A

FOUL AGAINST THE RANGER.

Auld relieved the pressure with a fine run—but it was all in vain. The whistle had gone for a foul against Bertie.

And the inside-left had to take treatment when the bother was sorted out.

Auld's genius was shown again with a wonderful ball that deceived the Rangers' defence, but Chalmers headed narrowly past.

Provan was booked in 20 minutes for a foul on Johnstone, who needed attention.

A great throw from Henderson let Johansen in for a shot but the danger was just cleared in time. What a tough game it was with tackles bringing sparks and angry looks.

Celtic grew more confident as the half went on—and well they might. They had more football up front, more venom, more ideas.

McNeill try

With the wind at their backs Celtic restarted with a terrific attack and from a corner a great McNeill header flew past the post.

A WONDERFUL HEADER—BUT WHY HADN'T RANGERS BEEN MARKING THE CELTIC CENTRE-HALF AT CORNERS?

In 17 minutes McBride had a chance when Chalmers dummied a cross, but Ritchie luckily saved the ball with his foot, and the ball was eventually scrambled clear.

Next Auld shot past, and now it was Celtic on the attack.

Some game. But back came Rangers and Simpson had to clear a Johnston cross.

Johansen scored a terrific goal for Rangers in the 70th minute McLean missed a Johnston cross then a Henderson shot was cleared off the line and Johansen came from nowhere to lash in a shot from just inside the box.

RANGERS: Ritchie; Johansen, Provan; Greig, McKinnon, Millar; Henderson, Watson, McLean, Johnston, Wilson.

CELTIC: Simpson; Craig, Gemmell; Murdoch, McNeill, Clark; Johnstone, McBride, Chalmers, Auld, Hughes.

● It's not the orthodox save for a 'keeper, but it was one good reason why Rangers won the Scottish Cup last night. 'Keeper Billy Ritchie sticks out a foot to save a net-bound shot from grounded Celt Joe McBride.

MIGHTY MILLAR IS A HERO

OH how Celtic have suffered for squandering opportunities!

They lost their chance against Liverpool by missing gilt-edged openings.

Last night they should have had the Scottish Cup booked for Parkhead long before that glorious goal by Kaj Johansen, 20 minutes from the end.

Even allowing for masterly goalkeeping by Bill Ritchie, the Steve Chalmers-led forward line should have shown dividends.

But whatever skills they had in the outfield were completely spoiled by poor finishing.

Master player

Rangers, in Jimmy Millar, possessed the master player.

Recall Ian McColl's great come-back to the Light Blues when he was drafted in for a Scottish Cup Final and made himself the outstanding player.

Here was a repeat performance by Millar. He was a great player in the first match, a still greater one in the replay.

Millar turned up in the right place at the right moment, in attack or defence. He was one of the few who could intelligently hold the ball to draw an opponent.

Strong tackling

Whenever I recall Rangers' latest triumph against their old rivals, I shall always think of Millar's craftsmanship, great-heartedness and seemingly inexhaustible store of energy.

And I shall recall his wonderful club enthusiasm, without which he couldn't, at his age, have played so magnificently.

It was not a game which produced much scientific football. In many respects it was a

WAVERLEY

repeat of Saturday—hard, tough and demanding perfect physical condition to stand up unflinchingly to the strong tackling.

Celtic, with the brainiest attacker in Bertie Auld, were the more cohesive in the outfield.

Didn't learn

BUT THEIR MOVES OFTEN BROKE DOWN AT THE VITAL MOMENT.

The fact that Joe McBride was injured just before the scoring of the victory goal and went to outside-left is no excuse.

Rangers' attack seldom got together.

Jock Stein has been quoted as saying: "We learn from defeat."

It seemed last night that some of his players had learned nothing from the first game against Liverpool.

If they had, they would have finished off their approach work in a manner more pleasing to their supporters who, today are suffering the pangs of sorrowful disappointment.

They were so sure of triumph, and now they have been brought to the sudden realisation that nothing is certain in this great game of football.

SOCCER ON MONDAY

THESE RANGERS HAVE GROWN UP

Talking about . .

. . . the difficulty in winning points at home. That's the theme after Saturday's First Division matches, for out of the seven League games played only ONE was a home victory. Even there the away team had some complaints to make about the result.

AT BROCKVILLE, Falkirk won 2-0 in a game against Ayr United which had one player sent off, four booked and a comment from Ayr boss Ally McLeod which went this way . . .

"I didn't like some of the things that went on out there. There was needle building during the game and it got out of hand. After all we have a reputation of being a well-disciplined club."

Falkirk boss Willie Cunningham, predictably, wasn't worrying over much. "It's a man's game and I didn't think it was bad . . . anyway we have the two points."

The only two points that went to a home team in the First Division.

We'll stay tops

At LOVE STREET, Eddie Turnbull's Aberdeen team won again away from home, following up that Ibrox victory.

It's this kind of win that must bring Turnbull a lot of satisfaction, for it shows that the consistency he has been searching for has arrived.

The 3-1 win has them at the top of the table with Celtic and also has the Pittodrie boss claiming:

"We can stay at the top. There is nothing to stop us. We are now 11 points ahead of what we were at this stage last year. That can't be bad."

Managerless St. Mirren hope to solve the problem left by Alex Wright's departure as quickly as possible.

They expect to have the post filled inside two weeks.

No atmosphere

AT CENTRAL PARK, it's getting to be a habit for Cowdenbeath to lose in front of their own fans. Says manager Andy Matthews: "We just don't carry luck at home at all. We have had three games here where we deserved to win or at least draw, but bad luck stopped us."

Motherwell scraped through to their one goal win in an atmosphere far removed from the glamour and the excitement of White Hart Lane.

Said manager Bobby Howitt: "There was no atmosphere at all especially after the game at White Hart Lane where there was so much excitement. It caused a bit of a slump in the team's play but we won and that suited us."

Teenage hero

AT RUGBY PARK, Kilmarnock and Morton drew 2-2 and Morton produced the game's talking point with two goal-keeping heroes.

In the first half it was regular 'keeper Lief Neilsen, then when he was injured, it was 16-year-old George Anderson who took over.

George had several fine saves, though he admitted: "That was the first time I'd ever played in goal and I was pretty nervous. It was coach Eric Smith who decided I should take over when Lief was hurt."

Killie still struggle to escape the injury jinx which has dogged them all season. When the team is allowed to settle, things could change for Walter McCrae.

AT BROOMFIELD, Airdrie fans are wondering what has hit them. The 2-1 defeat from Clyde was the third home defeat in succession . . . yet a month ago teams were scared to play there.

Manager Ralph Collins claims hopefully: "All we need is one win, just one, to bring the confidence back. We're in a rut at the moment but we'll get out of it soon."

Clyde fielded new signing John Flanagan from Partick Thistle and his form pleased manager Archie Robertson.

Flanagan himself was happy with the team's win and he said: "As the game wore on things seemed to go well."

THAT rainbow you see still lingering over Ibrox today is the glowing symbol of the new, bright, grown-up Rangers.

THERE'S BLUE for a well-blended team who played with spectacular success and a new-found poise.

THERE'S GREEN to signal them on to the main road which leads to even greater triumphs.

THERE'S YELLOW for the sands of Gullane where the sea breezes and the desert guerilla training turned out to be the ideal tonic for League Cup success.

Adulation

THERE'S RED for the faces of the critics (including myself) and the captains and cynics who gave them little chance against Celtic at Hampden.

So Rangers are bathing in adulation, the champagne of one of their sweetest victories, that never-to-be forgotten 1-0 win over Celtic to take the

By

HUGH TAYLOR

League Cup . . . and send the hoodoo that their old rivals had over them scampering in dismay.

Certainly it was a notable win, a well-deserved victory, with the eager Rangers at last turning on a variety of moves and lacing their superb running with the velvet touch so many thought they could never find.

Wisely, however, manager Willie Waddell says this is only the beginning. He's right. Only for the fanatical does a win over Celtic mean more than anything else.

EUROPE AT THE TOP IS THE TARGET FOR MODERN TEAMS.

And Rangers have still to show they can emulate Celtic and again become one of the great international names.

Saturday's win which had their fantastic support singing in the rain is almost certainly the pep pill they need to start them on their flight back to the top.

No one, not even the quiet Celtic fans could begrudge Rangers their win.

A story-book goal by 16-year-old Derek Johnstone . . . brilliant play by Alfie Conn, Willie Henderson and Willie Johnston . . . an inspiring captain's part by Ronnie McKinnon, standing in for the off-colour John Greig—these were the main features of the victory.

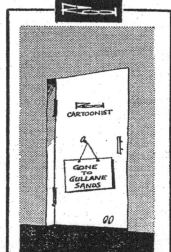

CARTOONIST

GONE TO GULLANE SANDS

Noble

It isn't often Celtic have to play second fiddle. But they had few players to compare with those of their exuberant rivals.

Jimmy Johnstone almost turned the tide and Willie Wallace (despite a sad miss) and Bobby Murdoch also played a noble part in rallying their team.

But the flaws which have marked several of Celtic's games, despite their imposing victory list this season, were obvious.

There are creaks in the defence and, up front, there is too often a loss of the smooth rhythm which made the Celts such a convincing side.

It is, of course, anything but the end of the world for Celtic. They are still after the big one, the European Cup. They have hopes of fielding stars such as Tommy Gemmell, John Hughes and Jim Brogan shortly.

A defeat by Rangers isn't relished at Parkhead . . . but manager Jock Stein knows victory for his men over the ancient foe isn't inevitable.

Defeat had to come sometime. Celtic's job is to acquire consistency, which may be achieved when the casualty list clears. Although they didn't deserve to win, Celtic weren't all that far away from a draw at Hampden.

So the praise goes to Rangers. Celtic have had glorious moments—for years. They can't really grumble if the shining Rangers take the headlines now . . . for Rangers were no longer a band of hope but a well-drilled, often inspired soccer orchestra.

What a pity the end was marred by the urchin trick of Willie Johnston of demonstrating his team's superiority by sitting on the ball . . . and the peevish attempt to get his own back by Jimmy Johnstone.

It's two against one . . . but young Derek Johnstone leaps between Billy McNeill and Jim Craig to head home Rangers' Cup-winning goal.

An 11-goal thriller . .

THE League Cup final may have attracted most of the glamour and attention—but New Kilbowie Park was definitely THE place for goals at the weekend.

Clydebank and Stirling Albion treated the fans to a real bonanza and it was Bankies who got the edge with a 6-5 win that smashed Albion's unbeaten away record.

Centre-half Jim Fallon threw away the chance of a hat-trick of penalties with a late spot miss, his first ever. But wee Jimmy Caskie scored two goals, as did Bobby Duffin and Joe Hughes for Albion. Duffin's tally included a penalty.

Partick Thistle unexpectedly dropped a point to Dumbarton, their League Cup quarter-final conquerors, at Firhill. The Boghead club

missed key forwards Roy McCormick and Brian Gallagher and Thistle led by a Frank Coulston goal until Kenny Jenkins equalised 12 minutes from time.

Albion Rovers stretched their best run in years by going eleven games unbeaten with a 2-2 draw against Raith Rovers at Starks Park.

The Coatbridge club have never looked back since their opening day defeat from East Fife at Cliftonhill and are now the only team in the Second Division undefeated away.

Raith scored first through a Benny McGuire penalty and led at the interval. But Rovers hit back with goals from Jimmy Johnston and Albert Rice. Pat Wilson preserved Raith's unbeaten home record with a last gasp equaliser.

Record Sport

Glasgow: 041-248 7000 . Dundee: 0382 27481
Edinburgh: 031-225 4275 : Aberdeen: 0224 52361

Those 13 captains were wrong.. Mr Waddell and a boy called Derek Johnstone got it right..

CELTS 0 'GERS 1

RANGERS are not going to be content just to sit back and admire the League Cup as it glitters in its showcase at Ibrox.

That was made obvious by manager Willie Waddell yesterday (writes KEN GALLACHER).

He stressed: "I want this to be the beginning for this Rangers' team. I want this to be the win that will show the way to more victories."

Waddell was glad that the grey years of failure had ended, delighted that the young players had repaid the faith he has in them ... BUT HE REFUSED TO BE CARRIED AWAY BY SUCCESS.

Instead he was already planning for the future. The League Cup win ensures Rangers of a place in the Fairs Cup again next season. To prepare for that, they will soon be in action against top European sides, including their old rivals Moscow Dynamo.

Last night Waddell revealed: "We have had an approach from Moscow Dynamo who want to play at Ibrox in the middle of November.

QUINN IS BOSS AT METHIL

PAT QUINN will tonight officially become player-manager of East Fife.

East Fife player Quinn, formerly of Motherwell, Blackpool and Hibs, was offered the job at the weekend (writes DICK CURRIE).

He will confirm his acceptance at tonight's board meeting.

The appointment is full time.

Quinn is a fully qualified S.F.A. coach and, with former Motherwell teammate John Martis, will be one of the Fifers' key men in the promotion race.

East Fife's previous manager, Bill Baxter, joined Raith Rovers just a week ago.

Stirling Albion have appointed former Dunfermline forward George Peebles as coach to their second team and signed 16-year-old right-half Ian Dair, of Woodhall Under-18 juvenile side.

Newspaper postage: Inland 4d., Overseas 3d.

Ibrox date for Moscow Dynamo

"I had intended playing top opposition once the League Cup was over with.

"This match against Moscow Dynamo is what we were lookin for.

"They haven't been at Ibrox since that game in 1945, although Rangers played them in Russia some years back.

"I will be looking into this closely this week. It seems like a good one for us."

The match would be a tremendous draw and a bonus to the fans.

Of the League Cup victory, Waddell said:

"I believe that this win can be an inspiration to the young players we have in the team.

"I really can't praise them too much. They've been worked hard this season and they have come through it magnificently."

Needed

He went on: "The win, though, isn't going to help only the young players. It'll be a fillip for the established players, too.

"It is what the Rangers have been needing ... and these boys have worked hard for this result."

That hard work will continue. There will be no letting-up.

Waddell declares firmly: "We must look on this as the break-through, as the start of something for the team. We have a lot more to do."

It could mean also that the Scottish team skippers who in Saturday's Record forecast a Celtic victory — 13-3 was the voting—will have a lot of re-thinking to do.

SOCCER'S newest boy bombshell, Derek Johnstone, revealed last night that he missed the sight which thrilled Rangers fans in the 106,263 crowd at Hampden Park ...

For the 16-year-old from Dundee did not see his header entering the net for the goal that shot him out of the unknown into a place in Ibrox history, writes ALEX CAMERON.

He said last night: "When Willie Johnston lifted the ball over I jumped by instinct. I got the ball with my head firmly enough, BUT AFTER THAT I SAW NOTHING.

"My view was blocked by Celtic's right back Jim Craig. Then I heard the most tremendous roar I've ever experienced. And I knew it was a goal."

Johnstone's widowed mother and brother Robert watched proudly in the stand. For 24 hours they had shared the secret that he was to be in the Rangers team as a twin striker with £100,000 star Colin Stein.

"There was no question of Derek being picked because John Greig was unfit," said Willie Waddell.

"Even if John had played, Derek was in the side and I told him so on Friday."

Johnstone began his soccer career as a 12-year-old centre half with Linlathen Junior

Hero who didn't see it happen

Secondary School in Dundee. Then he moved forward among the scoring action—and that's when Rangers began to take notice.

There is little danger of sudden fame spoiling him. Yesterday he went happily to Largs to train with the Scottish Youth party who will play in Iceland tomorrow ...

And it took a lot of prompting, even by his mates, to get him to chat about a scoring feat which every boy dreams about.

Dancing in the rain—that's Rangers' teenage goal ace Derek Johnstone as he waits to board the Scotland Youth team bus in Glasgow's George Square yesterday. Derek, naturally, is keeping that "golden" head dry.

Printed and Published by Scottish Daily Record and Sunday Mail Ltd., 67 Hope Street, Glasgow. C.2 for I.P.C. Newspapers Ltd., Holborn Circus, London. E.C.1. Registered at the Post Office as a newspaper.   © Scottish Daily Record, 197

THE IBROX DISASTER

4-Page 'Daily Record' Special

By DONALD BRUCE

THE disaster at Ibrox Park on Saturday is the worst we have ever known in British sporting history.

Even now, we cannot appreciate its ghastly enormity. The magnitude of horror as pathetic body piled on top of pathetic body in an unstoppable stampede of death on a stairway.

Ninety minutes before, 66 people had climbed that same stairway — full of New Year cheer, gay, laughing, happy, excited at the prospect of what has always been a feast of football from Glasgow's two biggest clubs, Rangers and Celtic.

Suffocated

An hour and a half later, they were dead — all of them — mangled, trampled on, suffocated, as joyous Rangers' fans, hearing about Stein's last-minute equaliser, went back UP the stairs to meet the thousands coming DOWN the stairs.

Someone tripped and fell. The rest piled on top, body after body, the iron stanchions broke, and there it was in all its simple, stark, awful horror — disaster at the big game.

The agonising cries of the dying, the wounded, the suffocated had to be heard to be believed. It could have been one of the more macabre scenes of the World War. Instead, it was the end of a football match — a sporting occasion, a festival of sport.

It is, unfortunately, not the first time we have seen horror and witnessed death at the big game.

Saturday's was the worst—have you ever seen so many sad-eyed, weeping people in Glasgow as you did on Saturday night as they waited on news of the names of the dead, fearing that they might be friends? But there have been precedents, although never on such a ghastly, massive scale.

Tripped

Almost ten years ago —in September, 1961, also at a Rangers v. Celtic game—a wooden barrier collapsed on the SAME stairway — the one leading to Harrison Drive and Copland Road — where Saturday's disaster happened. Two people were killed and 60 hurt.

The circumstances were almost identical. Someone tripped and fell, the huge crowd behind pushing to get down the stairs and out of the exits collapsed in a heap. The barrier broke, and the casualties piled up.

The wooden barrier was replaced with an iron stanchion, but only two years ago, on January 2, 1969, once again at Ibrox, once again at a Rangers-Celtic game, once again on the same stairway at what is known as the Rangers' end, a man tripped, a stanchion broke, and dozens of people were hurled to the ground.

Coincidence

Fortunately, no one died, but 24 people were hurt and taken to hospital.

Before Saturday, Britain's worst disaster was at Bolton in 1946 in a cup tie between Bolton and Stoke City when a barrier broke and 33 people were killed.

A testimonial match was played for the dependants.

Part of the retaining wall collapsed at Shawfield in 1957 in a match between Clyde and Celtic—a boy was killed—and in a Scotland v. England match at Ibrox in 1902 part of the west terracing gave way and 25 people were killed and more than 500 injured.

So the unfortunate precedents are there. It is an unhappy coincidence—and it can be no more than that— that most of the terracing terror at Ibrox in the past decade has happened on the same stairway.

Is it because it's the favourite exit because it's nearest to the Copland Road subway?

Control

Rangers Football Club have done everything possible to strengthen the stanchions, a crowd limit has been placed on the game by the police, so where do we go from here?

There is talk of licensing football grounds, but how can you licence for panic or for a stampede?

More stairways at the Copland Road end of Ibrox? There are two. More police to control the crowds as they stream from the ground?

The truth is that no one could forsee the freakishness of Saturday's flashpoint of disaster — Rangers' equalising goal after thousands of fans had already headed for the exits and turned back, some to their deaths.

Note: The worst ever disaster in football took place in Lima, Peru, in 1964, when the referee disallowed a goal in a match between Peru and Argentina. The crowd rioted, the police used tear gas, and in a stampede to get out 300 fans lost their lives and over 500 were injured.

DEATH AT THE BIG GAME

● Grim-faced Scottish Under-Secretary Alick Buchanan-Smith (centre), who was ordered by the Scottish Secretary to hold an immediate probe into the Ibrox disaster, leaves the City Mortuary accompanied by Glasgow's Chief Constable Sir James Robertson (left) and Lord Provost Sir Donald Liddle.

CROWD BROKE BARRIER

FENCE PUSHED OVER

FLASHBACK

● Ibrox, September 16, 1961. The same stairway where 66 people lost their lives on Saturday. In 1961, in a stampede after a man had fallen, the handrail in the middle broke, and the wooden fencing at the side (now replaced by iron stanchions) collapsed. Two died and 60 were hurt.

THE HORROR IN PICTURES   CENTRE PAGES

Record Sport IN EUROPE

WE WON THE CUP

We've done it! And last night in Barcelona's Nov Camp Stadium, Rangers' dream of Europe glory came true . . . at last. And skipper John Greig has the Cup Winners Cup to prove it.

● YOU can see the trophy tonight when Waddell's warriors parade it triumphantly at Ibrox. Gates open 6.30.

NOW RANGERS MAY FACE REPLAY

RANGERS, 3-2 victors over Moscow Dynamo in the European Cup-winners' Cup Final here tonight, face disaster and disgrace in their hour of glory.

Twice beaten finalists in the competition, they pulled off a magnificent win against the Russians. But now . . .

THEY COULD BE forced to REPLAY the final if a Dynamo protest is upheld . . .

THEY COULD BE BANNED from Europe next season because of the disgraceful pitched battles that raged

From KEN GALLACHER BARCELONA, Wednesday night

after the match between Rangers supporters and the Spanish police.

After incredible crowd scenes which delayed the end of the match, then developed into a vendetta between fans and police, angry Dynamo team manager Constantin Beskov stormed:

"WE ARE DEMANDING THAT THE MATCH SHOULD BE PLAYED AGAIN."

In the European Cup Inter Milan and Borussia Munchen Gladbach had to replay we feel it must happen again

"My team were intimidated by the Scottish supporters

"Seventy per cent of the Scottish fans were completely drunk and terrified my players.

"Before the start of the game, Szabo was hit by a bottle as he came on to the pitch. The team did not want to play and feared for their lives."

European Union officials in Barcelona would not

comment after the game but clearly the Russian protest will be given careful consideration.

And the possibility still exists that Rangers will have to play again and win again—before the Cup-Winners Cup is at Ibrox.

And even more probable is the threatened ban on Rangers playing in Europe next season because of the behaviour of their fans.

Three years ago they were warned by the European authorities after a riot at Newcastle. THIS WAS WORSE THAN NEWCASTLE!

The great Barcelona Stadium was still littered with broken seats, ripped cushions—all the weapons the fans had used in their fight with the police.

Said manager Waddell:

"We were happy with the way the fans supported us from the stand. But if we are to play in Europe then they must learn to behave."

And the Ibrox boss, close to tears, added: "They could crucify the club by this kind of behaviour They put our whole future at risk."

THE BLOODY BATTLE OF BARCELONA

CONTINUED FROM PAGE ONE

cushions and bottles on to the pitch. And in one charge the police held cushions in front of their faces as shields.

Late last night some top officials were blaming the Spanish police for not moving in quickly enough to halt the

trouble at the start.

When the Rangers team tried to come on with the Russians just behind them, the fans ran in a crazed show of adulation.

It took 10 minutes to sort this out and manager Willie Waddell had to plead with the fans.

He wrestled one off the track and back on

to the terracing with TV cameras beaming it all to 30 countries.

When Colin Stein scored Rangers' first goal, the 25,000 supporters from Scotland went wild. Thousands ran on to the pitch.

The same thing happened when Willie Johnston gave Rangers a 2-0 lead.

Just before the end of the game the fans misread a signal by Spanish referee Jose Ortiz de Mendible when he raised his hand to caution a player. They thought he was ending the match and on they came again in whooping droves.

But worst of all was that blood-bath finish.

When it was all over the police claimed 32 of their men were injured, one seriously.

The police could not say how many fans were injured.

Meanwhile out in the streets, the battles went on

One policeman had his face smashed open with a beer can.

He was left lying on

the ground with an eye hanging half out of its socket.

There were no arrests in Barcelona. A spokesman for the British Consulate said: "The police are being very lenient

But at resorts outside the city about 30 fans were charged with disorderly behaviour

PHONE GUIDE	GLASGOW 041-248 7000	EDINBURGH 031-225 4275	AYR 0292-62765	ABERDEEN 0224-52361	DUNDEE 0382-27481	INVERNESS 0463-33334

Printed and published by Scottish Daily Record and Sunday Mail Ltd, Anderston Quay, Glasgow, G3 8DA, for IPC Newspapers Ltd, Holborn Circus, London E.C.1 Registered at the Post Office as a newspaper. © Daily Record, 1972.

The goal that won the Cup

It's the goal that counted for so much . . . the goal that gave Rangers victory last night in Barcelona. Willie Johnston (left) jumps for joy as his shot beats Dynamo 'keeper Pilgui for Rangers third.

NOW–LET'S HAVE THE ENGLISH

By HUGH TAYLOR

IT ended gloriously . . . Another glorious goal by sharpshooter Peter Lorimer kept Scotland at the top in the Home Championship last night at Hampden . . .

But, oh dear, Scotland It's as well your fans haven't weak hearts. For once again it was a cliff-hanger of an international, a case of the boys in blue changing from villains to heroes.

The first half was a bore. Indeed, it might have been a disaster for Scotland.

For Wales surprised everyone by tearing into the attack and a most unusual Scottish defence had worries.

Manager Tommy Docherty had Pat Stanton at right back. Martin Buchan at left-back, with Billy McNeill and Bobby Moncur in the middle.

Apart from the brilliant McNeill, no one looked really happy and the Welsh attackers used the ball well.

If it hadn't been for rank bad finishing by the usually deadly Ron Davies and Alan Durban, Scotland would have been at least two down at half time.

And apart from Denis Law, the new hero of Hampden, Peter Lorimer, always anxious for a shot, and the brilliant Tony Green, our team looked short of pace, out of touch, and worried.

Once again the Doc dipped into his medicine bag and produced the proper tonic.

He took off the faltering Derby pair, Archie Gemmill and John O'Hare, and brought on Asa Hartford and Lou Macari.

That made a world of difference.

Golden

At last there was method, a touch of brilliance in the Scotland play. Fiercely our attackers hammered in, neatly the men in the middle began to dictate play.

But it seemed a goal would never come. Of all people, Lorimer missed a golden chance. So did skipper Bremner.

But Lorimer made amends in the 72nd minute. The persistence of Macari buzzing at England's heels paid off.

He hustled the Welsh centre-half out of his stride, the ball broke to Lorimer and from 15 yards and an acute angle Peter lashed the ball rocket-like last his Leeds mate. 'keeper Gary Sprake.

In the end Scotland

SCOTLAND .... 1 WALES 0
Scorer: Lorimer (72 minutes)

THE TABLE							
	P	W	D	L	F	A	Pts
Scotland	2	2	0	0	3	0	4
England	2	1	0	1	3	1	2
Ireland	2	1	0	1	2	1	2
Wales	2	0	0	2	0	4	0

deserved this win. And it could, with luck, have been much more convincing so much on top were we at the end.

The 21,332 crowd went home happy, but they'll be hoping that against England on Saturday, Scotland start as they finished—and there won't be a repeat of this alarming first half.

Wales played more briskly than Ireland and had star men in Durban and James, who came on for Hennessy.

But it was a magnificent finish by Scotland, with top marks going to McNeill, Green, Lorimer, Hartford, Macari and, of course, Law . . . Law, the inspiration, the man who now seems to own Hampden.

Skill

And it looks as though Green, Hartford and Macari must have strong claims for inclusion in the side to face England.

They brought speed and fire and no little skill to a team which, when it maintains real form for the entire 90 minutes will surely put us back on the map

Scotland—Clark, Stanton, Buchan, Bremner McNeill, Moncur, Lorimer Green, O'Hare Law Gemmill.

Wales—Sprake; Paige, Thomas, Hennessy England, Yorath, Durban, W. Davies G. Reece, R. Davies. Phillips

Referee—J. Lawther. Bangour.

Buchanan fight may be live on TV

By Dick Currie

SCOTTISH fight fans could see Ken Buchanan's World lightweight title fight against Roberto Duran of Panama in New York's Madison Square Garden on June 26 . . .

This is the good news I have for the fans this morning after talking to London millionaire Jarvis Astaire, boss of the Viewsport closed-circuit television company

It was Viewsport who outbid BBC and other TV companies to show the Joe Frazier-Cassius Clay World heavyweight title fight from New York throughout Europe 18 months ago.

Chance

"I have the TV rights for the fight and could show it in cinemas in Glasgow Aberdeen and Edinburgh." said 49-year-old Astaire last night.

"At the moment, I'm involved in negotiations regarding

Buchanan's title fight in New York. I think the Scottish fight public deserve a chance to see Britain's only World boxing champion

"I'm putting feelers out around London boxing circles to see if there is a demand for the fight to be shown in a West End cinema"

Buchanan. 26 once a joiner was a big success in clearly outpointing Canadian lightweight champion Al Ford at Wembley in March

The Edinburgh boy is also a big success in New York where he retained his title against the man from whom he won it—Panama's Ismael Laguna at the Garden in September.

Ken is now in full training for the Duran fight and yesterday he told me: "I'm delighted to learn that fight fans here could be getting a chance to see me defend my title in New York."

But Buchanan will not lack support on June 26 as John F. Condon, Publicity Director of the Garden, tells me:

"BUCHANAN IS TREATED AS A LOCAL KID HERE IN NEW YORK. HE'S GOT EVERYTHING GOING FOR HIM HERE."

The New Yorkers like Ken's frankness, willingness and confident style in and out of the ring.

Johnston, Stein clinch Cup for Ibrox men

Gers do it the hard way

From
Ken Gallacher
*Barcelona,
Wednesday.*

RANGERS won the European trophy they have searched for for so long—but the glory that should have been theirs was tarnished by the behaviour of their fans.

It was a night that no-one in European football will ever forget. a night of shame for the Scots who invaded the field at Barcelona at the end of the game.

But these same fans also robbed Rangers captain John Greig of the chance of being handed publicly the European Cup-Winners

Cup which he and his team mates had earned.

They had earned it the hard way—just as they have had to do everything the hard way in this tournament.

Sparkling

In a sparkling first half they looked as if they had the game won when they scored twice.

The first goal was a magnificent shot from centre-forward Colin Stein in 24 minutes.

And the second in 40

RANGERS........3,   MOSCOW DYNAMO........2

Scorers: Rangers—Stein, Johnston (2). Moscow Dynamo—Estrokov, Makovikov.

minutes came from a Willie Johnston header after a magnificent cross from Dave Smith.

And when Johnston added a third goal, and his own second. just three minutes after half-time. the game seemed won.

The fans—there must have been almost 25,000 in the ground—celebrated

wildly on the terracing.

They waved their banners. their Union Jacks. and their Scottish standards—but their celebrations had come too soon.

Trouble

For the redoubtable Russians refused to acknowledge defeat.

Desperately they made two substitutes. each time bringing on an attacking player.

Estrokov came on first in 55 minutes—and five minutes afterwards he had scored the goal which suddenly put Rangers in trouble.

Two minutes from the end, as the Russians

forced relentless pressure on Rangers defence, Makovikov scored a second goal for Dynamo.

It was an astonishing fight-back. Rangers, who had looked so certain to win, had seemed almost invincible, were suddenly in trouble.

But the main thing remained—Rangers have won the European Cup Winners Cup on their third appearance in the final.

Nothing can change that —although the hooligan fans certainly tarnished the victory by their behaviour.

It was not a night to pick out individual stars.

In that first half Rangers were magnificent—every single one of them—and after half-time they fought desperately against a Russian team which played with as much courage as any side I can remember in Europe.

Cool

In that spell when Rangers were in so much trouble, the coolness of Derek Johnston and Dave Smith and the brilliant goalkeeping of Peter McCloy have to be mentioned.

Just as earlier in the game the goal scorers, Colin Stein and Willie Johnstone, were the heroes.

But it was a tragedy that

this night of trial should have been spoiled by the fans.

For this should have been a night of celebration, it should have been a night of joy.

It should have been a celebration carnival for the Rangers fans who had waited so long for this European victory.

For the game. though, there can be nothing but praise.

Praise for the way the goals were scored, and praise too, for the way they refused to give in under that tremendous Russian fightback.

They lived dangerously to win this trophy—but they have won it.

At last the Ibrox trophy room will hold the European Cup Winners Cup.

And even the second half worries cannot take away the glory which was earned indeed in the epic battle across Europe.

It was just a tragedy for the thousands of decent fans who stayed in the stand and on the terracing that they could not see John Greag, that great Rangers captain. hold aloft the trophy that had eluded him for so long.

In a game of tremendous tension John Greig and Alex MacDonald were both booked by the Spanish referee.

But although the match was tough, it was not a dirty one.

Rangers—McCloy, Jardine, Mathieson; Greig, D. Johnstone, Smith; McLean, Conn, Stein, MacDonald, W. Johnston.

Dynamo—Pilgui, Basalaev, Dolmatov; Zhykov, Dolbanasov, Zhukov; Daidahyi, Jakubik. Sabo, Makovikov, Evruzhikin.

Referee—Jose Ortiz de Mendibil, Spain.

No. 1 for Rangers in Barcelona last night—and it's Colin Stein (left) evading a tackle to blast the ball past Dynamo 'keeper Pilgui.

The first of two goals for Willie Johnston as he rises between two Russian defenders to head in No. 2 for Rangers. Alex MacDonald (right) looks on.

Don wins title shot

SCOTTISH champion Don McMillan, 35-year-old Glasgow middleweight boxer, earned a crack at the British title with a fifth round win over Kevin Finnegan at the Bedfordshire Sporting Club last night.

Finnegan, younger brother of British and European light-heavyweight champion, Chris Finnegan, was odds-on favourite to win this final eliminator.

But the durable McMillan, who had won his previous

eight fights, seized what could be his last chance of a British title fight.

McMillan should now get a crack at champion Bunny Sterling for the British title.

The turning point came midway through the thrd third round when Finnegan was caught with a hard right hook. The punch opened a cut at the side of Finnegan's left eye.

Good work by his corner man repaired the damage but in the fifth round the cut was opened once more. At the end of the round referee Sid Nathan examined the cut and stopped the fight.

Daily Record

3p Friday, May 26, 1972 No. 23,878

20,000 FANS HAIL IBROX HEROES

REVELS IN THE RAIN!

THIS was it! The moment Rangers brought the European Cup-winners' Cup home to Ibrox—with 20,000 fans revelling in the rain.

On a red, white and blue-decked lorry, captain John Greig, his team-mates clustered around him, held the Cup aloft.

And slowly, proudly, the triumphant progress began—two circuits of the stadium.

| STORY BY KEN STEIN. | PICTURES BY ERIC CRAIG |

with cheering, cheering, all the way.

Many of the fans, just back from Barcelona, were still wearing souvenir sombreros.

They waved them and their banners and their scarves—and yelled themselves hoarse.

Before the team appeared, a loudspeaker announcement had warned that "stringent action" would be taken against anyone who invaded the rain-soaked pitch.

But, warnings or weather, nothing could dampen the good-natured enthusiasm of the crowd.

Earlier, Glasgow's Lord Provost John Mains had met Rangers chairman John Lawrence and the team when they flew into Prestwick Airport.

But all of that was just the curtain-raiser to the fantastic welcome at the stadium.

This was an Ibrox night of nights, a time to stand up and cheer.

And they did, 20,000 of them, like cheering had just been invented.

Police said later: "There was no trouble at the ground. Only two arrests were made —outside the stadium."

Willie's hat-trick —Back Page Follow, Follow—See Centre Pages

EXCLUSIVE ON THAT CUP VICTORY

MY TEAM RANGERS

By MANAGER JOCK WALLACE
Talking to Ken Gallacher

'I was happy for the players that we won . . . happy for all the backroom staff . . . and delighted that the fans have seen another trophy come to Ibrox.'

THE great thing for me about Saturday's victory at Hampden is that the players who have worked so hard all season have finished up with a reward for their efforts.

It would have been a tragedy for them if they had not won the Cup after that long, long unbeaten run.

They put in a tremendous effort—all of them—and to get the Cup at the end of it was what they deserved.

I am a great believer in having to win something before talking about achievements. As far as I was concerned we had achieved nothing this season unless we won the Cup on Saturday.

Magic

It's as simple as that . . . because people don't remember losers, no matter how good the losers might have been.

There were a lot of magic moments for me in that Final, in various things the lads did out there on the field where it mattered . . .

But the most memorable moment of all was in the dressing room afterwards. Because that's when John Greig summed it all up. He turned and said: "You asked for the Cup and there it is . . ."

No frills, no fancy talk, just "there's the Cup." And that's the way I like it

You see, we're a team at Ibrox—not just on the park but off it, too.

'You'd notice that the man I ran to on the field at the end was Greig because I know how much that Cup means to him.'

I know, at the top, that I can count on advice from Willie Waddell and Willie Thornton.

I know, as well, that I can rely on the whole training staff, the ground staff, the cleaners and even the women who do the laundry.

Skills

We have a team who play for each other. We have a system going on the field that calls for this from every player.

And whether they are newer lads such as Tom Forsyth and Quinton Young or old hands like John Greig, they know this.

We never ask anyone to do a job on the field

THEY ARE ALL PART OF THE IBROX TEAM.

Rangers to me don't just mean the players out on the park, they mean everyone connected with the club.

When you get that attitude going right through the club then you'll get things right on the field, too. I think we've shown that.

that is beyond his skills.

We want the players to play within the limits of their skills and within these limits we make any tactical adjustments we feel necessary.

These adjustments come with whatever style we set out to play . . . or whatever team we face.

Basically, though, what we want is the players to be ready to help each other out . . . and to play for the RANGERS.

If they aren't as committed to Rangers as I am—as I have been since I used to stand on the terracings at Ibrox—then they are no use to us.

We've worked hard at getting that attitude here and we're still working at it.

We laid down certain tactics for the Final and the players stuck by them. I was pleased by so many things . . . at the goals from Derek Parlane and Alfie Conn and Tom Forsyth . . . at the coolness of Derek Johnstone . . . at the leadership of John Greig . . . BUT, ABOVE ALL, AT THE TEAM EFFORT.

Derek Johnstone, of course, has so much skill. It may look, at times, that he has taken a chance with one of those bits of football in the box.

But I'd never try to change that, because it's the way he plays.

Mind you, if he lost a goal that way I would

probably get on to him.

If I have to single out one player from Saturday then it's Greggy.

You'd notice that the man I ran to on the field at the end was Greig because I know how much that Cup means to him.

Sting

He has suffered heartbreak and hammerings and this Hampden victory took some of the sting out of the other memories.

I'd like to say, too, how much I

appreciated Jock Stein's congratulations after the game.

He stayed at that tunnel to shake my players' hands then congratulated me. It was a great gesture from him.

If I had any disappointment at all on Saturday then it came at the end when we could not show the fans the Cup.

But the S F A have a rule which says we cannot come out with the Cup and we have to abide by the rules.

Now, though, I can thank the fans . . . they are the greatest support in the world.

I was happy for the players that we won . . . happy for all the backroom staff . . . and delighted that these fans have seen another trophy come to Ibrox.

This win doesn't mean the end of things . . . it's the beginning.

We will be working during the close season and we have one or two new players who will learn all about our training in the next month.

They have to be honed to our fitness and the work starts immediately. We are not going to rest . . .

CELTS WERE TOO CASUAL
By HUGH TAYLOR

HUNGER was the real spur in Saturday's dramatic Scottish Cup Final—the hunger of Rangers for an honour.

Just as I forecast—for once I was right—Rangers' determination and unquenchable spirit gave them the edge over Celtic.

And the story of a fine match was that Celtic seemed satisfied with previous success, not at all worried, while Rangers fought with all the purpose and single-mindedness of a hungry Benny Lynch.

Rangers deserved their 3-2 win, but they had a touch of luck, too. If it hadn't been for the injury to Jim Brogan, it's doubtful if Tom Forsyth would have been all alone when he scored the winning goal.

Brogan had just gone off, so there was

no-one to stop Forsyth as he strolled in to jab the ball over the line.

But the crucial difference in the outlook of the teams was shown when Rangers equalised that magnificent opening goal by Kenny Dalglish.

George Connelly was almost casual in his bid to stop Alex MacDonald on the Rangers' left. The wee Ranger beat the big Celt, over went the ball—and Derek Parlane headed it past Alistair Hunter.

Anyhow, it must be different next time. Now Celtic know Rangers can do it, are breathing down their necks for the big one —the league championship.

But chinks in the Celtic defence which manager Jock Stein must have felt had been sealed, opened up again. A face-lift in defence seems indicated

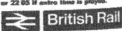

FOR SCOTLAND

barking on a new international career. I take it as a one-off thing.

If Willie Ormond picks me and then wants me for the next game then obviously I'd be delighted. But I'm not kidding myself it's a long-term move.

COMPETITION

I also feel my choice for Scotland reflects on my mates at Ibrox.

There would be no success for me without the others and I never like to forget that. JOHN GREIG IS FAR FROM BEING A ONE-MAN BAND.

As for Rangers, we needed Saturday's result, but I also think we deserved it over the 90 minutes.

Next Saturday when we play Celtic in the Premier League at Parkhead it will be completely different.

The Premier League has had the effect of stepping up competition. It is possible to recoup a defeat very quickly.

We will certainly be going all out next week to beat Celtic for the third time this season, but nobody at Ibrox will kid themselves that this will be easy.

A game between Rangers and Celtic is always something special.

However, my next job is to be ready to play for Scotland against Denmark on Wednesday.

I'm fit and rarin' to go. Never felt better, in fact.

HONOUR

Will I be captain? Let me get in the team first. If I were to lead Scotland out it would be a considerable honour, but I'm not even thinking about that.

Willie Ormond has to make these decisions and I'll accept whatever he says.

IT'S GREAT TO FEEL YOUNG!

John Greig

MAULE IN MIDDLE OF CUP ROW

By KEN GALLACHER

SCOTTISH League secretary Tommy Maule was at the centre of an Old Firm League Cup Final row last night.

For it seems certain that Celtic—beaten 1-0—will ask the League Management Committee why Scotland's top seven officials were ignored for the prestige Hampden final.

The leading men are those appointed to the FIFA international list —Bobby Davidson, John Paterson, Alastair McKenzie, John Gordon, Ian Foote, Rolo Kyle and Eddie Thomson. Next week at Celtic Park, Thomson will be in charge of the League game between the two teams.

Yesterday at Celtic Park, assistant manager Sean Fallon pointed out: "There are seven leading referees and they are all ignored. They are recognised as our top men, but when a big show game comes along they are ignored.

"It seems a strange situation when a FIFA-listed man is not in charge of a top game.

"This game was the first of the season to decide a team qualifying for Europe and there are only seven men recognised abroad as our best referees."

It is a reasonable point—though it could have been made before the match when the appointment was first announced. Now I would expect Celtic, who have director Tom Devlin as a voice on the Management Committee, to raise the matter officially.

Responsible

And the explanation must come from secretary Tommy Maule. Last night League President Bill Lindsay underlined that the full-time officials of the League appoint referees.

Added Lindsay: "That is something I defend completely. The secretary has the responsibility and it would be wrong for members of the Management Committee, who represent clubs, to take over this function."

Fallon did not criticise referee Bill Anderson's handling of the game. But clearly Celtic were unhappy about the performances of the man who was at one time on our FIFA list and then lost that position.

Their main anger surrounded the second half fouls by Rangers' defender Tom Forsyth.

For one, against Danny McGrain, he was booked. Minutes later he fouled Kenny Dalglish and that should have brought an ordering off.

Instead Anderson took no action.

That was his major error of judgment in a game which was never easy to handle.

The players sometimes behaved worse than those much maligned spectators . . .

As to the game, it was a poor one, and Fallon admitted.

"It was the worst final I can remember. We did not play well and I didn't think Rangers did either.

Face-lift

"I would have preferred to see a constructive rather than a destructive game.

"However, we will shake up the team a little for next week. There will be a face-lift and there will be a more adventurous approach."

Dive to glory . . . that's Alex MacDonald after his brilliant headed goal which brought the League Cup to Rangers. The stunned Celtic trio are Johannes Edvaldsson, Andy Lynch and Danny McGrain.

WALLACE DEFENDS FORSYTH

By HUGH TAYLOR

RANGERS manager Jock Wallace yesterday sprang to the defence of Tom Forsyth, whose tough tackling in the League Cup Final upset Celtic.

"Tom Forsyth is not a dirty player," said the Ibrox boss. "He doesn't go over the ball. He tackles for the ball every time.

"He just goes to get it, which is fair.

"Of course he goes in hard. IF HE DIDN'T, HE WOULDN'T BE HERE."

Treatment

Forsyth was booked for a foul on Danny McGrain and there were anger and retaliatory moves by Celtic players when Kenny Dalglish was bowled over by the Ranger later on—and no action was taken by the referee.

Meanwhile, Forsyth, who had to have six stitches put in a head wound after a collision with Colin Jackson should be ready for Saturday's next confrontation with Celtic at Parkhead.

Rangers, indeed, have a lengthy injury list. With Sandy Jardine, Quinton Young and Derek Johnstone all requiring treatment this week.

Rangers, naturally, were delighted to win 1-0—but Wallace agreed the match could have been better.

"I think both teams were tired," he said yesterday. "We have both played a lot of football and had mid-week games in Europe.

Physical

"Now, though, we have another meeting on Saturday and this will be a different affair altogether."

The splendid goal scored by Alex MacDonald was the one bright spot in a match which was too tense, too fast and too physical.

Certainly there was magic in the way MacDonald headed past the helpless Peter Latchford.

Otherwise, it was disappointing. Not a lunch-time feast.

Rangers probably deserved their victory because they were more aggressive, more powerful—AND MORE DETERMINED.

Or perhaps it's truer to say Celtic had more disappointing players than Rangers.

Remember

There were only a few flashes of Dalglish who, like Johannes Edvaldsson, didn't seem at peak fitness.

It wasn't until near the end that Celtic shifted into their old traditional gear—but by then it was too late.

Not a final to remember. And how we sighed for a touch of repose, of real artistry. How this match screamed out for someone to hold the ball.

But holding the ball in face of clanging tackles wasn't a risk I'd have willingly taken myself.

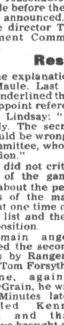

ANOTHER RECORD COLOUR EXCLUSIVE

3 IN A ROW

All-ticket plan after chaos at Hampden

THE SFA may now make big games at Hampden all-ticket after scenes of chaos at Saturday's Cup Final.

One angry fan said: "It was so bad there could easily have been another Ibrox disaster."

As Rangers and Hearts kicked off thousands of fans were still trying to get into the ground.

A bunch of supporters battered down a wooden gate. Thousands of others pushed and jostled at the turnstiles.

Blame

And when they finally reached the terracings—half-an-hour after the kick-off—hundreds turned and left because they could not see the field.

Last night Mr Rankin Grimshaw, president of the SFA, said: "The SFA will have to look into the possibility of making future big games at Hampden all-ticket."

But he blamed the fans for causing the trouble by arriving at Hampden too late.

HONOURS RIDDLE

By CHRISTOPHER BUCKLAND

No hold up — Sir Harold

THERE was growing mystery last night over ex-Premier Sir Harold Wilson's resignation list of honours.

Sir Harold hotly denied as "totally untrue" a report that names of proposed new life peers had been stalled by the three-man Political Honours Scrutiny Committee.

He added that he had received "No queries whatsoever" from them and had been told they had issued their certificate to all those falling within their jurisdiction.

But the chairman of the All-party committee, 78-year-old Lord Crathorne said last night: "Three names were sent back to Sir Harold because they had nothing whatever to do with us.

"They could be put forward under any category but they were not political."

Lord Crathorne added that nothing sinister was involved but said the list they had received should have been the final one.

"This has been going on ever since Easter and we have heard nothing back."

NAMES

The retirement honours list is a way an ex-Premier has of saying "thank you" to people who have helped him.

Last night Sir Harold said: "I have had no queries whatsoever from the committee following their meeting and I have been informed that their certificate was issued in respect of all the names which fall within their jurisdiction."

Tape measure beats 'victor' Hunt

BRITISH racing driver James Hunt beat all his rivals in the Spanish Grand Prix yesterday—but he lost the race.

He was disqualified because the rear end of his McLaren car was 1.5 centimetres too wide.

The race was awarded to world championship leader Austrian Nikki Lauda, who had come in second.

Because of the new technical ruling, which was introduced for the first time yesterday, Hunt lost vital points for the world championship—and £8000 in prize money.

Another driver, Frenchman Jacques Caffitte, was disqualified for the same reason.

A disappointed Hunt said: "It is a pity that the race had to finish this way."

★ **MEMORIES** are made of this!

Life is just great at the moment for Rangers manager Jock Wallace as he proudly shows off the trophies the Ibrox men have won this season.

They are the League Cup, Scottish Cup and the League Championship. But, as you will no doubt notice, there is a FOURTH trophy in our picture.

And what is that? It's a statuette of Sir William Wallace and the Rangers manager claims it is his lucky mascot. Who knows, if Wallace keeps on guiding Rangers to success there could be statuettes of Sir JOCK Wallace going around some day!

Among the legions of Ibrox fans delighted with Wallace's men is 11-year-old Martin Crosbie of 31 Queensway, Annan, Dumfries. His parents, though, aren't so happy. Martin slipped out of his home at 5 a.m. on Saturday and made the 90 mile trip to Glasgow where he saw Rangers beat Hearts 3-1 to win the Cup. The police were called out in a hunt for the missing boy, but he finally showed up when the Annan Supporters' Club returned him to his parents.

MARTIN CROSBIE

WALLACE'S WONDERS —PAGES 22, 23

Colour picture : ERIC CRAIG

EDITED, PRINTED AND PUBLISHED IN SCOTLAND

Edited, printed and published by Scottish Daily Record and Sunday Mail Ltd., Anderston Quay, Glasgow G3 8DA (041-248 7000). Registered at the Post Office as a newspaper. © Scottish Daily Record and Sunday Mail Ltd., 1976. A Mirror Group newspaper.

The S.F.A. are right

Rules must be obeyed

By ALEX CAMERON

THE SFA won a battle yesterday which could be as important as beating England at Hampden a week on Saturday.

Well, nearly !

They dug their heels in firmly against any suggestion of Derek Johnstone, Tom Forsyth and Colin Jackson, of Rangers, being freed for a gala night at Ibrox tomorrow or, indeed, of Willie Pettigrew playing for Motherwell tonight against Ayr.

Secretary Willie Allan said that the SFA ordered the players to report at 11 o'clock this morning to a Glasgow hotel. Or else.

The League wanted the players to be freed for the vital relegation matches but the conflict of opinions was catered for in the rules and the SFA very wisely insisted that these were carried out to the letter.

I can readily understand Dundee feeling peeved because their companions in distress, Ayr and Dundee United, are apparently meeting weakened sides.

But the rules clearly state that a match may be postponed if two or more players are required for an international.

Motherwell have no option but to play.

Don't think Willie McLean wouldn't have liked Pettigrew in his side. He wouldn't be human if he didn't want to help his brother Jim, at Tannadice, by thumping Ayr.

Willie Waddell, Rangers' general manager, said: "A club of Rangers' stature must have the reserve power to cope with a situation like this and especially when we have had players such as Sandy Jardine and Derek Parlane on the bench."

Very true.

Mess

Thank goodness the SFA laid down the law. Scotland would have been in a pretty mess had Scots clubs given the "V-sign" to the hierarchy

Willie Ormond had already said he wouldn't play Manchester United's Alex Forsyth, Lou Macari or Martin Buchan against Wales on Thursday if they play in the derby game against City tomorrow

It is certain they will, if fit, so Ormond would have been in an extremely embarrassing situation had the SFA not taken the stand they did.

EIGHT IN OLYMPIC SQUAD

SCOTLAND'S four new ABA champions have been named with other Scots for Great Britain's pool of boxers for the Montreal Olympics in July.

The four winners at Wembley on Friday were: John Bambrick (Edinburgh Transport), Billy Lauder (McTaggart and Scott), Eddie Burke (Woodside) and John Rafferty (Monkland), writes DICK CURRIE.

Other Scots to join them in Olympic training will be featherweight John Hutchison (Sparta), lightweight Tom McCallum (Sparta), light-welterweight Jim Douglas (Camperdown) and welterweight Steve Cooney (St Francis).

The first Olympic training programme is for May 21-25, but unfortunately some of the Scots will be unavailable as they fight against Hungary in Dundee on May 26.

The team is likely to be selected after the Great Britain-America international at Wembley next month.

Stecher's revenge

DOUBLE Olympic champion Renate Stecher, of East Germany, gained a revenge victory over British sprinter Sonia Lannaman in Split, Yugoslavia, yesterday.

Twenty-four hours after her surprise defeat by the 20-year-old British girl over 100 metres, the East German came storming back to take the 200 metres.

Dave Black won the 5000 metres in 13 minutes 31.7 seconds, while Brian Hooper took the pole vault with 17ft. 0¾in.

Dennis Coates and John Bicourt made it one and two for Britain in the 3000 metres steeplechase.

Great work John! Skipper Greig gets the first hug from manager Jock Wallace while Johnny Hamilton waits to get in on the act

Well done lad It's Martin Henderson's turn as Wallace greets his boys.

THE SURVIVAL STRAIN IS ON AYR

By IAN BROADLEY

AYR UNITED must beat Motherwell tonight at Somerset Park to escape relegation.

But they will be without four players—probably five—in their fight for survival.

Alex McAnespie, Dave Wells, Danny McDonald and Billy Paton are definitely out. And midfielder Gordon Cramond, who strained a groin in the 5-3 defeat from Celtic at Somerset Park on Saturday, is extremely doubtful.

Coasted

Ayr, though, have no intention of asking for another postponement. Manager Alex Stuart said:

"We've lived with the strain too long. I want to get it over with as quickly as possible. The pressure is getting to us now."

Yet, Ayr's Premier League place seemed assured as they coasted 3-1 in the lead with less than half an hour to play.

Added Stuart: "It was frightening the way we collapsed. My players stopped playing. They lost their concentration completely.

"I thought the penalty Celtic got turned the game. We were in control until that point.

"We know exactly what we've got to do against Motherwell."

'Well to end in style

By WALLACE MOORE

MOTHERWELL lost all hope of a UEFA Cup place when they went down 1-0 to Dundee at Dens Park.

They still had a chance of pipping Hibs for a place in the competition before the game, but a goal from Eric Sinclair ended their Europe bid and gave Dundee two vital points in their battle to stay in the Premier League.

The Fir Park side can do Dundee a favour by beating Ayr tonight and there is no doubt that Motherwell, who have given so much value for money and entertainment this season, would like to end the term on a winning note.

They had a chance to snatch an equaliser against Dundee, but Bobby Graham's sizzling header in the last minute was brilliantly saved by goalkeeper Thomson Allan.

Three Motherwell players—Willie McVie, Stewart McLaren and Peter Millar—were booked during the game.

McVie's offence was the strangest. He had his name taken when he appeared to try to remove or bend a corner flag before taking a last-minute corner.

Now the big centre-half is certain to appeal against the caution.

Can we have our Cup back?

By BOB PATIENCE

THE much-maligned Spring Cup is up for grabs at Firhill tonight . . . but not for keeps !

Surprisingly, the winners of tonight's Airdrie-Clydebank final will NOT be allowed to keep the trophy.

With the tournament doomed, it was expected that the winners would have a permanent memento of success. But not according to the League bosses.

I understand they will instruct the winners to return it after a year, because at a cost of about £250, it is too expensive to give away.

Managers Jackie Stewart and Willie Munro have been strong supporters of the competition and both are keen to win the trophy.

Said Stewart: "This Cup has provided the spark the team needed.

"We may be favourites, but we'll have a job on our hands. I've nothing but respect for Willie Munro.

"He has done a great job at Kilbowie and since both teams like to attack it should be quite a game. Naturally, though, we fancy our chances."

Munro is just as confident. He said: "It would cap a great season for us if we could add the Cup to the Second Division championship.

"If we play as we did against Dumbarton in the semi-final we can win."

THIS WEEK . .

The Europe finalists explain . . .

GOLDEN GOAL
Derek Johnstone
45 seconds
DETAILS TOMORROW

Did you win a date with your superstar?

IT'S ALL IN SUPER RECORD SPORT

ALL MY

KISSES FOR YOU!

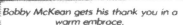

Bobby McKean gets his thank you in a warm embrace.

And, of course, the jubilant Ibrox boss had special words of praise for goalscorers Alex MacDonald and Derek Johnstone.

The boys have done me proud — says Wallace

By HUGH TAYLOR

RANGERS manager Jock Wallace relaxed yesterday after watching his team win the treble.

Then he said: "Shut up about me ... give the boys the credit."

Wallace, though, cannot sidestep the compliments that come his way. His team were in trouble earlier in the season when they won only one game in seven.

They took the League Cup, but then went out of the European Cup to St Etienne and the following Saturday they lost 2-1 to Hearts—their only League defeat at Ibrox during the season.

Rangers could have been in trouble. They could have let their heads drop and their spirits lower, but Jock Wallace didn't allow that.

Victory

"There was only one thing we had to do," he said. "We had to attack and that's the way we played it."

Wallace didn't try to defend and cover the gaps at the back. He was brave. He was courageous. And on Saturday he received yet another reward with his team's 3-1 Cup Final victory over Hearts. Derek Johnstone (2) and Alex MacDonald were the Ibrox goal heroes with Graham Shaw hitting the Tynecastle side's solitary effort.

Typically, Wallace tries to duck out of the limelight, but even the players don't allow him to do this.

They echo: "He's a great manager to play for. Tough at times, but a player's manager nevertheless."

Look at the decisions Wallace has made this season ... gambles that have paid off.

Last season Stewart Kenney was the Scottish international goalkeeper. Wallace drafted big Peter McCloy back into his first team this term and was rewarded with a string of shut-outs.

He dropped internationals Sandy Jardine and Derek Parlane and brought in the versatile Alex Miller and teenager Martin Henderson. Again his confidence was rewarded by these players.

WALLACE IS PROUD OF HIS BOYS—AND THEY ARE EQUALLY PROUD OF HIM.

The Ibrox boss was right when he said his team had to attack. He was proved absolutely correct when his side won the "Big Three" of League, League Cup and Scottish Cup.

And what about Rangers' future? Let Wallace sum it up.

"We take one game at a time. But we try to polish our play all the time, too," he said.

Their goal is the European Cup.

And Rangers, on the crest of the wave, might do it next season.

● And guess who predicted the winning scoreline at Hampden? No, it wasn't me, but—believe it or not!—my colleague Alex Cameron, who said Rangers would win 3-1 in Saturday's paper. Well, you've got to be right at least once in your life!

GALA NIGHT FOR RANGERS FANS

RANGERS fans will be treated to a gala at Ibrox tomorrow night when their heroes play their last League game of the season against Dundee United.

As a warm-up there will be a 30-minute confrontation between two former Ibrox line-ups that brought glory to the club. The 1948 and 1964 teams will face each other with a 7.15 kick-off. After that Rangers will be presented with the League championship.

All the ex-superstars will be on parade with big George Young as the referee. Look out for one of the linesmen. It will be your old reporter . . . in a green outfit? Hardly, I'm not committing suicide yet!

Rangers will be without Colin Jackson, Tom Forsyth and Derek Johnstone.

Now Celtic rely on the young brigade

SEAN FALLON will introduce more new faces at Tynecastle tonight, as he is convinced that Celtic's future rests with the young brigade.

Parkhead chairman Desmond White stated that the £90,000 signing of Johnny Doyle was the end of their bigmoney transfers.

And after Celtic had recaptured their vintage soccer in the second half rout of Ayr which ended in a 5-3 triumph, acting manager Fallon talked enthusiastically about his bright young babes.

He said: "I thought it was marvellous the way

Andy Ritchie, Tommy Burns, Roy Aitken, Roddy McDonald and latterly Rob Hannah refused to accept defeat.

"Even though they were 3-1 down they stuck to a task which might have daunted more experienced men.

"They deserved their victory.

"This was a transitional season for us.

We lost Billy McNeill and we needed players.

"Everyone got their chance and these boys certainly took theirs."

Doyle and Andy Lynch are doubtful for tonight, but Johannes Edvaldsson will return.

Incidentally, Celtic are calling up provisionally signed forward Willie Temperley, of Bo'ness United.

"I got the last one—but I've to wear a chain round my neck."

CAP FORM STEELE ENDED DOC'S DREAM

By KEN GALLACHER

JIM STEELE, the iron man of Southampton, stole the glory from Manchester United's international Scots at Wembley on Saturday.

He was a vital part of the team which shocked the Old Trafford youngsters.

It was Steele who subdued the exciting United attackers. Steele who shackled strikers Stuart Pearson and Sammy McIlroy.

He was the most commanding figure on the Wembley pitch.

The former Dundee defender has complained bitterly at being ignored by Scotland team boss Willie Ormond. If this is how he plays then his arguments for Ormond to watch him are valid.

Let's face it, the two strikers who faced him on Saturday will play in the Home International Championship—Pearson for England and McIlroy for Northern Ireland.

Tommy Docherty's boys, who have brought so much pleasure this season, failed to capture the excitement and flair they have shown before.

Perhaps the occasion was too much for some of them, while Southampton had experience to carry them through.

Afterwards at the team's party in a London hotel, the Doc admitted to me: "You can't take credit away from Southampton. It was their day. They played well and they deserved to get the Cup.

"When I took off Gordon Hill in the second half the first words he said when he got to the bench were

'I'm sorry, boss, what a day for me to have a stinker!'"

Now United are left without a major trophy. Still, they are in Europe and the Doc must settle for that.

Bobby Stokes scored the goal which gave the Second Division team the Cup

FOOTBALL TODAY

Premier League—Ayr United v Motherwell, Hearts v Celtic.

Spring Cup—Final—Airdrie v Clydebank (Firhill, extra time if necessary).

2nd XI Cup—Final—2nd Leg. Dundee v. Aberdeen (7 0).

Premier Reserve League—Celtic v Dundee United (7 0).

Scottish Amateur Cup—Semi final—Knockentiber v Cambus nethan Talbot (Rugby Park).

English League—Div. IV—Bradford City v Newport.

Mick Channon Testimonial—Southampton v Q.P.R.

Central Whitbread League—Div. A—East Kilbride v St. Rochs, Johnstone Burgh v Benburb, Rob Roy v Gleneairn, Cambuslang Rang v Pollok. Shettleston v Ashfield, Div B—Vale v Larkhall Th., Arthurlie v Renfrew.

Thorniewood v Stonehouse, Cumbernauld v Lanark United, Blantyre Vics v Dunipace Div. C—Shotts v Blantyre C. Kilsyth v St Anthony Neilston v Coltness Utd

Ayrshire District Cup—Second round—Beith v Kilbirnie Ladeside. Third round—Cumnock v Hurlford. Kello v Auchinleck Talbot

Ayrshire Whitbread League—Lugar Boswell v Annbank United Saltcoats Vics v Irvine Meadow, Muirkirk v Darvel

Scottish Welfare Cup—Semi final—Tennents v 200 FC (St. Roch's Park Provanmill, 7.15)

Football yesterday

Bill Shankly Trophy, Third Round—Stirling B.C. 2 Mariner 0

I'm a marked man, says McVie

By IAN BROADLEY

MOTHERWELL centre-half Willie McVie was ordered off for the sixth time in his career at Firhill.

His side went on to beat Partick Thistle 3-2, but last night McVie said: "I know I am a marked man, especially among the younger referees who want to make a name for themselves. I believe I am the new Willie Woodburn!"

Ex-Ranger Woodburn was, of course, suspended sine die by the authorities for indiscipline. McVie went on: "I'm no saint. I freely admit that, but football is a man's game. I don't go about breaking limbs.

"This is the first time I have been ordered off in two years . . . and the last time was for handling the ball.

"The only way my career can be saved is when the new disciplinary system comes into force next season. That way I would be dealt with automatically and the powers that be would get a chance to forget my face."

McVie's dismissal by Airdrie referee Mike Delaney in the 36th minute after two fouls on Partick striker Doug Somner was incredibly harsh.

Nature

Even Firhill officials sympathised with McVie.

Motherwell, an enlightened club who have done so much to try to reform soccer justice, will NOT fine McVie for being ordered off.

That is indicative of the trivial nature of the offences committed and the totally rigid attitude adopted by the referee who booked four other players.

Even with 10 men Motherwell were still capable of catching Partick with sucker punches. Ian Clinging, playing his first full game, added two goals which were enough for victory despite a late Thistle fightback.

Thistle boss Bertie Auld was furious at the setback to their bid for a place in Europe next season. He said: "My players acted like prima donnas. We had more spectators on the park than off it. They were disgraceful."

Auld intends bringing new signing Colin McAdam into his defence for tomorrow night's match with Rangers at Ibrox.

It's target Europe says Turnbull

By BOB PATIENCE

EUROPE is the target for Eddie Turnbull's exciting new Hibs—thanks to 12 goals and a hat-trick of victories within a week.

With four straight home matches against Ayr, Dundee United, Rangers and Partick Thistle coming up, Turnbull claims: "There is no reason why we cannot win a European place."

Hibs' fans seemed fated to a dull League run-in when their team was toppled from the Cup by Thistle. But, Turnbull's men have bounced off the ropes to establish themselves as the new hot shots of Scottish soccer.

Hibs were impressive in their three-goal spree against doomed Clydebank at Kilbowie. And Turnbull said: "It's all about confidence and hitting the back of the net.

Danger

"Earlier, we were playing well without getting goals. Then we went to town against St. Mirren and the team hasn't looked back. Everyone is working for one another and things are beginning to click."

On Saturday, Hibs were never in the slightest danger.

Two-goal Alisdair MacLeod was the man of the match. He is not one of the hardest workers in the game, but can take a chance as coolly as Jimmy Greaves. Bobby Hutchinson was the other scorer.

If it was a joy day for Hibs it was another depressing afternoon for Bankies. And after collecting over £200,000 in transfer fees, it is time the directors gave manager Bill Munro cash to re-build.

COST OF FRANK'S SUCCESS

By SANDY BEVERIDGE

FRANK McGARVEY lost £12 in the dressing room to a thief —but he still emerged smiling from Somerset Park at the weekend.

The disappearing cash could not dampen the St Mirren striker's feelings after he had scored the only goal of the match against Ayr.

Said Frank: "It may not have been the best goal I have scored, but it was probably the most important."

It certainly was for the 1-0 victory virtually ensures that Saints stay in the Premier League next season.

Paisley boss Alex Ferguson added: "That gives us a lifeline and it's up to us to grab it now."

Ayr's Alex Stuart confessed: "We deserved to lose. We didn't play as well as they did. But we will fight until the last game."

McNeill hit by injury pile-up

By WALLACE MOORE

ABERDEEN have been hit by an injury pile-up which could affect their title hopes.

Ian Fleming, who needed 12 stitches in a leg gash after the goal-less draw with Dundee United at Tannadice, is out of tomorrow's Premier League clash against Clydebank at Pittodrie.

Dom Sullivan and Duncan Davidson, also hurt in the game, could be struggling to make it, too.

Added to that is the fact that Joe Harper won't be risked unless manager Billy McNeill is 100 per cent sure his injury has cleared.

To make the Don's problems worse, reserve centre half Alex McLeish has an ankle in plaster after cracking a bone in the reserve game between the clubs.

However, McNeill refuses to concede that these injuries could end the Dons title challenge.

He said last night: "Obviously I was disappointed at getting only one point. However, a point at Tannadice is always good."

Repair it yourself

Tradesmen know that bodyfillers have to take the shocks and vibrations of the road, slamming of doors, dropping of boot lids. That's why they rely on David's ISOPON.

Free literature from David's ISOPON, FREEPOST, Northway House, London N20 9LR.

9 different Repair Paste and 3 Glass Fibre Kits from your accessory or hardware store.

david's ISOPON

SHODDY

OUCH! It looks like a painful moment for Rangers' Tommy McLean as Celtic skipper Andy Lynch makes a determined challenge to end a Rangers attack.

WHAT A BORE!

IT is bumptious English baloney to suggest their football is always better than our and, as was amply demonstrated at Wembley, it can even be worse.

"I have never gone along with the idea that the English club game is in a class of its own," said Scotland manager Ally MacLeod after watching a disappointing goalless League Cup Final between Liverpool and Nottingham Forest.

Liverpool should skate the replay at Old Trafford on Wednesday, but the fact that two teams of such talent could play for 120 minutes without scoring was really an insult to the 100,000 who paid £377,000 to watch.

Sure

MacLeod learned nothing positive. Kenny Burns played a super part for his team, but the Scottish manager would like to have seen him in a role which allowed him to be more constructive—as he is when David Needham is playing.

"I would like to see Forest in at least a couple more games," he said. "Brian Clough doesn't have any bad players, but I can take only 22 to Argentina so I must be sure they are right for the jobs I have."

Burns was effective, but it was in a defence which was over-run by Liverpool.

John Robertson looked good, but only in

No Wembley joy for Ally

By ALEX CAMERON

flashes. Can he depose either Willie Johnston or Arthur Graham, who can play on both wings?

MacLeod will not decide until after the Home Internationals for he is likely to produce a squad of 28 for these games and finalise his World Cup party afterwards.

Archie Gemmill, whose presence was sadly missed by Forest, is likely to be in that party, as is Kenny Dalglish who was excellent even if he did miss chances for Liverpool.

Thrilled

The Anfield men were easily the better side. They made mincemeat of Forest after the first-half and Brian Clough said: "If I were Bob Paisley I'd find it hard to explain why we hadn't won. I'm thrilled we held such a great team."

Clough was again unpredictable. He didn't raise his backside off the bench when the teams prepared to go into extra time. "I felt there was nothing I could do to help them," he explained.

Eighteen-year-old goalkeeper Chris Woods was the Forest hero. He was a brilliant stand-in for cup-tied Peter Shilton who won England's Player of the Year award last night.

Another of Forest's Cup Final stars, Tony Woodcock, was voted Young Player of the Year.

A final note of comfort to the thousands who were bored at Hampden. It took Ally MacLeod four hours to get through the match traffic to central London.

JOHN ROBERTSON . . . good in flashes.

KENNY BURNS . . . was effective.

ANOTHER CHANCE FOR SAINTS' DOCHERTY

ST. MIRREN'S teenage star, Brian Docherty, gets the chance at Tannadice tonight to stake his claim to a Scottish Youth team place.

Docherty, included in the youth trials but unavailable later because of club commitments, is back for the match against the Dundee United Under-20 side.

Says Youth team coach Andy Roxburgh: "I will be having a look at the boy. But in many ways it's a trial for a lot of them for so much can happen to kids of this age between playing well six months ago and today."

Roxburgh hopes to arrange a final warm-up match against Manchester United's kids before the European Youth Tournament finals in May in Poland.

CELTIC v. RANGERS

Sat. 25th March 1978
Kick-off 1.00 p.m.

ALL TICKET MATCH

Stand and Ground Tickets will be on sale at Lumley's, Sauchiehall Street, and the Celtic Development Pools Office, West Nile Street.

Ground Tickets will also be on sale in the usual Rangers Agencies.

TODAY'S SOCCER EXCLUSIVE IS ON PAGE 29

SHOWPIECE!

Nerve-ridden Old Firm in a Final flop

By KEN GALLACHER

AFTER the sad, shoddy showpiece which served as the League Cup Final, I feel mightily relieved that the Old Firm will not be together in the season's remaining glamour game at Hampden in May.

Because I want to see a Scottish Cup Final which has dignity, a sense of occasion and an abundance of good football.

I do not want to see yet another nerve-ridden battle between two teams who have been overtaken by the almost unbearable tension which surrounds these Celtic-Rangers clashes.

Dignity

The Premier League, with the four club clashes every season, and the continued domination of the domestic scene by the Old Firm has intensified the pressures.

There was little good football played on Saturday, still less dignity surrounding the game, and no sense of occasion at all!

It was a bad advertisement for our national sport made all the worse by the fact that the players out there on Hampden can play much better than they did.

There are half-a-dozen I would exempt from that—Sandy Jardine, Tom Forsyth and Gordon Smith for Rangers, and Alan Sneddon, Roddy MacDonald and George McCluskey for Celtic.

The two goalkeepers, but for vital errors—one each by Stewart Kennedy and Peter Latchford—which brought goals, might have joined the list. Otherwise, the game was a catalogue of errors and frayed tempers and below-average performances.

In the end, Rangers edged through and are now on course for that "treble," especially after the help given them by Dundee United on taking a point from Aberdeen on Saturday.

They can win it, too, but there remains a doubt over that Ibrox defence. They have made a habit of losing bad goals—the equaliser from Johannes Edvaldsson js just one of several this season.

Bruising

Manager Jock Wallace was delighted to get the game over and the Cup won.

"It was a bruising, physical game," he admitted, "and we had to fight hard, but we deserved to lift the Cup. At least, I thought we did.

"It was especially good to see Davie Cooper and Gordon Smith get the goals in their first Final."

Smith had a superb game. His strong, intelligent runs brought danger to Celtic all through the game.

At Celtic Park, Jock Stein was left to contemplate his first-ever season without an honour being won by his Celtic team. Although, of course, they won nothing two years ago when Sean Fallon was in charge.

Heart

He was clearly disappointed, but took heart from the displays of his younger players. "Alan Sneddon, George McCluskey, Roddy MacDonald and Roy Aitken played really well for us.

"Really, there was very little between the two teams and I thought that we did deserve at least another game."

I did, too. But I'm glad we don't have to sit through it all again.

... AND SOME YOU LOSE!

★ TOP. It's the catch of the day as Celtic keeper Peter Latchford easily outjumps Alex MacDonald to break up a Rangers attack.

★ LEFT. It's the miss of the match as Latchford fails to hold a high ball in a challenge with MacDonald and the ball breaks free to allow Gordon Smith to score the winner.

Russell DID get a medal

SPINKS' ONE-WAY LUCK...

SATURDAY night and Sunday morning won't ever be the same again for Leon Spinks, the man who beat Muhammad Ali for the world heavyweight boxing title.

In a weekend he won't forget in a hurry, Spinks was . . .

STRIPPED of his title by the WBC on Saturday night for refusing to fight official challenger Ken Norton, who was named champion in his place.

ARRESTED early yesterday morning in St. Louis for driving the wrong way on a one-way street. Spinks, who was not carrying a driver's licence—an offence in America—was released on £350 bail.

BOBBY RUSSELL the 21-year-old Rangers star who missed the League Cup Final after playing in all the other games in the tournament, did leave Hampden with a medal.

The slim Russell, left out because he had not shaken off the effects of 'flu, was given his medal by World Cup man Sandy Jardine.

Counted

And yesterday the youngster said: "I felt great after the game when Sandy came over to me in the dressing room and handed me the medal he had just won.

"Obviously the lads knew I was disappointed at missing the match and it seemed that everyone wanted to give me a medal. But Sandy gave me his and I'll never forget that.

"It helped me get over the disappointment—though, really, seeing Rangers win the Cup was the most important thing of all. That's what counted for all of us."

Rangers manager Jock Wallace said: "All the lads appreciated how young Robert felt. But Sandy was the first to say he would give him his medal.

"I thought a lot of him for doing it, but it's just the way we try to be at Ibrox."

FORMER A B A lightmiddleweight champion, Charlie Malarkey, tops the bill at the St Andrews Sporting Club, in Glasgow, tonight.

Malarkey tops bill

Malarkey, beaten once as a professional, meets experienced Tony Burnett, of Cardiff.

But fight of the night should be the bantam clash between comeback man Tony Kerr, of Aberdeen, and former English amateur internationalist Muhammad Younis, from Wednesbury, over eight rounds.

Kerr beat Younis in Birmingham three weeks ago.

Completing the bill, new professional Mike Reid, from South Queensferry, meets Tony Bogle, of Bradford, over six rounds.

JACK NICKLAUS marked up his 65th victory on the American circuit yesterday by winning the Tournament Players' golf championship in Jacksonville, Florida.

And Nicklaus didn't need his customary magic to clinch the title. Big Jack, who had played the inward half in 30 in each of his last two events, won this one by a single shot with a three-over-par 75 in the final round.

It's No.65 for Nicklaus

His 289 total—one over par—was the highest winning aggregate on the tour since Mark Hayes won this championship a year ago.

Lou Graham, who also finished with a 75, was second with Lon Hinkle third on 291.

RIOCH TO MISS JUST ONE GAME

By RECORD REPORTER

BRUCE RIOCH will miss only one game for Derby County as he attempts to convince Scotland manager Ally MacLeod that he is still the man to lead our World Cup challenge.

Rioch believed he had topped 20 disciplinary points and faced a possible four-match ban when sent off against Birmingham on Saturday.

But referee Peter Reeves, of Leicester, confirmed later that he had sent the Derby man off for "two bookable offences" and the only punishment for that is a one-match automatic suspension.

Already on 19 penalty points, Rioch could not have afforded the extra points added for a sending-off offence.

Rioch's form, and that of team-mate and Scotland colleague Don Masson, must be worrying MacLeod.

Masson was taken off midway through the game against Birmingham, and with another of his midfield men, Asa Hartford, also in disciplinary trouble, MacLeod has a few worries he could do without as he builds up to the trip to Argentina.

Rioch was one of six players sent off in England, taking the total for the season to 104.

mailsport

GREIG'S GREATS

Celebration time for Rangers and captain John Greig is raised shoulder high to acknowledge the cheers of the fans. The other happy Ibrox stars are (left to right): Gordon Smith, Colin Jackson, Derek Johnstone, Sandy Jardine, Tom Forsyth, Kenny Watson, Peter McCloy, Davie Cooper, Bobby Russell and Alex McDonald.

Picture by Dave McNeil

RANGERS have won the league championship for a record 37th time.

Manager Jock Wallace poured champagne for his players in the dressing room—then told me: "I never had any doubts we'd do it."

Early goals from Colin Jackson and Gordon Smith brushed aside the challenge of Motherwell before 47,000 singing, chanting fans at Ibrox.

And they roared their delight as John Greig led the players in a lap of honour after their 2-0 victory.

Added Wallace: "Though this is the second time we've won the Premier Division title in three years I

By ALLAN HERRON

think I've had more satisfaction out of this one.

"No one at Ibrox can remember the last time we clinched a championship at home. When

you win it before your own fans it's something special.

"I always said that the team that played the best football throughout the season would

win the title—and we proved we're the best side today.

"This was a team job. I'm not going to pick individuals. I've stayed with the same players even when we struggled

a wee bit, and in the end they won it.

"I'm delighted—a very happy man. But now we've got to prepare for the Scottish Cup."

Rangers will travel to Largs on Thursday to do their final preparations for Saturday's Cup Final with Aberdeen at Hampden. They have no injury problems.

Rangers, who have now qualified for the European Cup next season, bid for the "treble" at Hampden having already won the League Cup and now the Championship.

Aberdeen, who now automatically qualify for the Cup Winners' Cup next season, drew 1-1 at Easter Road against Hibs.

Manager Billy McNeill said: "It's been a great effort, but we didn't quite make it."

A day of joy for champion Rangers

HAPPY HEARTS ARE BACK

THOUSANDS of delirious Hearts supporters invaded the field at Arbroath yesterday when the final whistle went to signal the Edinburgh club's return to the Premier League.

The fans danced a victory jig on the pitch and police had to form a cordon at the entrance to the players' tunnel as the celebrating fans surged forward to see their heroes.

When the Hearts team came out of the dressing room to take a bow, the

By BILL MILLAR

excited fans broke through the police cordon and the players had to make a hasty exit.

But police quickly restored order and the chanting fans soon made their way from the ground.

While the celebrations were going on, Hearts manager Willie Ormond admitted that he had not known that Dundee had beaten Morton 3-2—a result that meant Hearts had to win to clinch promotion.

The delighted manager

said: "Thank goodness that's the tension over. Maybe now we will be able to get some sleep. It's been a tremendous season and I'm delighted for the players and their fans—they deserved promotion."

Ormond has already begun his plans to prepare Hearts for the Premier League and after yesterday's crucial win he revealed that he had signed a new player—Frank Liddell of Alloa.

Liddell, a centre half, was

a part-timer with Alloa, but he will go full time when he joins up with his new club-mates at Tynecastle on Monday.

So it's Morton and Hearts in the Premier Division next season with Ayr United and Clydebank relegated. Morton won the First Division championship on goal differences.

Clyde crushed Stranraer 4-0 at Shawfield to take the Second Division Championship on goal difference from Raith Rovers. As they go up, Alloa and East Fife are relegated to the Second Division.

Edited, printed and published by Scottish Daily Record and Sunday Mail Limited, Anderston Quay, Glasgow G3 8DA (041-248 7000). Registered at the Post Office as a newspaper.
© Scottish Daily Record and Sunday Mail Limited 1978. A Mirror Group newspaper.

mailsport

WELCOME HOME

By ALLAN HERRON

RANGERS......2 MOTHERWELL.....0 (H.T. 2-0)
Scorers: Jackson (5min), Smith (19). Attendance: 47,000.

MANAGER Jock Wallace ran on to the field to put a bear hug on skipper John Greig, Cliff Richard sang "Congratulations" over the tannoy and the punters went berserk around the ground.

Rangers were champions of Scotland for the 37th time in their history—and now tackle the mountains of the European Cup once more.

Their 2-0 victory over Motherwell was decisive. It didn't have to carry too much distinction as Roger Hynd's side offered little resistance.

Exciting

The lap of honour from the Rangers' players, led by the bionic man himself, was probably more exciting to the 47,000 crowd than the match.

Any doubts about Rangers winning the match AND the championship were killed in five minutes by centre half Colin Jackson.

After Willie Watson had been lectured for a rather spectacular tackle on Davie Cooper, referee Tom Muirhead allowed John Greig to take the free-kick.

It floated left to right into the Motherwell box, and there was Jackson with Derek Johnstone right at his shoulder to knock the ball over the goal-line with a flick of the head.

OH DEAR, WHERE WERE THE MOTHERWELL DEFENDERS?

Though Peter McCloy made a good save from Stewart McLaren in 11 minutes, when he beat down his powerful right-footer from 12 yards, there was only going to be one winner.

Bad defensive play by Motherwell allowed Rangers in again in 19 minutes when Derek Johnstone, from a tight angle on the left, was allowed to whip the ball low across the goal area.

'Keeper Stewart Rennie missed it, leaving Gordon Smith the simple exercise of flicking the ball over the goal-line.

To lift the game into any real category of excitement we really needed a goal from Motherwell.

Demanded

But it was not to be, though they should have been given a penalty in 23 minutes when Tom Forsyth blatantly fouled Lindsay.

HOW THE REFEREE COULD INDICATE A DIVE COMPLETELY BAFFLED ME.

Rangers always looked like sticking in a few more goals, but they didn't quite get the angles right, though before half-time Alex MacDonald hit the crossbar and Johnstone had blistered a right-foot shot wide.

Gordon Smith hit the Motherwell post in 60 minutes then hit the 'keeper with the rebound as the game moved on, and we had a couple of really fine saves from McCloy.

The Motherwell manager, Roger Hynd, put on his two substitutes in the second-half in an attempt to shake up his squad, but it made no difference.

It certainly didn't surprise anyone when Willie Pettigrew was replaced in 73 minutes, as he never once got himself into a striking position and was completely taken out of the game by the Rangers' defence.

Only when the game ended did the fans really come to life. They demanded a lap of honour —and got it, and nobody was running stronger round that track than John Greig. What a season he's had.

RANGERS (4-2-4): McCloy; Jardine, Forsyth, Jackson, Greig; Russell, MacDonald; McLean (Watson 581), Johnstone, Smith, Cooper. Not used—Parlane.

MOTHERWELL (4-3-3): Rennie; Watson (Millar 566), Stevens, McLeod, Kennedy; Mungall, Clinging, McLaren; Pettigrew (Sommerville 873), Lindsay, Marinello.

Referee: T. Muirhead, Stenhousemuir.

After a long, hard slog the title goes back to Ibrox.

Heading for the title ... and it's Colin Jackson beating Motherwell's Stuart McLaren and his own team-mate, Derek Johnstone, to score Rangers' first goal.

Celtic out of Europe

By TOMMY MACK

ST. MIRREN................3 CELTIC................1
(H.T. 1-1)

Scorers: St. Mirren—Fitzpatrick (36 mins.), McGarvey (65), Bell (86); Celtic—Glavin (pen. 31). Attend.: 13,026.

SUPER Saints turned on a spectacular display to dash Celtic's hopes of appearing in Europe next season.

It's the first time for 17 years that Celtic have not qualified for any of the major tournaments. In fact, the Paisley youngsters looked more likely candidates.

They ran the Parkhead side ragged, with every one of their players showing an attacking zest and skill that Jock Stein's men couldn't match. It was a wonderful climax to their first Premier League season.

Celtic had gone ahead with a hotly disrupted penalty by Ronnie Glavin. Referee Bill Mullen had signalled for a corner kick after George McCluskey had seemingly rammed the ball past the post off defender Ian Munro.

But the linesman had signalled for "hands" and the referee changed his mind to give Celtic the spot kick.

Five minutes later Saints equalised when Fitzpatrick took a McGarvey pass to crash a low drive past Latchford. Then McGarvey scored one himself in 65 minutes.

His overhead kick was blocked but he wheeled round to whip the rebound beyond Latchford.

And Saints substitute Dougie Bell completed a great season for Saints with his side's third goal four minutes from the end.

Celtic threw on Joe Craig for skipper Andy Lynch in a late, desperate bid to pull the game back—but it made no difference.

ST. MIRREN—McCulloch, Beckett, Dunlop, Copland, Munro, Fitzpatrick, Stark, Richardson (Bell, 882), McGarvey, Bone, McGarvey. Sub—Torrance (not used).

CELTIC—Latchford, Sneddon, Strachan, McDonald, Lynch (Craig 878), Aitken, Mackie, Conroy, Glavin, McAdam, McCluskey. Sub—Ward (not used).

Ref.—W. Mullen (Dalkeith).

THE STRAIN GAME

By DON MORRISON

EASTER ROAD has been the final scene of the past two Premier League championships but this time it was not to be.

For, irrespective of what was happening at Ibrox, Aberdeen just could not break the anxiety and tension which riddled their play as they went for the win they needed against Hibs.

It looked as if they just might have made it in 79 minutes when substitute Ian Scanlon put them ahead, but the dream crumbled again when, with three minutes to go, Arthur Duncan headed Hibs to a share of the points.

However, the Edinburgh men were not a willing sacrifice—far from it. Only

Hibs robbed as pressure tells on Dons

HIBS.............1 ABERDEEN.............1 (H.T. 0-0)
Scorers: Hibs—Duncan (87 mins; Aberdeen—Scanlon (79). Attendance—11,300.

superb goalkeeping by Bobby Clark, which was spiced with a little luck, stopped Hibs winning.

Wild

With the tackling razor keen and the marking so tight, it was difficult for either side to build on their unquestioned skills. But the thrills, spills and near things were more than compensated for that.

Before the two late goals, Hibs' striker, Gordon Rae came closest to scoring when he charged down a wild clearance by Dons defender, Willie Garner.

As Clark advanced, Rae hit his first shot off his legs and then smashed the rebound off the keeper's back and the ball spun for a corner kick.

It was a real break for Aberdeen, but one which Clark deserved as he had made some class saves.

In seven minutes he brilliantly parried a swerving 20 yards shot from Ally MacLeod and then he easily touched a Duncan shot over the bar.

So what of Aberdeen?

With both Fleming and Harper in the tight grip of Stewart and McNamara they gave 'keeper Mike McDonald few problems.

It was big defender, Willie Garner who gave him his hardest moment a shot which McDonald fingertipped over the bar.

Some of the strain and tension also showed when Harper tackled McNamara —and sent him spinning into the trackside wall.

In a bid to break the stalemate, Dons sent in Ian Scanlon to make his first-team debut. And what a start he made.

Stroke

He took a Davidson pass to push the ball round McDonald, run on and stroke it into the net.

It was a goal which had the Dons dancing in delight.

But their joy was short-lived as a long cross from Brownlie found Duncan's head popping up in the crowded goal-mouth to give Hibs the share of the points they fully deserved.

HIBS (4-3-3)—McDonald; Brownlie, McNamara, Stewart, Smith; McLeod, Bremner, Duncan; Murray, Rae, Higgins. Subs—Carroll and McGhee (not used).

ABERDEEN (4-3-3)—Clark; Kennedy, Garner, Miller, Ritchie; Sullivan, McMaster, Jarvie; Davidson, Fleming (S. Scanlon, 78 min.), Harper. Sub—McLelland (not used).

Referee—J. M. B. Foote (Glasgow).

DUNDEE UNITED............5
PARTICK TH............2
(H.T. 3-0)

Scorers: Dundee Utd—Wallace (16 min.), Addison (20, 35), Stewart (58), Kirkwood (79). Partick Th.— McAdam (54), Somner (64). Attendance—3546.

DUNDEE UNITED found their scoring touch in time to clinch third place in the Premier League.

World Cup 'keeper Alan Rough had no chance with the goals.

Thistle had a good spell after the interval, but their chances were ended in 53 minutes when Alex O'Hara was ordered off.

The ex-Ranger was sent off after he clashed with George Fleming.

Gordon Wallace scored

THISTLE'S HOPES GO WITH ALEX O'HARA

the first in 16 minutes with a superbly judged glancing header from a Paul Sturrock cross.

The first of Derek Addison's double which followed was surely United's goal of the season.

Bourke dummied a Fleming cross and Addison hit the ball powerfully past Rough from 20 yards.

His second wasn't bad either, a flying header from another cross by Sturrock.

A couple of times in the second half Thistle looked as though they might come back, but United always had plenty in hand.

Colin McAdam made it 3-1 with a close-in header from a Craig free kick, but young Raymond Stewart restored United's three-goal advantage

Immediately after O'Hara's ordering off, Doug Somner made Thistle's second, but substitute Billy Kirkwood made it 5-2 with 11 minutes left.

Holt (United) and Somner (Thistle) were booked.

CLYDEBANK......0   AYR UNITED......2 (H.T. 0-1)
Scorers: McLaughlin (44 mins., pen.), Cramond (49). Attendance: 1000.

AYR said goodbye to the Premier League with a victory—over the club with whom they take the drop into the First Division.

And of the two, Ayr look the more likely side to make a quick return.

They dominated Clydebank in the first half, but couldn't get the ball past Jim Gallacher until a minute from the break.

A bad error by John McCormack let Brian McLaughlin clear, only to be pulled down by the goalkeeper. The ex-Celtic man took the spot kick himself and netted easily.

Ayr finished the game

AYR TURN ON STYLE

with a goal from Gordon Cramond in the 49th minute. He worked a great move with young Robert Connor

CLYDEBANK (4-3-3)—Gallacher; Gourlay, Fallon, McCormack, Abel; Houston Geighan McColl (Bradbury 873), Gervaine (Colgan 879); Miller, O'Brien.

AYR UNITED (4-3-3)—McLean; Wells, McColl, McAllister, Connor; Kelly (Fleming 885), Phillips (McCulloch 580), McSherry; McLeland, McLaughlin, Cramond.

Ref.: K. Stewart, Glasgow.

mailsport

CLEANEST SWEEP

THE CLINCHER . . Rangers' No. 9 Derek Johnstone, surrounded by Aberdeen players, sees his thundering header beat Dons 'keeper Bobby Clark for the Ibrox men's second goal.

HIGH AND DRY . . that's Rangers' 'keeper Peter McCloy as he dangles from the crossbar after Aberdeen's Steve Ritchie has scored with a freak shot.

Roger and out Arsenal!

DON MORRISON at Wembley

JOHN WARK jumped higher than anyone at Wembley to greet the goal which gave Ipswich their first-ever English Cup win.

The Glasgow-born Anglo may have had no hand in the 77-minute goal, but having already twice hit woodwork his relief was understandable.

Direct

But while the deadlock-breaking goal brought delight to one Scot, it brought despair to another, for it was a panic-stricken clearance by former Aberdeen star Willie Young which paved the way for Roger Osborne's match-winning goal.

It was a goal long overdue. Ipswich totally deserved to beat the Gunners in a final which was always a fascinating contrast in styles.

Arsenal, relying on the ball skills of Brady and the unpredictable Hudson, tried a slow, patient build-up—and it didn't work.

Ipswich were more direct, driven on by the energetic Wark and with Paul Mariner a hard-hitting spearhead.

Pat Jennings was by far the busier 'keeper and carried the luck of his countrymen when the ball was twice struck out of his reach and both times rebounded into play from almost exactly the same spot on his right-hand post.

But the all-important goal first, and in the best Cup-tie traditions it was set up by youngster David Geddis, a late replacement for top scorer Trevor Whymark.

Breaking on the right, he hammered in a low cross which Young blocked but could not tame. Osborne had the simplest of jobs to stick it between the posts from 10 yards.

Miss

Ipswich, while always looking the better side, had found the defensive trio of Irishmen Jennings and David O'Leary and Scot Young a tough one to crack. And luck certainly didn't seem to be handing them any favours.

In 51 minutes winger Clive Woods let Wark in, but from 25 yards his shot smacked against the post, Mariner shooting wildly wide with the rebound.

In 71 minutes Woods set up Wark again, and again he hit woodwork.

While Ipswich were making and scoring chances, moments of pleasure for Arsenal fans were few and far between.

Striker Malcolm MacDonald was a particular disappointment. I cannot recall even one occasion when he unshackled himself from Irishman Allan Hunter.

ARSENAL..........0 IPSWICH TOWN........1
(H.T. 0-0)

Scorer—Osborne (77 mins). Attendance—100,000. Receipts—£500,000.

TEAM RATINGS	
ARSENAL	
JENNINGS	5
RICE	3
O'LEARY	5
YOUNG	3
NELSON	3
BRADY	2
(RIX S66)	
HUDSON	2
PRICE	3
SUNDERLAND	2
STAPLETON	1
MACDONALD	1
IPSWICH	
COOPER	5
BURLEY	3
HUNTER	5
BEATTIE	4
MILL	4
OSBORNE	3
(LAMBERT S79)	2
WARK	4
TALBOT	5
GEDDIS	3
MARINER	2
WOODS	2
Referee: D. NIPPARD, Christchurch	4

LATE NIGHT EXTRA

£500,000 PAY-OFF FROM ENGLISH FINAL

THE English Cup final at Wembley drew a record-breaking half million pounds at the turnstiles.

There were 100,000 fans at the Ipswich-Arsenal encounter, and the supporters found themselves confronted for the first time by the new fence which is all the way round the stadium . . . it's 10ft high, with spikes facing inwards towards the terracings.

Perhaps that's why referee Derek Nippard and his linesmen were allowed to do a lap of honour ahead of the Ipswich players at the final whistle.

Hull. Bremner joined Hull, who have just been relegated from the Second Division, for £25,000 from Leeds in September 1976. He intends to retire from English League football.

SCOTLAND striker Joe Harper will play in tomorrow night's testimonial game for Ayr United defender Alex McAnespie.

Harper will join an Old Firm Select which includes

BILLY BREMNER, the 35-year-old former Scottish international, has been given a free transfer by

Gordon Smith, Roy Aitken, Johnny Doyle and Peter McCloy. The opposition will be provided by an Ayr United/Kilmarnock Select.

Before the game, which starts at 7.30, there will be an Old Crocks match refereed by Scotland manager Ally MacLeod. It starts at 7 p.m.

BOB PAISLEY of Liverpool was yesterday named manager for April by

the Bells Scotch Whisky awards panel. Paisley, manager of the year in 1976 and 1977, is a leading candidate for the 1978 award which will be announced in Glasgow on May 19.

MALCOLM ALLISON is to remain in charge of Plymouth and will be signing a three-year contract as manager-coach in the next two weeks.

HIBS have signed forward Willie Temperley who was freed by Celtic at the end of the season.

mailsport

Allan Herron at Hampden

OF THEM ALL

WHAT A HAT-TRICK . . Rangers skipper John Greig grasps the Cup and shows how he feels about the club's third treble success since he joined them. Team-mates Forsyth, Jackson, MacDonald, Smith and manager Jock Wallace complete the picture.

RANGERS swept the board, leaving Aberdeen bemused and bewildered, with a Hampden Cup victory that had a style, method and control which made their success almost inevitable before the interval had been reached.

They took the Scottish Cup for the 22nd time in their history, and swept to the treble of the Championship, the League Cup and THE Cup, for a record fourth time, with such assured purpose and poise, that it makes the score-line look a little ridiculous.

Aberdeen, always struggling with their rhythm, never looked like winning this bloodless occasion where the lack of goalmouth incident made it all a bit unreal for long stretches of play.

That great little Cup campaigner Alex MacDonald tore the heart out of the Dons after 34 minutes with the kind of goal that only a player of exceptional reflexes can score.

It began with a bit of ball control from the elegant Derek Johnstone at the edge of the Aberdeen box, when the big man turned away from the target looking for a man to take it from him.

He spotted the drifting, floating Bobby Russell on the right side, and fed him.

Russell, who had his finest 90 minutes in a Rangers strip, floated the ball goal-wards with his left foot and before anyone could spot the danger, MacDonald had moved.

He sprinted towards the ball to get his head at it, and beat Bobby Clark.

The Dons 'keeper managed to get his hand to

Punished

Sandy Jardine was in World Cup form. John Greig looked good for another five years. Tommy McLean and Derek Johnstone were the best front men on view.

It was therefore no great surprise to the 61,563 crowd when Rangers scored again in 58 minutes.

Jardine and McLean who had punished the deficiencies of Aberdeen left-back Steve Ritchie, worked the old one-two on the right, leaving McLean to drift the ball across goal with his left foot.

Derek Johnstone rose

the ball, but couldn't stop it squirming over the line.

Right there, we all felt Rangers had won it, as they grew in stature and confidence.

Bobby Russell was hitting his passes, long, short or delayed with almost sadistic pleasure as the men from the north turned and tired in anguish.

THIS BOY IN A MAN'S BOOTS FULLY DESERVED HIS "MAN OF THE MATCH" CHEQUE OF £100 AWARDED BY YOUNGER'S TARTAN SPECIAL.

Colin Jackson, whose form has worried Rangers' fans this season, was a tremendous figure in defence, winning the battle against the restless Joe Harper.

Brilliant Russell makes sure the Cup goes to Ibrox

RANGERS 2   ABERDEEN 1   (H.T. 1-0)
Scorers: Rangers—MacDonald (34 min.), Johnstone (58). Aberdeen—Ritchie (85). Attendance—61,563.

clear to thunder the ball high in the net with the kind of header which made him Scotland's Player of the Year.

A devastating goal. The Aberdeen heads went down, and they didn't lift until Ritchie hit an unbelievable goal five minutes from the end.

This goal, which came too late to have any effect on the result, completely baffled everyone, including the scorer!

He thrust his boot at a short pass from John McMaster in a real goalmouth scrimmage, mishit

it, sending the ball spinning up in the air over the head of Peter McCloy.

It then dipped, hit the crossbar and slipped over the line. McCloy looked disgusted, and no wonder.

But the game had been over long before that. Rangers quickly took control again and played out time.

Bright

If the whole affair did not turn out to be the classic everyone expected from the two best sides in Scotland, this was surely because Rangers had so

much of the game, and Aberdeen's challenge was terribly disappointing.

It had looked like a bright start for Aberdeen, and their £15,000 colourful fans on the terracing when John McMaster hurtled a tremendous 25-yards shot at the Rangers goal in just two minutes—and missed by a fraction.

Dons looked eager and fairly confident in those early minutes as Jarvie, Sullivan and Harper stuck the ball about with a lot of accuracy.

But the lack of response from Fleming, Davidson and Ritchie began to have its effect, and the great talent of Russell was blooming all the time.

In short, Aberdeen had too many players off form.

Rangers were the better side man for man, and as a team.

Great

They didn't have a weakness in this their 33rd Scottish Cup Final.

Indeed Rangers might have had one or two more if they had got any reasonable break of the ball.

So Aberdeen's great unbeaten run of 23 games ended before their biggest audience of the season.

Hampden belonged to Rangers, the team that kept rising to the big occasion every time they were challenged this season. Jock Wallace should be a happy man this morning.

TEAM RATINGS

Rangers (4-2-4)		Aberdeen (4-3-3)	
McCloy	4	Clark	3
Jardine	4	Kennedy	3
Jackson	5	Garner	3
Forsyth	4	Miller	4
Greig	4	Ritchie	2
Russell	5	Sullivan	2
McDonald	4	McMaster	3
McLean	4	Jarvie	2
Johnstone	4	Fleming	2
Smith	3	Sub. Scanlon (56 mins.)	2
Cooper	3	Harper	2
Sub. Watson (77 mins.)	2	Davidson	1
Not used—Robertson		Not used—McClelland	
Referee : B. R. McGinlay (Glasgow)			5

FAIRGRIEVE

Time to stop this treble threat

IT is important to Rangers that they have won the treble, but it is much more important to Scottish football that they should not do so again—at least for some time.

Monopolies are unhealthy. This applies to sport just as much as it applies to commerce.

I made this point, and it was not appreciated then, either, when Celtic were winning everything in sight.

I make it again now, because there is a very real threat—or promise—according to one's outlook that Rangers are on the verge of a period of embarrassing dominance.

Of course, it matters enormously that standards should rise rather than fall. We do not want Rangers to play less effective football.

We do, I trust, want the competition to become more significant.

Nerves

Celtic may return, who knows? As one who said last October that they would win the League, I am probably not the best man to give an inspired opinion.

So what of the rest? No inspiration here either, but I did have high hopes of Aberdeen. In yesterday's mediocre Cup final, however, they supplied most of the mediocrity and Rangers supplied the moments that mattered.

It could be that Aberdeen's nervous system failed and that is Billy McNeill's problem.

The point is the Ibrox nerves seemed in fine shape, even if the skills were scarce. It was once said of Rangers that they took a goal of a start into every match, simply because they WERE Rangers . . . we'll forget referees for a minute.

Wrong

The theory was based, not so much on their victories as on their refusal to take the prospect of defeat seriously.

Whether this theory is right or wrong, they may well have won yesterday's Scottish Cup because they did not think they could lose, whereas Aberdeen merely hoped they would win.

Between these two attitudes, you will agree, there is one hell of a difference.

SOFTLY, SOFTLY...

A PERSISTENT story—perhaps beyond mere rumour—says that Celtic have made a bid for one of Edinburgh's most talented players.

I will not name the player involved, because this is precisely the kind of story which—in a newspaper—is called "tapping."

It may not be true, though I suspect it is. To give details, though—rumour or otherwise—would simply unsettle the player.

I await developments with interest. If there are no developments, that's all right.

Carrying the can

I AM one of those who think Ally MacLeod should have chosen Andy Gray for the final World Cup 22, because i doubt whether any defence on earth could have coped—ot a free-kick, say — with Jordan and Gray, to say nothing of McQueen coming up like a Chieftain tank on stilts.

But I am assuredly not one of those who would dream of blaming Ally for a decision which must rank as among the most difficult he has ever had to make.

As any football writer — any journalist — knows, it's easy to criticise, but maybe not so easy to criticise fairly. Ally carries the can. I don't.

P.S. Known acquaintances and unknown enemies may be assured that, despite the above paragraph, I am not going soft. It is charity, not old age, that's creeping in.

CORONARY HEARTS

LEARNED medical men say, after an exhaustive survey, that the citizens of Edinburgh are more prone to coronaries than their Swedish counterparts, because they are shorter, fatter, more addicted to cigarettes, more fond of bevvy.

They may well be right. But how many Swedes support Hearts?

JOHN FAIRGRIEVE

Alex Cameron on the line from Munich

Malmo's cash boost

ALRIGHT

CLOUGH

HOUGHTON

NOTTINGHAM FOREST arrived last night for the poor man's European Cup final minus manager Brian Clough who returns this morning from the sunshine of Crete to join his team.

Forest, two and a half million pounds in debt when they finish their new stand in November, are favourites to win the big game at the Olympic Stadium and will pay a bonus of £2500 to each player if they win.

Malmo of Sweden, who fly in today have a rich banker chairman but a shoestring income from an 8,000 following. Yet they will pay twice the rewards of Forest if they upset the odds.

Memories

Forest are in the competition for the first time and if they become the 13th winners it will be one of the greatest performances of all.

Four Scots are likely to line up with million-pound Trevor Francis. They are skipper John McGovern, Archie Gemmill, John Robertson and Kenny Burns whose

6I don't want to get into any conflicts with Brian Clough. He's a nice bloke, I think.**9**

—Malmo boss BOB HOUGHTON

fitness will not be judged until the great one examines the pros and cons.

Munich has laid out every available red carpet for the teams and a small army of reporters. The city, dotted with soaring high-rise buildings, has solemn sporting memories which will never be erased.

They cannot forget that a brilliant Manchester United team was wiped out here and at the Olympics terrorists brutally killed 13 members of the Israeli team.

Reaction

Malmo will live at The Hilton where you take out a mortgage before nodding to the doorman. Forest will content themselves with less sumptuous lodgings.

In Malmo yesterday English coach Bob Houghton said: "Frankly we would rather have played Cologne. Their style would have been better for us than Forest's.

"I know Brian has been getting all the Press but that doesn't bother me. I would rather get goals. In saying this I don't want to get into any conflicts with Brian Clough. He's a nice bloke, I think."

The managers have one factor in common. Both have been sacked—Clough by Leeds and Houghton by Maidstone.

Houghton would say nothing yesterday about his reaction to reports of an offer to manage Derby but the odds are that he will turn it down.

He is paid £25,000 a year by Malmo and is treated like a lord. The local fans call him "The Man from the Sky" because they think he has performed miracles.

A GOAL—AT LAST ! Hibs' Tony Higgins turns away after putting his side ahead in the second replay after successive goalless draws. At the end of the night there were five goals scored . . . and Tony wasn't so happy.

TODAY'S SOCCER CARD

International—Rep. of Ireland v. Argentina.
Amateur Cup Final—Crosshouse Wav. v. Chapelhall (Hampden, 7.30).
Whyte & Mackay Cup—Lesmahagow v. Cumnock (at Pollok).
Ayrshire Drybrough Cup—Largs v. Darvel (at Hurlford).
Scarlett Cup—Kilbirnie v. Irvine Vics.
McCrae Cup—Maybole v. Kello, Kilwinning v. Ardrossan.

. . . AND YESTERDAY

Scottish Cup Final (second replay)—Rangers 3, Hibs 2 (after extra time).
Ayrshire League—Lugar 3, Annbank 0; Auchinleck 1, Beith 0.
Central League—Baillieston 0, East Kilbride 3; Shettleston 1, Cumbernauld 0; Glencairn 0, Pollok 2; Petershill 1, Yoker 1; Vale of Clyde 1, Wishaw 3; Blantyre Celtic 4, Royal Albert 1.
Renfrew Juniors Trophy (semifinal)—Harmony Row 2, Williamsburgh 1 (after extra time).

GET READY FOR TWO-MAN SHOW

By JACK ADAMS

WORLD CUP champions Argentina face one final test before they clash with Scotland at Hampden Park on Saturday.

Tonight at Landsdowne Road, the South American stars meet the Republic of Ireland in what could turn out to be a two-man show. For displaying their enormous skills in opposition will be Dublin's Liam Brady, the pride of Ireland, and Deigo Maradona, the 18-year-old genius who has suddenly burst into the Argentina soccer scene.

Change

Apart from the appearance of this pair, who have the elegance and control to captivate any crowd, tonight will see the farewell as an international of Johnny Giles, who has dominated the Irish game for two decades.

Meanwhile, the Republic make one change from the side beaten by West Germany last week. Mick Walsh, the QPR striker, comes in for Gerry Ryan, who is unavailable because of American commitments. Teams:

REPUBLIC OF IRELAND—Peyton (Fulham), Gregg (Bohemians), Martin (Newcastle), O'Leary (Arsenal), Mulligan (West Brom), Giles (Shamrock), Brady (Arsenal), Grealish (Orient), Walsh (QPR), Stapleton (Arsenal), Givens (Birmingham).
ARGENTINA (probable)—Fillol, Olguin, Villaverde, Passarella, Tarantini, Barbas, Gallego, Maradona, Houseman, Luque, Ortiz or Valencia.

● Don't miss World Cup star Osvaldo Ardiles' exclusive look at Scotland this week.

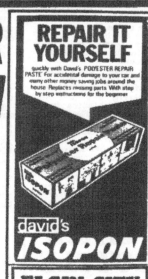

RECORD SPORT BRINGS YOU THE HAMPDEN ACTION

ON THE NIGHT!

Marathon men make it magic

RANGERS completed a Cup double at Hampden last night when a 5½-hour battle against Hibs ended with Derek Johnstone holding aloft the Scottish Cup.

And on the rain-soaked Hampden pitch the players finally got it right. This was an unforgettable final that flourished in an atmosphere which was against great football.

There was teeming rain, a Hampden stadium with only 30,000 fans, yet how this game will be talked about.

It was the last of the three clashes and it was by far the finest. Judged on its own, it was a memorable and dramatic final marred only by some strange refereeing decisions from Ian Foote.

Rangers won, but how Hibs fought them before falling to the Scottish Cup jinx which has dogged them for most of this century.

And it was that jinx which finished their hopes with only 10 minutes of extra time remaining.

Dave Cooper moved down the left wing took the ball clear of the Hibs defence and then sent it across goal. The ball beat Jim McArthur and behind him Arthur Duncan raced in to head clear with Gordon Smith and Derek Johnstone ready to challenge.

Command

The ball spun from his head and raged into his own net. Duncan collapsed on the goal-line knowing, as well as anyone in the stadium, that the last dice had been thrown in this seemingly never-ending final. It was a tragic finish for Hibs.

In the first-half they had taken

RANGERS.........3 HIBS.........2
(After extra time)
Scorers: Rangers—Johnstone (42min., 61), Duncan (o.g. 110). Hibs—Higgins (16), MacLeod (pen., 78). Att.—30,602.

By KEN GALLACHER

the lead through a Tony Higgins goal in 16 minutes. Not only taken the lead, but taken command of the game, too.

They played with confidence and assurance and Rangers struggled until half-way through the first half when a tactical switch from John Greig repaired the damage.

Ally Dawson moved to the right to mark Higgins, Sandy Jardine joined Colin Jackson at the heart of the defence, and Derek Johnstone went up front alongside Derek Parlane.

Three minutes before half-time a Tommy McLean shot skidded along the Hampden turf. Jim McArthur went down to cover it, allowed the ball to squirm away from him, and Johnstone was there to touch it over the line.

THAT GOAL CHANGED THE GAME TREMENDOUSLY.

In the second half Rangers were the team with confidence, the team who made chances. And in 61 minutes they deserved to go in front. It was a good move and a good goal.

Sandy Jardine found Man of the Match Bobby Russell on the right. The slim midfield man sent the ball into the Hibs box and Johnstone hooked a shot past the keeper.

There could have been other Rangers goals around then, but when they missed the chances it didn't seem to matter because they were so much in control.

Penalty

Suddenly, in 78 minutes, the game changed again. Substitute Bobby Hutchinson, just minutes on the field, went down in a Jackson tackle. Referee Foote waved away Rangers protests, gave a penalty, and Ally MacLeod stepped up to score.

The game moved once more into extra time—bringing more controversy with it.

In 104 minutes Rangers were given a 'soft' penalty when Parlane went down after a Duncan challenge.

Substitute Alex Miller took the kick but McArthur dived to his right and saved it. When a Smith goal was disallowed for offside almost immediately afterwards it looked as if the teams would be back at Hampden on Thursday.

Then came the glorious run from Cooper and the tragic ending for Hibs.

With so much at stake there was total commitment and five players were booked—Johnstone, Parlane and MacDonald of Rangers and Hibs McNamara and Brazil.

Ally Dawson, Bobby Russell and Derek Parlane in extra time were good players for Rangers last night.

For Hibs, Jackie McNamara was superb throughout, while Tony Higgins, Colin Campbell and Gordon Rae excelled in the first half.

Rangers now go into the European Cup Winners' Cup with Celtic, of course, going into the European Cup. Dundee United and Aberdeen will play in the UEFA Cup.

RANGERS: McCloy, Jardine, Dawson, Johnstone, Jackson, Watson, McLean, Russell, Parlane, MacDonald, Cooper. Subs—Miller, Smith.

HIBS: McArthur, Brazil, Duncan, Bremner, Stewart, McNamara, Rae, MacLeod, Campbell, Callachan, Higgins. Subs—Brown, Hutchinson.

Referee: L Foote, Glasgow.

Rangers go in front for the first time as Derek Johnstone beats George Stewart to hook in the Ibrox team's second goal.

The flying Rangers . . . Derek Johnstone and Alex MacDonald dive at the same time to meet a cross. Arthur Duncan, Davie Cooper and George Stewart watch the effort go wide.

SPORTSPOTS

Glavin may move South

By JIM BLAIR

RONNIE GLAVIN, Celtic's "forgotten man," may resume his football career in England next season.

The 27-year-old midfield player, capped once by Scotland, travels south today for transfer talks with Barnsley.

The English Third Division club have already been in touch with Celtic and the ambitious Allan Clarke, player-manager of the Yorkshire club, is anxious to sign Glavin.

Glavin—bought for £80,000 from Partick Thistle over four years ago—hasn't figured recently in Celtic's first-team plans.

But Barnsley's move may prompt Queen's Park Rangers boss Tommy Docherty, who has already been credited with an interest, to make a bid.

Meanwhile, Liverpool yesterday clinched the £200,000 deal for Israeli defender Avi Cohen.

★ Junior talent spotters will be out in force at Hampden tonight for the Scottish Amateur Cup Final between Crosshouse Waverley and Chapelhall. Crosshouse were beaten 3-2 by Cambusbarron Rovers at Hampden last year, while Chapelhall are making their first appearance in the final.

● Cumnock midfield player Jim Doherty looks set to sign for English Second Division club Notts County. A signing fee of around £3000 has been agreed and the clubs await the player's decision.

● Scotland's David McGill and Billy Moseley of South Africa, were joint leaders after the first session of the Kodak Masters bowling pairs event at Hartlepool yesterday.

● Rosie Casals (US) and Wendy Turnbull (Australia) beat Aussies Evonne Cawley and Kerry Reid 6-2 7-5 in the final of the West German women's tennis championships.

● Algirdas Notskus (Russia), won the opening stage of the 1100-miles Milk cycle race at Basingstoke yesterday.

● Former Morton goalkeeper Neil Mooney lines up for the Danish League Select against West Brom in Odense tonight.

Tame finish from Scots

From SANDY BEVERIDGE

SCOTLAND........2 DENMARK........1
Scorers: Scotland—McBride (9 mins), Simpson (76). Denmark—Petersen (15).

SCOTLAND won their final section match of the European Youth tournament in Austria last night thanks to a late goal by Aberdeen's Neil Simpson.

But the victory won't give them a place in the semi-finals. Saturday night's defeat by Bulgaria and Bulgaria's 4-1 win over Poland last night put paid to our hopes.

Not even an early goal by Everton's Joe McBride could pep up the Scots last night.

The Danes hit back in 15 minutes when Jan Petersen shot past Campbell Money.

Scotland (4-2-4): Money (St Mirren); Dornan (Aberdeen), McGlinchey (Hibs), McAveety (Berwick), Lorimer (Dundee Utd); Cowie (West Ham), Simpson (Aberdeen), Walsh (Notts Forest); McKay (Rangers), Milne (Dundee Utd), McBride (Everton).

Ref.—J. Brennstad, Norway.

The Hampden drama...captured

COOPER

★ GOING IN . . . that's this low shot from John MacDonald as his effort sweeps past the helpless Dundee United goalkeeper Hamish McAlpine for the Ibrox side's third goal in their impressive runaway triumph.

ENGLAND v. BRAZIL

★ GOING UP . . . that's the arms of Ibrox two-goal hero MacDonald as he accepts the cheers of the Rangers fans at Hampden.

SPORTS COMMENT

Deadly elegance

Brazil are back at their best

ENGLAND.....................0   BRAZIL.....................1

Scorer—Zico (11 min). Att. 75,000. Receipts £480,000.

KEN GALLACHER at Wembley

ENGLAND trudged wearily from Wembley after their third game in succession without a victory for their supporters.

After a defeat from Spain, a drab draw with Rumania, they lost last night to the masters from Brazil.

There was just one goal in the game, but it was a superb one, scored by Zico after 11 minutes.

England might have managed a draw with a last-gasp shot from Peter Withe which struck the inside of the post, ran along the goal-line and then came clear— BUT IT WOULD HAVE BEEN MORE THAN THEY DESERVED.

Disgraced

For this was a night when the Brazilians decided to show once more that no other country can match their grace, their flair, and their magnificent skills.

If a second goal had been allowed to stand when Reinaldo had the ball in the net after 17 minutes then manager Ron Greenwood's team might have been disgraced.

But the Austrian referee forgot about the advantage rule and awarded a foul after Alvin Martin had unsuccessfully tried to stop the Brazilian striker.

It was, of course, a patchwork England team. Greenwood had been hit by call-offs, and it was obvious from the beginning that the Brazilians could outclass the home side.

They flicked the ball about with ease, strutted around the field with an inborn arrogance, and finished with venom when it mattered.

It mattered in that 11th minute when Edevaldo sent the ball through to Zico. The midfield man had thrust himself forward into the penalty box. He was clear of the England defence when he lashed a low shot past England's skipper for the night Ray Clemence.

It was a marvellous goal and six minutes later the second one, equally well constructed, would have finished England if the referee had not blundered.

In fact when the goal was disallowed England seemed to lift themselves. They had a good spell and Terry McDermott had a shot held by Valdir and then Peter Withe had a header blocked by the 'keeper.

The one England player who seemed to trouble the Brazilians was Peter Barnes. He switched wings and always he was able to give problems to the defenders.

Towards the end of the first half he was barged by Eder and at the start of the second, scythed by Socrates. And it was Barnes who burst through to test Valdir in 48 minutes with a shot which the 'keeper was happy to push for a corner.

At the start of the second half England looked good. But, almost as if they sensed a revival, the Brazilians asserted themselves again.

Post

In 57 minutes Eder and Reinaldo combined exquisitely in the penalty box and the move ended with the winger shooting to the side net.

A minute later it was Eder again with a thundering shot which deceived Clemence before striking the top of the crossbar.

It was almost into injury time when Withe hit the post—but Brazil had deserved their victory.

England—Clemence (Liverpool), Neal (Liverpool), Sansom (Arsenal), Robson (West Brom), Martin (West Ham), Wilkins (Man United), Coppell (Man United), McDermott (Liverpool), Withe (Aston Villa), Rix (Arsenal), Barnes (West Brom). Subs—Mills (Ipswich), Lukic (Leeds), Osman (Ipswich), Brooking (West Ham), Francis (Notts Forest).

Brazil—Valdir, Edevaldo, Oscar, Luisinho, Cerezo, Junior, Isidoro, Socrates, Reinaldo, Zico, Eder. Subs—Paulo, Sergio, Getulio, Edinho, Victor, Renato.

Referee—Erich Linemayr (Austria).

SHAME OF ENGLISH RETREAT

THE British Football Championship was yesterday thrown into such diabolical confusion that there is a sound case for abandoning it.

First of all England refused to sell tickets for the Wembley match to Scots. And now, virtually at the eleventh hour, they have run up the white flag and said they will not play in Belfast.

The decision was taken yesterday and was followed with the usual apologetic smokescreen of meaningless platitudes. Anyone who wants to steer clear of the troubles in Belfast is entitled to do so. But consider this:

The Government was satisfied with the RUC's assurance on the security of the England team and wanted them to go.

The game has been arranged for two years and the cancellation came four days from the kick-off.

The English FA say there is no chance of a re-arrangement. This isn't really surprising, but the timing was entirely England's.

They have botched up the championship, peeved the Irish and disappointed even Wales who are the only country with whom England's pompous Footering Association seem happy.

England restored football links with Northern Ireland in 1975. And their secretary Ted Croker said, with what can only be construed as arrogance or a complete lack of knowledge, that it "might help a speedy solution to the province's troubles."

Croker admitted the cancellation was based on newspaper and TV reports, although none has suggested England would be in danger of a terrorist attack.

IT IS A PANIC MOVE WHICH WILL HELP NO ONE.

ALEX CAMERON

in words and pictures by the No. 1 section

MAGIC SHOW!

Davie the hero for Rangers

RANGERS won the Scottish Cup at Hampden last night—and Davie Cooper graduated as Master of Soccer Arts.

United, and forecasters like myself, were sliced into little pieces, but the majority of Hampden's 43,099 replay audience left in ecstasy.

It was a memorable 90 minutes. A dramatic form about-turn and as convincing a victory as Hampden has ever seen in the national tournament.

Bright

Hampden was a sea of blue-and-white scarves as young skipper Ally Dawson took the Cup—the 24th time it has gone to Ibrox.

And it was certainly on merit, a point conceded by the sorely forlorn United players who thought they were on the brink of their first-ever win.

Rangers' prestige was restored on this night of style, of dash, of high-class artistry. And Scots soccer said good-bye to the season with the kind of flourish our ailing game needs.

United never approached the heights of which they are capable. They searched for inspiration after a good start, but none came, except for one bright passage in the second half.

John Greig's changed team choice turned out to be an inspiration.

Saturday's substitutes—the exciting, elegant Cooper and the devastating John MacDonald—were superb, with MacDonald grabbing two of the goals and Cooper one.

But it was Cooper who really wobbled and finally dis-united the men from Tannadice.

He ran, weaved, dribbled, passed and shot in a tantalising combination of knockout skills.

This was Cooper's finest match, and it came at a time when Rangers needed it most of all.

Fight

The goal which virtually finished United had all the brilliance of a Cup Final replay winner.

Rangers were leading 2-1 and there was the semblance of a fight coming from tangerine-shirted United.

The casual-looking Cooper gathered the ball a few yards outside the penalty area. He spotted MacDonald and saw that a pass on the inside of the luckless John Holt would render the full-back useless and give his team mate a scoring chance.

The ball travelled 25 yards. MacDonald controlled it quickly, ran towards Hamish McAlpine and shot a goal which Rangers fans will remember for a long time.

That bit of sheer class put the stamp on the match, on Rangers success hopes and the fact that United were to be Cup Final losers for the second time in their history.

Full-back Holt had an unhappy match. In 10 minutes he made to clear the ball upfield, but sliced it square across the penalty

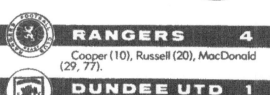

RANGERS	4
Cooper (10), Russell (20), MacDonald (29, 77).	
DUNDEE UTD	1
Dodds (23).	Attendance: 43,099

By ALEX CAMERON
Sportswriter of the Year

area to the feet of that man Cooper.

He advanced on McAlpine and flicked the ball over him and into the far corner of the net.

Ten minutes later Holt fouled Cooper. The Rangers winger took the kick himself, and with great precision laid the ball right at the feet of Robert Russell, who came running in at an angle to volley goal No. 2.

United needed a goal badly at this point. And they got it from an excellent cross by Eamonn Bannon and a flick by Paul Sturrock to Davie Dodds.

Dodds was on his own, and the Rangers defence could do nothing about it as he shot what turned out to be United's only goal.

Six minutes later we had that marvellous piece of Cooper excellence which set up MacDonald's third goal for Rangers.

And going into the second half nobody gave United much of a chance.

There was only one other goal. And it went to Rangers 13 minutes from the end.

The busy Ian Redford passed into the penalty area

and MacDonald went for it quickly. Dave Narey was near him, but the Rangers players had no doubts about the scorer.

Referee Ian Foote retired after the game as a grade one referee in Scotland. In his book were the names of Ally Dawson, Tom Forsyth, Gregor Stevens (Rangers), and Derek Stark and Paul Sturrock (United).

But in Foote's memory was a game he'll find difficult to forget.

Rangers—Stewart, Jardine, Dawson, Stevens, Forsyth, Bett, Cooper, Russell, D. Johnstone, Redford, MacDonald. Subs.—McLean, McAdam.

Dundee Utd.—McAlpine, Holt, Kopel, Phillip, Hegarty, Narey, Bannon, Milne, Kirkwood, Sturrock, Dodds. Subs—Stark, Pettigrew.

Referee—I. Foote, Glasgow.

Hampden tantrums . . . Rangers defender Tom Forsyth and Dundee United substitute Derek Stark don't quite see eye-to-eye after a confrontation.

ENGLISH CUP FINAL LATEST

"It's somebody offering us Hampden Park to play Northern Ireland . . ."

WEMBLEY WOE

Players fear cramp danger

THE injury problems of Tottenham and Manchester City are beginning to clear up for the English Cup Final replay tomorrow night.

But both managers must be worried about the possibility of cramp affecting their players.

For Saturday's extra time was such an ordeal for both sets of players there is no guarantee they will be able to take the strain on Wembley's testing turf.

Worry

Tottenham skipper Steve Perryman, one of Saturday's cramp victims, said: "Any strain makes you anxious, because you want to be in tip-top condition when you go into the game."

Although, like the other Spurs casualties, Perryman expects to be fully fit by tomorrow, team-mate Chris

Hughton voiced the fears of the other players. He said:

"There's always the worry that we might suffer again—five days is not long enough to recover from a game like Saturday's.

"That Wembley pitch is a real killer. It takes its toll on your legs."

Tottenham's other injury worries—Glenn Hoddle, Graham Roberts, Tony Galvin and Garry Brooke—have all

cleared, and manager Keith Burkinshaw expects to name his team today from the same 12.

City's Dennis Tueart is standing by to step into the side if Kevin Reeves, Dave Bennett or Gerry Gow fail fitness tests. If all the players report fit the team will be unchanged, but Tueart will be substitute.

Maine Road boss John Bond said: "We will not be training again before the final. We will just be taking a walk in the park near our London hotel."

● Bobby Murdoch has been unanimously approved by the Middlesbrough board as manager of the club.

And the former Celtic and Boro star hopes the success of Jock Stein and Jack Charlton will rub off in his new career.

"Jock is the greatest manager I've played under. Jack is an outstanding tactician. I learned a lot from both."

EURO NEWS

★ Want to buy a ticket for tonight's big game?

The European Cup Winners' Cup Final between Carl Zeiss Jena, of East Germany, and Russia's Dinamo Tbilisi is being televised live to 41 countries.

But so far only 2025 of the 70,000 tickets on offer have been sold.

The severe lack of local interest arises from the fact that the clubs—the so-called cream of Soviet soccer—clash at Dusseldorf . . . in West Germany.

SOCCER TODAY

English Div. 1—Ipswich Southampton.

MacLeod Cup—First round—Coltness Utd v Bellshill.

Central League—Forth v Perthshire, Rob Roy v Cumbernauld, East Kilbride v Renfrew, Lesmahagow v Port Glasgow, Glencairn v Shotts, Blantyre Vics v Maryhill, Petershill v Kilsyth Rangers, Neilston v Dunipace, Lanark Utd v Shettleston, Yoker v St Anthony, Royal Albert v Thorniewood.

Ayrshire League H—Maybole v Kello.

★ ◉ ★ *The section with picture power covers*

BETTER LATE

THE ONE THAT GOT AWAY ... and rightly so. Paul Sturrock's shot is on its way into the net, but the camera clearly shows that his Dundee United team mate John Holt is offside and interfering with play as Rangers keeper Jim Stewart attempts to save.

"It wasn't really his fault he was caught off-side..."

Forget it says Jim

MANAGER Jim McLean accepted last night that all Dundee United's Cup problems did not stem from Paul Sturrock's disallowed goal.

As he brought his disconsolate squad together for tomorrow's UEFA Cup clash with Winterslag, McLean remained tight-lipped over the most controversial moment against Rangers.

But I believe the feeling in the United camp now is that on two occasions they have come out on the wrong side of controversial decisions against Rangers.

Excuses

In a League game at Tannadice last season a Davie Cooper goal was allowed to stand — even though United were convinced that another Rangers player was interfering with play.

All McLean would say of the

★ DUNDEE UNITED were told when they arrived in Belgium last night there is a doubt about their UEFA Cup-tie against Winterslag tomorrow night.

Winterslag's Belgian First Division match against Cercle, of Bruges, scheduled for Saturday, was postponed because the pitch was waterlogged.

And an official of the Belgian

By WALLACE MOORE

incident last night was: "If people want to look for excuses for our defeat they are there."

Significantly, though, he added "The matched proved we still have work to do here at Tannadice. Not enough players played well against Rangers and we didn't take advantage when we had the game by the throat."

But the last thing United can afford is to dwell on the misfortune.

club said last night: "If we have any more heavy rain there is a chance that the ground will be unplayable for the European tie.

"However, we would attempt to find another ground in this area which is playable."

The alternatives are the First Division ground at Beringen, (13 miles away) and Second Division Diest (25 miles away).

On the charter flight from Leuchars yesterday, McLean told me:

"We have to pick ourselves up and be positive. We have to take the chance to come back from a bad result by getting a good one."

There was a last-minute change in the United party. Goalkeeper John Gardiner had to be raised from his Sunday morning lie-in.

Andy Graham, who had been the stand-by for Hamish McAlpine, was unwell.

PITTODRIE NEWS ... Ian Broadley reports   **DENS PARK LATEST ... Jack Adams reports**   **EASTER ROAD AFTERMATH ... Jim Kean reports**

ABERDEEN must swiftly solve their erratic goal-scoring form or accept that the Championship isn't a realistic target.

Their failure to score in the draw with relegation threatened Airdrie at Pittodrie means the Dons have managed just 20 goals in 14 league matches.

Yet in five UEFA Cup ties against quality opposition, they have scored 12.

Last night manager Alex Ferguson admitted; "I just don't know the reason. Airdrie came to play it tight and the responsibility was on us to break them down.

"But Ipswich and Hamburg didn't exactly give us a free hand in attack yet we managed three goals against both at home.

"I was very disappointed with our performance against Airdrie. We created only one chance.

"There was a reaction after beating Hamburg, particularly

DONS IN TARGET RIDDLE

among the younger players. They suffer a physical and psychological reaction after involvement at the highest level."

What Ferguson left unsaid was the shocking attendance of just 8006 a pathetic number following the full house against Hamburg. If Aberdeen are to retain their top players they must be better supported.

The only bright spot to emerge for the Dons was the comeback of Alex McLeish who felt no adverse effects after his serious ankle injury.

DUNDEE'S 4—1 win over Morton could be their most important result of the season.

Because it not only took them off the bottom of the league, it also brought them back in touch with the four other teams in most danger of relegation.

The Dens Park side deserve a lot of credit for the way they went about gaining their first home win since September 19.

It was a dream start with a goal from Davie Bell in 77 seconds, and built on that was a second from Peter Mackie in nine minutes.

And when Morton pulled themselves into the game with a goal by Roddie Hutchison and took control of the play for 20 minutes, Dundee showed determination and courage that could keep them in the Premier League.

They came back to score twice more through Sinclair and Ferguson. Morton's normally solid defence just fell apart.

Manager Benny Rooney said:

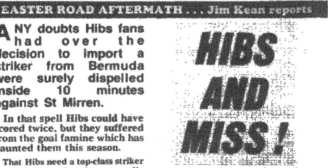

"The keeper and the back four must carry the can."

Dundee boss Donald Mackay said: "That result and the others at the weekend help us but we still have a long way to go."

Tommy Craig could help them along the road. The ex-Scotland midfield man will train at Dens this week with a view to signing from Swansea.

The only blot on Dundee's win was the strange ordering-off of Scotland youth cap, Ray Stephen, for an offence seen only by the linesman.

ANY doubts Hibs fans had over the decision to import a striker from Bermuda were surely dispelled inside 10 minutes against St Mirren.

In that spell Hibs could have scored twice, but they suffered from the goal famine which has haunted them this season.

That Hibs need a top-class striker is as plain as the cigar normally found in Bertie Auld's face and the player can come from Timbuctoo— as long as he can score goals.

Injured

"That's four times we've played St Mirren this season," lamented Auld. "Each time we've looked the better side, made more chances but still haven't scored a goal."

Up to a point there was nothing wrong with Hibs' play. Their defence was seldom in trouble and in midfield Bobby Flavell did enough to earn about everyone's man-of-the-match award.

HIBS AND MISS!

But he went off injured in the second half and it was left to his replacement, Derek Rodier, to sum up a frustrating 90 minutes.

Billy Thomson pushed away an Alan Sneddon shot and as Rodier's cross came over it was headed over his own keeper by Billy Stark. Instead of dropping into the net the ball landed on top of the bar and bounced to safety.

From a Paisley point of view the match could have been better but a point gained away from home is never to be sneezed at in the Premier League.

THAN NEVER !

Ibrox men get it right

THE League Cup is in the Ibrox trophy room this morning because Rangers wanted it more than Dundee United.

And critical decisions by John Greig were as important in the end as one by referee Eddie Pringle which knocked the heart out of United.

They threw in the towel in the manner of a boxer resenting a belt on the chin after being better for two thirds of the Hampden final.

Drama

Yet Rangers won 2-1, qualified for Europe with superb team determination, and, finally, a floated shot by sub Ian Redford two minutes from the end.

The sink-or-swim drama in the dug outs was deadly. Greig, who slammed his players viciously at the interval for bad play, said: "We were upset in the first half by that injury to Derek Johnstone.

"The players must have wondered what was happening as it took 10 minutes to patch up a gash on his forehead.

"It was a worthwhile risk in my view.

"I told Gregor Stevens to mark Davie Dodds in the second half and gave Sandy Jardine a free role to construct behind the three backs.

"Ralph Milne scored quickly, however, and I wondered if I should take off a defender and plunge everything into attack. I decided to leave things for a while.

Knock

"Then Paul Sturrock's 'goal' was disallowed and this became the turning point. Davie Cooper equalised with one of his bending shots off a free-kick and we needed defenders to consolidate.

"However, 1-1 wasn't good enough. When goals aren't coming a change should be made. That's why we have substitutes.

"Gordon Dalziel had a good match, but the laddie was limping from a knock. The change, therefore, was to put

THE WINNER . . . Dundee United 'keeper Hamish McAlpine is beaten by a lob from Rangers substitute Ian Redford just outside the box. Redford's team-mate John MacDonald looks offside here, but was certainly not interfering with play.

ALEX CAMERON'S Hampden verdict

on Ian Redford for him.

"SOME FANS DIDN'T LIKE THIS, BUT I'VE GOT TO MAKE THE DECISIONS."

He added: "Switches don't always come off, but this one certainly did when Ian scored with that floater over Hamish McAlpine.

"Pleased? I was delighted particularly for the players and the fans."

United were sorely disappointed. They thought a super shot by Paul Sturrock was a scorer and would have given then a 2-0 lead.

However, though Mr Pringle didn't have a good match, he was right to rule that John Holt was offside and interfer-

ing with play. TV pictures later showed that Holt was in line with the flight of the ball.

Despite criticisms, Rangers went through the League Cup unbeaten in 11 games which is a splendid performance.

"Some of the pressure is now off with a UEFA place assured for next season," added Greig.

"But I've already made the point to the players that the Cup and the League are still there to be won with the chance of even more important European games.

"Youngsters such as Dalziel, Billy Mackay and Kenny Black have had a taste of what is expected of a Rangers player. There are others who may get a chance this season, but I still say it is difficult to bring in a lot of youngsters and still get results consistently.

"Rangers played badly against Partick Thistle in the League, but look at the improvement since. The benefit of the performance at Parkhead a week ago rubbed off on the League Cup Final display.

Style

"We realise at Ibrox that supporters want something more than just a result. There must be style and excitement to go with it."

I thought the man who made Rangers tick was Robert Russell. In the second half he began to counter Eamonn Bannon and pass the ball well.

And Colin Jackson gave a really excellent display throughout even though the quick-fire Sturrock should have scored a couple in the first half and put United on Easy Street.

FIRHILL ACTION . . . Jim Blair reports

STAND-BY CELT

Nick sits it out

CELTIC fans who rate Charlie Nicholas too good a player to be sitting on a substitutes' bench won't get any arguments from manager Billy McNeill!

However, recently last season's superkid — and the current Young Player of the Year — has had to settle for a stand-by place in the Celtic side.

Again he played a substitute's role in the 2-0 victory over Partick Thistle.

Nicholas has featured from the start in only seven of Celtic's 14

NICHOLAS   McCLUSKEY   ROUGH

Premier League games, scoring three goals.

So how has the 19-year-old striker reacted to going from being a feature artist to a supporting act?

"No problems," McNeill told me. "I reckon Nick has put more into his game as a result of being in and out of the side.

"Last season George McCluskey was in a similar position, and it most certainly benefitted him.

To my mind McCluskey is the most skilful front-player in Scottish

"Obviously Charlie Nicholas is too good a player to be sitting on the bench every week . . . but it's comforting to know that I've three good front players when you include Frank McGarvey."

To underline McNeill's point about McCluskey, he contrived to score the best goal I've seen all season.

football, and he proved that by inventing space from a Dom Sullivan throw-in in 25 minutes before firing an unstoppable shot high past Alan Rough.

The goal which killed the game came on the hour when a Davie Provan cross-shot was deflected past Rough off the shins of defender Andy Dunlop.

Celtic, meanwhile, improve on and off the park. Tomorrow Danny McGrain makes yet another move towards first team fitness when he plays against Queen's Park at Hampden.

Tommy Burns, who in McNeill's words has made remarkable progress from his leg injury, may appear as a substitute.

IT'S RANGERS

PENALTY No. 1 . . . Ally McCoist sends Celtic 'keeper Pat Bonner the wrong way from the spot to put Rangers 1-0 ahead.

PENALTY No.2 . . . this time Bonner parries McCoist's extra-time spot-kick, but the Rangers striker followed up to shoot the winner.

MILK CUP FINAL ACTION...JIM BLAIR REPORTS FROM WEMBLEY

★ GOAL No. 2 . . . Ally McCoist leaves Celtic 'keeper Pat Bonner lying in despair as he dashes away to celebrate putting Rangers two goals ahead at Hampden.

ACTION REPLAY

TOP MAN . . . Liverpool's Ian Rush with the Player of the Year award in London last night.

LIVERPOOL are keeping their manager Joe Fagan waiting for his first trophy . . .

For they were held to a goalless draw by arch rivals Everton in a marvellous two-hour Milk Cup marathon at Wembley.

Winners of this competition for the past two years — when they beat Spurs and Manchester United after extra time — Liverpool had to fight for everything against a spirited, competitive Everton team inspired by midfield player Peter Reid.

Everton showed from the start that they were not prepared to let Liverpool settle — and were quick to play the ball up front in an effort to commit central defenders Mark Lawrenson and Alan Hansen.

In fact, they should have been awarded a penalty in seven minutes following a mistake by eccentric Liverpool goalkeeper Bruce Grobbelaar. Adrian Heath shot as he lay on the ground only to see Hansen juggle the ball clear with his thigh and left hand.

Midway through the first-half Liverpool got their act together and forced four successive corners.

But 35-goal Ian Rush, a one-time Everton fan, only had one shot to show for his first-half efforts, and that was blocked by Everton keeper Neville Southall.

Everton's efforts in that first-half seemed to have sapped some of their strength and enthusiasm after the interval.

And with Dalglish only showing in flashes, it was left to Graeme Souness to inspire Liverpool.

However, it just wasn't Rush's day — and in 65 minutes he unbelievably hooked the ball over the crossbar from inside the six-yard area.

As expected, Liverpool were the first team to show in extra-time. Four minutes had gone when Southall had a marvellous diving save to prevent Rush putting Liverpool in front.

By this time Liverpool were dominating the proceedings and a goal looked very much on the cards.

Ronnie Whelan did manage to get the ball in the net in the second period of extra-time, but the "score" was ruled offside.

Near the end of this enthralling match Liverpool again had the ball in the net — and again the standside linesman flagged for offside.

The replay will now take place on Wednesday at Maine Road, Manchester.

Ian Rush did have something to celebrate last night — he won the English PFA Player of the Year award. He finished well clear of Anfield skipper Graeme Souness and third-placed Bryan Robson, of Manchester United.

Fagan waits for glory

EVERTON	0

Attendance: 100,000. Receipts: £670,000.

LIVERPOOL	0

(After extra time)

Everton — Southall; Stevens, Bailey, Ratcliffe, Mountfield, Reid, Irvine, Keith, Sharp, Richardson, Sheedy. Sub., Harper.

Liverpool — Grobbelaar; Neal, Kennedy, Lawrenson, Whelan, Hansen, Dalglish, Lee, Rush, Johnston, Souness. Sub., Robinson.

Referee — A. Robinson, Portsmouth.

FOOTBALL TODAY

Reserve League—Celtic v. Motherwell, Falkirk v. Queen's Park, Hamilton v. Ayr.

FIXTURES CHAOS . . . WALLACE MOORE reporting

LEAGUE SET TO BURST

THE postponement of the Dundee United v Aberdeen League game may lead to an extension of the season.

Scottish League secretary Jim Farry confirmed yesterday that the management committee are reviewing the situation.

Farry said: "The question of an extension arises but that is not such a simple answer.

"The Scottish Cup Final (May 19), the Scotland v England international (May 26) and the France v Scotland game (June 1) all complicate the issue.

With the League season due to finish on May 12 — only seven Saturdays left — United face a minimum of 16 games, 13 in the League, two in the European Cup against Roma and the Scottish Cup quarter-final replay against Aberdeen at Tannadice on Wednesday.

Aberdeen have one less League game but are similarly committed in Europe against Porto. In addition, the winners of the Tanna-dice replay will face a Scottish Cup semi-final against Dundee on April 14.

United's Europe opponents Roma drew 0-0 at Ascoli yesterday.

Aberdeen boss Alex Ferguson meanwhile confirmed that the club have now received written offers of around £750,000 for Strachan on behalf of Italian clubs Verona and Genoa.

Aberdeen's Euro rivals Porto beat Farense 7-1 in their Portuguese League match.

"Could you put it in a CUP..?"

HAMPDEN PHOTO TEAM

ERIC CRAIG,
ROBERT HOTCHKISS,
KEN FERGUSON

IN PARADISE!

RANGERS threw Celtic out of Paradise yesterday with a League Cup-winning hat-trick by Ally McCoist.

They won dramatically at Hampden, routed forecasting pundits and left Celtic in an ill-mannered rage at what they considered to be referee injustices.

It was a display of nerve, determination and persistence by Rangers which was orchestrated over 120 minutes of hard, unclassical slogging by the superb Robert Russell.

Maximum

Rarely has one player done so much for so many in a controversial final which, in the end, Rangers deserved to win.

Referee Bob Valentine awarded three penalties—two to Rangers, one to Celtic.

A goal following one of them sealed the game for Rangers and the other gave Celtic a 2-2 leveller which pushed proceedings into extra time.

Rarely has Hampden seen such drama mingled with the stubborn soccer mediocrity usually stemming from a collision of the Old Firm.

Eight players were cautioned and I cannot say I agreed with every booking. They were Mark Reid, Jim Melrose and Roy Aitken of Celtic, and Sandy Clark, Russell, John McClelland, Dave McPherson and McCoist of Rangers.

It was Aitken's booking a minute from the end in an incident with McCoist which finally upset Celtic players to an extent that some were thoroughly and inexcusably unruly.

Ignored

A senior policeman had to step between protesting players and referee Bob Valentine as he waited for the touchline for the presentation ceremony.

However aggrieved Celtic players may have felt about Mr Valentine's match-handling, there was no excuse for such provocative behaviour which the referee will, apparently, NOT report to the Scottish League.

It was a shame that this scene marred the end.

For there were outstanding players on both sides and all

Silver lining —thanks to mighty Mac

 RANGERS 3
McCoist (44 min pen, 61, 104). Att: 66,369.
CELTIC 2
McClair (67), Reid (89 pen). After extra time.

ALEX CAMERON'S HAMPDEN VERDICT

26 gave absolutely maximum effort.

The super Celt was Tommy Burns. After a slow start he ended by nearly tilting the balance in Celtic's favour.

Agatha Christie could not have scripted more thrills or improbabilities as the match unfolded.

It was 2-2 at the end of the 90 minutes and in the first period of extra time Valentine penalised Roy Aitken a couple of steps inside the box for fouling McCoist.

There was no doubt about the award in my view. McCoist took the kick and Pat Bonner lunged to his left — having previously gone

the wrong way for the first spot award.

He stopped the ball but couldn't hold it and McCoist followed up to score.

And so the Cup went from the Parkhead trophy room to Ibrox.

Rangers' first penalty claim was in 23 minutes but Valentine ignored Tom McAdam's challenge on John MacDonald and little happened until a minute from half-time.

Murdo MacLeod tackled Robert Russell and there seemed no argument about the penalty from which McCoist opened the scoring.

The second Rangers goal in 61 minutes looked like the winner to all of us, including

the Rangers team—but not to Celtic

Roy Aitken and Sandy Clark chased a huge wind-assisted kick-out from Peter McCloy.

Clark managed to get his head to the ball and nudge it to McCoist. From that moment Pat Bonner had no chance.

This was where Celtic showed their mettle — although not quite enough of it to win.

In fact, a foul on Burns just outside the penalty area in 67 minutes led to the best goal

Burns decided to take the free-kick himself. He paused over the ball then flicked it over the shocked Rangers line-up.

Paused

Brian McClair ran clear to swivel and finish off as good a "dead-ball" goal as anyone could care to see.

The match was 90 seconds into injury time when Celtic equalised.

McCoist was involved again —but this time conceding a penalty for a tackle on MacLeod.

The pressure on Mark Reid as he moved forward to take the kick must have been very nearly unbearable.

But he showed not a flicker of doubt as he slotted the ball away from McCloy.

Rangers looked the more likely to tire in the extra-time. Instead they were more purposeful than Celtic for most of the exhausting 30 minutes.

They snatched their winner with 16 minutes to go and, close as they came to it, Celtic could not equalise for a second time in the game.

RANGERS: McCloy, Nicholl, Dawson, McClelland, Paterson, McPherson, Russell, McCoist, Clark, MacDonald, Cooper. Subs —McAdam, Burns.

CELTIC: Bonner, McGrain, Reid, Aitken, McAdam, MacLeod, Provan, McStay, McGarvey, Burns, McClair. Subs — Sinclair, Melrose.

REFEREE: R. B. Valentine, Dundee.

SMILES BETTER... Ally McCoist grins and bears the weight of beaming Sandy Clark as delighted Davie Cooper joins in the glee after McCoist's second goal.

Goal hero McCoist talks to Rodger Baillie

RANGERS' hat-trick hero Ally McCoist left Hampden loaded with rewards for the League Cup goals that helped put him in the soccer history books.

It was the first hat-trick in an Old Firm Final since Celtic centre Billy McPhail scored three in the famous 7-1 defeat of Rangers in 1957.

Happy Ally collected his winner's medal and was presented with the match ball as a souvenir of the greatest day in his football life.

Bonus

He also picked up a gold watch, the prize given to the player who scored the last goal in yesterday's match.

But he missed out on one of the major awards from the sponsors, Skol Lager. Rangers would have collected £10,000 if Ally's three goals had come in the first 90 minutes. Extra time goals didn't count for that bonus.

However, it didn't bother the 21-year-old,

ALLY DELIGHTED TO BE SPOT ON

who as well as grabbing Rangers' second goal, was at the centre of all the penalty action, scoring from two of them and conceding the spot kick from which Celtic scored.

McCoist, signed from Sunderland last year, was linked with his old club a few months ago, and he admitted: "All that transfer talk was unsettling. I only wanted to play for Rangers, and play well.

"I'm just delighted to have played a part in this success. And I'm happy for the manager

Jock Wallace, and for the man who signed me, John Greig.

"The last time I scored a hat-trick was for St Johnstone against Berwick Rangers. There were a few more people watching this time."

He explained why he replaced regular spot-kick expert Davie Cooper, and took the gamble that paid off.

"I was feeling good, so I shouted to Davie I would take the kick when we got the first penalty, and he waved to me to go ahead."

He joked about his long run-up. "I heard a

few shouts as I was going to take the kick. I should have had ear muffs on".

Rangers boss Wallace, a winner again only four months after his return to Ibrox, picked out Bobby Russell as man of the match.

"He had a tremendous game, and was the outstanding player.

"Craig Paterson did well also. He had a good game agaist Linfield last week and we decided to take a chance on him."

Advantage

Wallace added: "I delayed announcing the line-up because I wanted to psyche the players up. We had our main tactics talk on Saturday night, not that they paid much attention when they got on the park".

Ibrox skipper John McClelland, who collected his first winner's medal in four attempts, said: "I thought the advantage had swung to Celtic when they scored that equaliser, but we just had to get on with it.

"And I felt that the first goal in extra time would settle it."

RECORD SPORT

PRICELESS

SKOL CUP FINAL SPECIAL

Ferguson

DUNDEE UNITED..0
(H.T. 0-1)

RANGERS..............1

Ferguson (44). Attendance—44,698.

THE SKOL CUP was draped in blue and white ribbons last night thanks to a super goal by Iain Ferguson.

Jock Wallace's most expensive signing therefore kept the League Cup at Ibrox for the second year running in a fleeting moment of high drama 15 seconds from half-time.

Dundee United's Rangers jinx had struck again, and the ball came off the right foot of a player schooled just along the road from Tannadice.

It was a mediocre final for the connoisseur but as nearly 40,000 of the Hampden crowd were cheering Rangers, most went home happy.

Oddly, it was not a question of United losing their nerve against the team they seem incapable of beating on big occasions. Rangers merely snatched with more speed, accuracy and panache one of the match's rare chances.

Spirited

Most efficient man on the pitch—and the only one not getting a share of the sponsors cash—was referee Brian McGinlay. He kept a firm clamp on a game which could have become over-tough.

He took the names of Robert Russell, Dave McPherson and Davie Cooper of Rangers and Paul Hegarty and Richard Gough of United.

Although United made spirited efforts, if in flashes, in the second half, Rangers deserved to win. They kept their cool, with Cooper causing United most worry.

As the Rangers players jumped on each other with joy at the finish and Jock Wallace rushed on to shake hands with them, the United men stood sadly aside, beaten yet again by Rangers.

United were baffled by the defeat and would not use as an excuse the fact that Ralph Milne, doubtful before the game, had to be replaced after only 10 minutes by Stuart Beddie.

In the final 15 minutes Rangers substituted Robert Prytz for Russell and Clark replaced John Holt in United's team.

Rangers final throw of the dice was to bring on Dave

HERE WE GO . . . Rangers striker Iain Ferguson splits Dundee United defenders Dave Narey, left, and Richard Gough to score the all-important goal yesterday.

FLOORED . . . Rangers defender Dave McPherson, who was awarded the Man of the Match prize, upends United striker Paul Sturrock.

WORLD CUP QUALIFYING MATCH

SCOTLAND
v. SPAIN

HAMPDEN PARK, GLASGOW—Kick-off 8 p.m.
14th NOVEMBER, 1984

ADMISSION TO THIS MATCH WILL BE AS FOLLOWS:

BY TICKET ONLY

South Stand (centre) £10.00	South Stand (wings)...........£8.00
Enclosures.........................£3.50	Terracing (covered)...........£3.50

Terracing (uncovered).................£3.00

Tickets will be on sale from today onwards at the SFA Offices, 6 Park Gardens, Glasgow, from 9.30 a.m.-4 p.m. daily (Saturday, 9.30 a.m.-12 noon) and at the following agencies:

Glasgow:
Scottish Football League, 188 West Regent Street, G2. Queen's Park FC, Hampden Park, G42. R. M. Bell, 1507 Dumbarton Road, G13. A.T. Mays, 335 Duke Street; 37 Dunkenny Square, Drumchapel, G15; 537 Victoria Road; The Pollok Centre, 45 Cowglen Road. Royal Stores, 1016 Pollokshaws Road, G41. W. Marley, 7 Grantlea Terrace, Mount Vernon, G32.

DUNBARTONSHIRE:
G. Langland, 18 High Street, Dumbarton.

LANARKSHIRE:
A. T. Mays, 187 Main Street, Coatbridge; 24 Main Street, Wishaw; 26 The Plaza, East Kilbride; 74-76 Quarry Street, Hamilton; Merry Street, Motherwell.

RENFREWSHIRE:
A. T. Mays, 74 Causeyside Street, Paisley, 4 County Place, Paisley; 56 West Blackhall Street, Greenock.

AYRSHIRE:
A. T. Mays, Dockhead Street, Saltcoats; 15 Rivergate, Irvine; 20 Bank Street, Kilmarnock; 5 Alloway Street, Ayr.

STIRLINGSHIRE:
Bairnspool, Brockville Park, Falkirk. Scottish & Universal Newspapers Ltd., 40 Craigs, Stirling.

FIFE:
Brown's Bazaar, 51-53 High Street, Kirkcaldy.

TAYSIDE:
Dundee FC Shop, The Keiller Centre, Dundee. Saintspool, 31 North Methven Street, Perth. Scottish & Universal Newspapers Ltd., 36 Tay Street, Perth.

EDINBURGH & DISTRICT:
A. T. Mays, c/o John Menzies Holdings Ltd., 107 Princes Street, Edinburgh; Leith Athletics, 208/210 Leith Walk, Edinburgh; 1 Meadowbank Avenue, Edinburgh; 9 Drum Street, Gilmerton, Edinburgh; The Forum Shopping Centre, Wester Hailes, Edinburgh.

Postal applications, enclosing the correct remittance and a stamped, addressed envelope, will be accepted for all prices of tickets except £10, and should be sent to the SFA, 6 PARK GARDENS, GLASGOW, G3 7YF.

HATELEY'S GOLDEN WINNER

INTER TAKE A TUMBLE

AFTER their 3-0 UEFA Cup success over Rangers, Inter Milan were brought down to earth yesterday.

They lost the Milan derby 2-1 in front of a capacity 80,000 crowd with England striker Mark Hateley grabbing AC Milan's winner — his fifth goal in seven matches.

Threat

Inter's Liam Brady and Karl-Heinz Rummenigge were strangely subdued but livewire striker Sandro Altobelli was a constant threat apart from scoring Inter's goal.

Graeme Souness experienced joy, agony and then relief in Sampdoria's 2-2 draw with Torino in Genoa.

Scotland's World Cup skipper scored a first-half goal, missed a penalty—his second failure in three games — and then celebrated gleefully as Trevor Francis hit an injury-time equaliser.

In Spain, Steve Archibald's goal famine continued yesterday as unbeaten Barcelona won 2-1 away to Atletico Madrid.

He last hit a league goal in his debut against Real Madrid eight games ago.

But yesterday's victory earned him a £1000 bonus.

RECORD SPORT

BOY BLUE
pounces to repay Rangers

ALEX CAMERON at Hampden

Mitchell in place of Ferguson who looked unhappy to spend the last 10 minutes on the bench.

However, he could think back to his smashing Cup-winning goal seconds before the interval whistle.

Cooper began to move with a pass for Russell. He switched it on to Redford who squirmed through in a very tight position to Ferguson. The ex-Dundee striker took a step forward and sent the ball swirling unmistakeably into the net.

In the first half a left-foot shot by Russell which hit the side netting in 25 minutes and a 35-yard blaster from Eamonn Bannon a minute later were the best attempts.

But there could have been a penalty when McPherson appeared to push Paul Sturrock in the box. The referee ignored this as well as appeals by McPherson.

Europe

United had a better second half. They began to get passes together as they hadn't managed to in the first 45 minutes. And after five minutes both Kirkwood and Beedie had chances before John McClelland kicked the ball away close to the line with Davie Dodds near him.

Victory means that Rangers are automatically into Europe next season — 10 days before they make a formal exit from this season's UEFA competition against Milan.

NONE WAS REALLY BRILLIANT IN THE 90 MINUTES BUT DAVE McPHERSON WAS GIVEN THE SPONSORS MAN OF THE MATCH AWARD.

United must have felt on the bus run home that they had given everything. Why they should go out to Rangers consistently remains a mystery.

■ I'VE won the Cup ... Rangers goal hero Iain Ferguson can't contain his joy after tucking away the Skol Cup Final winner **Pictures: ERIC CRAIG.**

★ THE TEAMS

Dundee United—McAlpine, Holt, Malpas, Gough, Hegarty, Narey, Bannon, Milne, Kirkwood, Sturrock, Dodds. Subs— Beedie, Clark.

Rangers — McCloy, Dawson, McClelland, McPherson, Paterson, Redford, Russell, Fraser, Ferguson, McCoist, Cooper. Subs—Mitchell, Prytz.

Referee—B. McGinlay, Balfron.

"I think he's very pleased—he gave me a happy growl..."

FOOTBALL TODAY

Reserve League—Dumbarton v. Dundee, St. Mirren v. Aberdeen, Clyde v. St. Johnstone.

BP Youth Cup (first round)— Motherwell v. Hamilton.

SPOTLIGHT ON YESTERDAY'S GAME DOWN SOUTH

Back in business

LIVERPOOL appear to have cured their bout of soccer hiccups.

That was the main message to emerge from yesterday's victory over Nottingham Forest at the City Ground.

It was almost as though the indignity of starting a match in the bottom three of the table for the first time in 20 years made them react like aristocrats who feel insulted — with a mixture of cold disdain and sheer determination.

With Ian Rush up front to create his unique brand of opportunist menace once again and Mark Lawrenson restoring authority to the

NOTTM FOREST.............0 LIVERPOOL.............2

Scorers — Whelan (36 mins), Rush (51). Attendance—19,838.

midfield confidence flooded back for Liverpool.

The victory was only their third in 12 League outings this season.

AND KENNY DALGLISH WAS THE ARCHITECT.

He provided the crosses for both Liverpool's goals to show that, at 33, he can still be a handful for any defence.

Clever

The first came after 36 minutes when Dalglish eluded a tackle from Kenny Swain and hooked in a superb cross for Ronnie Whelan to head past Steve Sutton.

Forest could hardly put a telling move together throughout and Liverpool completely controlled the game.

They scored a second after 51 minutes. Phil Neal shrugged off a tackle by Steve Hodge and slipped a clever ball to Dalglish. He ran into the penalty area and pushed a cross into the path of Ian Rush who bundled the ball in from six yards for his first League goal of the season.

Forest suddenly raised their game after an hour.

But it was too late

KENNY DALGLISH ... set up goals

OFF THE RECORD

JIM BLAIR'S OFF-BEAT LOOK AT SPORT

IT'S surely a commentary on televised football that managers are constantly brought into play as so-called linkmen.

For instance, Aberdeen boss Alex Ferguson formed an entertaining double-act with Archie Macpherson for the BBC Scotland transmission of the Skol Cup Final ... and they hardly paused for breath.

I'm sure if they spoke as much in the house during a week as they did for 90 minutes at Hampden, their wives would be delighted!

Seriously, while their comments did overlap on occasions, I did feel Fergie was anxious not simply to play pat-a-cake, knowing the BBC cheque is in the post.

His pertinent observations included a back-handed compliment for referee Brian McGinlay . . . *"WHEN HE WANTS TO BE, HE IS THE BEST REFEREE IN THE COUNTRY."*

He criticised Davie Cooper for wandering into the middle during the match . . . "He's a naturally left-footed left winger — and that's where I like to see him play for Scotland."

Challenge

The fact that Alex Ferguson is Scotland's coach should not be lost on viewers . . . or Davie Cooper for that matter.

Dundee United's international striker, Paul Sturrock, wasn't missed either when he went down in the Rangers penalty box in the first half, the inference being the player's action owed more to Jacques Cousteau than a foul challenge.

Straightforward opinion is always preferred to cotton-wool conversation and certainly neither Archie nor Fergie bodyswerved John McClelland's reluctance to hold the old League Cup aloft.

Instead he passed the "parcel" to Davie Cooper.

While Fergie was an

obvious fill-in football voice for BBC, I thought ITV boobed by plonking Manchester United's Ron Atkinson down beside Brian Moore for the Nottingham Forest—Liverpool match.

Having watched his own side concede five goals at Goodison against Everton, I thought he was the last person to criticise anyone else's defence 24 hours later.

A bit like advising someone to take care crossing the road after you've been knocked down by a bus!

Certainly there is no shortage of football personalities prepared to chunter on radio and television. If snooker follows suit, it's only a matter of time before Ted Lowe is joined by Cannon and Ball!

HEAR.. WHAT'S THIS DOUBLE TALK?

KENNY— SIMPLY YEARS AHEAD

KENNY DALGLISH'S form in the 2-0 win at Nottingham Forest is recurring proof that he, like Liverpool, will not be written off.

At 33, and with a record 95 caps for Scotland, Dalglish—surely one of the best-ever buys in football — got a further international boost over the weekend.

Tommy Docherty, who gave Dalglish his first-ever game for Scotland, reckons King Kenny's future is as an Under-21 player!

Now manager of Wolves, the Doc is convinced that

Dalglish should be appointed player-coach of Scotland's Under-21s after the Mexico World Cup.

"His influence as an over-age player would be tremendous for young players," the Doc enthused. "Just for kids to be in the same side would be a fantastic boost.

"KENNY IS THE COMPLETE PRO.

"Players such as Dalglish and Graeme Souness mustn't be discarded once they fall out of international football. They have too much to contribute."

JONES WRAPS IT UP

WHEN RAF corporal Steve Jones completed the world's fastest marathon (2hrs, 8mins, 5secs) in Chicago recently, American journalists marvelled at his time.

It was only his second marathon—and the only one he has completed — yet he knocked eight seconds off the world-best time.

Perhaps the most amazing statistic is that the fastest mile he ran was at the 23rd-mile stage. Whereas he took 4mins 55secs for the first mile, he knocked 14 seconds off that with just over three miles to go.

My personal Marathon time is two minutes ... and that's just to get the wrapper off!

McMINN HURT

RANGERS' £100,000 signing Ted McMinn could be out of action for the next three weeks. He was injured in the reserve match at Ibrox which Celtic won 1-0, and detained in hospital overnight with a leg injury and concussion.

RECORD SPORT

5

SHAME ON YOU

Scorers: Celtic—McClair (70 min.). Rangers—Durrant (62), Cooper (84, pen.). Attendance: 74,219.

Hot-heads hand it to Rangers

DISGRACEFUL indiscipline lost Celtic the Skol League Cup at Hampden yesterday, and none could have an ounce of sympathy with them as they watched Rangers collecting the silverware for the 14th time.

The SFA must surely act on the shameful Final shambles. Seven Celts were booked — plus three Rangers players—and then Mo Johnston was sent off. Tony Shepherd also got a red card, but remarkably was allowed to continue when it turned out he had done nothing wrong.

It was the rowdiest finish to a Cup Final, in which the entertainment had been good but not brilliant, that I can remember. The rowing involving Celtic players when Johnston was ordered off for an off-the-ball incident with Stuart Munro in the last two minutes was simply shocking.

The score at this point was 2-1. Davie Cooper had tucked away a controversial 84th-minute penalty, and Celtic, the better team, could see victory slipping from their grasp after fighting back from being one down.

Religious

While Ranger Ally McCoist was being booked after lying on the ground apparently injured, linesman Arthur Wilson, of Rosyth, saw an incident between Munro and Johnston.

He flagged referee Davie Syme who called both players to the side and checked with the linesman they were the correct two. He cautioned Munro, but had to send Johnston off as he had already been yellow carded after a tangle with Jimmy Nicholl, who was later nabbed himself for fouling Brian McClair.

Johnston crossed himself as he ran off, even though Celtic players were told only a couple of weeks ago to stop making religious signs. All hell then broke loose and Syme wrongly showed the red card to Shepherd in the midst of the kind of melee expected in a pub at closing time.

It then became very nearly a pitched battle which was stopped only by manager Davie Hay running to the line and pushing his players back. Three senior policemen moved towards the incident. Syme called his linesman to his side and stood on the line, hands behind his back with the red card still visible.

Sordid

Some kind of order was eventually restored so that the game could be finished. But it is awful that once again the talking point of an important match is not the football, but sordid incidents arising from it.

RANGERS DESERVED TO WIN IF ONLY BECAUSE THEY KEPT THEIR COOL ON SUCH AN EXPLOSIVE OCCASION.

Three of the early cautions were for fouls on Davie Cooper who, although he once or twice exaggerated his fall, was badly treated. So it was ironic that Cooper swept away a penalty to win the game after jersey-pulling conflict between rival skippers Roy Aitken and Terry Butcher.

Rangers played minus injured player-

SEEING RED . . . Hampden referee David Syme shows Celtic's Mo Johnston the red card after an incident with Rangers' Stuart Munro, then turns his attention to Tony Shepherd. This time the Celt was shown the red card, but allowed to stay on the field.

RODGER BAILLIE at Douglas Park

INJURY-HIT Aberdeen could have striker Joe Miller back in the League team against Dundee this week.

Miller set for recall

Miller has been out for six weeks since damaging his hand opening a bottle filled with cash at a charity function.

After Dons' 1-0 victory against bottom-of-the-League Hamilton at windswept Douglas Park, manager Alex Ferguson said: "We will arrange a special fixture this week to sharpen Joe up for a possible first-team comeback."

Now there's a light at the end of Aberdeen's injury tunnel. For Neil Simpson, out for seven months, is

also set to start a comeback campaign.

Despite their troubles, the Dons are only five points behind joint League leaders, Dundee United.

But this young Aberdeen side have one major failing—they don't go for the jugular when they're on top.

It took a world class save by Jim Leighton to stop Hamilton's Adrian Sprott equalising Jim Bett's goal.

WALLACE MOORE at Dens Park

THE huge sigh of relief from Dundee represented the greatest moment of atmosphere in their 3-0 defeat of Falkirk at Dens Park.

The club, with ambitions of qualifying for Europe this time after two narrow failures, could not have afforded another defeat hard on the heels of losing a total of seven goals to Celtic and St Mirren in successive games.

They got there in the end in a match watched by only 3715—but Falkirk gave them many anxious moments even after Graham Harvey put Dundee in front after just eight minutes.

Dundee boss Jocky Scott said: "We badly needed to win to stop

DUNDEE SO GRATEFUL

our slide and I am grateful we did.

"But we allowed Falkirk to dictate for a long time when we should have been burying them after the early goal."

Ian Angus and substitute Colin Hendry made the game safe for Dundee by adding second half goals.

But they finished with another headache over midfield man John Brown, who suffered a recurrence of a knee injury.

JIM BLAIR at Fir Park

HIBS slumped to their seventh defeat of the season and third-bottom place after the 4-1 defeat by Motherwell at Fir Park.

After a match played in gale-force conditions, manager John Blackley said: "We've blown hot and cold this season . . . and when we blow cold, it's bloody cold!

"Against Motherwell, anything that was played into the area caused us problems. Alan Rough had some fine saves — but they resulted from his not getting to the ball in the first place."

Blackley then admitted he had made a bid for another goalkeeper, but would not reveal his identity.

Motherwell boss Tommy McLean

Blackley's icy blast

was as pleased as Blackley was disappointed. He saw his side lead 3-1 through first-half goals from Tom McAdam, Ray Farningham and John Reilly, with Gordon Chisholm scoring for Hibs.

McLean said: "Besides scoring four goals we hit the crossbar three times."

Man of the match Andy Walker scored a last-minute penalty after Gordon Rae had brought down Reilly.

RECORD SPORT

CELTIC!

SEEING BLUE...referee Syme awards the penalty which won the game for Rangers, much to the delight of Ibrox striker Ally McCoist.

DAVID SYME wrote the Skol Cup Final book. And no doubt when we see the film version again it will look like the Nasty Video of Scottish Football.

I know it's difficult to put aside 10 name-checks and Mo Johnston's late ordering-off, but for the most part of the 90 minutes this was a pulsating, pacey Final.

Around 40 million viewers throughout the world watched this Old Firm head-to-head ... and I'm told the football punters in Venezuela thought the referee had gone Caracas when he started flashing yellow cards.

They should talk. Over there a popular pastime is shooting referees. This isn't allowed in Scotland as the referee is already an endangered species.

Rangers got the result without playing to their capabilities. The fact that Celtic were the better team over the piece will be little or no consolation.

However, the discipline of the Celtic side was appalling ... even to the extent that Johnston purposely blessed himself after being sent off. In the cauldron of an Old Firm atmosphere that is nothing short of incitement to riot.

Best

Dundee United manager Jim McLean, whose job it was to officially interrupt Archie Macpherson, made plenty of professional points without getting his grammar right.

But McLean did pay tribute to both teams in that they both went out with a positive attitude. Me? I thought that was how cup finals were won.

To be fair, I think Jim McLean is one of the best coaches in Scottish football. But as a football commentator he does make mistakes —something he finds hard to forgive if you happen to be a football writer!

Mac letting slips show

★ LIVERPOOL player-manager Kenny Dalglish didn't mince words after the 4–1 defeat at Luton. He said: "We got what we deserved—absolutely nothing."

Meanwhile Luton boss John Moore made yet another manic managerial decision when he refused to let Town's hat-trick striker Mike Newell speak to the Press. He said: "The game is about teams not individuals." Only one individual in his team scored a hat-trick against Liverpool.

THISTLE HOME FROM HOME

PARTICK THISTLE'S great revival has given a belated injection of Jags appeal in and around dear old Maryhill. Unbeaten in their past seven matches — and only eight points off the First Division pace despite being fourth bottom — Thistle are on the verge of Scottish football history.

For on Wednesday they play Dunfermline in the first of FOUR successive home matches...although that's not strictly accurate. The match sandwiched between Airdrie and East Fife at Firhill is an "away" game against Clyde, their official lodgers. Only Thistle could play away from home at home.

HEARTS' MISERY

ALEX CAMERON at Hampden

manager Graeme Souness and their handicap seemed to be more severe than that of Celtic, who couldn't field the injured Tommy Burns. In addition, neither Cammy Fraser nor Ted McMinn was replaced by David MacFarlane in 73 minutes.

Celtic had the edge in the first half, although Rangers, with less of the ball, were still dangerous. A good Celtic move ended with a McClair shot across goal which Chris Woods held. He went on from that to have his best game for Rangers.

Pat Bonner tipped a magnificent Fraser free-kick on to the bottom of his left-hand post. And Aitken galloped half the length of the park to set up Johnston who slammed in a shot which Woods touched against a post.

There were a series of such goal tries, but the match had the look of a goalless draw until

Ian Durrant grabbed his second goal in successive Old Firm games. He slotted the ball away in 62 minutes off a Fraser free-kick.

When Celtic levelled it was one of the best goals seen at Hampden in a decade. McClair hit the ball fiercely from 16 yards, an instinctive right-foot shot which swirled high into the corner of the goal.

IT WAS THE KIND OF GOAL WHICH SHOULD HAVE BEEN A MATCH-WINNER, BUT CELTIC WENT ON TO LOSE IN INDIGNITY.

The roll of dishonour reads: Yellow cards— Aitken, McInally, Johnston, Whyte, Grant, Bonner, Archdeacon (Celtic); Nicholl, McCoist, Munro (Rangers). Red card — Johnston (Celtic).

Celtic—Bonner, Grant, MacLeod, Aitken, Whyte, McGhee, McClair, P. McStay, Johnston, Shepherd, McInally. Subs—W. McStay, Archdeacon.

Rangers—Woods, Nicholl, Munro, Fraser, Dawson, Butcher, Ferguson, McMinn, McCoist, Durrant, Cooper. Subs—MacFarlane, Fleck.

Referee—D. Syme, Rutherglen.

"It's full of yellow cards."

RESULTS

Skol Cup Final—Celtic 1, Rangers 2.

English Div. One — Manchester City 1, Manchester Utd. 1.

JIM KEAN reports

IF DUNDEE UNITED needed a warm-down at Tynecastle, Hearts' thoughts were probably more in line with a lie down...

To get over the shock of only getting a point.

For the second time this season they turned in a five-star performance against Dundee United.

And the fact that they at least managed to get one point this time didn't seem much consolation to anyone.

Adamant

The timing of Paul Sturrock's two goals — right on half-time and full time — clearly hurt.

But it was the manner of the second which took up most of the after-match conversation.

Manager Alex MacDonald and his players were convinced Sturrock was offside.

Not surprisingly the player said he wasn't and unfortunately for Hearts, referee Kenny Hope and his linesman agreed.

"I'm very disappointed at

losing the two goals," said MacDonald.

"We out-played them and, in the end, it was things beyond us which cost us a point."

But if Hearts felt hard-done-by with the late equaliser, United were equally adamant that it wasn't a penalty when Sandy Clark was brought down and Gary Mackay put the home side in front for the second time.

There was nothing dubious

about Hearts' first goal, a glorious drive from John Colquhoun.

United didn't look like scoring until Brian Whittaker missed a cross from the right and Sturrock pounced from close in.

There was almost as much incident after the game with Hearts' refusal to allow United back onto the pitch and the news that the Tynecastle club are to pay Aberdeen's share of the Cup Final ticket mix-up.

Chairman Wallace Mercer is going against the wishes of his fellow directors to do so.

Dickson blows it for Bankies

CLYDEBANK'S Joe Dickson won't score many better goals than the one he got at Kilbowie on Saturday...what a pity it was for St Mirren.

Dickson's second half blunder gave Saints a 1-1 draw, which was a fair result in very windy conditions. Three minutes earlier another mistake, this time by Saints' Peter Godfrey, had let Lex Grant put Clydebank ahead, writes DICK CURRIE.

Kilbowie defender Dickson is now beginning to think that the Paisley team are a jinx to him. The last time he played against them he was ordered off.

"The equaliser sure was a smashing goal," joked Saints manager Alex Miller afterwards. "But really I didn't think we deserved to lose after getting on top in the second half."

UPDATE

★ Diego Maradona handed Roma their first home defeat in 10 years yesterday.

The Argentinian ace struck the only goal for Napoli just after half-time.

Napoli are now equal with Juventus at the top of the Italian League on 11 points.

Gary Lineker smashed in two and Mark Hughes broke a 13 game goal drought yesterday as Spanish League leaders Barcelona powered to a 4-0 win against Las Palmas.

PEDIGREE STUFF!

IT was labelled and marketed as the downtown bone-crunching battle of the underdogs.

But for the 32,440 crowd at Maine Road — the lowest ever for a Manchester derby —it was pure pedigree stuff.

The only losers were the 10 million armchair fans who were unable to savour the atmosphere of a classic encounter which was being

MAN. CITY...................1
MAN. UNITED.............1

Scorers: City — McCarthy (50 mins.). United — Stapleton (46). Att—32,440.

televised live for the first time.

City, with new signings John Gidman, Tony Grealish and Imre Varadi making their home debuts, were more than equal to their neighbours.

But only two saves by Perry Suckling from Norman Whiteside in the dying minutes prevented United from snatching victory.

City were caught napping a minute after half time when Frank Stapleton headed home a Peter Barnes free-kick to put United in front.

But City battled back to equalise four minutes later with a powerful header by Mick McCarthy from Neil McNab's centre.

RECORD SPORT

BLUE  CHIP

WE'RE THE CHAMPS . . . Terry Butcher and Chris Woods lead their team-mates in a dressing room celebration.   Pictures: ERIC CRAIG

Title joy—after a moment of anguish

WHO ME . . ? Graeme Souness can't believe he is being sent off to spend the rest of the game in the stand with chairman David Holmes.

CHAMPIONS

Rangers plan £1m signings

RANGERS will plunge into the transfer market soon in a £1 million-plus revamp of their championship-winning team.

They will compete in the European Cup next season for the first time in nine years and Graeme Souness is desperate to do well.

His first spending could be £600,000 for Mark Hateley from AC Milan — but ignore rumours and reports that goalkeeper Chris Woods will be moving back south.

Souness also needs to bolster the right side of the team and could try again for £450,000 Eire international Ray Houghton, of Oxford.

The influence and experience of Souness has been paramount in Rangers' success. He has orchestrated them like a poker player and when he turned over his cards, most have been aces.

He admits he is still learning management and will be big enough to correct mistakes next season.

Inspired

A 1-1 draw with Aberdeen in a miserable, spoiling feud in which Souness himself was sent off for the second time this season—and a shock defeat for Celtic — put Rangers four points ahead.

Delighted Ibrox supporters massed on the Pittodrie pitch at the end and broke down a set of goalposts.

This, however, was the happier side of a mean and nasty 90 minutes in which every decision of referee Jim Duncan — however trivial — was challenged.

Duncan issued nine cautions, and I thought he booked Jim Bett twice. However, Dons boss Ian Porterfield later claimed that Neil Simpson had been yellow-carded with Bett.

Souness's 31st minute ordering off for a challenge on his marker, Brian Irvine, could have been the game's turning point.

But inspired by Terry Butcher—who headed a 40th minute goal — and Graham Roberts, Rangers held on

BUTCHER'S CLEAVER . . . Rangers skipper Terry Butcher roars his delight after scoring his vital goal —and Ally McCoist is equally ecstatic

ALEX CAMERON
.. on the end of a nine-year wait

PREMIER LEAGUE							
	P	W	D	L	F	A	Pt
Rangers	43	30	7	6	84	20	67
Celtic	43	27	9	7	90	40	63
Dundee Un	42	24	11	7	65	34	59
Aberdeen	43	20	16	7	60	29	56
Hearts	42	20	13	9	62	42	53
Dundee	43	17	12	14	67	54	46
St Mirren	43	12	12	19	36	50	36
Motherwell	43	10	12	21	42	64	32
Hibernian	43	9	13	21	42	69	31
Falkirk	43	6	10	25	30	67	26
Clydebank	43	6	12	25	34	91	24
Hamilton	43	6	9	28	36	86	21

after Irvine levelled just before half-time.

Jimmy Phillips came on to help the defence, replacing striker Robert Fleck.

Aberdeen are now sure to be in Europe next season and, on Saturday's evidence, are better than recent results suggest.

SOUNESS, OF COURSE, SHOULDN'T BE SENT OFF. IT IS THE WORST POSSIBLE EXAMPLE — AND HE KNOWS IT.

However, he is a target and resents the harness of a defender detailed to stop him. As manager and player

he may be too involved in the overall hype.

In a match so tense, is it reasonable to ask the determined midfielder to bear the added burden of management?

On his ordering off, he said: "I felt sick . . . but I want every Rangers player to be a winner and football is a physical game.

"There's no way, as long as I am manager, that we'll stop being physical. We won't change.

"It would be wrong to talk of our fans being specially

marvellous at Pittodrie. They've been that way all season.

"The Rangers club belongs to them. A lot of money has been earned this season and it will go where it benefits our supporters.

"I ALWAYS THOUGHT WE'D WIN THE TITLE. WE DESERVED TO GET IT."

Souness's worst memory this season is of losing to Hamilton Accies in the Scottish Cup.

For their temerity they will play in the First Division next season!

We're on our way!

YOU ain't seen nothing yet! That was the verdict yesterday from Rangers' expensive imports Terry Butcher and Chris Woods.

The England international double act have been major influences in the Ibrox club's season of glory — and they reckon there is more to come.

Skipper Butcher, signed from Ipswich for £750,000 last July, said: "It has been an unbelievable year, but this is only the start.

"We are now in the European Cup next season and I believe we have what it takes to go a long way in that competition.

"This year's experience will be of enormous benefit, and the management may have strengthened the squad still further by the start of the new season."

His views were echoed by goalkeeper Chris Woods, the £600,000 buy from Norwich, who said:

"Considering we trailed Celtic by nine points before Christmas, and are now four ahead of them going into the last match, it just shows the sort of team being built at Ibrox."

Butcher believes the signing of Graham Roberts from Spurs "to add some steel in the defence" was the turning-point of the season, while Woods thinks it was beating Celtic in the Skol Cup Final, and "removing a lot of the pressure from us."

In a matter of months, a leaking defence which lost 45 goals in 36 League matches last year, has been repaired by Woods, Butcher and Roberts.

PARKHEAD TITLE GLOOM...JIM BLAIR reporting

CELTIC COME A CROWN CROPPER

JIMMY GILMOUR *. . . celebrations*

CELTIC'S season disintegrated completely when they lost to Falkirk at Parkhead.

For the Brockville side, the result meant survival in the Premier League.

For Celtic, it cemented a disastrous day which saw them lose their Championship to arch-rivals Rangers.

So upset were the Parkhead support that manager Davie Hay was offered a choice of scarves to wear, and police were called when fans demanded an after-match "interview" with chairman Jack McGinn.

The irony for Celtic was that the man who scored the late winner for Falkirk was Jimmy Johnstone's nephew. And Jimmy Gilmour, currently on the transfer list, was almost apologetic when he described his goal.

"I felt a bit like Denis Law did when his goal for Manchester City put Manchester United into the Second Division," he said.

"I'm a life-long Celtic fan — and before the match my uncle warned me not to do any damage!"

Actually, the damage was done after only 40 seconds. Falkirk showed up the

glaring frailties in the Celtic defence when Sam McGivern toe-poked a goal.

Celtic's equaliser owed much to the indecision of the referee and his farside linesman — Falkirk's Jim Kerr clearly handled the ball OUTSIDE the area.

The linesman didn't flag for a penalty, the referee pointed outside the box and then changed his mind after Roy Aitken's protests. It let Brian McClair slot his 41st goal of the season.

Celtic have lost 40 goals this season while Rangers have conceded 17 fewer. That is surely a case for a new defence.

FACT FILE

■ Brian McClair's consolation goal for Celtic against Falkirk took his Premier total for the season to 35, and with one game remaining he leads the chase for the top honour in the Euro Golden Boot awards. His British challengers are Rangers' Ally McCoist with 33 goals, and Clive Allen, of Spurs, on 31.

■ Rangers boss Graeme Souness becomes the second Premier man to collect two red cards in League games. John Robertson, of Hearts, shares the dubious honour. In the First Division, Mark Shanks, Queen of the South, also has two, while in the Second Division, Cowdenbeath's Willie Paxton can claim a hat-trick of red cards.

GOLDEN SHOT
41 — McClair (Celtic); 35 — McCoist (Rangers); 30 — Sludden (Ayr); 28 — Brown (St Johnstone), Ferguson (Dundee United).

TEAM SCORE
	L	SKSC	Euro	Tot	Ave
Morton	86	2 4	0	94	2.04
Celtic	90	9 3	5	107	1.91
Rangers	84	12 0	8	104	1.89
Raith R.	69	0 13	0	82	1.82
Dundee U.	65	7 10	12	94	1.51

SHUT-OUTS
	P	GA	SO	Ave
Woods (Rangers)	53	32	28	52.8%
Thomson (Dun.)	58	40	29	50.0%
Graham (Stirling)	40	29	19	47.5%
Leighton (Abrdn)	47	35	21	44.6%

CARD INDEX
	P	Yellow	Red
Aberdeen	51	67	4
Celtic	56	54	2
Clydebank	50	58	2
Dundee	53	47	1
Dundee Utd	62	61	1
Falkirk	44	62	2
Hamilton	47	64	4
Hearts	52	52	5
Hibs	49	57	0
Motherwell	51	43	2
Rangers	55	59	7
St Mirren	49	50	6

FOOTBALL TODAY

English Div. 1 — Aston V. v. Sheffield W. Leicester v. Coventry (7.45), Liverpool v. Watford, Man City v. Nott. For., Newcastle v. Charlton, Norwich v. Everton, Q.P.R. v. Arsenal (11.30), Southampton v. West Ham, Spurs v. Man. Utd. (11.30).

English Div. 2 — Barnsley v. Huddersfield, Bradford v. Brighton, Crystal P. Portsmouth (12.0), Leeds v. West Brom, Plymouth v. Stoke, Reading v. Derby, Sheff. Utd. v. Ipswich.

English Div. 3 — Blackpool v. Chester, Bolton v. Doncaster (7.30), Bristol Rov. v. Brentford, Chesterfield v. Darlington, Fulham v. Bournemouth (12.0), Middlesbrough v. Mansfield (7.30), Notts County v. Bury (7.30), Port Vale v. Newport (7.30), Rotherham v. Carlisle, Swindon v. Gillingham, Walsall v. Bristol City, Wigan v. York.

English Div. 4 — Cardiff v. Northampton, Colchester v. Aldershot (11.0), Crewe v. Burnley (7.30), Exeter v. Wolves (11.0), Hartlepool v. Preston, Hereford v. Swansea, Lincoln v. Scunthorpe, Orient v. Torquay (7.30), Peterborough v. Stockport, Rochdale v. Halifax, Wrexham v. Tranmere (3 p.m. KO unless stated).

Premier Res. League — Aberdeen v. Clydebank (3 p.m.), Scottish Res. League — Morton v. QOS; Raith R v. Dunfermline.

West of Scotland Cup Third round — Pollok v. Ardrossan W.R. Western League — Largs v. Beith, Lugar v Maybole, Cumnock v Ambank, Glenafton v Craigmark. Trophy Centre League — Shotts v Forth. Petershill v Baillieston, Shettleston v Glasgow, Larkhall v Cumbernauld, Glenboig v Arthurlie, Rob Roy v Lesmahagow, Stonehouse V v Bellshill, Wishaw v St Rochs; Carluke R v Blantyre C (all at 7.15 p.m.).

Scottish Amateur Cup Under 12 Semi-final — Cathkin U v Bill U (Douglas Park, Hamilton 7.15).

RECORD SPORT   5

CUP FINAL Special

★★ No real losers in this
MEDALS

ON THE SPOT ...Aberdeen's Willie Falconer is sent tumbling by 'keeper Nicky Walker for the first half penalty which put the Dons into an early lead.

ON THE BALL ...Ian Durrant of Rangers times his run to perfection past Alex McLeish (left) and Peter Nicholas to put Rangers 2-1 ahead.

Spot miss torture will haunt Peter

RODGER BAILLIE SPOTLIGHTS THE SUDDEN-DEATH DRAMA

THE agony and the ecstacy of scoring and missing in a Cup Final penalty shoot-out made soccer history at Hampden.

For in Scotland's first-ever Cup Final penalty decider, it was Ian Durrant who scored the winner for Rangers, and Peter Nicholas who missed the spot-kick that lost the Skol Cup for Aberdeen.

The drama had been almost too much for the players, never mind the 71,961 fans and the watching millions on TV.

Nicholas was inconsolable after he missed Aberdeen's second penalty, and when it was Durrant's turn, neither Ibrox skipper Graham

Roberts nor keeper Nicky Walker could bear to look.

However, after the game it was revealed that Nicholas was not even in line to take one of the Dons penalties.

Explained Aberdeen boss Ian Porterfield: "Joe Miller should have been one of our penalty kickers but he was feeling the effects of an injury so Peter was drafted in."

Welsh international Nicholas admitted: "I didn't really want to take the penalty. I had a bad experience at Luton last season when

I missed two of them. Having said that, I'd take another if I had to.

"IT'S AN AWFUL FEELING, BUT I FELT WE REALLY SHOULDN'T HAVE NEEDED TO GO TO PENALTIES ANYWAY."

Ian Durrant, voted by journalists as the sponsor's 'Man of the Match,' clinched the Cup for Rangers with his side's fifth spot kick.

He said: "I was a bit nervous, because I was taking the last penalty and it seemed such a long wait."

It was the first penalty he had taken in more than a year.

Durrant whose winner's medal will be an early birthday present—he will be 21 on Friday—was praised by manager Graeme Souness.

"HE WAS TREMENDOUS. HE JUST GOT STRONGER AS THE GAME WENT ON."

Only two weeks ago the youngster asked for a transfer but Ian said: "It was a heat of the moment situation. I'm just glad now it's sorted out."

Rangers winger Davie Cooper, who scored his side's first goal and second penalty, also goes in the history books.

His seventh League Cup winner's medal creates a new record that puts him one ahead of Celtic boss Billy McNeill.

★ ★ SOCCER ROUND-UP . . . ALL THE LEAGUE ACTION—PAGE 37

classic Hampden shoot-out ★ ★
OF HONOUR

Non-stop Durrant the hero

THIS was a unique Hampden Cup Final because everyone won something very special.

RANGERS snatched the trophies in a tight-rope penalty shoot-out with poor Peter Nicholas cannoning the ball off the crossbar.

ABERDEEN won the admiration of all with an astonishing fight-back after being down 2-1 to take a 3-2 lead nine minutes away from extra time.

THE FANS in the ground and watching on TV saw one of the truly finest finals this great sporting acreage has hosted.

And, thankfully, although Alex McLeish and Willie Miller were cautioned, it was a very mannerly occasion.

Skills

It was very nearly regrettable that after 120 minutes of a brilliantly tied final it had to be settled in a penalty duel.

Penalties, however, are one of the game's skills and Rangers had the good luck to win the right to have them fired in at their end.

THE CRUCIAL KICK WAS ABERDEEN'S SECOND.

Welshman Nicholas, experienced and one of the game's better players, set out on a short run-up with whistles and jeers ringing in his ears.

He slammed the ball upwards but it skimmed the top of the bar and continued its flight path towards the frenzied Rangers fans.

Nicholas was in a state of abject despair.

Rangers had been put into a shoot-out lead by Ally McCoist and Davie Cooper with Jim Bett scoring the first for the Dons from a penalty.

Robert Fleck and Trevor Francis scored two more and sub Peter Weir and John Hewitt made it 4-3.

Appropriately, it was left to Ian Durrant to slot in the winner because he was the outstanding player in this Titanic game which restored sanity and respectability to Scottish soccer.

Durrant was an old-fashioned half-back, running powerfully, dictating, passing, creating and shooting. And even when, in the extra 30 minutes, his stockings dangled at his ankles giving away his sheer exhaustion.

There were fine goals and debatable ones. Misses to argue over, and a couple of decisions by Bob Valentine to discuss, although this didn't in any way dent his overall rating which was excellent.

Rarely can two teams in a competition so important have been so close—and yet so far away at the prize-giving.

When Alex McLeish chipped a perfect pass to the feet of Willie Falconer, putting him clear of the defence, the youngster decided against lobbing Walker and ran round him.

The only thing left for the beaten Walker to do was pull him down. The penalty was taken by Bett. He placed the ball to Walker's right ... and in the shoot-out placed the ball to the keeper's left.

Brilliant

Around this time the Dons were buoyant. Falconer failed to take a chance, and a McLeish shot was stopped on the line by Derek Ferguson.

Then it was Rangers' turn to think they had won in a somersault.

Davie Cooper hit the ball into the net brilliantly from a free-kick outside the penalty area. He hit it so well, I question if a defender, including Leighton, moved.

Five minutes from half-time, with Rangers really turning the screw, Durrant right-footed Rangers 2-1 ahead. It looked good for the Ibrox team.

Ten minutes into the second half, the surprise Dons choice Neil Simpson was replaced by Weir, but he had done a serviceable job after being out for so long injured.

Walker made his one real error when Hewitt levelled at 2-2 in 72 minutes. The keeper was on his way out to meet a Joe Miller cross but changed his mind. This left Hewitt with room to shoot, which he did with deadly effect.

Falconer headed the Dons into a 3-2 lead when the ball was directed to him by Bett from Miller's cross.

And then to the 85th-minute 3-3 leveller, in which Graham Roberts showed all the qualities of a battling captain in the way he moved upfield to win the ball in the air. It finished in the back of the net off Fleck's left foot.

And so into the goalless extra time and the match-settling penalty shoot-out.

A GREAT GAME AND ALL OF IT A VERY PLEASANT MEMORY.

RANGERS 3
ABERDEEN ...3

After 90 minutes and extra time 3-3; Rangers won 5-3 on penalties.

Scorers: Rangers — Cooper (21 min), Durrant (40), Fleck (85). Aberdeen — Bett (8, pen), Hewitt (72), Falconer (81).

ALEX CAMERON
The Final Verdict

EXTRA SPECIAL ... the goal that sent a classic Skol Cup Final into overtime. Dons defender Stewart McKimmie is helpless as Robert Fleck, shadowed by team-mate Ian Durrant, fires Rangers' third past Jim Leighton.
Pictures: ERIC CRAIG and KEN FERGUSON

RANGERS: Walker; Nicholl, Munro, Roberts, Ferguson, Gough, McGregor, Fleck, McCoist, Durrant, Cooper. Subs. — Cohen, Francis.

ABERDEEN: Leighton; McKimmie, Connor, Simpson, McLeish, W. Miller, Hewitt, Bett, J. Miller, Nicholas, Falconer. Subs. — Weir, Grant.

Referee: R. B. Valentine, Dundee.

"It was a great success — maybe we should START with the penalties!"

"SCO LEAGUE"

SNOOKER ... GREAT SCOT'S £60,000 TITLE TRIUMPH

HENDRY'S POT!

TAYLOR ... "he was brilliant"

STEPHEN HENDRY became snooker's youngest major tournament winner and the season's richest at Reading last night.

The 18-year-old Scottish champion crushed Dennis Taylor 10-7 in the Rothmans Grand Prix, picking up a £60,000 cheque.

IT BROUGHT HIS BANK BALANCE TO £122,000 IN EIGHT WEEKS.

Starting the tournament as a 40-1 outsider, he took the scalps of World No 1 Steve Davis, No 7 Tony Knowles, and England's young pretender John Parrott 9-7 on his way to the final.

And he crowned it all with a dazzling victory over Ireland's ex-world champion.

Sporting Taylor, who never gave up, stated: "When Alex Higgins came over here as a teenager I played against him. Stephen is every bit as brilliant.

"SOME OF THE SHOTS HE PLAYED WERE UNBELIEVABLE.

"He's great for the game. He's just what snooker has needed, and he has come along at the right time. It's done a world of good for snooker in Scotland."

Struggle

Hendry was watched by his father Gordon, mother Irene and younger brother Keith.

He admitted: "Winning for Scotland was tremendous. It was a struggle and when I was 4-1 down I had a 'kick' on the red and was really sick.

"After the interval when I made it 4-4, I started potting and really came into the game.

"I played well but only in patches and towards the end I had a struggle getting over the line.

"I STILL CAN'T GET OVER MY VICTORY AND I KNOW THERE ARE A LOT OF PEOPLE IN SCOTLAND RIGHT BEHIND ME."

The opening frames throughout the tournament have been a jinx for the modest Scot, but although Taylor moved 4-1 clear he was made to dance a Scottish reel!

★ ★ BOXING SPECIAL ... BUGNER'S NIGHT OF SHAME—PAGE 36

⚽ ⚽   **THE SKOL CUP FINAL**   Dons agony

IT'S BLUE

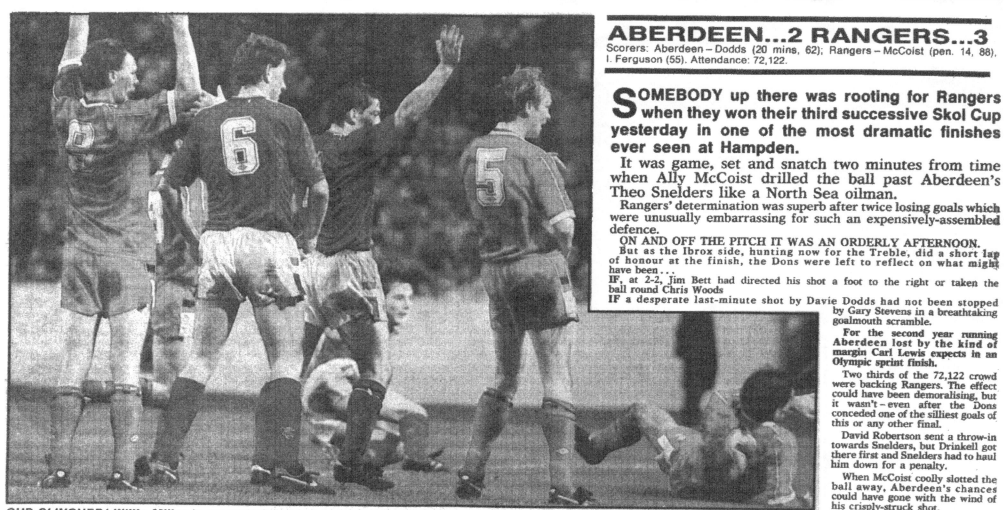

ABERDEEN...2 RANGERS...3

Scorers: Aberdeen – Dodds (20 mins, 62); Rangers – McCoist (pen. 14, 88), I. Ferguson (55). Attendance: 72,122.

SOMEBODY up there was rooting for Rangers when they won their third successive Skol Cup yesterday in one of the most dramatic finishes ever seen at Hampden.

It was game, set and snatch two minutes from time when Ally McCoist drilled the ball past Aberdeen's Theo Snelders like a North Sea oilman.

Rangers' determination was superb after twice losing goals which were unusually embarrassing for such an expensively-assembled defence.

ON AND OFF THE PITCH IT WAS AN ORDERLY AFTERNOON.

But as the Ibrox side, hunting now for the Treble, did a short lap of honour at the finish, the Dons were left to reflect on what might have been...

IF, at 2-2, Jim Bett had directed his shot a foot to the right or taken the ball round Chris Woods

IF a desperate last-minute shot by Davie Dodds had not been stopped by Gary Stevens in a breathtaking goalmouth scramble.

For the second year running Aberdeen lost by the kind of margin Carl Lewis expects in an Olympic sprint finish.

Two thirds of the 72,122 crowd were backing Rangers. The effect could have been demoralising, but it wasn't – even after the Dons conceded one of the silliest goals of this or any other final.

David Robertson sent a throw-in towards Snelders, but Drinkell got there first and Snelders had to haul him down for a penalty.

When McCoist coolly slotted the ball away, Aberdeen's chances could have gone with the wind of his crisply-struck shot.

Yet they came back twice – if not from the dead, pretty close to it – before they were finally

CUP CLINCHER! Willie Miller is grounded and helpless as Ally McCoist grabs Rangers' late winner. Getting a close-up of the goal which separated the sides are Davie Dodds, Terry Butcher, Kevin Drinkell and Alex McLeish.

SPOT PRIZE! McCoist drills home a penalty after an outbreak of panic in the Dons defence when Theo Snelders pulled down Kevin Drinkell.

THE THIGH'S THE LIMIT! It's goal No. 1 for a delighted Davie Dodds as Aberdeen team-mate Alex McLeish joins the Hampden celebrations. Rangers keeper Chris Woods was left stranded after failing to cut out a corner in the first half . . . and the ball cannoned off Dodds' leg into the net.

again in another furious Hampden finish

HEAVEN!

Ally grabs the glory clincher

BY ALEX CAMERON

Pics: ERIC CRAIG, RICHARD PARKER

wheeled into the mortuary, too late for the kiss of life.

Davie Dodds was the next most profitable player to McCoist, with a goal which bounced off his thigh and a second which nearly matched the best of the game by Ian Ferguson, who had his finest 90 minutes for Rangers.

A mere six minutes after the penalty, Aberdeen equalised. The entire Rangers defence seemed to be watching Alex McLeish when John Hewitt sent over a corner.

Woods missed the ball and it flew in off Dodds' thigh.

Aberdeen risked playing Neil Simpson after his horrific tackle on Ian Durrant two weeks ago.

Predictably, he was jeered. He treated the ball like a hot potato until he went off in the second half.

I still wonder if the Dons were wise to play him as he was more restrained than usual.

At half-time it was 1-1, and for a spell in the second period it looked as though fatigue had taken over.

But Rangers went ahead again in 55 minutes when a Stevens throw set up Ferguson's super strike.

FERGUSON WILL SURELY NOW BE FULLY ACCEPTED BY THE RANGERS FANS.

When McCoist hit the top of the bar a second after this, every Light Blue supporter agonised. A goal then would have finished it.

Instead, the bold Charlie Nicholas set up another leveller with a classy diagonal pass to Bett. His cross to the far post was perfect for a scoring header by Dodds.

And so to the finishing drama that brought McCoist's superb goal from a Mark Walters corner – and a noise eruption which was a mixture of relief and joy.

Dons Connor and Robertson and Ranger Ferguson were booked by referee Smith, who did well.

Aberdeen – Snelders, McKimmie, Robertson, Simpson, McLeish, Miller, Nicholas, Bett, Dodds, Connor, Hewitt. Subs – Irvine, Grant.
Rangers – Woods, Stevens, Brown, Gough, Wilkins, Butcher, Drinkell, I Ferguson, McCoist, N Cooper, Walters. Subs – Munro, D Ferguson.
Referee – G Smith, Edinburgh.

ABOVE ... Man of the Match Davie Dodds grabs his second goal, leaving Rangers keeper Chris Woods totally helpless with a floating header from Jim Bett's measured right-wing cross.

BELOW ... Hampden hit specialist Ian Ferguson, hidden among a throng of players, gives Rangers a leg up as he grabs the goal of the game against Aberdeen with a spectacular hook shot.

CHEERS, RANGERS

● FROM BACK PAGE

attacks the next.

"I just hope he scores in the Scottish Cup Final next May."

New signing Kevin Drinkell was also given a pat on the back.

"He played like an old pro, took on defenders and worked so hard," added Souness.

Drinkell and Ferguson were two of seven Ibrox players picking up their first honour with Rangers. The others were Gary Stevens, John Brown, Ray Wilkins, Neale Cooper and Mark Walters.

But Souness was unhappy about the two goals his side conceded, both scored by striker Davie Dodds.

Worst

He said: "It's the worst I've seen the defence play for ages. I like to think it's the strongest part of my team, but it wasn't like that in this game.

"I WON'T LISTEN TO ANY ARGUMENTS FROM THEM."

It's the fourth trophy Rangers have won out of the seven they have competed for in the three seasons since Souness took over at Ibrox.

And it already guarantees them a place in Europe next season.

Disappointed Dons boss Alex Smith praised his players: "They have been under a lot of pressure

because we won the League match two weeks ago.

"But I'm very proud of them and for the way they accepted the defeat at the end."

He picked out Neil Simpson, whose tackle on Ian Durrant a fortnight ago made him the target for a constant succession of jeers from Rangers fans.

Said Smith: "Many wouldn't have been able to have handled that situation. He took responsibility and I'm proud of him."

Simpson was subsituted in the second-half because of injury.

Smith looked back with regret on Jim Bett's vital miss – just before McCoist hit the winner.

He said: "In fairness to Jim, the keeper made it very hard for him because he narrowed the angle.

"But even after Rangers third goal we were unlucky not to equalise again."

For the first time ever, an after-match drug test was held at a major final in Scotland. Two players on each side were picked at random to be tested.

■ Scotland boss Andy Roxburgh saw World Cup rivals Cyprus and France draw 1-1 in Nicosia. The Cypriots got their surprise point with a late penalty. Roxburgh will watch Cyprus again before Scotland meet them on February 8 at Limassol.

 PAT BACK TO GIVE CELTIC NEW HEART   – Page 33

Now the nightmare's over for

END OF MY

TERRY BUTCHER

talking to the Record

Fly the flag — I'm back in the groove

By RODGER BAILLIE

RANGERS skipper Terry Butcher spoke for the first time after Rangers' title win about the fears he had for his future.

This was comeback season for the big England international – an ever-present in the Ibrox march to the Championship – after his leg break.

As he sipped champagne from a paper cup, he admitted: "I did have a few doubts, for I found it hard to get back into the groove.

"My first game was a pre-season friendly at Raith Rovers, and I wasn't too pleased with my form.

"But I worked hard, especially on my partnership with Richard Gough. We have a natter every day in the dressing room and he certainly deserves his Player of the Year title."

Butcher talked about Rangers' title win – achieved through the 4-0 victory over Hearts and the no-scoring draw between Aberdeen and Celtic – and revealed:

"I DIDN'T THINK WE WOULD DO IT TODAY. OUR PRIORITY WAS TO GET TWO POINTS.

"The fans were shouting so much, we really didn't know what the score was at Pittodrie."

Resolve

Butcher added: "All credit to Celtic for their double last season, they had a great season.

"But it was hard for us to take that our main rivals had won the Double.

"It made us resolve to do well this season. Now we've a chance of the Treble, and it's down to one game."

He praised the squad when he said:

"It's a very happy dressing room.

"It's not just been about 13 players in any one game.

"We've had players come in such as Ian McCall, who scored against Hibs, and aren't headline-grabbers."

This was emphasised by manager Graeme Souness when he praised sub Tommy Cowan.

"He's what football is all about.

"He loves playing, and he would be the same if he was wearing the strip of his local amateurs."

Butcher has been a hugely successful part of

AYE-AYE, SKIPPER! Hat's the way to do it as captain Terry Butcher celebrates Rangers' Championship win

AYE-AYE, BOSS! Glory is the order of the day as Graeme Souness ensures injured hero Ian Durrant also gets in on the act

AYE-AYE IBROX! The title's in the bag and the prize guy trio of Richard Gough, Chris Woods and Terry Butcher have that three and easy feeling as they take a bow before their legions of adoring fans

Pictures: ERIC CRAIG

★ Another crate of sparkling bubbly is heading Rangers' way.

They need four more goals to win Record Sport's champagne prize for being the first team to hit 100 in domestic action.

Their total so far, inclusive of European games, is 102.

Rangers also lead in the shut-out battle.

Keeper Chris Woods has the best percentage with 57.1.

★ ★ ROXBURGH'S WORLD CUP WARNING FROM FRANCE – SEE PAGE 33

Captain Courage

FEARS!

DOUBLE TOPS! There was no flagging by Tommy Cowan and Derek Ferguson as the League title celebration party kicked off in earnest at Ibrox

CHAMPIONS

	P	W	D	L	F	A	Pts
Rangers......	33	24	4	5	58	22	52
Aberdeen....	34	17	13	4	48	25	47
Dundee Utd	33	16	11	6	44	23	43
Celtic..........	34	19	4	11	64	44	42
Hibs............	34	13	8	13	36	34	34
Hearts..........	34	9	11	14	34	41	29
St Mirren....	34	11	7	16	38	52	29
Dundee........	34	9	9	16	32	45	27
Motherwell.	34	7	11	16	34	43	25
Hamilton.....	34	4	2	28	16	75	10

the new Rangers "Iron Curtain" defence, and their title success has been based on Fortress Ibrox.

They have the best home League record in Britain, with just three points dropped at home in one defeat from Dundee United and a draw against Hibs.

The worry for the nine other Premier clubs is how they can overcome this Ibrox barrier, with a packed stadium which will soon be even bigger.

Denied

The four goals against Hearts were split between the new English buys this season, Mel Sterland in the first half and Kevin Drinkell after the break.

Rangers officially denied suggestions that Sterland would move back to his native Yorkshire with Leeds United.

And the player didn't sound like a man on the move when he said:

"I'm looking forward to next season. I've had trouble with injuries and pre-season training will sort that out."

Now Rangers will change their line-up and bring in some of their younger players, starting against Dundee United at Ibrox tomorrow.

"We deserved it. We were the best team money can buy..."

SFA SLAM WAR TALK

ERNIE WALKER yesterday slammed talk of a war between Rangers and the SFA.

As new measures were announced to curb officials in dug-outs, the SFA supremo told me in Paris: "It is nonsense to talk of war.

"And to be fair to Rangers, none of their officials has been quoted as saying there is a war.

Rubbish

"The SFA have administered football justice for more than 100 years and will go on doing so.

"The clubs are the association – Rangers, Dundee United . . . all of them. If they think rules are wrong there is a democratic way to try to change them.

"And it's certainly utter rubbish to suggest that, when deciding punishments, the Disciplinary Committee took into account Rangers' withdrawal of Ibrox as a venue for the FIFA Youth Tournament."

Antics

However, the SFA are so determined to stamp on dug-out antics that automatic punishments have been fixed.

"These will be a £1000 fine for the Premier League, £500 in the First Division and £300 in the Second.

With the fines there will be a year-long ban.

ALEX CAMERON

ABERDEEN will today launch a Continental man-hunt for new talent.

The Dutch FA's official agent met manager Alex Smith after the 0-0 draw with Celtic at Pittodrie.

And his top priority is to find a winger.

Keeper Theo Snelders was taunted throughout by Celtic fans on Saturday because of his call-off from the Dutch team.

But he handled the pressure magnificently and defied Celtic.

Striker Andy Walker will be out for a couple of weeks with an eye injury and Billy Stark needed five stitches in a head wound.

But both will be ready for Celtic's final fling.

Who is the lucky lad?

GRAEME SOUNESS made it a day to remember for a little boy in the huge crowd when he presented him with a ball in exchange for his scarf.

The magic moment came during the title-winning celebrations and Souness said later: "I spotted him because he had a black eye."

Do YOU know the identity of the little lad? If you do, get in touch with the Record. We want to meet Rangers' luckiest fan. You can reach us on:

041-242-3200.

★ ★ SAD DUFFY'S SO SORRY – SEE PAGE 32

HOME IS THE HERO . . . ex-Celt Kenny Dalglish slips the ball past Pat Bonner for Liverpool's opener. Picture: ANDY HOSIE

SWEET CHARITY

Parkhead gift goals as Kenny returns

CELTIC 0 LIVERPOOL 4
Scorers – Dalglish (20 mins), Aldridge (62, 75), Rush (82).
Attendance: 60,437.

RODGER BAILLIE at Parkhead

KENNY DALGLISH was crowned king of soccer again yesterday as he made his farewell appearance at Parkhead as a player.

And he left 60,000 fans wishing they could turn the clock back on an occasion drenched with emotion as his Liverpool players, numbed by the horror of Hillsborough, managed to turn their attention back to football.

BUT THIS WAS KENNY'S DAY.

It ended with thousands of supporters refusing to move until he took a farewell bow – and he returned in a Liverpool track suit with a Celtic scarf draped round his neck.

Really it was hard to believe that it was 19 years to the month since he made his debut for Celtic.

HE STILL LOOKED GOOD ENOUGH – EVEN TO PLAY AGAIN FOR SCOTLAND.

Stroll

And it was nice to see him smile once more, possibly for the first time in a fortnight, as he dismissed any chance of a comeback when he joked:

"You only get selected on merit, and I don't think I'm good enough."

He played only 56 minutes, but during that time he snapped the first goal in 20 minutes when he pounced on a John Barnes shot that had bounced off Pat Bonner's body.

Celtic's best first-half chance was a Tommy Coyne effort blocked by keeper Bruce Grobbelaar in a match that was no Sunday stroll.

Liverpool's running off the ball was an object lesson to any team, and they were pretty lethal when they were on it as well.

Destroyer Barnes had a part in all four goals. He set up self-confessed Celtic fan Ray Houghton after 62 minutes with another shot which came back off Bonner for sub John Aldridge to score.

Thirteen minutes later Bonner could only claw away a Barnes shot and Aldridge, who had been so depressed last week he said he might never play again, headed the third.

Eight minutes from time Rush lobbed the Celtic keeper for a fourth.

Celtic came close with a second-half Mark McGhee header which spun off the bar, but the effort of two games inside 24 hours took its toll.

The lasting memory was of the entire ground turned into a sea of green and white and red scarves as the fans sang "You'll never walk alone.".

Dalglish summed it up:

"THE SCORE-LINE WAS IRRELEVANT."

Worried

Celtic boss Billy McNeill wasn't so charitable to his own team when he said:

"The fans were wonderful. It's not them that worries me, it's the team.

"We had benign defending, and we had slackness and carelessness that would have been punished in any game never mind by a team with Liverpool's class of player."

Both Tommy Burns and Joe Miller, carrying knocks from the Dons game, were substituted by Dave Elliot and Derek Whyte.

Celtic: Bonner, Grant, Rogan, Aitken, McCarthy, Burns, Stark, McStay, Coyne, McGhee, Miller. Substitutes: Baillie, Balmer, Fulton, Elliot, Whyte, Andrews.

Liverpool: Grobbelaar, Gillespie, Burrows, Nicol, Venison, Hansen, Dalglish, Houghton, Rush, Barnes, McMahon. Substitutes: Aldridge, Beardsley, Ablett, Whelan, Staunton.

Referee: R. B. Valentine, Dundee.

★ HOTLINE ★
● Our exclusive fans' phone-in is on Page 33

SUNDAY

Ace Gough extra special as he grabs glory for Rangers

CELTIC

PAT BONNER: Usually hero of the Celtic defence, but fumbled his way round his penalty box. Partly to blame for Rangers' winner. ★★

PETER GRANT: Played with his usual commitment and purpose both in the back four and in midfield after second half switch. ★★★

DARIUSZ WDOWCZYK: No. 3 jersey but operated in middle of defence. Found it hectic. ★★★

STEVE FULTON: Enjoyed his best spell in the first-half with some great passes, but fell out of the action. Subbed 76 minutes. ★★★

PAUL ELLIOTT: Commanding in defence and took part in plenty of attacks. ★★★

ANTON ROGAN: Stretched by Mark Walters but stuck to the task and found time to go forward. ★★★

JOE MILLER: Not his day. He never managed to put Rangers under pressure. Subbed in 59 mins. ★★

PAUL McSTAY: Worked so hard to spark his team into attack, and also help out in defence. ★★★★

JACKI DZIEKANOWSKI: Worried Rangers' defence on occasion, but missed one of the best chances of the game. ★★★

GERRY CREANEY: Can be well pleased with his Old Firm debut. Dangerous in first-half. ★★★

JOHN COLLINS: He also worked well, shuttling between defence and attack, to get Celtic going. Few scoring chances. ★★★★

CHRIS MORRIS: Replaced Joe Miller. Partly at fault at winning goal. Did reasonably well. ★★★

JOHN HEWITT: Replaced Fulton. Helped to stop the runs Gary Stevens was making. ★★★

REFEREE: Jim McCluskey tried to keep game flowing and helped make sure it never exploded. ★★★

RANGERS

CHRIS WOODS: Made vital first-half saves when Celtic looked to be getting on top. ★★★★

GARY STEVENS: Impressive going forward where his runs caused Celtic many problems. ★★★

STUART MUNRO: Recovered from the display against Red Star to snuff out Joe Miller. ★★★

RICHARD GOUGH: Slightly shaky at the start but came on to a powerful display. ★★★★

NIGEL SPACKMAN: Worked harder than anyone. Not showy but covered much ground. ★★★

JOHN BROWN: Another who shrugged aside the nightmare in Belgrade but 'lost' Paul Elliott at Celtic's goal. ★★★

TREVOR STEVEN: Forced to work deeper than usual, but still sprayed perfect passes. ★★★

TERRY HURLOCK: Helped out with midfield effort, but was lucky to escape caution for tackle on Fulton. Subbed 63 mins ★★

ALLY McCOIST: Few real goal chances, but helped set up equaliser. Subbed 98 mins ★★★

MARK HATELEY: Should have scored early on, but was involved in the equaliser. ★★★

MARK WALTERS: Celtic could never take their eye off him. Not all his moves came off, however. ★★★★

IAN FERGUSON: Brief appearance but with fresh legs among some very tired players, produced some good runs and passes. ★★★

PIETER HUISTRA: Replaced Hurlock. Didn't look out of place in his first Old Firm game and worked hard. ★★★

CELTIC.................1

Elliott (52).   Attendance: 62,817.

RANGERS 2

Walters (65 mins), Gough (105)

After extra-time

RANGERS won the Skol Cup for the fourth time in five years yesterday ...

And the Hampden presentation ceremony was the only obvious difference between two heroic teams.

It was a superb 120 minutes, with Rangers finally triumphing over adversity off and on the pitch to snatch a record 17th League Cup trophy that assures them of European football next season.

Rarely has a game see-sawed quite so dramatically and ended with so little between the sides on play.

There was even a pre-match party piece from the Celtic fans, with a sea of red stars held high to remind Rangers of their midweek Euro setback.

But in the end, the men from Ibrox turned out to be the shooting stars.

Paul Elliott hurled Celtic into a dramatic 52nd minute lead; Mark Walters levelled and then halfway through extra-time, Celtic's defence blundered badly and skipper Richard Gough grabbed the winner.

So the trophy, bedecked in red white and blue, was held aloft on the pitch afterwards by the victorious skipper – and then manager Graeme Souness led his players on a victory jig across the park.

Freak

It was a joyous scene for a team who were at the wrong end of two arguable and crucial refereeing decisions, and had to play without Mo Johnston and Terry Butcher.

Johnston was the surprise omission because of a groin injury and it was decided Butcher's match fitness might have been suspect after missing seven first team matches.

The game was in the best traditions of the Skol Cup Final – frothing over with determination, skill, and let it be said, sportsmanship.

The winning goal was a freak, but it sent scorer Gough hurdling the advertising boards in his excitement, waving to the jubilant Rangers crowd.

Gary Stevens hit the ball firmly, fiercely and accurately, high into the area.

Elliott and Hateley failed to connect with headers and sub Chris

★ ALEX ★
CAMERON
at Hampden

Pictures by ERIC CRAIG

Morris tried to shepherd the ball to Pat Bonner.

But Gough rushed in from behind Morris and got between the defender and keeper to slot the ball away for a goal which took a tantalising time to come.

So this titanic tie was settled by errors and opportunism as Rangers kept their cool ...

● DESPITE a rejected penalty claim in 19 minutes when Ally McCoist tumbled as he was challenged by Bonner on the fringe of the penalty area.

● DESPITE a hint that Joe Miller elbowed the ball to control it as it came over from a John Collins corner kick on the lead-up to Elliott's goal.

In the first incident, referee Jim McCluskey, who had a good first major final, signalled that McCoist had thrown himself.

In the second, he ruled the ball had come off Miller's chest.

Anyway, Dariusz

● Scottish Television, prevented by the Old Firm gag from any interviews, signed off its live programme with the Cliff Richard song: "It's So Funny That We Don't Talk Anymore."

PIPPED AT THE POST ... Richard Gough nips in between Pat Bonner and Chris Morris at the back post to give Rangers an extra time Skol Cup victory.

Skol sizzler in the rain

BEST!

HIGH AND MIGHTY . . . Celtic's star man Paul Elliott in a tough aerial duel with Rangers striker Mark Hateley.

Wdowczyk fired in a shot that looked to be going wide, but six feet two inch Elliott made a startling stoop to send the ball swirling away from Chris Woods into the goal.

Rangers' equaliser was finished off perfectly by the dazzling Mark Walters.

Mark Hateley leaped high to head the ball down to Ally McCoist.

McCoist tried gamely to control it, couldn't, and it rolled into Walters' path for him to finish off with a dramatic right foot shot.

The game was packed with ifs and buts.

● IF Nigel Spackman had passed to Hateley instead of shooting seconds from half-time, Rangers would almost certainly have led then.

● IF Jacki Dziekanowski had shot quicker after a great run and pass from Anton Rogan in 92 minutes, Celtic would have gone 2-1 in front.

Chris Woods had three good saves on the ground from Gerry Creaney, Dziekanowski and skipper Paul McStay.

At the other end, Pat Bonner looked unusually uncertain and even tumbled over the advertising boards as he was challenged by McCoist.

Both managers made changes to try to break the 1-1 deadlock.

Chris Morris came on for Miller in 59 minutes and four minutes later Pieter Huistra took over from Terry Hurlock.

Stamped

Fourteen minutes from the end John Hewitt replaced Steve Fulton and then Ian Ferguson came on for McCoist – although Hateley went off first, thinking his number had been held up.

Hurlock and Hateley (Rangers) and Celtic's Dziekanowski were yellow-carded, but for routine offences.

Referee McCluskey stamped on any trouble, but in the furious pace of the match the players found time only to pursue the ball.

It was a truly great game, one of the best Old Firm matches I've seen.

FACTS AND FIGURES

CELTIC		RANGERS	
SHOTS ON TARGET	12	SHOTS ON TARGET	9
OFF TARGET	8	OFF TARGET	4
CORNERS	7	CORNERS	11
FREE KICKS	17	FREE KICKS	29
AGAINST	29	AGAINST	17
GOAL KICKS	13	GOAL KICKS	10
OFFSIDE	8	OFFSIDE	3
CAUTIONS	1	CAUTIONS	2

GOUGH GLORY

From Back Page

Elliott put Celtic ahead said: "We've had a hectic time, but considering Celtic didn't have a mid-week match we matched them all the way.

"It was a tribute to our pre-season training that we were able to last so well."

Rangers boss Graeme Souness said: "Players in my team who had a point to prove.

"In my book this team showed the most character in my time at the club.

"Considering the week we've had, starting with the loss of Oleg Kuznetsov and not playing well in midweek, the criticism the players received did us a favour."

Disaster

Souness revealed that Mo Johnston had been left out on medical advice with a hamstring injury.

He also said that deposed captain Terry Butcher had been close to playing, but he decided to stick with the back four who played.

For apart from the Belgrade disaster, they hadn't lost any goals.

Souness praised Celtic's contribution but added: "We were just a bit too hot for them."

Celtic manager Billy McNeill congratulated his rivals, but said:

"I was disappointed at the way we lost the goals. I thought when we opened the scoring it would be our day."

And he added: "We had a chance in extra time that would have made life awkward for Rangers but we didn't take it."

Dempsey KO angers fans

CELTIC fans united in condemnation of Brian Dempsey's removal from the Parkhead board at the weekend.

Ian McGuigan, from East Kilbride, stormed: "It's a disgrace. Dempsey was going to take Celtic out of of the dark ages."

Joseph Colqhoun, Clydebank, said: "I'm both surprised and disappointed by Dempsey's departure. He was too far-thinking for Celtic.

"Now he has gone and I'm disgusted. The timing – just before the Skol Cup Final – could only be described as pathetic."

★ ★ ★ ★ ★

Pat McKeesick, from Dalkeith, chipped in: "Brian Dempsey could have been great for Celtic.

"He is obviously much too progressive for a club who should be one of Europe's biggest.

Joe Connelly, from Glasgow, complained :I would like to compliment Celtic on their diabolical timing. Brian Dempsey is a genuine man, a real professional who put his heart into Celtic."

At the other side of the fence, Rangers season ticket holders were not chuffed at being unable to get tickets for yesterday's game.

Henry Paterson, from Alloa, moaned: "I paid £240 for my main stand season ticket yet I could not buy a brief for the Skol Cup Final."

Jim Cliff, from Galston, Ayrshire, said:"My season ticket cost me £155 but I had to watch the match on television.

"Where's the reward for the fans who put their faith – and cash – in Rangers?

★ ★ ★ ★ ★

William Hatch, from Bishopbriggs, is another reluctant armchair fan.

He said: "There must be hundreds of season ticket holders who are disgusted at missing the match. Surely there should be some kind of priority?"

Wallace Mercer is off Alex Frew's Christmas card list following Hearts' decision to increase admission prices for the Euro tie with Bologna.

Alex, from East Kilbride – who also happens to edit a fanzine magazine, said: "There were only 10,000 at the game.

"If the prices had not been so steep, the crowd would have been twice that size."

★ ★ ★ ★ ★

Paul Reid, from Perth, reckons that St Johnstone are not being put in the picture . . . not by the TV people anyway.

"I know the cameras were at our home game with Rangers, but we're not getting a fair deal.

"BBC covered Saturday's game between Airdrie and Falkirk and I have nothing against the First Division getting a fair crack of the whip.

"But the cameras should have been at Tannadice. It was a superb game."

★ ★ ★ ★ ★

Hampden may not be the greatest football stadium on earth, but it was the place to be yesterday.

And for once, 'HOT-LINE' callers were united in their view that the Skol Cup Final was a cracker.

Derek Johnson called from Glenrothes to say of Rangers' turbo-charged 2-1 win over gallant Celtic: "It was everything you expect of a cup final. Two good teams, all-out effort and loads of excitement."

★ ★ ★ ★ ★

Paul Elliott was generally rated the outstanding player on the field, but Hamish Whiteford, of Bannockburn, stated: "Elliott certainly put himself about. But I think the top player was Anton Rogan, who never stopped trying."

What about this for a novelty . . . PRAISE for a referee.

Stephen Blake, from Ayr, reckons that Jim McCluskey played a significant role in the success of yesterday's final.

"The ref was excellent. He kept firm control and let the game flow."

★ ★ ★ ★ ★

But Barry Brown, Shawfield, claims instead that McCluskey boobed. "Bonner fouled McCoist in the box and it should have been a penalty."

Archie Hyslop, Saltcoats, had this to ask of Celtic boss Billy McNeill: "Why replace a forward, Miller, with a defender, Morris, when you are 1-0 up and in control of the game?"

Robert Pellegrine, Ardrossan enjoyed the game. But describes Hampden as a disgrace. "I got soaked to the skin, my white training shoes are now black.

"Hampden really is in a mess . . . and what's more, I had to park my car about a mile from the ground."

JOHN DOCHERTY takes your calls

"It happened BEFORE the game . . ."

CELTIC'S NEW Mr BIG

From Back Page

had called for a share-poll. So Dempsey was out.

"It wasn't a reactionary move," White said. "Nor are we shutting the lid on the progress which is essential.

"We've got to make the right decisions and my view – I hope the board will support me in this – is that we must have the best possible advice on all our plans."

The club is £3 million in the red and carries forward a loss of £800,000 with no upsurge in cash fortunes predicted.

Early this week White will

ask the other directors to approve appointing a high-powered chief executive with a strong business knowledge as well as experience in the sport and leisure industry.

SUCH A MAN WILL NOT BE EASY TO FIND.

Jim Farrell, who has been on the Parkhead board for nearly 26 years, made this point strongly when Dempsey was booted.

Dempsey had outlined plans to build a new complex on 110 acres at Robroyston, but some directors were not convinced the club could

afford the phone-number figures quoted.

White's new era must as a priority provide a home for Celtic in the next century which will at least match Ibrox.

They will NOT move to Renfrewshire, but a link-up with a new venture at Strathclyde Park is a possibility.

Celtic fans want the club to compete with Rangers – and not just on the park.

White is aware that the removal of Dempsey was a major step.

If it is to be a forward one he must DO the right things as well as SAY them.

EXCLUSIVE: How the Ibrox boss
MY WAY FOR

MARK HATELEY FAN CLUB

"Guess what— Ally McCoist has just joined . . ."

VICTORY DOUBLE ACT . . . goals hero Mark Hateley and manager Walter Smith are the Rangers prize guys.

Walter Smith
TALKING TO YOUR RECORD

Interview: ALEX CAMERON

"I'VE HEARD it said that I'm a nice guy. I'm not abrasive, but you don't run players at the top level - as I've done with Rangers and Dundee United - by being nice all the time.

I'll manage Rangers in much the same way as Graeme Souness, except that I'll put my own personality into the job.

Graeme's public image isn't all that he is, and it's much the same with me.

It's been said I did most of the work while Graeme was at Ibrox. That's not the case.

The hardest job is motivating players, discipline, and dealing with matters like contracts. These things are not the responsibility of the assistant manager.

I handled the training, but Graeme did the hard bits, which are now my worry.

Graeme deliberately kept himself away from the squad at times, so as not to get too close to them.

Booted

It didn't mean he wasn't doing anything, although even players have been fooled.

It's not possible for a manager at this level to be among the players all the time. Graeme didn't do this and neither will I.

Frankly, I always felt that if Graeme left Ibrox I'd have to go with him. Every manager knows the risk of getting the sack!

If Graeme had been booted I wouldn't have stayed on - but, of course, he went because he wanted to.

It was a surprise, but it was his decision.

Things have been said about Graeme's waygoing. Supporters felt let down. But for a manager to win four Championships in five seasons is outstanding.

I took over for the last four games, but we only carried on in the Souness way. He's been involved in everything.

Treble

He's given the fans success that they've never had before. This is what should be remembered.

My immediate reaction after helping complete a hat-trick of titles was how nice it would be to win the treble.

I want to see us imposing ourselves more in

Mark's goals target

THE Rangers player with the widest grin was two-goal hero Mark Hateley.

It took his goals tally for the season to 15 and he promised: "I want to score more next season. It's not enough."

It's his second championship medal - he's already won with French club Monaco.

System

He said: "It didn't really worry me I couldn't win over the fans when I came to Rangers at first.

"I know Ally McCoist was the fans' favourite.

"But it wasn't me that kept Alistair out, it was the system the team were playing.

"It had to be a target man and one other, and I'm the target man."

Hateley, who will be 30 later this year, has three years of his contract still to run and he joked:

"I'll be an old man by the time that's over."

WE'RE THE TOPS . . . Rangers' Walter Smith and striker Mo Johnston are feeling smiles better at the final whistle.

SKY'S THE LIMIT FOR FALKIRK - FIRST DIVISION ON PAGES 30, 31

EUROPEAN ACTION
Final lift for Barcelona

BARCELONA, who meet Manchester United in the European Cup-Winners Cup Final in Rotterdam on Wednesday, clinched the Spanish title yesterday . . . without kicking a ball.

Second-placed Atletico Madrid lost 2-1 to Real Sociedad - John Aldridge got the winner - and are now nine points behind with four games left.

It's Barcelona's first title since Terry Venables led them to glory in 1985.

WE THOUGHT WE'D BLOWN IT

RODGER BAILLIE ON NIGEL SPACKMAN'S GLORY DAY

NIGEL SPACKMAN, Rangers' stand-in captain, admitted: "We thought we'd blown our title chances."

Minutes after he led the team on a dance round Ibrox he talked about the players' anguish.

Spackman, who took over as skipper when Terry Butcher left and

"After we lost three goals at Motherwell it flashed through our minds maybe the title had gone," he said.

Richard Gough was hurt, added: "It's been a wonderful season for me.

"To captain Glasgow Rangers on the day they won the title is one I'll always remember.

"I've played in Cup Finals at Wembley and won a championship medal with Liverpool.

"But I've never known an atmosphere like that at Ibrox. These fans were wonderful."

plans to build on that title treble ⚽⚽

RANGERS

Graeme was involved in everything

The treble will be my first target

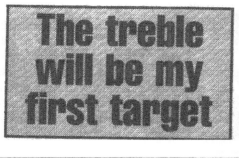

NO SHORTAGE of candidates for the Hotline bad fire this week! The Celtic board, Chief Executive Terry Cassidy, Billy McNeill, Gerry Creaney, even . . .

Plus ITV, BBC, Radio Clyde and, of course, the dear old referee.

And one Dons fan actually savages Aberdeen! Okay, we'll start with him.

Come in **Gordon Law, Aberdeen.** "I'm not surprised we lost to Rangers. We had a jitterbug in goal and a powder-puff midfield led by Mr Nowhere Man Jim Bett."

★★★★★

Dons fan **George Chambers, Aberdeen,** said: "I'd like to congratulate Rangers on winning the Championship.

"They handled the pressure better on the day. But I still felt the allocation of 3000 tickets instead of giving over the Broomloan Road Stand to Aberdeen fans had an effect on the outcome."

★★★★★

Gordon Nugent, Kirkintilloch reckoned Brian McGinlay denied Rangers two penalties for challenges by Alex McLeish on Mark Hateley early in the first-half.

Meanwhile **Bobby Mills, Denny,** accused Big Alex of being the new Willie Miller!

"He sarcastically applauded the Rangers supporters when he fouled Mark Hateley.

"And as for Jim Bett indicating he had Mark Walters in his pocket, tell him Mark has a Championship winners' medal in his!"

★★★★★

George Gardner, Whitburn, congratulated Mark Hateley on winning over the Rangers fans.

★★★★★

Derek Taylor, Peterhead, had a telly complaint.

"BBC 1 ruined Sportscene by showing the two Rangers goals on the News five minutes before

Up in powder puff of smoke

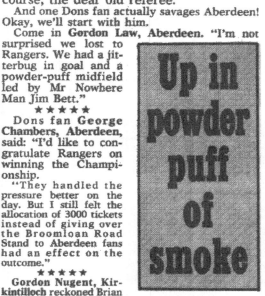

the programme started – for the benefit of **ENGLISH** viewers."

★★★★★

Joe Bruce, Camelon, Falkirk, switches TV channels.

"The ITV News didn't even mention Rangers winning the Premier League, so what chance did Falkirk have of getting a mention.

"I was pleased we went up as champions as it has shut up the critics who accused us of reorganising our way to promotion."

★★★★★

Andrew Black, Bannockburn, complained about the prices for the Scottish Amateur Cup Final.

"I had to pay £3 each for a seven-year-old and a 10-year-old – the same price as an adult.

"I thought it was scandalous."

TICKING OFF FOR CELTIC

★ FIRST to open the ticking Parkhead parcel is **Ian Grant, Rosebank, Falkirk.**

"I've been a critic of Billy McNeill, but the treatment he is getting at present is a damned disgrace.

"This season we have been the laughing-stock of Scottish football on and off the park.

"The club has had nothing but bad publicity since Terry Cassidy joined the club."

★★★★★

Not so says, **Jim Kirk, East Kilbride.** "I have no sympathy for Billy McNeill.

"He knew the type of directors he was dealing with when he returned to the club."

★★★★★

Brian McArthur, Perth, hits out at Gerry Creaney for helping a Celtic hooligan back into the stand at McDiarmid Park on Saturday after he had had a kick at St Johnstone's Don McVicar.

"Creaney should have handed him over to the police," he said.

★ **GOALDEN MOMENT** . . . Mark Hateley (No 9) heads past keeper Michael Watt for Rangers first goal.
Pictures: CRAIG HALKETT

Europe, but the treble will be our first target.

We're reasonably settled now, and when Oleg Kuznetsov and Trevor Steven and our other better players are fit again, we'll be better placed to have a wee run in Europe.

We'll need luck in the draw, of course. That's essential at this level.

Kuznetsov left after the game for two weeks at home in Kiev, then he'll go to Greece for a fortnight's holiday before training with Kiev.

He'll be fighting fit for the new season.

The hardest thing for me will be how to handle criticism. I was assistant to Jim McLean and then to Graeme. But the buck stopped at them.

If fault-finding is justified I'll accept it, but when it's done for the sake of it I don't know how I'll react.

Criticism hurts, but as an assistant I haven't had too much of it.

However, after five years at Ibrox I know what to expect. Success is a must.

Yesterday was a great day for Rangers and the fans.

We were playing without a lot of players of genuine quality. It had to be backs to the wall stuff.

Best

Lads like Nigel Spackman, who doesn't get a great deal of publicity, have been terrific.

Terry Hurlock's come in and done a good job as have others like Mark Hateley and Gary Stevens.

Mark's two goals against Aberdeen were smashing, particularly his first, which was a great header off our best move of the game.

I was really confident that, given a break, we'd win the match.

The reserve of grit that Rangers have – and Celtic are in the same category – can be underestimated. ❞

HEADSTRONG
Ibrox men in right frame of mind

RANGERS won their fourth championship in five years because they rediscovered self-belief.

Doubters were swept aside in the fury of a game in which pounds, prestige and position were the prizes.

Aberdeen flunked it. They were red shadows. Wobbly in defence, grey in midfield, disappointing up front.

How much they were intimidated by the 33,000 Rangers fans is hard to tell. But once Peter van de Ven and Hans Gillhaus missed chances, the Northern Lights were dimmed.

Mark Hateley, the target man for jeers from the fans as well as passes from his team-mates at the start of the season, was the hero with two cracking goals with head and foot.

And defender Gary Stevens had one of his best games for Rangers.

Hateley, was lucky that referee Brian McGinlay didn't penalise him for a first-minute challenge on keeper Michael Watt.

Rangers TWICE had to reorganise, when Tom Cowan and John Brown

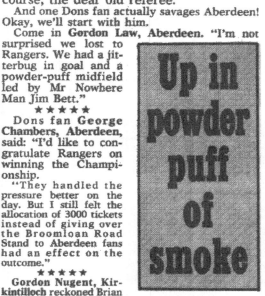

GARY STEVENS

ALEX CAMERON'S VERDICT

hobbled off to return only for the celebrations – walking with sticks.

But the team didn't crumble.

Alex McLeish and Stewart McKimmie tried to halt Rangers but had little support.

"It was a battle from the first minute to the last," said a disappointed Aberdeen boss Alex Smith.

"We missed two chances which could have turned the game for us.

"The first goal was bad from our point of view – Rangers hadn't done anything at that stage. And the second was WORSE!"

Aberdeen's other bad luck was an injury to Eoin Jess.

⚽⚽ CELTIC FANS SAY THANKS A BUNDLE ON PAT'S BIG DAY – PAGE 28

12 SPOTLIGHT ON THE BOSS WHO BECAME

THE YEAR

PREMIER LEAGUE
PREMIER DIVISION

	P	W	D	L	F	A	Pts
Rangers	41	31	5	5	96	29	67
Celtic	42	25	10	7	85	40	60
Hearts	41	26	7	8	55	34	59
Aberdeen	42	17	13	12	54	39	47
Dundee Utd	42	17	13	12	63	49	47
Hibernian	42	15	16	11	50	43	46
Motherwell	42	10	14	18	41	57	34
Falkirk	42	12	10	20	53	70	34
St Johnstone	42	13	8	21	50	71	34
Airdrie	41	13	7	21	48	66	33
St Mirren	41	5	11	25	29	70	21
Dunfermline	42	4	10	28	21	75	18

Boys in blue grab No.4

★ By ★
WALTER SMITH

I WASN'T sure we had clinched the title until somebody behind me in the Ibrox stand said Dundee United had scored a last-gasp second goal against Hearts.

What a great feeling that wee bit of news gave me and what a smashing atmosphere it helped to create as Rangers did a lap of honour. It was great to be part of it.

Optimists among our fans are already talking about winning the title another six times in a row – to beat Celtic's run of nine.

Steady on! I'd like to think this could happen but winning margins in championships are never great. That underlines the problems.

This year's title battle would have been very different if Celtic had won their home games with us instead of losing 2-0 and 3-1.

Rangers would have 63 points this morning and the Celts 64.

Don't let me spoil the fun for our fans, of course. I simply want to be realistic and not let our thoughts run riot.

Hazards

Ten in a row is a nice target but there are more hazards now – the glut of games, turnover of players etc – than when Celtic got nine.

I know how happy the support feels because I've been a fan since the age of four.

When I was a Dundee United part-timer and apprentice electrician I hitched to Newcastle to see Rangers in the old Fairs Cup.

Now I'm the boss and my team has won the League and is in the Cup Final in my first term.

The final with Airdrie on May 9 demonstrates what we have to guard against. The fans think we've won already which simply isn't true.

Awkward

The majority seem to think we'll win the Cup no problem. Happily, my players are used to this and pay no attention.

Say what you like about Airdrie, they're successful and that makes it awkward for us going to meet them.

Of the leading sides I wasn't surprised that Aberdeen ceased to be challengers weeks ago.

They lost their back four with injuries for quite a period and it was too much.

I expected Hearts to do well and they were leading the League for a spell. I suppose they hoped we would drop

★ *CHEERS! Assistant boss Archie Knox toasts manager Walter Smith after Rangers had clinched the title by beating St Mirren 4-0 at Ibrox.*

Pictures by CRAIG HALKETT

BLUE-EYED BOY ALLY WRITE CHOICE

FROM BACK PAGE
would give me a chance if I deserved it – and he did.

"There's been a lot of talk over the years about me leaving Ibrox but I never ever thought I would. I didn't want to go.

"The lap of honour at the finish was special.

"I didn't think the celebrations when we beat Aberdeen could be beaten. I was wrong.

"Saturday's party was just terrific."

McCoist will be named Player of the Year by the Football Writers' Association at a dinner in Glasgow on May 3.

"I am absolutely thrilled," he said . "This is one of the biggest honours that can come to any player and I have to thank my team-mates for making this a great season for me.

"A lot of great players have won this award and I feel privileged to join them."

McCoist is the sixth Rangers player to win the award, the last being Richard Gough three years ago.

By then he may have added to his 31 League goals and clinched the Golden Boot for top Euro marksman.

His closest rival is Jean Pierre-Papin, of French side Marseille.

BLUES BROTHERS . . . Ian Durrant and team-mate Pieter Huistra salute the Huistra goal which sealed a 4-0 win for Rangers.

I'LL NEVER FORGET!

DAVID MURRAY

Now fans want ten in a row – but it's not that simple

GOAL-DEN GARY ... Alexei Mikhailichenko hugs scorer Gary Stevens as Stuart McCall looks on.

ALEX CAMERON'S BIG GAME VERDICT

Consistent Gary's a big shot

GARY STEVENS, most decorated Rangers star, thinks Smith's era has produced "possibly the best" of the four title-winning teams in which he's played.

Rangers have set a high standard and it's up to the others to match it.

Chairman David Murray said the team now bears the Walter Smith stamp and has "ended the Souness reign."

It will take much hard work – and cash – to sustain. Whether they are yet good enough to win a major European honour is arguable.

But given luck in the draw they'll do well.

Stevens had a key role on Saturday with a smash-hit goal in the 4-0 defeat of St Mirren.

Only his second of the season, it was put away spectacularly.

Apart from four Scots' title medals, Stevens won two with Everton and was also a winner in the English and European Cup Winners Cups.

RICHARD GOUGH

Loyal

At £1 million four years ago, he is the best value Rangers have had in a big transfer.

Ibrox skipper Richard Gough said the reason for Rangers fourth League success in a row was "consistency" – the very thing which is epitomised by Stevens.

He has a standard which he never falls below. The next winger to make a fool of him will be the first.

Stevens, who could be recalled by England today to play the CIS next week, added: "New lads coming to the club keeps you on your toes. The competition is fierce."

Winning the League and reaching the Cup Final has been a team effort.

Walter Smith has been loyal to those who've come in and done well.

The best example of this is John Brown who knows Oleg Kuznetsov is ready and eager to take over in defence.

Brown gives the impression that dying for Rangers would not be out of the question.

But the player most likely to emerge to do even better things next season is the classy Alexei Mikhailichenko.

He set up McCoist's second goal – Ally thought it was his best of the season – and set up Pieter Huistra to score the fourth.

Keeper Andy Goram, winning his first medal, laid on McCoist's first with a long kick-out.

Saints boss Davie Hay said: "Rangers could have scored more.

"They are worthy champions."

KUZNETSOV

Oleg Kuznetsov could be restored to Rangers' champion team on Thursday at Motherwell.

Kuznetsov has played in only 17 games since he moved to Ibrox in October, 1990 – mainly because of an early knee injury.

Manager Walter Smith said: "I hear and read stories he's moving – but where? The speculation never includes this.

"Oleg's out of the team and he doesn't like it. I'd be annoyed if he did.

"Any good player who's not in the top team should be upset."

Richard Gough and Stuart McCall will not play against Motherwell on Thursday.

Both are on 10 penalty points and can't risk missing the Scottish Cup Final due to suspension.

Interviewer: ALEX CAMERON

points while they were on a winning run.

I also feel that in the second half of the season Celtic played a brand of football which was as good as any we've seen from a visiting team in the past few years.

If Joe Jordan, Liam Brady and Willie Miller get the backing of their clubs in the close season they'll sustain a strong challenge next time.

The pressures I've felt have all been about not letting down chairman David Murray.

He told me the day after Graeme Souness went to Liverpool that the job was mine. He could easily have picked someone else.

It couldn't have been an easy decision but the positive way he made it lifted my confidence.

I don't feel a manager can change his personality. I certainly haven't done so after serving under Graeme Souness, Jim McLean and Alex Ferguson.

Sure, I picked up tricks of the trade from

them but I'm still the guy I was a year ago.

When we lost the Skol Cup early on, it gave me a jolt.

I wondered if, having been forced to make so many changes, it was going to rebound.

In the summer, I'll be back in the market to sign maybe two players.

Rangers must have the best. This is essential because the demands on our squad will be even greater next season.

In the first few weeks

they may be playing in the League and Skol Cup and the World Cup for Scotland, England, CIS and Holland.

The signings I made last season have done well. Andy Goram and David Robertson are now used to the demands of being a Ranger and perform consistently.

Alexei Mikhailichenko has taken a little time to settle but in 23 matches he's scored 10 goals.

He'll become even better once he fully adjusts to our game.

Target

Stuart McCall, Dale Gordon and Paul Rideout came from the English First Division so the change has been drastic for them.

My target for the future is simply to be successful and continue to play football which entertains.

We're only four goals off the ton and I hope we can achieve this in our closing games.

Trev's title trot

Trevor Steven hasn't missed out on a title party by leaving Ibrox.

The former Ranger's Marseille team need only a point from two games to clinch their fourth French flag on the trot after winning 3-0 at Monaco.

Their star hit man Jean-Pierre Papin won't be staying on to help Marseille try to go one better than St Etienne and win five titles.

He's going to Italy and AC Milan where a three-year deal could net him close £10 million.

GRIN AND

Scottish CUP FINAL Special

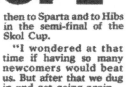

ALEX CAMERON reporting

RANGERS won the Tennents Scottish Cup in a Hampden Final that pleased nearly all loyal fans.

But carping TV neutrals had shock allies – the Ibrox artistocrats themselves.

They wanted to finish with a rhapsody to salute their fans. And freely admitted yesterday that this hadn't happened in a nervously tuneless 25th Final win.

"It could be one of the worst games I've ever played in," said Gary Stevens, who went off yesterday with England to Hungary.

"*We badly wanted to win with style. In fact, the players had their heads down in the dressing-room even though we'd just won the Cup.*

"If it had been a good game it would have meant an awful lot more to us."

Regardless of this, Ibrox fans danced in Copland Road over the first double for 14 years.

And gallant Airdrie were out on the streets convinced a 2-1 defeat was a moral victory.

"I think we'll forget about the way we played," added Stevens. "There was too much long stuff and we lost our way a bit.

"But the lads up front – Mark Hateley and Ally McCoist – came up with the goods and the game looked dead buried.

"We were really on a hiding to nothing. Everybody expected us to win by a big score.

Coast

"I never thought this was on after watching Airdrie beating Hearts in the semi-final.

"In fact, I would have preferred to play Hearts. Airdrie make it very difficult."

Skipper Richard Gough added: "We didn't play well but we won the Cup and that's what matters.

"We wanted to play well but didn't. At 2-0 we may have tried to coast a bit.

"*People said we'd win by three or four, but we knew deep down it wasn't going to be like that.*

Furious

"Winning the double means a lot and it's a good day for the club and manager Walter Smith."

Sub Andy Smith's stunning 80th minute fight-back goal really shook Rangers.

Airdrie suddenly had the look of Davids shaping up to Goliath.

It was certainly close but Rangers deserved to win despite the furious finish.

Stevens confessed he had a foot in the Airdrie goal.

"Smith volleyed the ball and it scraped off my studs and moved two or three feet to Andy Goram's left and ended in the top corner," he said.

The Diamonds were on their best behaviour.

THAT WINNING FEELING . . . Airdrie's Chris Honor and keeper John Martin can do nothing about Ally McCoist's Hampden winner.

TWO MORE FOR EUROPE

MIKHAILICHENKO

FROM BACK PAGE
more a factor as people want Rangers to prove they're winners outwith the domestic sphere," he elaborated.

"We're becoming more conscious that we must start to do something again.

"In the Champions Cup we'll be against the best in Europe.

"*We've been unlucky in the past to meet one of the eventual finalists – like Sparta Prague – in the early rounds.*

Form

"I don't think we're far away from being able to field a team who can do well outside Scotland.

"Scottish clubs are always under a wee bit more pressure than a lot of other countries because some players are in four competitions.

"We play in the League, League Cup, Scottish Cup and a few will be involved in the World Cup.

"So it's difficult to hit form in the early part of the year because of the number of matches."

Smith is pleased that Alexei Mikhailichenko has now settled into the side.

"He's scoring good goals and that's vital because he replaced Mark Walters who was giving us 10 or 12 a year.

"Our start to the season was generally good, despite losing to Hearts in our first away game.

"Around October came our worst period when we lost to Aberdeen at home,

then to Sparta and to Hibs in the semi-final of the Skol Cup.

"I wondered at that time if having so many newcomers would beat us. But after that we dug in and got going again.

"If our bad spell hadn't come at this time we might even have done better in Europe.

"We've played well and scored a lot of goals which pleases me because the onus is on us to attack home and away.

Target

"I admit the statistics of having lost only two games away yet THREE at home are peculiar.

"But we took the title and that is always the target. Cup success is a bonus."

The Rangers players not on international duty will fly today for a week in the sun at Monaco.

THAT SINKING FEELING . . . Martin is grounded as Mark Hateley steers home David Robertson's cross for the opener.

PICTURES BY CRAIG HALKETT and IAN TORRANCE

BEAR IT BLUES!

Ibrox rhapsody never happened

PANIC MEASURE . . . Andy Smith's cracking volley that guaranteed a nail-biting Hampden finale for Rangers.

Smith's sparkler had 'em rattled

GOAL-ACE Andy Smith gave Airdrie fans something to sing about.

His fifth goal in the Cup was the best of the three.

It also sparked off a fight-back which rattled Rangers.

The 23-year-old, who cost £15,000 from Peterhead nearly two years ago said:

"I volleyed the ball without thinking and was delighted to see it going into the top corner.

"If Gary Stevens is claiming the goal for a deflection he can forget it. It's mine!

"We started to believe in ourselves because we hadn't scored against Rangers all season.

"Wes Reid came close as well and Rangers were pleased to hear the final whistle.

"Next season will be the same for us — we'll have to fight to stay in the Premier League.

"When I first came to Airdrie playing in the Premier League was my only target.

"Having scored in the Final I don't know what to expect next."

Their man-marking upset Rangers but the most policed, Hateley and McCoist, still scored.

Hateley snatched the first when Davie Kirkwood fell as the ball was in flight from Nigel Spackman.

David Robertson was given time to aim carefully as he squared the ball into the penalty area.

Sweeper Paul Jack ran to meet him but the ball went under his foot and Hateley swept it grandly into goal.

Airdrie marker Gus Caesar was for once posted missing.

McCoist's goal just before half-time was the result of a splendid quick forward pass by Stuart McCall.

Again the Airdrie system broke down and Walter Kidd may have wondered why.

The Rangers millionaires are racing away from the others on all fronts. It was a tremendous show by Airdrie to nearly match them.

Alex MacDonald is the pied piper of Broomfield. The Airdrie players don't question his judgment.

"Both Rangers' goals were easy," MacDonald said. "Losing the second just before half-time was a nightmare.

"Andy Smith's goal was the best of the match and gave our supporters something to shout abut — which is the most important thing to me.

"I'm disappointed but still delighted about the effort and team spirit of the players.

"I hope we can achieve half as much next season."

SPORTS HOTLINE

RODGER BAILLIE taking your calls

SCOTTISH soccer has reached the end of the long and winding road for this domestic season.

But **Hotline's** snipers predictably were waiting to stage an ambush at the finishing post!

Mount Florida resident **Robert Dickson** was first on the attack, for he wants Hampden closed.

"The SFA's decision to retain Hampden as the national stadium shows no consideration for the local residents. Where I live fans were urinating in closes and fences were broken down.

★ ★ ★ ★ ★

Rangers had a major off the field problem with their ticket allocation from the SFA, which was smaller than their giant army of fans required.

And hell hath no fury like a ticketless fan left out of the Cup Final.

Ardrossan's **Harry Herd**, secretary of the local supporters association, claimed: "The usual fat cats who never watch any other match had tickets for the Cup Final.

"Yet good fans were left without tickets."

★ ★ ★ ★ ★

Andrew Peace from **Uphall, West Lothian** said: "I've not had my cheque back from Rangers, never mind a ticket.

"I don't know why the SFA don't just split the allocation between the competing teams, instead of worrying about other club's supporters.

"I don't imagine many Celtic fans wanted to watch Saturday's game."

★ ★ ★ ★ ★

Campbeltown's James MacDonald isn't happy either.

"My family have four Premier Club tickets and three debenture bonds and we couldn't get a ticket," he moaned.

★ ★ ★ ★ ★

Rangers fan **Alan Beattie** from **Lanark** has praise for the staff in the Airdrie ticket office.

"About 300 of us queued for more than three hours at Broomfield on Friday for tickets," he said.

"I'd like to thank the staff for coming out and giving us cups of soup."

★ ★ ★ ★ ★

From **Invergordon**, a furious **Henry Miller** blasted the SFA.

"Their Cup Final programme cost £2 and was an absolute rip-off.

"The Rangers team picture had Mo Johnston, Mark Walters, Trevor Steven and Terry Hurlock in the line-up.

"Surely they could find an up-to-date picture."

★ ★ ★ ★ ★

Still on charges, Rangers fan **Ralph Craig** of **Newtongrange** hit out at the SFA's ticket pricing policy.

"They charged £8 for a seat in the covered enclosure and upped it to £12 for the final. That's a bit steep."

★ ★ ★ ★ ★

Edinburgh's Marion Grant isn't too charitable about Rangers skipper Richard Gough.

"I was surprised he didn't hand the Cup along the line of players after the presentation.

"It's so long since Rangers have won the trophy, maybe they've forgotten what usually happens."

★ ★ ★ ★ ★

Former referee **James Marshall** of **Torphichen, West Lothian**, reckons he spotted a Hampden incident everyone else missed.

"Owen Coyle was definitely in an offside position when Andy Smith scored for Airdrie."

★ ★ ★ ★ ★

But, surprise, surprise, **Alan Fisher**, from the deep blue territory of Ibrox, praises Cup Final referee Douglas Hope.

"I thought he had a tremendous match. It's only right he should get a pat on the back."

★ ★ ★ ★ ★

The Cup Final wasn't the only topic to upset the callers.

James McKay of **Alexandria** is furious at Clydebank's decision to release veteran keeper Jim Gallacher.

"It's a disgraceful decision. He should have been put on the coaching staff right away."

★ ★ ★ ★ ★

Long-range Hibs fan **Ronnie Mann** phoned from Stranraer to complain: "What justification does Andy Roxburgh have for bringing Pat Nevin back into the Scottish squad?

"Nevin has never done anything for Scotland. Hibs midfielders Mickey Weir and Pat McGinlay surely deserve a chance."

★ ★ ★ ★ ★

John Riggans of **Nitshill** thinks he has the answer to St Mirren's current search for a new boss.

"They should bring back Tony Fitzpatrick."

★ ★ ★ ★ ★

Hamilton fan **Alex Stewart** from **Blackwood, Lanarkshire** finds it hard to stomach Airdrie's success.

"It's only a season since we were both in the First Division, but look how they've streaked ahead.

"We could be in their position if the board spent cash on the team."

Absence makes Bears groan louder

MARK WALTERS   **MO JOHNSTON**

SKOL CUP FINAL

(12)

A GAME

By ★ ALEX CAMERON

JUBILANT Rangers snatched back the Skol Cup at Hampden yesterday...

As Aberdeen handed it to them on a plate with two golden goofs.

The second and deciding freak came off luckless Gary Smith's head six minutes from the end of an exhausting extra-time session.

It couldn't have been more welcome for Rangers – or more agonising for the Dons.

RANGERS 2 ABERDEEN 1

After extra time

Scorers: Rangers – McCall (13 mins), Smith (o.g. 114). Aberdeen – Shearer (62).   Att: 45,298

The game certainly deserved a better ending.

But Smith knew in a flash he had unwittingly lost a Final he, more than most, had tried to win skilfully.

His utter dejection was not helped by the fact that a reckless passback by David Winnie led to Stuart McCall's 13th-minute opener.

Theo Snelders, taken by surprise, tried to chest the ball away but it spun to McCall, who was in no mood to squander such an easy chance.

The Dons had the consolation of a belting right-foot equaliser by Duncan Shearer in 62 minutes.

And the chance was set up by Winnie to balance the full-back's personal account.

It was hardly surprising that Under-21 international Smith, and a host of his team-mates, sprawled on their backs like war casualties when Rangers got the dramatic 114th-minute winner.

Upset

Only yards away, Rangers players tussled so anxiously on the ground to congratulate ex-Don David Robertson, he could have been Madonna!

Rangers certainly had winners' luck, but in the final tally-up they had many more goal attempts...

AND ON SHEER PRESSURE, MERITED THE VICTORY.

It will be hard for the Pittodrie outsiders to swallow this, having been only six minutes away from the prospect of a major upset.

Desperate

Robertson was ecstatic because, though he fired the ball fiercely, it was really an optimistic cross-cum-shot pleading for a finisher.

Smith lunged for it just ahead of Mark Hateley – the act of a desperate defender.

The ball could have gone forward to safety or round the post.

But on this day of awful luck for the Dons, it whirled into the corner giving Snelders not even a dog's chance of saving it.

That was the end, the grand but luckless finale to a game which had looked sure to go into a penalty shoot-out.

And fast-tiring Rangers, frustrated and just a little bamboozled that a tide of pressure failed to produce a winner, will rarely be more grateful.

Although it was the score I predicted, the

OH GEE WHAT HAVE I DONE! The unfortunate Gary Smith and Aberdeen team-mate Alex McLeish are down and out as Rangers Mark Hateley, Ally McCoist and Dale Gordon celebrate the Skol winner at Hampden.   Picture CRAIG HALKETT

EXTRA SPECIAL — BUT AGONY FOR GARY

From Back Page

we deserved to win."

Now Rangers have a new worry for the return leg at Leeds next week.

For skipper Richard Gough went off with a recurrence of his groin injury, and Trevor Steven made a bitter after-match attack.

Smith said: "I hope they're fit for the Leeds game. We'll know better in 48 hours."

Man of the Match Stuart McCall scored Rangers' first goal – after Aberdeen keeper Theo Snelders was caught out by the new passback rule – and Duncan Shearer equalised.

Aberdeen boss Willie Miller made a bitter after-match attack.

"A team like Aberdeen always has to put up with a lot in Glasgow," he said.

"I won't elaborate. The players know it, I know it and it was there for everybody to see."

Miller was obviously unhappy at the passback rule confusion which caused the first goal.

He claimed: "We were punished again in the second half after a tackle was seen as a passback.

"This law needs to be clarified."

Miller defended Gary Smith.

"It was a good cross and he just got a touch, but these things happen. He had an outstanding game."

Rangers defender David Robertson, who set up the winner against his old team, said:

"Eoin Jess tried to close me down, but I got in the cross and as Mark Hateley

went for it Gary Smith got the slightest touch."

Rangers boss Smith singled out Ian Ferguson, saying: "He's got back his stamina and strength.

"If he'd got a goal from the shot that hit a post, it would have been one of the best ever seen at Hampden."

Dons ace Shearer won a luxury weekend for two at Gleneagles Hotel from the sponsors. As own goals don't count, his was the game's last score.

He was whisked to the airport to head for Kiev where he'll join the Ukraine squad for international duty this week.

Pieter Huistra wasn't considered for Rangers due to injury.

Alexei Mikhailichenko didn't have time to grab his winner's medal.

DONS SHOOT THEMSELVES IN THE FOOT 13

OF TWO GAFFES

And Rangers clean up

STAR TURNS . . . Man-of-the-Match Stuart McCall and Ian Durrant get to grips with the silverware after Rangers' Hampden triumph

Dons were better and more resilient than I expected.

It was difficult not to feel sorry for them.

Rangers, clearly suffering a Euro hangover after their exertions against Leeds, weren't as sharp as they had been against the English champions.

Bounced

But the fact that they had two fresh men on the bench worth nearly £3 million – Alexei Mikhailichenko and Dale Gordon – demonstrated the difficulty clubs like Aberdeen face.

Hampden was awash with red, white and blue as the Cup was handed over to sit alongside the League trophy and the Scottish Cup in the Ibrox trophy room.

It was the last match before the bulldozers move in to dolly up Hampden.

And this may have added a little more spice to the victory lap by Rangers.

Both teams used their two subs – Lee Richardson taking over from injured Roy Aitken in 25 minutes and Scott Booth replacing Jim Bett in 61.

Richard Gough, who didn't look fully fit, was replaced by Mikhailichenko in 64 minutes and, shortly before, Dale Gordon took over from limping Trevor Steven.

Ian Durrant, McCall, Ian Ferguson, John Brown and Dave McPherson were the top Rangers.

Take away his badluck goal and Smith was the top Don, followed by Snelders, Alex McLeish and Eoin Jess.

There had been bags of action.

A Ferguson shot bounced off a post before McCall's opener.

Refused

And Jess nearly grabbed an equaliser soon after.

He left Gough on the ground behind him but Andy Goram moved out just far enough to narrow the angle and save.

A 20-yard shot by Ally McCoist was held on the ground by Snelders – one of several good saves.

When Mikhailichenko came on, he had four shots at goal and from one Snelders had another great save.

Snelders was booked when the referee debatably ruled that McLeish had passed back.

The Dutch goalie refused at first to give the ref the ball for an indirect free-kick.

Three others yellow-carded in a match firmly handled by Dougie Hope were Richardson of Aberdeen, and Gordon and Hateley of Rangers.

Hampden match facts

★ RANGERS ★	
Goals	13:50 and 114:15
Shots on target	11
Shots off target	19
Corners	13
Throw Ins	27
Free kicks	20
Pass backs	19
Goal kicks	10
Offside	3
Cautions	2

★ ABERDEEN ★	
Goal	62:10
Shots on target	3
Shots off target	7
Corners	2
Throw-ins	26
Free kicks	11
Passbacks	8
Goal kicks	25
Offside	6
Cautions	2

■ Game duration: 121 minutes, 20 seconds. Actual playing time: 76.03. Stoppages: 10.

Ally's the top hit man

ALLY McCOIST was off target yesterday – but he still finished top Skol marksman.

The Rangers hit man failed to equal his best-ever League Cup tally of nine, but his eight Skol goals put him three clear of Aberdeen's Duncan Shearer and Gerry Creaney of Celtic.

Rangers were top Skol scorers with 18 and the total of 130 was the highest for the knock-out system in the sponsored competition.

■ BERWICK Ranger Graeme Davidson won the first-ever Skol Sprint before the big match. He earned £3,000 by being fastest man in the 60 metre dash.

RANGERS

ANDY GORAM: He had a great first-half save from Jess and had no chance with Duncan Shearer's goal. ★★★

STUART McCALL: Snapped up first-half goal well and operated effectively in midfield and right back. ★★★

DAVID ROBERTSON: Powerful contribution with runs down the left – one of his crosses led to the winner. ★★★★

RICHARD GOUGH: He found Eoin Jess a hot handful in that first half. Substituted in 64 minutes because of injury. ★★

JOHN BROWN: Rangers' defence anchor in the first half, he battled valiantly after knee injury early in the second. ★★★

DAVE McPHERSON: Moved from right back to centre half in defensive shuffle and did well. Danger up front at set-pieces. ★★★

TREVOR STEVEN: Wide right role, he produced some good moves but not enough of them. Substituted after 57 minutes. ★★

IAN FERGUSON: Great first-half shot hit the post and he worked so hard throughout to get his side moving. ★★★

ALLY McCOIST: Kept as quiet as possible by the Dons defence, with only the chance of three shots on target. ★★

MARK HATELEY: A day when his flicks and feints didn't come off, until he forced the Dons into that o.g. unhappy ending. ★★

IAN DURRANT: Yet again he was at the heart of so much of all that was the best in Rangers' play. ★★★★

ALEXEI MIKHAILICHENKO: Came on after 64 minutes. The most effective of the four subs, with one great shot. ★★★

DALE GORDON: Tried hard to set up chances but few of them came off. ★★

ABERDEEN

THEO SNELDERS. Involved in the mix-up at the first goal, but recovered with some wonder saves. ★★★

STEPHEN WRIGHT. Kept his cool under pressure, and produced one great tackle to foil Mikhailichenko. ★★★

DAVID WINNIE. Also played a major part in the first-goal cock-up, but atoned by setting up the equaliser. ★★

BRIAN GRANT. Worked hard but didn't manage to get forward enough to trouble Rangers. ★★

ALEX McLEISH. Another superb game from the man who has made more comebacks than Sinatra. ★★★

GARY SMITH. The best defender – what a tragedy for him that his own goal settled the final. ★★★★

ROY AITKEN. Didn't have long enough to impress himself on the game before going off injured in 27 minutes. ★★

JIM BETT. Some deft touches, but the gamble of playing him after such a long absence didn't pay off. ★★

EOIN JESS. Wonder first half when every time he touched the ball he was a danger to Rangers. ★★★★

DUNCAN SHEARER. Great strike for the equaliser, but not enough overall pressure on goal. ★★★

MIXU PAATELAINEN. Another who could have troubled Rangers more than he did over the 120 minutes. ★★

LEE RICHARDSON. Neat touches but didn't create enough chances. ★★

SCOTT BOOTH. Replaced Bett in 61 minutes, and battled bravely despite an obvious extra-time injury problem. ★★

CUP COLOUR SPECIAL...Pages 32 and 33

SIMPLY CHEERS AHEAD .. BOSS REVEALS SECRET

WE'VE LOADSA

★ ALEX CAMERON
ON THE CUP AFTERMATH

RANGERS will spend millions this summer on players . . .

But they clinched their fifth Treble with a quality money can't buy – bottle!

And manager Walter Smith said fiercely: "It's been said our Treble is bad for football but if it is, it's not our fault."

No team, including Aberdeen, can touch their battling spirit which skipper Richard Gough says is brought about by "togetherness".

It's a priceless mix of guts and skill which Rangers have proved in domestic and Euro matches.

They deserved to win an exciting Tennents Scottish Cup Final 2-1 after a shaky start and tightrope finish.

From chairman David Murray all the way down, Rangers are more with-it than any of the others.

THEY'RE ON CLOUD NINE AND ALONE IN A STRATOSPHERE OF THEIR OWN MAKING.

The irony of winning at Parkhead in the last match before the Jungle is made all-seated was not lost on Celtic fans who were less than pleased.

Rangers' roller-coaster is in full swing with the only bleak spot the fact that Andy Goram left for Los Angeles yesterday for a knee operation.

Mark Hateley will be in a Glasgow hospital tomorrow being treated for a mild thigh problem and Stuart McCall will have an op next week.

Smith spoke jovially in the Ibrox Blue Room yesterday – and didn't forget to pass credit to assistant Archie Knox.

"Rangers are expected to win trophies but it's pressure I can live with," said Smith. "It's not doing us any harm.

"*If we're the only team having to cope with this, the others should look at themselves and accept a share of it as well as us.*

"If we're to take all the pressure, others must think we'll win all the time.

Passion

"Archie took the lads to Monaco for a short break before the Final.

"*I don't know what he did with them but it worked!*"

Aberdeen failed because they lost their urgent passion – but not their pride – in the second part of the first half and for 25 minutes after the break.

Ian Durrant, the passer, and Stuart McCall, the runner, did more than any others to ensure Rangers snatched the Treble.

The game was a grand splash of the cavalier football customers want to see.

Aberdeen were unlucky but also nearly as inept at taking scoring chances as AC Milan in the Euro Final.

Their top man, Brian

★ HIT AND MISS! Rangers hero Neil Murray (above) shoots for goal, and, (below) beats Aberdeen keeper Theo Snelders with the help of a deflection, to Ian Durrant's delight.

MILLER SALUTES DONS BATTLERS

BEATEN Cup Final boss Willie Miller spoke last night of his pride for his team.

"We had a lot of territorial advantage and did very well in the first 25 minutes," he said.

"We created a few openings by getting round the back of their defence.

"However, we never had a striker in the right place.

"When we lost a goal we fell out of it a bit to half-time. After we scored we pushed them hard but needed the wee breaks and the right bounce of the ball.

"If we had taken them into extra time we had a real good chance of going on and winning. We were looking fresh.

"We had to go for it 2-0 down and we got a goal soon after Eoin Jess came on.

Happy

"I'm very happy with what my players have given throughout the season.

"Choosing a team was difficult and there'll be a lot of unhappy players because they've all came in and did well.

"I congratulate Rangers on a very good season having competed well in Europe and won the treble."

Pictures: CRAIG HALKETT

BOTTLE!

Just don't blame us for it says Smith

LEE'S PLEASED! Aberdeen goal hero Lee Richardson turns away to celebrate, but there's dejection on the face of David Robertson.

Grant, hit a post in the first minute but the Dons exerted so much pressure their fans were entitled to wonder why the cupboard was bare.

My forecast was wrong because I thought Rangers were a worn-out team after winning the Skol Cup, League title and nearly reaching the European Cup Final.

Worried

I was in good company because Smith admitted:

"After we clinched the League title at Airdrie some players had only a few games and some not at all. It worried me.

"When Neil Murray scored we were starting to play a bit and finished the stronger at half-time.

"The second half was reasonably even and then the Dons tried to get back into the game.

"At that stage we had to defend well but we were tired."

Of course, it would be better if the honours were spread. But merit is the only guage and Rangers are out front.

If there was any haggle about bad luck for the Dons – and there was some – no one could dispute that Hateley's winner was as fine a goal as Parkhead has seen for a long time.

Durrant made a great running pass which looked even better to Smith on TV.

Hateley hit the ball as though he never wanted to see it again and it whipped between Theo Snelders' legs and over the line.

This over-ruled the hard luck of Brian Irvine re-directing a Murray shot which otherwise would have gone past.

Murray claimed the goal and reasonable people will give him it. But technically the "credit" should go to Irvine.

Irvine's misfortune was not helped by the fact that he had just made a rash swing at the ball to try to clear and landed it conveniently at Murray's feet.

"Having started so well it was disappointing to lose the opener in the way we did," said skipper Alex McLeish, without rubbing salt in his team's wounds.

"Brian hitting a post and another couple of goalmouth incidents raised our hopes.

Admitted

"But it's easy to say that. We had to show up as Rangers have done this season.

"We made a go of it in the second half and Rangers sat back a wee bit when we scored.

"The ref admitted there had been a handling incident but didn't think it was deliberate.

"It was disappointing but we'll be back for the Final next year – and if I'm good enough maybe I'll be back, too."

Should Willie Miller have brought on Eoin Jess sooner?

The Dons manager explained that he knew the maximum time it would be fair to ask of Jess after breaking a leg.

That was why he left his appearance to the 73rd minute when it seemed a half-time gamble would have been more appropriate.

The in-off jinx which so often haunts Cup Final players was balanced, although not as crucially, when a Lee Richardson shot clicked off John Brown and left Goram with no chance.

Referee Jim McCluskey handled the game well.

There was very little argument even about two penalty claims.

The first was for handling – I thought by David Robertson – which was correctly ignored.

The second was when a pair of arms wrapped round Scott Booth as he ran into the area.

But it was one of the least contentious finals despite the pace.

RANGERS IN FINE FURY!

FROM BACK PAGE
Final, the Committee's ruling was hushed up until yesterday in case the news affected Rangers' chances.

The bust-up in January was as bitter as any between two clubs in recent years.

Speculation

Chairman Murray confirmed that Rangers had made a £2.5 million offer for 21-year-old 6ft 3ins Ferguson.

But Jim McLean denied this to the Daily Record and then was forced to admit: *"I told the Record a lie."*

He claimed he had done so only to maintain confidentiality over Rangers' move.

Murray insisted he had spoken out because of speculation and simply "wanted to put Rangers fans in the picture."

United also sent a lawyer's letter to London agent Denis Roach.

They demanded an apology over a claim that United had said the youngster "would never kick a ball again for United or anybody else."

Roach also consulted a top Scots QC about the legality of Ferguson's contract, which would have tied him to Tannadice until 1998 before United said they would consider offers.

Hoped

Ferguson hasn't played since he broke a toe in a Dundee pub brawl.

United exonerated him from blame, but warned:

"In future he must be more careful of his choice of company."

Andy Roxburgh had hoped Ferguson would be fit in time to play in the World Cup match in Estonia.

But the last chance to prove his fitness was United's final league game with Aberdeen – and he wasn't ready.

● Chelsea chairman Ken Bates who watched the Cup Final, is also interested in Ferguson and can't be ruled out of the race to sign him.

SPORTS HOTLINE

RODGER BAILLIE TAKES YOUR CALLS

THE red, white and blue ribbons have been tied on the Tennents Scottish Cup, but even a treble haul couldn't keep all Rangers fans happy.

And Aberdeen supporters weren't too amused after seeing the Ibrox side clinch their first treble since 1978 at the first Scottish Cup Final to be held at Parkhead for 70 years.

Brian Marshall, of Lennoxtown, was one of the happier callers.

"People can snipe at Rangers as much as they like, but the record books show they have won Scotland's three major trophies.

"As far as I'm concerned, and thousands more like me, they're simply the best!"

★ ★ ★ ★

However, Aberdeen supporter Brian Cowe, who travelled to the final from Fraserburgh is still upset.

"The Dons were robbed. Referee Jim McCluskey was a joke the way he turned down blatant penalty appeals."

★ ★ ★ ★

He wasn't the only caller in the complaints corner.

Paisley's Gordon Berry, Wishaw's Peter Hughes and Robert Cross, of Port Glasgow, all phoned on the same topic.

They claimed TV showed Rangers players singing sectarian songs during the after-match celebrations.

Shame

Cross said: "David Murray has done so much to try to change Rangers' sectarian image. It's a shame his players let him down by returning to the bad old days."

★ ★ ★ ★

James McEwan, of Mosspark, didn't like what he saw from his armchair view.

"Aberdeen's players moaned constantly at the ref. If they had done as well with their feet as they did with their mouths they would have won 10-0."

★ ★ ★ ★

Steve Duffus is an exiled Scot who lives in Crewe, and he would have liked any kind of TV view. "What a disgrace! We only saw 10 minutes of Scottish Cup highlights on TV in England."

★ ★ ★ ★

Sighthill's Jimmy Neil is an unhappy Rangers season-ticket holder.

"I didn't get a Cup final ticket, nor did I get one for last year's final or the Skol Cup Final. I realise Rangers don't get enough tickets for everyone, but surely they could work a rota system."

★ ★ ★ ★

Some Rangers fans didn't like the choice of Parkhead as the venue, and Ronnie Harper, of Girvan, felt he was short-changed at the end.

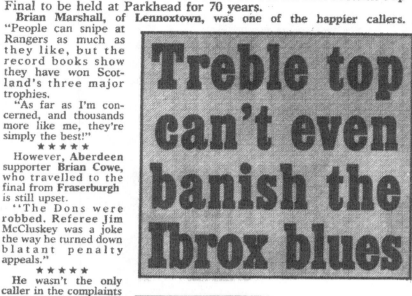

Treble top can't even banish the Ibrox blues

JIM McCLUSKEY ...final ref

"I paid £14 for a seat in the front row of the stand. But none of us could see the Rangers players lap of honour because of the number of stewards and policemen round the track."

★ ★ ★ ★

Joseph Milligan, of Ardrossan, had a ticket for The Jungle and he has an unhappy Cup final memory.

"I got there at 2.25, but didn't get into the ground until 3.20.

"When I complained to a policeman, he told me to contact the SFA and Celtic."

★ ★ ★ ★

Rangers fan Derek Clarkson, of Stewarton, has nothing but praise for the Celtic staff.

"I was supposed to have a ticket left for me, but the arrangement fell through.

"The Celtic stewards couldn't have been more courteous and polite, and gave me a spare complimentary left by an Aberdeen player."

★ ★ ★ ★

Tommy Smith, of Auchenshuggle, didn't agree with Jim McLean's player ratings in Saturday's Daily Record.

"I don't know how he could put Alex McLeish and Brian Irvine ahead of Richard Gough and rate Brian Grant and Paul Mason better than Ian Durrant.

"He got his answer during the game."

★ ★ ★ ★

The sight of the Cup final at Parkhead – without Celtic playing – was too much for Jim Cassidy, of Bonhill.

"I'm green with envy. Rangers and Aberdeen fans had fun in the sun and our team can't fill the ground.

"We can't keep our best players, with John Collins and Peter Grant being allowed to go."

★ ★ ★ ★

Sighthill's John Kelly is also worried about Collins' future.

"It looks as if we'll flog our best player yet again. I think the fans would rather see Paul McStay leave.

"It would be even worse if Collins joined Rangers. That would be the final insult."

★ ★ ★ ★

Just in case SFA Chief Executive Jim Farry is patting himself on the back for a successful Cup final, he didn't please James Robertson, of Linlithgow.

"I've never seen a more glum face at the trophy presentation.

"The final is supposed to be a joyous occasion, but he looked as if he was at a funeral!"

SUPERSUB McCOIST SETS
LEAGUE CUP FINAL SPECIAL
ALLY'S

SILVER LINING ... Ally McCoist fires in Rangers' Cup winner with a spectacular overhead kick

I'VE DONE IT! Supersub McCoist turns towards the Hibs goal to see his shot flashing into the net despite a despairing attempt by Jim Leighton to reach it

HIBS 1 RANGERS 2

Scorers: Hibs – McPherson (og 59 mins). Rangers – Durrant (55), McCoist (81). Attendance – 47,632.

ALLY McCOIST snatched the most golden goal of his glittering career to win the League Cup for Rangers at jam-packed Parkhead yesterday.

Such a thing could only happen to magic McCoist in a game of Titans which gave the Ibrox side their 19th victory in the competition.

The score was tied at 1-1 when Walter Smith decided with 31 minutes to go that it was time to unleash McCoist in place of Pieter Huistra.

The Dutchman looked bitterly unhappy as he went off but was delighted as he saw McCoist snatch victory with a brilliant overhead kick nine minutes from the end.

McCoist, just back after months on the injury list, made such an acrobatic jump for the ball it would have won him a gold medal in Olympic gymnastics.

He has now broken the record he shared with Davie Cooper by winning his eighth League Cup winner's medal.

His seven previous successes were against Aberdeen (3 times), Celtic (3 times) and Dundee United.

Rangers fans were overwhelmed with joy. Although their team made more chances, the game was always balanced on a tightrope.

But there was no safety net for gallant Hibs when David Robertson hurled one of his special throw-ins from the left in line with the penalty box.

The ball swirled into the air and a cluster of players went for it but couldn't control it. Steven Tweed may just have got his head to it, enough to send it on to McCoist.

Golden-booter McCoist took it on his chest, with his back to goal, then sent the ball away from Jim Leighton's despairing dive.

It was a marvellous piece of play by McCoist, with Leighton blameless.

Few would dispute that Rangers deserved the win.

It was a display of steel

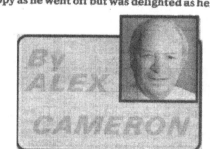

By ALEX CAMERON

Pictures: CRAIG HALKETT, RICHARD PARKER and DAVID CRUICKSHANKS

A RECORD WITH WONDER WINNER

8-SOME REEL !

ALL SQUARE ... Kevin McAllister signals to Hibs fans after Rangers' Dave McPherson heads Keith Wright's shot into his own net, to the anguish of David Robertson

THE FINAL STATS

HIBS

Goals	1
	(58min 58sec)
Shots on	6
Shots off	4
Corners	3
Throw-ins	25
Free-kicks	16
Pass-backs	6
Goal kicks	13
Offside	6
Cautions	2
	(Wright, O'Neill)

RANGERS

Goals	2
	(54m 57s, 81m 30s)
Shots on	6
Shots off	13
Corners	10
Throw-ins	15
Free-kicks	17
Pass-backs	10
Goal kicks	11
Offside	4
Cautions	0
Game stoppages	6
Duration	96m 24s
Actual play	63m 35s

★ The 47,632 crowd sent the competition total to 356,022 – an increase of just under 50,000 against last season.

The 37 ties produced 110 goals, with Celtic's Frank McAvennie leading marksman on five goals.

Five players registered hat-tricks, and Partick Thistle's Ian Cameron was top scorer in a single tie, with four goals against Albion Rovers.

Crime department – 62 players were booked and six red-carded.

HIBS

8 JIM LEIGHTON: Succession of good saves to keep Rangers out, apart from one mistake. No chance with the goals.

6 WILLIE MILLER: Started well against Huistra, but as the game went on the Rangers winger caused him more trouble.

6 GRAHAM MITCHELL: Up against Rangers' most dangerous player, Trevor Steven. One chance – took it like a defender.

6 DAVID FARRELL: Good long balls that troubled Rangers, and battled hard in that over-crowded midfield area.

7 STEVEN TWEED: Great rescue act in the first two minutes to stop Rangers grabbing a quick goal. Hibs' defensive hero.

6 GORDON HUNTER: Man-for-man on Mark Hateley, and did as well as anyone can against Rangers' ace hit man.

8 KEVIN McALLISTER: Switched from right to left to try to catch out defenders. Great display, but should have scored.

7 BRIAN HAMILTON: Hard battle with his former St Mirren team-mate, Ian Ferguson, in that rugged midfield.

7 KEITH WRIGHT: He showed marvellous determination to get the ball across for the equaliser. Made the goal out of nothing.

6 DARREN JACKSON: Kept quiet by Rangers' back four. Well into the second half before he got his first shot. Subbed.

6 MICHAEL O'NEILL: Operated in the old inside-left position, but failed to provide a regular supply for his strikers.

5 GARETH EVANS: Replaced Jackson and had one great effort – but found he had to make his own chances too often.

Subs not used – Beamont, Reid (g).

RANGERS

7 ALLY MAXWELL: Good saves by the Rangers keeper, but appeared reluctant to come off his line at crucial moments.

6 GARY STEVENS: Unhappy spell in the second half when he made crucial errors, but did well to clear from Evans.

6 DAVID ROBERTSON: Always keen to move forward, but found McAllister so hard to pin down in the second half.

7 RICHARD GOUGH: Effective as ever, until Hibs got their equaliser and then he had a shaky spell. Finished strongly, however.

7 DAVE McPHERSON: Disaster for him with an own goal. He had looked so much in command until then, but recovered well.

6 STUART McCALL: As always, all over the park. But his lack of match practice told with not as much dominance.

8 TREVOR STEVEN: Answered his critics with his best display of the season, and most of Rangers' pressure came from him.

7 IAN FERGUSON: The midfield anchor man who put in a power of work to blunt Hibs' efforts to take control.

8 IAN DURRANT: Marvellous piece of up-front play for Rangers' first goal which showed yet again his class.

7 MARK HATELEY: Always a handful for Hibs, but they managed to blunt his goal menace with a few near things.

6 PIETER HUISTRA: Started slowly, but did get in some telling crosses. Not enough on a regular basis, however. Subbed.

8 ALLY McCOIST: Soccer showman back on the biggest stage the way only he can – with a spectacular goal.

Subs not used – Mikhailichenko, Scott (g).

REFEREE – Jim McCluskey, Stewarton.

---

by Hibs and a pity there had to be a loser.

It had most of the good things in football, including a bit of controversy to keep the fans arguing.

It was a shame that the wee green devil Kevin McAllister had to be on the losing side.

He ran and ran and did everything possible to sway it in Hibs' favour.

Deadlier

It was a pity that Leighton had to lose two goals. He was blameless each time and made only one mistake in the game.

Justice took a long time in coming but in a superb battle Rangers emerged the deadlier side.

Hibs were certain they should have had a penalty just before half-time.

Keith Wright broke clear and Ally Maxwell dived despairing at his feet. Wright stumbled and crashed to the turf.

But Ally Maxwell claimed he hadn't touched him and TV pictures backed this up.

It was good refereeing by Jim McCluskey, who right away booked Wright for feigning a foul.

Richard Gough was immense, Stuart McCall never relented and Trevor Steven had one of his best matches.

The decision to play Ian Durrant from the kick-off was a surprise – but it was certainly the right one.

He broke the deadlock in 55 minutes with a super move involving a couple of one-two passes, first with Ian Ferguson and then with Mark Hateley.

The striker's final pass was perfect and Durrant ran on to lift the ball over Leighton.

Having waited patiently for goals, it was a surprise when Hibs levelled only four minutes later after the Rangers defence blundered.

Control

Richard Gough played the ball to Gary Stevens who tried to return it but misjudged.

Keith Wright gathered the ball on the byeline and when he shot, Dave McPherson turned the ball into his own net.

Hibs refused to lie down and it was greatly to their credit that they looked organised and in control of themselves right to the end.

Ironically, McAllister had the best chance for Hibs in only 25 minutes.

Darren Jackson gave him a superb ball on the left of the six-yard box.

The linesman's flag flickered up but McCluskey waved him aside. McAllister may have thought he was offside, hesitated and hit the side netting.

The game was littered with good saves by Leighton.

In 16 minutes he dived to touch the ball out.

In 44 minutes he pushed out a Huistra shot and was lucky when Ferguson struck the rebound over the bar.

But this was ageless Leighton's only mistake in a game in which he had much more of the action than Maxwell.

The second-half started with him holding a shot from Steven and a Huistra header hit a post.

Leighton surprisingly denied he had touched the ball when a corner was awarded.

He should have been proud that the referee gave him credit for such a good piece of work.

Memorable

With 15 minutes to go Alex Miller took off Jackson, who had been doubtful before the match, and put on Gareth Evans.

It nearly worked with Evans just beaten at the far post in a jump with Stevens.

It was a memorable final but indelibly printed in the minds of all who saw the match will be that super scissors movement by M'lord McCoist.

MORE SUPER CUP FINAL ACTION ON PAGES 32, 33 and 37

MONDAY October 25 1993

YOU LUCKY B!

That's Smith's salute to McCoist the match-winner

RANGERS boss Walter Smith last night hailed Ally McCoist's marvellous League Cup Final winner.

"He's a lucky b★★★★★★. But he'll go through life like that, and there's no point in me trying to change him."

McCoist struck with a spectacular over-head kick nine minutes from time to beat Hibs 2-1 and add to Ian Durrant's earlier goal.

Smith led his over-joyed back-room boys in a dance of joy on the Parkhead track.

Ally captured a record-breaking eighth League Cup winner's medal.

As he proudly clutched that medal, which now gives him

RODGER BAILLE reporting

one more than former Ibrox team-mate Davie Cooper, the striker joked:

"Maybe it's the manager that's lucky. He put me on after all."

It was his first competitive goal since the horror of his leg break playing for Scotland

Turn to Page 32

PRIZE GUYS...Rangers goal heroes Ian Durrant and Ally McCoist proudly show off the League Cup after the 2-1 victory over Hibs. Picture: CRAIG HALKETT

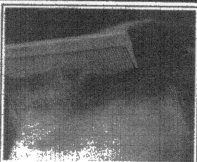

43

Published By Scottish Daily Record and Sunday Mail Ltd. (041-248-7000) and printed by Anderston Quay Printers Ltd., Anderston Quay, Glasgow G3 8DA. Registered at the Post Office as a Newspaper. ©Scottish Daily Record and Sunday Mail Ltd. 1993. A Mirror Group Newspaper.

9 770956 806018

EDITED, PRINTED AND PUBLISHED IN SCOTLAND

Sports RECORD

GR-EIGHT!

Hat-trick hero Gazza kicks off Gers flag party

By KEITH JACKSON

PAUL GASCOIGNE produced one of the greatest performances Scottish soccer has ever seen to make it eight in a row for Rangers.

The £4.3 million Geordie grabbed a sensational hat-trick as Walter Smith's side beat Aberdeen 3-1 to clinch the title.

Gascoigne's breathtaking one-man show started when he cancelled out Brian Irvine's opener with a stunning solo effort.

And he capped it all with a 70-yard run before hitting number two in 80 minutes, then bagged the third from the spot with just four minutes to go.

In the emotion-packed scenes which followed, Gascoigne was held aloft by his team mates clutching the match ball and given a staggering standing ovation from the adoring Ibrox fans.

And he broke down in tears as he hugged Gordan Petric on the touchline before skipper Richard Gough hoisted the trophy which sends Rangers back into the Champions Cup next season.

Legend

Gascoigne later branded his virtuoso performance the best day in his career.

But there were tears of misery for Ally McCoist on the lap of honour – fuelling rumours that this was his last ever appearance at Ibrox.

The strike legend – who is out of contract this summer – came off the bench with half an hour to go.

But he was more subdued than ever as the title celebrations raged on.

8-IN-A-ROW SPECIAL – Pages 48,49,50,51

18 Published by Scottish Daily Record and Sunday Mail Ltd., (0141-248 7000), 40 Anderston Quay, Glasgow G3 8DA and printed by Saltire Press, a trading division of Scottish Daily Record and Sunday Mail Ltd. Cardonald Park, Glasgow G51 4EA. Registered at the Post Office as a Newspaper. © Scottish Daily Record and Sunday Mail Ltd., 1996. A Mirror Group Newspaper.

9 770956 806018

BERT'S PAR-TY HAT

12 PAGE WINNER STARTS ON P 21

8-IN-A-ROW++8-IN-A-ROW++8-IN-A-ROW++8-IN-A-ROW

TEARS OF A

UP-ROAR ... Gazza sent sparks flying at Ibrox with his dazzling display and Brian Irvine was helpless to stop the second goal

GAZ MARK ONE ... Gascoigne side-steps helpless Windass en route to his stunning first goal

8-IN-A-ROW++8-IN-A-ROW++8-IN-A

CROWN

Gazza's war cry as he lifts title medal at last

PAUL GASCOIGNE has waited all his life for the day he had yesterday.

A glittering career with millions in the bank and a lifestyle to match meant nothing without a championship medal to show for it.

In front of 47,000 fans and millions watching on television, Aberdeen threatened to take his first League gong away from him.

So the English genius flicked a switch and produced possibly the most dazzling individual display EVER seen at Ibrox.

Gazza scored two individual classics and a penalty to hand Rangers their eighth title in a row.

At the end he broke down and sobbed on the shoulder of Gordan Petric.

Sparks

We've seen it before. But this time the tears were of pure undiluted joy.

Aberdeen were expected to come to Ibrox like sheep to the slaughter but after 19 minutes it was the Rangers fans who were bleating.

Brian Irvine hammered home from close range – and it turned out to be the worse thing he could have done.

Quite simply, he sent Gazza into overdrive.

You could almost see the sparks flying from his boots as he single-handedly set about Roy Aitken's men.

Within two minutes, the Geordie had dragged Rangers level with a solo effort that nearly took the roof off every stand in the ground.

He collected a short Brian Laudrup corner 25 yards out and shimmied away from Billy Dodds towards the box.

Magic

Dean Windass was sidestepped as he tried to cut off Gascoigne, and as he was still trying to find his way back into the ground, the Rangers midfielder drew Michael Watt out.

The keeper seemed to have his angles right, but Gascoigne quickly pinged the ball over his hands into the roof of the net.

Rangers piled forward for the next hour without breaching the Irvine-inspired Dons defence.

And it all produced so many tense, nervous headaches in the stands that you'd have thought the game had been sponsored by Dispirin.

Then with ten minutes left, Gascoigne provided the antidote with a moment of magic that will be talked about for decades.

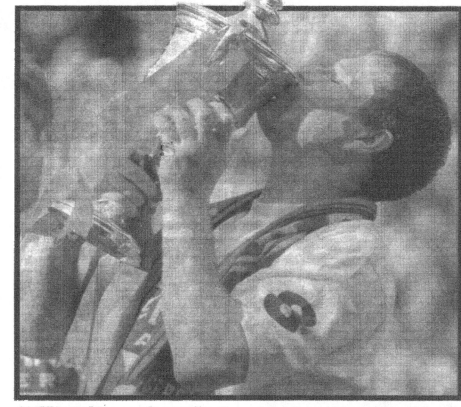

SHEER KISS ... as Gazza finally celebrates a championship win

RANGERS	3
ABERDEEN	1

From DAVID McCARTHY at IBROX

He robbed Windass of the ball ten yards inside the Rangers half, swerved over the half way line past two tackles and deep into Dons territory.

Aberdeen backed off, and kept retreating, expecting Gascoigne to pass to Laudrup.

But Gaz stormed into the Dons box and unleashed an unstoppable shot from 12 yards that left Watt rooted to the spot.

For the next five minutes Gazza was running around waving at the fans, punching the air and dancing about while play raged on around him.

In the entertainment stakes it was Prince, Frank Sinatra, Oasis, the Bolshoi Ballet and the Moscow State Circus rolled into the one blue jersey.

And when Paul Bernard sent Gordon Durie tumbling inside the box with four minutes left, not even substitute Ally McCoist had the nerve to deny Gascoigne his hat-trick.

He sent Watt the wrong way and ran to the Rangers end with his jersey over his head.

That goal sealed the eighth title and sparked the craziest celebrations yet.

Trauma

And you couldn't blame the Geordie for blowing a fuse.

He's played for Newcastle, Spurs and Lazio – all massive clubs – but never won a League title with any of them.

He came to Rangers to sort that out and yesterday all the tears and trauma of his run-ins with referees were forgotten.

Even whistler Les Mottram got in on the act by handing him the ball at the end.

The Geordie then treated his audience to a bit of keepy-uppy in the centre circle.

By that time, Aberdeen were long gone up the tunnel.

But for 80 minutes they produced enough spirit to suggest Rangers might have to go to Kilmarnock next week to win the league.

Walter Smith's men created a barrow load of chances and hit the woodwork twice.

And Andy Goram was forced into a fine fingertip save to stop a Windass header.

But Gascoigne ended the doubts with ten magical minutes.

Player of the Year? DEFINITELY.

The most talented individual ever to have played in this country?

You wouldn't find many of the 47,247 fans at Ibrox yesterday who would argue.

RANGERS: Goram, Steven (Petric), Robertson, Gough, McLaren, Brown, Durie (Durrant), Gascoigne, Andersen (McCoist), McCall, Laudrup.

ABERDEEN: Watt, McKimmie, Smith, Rowson, Irvine, Inglis, Bernard, Windass, Booth (Kpedekpo), Dodds, Glass.

REFEREE: Les Mottram, Forth.

Pictures: CRAIG HALKETT and GRAHAM STUART

HOW THE CUP WAS WON

MINUTE BY MINUTE by GORDON WADDELL

56 secs: Hearts' defence is tested instantly as John Brown flights a long ball for Gordon Durie to control on the edge of the box but his second touch lets him down and Gilles Rousset mops up.

4 mins: Jambos skipper Gary Locke falls to the turf clutching his right knee after catching his studs. He hauls himself up to soldier on.

7 mins: The game's over for Locke as he collapses in pain and is stretchered off. Alan Lawrence comes on.

14 mins: Gazza shows his first flash of temper as he wins a couple of tough tackles in the middle but is bundled over by Gary Mackay.

17 mins: Surprise pick Ian Ferguson almost snatches the opener as he volleys a delicate David Robertson chip but Rousset saves.

21 mins: Ferguson is booked for clattering Steve Fulton.

25 mins: Alex Cleland joins him in Hugh Dallas's book for chopping down Allan Johnston.

30 mins: Paul Ritchie intercepts as Brian Laudrup and Robertson carve out a chance for Durie.

37 mins: Killer first goal. Durie lobs the defence, Laudrup's electric pace takes him into the box and he meets the ball on the drop 14 yards out and drills it across Rousset and into the keeper's bottom right hand corner.

41 mins: Cleland crosses from the right and Rousset, unbelievably, claws away Richard Gough's header.

44 mins: Ritchie is lucky to escape with a yellow card as he chops Gazza on the edge of the box.

45 mins: Durie blows another great chance as he rounds Alan McManus, Pasquale Bruno and Rousset but runs the ball over the bye-line.

49 mins: Every keeper's nightmare comes true for Rousset. Laudrup fires in a harmless looking cross from the right but, as the Frenchman stoops to collect, the ball squirms through his hands AND legs and it's 2-0.

52 mins: Hearts' defence is in shreds as Ferguson grazes the bar with a header.

55 mins: Durie escapes a booking after giving it a bit of Swan Lake in a penalty box challenge from Bruno.

59 mins: Jim Jefferies throws on striker John Robertson for Bruno in a bid to pull the game back.

67 mins: A magnificent eight pass move ends with Laudrup crossing for Durie to ram home the third.

76 mins: John Colquhoun gives the Jambos a glimmer of hope with a superb strike past Andy Goram from 22 yards.

79 mins: Laudrup almost bags his hat-trick after dancing past four inside the box but is denied by a brilliant double stop from Rousset.

80 mins: The Dane tees up Durie's double and No.4.

86 mins: Final nail in the coffin. Laudrup floats in a cross and Durie heads it home for only the third ever Cup Final hat-trick.

HAT'S THE WAY TO DO IT . . . Two goal-hero Laudrup heads off to celebrate Gers' 5-1 win after, inset, setting them on their way with a superb opener

FOR CRYING

GAZ PACKS A PUNCH . . . Paul Gascoigne salutes Blues fans

| HEARTS..... | 1 |
| RANGERS... | 5 |

IAIN KING at HAMPDEN

IN years to come they'll simply call this the Laudrup Final.

One man's lavish talent left Hearts broken and weeping at Hampden.

Great Dane Brian crafted three goals for Gordon Durie and helped himself to two as he orchestrated an afternoon of torture for his rivals.

It was a day that turned on a critical blunder from Gilles Rousset when he let Laudrup's weak cross slither from his grasp and trundle through his legs to put Gers two up.

The Double was tied up in red, white and blue ribbons and after that it was an exercise in Hampden humiliation.

Man of the Match Laudrup was left to bask in the glory and he said: "We could have scored EIGHT or more.

"The second goal was critical, we were very comfortable after that. Now we have the Double – what a great achievement."

Sympathy

French cult hero Rousset will never be allowed to forget that nightmare moment and the Ibrox idol had words of sympathy for the dejected Jambos keeper.

He admitted: "I felt for him because at that stage of the game it was so important.

"He has been tremendous all season but that just shows he is human, we all mistakes.

"Unfortunately for Gilles and Hearts he made his in the Final.

"After his error it was fun for us. Now I feel that with Doubles behind us my close pal Peter Schmeichel and I will take some stopping at Euro 96!"

Hearts boss Jim Jefferies had made careful Final plans all week but he saw them ripped apart after just seven minutes when skipper Gary Locke's world collapsed around him.

Locke's enthusiasm took him tearing towards a midfield tackle with Stuart McCall and he appeared to catch his studs in the turf.

He limped on with a badly twisted knee that now looks certain to count him out of Scotland Under-21s Euro semi-final with Spain on May 28.

Locke eventually slumped again and you felt choked for him – he beat the ground in pain and frustration as the stretcher came towards him to end his Final before it had really started.

Hearts had looked consumed with nerves early on but settled before David Robertson's clever lofted pass carved them apart in the 17th minute.

Surprise choice Ian Ferguson's left foot volley on the run was arrowing for the far corner but Rousset swooped to save.

The Gers midfielder had clattered, commanded, breenged and battled his way through the early skirmishes and he was eventually booked for decking Stevie Fulton.

Gradually, Hearts were banishing their fears and Alan Lawrence, the early replacement for their stricken skipper, tested Andy Goram with a 25-yarder.

Alex Cleland then picked up Gers' second booking as the quick feet of Allan Johnston left him bewildered on the touchline.

But Gers turned up the heat and Rousset pawed at a Paul Gascoigne free-kick before charging from his goal and watching with relief as Laudrup's shot was scrambled clear.

Eight minutes from the break, though, Laudrup's aim was unerring as he rapped Rangers in front with a finish of quality.

Durie's pass spreadeagled the Hearts defence and the Ibrox idol raced away to home in on Rousset, the ball sat up invitingly

UP FOR THE CUP . . .delighted Archie Knox and Walter Smith celebrate a glorious double

OUT LAUD

Bri leaves Hearts weep at the knees

and a sweet volley directed the opener into the corner.

Jambos were reeling now and they were almost dead and buried when Richard Gough rose majestically to power in a header from Cleland's cross – Rousset's save at full stretch kept them in it.

Then came a moment of crackling controversy when I believe referee Hugh Dallas BOTTLED out of giving Hearts kid Paul Ritchie a Hampden red card.

John Brown's through ball left Gascoigne racing clean through and Ritchie, clearly the last man, hacked the Geordie genius down just outside the box.

Destroyed

Somehow he survived with a yellow card and Gazza's free-kick was easily saved before Durie blew a golden chance right on the break.

His power and poise took him clear of his markers and round Rousset but instead of slotting home with his left foot he lost control with his right and the opportunity was gone.

But four minutes after the break Rousset's howler ripped the Heart out of the Jambos and Gers produced one of the goals of the season to tie it all up.

Eight passes were crafted together to tear the Jambos to shreds and when Gascoigne's ball freed Laudrup on the left the ammunition was deadly.

The cross speared in and Durie swept in front of his marker to steer a classic volley

away from Rousset – now a picture of misery.

Jambos finally snatched a 76th minute goal when John Colquhoun crashed home a superb shot from 22 yards but even that crumb of comfort didn't last long.

Gers simply poured forward again and Laudrup delayed the pass until the perfect moment to set up Durie and he evaded Rousset to gleefully prod home the fourth.

Four minutes from time Durie feasted on Laudrup's supply once more as he galloped in at the far post to head home another exquisite cross to complete the final act of a footballing murder.

Gers boss Walter Smith was left to reflect: "The second goal set the tone for us and after that we hit them on the break in spectacular fashion.

"People ask where the motivation to keep winning comes from but I have players who react to challenges and I'm delighted for them. Laudrup's overall performance was outstanding."

Jambos manager Jeff, dignified in defeat, could only survey the wreckage and he said with a rueful smile: "We were destroyed.

"We lost our discipline but I will never criticise the players because they have had a great season.

"Rousset was distraught in the dressing-room but he is one of the biggest reasons we got here.

"That was a very bad day at the office."

For Double kings Rangers – the stars who come up with the goods when the chips are down – it was business as usual.

LOCKE ... Heartbreak

COLQUHOUN... consolation

 HEARTS

GILLES ROUSSET – Had brilliant saves from Gough, Ferguson and Gascoigne, but blundered badly with the second goal which deflated his team and allowed Rangers to run riot. (5)

GARY LOCKE – Went down injured after just four minutes clutching his right knee and was eventually replaced a few minutes later. A tragedy for the young skipper in what should have been the greatest day of his life. (2)

PAUL RITCHIE – Should have been red-carded for a foul on Gascoigne but, that apart, made a couple of brilliant last-gasp tackles on Durie early on. (6)

ALAN McMANUS – The youngster didn't let himself down on the biggest stage of the season, but did get dragged out of position a bit too often. (6)

DAVE McPHERSON– Found it difficult to combine his role of attacking and defending on the right hand side. Blameless for any of the goals. (5)

PASQUALE BRUNO– Had a brilliant start with some vital tackles which he made look easy. Lost it a bit later on and was replaced by Robertson. (6)

ALLAN JOHNSTON– Started up front but dropped into midfield to stop Gazza after Locke's injury. Failed to live

up to his pre-match reputation in what could be his last game for the club. (6)

GARY MACKAY – Ran himself into the ground, but found it too much trouble containing Gazza and Co in the midfield. (6)

JOHN COLQUHOUN– Up front on his own for long spells which made it hard for him to produce. Gave away a lot of needless fouls, but his goal was magnificent. (6)

STEVE FULTON – Tried his damnedest, but it just didn't happen for him. Had few options available to him when he had the ball. (5)

NEIL POINTON – Worked hard and hardly lost a ball in the air. However, he didn't see enough of it to cause any damage. (5)

ALAN LAWRENCE– Replaced Locke. Forced Goram into his first save of the match after 23 minutes and looked by far the Tynecastle side's most dangerous player. (7)

JOHN ROBERTSON– Came on from the bench at 2-0 to and snatch a goal but he'd have been as well staying on the bench as nothing came his way. (3)

Sub. not used: Hogarth

 McPHERSON... on the receiving end

RANGERS

ANDY GORAM – Had so little to do he could have picked his line for tomorrow's race meeting from his 18-yard box. No chance with Colquhoun's superb strike (7).

ALEX CLELAND– Never got a minute's peace from the Hearts players who went at him as he struggled to cope, especially with Pointon. Unfortunate to be booked for challenge on Johnston (6).

DAVID ROBERTSON– Attacked more than he defended which suited him right down to the ground. Caused McPherson problems down the left and came close to scoring twice (6).

RICHARD GOUGH – Strolled through the final before going up the Hampden stairs to collect his 12th trophy as Ibrox skipper. Didn't let his men sit back and urged them to keep pressing for more goals (8).

ALAN McLAREN – A couple of dodgy tackles which he was lucky to get away with. Covered a lot for Cleland when the full-back was exposed and that was vital in Rangers' tactics (7).

JOHN BROWN – Charged forward in spells looking for a goal as Rangers piled on the pressure and performed well at the back when needed (6).

GORDON DURIE – The hat-trick hero ran Hearts ragged in the second half. Lapped up

first-class service from Laudrup and gave his Euro 96 hopes a massive shout (8).

PAUL GASCOIGNE – Always involved in the play and was in the middle of a few crunching early tackles. Treated us to his usual tricks and flicks (8).

IAN FERGUSON – A surprise starter, he played in his usual way of stopping the opposition ball players with whatever tactics he fancied. Rightly booked after 20 minutes for chopping Fulton (5).

STUART McCALL – Never missed a tackle and must have run at least 20 miles. Happy to let his mates grab the limelight and that's what makes him so valuable (7).

BRIAN LAUDRUP – Started the rout with the opening goal. Added the crucial second and laid on Durie's hat-trick as he turned on a spectacular one-man show. Man of the Match, deservedly (9).

IAN DURRANT – came on for Ferguson with just two minutes remaining and received his usual hero's reception from the Rangers fans. Subs not used: Petric and Andersen.

REF HUGH DALLAS – Not a bad final but should have sent off Ritchie. Stopped play for niggly things when he could have let it flow (6).

McLAREN ... kept things tight at back

THE SPIRIT OF SCOTTISH FOOTBALL

BELL'S LEAGUE CHAMPIONSHIP

"A double rum and c..c..co.. oh just a lemonade"

contents

WE WEREN'T SUPER PALLY

SLAPPY DAY ... raging McCoist homes in on Gazza before giving him a smack on the head

ROWING Rangers goal **R**aces Paul Gascoigne and Ally McCoist shocked millions of TV fans with a bitter bust-up during the Coke final yesterday.

They clashed in the first half, viciously mouthing off at each other before McCoist smacked his team-mate on the back of the head – an act that earned him a lecture from ref Hugh Dallas.

And the simmering stars exploded again in the dressing-room at half-time as Walter Smith's treble-chasing side went to war on each other.

But Parkhead matchwinner Gazza revealed that those rammies are the reason Rangers are the country's most successful team.

He said: "I said something to Ally

Headbanger Coisty rattled

By DAVID McCARTHY

and he wasn't happy and came over to me.

"There was also a lot said at half-time involving a lot of people.

"The gaffer was a happy man – not. The sparks were flying and I was copping it as well.

"Of all the clubs I've been with, Rangers have the most arguments at half-time. It's because we are full of guys who want to be winning at half-time and full-time and it's great to see that."

Gers skipper Richard Gough revealed the extent of the half-time bust-up – and pointed to record breaking striker Coisty as the MOST hyped-up battler.

McCoist shattered another

record as he picked up his NINTH League Cup winner's medal – his double took him to 50 goals in the competition, past Gers legend Jim Forrest.

Gough said: "Our dressing-room was like a war zone at half-time. We were winning 2-1 but not playing well and plenty of things were said.

"But we're like that at this club. I've had one or two flashpoints in training – and Ally McCoist has been the man involved.

"He has the reputation of being a happy-go-lucky guy, but he has a depth of desire and hunger that got him two more cup final goals."

Gascoigne's double paid back the first instalment of the debt he owes Rangers by winning the Coca-

Cola Cup. Gazza feared he could have been kicked out after admitting beating his wife last month – but the club stood by him and he repaid them big-style by delivering the first trophy of the season.

Now Gascoigne believes he's getting his head sorted and recapturing the form that can drive Rangers towards the treble.

He said: "In the last few weeks I have been very nervous and have not been myself – you all know why.

"But I'm coming to terms with what happened, though my personal life is still private.

"The counselling IS helping and I can concentrate more on football, which is important.

"I'm delighted with my two goals. My first goal against Celtic was special for me but the first

KICK-OFF

With Alan McMillan

FERGIE

I've heard people say you can still feel the presence of former manager Alex Ferguson around Pittodrie – but here's the photographic evidence which suggests it goes much deeper than that. For some reason, Aberdeen coach Drew Jarvie has started to look like Fergie. He has even perfected the famous tight-lipped, hang dog expression that comes into play whenever a game hasn't gone exactly to plan. Very spooky!

JARVIE

Ayrshire junior footballers are pure mental – but this has nothing to with declining standards of social behaviour in the last couple of decades.

They've been mental far longer than that. And if you want proof, here's a report I came across of an SJFA Rough Play Committee probe into a Glenburn Rovers v Kilwinning Rangers Scottish Cup tie at Prestwick way back in October, 1933.

Ref Gribben sent off five and abandoned the game when Kilwinning called their last eight men from the field.

Messrs J Aird and J Kenmuir, of Kilwinning, were the main villains.

Aird was fined one shilling, banned for 14 days and ordered to pay for repairing the glass on the ref's watch.

Kenmuir was fined five shillings, banned for a month and ordered to pay for a new shirt for the ref, whose match attire had been ripped from his back.

And refs today think THEY have a hard time!

JACKETS OFF FOR BATTLE

OH to be a fly on the wall when the SFA are discussing where not to play against Estonia.

Cyprus? Too far. Poland? Too cold. Azerbaijan? Too hard to spell. Turkey? Did you SEE *Midnight Express*?

They don't want to go anywhere remotely warlike, so the rule is that if Kate Adie's been there, it's out.

Personally, I feel that playing the game at all will be the biggest mistake since Andy Goram turned up at a tupperware party asking to buy clothes for his tupp.

We've spent a fortune taking a squad of players and officials to play them already – doing it again would be an obscene waste of money.

Swearing

I suggest we abandon the idea completely and find another way to decide who gets the World Cup points.

How about a game of heidy fitba between Jim Farry and the president of the Estonian FA?

Ten half-time, 21 the winner, jackets for goalposts and any disputes about whether a ball was inside, outside or over the jackets to be settled in the usual way – much shouting and swearing until someone gives in.

The fact that Faz doesn't swear – "nobody at the SFA swears, we have a young female staff and we don't indulge in that" – could be a problem. However, we'll just appoint a manager to do his swearing for him. I understand one or two of them have indulged in the odd sweary word.

Of course, some people will think a game of heidy fitba for vital points is a bit risky.

Nonsense! We invented the game, so we can't lose.

The only problem would be finding a venue.

Cyprus? Too far. Poland? Too cold ...

You'd think it would be difficult to confuse a wee, fat striker with a big, skinny defender – but the PR lady at Dave McPherson's book launch managed it. John Robertson wondered why she was asking him how *A Tale of Two Cities* had turned out and what he thought of the cover, but the penny finally dropped when she asked him to go and talk to the press about it ... she thought he was the author. A strange mistake to make – Robbo couldn't get a game at centre-half for Subbuteo.

Are Queen of the South trying to take over the world? Last week I told you that their huge staff list in the Scottish League Review included EIGHT coaches. I have now been sent a copy of Queens' most recent match programme from Darren Manley, of Dumfries, and the number of coaches at Palmerston has now gone up to a staggering THIRTEEN. At this rate the players will soon have one each.

BLIMEY – WOT A PITCHA!

★ Some people are born smooth, others achieve smoothness. Big Mark Hateley is obviously in the latter category judging by this picture of his teenage days at Coventry City. It's just typical, isn't it? The photographer's coming to training to do some snaps and that's the very day your curling tongs go haywire. Ach well, it could be worse ... you could be going bald.

KISS IS THE LIFE ... Ally and Gazza are mates again as the party starts

me admits Gazza

one today meant as much because Hearts were on a real high, having got back to 2-2."

Skipper Gough bows out at the end of this season but insists he wants the treble for Rangers. He said: "This isn't about Richard Gough. It's about Rangers trying to win every competition they enter."

Both Gough and Gazza heaped praise on battling Hearts.

Wondering

Gough said: "They'll be sitting in their dressing-room wondering how they lost that match.

"Hearts had ALL the better players on the day – Weir, McCann and Cameron were outstanding.

"But the bottom line is that we won the trophy, even if we didn't play as well as we had hoped to on the day."

Gascoigne added: "A lot of teams would have folded after going two down to us so early, but they showed a lot of spirit and deserve credit."

Gers gaffer Smith said: "Paul's been under pressure for the past few weeks. I don't think ANYBODY who has watched him could say otherwise.

"But he scored two terrific goals today and his average of goals this season is very good for a midfielder.

"We needed him today and we got a performance from him.

"Ally McCoist also made another important contribution – but he can do that even when he's not fully fit.

"If you can get the ball to him inside the box he'll always get you a goal.

"His first was typical and the second goal was a real poacher's strike."

But Smith admitted the seven-goal thriller had shredded his nerves.

He said: "Imagine it was very good to watch – if you are not a manager!

"*Jim Jefferies and I could complain about losing so many goals, but it all made it a great game.*

"It took some of Paul Gascoigne's best tricks to get us out of a difficult situation because Hearts were by far the better team at the time."

German midfielder Jorg Albertz was delighted to pick up his first medal in Scotland.

Unbelievable

He said: " I'm very happy to have won my first medal with Rangers and now I'm looking forward to the rest of the games.

"We started very well and went 2-0 up but Hearts also played very well.

"*When they scored their second I thought 'Oh, what's going on here?' But, thankfully, Gazza turned it round again. He was unbelievable.*

"That's three times I've played at Parkhead and three times I've won so it's a good place to play for me."

DERBY OF THE DECADE ++ DERBY OF THE

GOUGH: THE

WHERE THE WAR WAS WON

KERR v DIBBLE

ANDY DIBBLE has been on loan more often than Ally McCoist's car keys but the Welshman looked confident.

He made the first save of the match when he blocked a shot from the onrushing Cadete.

The first noteworthy thing Stewart Kerr had to do was pick the ball out of his net after his defenders left him defenceless.

But he did well to save bravely at Laudrup's feet before being booked for his part in the scuffle which saw Hateley ordered off.

While Celtic pressed for the equaliser, Dibble was really only called upon to deal with crosses.

But Kerr produced a great save to deny Jorg Albertz.
Verdict: KERR

STUBBS v GOUGH

THIS was Richard Gough's final Old Firm match, while Alan Stubbs was signed to be the cornerstone of a new Celtic era.

But Gough looked easily the more accomplished player. Stubbs was done for pace by Laudrup in the 10th minute which set up a chance for Durrant, and he was at fault at Rangers' goal, allowing Durrant to steal in front of him.

Gough showed the leadership qualities missing in Rangers' cup defeat. A vital block to Di Canio's driven cross in 39 minutes typified his contribution.

Gough was booked for a foul on Di Canio before he and Stubbs were substituted simultaneously in the 63rd minute.
Verdict: GOUGH by TKO

DI CANIO v LAUDRUP

CLOSE control by Paolo Di Canio caused Rangers problems and Durrant and Gough were booked for fouling him – while Ferguson should have been.

The Italian often wanted an extra touch and twice squandered chances because of that.

He crashed an astonishing 25-yard volley against the bar at 0-0 before being booked for dissent.

Brian Laudrup's skill created a chance which Durrant blew and that was his only first-half contribution until he prodded Durrant's lob over the line in 44 minutes.

The Dane forced a fine save from Kerr and his speed on the break led to the foul which saw Mackay red-carded.
Verdict: LAUDRUP on points

CADETE v HATELEY

MARK HATELEY was out to rekindle old glories. Jorge Cadete aimed to prove a stilletto was deadlier than a club.

The Portuguese star left Bjorklund for dead as he created a half chance for Grant, but Hateley won a series of free-kicks and came close with a looping header.

Cadete's pace caused Rangers problems and he produced a fine block from Dibble.

Hateley's spoiling challenge on Annoni helped set up the goal but he blotted his copybook by stupidly being sent off for appearing to head-butt Kerr.

Cadete didn't enjoy the best of service.
Verdict: CADETE (for going the distance)

LAUD HAILER ... Rangers star Brian Laudrup beats Malky Mackay to grab the Ibrox glory-hunters' match-winner at Parkhead

RICHARD GOUGH has played in every crucial match through the nine years of Rangers' title stranglehold.

But he reckons yesterday's stormy showdown topped the lot.

It was the last Old Firm clash that USA-bound Gough will ever play in. And that made victory all the sweeter.

He said: "This was arguably the biggest game in the club's history and it's a fantastic result for us.

"It doesn't mean that the championship is over, although

By KEITH JACKSON and EWING GRAHAME

there will be people who'll say that it is.

"Celtic were the hungrier side when they won the Scottish Cup-tie but it says a lot for our players' character that we came back and I was proud to be part of it."

Subdued

Gough limped off in the 63rd minute with a recurrence of his calf injury and hobbled into the after-match Press conference on crutches.

He admitted: "I was stiff before this match but I had a word with the gaffer because this was not a game I was going to miss. The last

time I lost here was in 1991, so I've had a good six-year run at Parkhead.

"It's been a lucky ground for me and I hope it is just as lucky for Rangers in the future.

"Our main objective when we came here was to keep a clean sheet. We knew if we did that we would at least keep our five-point lead.

"And if we do go on to get the nine titles, Andy Dibble will be well remembered by the fans for the part he played today.

"What a situation it was for him to come in and play here! He's been playing in the Manchester City THIRD team and he comes straight in to this. He's an experi-

enced goalkeeper but thankfully he didn't have too much to do. Celtic seemed strangely subdued and we expected a lot more pressure than we were put under."

But spare a thought for Dibble this morning.

The poor guy is waking up in a hotel room in a city he doesn't know and he must be thinking the world has finally gone mad.

Occasion

The Welshman won't have seen anything like this before – and it's doubtful he'll ever wish to again.

What a game to make your debut for Rangers!

Some would say it was the biggest Old Firm derby of all time. Not many would argue.

And, unfortunately, the importance of the occasion brought out

everything that's mad, bad and dangerous about the most bitter rivalry in football.

This wasn't sport. This was WAR. The first shots were being fired long before most of the 50,000 foot soldiers were even in position in their trenches.

Rangers had suffered heavy losses.

Andy Goram would be missing in action, along with David Robertson.

It meant Dibble was to be thrown into the firing line for one of the most savage battles ever in an age-old conflict he knows nothing about.

He was just about to find out.

At 2.55, as sheets of rain swirled and swept their way across the battlefield, the guy in the Parkhead DJ box played *You'll Never Walk*

GREATEST

That win topped the lot says Gers skipper

ALL-TIME HIGH ... Laudrup turns to the ecstatic Rangers fans – but it's sheer agony for Enrico Annoni

Alone. Dibble wouldn't have been able to see the awesome visuals in the stands from deep down in the bowels of the stadium. But you can bet the vocals would have had the hair standing up on the back of his neck.

There was ANOTHER new boy beside him – the familiar face of Mark Hateley.

But at least he knew exactly what he was getting himself into as he ran out that tunnel to take his place in the derby of the decade.

Untouched

Hateley wouldn't have batted an eyelid as he stood waiting for kick-off and watched Ian Ferguson chasing bunches of balloons across the turf.

One by one Ferguson picked off the green ones – leaving the white and orange untouched.

It would all have been lost on poor old Dibble.

Afterwards he was still trying to come to terms with it all as he said: "The atmosphere was unbelievable. I've played in Manchester derbies, but the atmosphere at them was nothing like today.

"It was hard coming in for Andy Goram because he is one of the best keepers in Europe, if not the world, and I knew I had to match his standards.

"I didn't have that much to do, but I didn't make any mistakes which was the main thing.

"This was HUGE – I possibly didn't realise how big a game it was until I ran out onto the field."

By the time the whistle sounded on the match which will no doubt clinch the title for Rangers, the noise inside Paradise was deafening.

But you wonder exactly what must have been going through Dibble's mind as Glasgow's giants went to war.

First Hateley – who should have known better – was sent packing, then he was followed by Malky Mackay.

Chanting

Paolo di Canio was lucky not to follow them, then a posse of players were caught up in the mayhem at the final whistle.

Eventually, it calmed down as the players disappeared up the tunnel and the Rangers fans started chanting for TEN IN A ROW.

See you next year then, Andy, same time, same place!

> **❝ I knew this was a huge game..I just didn't know how huge ❞**
>
> **– ANDY DIBBLE**

Pictures: CRAIG HALKETT and GRAHAM STUART

NINE IN A ROW++NIN IN A ROW++N IN A

CRYING GAME ... Walter Smith led the cheers on the final whistle while departing skipper Richard Gough choked back the tears, but it was scrum night all round for the Gers, who indulged in a post-match huddle

Pictures: IAN STEWART and GRAHAM STUART

CLOUD 9

Party time as sky-high Gers wrap up the title

SILVER DREAM MACHINE ... the party's just beginning for Rangers' glory boys

TANNADICE was rocked to its foundations last night.

Songs of triumph drifted up over the stands and across Tayside. There may have been only 6000 of them but Rangers' fans made themselves heard.

In fact, so loudly did they sing they were probably heard back in Glasgow as their heroes paraded the championship trophy around Dundee United's home.

Sportingly, many of United's fans stayed in their places and applauded Rangers' players, who were lead by their captain, Richard Gough, even though a calf injury denied him the opportunity to end his Rangers career with his boots on.

Gough, of course, leaves today to begin a new life in America. Even though he's one of the most strong-willed individuals in the business Gough was choked as he accepted a ninth successive title.

This was his last stand, his final farewell and he wanted to linger. He wanted to enjoy his last sight for a while of the fans who have supported him for the last 10 years.

Walter Smith sprang from his place in the dug-out as soon as the final whistle sounded and he hugged his players before turning to scan the stands for a sighting of his two sons.

Gifted

It would have been ideal had Rangers clinched the title on home soil two days earlier when Motherwell forced them to put the champagne back on ice but last night the drinks flowed. Nine titles and a place in history along with Celtic whose mark has now been equalled.

Rangers fans sang of 10 in a row but Ally McCoist, who has featured in all nine championship runs, said: "Let's just enjoy this triumph."

It was all heady stuff and so long as Rangers can continue to attract players as wonderfully gifted as Brian Laudrup and Paul Gascoigne it is entirely possible they could go on and collect more glittering prizes.

It was appropriate that Laudrup should be the one to signal the beginning of a joyous riot. The Dane nodded Charlie Miller's cross into the net after 11 minutes and that was it. Party time.

United, unbeaten at home since Christmas, were far from overcome but they couldn't get themselves upfield often enough with any real threat and for the second time they saw Rangers clinch the title by 1-0 at Tannadice.

Rangers, in fact, could have scored more than one goal, which was their 124th of the season, but Gascoigne

DUNDEE UNITED	0
	Att: 12,000
RANGERS	1
Laudrup (11)	

By JAMES TRAYNOR

and Charlie Miller both saw shots smack posts. In the end it didn't matter.

The Ibrox side were champions again and Smith was one of the last to leave the scene of the triumph. Before going he accepted the trophy with one hand, the other in his pocket.

Joe Cool, he was, but he would probably have been more like Mr Rubberlegs as Wednesday night flowed into Thursday morning.

It had been a long haul and there were times when Rangers appeared to be running on empty but in those matches they proved that even when they drop below their own standards they are still the best side in the country.

So determined were all of Rangers' players to be part of an emotional evening that Gascoigne refused to be substituted until the last minute.

Smith wanted to take him off and send on Derek McInnes, who had stripped off his tracksuit, but the English interna-

tionalist gave his gaffer a rubber ear before eventually trudging off.

Gascoigne's refusal to obey instruction from the management will be dealt with at a more appropriate time.

But although he was cut down a few times by Jim McInally and Ray McKinnon he remained remarkably calm.

HE HAD TO CONSERVE ENERGIES FOR THE CELEBRATIONS.

Laudrup, who had taken his tally to 20 goals for the season, also left the pitch and his place was taken by McCoist, who simply had to be a part of the party. After all, without the striker's contributions Rangers would not have achieved this remarkable feat.

Stunned

Yet last night had started dismally for Rangers when Gough failed a late test as did Mark Hateley. Also, Jorg Albertz was fit only to sit on the bench and as the teams emerged the skies, which had been a brooding grey all night, opened.

The rain tumbled heavily and Rangers fans looked stunned as they searched in vain for Gough and Hateley.

However, Laudrup lifted them quickly and the smiles on their faces were so bright they wouldn't have needed to switch on their car headlights on the way home.

They have still to play Hearts at

Tynecastle on Saturday but Edinburgh is also a good city in which to party and no doubt Rangers fans will prove that.

United did contribute to the evening and they came close on a few occasions in the first half but Andy Dibble did not have a great deal to do and in the second period, when the pace slowed, Gascoigne and Laudrup were able to impose themselves even though they looked weary.

Gascoigne's angled drive which hit Sieb Dykstra's right-hand post and Miller's thunderous volley which almost destroyed the keeper's other post were the highlights although United will still insist they were denied a couple of penalty claims.

Five players, United's Lars Zetterlund and Laudrup, Gordan Petric, Alan McLaren and Craig Moore, of Rangers, were booked in a game which was fiercely contested but never foul.

Rangers had been staggering in recent times but again, when they had to, they responded. They are worthy champions.

DUNDEE UNITED. – Dykstra, McInally, McKimmie, Pressley, Perry, Pederson, Olofsson, Zetterlund (Dolan 67), McSwegan, McKinnon, McLaren (Winters 75). Sub not used: Black.
RANGERS – Dibble, Cleland, Robertson, Petric, McLaren, Bjorklund, Moore, Gascoigne (McInnes 90), Durie, Miller, Laudrup (McCoist 90). Sub not used: Alberts.
Referee – S Dougal, Burnside.

BEAR HUGS ... Ally McCoist celebrates with Walter Smith

Fitting tribute for Bri

By KEITH JACKSON

ALLY McCOIST was one of the few players at Tannadice with the right to score the nine in a row clincher.

But the strike legend couldn't argue with the man who headed Rangers into the history books.

Brian Laudrup's 11th minute strike clinched a record-equalling triumph – and that seemed fitting.

Laudrup is probably the greatest player ever to pull on a blue shirt – and tops the list of nine in a row heroes.

Golden boy Coisty said: "I don't think anyone can grudge him that goal.

"At times this season he's been absolutely breathtaking and hopefully this will be recognised when you guys vote for player of the year."

The Dane showed his delight as he grabbed Paul Gascoigne and the trophy and raced to start up a Celtic-style celebratory huddle.

Richard Gough was watching from beside the Tannadice tunnel with a lump in his throat the size of a Mitre 5.

He said: "Brian was tremendous again tonight, but then, for the last three seasons he's been exceptional.

"It was a good omen when Brian scored with his head because he doesn't even head the ball in training!"

For McCoist – one of the few to have been at Ibrox throughout the historic run – time may be running out at last.

But he said: "I'll sit down with the manager and the chairman and have a chat about my future.

"I haven't made my mind up yet and I'm not going to say anything daft.

"That's for another day – tonight is all about enjoying nine in a row. This tops the lot – it is as sweet as our previous victories, if not sweeter.

"When Celtic achieved nine in a row it really was something special. I take my hat off to them because they were a great and wonderful team.

"The pressure on us was colossal to do it and if we had failed we would have been known for all time as the team who DIDN'T win nine in a row."

HOW THEY RATED

ST JOHNSTONE

MAIN: Looked assured throughout and made three excellent saves from Kanchelskis. Put his 1991 cup final disaster firmly behind him.

8

McQUILLAN: Steady at the back, but was unable to add any serious weight to the Saints attack.

6

DASOVIC: Competed bravely with Rangers' highly-rated midfield and possibly just edged the battle. Superb 20-yard shot for Saints' goal.

8

KERNAGHAN: Defended well, but was powerless to stop the Rangers goals.

7

SCOTT: Some good touches throughout, but he and Albertz tended to cancel each other out.

6

O'NEIL: Lively as always, helped make sure the Saints midfield was never over-run.

7

O'BOYLE: Well checked by Hendry, but the Irish striker battled for scraps throughout.

6

KANE: Another influential display in midfield, his experience ensured that van Bronckhorst wasn't given too much space.

7

BOLLAN: Kept Kanchelskis in check until late on, but was unable to compete for pace with the Russian when he set up the opening goal.

6

DODS: Allowed Wallace little space and unsurprisingly cleared everything in the air.

7

SIMAO: Saints' most dangerous player, ensured that things didn't get too easy for Rangers at the back. Will never understand why ref Dallas blew for half-time as he broke free.

8

THE CAAT'S

HIGH-HO SILVER: Skipper Lorenzo Amoruso and match winner Jorg Albertz play it for laughs with the League Cup

DICK ADVOCAAT stood, collar up, hands shoved deep into his coat pockets, and shared a quiet word with his assistant manager.

All around him Parkhead was shaking to a noise which has not been heard in Glasgow for 18 months.

It was the sound of Rangers' celebrations.

He had brought them this moment but he seemed reluctant to share in their joy.

Perhaps it was because his side had won their first trophy without ever having to find top gear.

Progress

Then again, perhaps this little Dutchman has much bigger plans for his team.

If so, he can be quietly pleased with the progress which has been made in his short tenure and which, yesterday, manifested itself in the shape of the League Cup.

It was not a spectacular win by any manner of means against a St Johnstone side which had travelled south in no mood to repeat recent capitulations against Advocaat's lot.

But goals from Stephane Guivarc'h and Jorg Albertz were enough to claim the season's first silverware and further signal an ominous sign of intent from the city's south side.

Peculiar

St Johnstone left with their pride intact, but Rangers, in truth, had cruised towards a trophy they have now won 21 times.

It must be said that there was something peculiar about this cup final before it had even begun – the number of empty green seats around the stadium come kick-off time.

It was clear that those who care most about the finalists had not been entirely convinced that it was worth parting with hard-earned money to watch them compete for a trophy which appears to have lost a lot of its appeal.

Those who had made it down from Perth, however, seemed determined to enjoy their first cup final in 29 years.

They arrived in the east end of

THE BIG MATCH AT A GLANCE

By IAIN CAMPBELL

3 MINS: Rod Wallace shoots past after Barry Ferguson's corner was only partially cleared.

5 MINS: Jorg Albertz shuts out a Simao cross after the Portuguese star had beaten the offside trap.

6 MINS: Stephane Guivarc'h slams Rangers ahead from 12 yards after Andrei Kanchelskis cut back a superb Sergio Porrini pass.

7 MINS: Nick Dasovic hauls Saints level with a superb left-foot drive from 20 yards after Alan Kernaghan headed the ball down on the edge of the area.

11 MINS: John O'Neil wastes a good chance by shooting weakly from the edge of the area after a good build-up from Kane, Dasovic and O'Boyle.

23 MINS: Main saves at Kanchelskis' feet as the Russian chases a Colin Hendry through ball.

26 MINS: Main makes another superb save, sprinting from his line to defy the Russian again, after Ferguson had split the Saints defence.

29 MINS: Guivarc'h heads just over following a Wallace cross.

36 MINS: Albertz sweeps Rangers ahead with an untypically measured shot into the corner of the net after Guivarc'h had cleverly turned a Ferguson pass across the edge of the area.

43 MINS: Dasovic earns the first yellow card after a body check on van Bronckhorst.

45 MINS: Referee Hugh Dallas infuriates the Saints fans by blowing the half-time whistle with Simao ready to sprint clear from his own half.

54 MINS: Kane misses a decent chance after a Philip Scott cross was dummied by O'Boyle, shooting the ball just wide.

65 MINS: Ian Ferguson comes on for Albertz.

68 MINS: Van Bronckhorst rifles a 25-yarder just wide of Main's goal.

74 MINS: Nathan Lowndes replaces George O'Boyle.

80 MINS: Brilliant full length save by Main stops Kanchelskis' volley tearing into the back of the net.

Pictures: CRAIG HALKETT

WHISPERS

Dutchman's first trophy nothing to shout about

PARADISE FOUND: Rangers boss Dick Advocaat didn't get too carried away with his team's League Cup Final success at Parkhead, but the same couldn't be said for Rod Wallace, a bewigged Andrei Kanchelskis and Arthur Numan who were quickly into party mode

HOW THEY RATED

RANGERS

NIEMI: The Finnish keeper had no hope with Dasovic's goal but had little to do apart from that. **6**

PORRINI: Brilliant pass to Kanchelskis to set up Rangers' first goal. Supported his attack willingly and defended well. **7**

AMORUSO: In danger of becoming the weak link in the Rangers side. Had a nightmare spell when he made eight passes to Saints players. **5**

HENDRY: Did everything that was required at the back. No sign that talk of a return to Blackburn is worrying him. **8**

NUMAN: Still not at his best Holland form, but rarely troubled at the back. **6**

B.FERGUSON: Made usual shrewd passes but didn't dominate the match the way he might have wanted. **7**

KANCHELSKIS: His pace troubled Bollan when he got the service. Was Gers' most dangerous man. **7**

BRONCKHORST: Seemed to spend his time taking set-pieces. Happy to flit in and out of the match. **6**

GUIVARC'H: Looked dangerous every time he got the ball. Scored the first and set up the second. **8**

WALLACE: Buzzed around as always, but was upstaged by fellow striker Guivarc'h on the day. **7**

ALBERTZ: Scored Rangers' winner after some great link-up play, but was casual at times in a fairly subdued performance. **6**

RANGERS 2
Scorers: Guivarc'h (6 mins); Albertz (37)
ST JOHNSTONE 1
Scorer: Dasovic (8 mins)
Attendance: 45,533

By KEITH JACKSON

Glasgow in good voice and hoping they would have even more to sing about on the way home.

They tried their best to lift the Celtic Park gloom but the whiff of freshly-waxed Barbour jackets hung heavy in the air around the main stand and so made the occasion stranger still.

Many of Perth's finest gave the impression this was the first time they had experimented with football as they stood around slack-jawed, waiting for it all to begin.

All around them, those who prefer a dash of red with their blue and white, seemed almost too embarrassed to show any great level of excitement.

Strange, really, because in terms of trophy successes they'd had nothing to celebrate since May 1997.

Yes, it was an odd atmosphere in which to play a cup final.

Thankfully, the players were about to change all that by ensuring that this was to be no ordinary cup final.

It took only a few minutes for the 45,000 who had made it into Parkhead to become totally immersed in this match.

Rangers started brightly with a Giovanni van Bronckhorst shot deflected behind for a corner kick.

From the resulting set-piece, little Rod Wallace saw his shot ricochet just wide of Alan Main's net.

Even after such unwelcome early activity in and around their penalty box, St Johnstone did not appear overwhelmed by the task with which they were faced.

Stunning

But with just six minutes on the clock they were to have good reason to fear for their safety as the side which had smashed seven past them at McDiarmid Park suddenly struck again.

The goal was something of a disaster for Main.

He appeared to be glued to his line as Andrei Kanchelskis darted round defender Gary Bollan to collect a superbly flighted ball from Sergio Porrini.

The goalkeeper allowed Kanchelskis to progress all the way to the byeline and from there the Ukrainian rolled the ball into the path of Stephane Guivarc'h who smashed the ball past the Saints keeper for the third time in his short Ibrox career.

Right about then, the St Johnstone people looked to the skies and wondered if it wasn't time to head off up the road.

Thankfully, Nick Dasovic was to provide them with a quite stunning answer.

Within two minutes Sandy Clark's side were level and we did indeed have a cup final on our hands.

Dasovic does not score often but when he does his goals tend to be memorable – and the Canadian will not forget this one in a hurry.

Fellow-midfielder Paul Kane sent the ball floating in his general direction from a free-kick out on the St Johnstone right.

Alan Kernaghan rose to nod the ball down to Dasovic on the edge of the Rangers box and with one vicious swipe of his right boot the ball was dispatched at high velocity into the roof of Antti Niemi's net.

Suddenly, the St Johnstone support felt more comfortable in these strange surroundings, but more importantly, so did their players.

Dasovic and Kane, in fact, began to enjoy themselves in midfield and for long periods, Saints threatened to out-pass a team who major in such a game.

After one electric exchange in the centre circle Phil Scott was sent scampering through the heart of the Rangers defence.

But the former Scotland Under-21 seemed slightly spooked by it all as he eyed the advancing Niemi and shot weakly into the keeper's arms.

Still, the fact that he had even got himself into such a situation further heartened those who had previously feared for the safety of a Saints side who had lost 11 goals in their two previous encounters with Rangers.

Rangers appeared taken aback by the speed and guile of their rivals and were finding it almost impossible to forge a way through.

Genuine

Then, in the 36th minute, they turned to the one man in their team capable of blasting a hole in even the most resilient of barriers. They turned to the brute force of Jorg Albertz.

The German, though, played a wonderfully subtle part in the build-up, stepping over a Barry Ferguson pass and allowing it to roll through to Guivarc'h.

With one touch Guivarc'h had stroked it back into the path of Albertz and there was little doubt about what would follow.

Main, as many have done before him, dived to his left, more in hope than genuine expectation, but the ball had exploded behind him before he even hit the ground.

He did not know it at the time but his dream was over already. There were still nine minutes to half-time but there would be no way back.

Ten minutes after the re-start, the outstanding Kane was to miss Saints last half-chance, firing wide of Niemi's right-hand post after George O'Boyle had failed to connect with a scissors kick.

From that moment on, Rangers were rarely in trouble and it was Main who had to make the save of the match in the 81st minute when he brilliantly turned a scorching Kanchelskis volley over his crossbar.

Saints pressed until the end but could not force Niemi into any kind of serious action.

Rangers had a trophy to collect, Dick Advocaat's first in his new job. It will not be his last.

SWEET VICTORY

Gers rise to the challenge and land historic triumph

McCANN OF THE MATCH: Rangers' two-goal hero Neil McCann laps up the cheers after his second strike put the seal on his side's title success

GIVEN the madness which descended on the east end of Glasgow last night it is perhaps necessary to remind ourselves a championship was won and lost.

Rangers won their 10th title in 11 years but for the first time in the Govan club's history the top domestic prize was clinched on the soil of their greatest rivals.

As night fell and a darkness descended on Jozef Venglos's side, Celtic Park belonged to Dick Advocaat and Rangers.

As Advocaat hugged his right-hand man and fellow Dutchman Bert van Lingen like long-lost brothers and their players celebrated wildly it was possible for a short time to forget the shameful scenes during the match.

Chilling

Maybe because there was more than a championship at stake, with Celtic determined not to be cast as stooges, while Rangers strove to claim a special place in the game's folklore, the fans were more on edge than normal.

Even before the kick-off there was an uneasy feeling about the place and after half an hour a genuinely chilling malevolence spread through the ground.

It was around that time, with Rangers one goal ahead thanks to the ever-improving Neil McCann, that Stephane Mahe lost all control.

The Frenchman set an appalling example and if he is not severely punished by his own club – never mind outside authorities – then we will know there is no hope for this game of ours.

His composure, in fact, began disintegrating early in the game when he was cautioned after a reaction to a

CELTIC	0
RANGERS	**3**

By JAMES TRAYNOR

challenge which wasn't even his. Paul Lambert downed Rod Wallace but Mahe protested stupidly at the foul given against Celtic.

It was obvious then that a dangerously fragile temperament was already seriously overloaded because of the tension sweeping down from the steep tiers holding 59,918 highly-charged supporters.

Even so, Mahe's response after McCann had tackled him in 31 minutes still caused shock.

The defender made to lunge at his attacker and referee Hugh Dallas reached again for a yellow card before producing the red one.

Mahe should have had the sense to go as quietly as possible but he had been deserted by all reason.

He was like a man possessed and it was several minutes before some kind of order could be restored as players from both sides pushed and jostled.

Hatred

All around the ground fans were on their feet, the vast majority of them now convinced some kind of injustice had been perpetrated against Celtic.

There is no doubt Mahe's ridiculous and irresponsible remonstrations stoked the hatred which is always brought to these occasions.

It was not long afterwards when Rangers had won a free-kick deep on the right inside Celtic's territory that a fan breached the security cordon around the pitch and tried to get at Dallas.

The would-be attacker was caught and dragged away but then the referee was struck by a coin and he required treatment to a head wound.

After the blood had been wiped and he had recovered, Dallas's next decision was to award Rangers what appeared to be a soft penalty after Vidar Riseth had cut across Tony Vidmar.

Celtic protested but Jorg Albertz was already deciding how he would blast the ball into Stewart Kerr's net.

The German did exactly that but only after a second fan had managed to get on the field of play.

A third idiot would get beyond the security men and a fourth was caught just as he tried to get over the barrier before players were able to concentrate fully on the game again.

McCann's goal had been set up for him by Wallace, who was sent off in 75 minutes after he had made a threatening gesture when fouled by Riseth.

Strange

Wallace had already been booked and he had to go while Riseth was cautioned.

However, the Norwegian was also dismissed after he lunged into Claudio Reyna.

In total Dallas, who did seem to make a series of strange decisions which favoured Rangers, issued 10 bookings in a match played against a poisonous backdrop and watched by tens of millions throughout Britain and a number of foreign countries.

McCann scored Rangers' third goal after Jonatan Johansson, who had taken over from Gabriel Amato, played him into Celtic's box. McCann went around Kerr and scored easily.

However, from the moment McCann scored his first goal a nightmare was unfolding for Celtic, who had been hit badly by injuries.

There was no Craig Burley, Regi Blinker was still missing as were Lubomir Moravcik, Johan Mjallby, Jonathan Gould, Tom Boyd (suspended) and Marc Rieper and Venglos had to take drastic action.

He gave Scott Marshall, brother of former Celtic keeper Gordon, his first game since arriving on loan from

ON FOREIGN SOIL

HAMMER BLOW: Jorg Albertz scores No.2 from the spot to put the champers on ice for Rangers

THREE'S A ROUT: Neil McCann breezes round Celtic keeper Stewart Kerr on his way to scoring his second

I'M THE ONE: Penalty hero Jorg Albertz salutes the fans after firing in his goal

Southampton and the defender must be wishing he had never made the journey back north.

He didn't have a good debut and was unable to do anything about McCann's flashing runs and close control.

Venglos's bench told the story of his troubles because there were three teenagers – Mark Burchill, Barry John Corr and Colin Healy – sitting there along with Tommy Johnson, who hasn't kicked a ball for Celtic since the days of Tommy Burns.

Celtic simply couldn't cope and even though they still had Henrik Larsson he continued to play like a mere mortal.

When Advocaat scanned Celtic's line-up he must have known he would have the last laugh at Celtic Park where he had suffered back in November when Celtic had beaten Rangers 5-1.

The triumph also allowed Rangers to steal a psychological advantage for the Tennents Scottish Cup final later this month when more than 50,000 Old Firm fans again will come together, this time at the new Hampden.

Noise

Hopefully tempers will have subsided by then because Scottish football can do without another display of such hatred and intolerance.

The din at five minutes after six which split the the air over Celtic Park signalled the significance of this encounter and when Celtic went into their huddle seconds before the ball started rolling in earnest, the noise must have carried over all of Glasgow.

However, Celtic's fans were silenced after only a couple of minutes when Rangers surged forward and Albertz was allowed to gallop into shooting distance.

He didn't release the trigger and instead slipped a pass to McCann whose shot was blocked by Mahe, although the ball broke loose and bounced off Rico Annoni before landing in the arms of Kerr.

Stefan Klos was also tested early but he was equal to the task and punched clear Morten Wieghorst's corner from the left even though he was under pressure from Marshall.

A few minutes later Celtic brought the pace of Harald Brattbakk into force and suddenly the lack of speed in Rangers' defence was exposed.

Lorenzo Amoruso had to lean heavily and illegally on Brattbakk to prevent him from sprinting towards Klos and although Larsson took the free-kick Rangers cleared.

Giovanni van Bronckhorst took possession, brought Wallace – who had appeared unmarked on the left-hand side – into play and the little striker, playing just off the front line, raced into Celtic's box.

He clipped the ball back into the path of McCann, who jabbed out a leg and prodded the ball into the net.

Only 12 minutes gone and Celtic were behind and facing a huge test of their character but even allowing for their injury problems they failed miserably.

Mark Viduka tried to menace with his power play but on the whole Amoruso and Colin Hendry coped comfortably although Wieghorst, released by Viduka, should have scored instead of hitting the ball a foot wide of Klos's right-hand post.

Bizarre

While the players were indoors trying to catch their breath after a frantic first half even by Old Firm standards, the groundstaff were busy picking up the missiles which had been thrown on to the pitch.

Kerr was booked in 52 minutes after a bizarre error. He rolled the ball in front of him as he trotted out of his box to start a move, but he dithered and McCann pounced.

The winger blocked the clearance and the ball bounced into Kerr's arms but he was a yard out of his area.

Amato could have punished him further from the free-kick but Kerr got his body behind the shot and was relieved to see the ball soar into the air and over his bar.

A few minutes later Brattbakk was clear on the edge of Rangers' penalty area and sent in a good low shot which Klos did well to knock away and then, at the opposite end, McCann wriggled away from Lambert and should have done more than shoot straight at Kerr who saved with his legs.

If the first half was frantic the opening to the second spell was utterly chaotic but in the end Rangers deserved their triumph and the title.

DREAM TEAM MAN OF THE MATCH: *McCann (Rangers).*

Pictures: CRAIG HALKETT, ROB CASEY and MARK RUNNACLES

CELTIC
MAN BYMAN

JONATHAN GOULD **7**
The big Englishman turned in another accomplished display between the sticks and made some important stops towards the end of the first half.
His save from Vidmar just after the break was also top drawer and he had no chance with the Wallace goal.

STEPHANE MAHE **6**
A sinner the last time the teams met, the Frenchman was on his best behaviour at Hampden. Didn't do much wrong and defended reasonably well before being replaced by Phil O'Donnell.

JOHAN MJALLBY **6**
Had a fascinating duel with Amato, with honours just about even after the 90 minutes.
However, he won't fancy watching too many replays of the incident when the Argentine stitched him up with an outrageous piece of skill on the touchline.

ALAN STUBBS **7**
One of Celtic's better players, the big defender will be disappointed to end his career on such a low note. Stubbs mopped up almost everything at the back and came close to getting himself on the scoresheet from set pieces a few times.

TOM BOYD.......**8**
Celtic's best player, the skipper didn't deserve to be on the losing side on Saturday afternoon. Boyd did an excellent man-marking job on Neil McCann and was an inspiration.

ENRICO ANNONI **6**
The Italian was handed the task of stifling Rod Wallace and did his job reasonably well. However, pace has always been the former Roma defender's Achilles heel and it was cruelly exposed a few times in the wide open spaces of Hampden. Replaced by Tommy Johnson on the hour mark.

PAUL LAMBERT **7**
The best of a mediocre midfield bunch, the Scotland star was unlucky not to open the scoring at the new national stadium when his 30-yard effort came crashing back off the crossbar in the first half. Rarely wastes a pass and is one of the few Scots who could walk into any English Premiership side.

MORTEN WIEGHORST..........**5**
Handed an unfamiliar slot on the right-hand side of midfield, the role soon looked alien to the big Dane, who contributed nothing in either defence or attack.

REGI BLINKER **4**
Lucky not to be red-carded for a disgraceful two-footed lunge on McInnes, the little Dutchman was a passenger for the entire match. The occasion seemed too much for him and he was largely anonymous, particularly in the second half.

PHIL O'DONNELL..**3**
Couldn't force his way into the match when he replaced Stephane Mahe, O'Donnell's Parkhead career ended on a low note before his summer move to Sheffield Wednesday.

LUBOMIR MORAVCIK **5**
Starting only his second game after a four-month absence with a hamstring injury, the Slovak didn't even look half fit. Playing in a free role behind Larsson, he never really got into the game and was a major disappointment.

HENRIK LARSSON...................**6**
Scotland's Player of the Year gave his all but just couldn't find a way past the outstanding Hendry and Amoruso. Had little support up front and the burden of carrying Celtic almost single-handedly for much of the season finally took its toll.

SUBS - TOMMY JOHNSON......**5**
Preferred instead of young Mark Burchill, the striker was hardly noticed when he came on for Annoni. **PHIL O'DONNELL** see above.

BACK FOR GOOD: Rod Wallace hitches a lift from Ian Ferguson as the party starts

NEW DAWN,

Stunning stadium only makes match look more dreary

THEY say the cost of rebuilding Hampden comes to approximately £52million. A mere drop in the football business's financial ocean.

In fact, the pennies spent on refurbishing the Grand Dame of Scottish football amount to little more than loose change when set alongside the spending of Celtic and particularly Rangers over the last decade.

Yet, there we all were, spruced up and sitting in the shiny new Mount Florida amphitheatre which Jim Farry built, watching the same dreary old stuff played out by two of the game's most ancient rivals.

The more things change the more they remain the same.

There was atmosphere and, yes, there was an air of expectancy, but it would have been a strange Scottish Cup Final indeed if the natives had remained subdued on such an important afternoon.

The sponsors, Tennents, did their bit and the SFA tried hard, but cup final day passed with the feeling that something was amiss.

You know what, the vital missing ingredient just might have been quality football.

Also, the outcome of the 114th playing of this final may have been decided before a ball was kicked because Dr Jozef Venglos's selection was the wrong one.

Venglos's set-up was wrong and his refusal to recognise Mark Burchill is a serious weakness.

Judgment

Burchill's pace could have helped unnerve Rangers' central defence, but for some reason this was not a game to suit the striker. How do we know this?

Venglos told us, but the bottom line is he made another error of judgment which was compounded when he put only two outfield players, Tommy Johnson and Phil O'Donnell, on the bench with keeper Stewart Kerr.

Having left him out of the starting 11, Venglos most certainly should have had Burchill in the dug-out, not in the stand.

Many Celtic fans just can't follow Venglos's logic and are growing weary of his philosophical ways and musings. Last year they were champions, this year, nothing. Venglos can't continue to shrug-off that truth.

Thankfully the afternoon was violence-free and we were spared the embarrassments which damaged our game – no, that's not quite accurate as our entire society suffered – last time these two sides were allowed out to play together and that terribly nice man Donald Dewar was there to present the prizes to the winners.

The First Minister was all smiles

| CELTIC | 0 |
| RANGERS | 1 |

By JAMES TRAYNOR

as he handed over the cup to Rangers captain Lorenzo Amoruso, but then it was the first time in a while that our Donald had been seen in public without his new sidekick, Jim Wallace of the Lib Dems, who could be seen as the political equivalent of Partick Thistle.

They are pretty hopeless, but for some unknown reason command an importance they don't deserve.

It wouldn't have been surprising if the lid tumbled from the cup as Amoruso lifted it and Wallace popped up looking for Donald, the man who has given him credence and status the electorate refused to.

Speaking of Dewar, perhaps he could step in for the injured Colin Hendry, who won't travel to the Faroe Islands and Czech Republic with Scotland because of injury sustained in Saturday's 1-0 win against Celtic.

After all, did not former SFA chief executive Farry once suggest that Tony Blair's mate could play centre-half for Scotland?

Long before the end of the final it was clear Johan Mjallby couldn't play central defence either.

Sharp

The huge Swede with the spiky hair and sharp temperament was toiling and unable to chase after anyone who wanted to run by him.

Long before the end, and in common with his look-a-like Dolph Lundgren, he was reduced to B-movie acting.

Mjallby gave an Oscar-winning performance of a lumbering hulk while players around him, usually Gabriel Amato and Rod Wallace, darted and turned with a fluency that seemed to baffle the Celt.

At the opposite end of the pitch Amoruso was playing his finest game for Rangers and making even critics like myself think again about him.

He was immense and, from early on, he made it clear he was ready to lead Rangers to the treble.

Colin Hendry stood tall beside

❝ The missing ingredient

TENNENTS SCOTTISH CUP 3

SAME STORY

ROD OF IRON: Rod Wallace secures his place in Rangers legend by steering the Cup Final winner over the shattered Jonathan Gould at Hampden

him and they formed a barrier against which Henrik Larsson, again a shadow of his former self, and Lubomir Moravcik flitted in and out of the action only threatening to inflict damage.

Other players, for example Morten Wieghorst, didn't even do that much.

It was Rod Wallace who secured victory for Rangers minutes into the second half when dreadful defending allowed him to pounce after Tony Vidmar had driven the ball in from the left.

The delivery passed Wallace but Neil McCann, who had been shadowed well by Tom Boyd until this point, lunged and stabbed the ball through to the little striker who smacked it into the net.

Enrico Annoni, who was supposed to be dealing with Wallace, stood stranded a yard away and Rangers' fans went wild while Celtic's people fell silent.

They had watched Rangers dominate the first half even though Paul Lambert's fierce long-range shot thumped Stefan Klos's bar. Now they were a goal behind.

It looked ominous, especially with Regi Blinker wandering around without offering much assistance – apart from a nasty tackle born of frustration on Derek McInnes – to Lambert.

Yet Venglos's side enjoyed more of the ball in the second half but couldn't apply a finishing touch.

There was one moment soon after Rangers' goal when Larsson failed to get his head to a cross as Klos stayed on his line.

Five or six weeks ago he probably

would have, but Larsson's club season ended far too prematurely.

He may have become a victim of fatigue, but before we give him the benefit of the doubt perhaps we should wait and see how he plays for his country against England at Wembley on Saturday.

Celtic created more openings in the second period than in the first, but they always ran into Amoruso and Hendry, who refused to leave the pitch before the end even though in agony because of a groin strain, standing almost shoulder to shoulder in defiance.

Courageous

Even when they did get the ball beyond these twin pillars they were blocked by Klos, who made some excellent saves and he, too, had his best match for Rangers.

The referee, Hugh Dallas, also performed well and he made what might have been the most courageous decision of his career when, after 87 minutes, Lambert drove a stinging shot towards goal and the ball came back off Amoruso.

Everybody in the stadium, including Rangers' fans thought the Italian used an arm to block the shot. Dallas thought otherwise.

He gave Celtic a corner and their fans rose up against him. Thankfully no one threw any coins or tried to get on the pitch, but video evidence later proved Dallas's call had been spot on.

It wasn't the referee who cost Celtic this final, although their fans will disagree.

Perhaps they should start looking more closely at their head coach.

HUGGY BEARS: Van Bronckhorst, Ferguson and Albertz clinch at the final whistle

was quality football 9

BILLY'S HAPPY ENDING

Double strike caps a night to savour for the smiling assassin

STRIKE ONE: Billy Dodds ignores the tight angle to shoot Rangers ahead

STRIKE TWO: Stephen Robertson has missed the ball, leaving Dodds a tap-in

BILLY DODDS spent almost an entire career believing nights like these were meant for someone else.

But a four-month fairytale was completed last night for the 31-year-old as he returned to one of his former places of employment and scored the two goals that marked the deliverance of another SPL title to Ibrox.

In a match riddled with nasty tackling and bad-tempered incidents, Dodds, a man who has always played with a smile on his face, scored a goal in each half to ensure the championship party went with a bang.

Greasy

While the action itself may have been forgettable, this is one game that will live on long in the memory of Dodds who used to dream of such nights as he grew up in Ayrshire.

He obviously wanted to savour the moment because he was last man off the pitch, weighed down by at least a dozen scarves.

Rangers emerged to familiar chants of "champion-ees" from the small band of their fans who had arrived unfashionably early for the party.

They were quickly to learn that Dodds had recovered from the hamstring strain and was in an unchanged side.

Sandy Clark gave 17-year-old Keigan Parker his first start in

ST JOHNSTONE 0
RANGERS 2
By KEITH JACKSON

a Saints attack minus suspended Graeme Jones and the injured Nathan Lowndes.

Rangers started off as if they meant business, with midfield player Barry Ferguson looking particularly fired up.

Saints struggled to manage any meaningful possession in the opening minutes and their frustration manifested itself in an eighth-minute booking for Danny Griffin for clattering into Jorg Albertz.

The German was not seriously damaged and it was from his well-disguised pass that Rod Wallace was given his first real sight of goal.

As the little striker pulled back the trigger, though, Darren Dods powered in to make a timely, sliding block.

The greasy surface didn't help everyone, however, and Lorenzo Amoruso was next into Mike McCurry's book when he launched himself into a skid that almost ended with little Kieran McAnespie taking an unexpected place in the front row of the main stand.

Saints worked feverishly to find their way into this game and as the half wore on began

making progress towards the goal of Stefan Klos.

John O'Neil tried his luck from 30 yards after running on to a misplaced Amoruso headed clearance but his shot squirted harmlessly wide of the target.

Although spending much of the time in Rangers' half, Saints were short of ideas on how to make possession count.

When Amoruso conceded a free-kick just outside his own penalty area and then risked a second yellow card by booting the ball away in disgust, Rangers went unpunished.

First ref McCurry turned a Nelson and then Griffin wasted the opportunity by overcooking his delivery and sending it over

the heads of the cluster of players at Klos' back post.

Keith O'Halloran was next up when the ball broke to him after another Perth attack perished on the edge of the Rangers box but his sweetly-struck shot was always rising.

You began to sense that if St

Johnstone kept wasting such opportunities, they would be made to pay when the visitors were fully into their stride.

Parker was left holding his head in his hands after blasting high and wide under pressure from Scott Wilson.

It was a clever pass by O'Neil that had picked him out and it deserved a better finish.

Sure enough, not long after that miss, Rangers sneaked up the other end almost unnoticed to grab a 42-minute lead.

It was another stiletto-like pass from Albertz that did the damage, cutting through the home defence and allowing Dodds to make his way into the six-yard box. The hitman still

had work to do but from an acute angle he somehow managed to spin and send a wonderful shot past Stephen Robertson who had dived a little too quickly.

It was a spectacular finish from the Scotland striker – his 10th Rangers goal in just 12

starts – and it could not have come at a more crushing time for St Johnstone who had looked as if they were starting to believe in themselves.

Wallace, who had suffered an ankle injury early in the first half, was removed from the action at half-time – but sub Seb Rozental wasted little time in making his presence felt.

He pulled the strings in a sweeping counter-attack in 55 minutes, feeding Andrei Kanchelskis on the right, then cutely stepping over the Ukrainian's cross to allow Amoruso a crack at goal.

The big defender, whose surge from the back had started the move, was now in unfamiliar territory, though, and his effort skidded wide.

Ferguson also missed a decent chance, heading wide from a Kanchelskis corner, before Rozental sliced through Saints again to set up a second goal for Dodds.

This time the Chilean showed a good burst of pace to collect a Claudio Reyna pass before it crossed the byeline. He then showed a delightful touch as he floated the ball back across the six-yard box, out of the reach of the diving Robertson and into the path of Dodds who had only to raise a boot to nudge it over the line.

The goal did little to cool a few tempers, which had been simmering from the off, and in 66

minutes McAnespie brought the game to boiling point with a shocking tackle on Giovanni van Bronckhorst that left the Dutchman writhing in agony.

McAnespie was booked, as was Ferguson who had reacted furiously to the challenge, sparking an ugly flare-up.

Van Bronckhorst, meanwhile, got back to his feet but only long enough to see Neil McCann stripped and ready to replace him on the sidelines.

Claudio Reyna then exacted retribution on McAnespie with a late tackle and he, too, was booked for his trouble.

Crunching

McAnespie was himself removed from the fray by Clark in 77 minutes and replaced by Irishman Gerry McMahon whose first contribution was a crunching foul on Albertz for which he, too, was booked.

Rangers had also replaced Kanchelskis with Tugay and the Turk almost made it 3-0 with 10 minutes to go but his shot – following some clever link-up play between McCann and Numan on the left – was blocked on the line by Gary Bollan.

Dodds should have completed a hat-trick in 86 minutes but headed a McCann cross wide of Robertson's left-hand post.

Still, there was little need for him to take the match ball from McDiarmid Park.

He already had his memories ... and his new collection of scarves, of course.

DREAM TEAM MAN OF THE MATCH: *Dodds (Rangers)*

THE MATCH STATS

ST JOHNSTONE		RANGERS
0	Goals	2
1	Shots on target (incl Goals)	2
6	Shots off Target	10
0	Blocked Shots	5
2	Corners	7
20	Fouls Conceded	12
2	Offsides	6
4	Yellow Cards	4

Pictures: CRAIG HALKETT and ROB CASEY

Sports RECORD

Viduka lashes back at walk-out claims

FURIOUS Celtic striker Mark Viduka last night hit back at claims that he has walked out on the club for a second time.

Viduka believes someone is out to blacken his name after weekend claims that he had stormed out of

EXCLUSIVE
By KEITH JACKSON

Parkhead in a huff after being left out of Kenny Dalglish's team for the 1-1 draw with Hibs.

The Australian, speaking from his sick bed at

home in Bothwell, angrily rejected claims that he missed training on Friday after going out on a bender.

And he revealed the only reason he didn't stay around on Saturday to watch his team-mates concede the title was because he was

ordered to return to bed by the club's medical staff.

Viduka said: "I am absolutely amazed at these claims. It's total bull****. I can't believe

Turn to Page 40

8-PAGE TRIBUTE TO THE Champions 2000 / **COULTHARD'S SILVER DOUBLE** **PAGES 38,39**

CHEERS

Gers celebrate two in a row – as Dick starts making plans for three

DICK ADVOCAAT celebrated his second successive SPL title at McDiarmid Park last night and immediately turned his thoughts to making it three in a row.

The Rangers manager watched, arms folded, from his dugout as his players embarked on

By KEITH JACKSON

a lap of honour following their 2-0 win over St Johnstone which has left them a staggering 20 points clear at the top of the table with five games to go.

It was party time in Perth for the Ibrox club, which has now claimed 11 of Scottish football's last 12 league flags.

But before the last of the Rangers fans had even begun making their way back **Turn to Page 40**

BREAKING OUT THE BUBBLY: Lorenzo Amoruso starts the celebrations at Perth last night to the delight of Dick Advocaat

---

Published by Scottish Daily Record and Sunday Mail Ltd., (0141-248 7000), 40 Anderson Quay, Glasgow G3 8DA and printed by Saltire Press, a trading division of Scottish Daily Record and Sunday Mail Ltd. Cardonald Park, Glasgow and MCP Ltd, Oldham and Watford. Registered at the Post Office as a Newspaper. © Scottish Daily Record and Sunday Mail Ltd. 2000. A Trinity Mirror plc Newspaper.

mailsport

THE LOVEN CUP

Goal hero was praying for end

By EUAN McLEAN

GOAL hero Peter Lovenkrands prayed for the final whistle to sound BEFORE his last-gasp Scottish Cup clincher – because he was too tired to play on.

The Danish striker sealed an injury time 3-2 win for Rangers at Hampden, the first time in 41 Old Firm games a team has come from behind to win.

Before heading back to Ibrox for a knees-up, exhausted Peter revealed he wanted Hugh Dallas to blow for full-time with the sides locked at 2-2.

He said: "I felt too tired to run any more. I managed to make it to Neil McCann's cross, hit the ball and my momentum carried me forward. I didn't see where the ball had gone.

"That was a nervous moment but then I heard the fans shouting and realised it was in the net. I was so happy all I could think of was to run towards

● TURN TO PAGE 83

COURT GERSTER: Lorenzo Amoruso

WIN TICKETS TO SEE EURO FINAL

Page 72

HENDRY SOCKS IT TO THE ROCKET

Page 63

Published By Scottish Daily Record and Sunday Mail Ltd. (0141-309 3000), 1 Central Quay, Glasgow G3 8DA and printed by Saltire Press at Cardonald Park, Glasgow G51 4EA. Registered at the Post Office as a Newspaper. © Scottish Daily Record and Sunday Mail Ltd. 2000. A Trinity Mirror Group Newspaper.

THE WINNER

PICTURE: KENNY RAMSEY

NOW FOR THE TREBLE

Final hero Lovenkrands tips Gers to hog the glory

PETER LOVENKRANDS launched Rangers towards their second successive CIS Cup triumph then insisted Alex McLeish's men can win the Treble.

The Danish winger, who scored twice against Celtic in last season's Scottish Cup Final, returned to Hampden to destroy their dreams again.

Lovenkrands made the opening goal for Claudio Caniggia then took his personal tally against Celts to six with the winner in the 2-1 victory.

Now the youngster has set his sights on retaining the Scottish Cup and

By DAVID McCARTHY

ripping the SPL championship from Martin O'Neill's grasp.

He said: "We have won one trophy now and we are capable of winning the others. We will definitely go for it."

Lovenkrands hopes his performance will speed up contract negotiations which have dragged on for months.

He added: "I just want to be playing football well for the first team and I am sure if I can get back my form the contract will come."

Ibrox boss Alex McLeish is also targeting three trophies. He said: "We have got a chance of the Treble as opposed to last season when we trailed in the league."

CIS CUP SPECIAL: PAGES 3, 8, 9, 10 AND 11

LOVE IS ALL AROUND: Peter Lovenkrands nets Rangers second goal past Rab Douglas, top, then does a cartwheel before being congratulated by team-mates Ricksen, Arteta and Mols

I started to have doubts over Peter ..today he proved that I was wrong

Eck full of praise for Danish goal hero

BRAVE FACE: Thompson

Tommo: We can bounce back at Anfield

By JAMES TRAYNOR

ALAN THOMPSON refused to concede Celtic's season is in danger of falling apart after the Hampden defeat.

Disappointment was clearly etched on the wingback's face as he tried to banish the nightmare scenario of a dramatic CIS Cup Final but he insisted Celtic can still hit the heights.

He stressed Celtic must start thinking positively again as they turn to Thursday's away leg of their UEFA Cup quarter-final tie against Liverpool.

Thompson said: "Thursday night's game is now huge. We'll be ready for it even after this defeat.

"It's not as though we were played off the pitch or were never in the game so I don't think we will have a bad reaction.

"It wasn't a bad performance by us ahead of a huge game and once the whistle goes at Anfield we'll be ready."

Slipped

But before Thompson consigned the final to the darkest recesses of his mind he made it clear Celtic are convinced some blundering officials had as much to do with the setback as Rangers.

While Martin O'Neill was busy listing what he felt were mistakes by referee Kenny Clark and his team, Thompson had the main standside linesman David Doig in his sights.

Four minutes after Henrik Larsson scored, the striker slipped a pass to John Hartson who blasted home what should have been the equaliser.

However, Doig flagged for offside, even though the Welshman had timed his move to perfection.

Thompson said: "I'm not saying that cost us the cup but it did cost us a very good chance of going on to win it.

"*I hope the linesman watches the game again and realises he made a rip-roaring error in a cup final.*"

Thompson also had words of comfort for Hartson, who missed a late penalty.

He said: "John and Henrik had a few words although I don't know what was said but John missed and I really feel for him.

"I just hope he bags a goal or two on Thursday instead."

ALEX McLEISH was loathe to admit it but somewhere lurking in the back of his mind may have been the fear that Peter Lovenkrands was a one-season wonder.

The Danish youngster destroyed Celtic last term with his pace and precision in front of goal, scoring five times including the two that won the Scottish Cup in May.

This term, though, Celtic seemed to have sussed Lovenkrands out. He hadn't kicked a ball against them and last week at Parkhead he produced his worst Old Firm performance of his career.

McLeish was surely tempted to ditch him yesterday but the manager kept faith and Lovenkrands repaid him spectacularly.

He ran Celtic, and Johan Mjallby in particular, ragged. He had a shot cleared off the line at 0-0, forced Rab Douglas into the blocked save that left Claudio Caniggia a tap-in for the opener, then scored the goal that ultimately allowed his team to hang on to the CIS Cup.

Rangers were forced to hang on for dear life when Celtic bit back at them bravely and brilliantly after the break.

Heroes

Henrik Larsson jabbed a shot of adrenalin straight into their weary limbs by scoring early enough in the second half to give them reason to believe a salvage mission was possible.

But an offside decision and a missed penalty kick later, Celtic's dreams were dead and Rangers boss McLeish had reasserted his grip over this fixture.

He thought all his players were heroes but some were more than others. And Lovenkrands topped the lot.

McLeish said: "I was beginning to wonder about him before today because in the last two or three Old Firm games, Celtic have kept him quiet. But he showed how dangerous he can be today.

"I thought in the first half we were fantastic and we thoroughly deserved the lead we had. In the second half, Celtic had the ascendancy and maybe it is a human trait to try to hang on to what you've got.

"*You've got to credit Celtic as well because I thought some of their players might be dead on their feet. Instead they became a threat.*"

Lovenkrands admitted the Rangers team owed their fans a performance after last week's Parkhead defeat.

He said: "Everybody wanted to prove something today and I think we did that. I felt very good and I think we were mag-

CUP FOR IT: Alex McLeish was absolutely delighted that his side took the CIS Cup for the second time in a row

Pictures: CRAIG HALKETT & ROB CASEY

By DAVID McCARTHY

nificent in the first half. We showed that we can play good football."

McLeish believed the tie was going into overtime when Lorenzo Amoruso was judged to have fouled Bobo Balde inside the box – but he insisted his team would have had the advantage because of Neil Lennon's red card in the dying minutes.

The Rangers boss said: "My gut instinct was we were going to extra time but I was trying to take positives from it and one was that we were going into it with an extra man. I thought we could have made that count. Thankfully we didn't have to and now we can look ahead to the rest of the season."

While there was delight in the Rangers camp, there was only despair laced with disgust in the Celtic dressing room.

Martin O'Neill clearly believed his team's chances of success had been ruined by the chopping off of Hartson's goal at 2-1. He also reckoned Lennon was harshly treated and Amoruso, who'd been booked previously, should have walked for his trip on Balde that led to the penalty.

While the last two of his three views were undoubtedly seen through green-tinged glasses, there's little doubt Hartson was onside for the goal that was disallowed.

Emotional

The manager found time to praise his players. He said: "I thought they were magnificent and I am proud of them. They could have wilted at half-time but they had the will and desire to go again and that was just incredible.

"They were cheered off at the end and they deserved it."

O'Neill was quite emotional. Then again, he usually is. But these fixtures grab at the senses and shake them until you hardly know what day of the week it is.

Michael Mols summed that up quite perfectly. Finally, the Rangers striker got to play in a cup final, having missed the last three through injury or non-selection.

His joy was unconfined at the final whistle but when he saw his little boy after he'd collected his medal, the dam broke and tears flowed. He hugged his son and wouldn't let go, even as his team-mates called on him to join their lap of honour.

There might have been 30,000 fans left in the stadium but as far as Mols was concerned, he and his kid were alone.

That's what winning an Old Firm Cup Final does to a man. Seeing O'Neill looking pale and drawn, barely keeping his emotions in check, showed what losing one can do to a man.

PENALTY

Arteta keeps his cool to land the title with spot-kick

BY JAMES TRAYNOR

RANGERS.................6
DUNFERMLINE..........1

HEADING FOR GLORY: Derek Stillie fails to prevent Shota Arveladze grabbing Rangers' third with a diving header

MOLS SKINS 'EM: Michael Mols hits No.1 in three minutes

DAIR DEVIL: Jason Dair stuns Gers fans with an equaliser

PERFECT DUTCH: Ronald de Boer soars into the air to connect with a Neil McCann cross and head in the fourth goal

ALEX McLEISH disappeared under a sea of bodies yesterday as Rangers refused to buckle on a Sunday bursting with nerve-jangling drama.

With the Old Firm tied on points and goal difference it was always going to be a day of heavy tension, but no one could have expected this level of anxiety, despair and ultimately, for Rangers and their fans, unbridled joy.

As the afternoon progressed and the goals flew in at Ibrox and also Rugby Park where Celtic beat Kilmarnock 4-0 the SPL championship had gone one way and then the other. It was almost too much for some and in the closing seconds when Rangers won a penalty many fans and players couldn't watch as Mikel Arteta steadied himself.

Rangers, 5-1 up, needed another goal and having missed three penalties in their previous two matches it was no certainty they would score. Arteta breathed in deep, looked at Derek Stillie, trotted up and sent the Dunfermline keeper the wrong way.

Finally it was over, on the last day and at the last moment McLeish's side broke Celtic's hold on the title and also their great rivals' hearts.

Rangers won the title by a single goal and for McLeish it was almost too much. At last the weight of expectation was removed from his shoulders and for the first time in months he was able to breath properly without his chest hurting.

The tension, which had wrapped itself around this young manager like an iron corset, was ripped away and he realised he had just become a real, bona fide, genuine hero.

In a season which had promised so much for Celtic it was McLeish's side who stayed the course, but only just. It was Rangers who had barely enough left to get to the summit and although arguments will rage about which manager, McLeish or Martin O'Neill, has had the best campaign, only one of them can produce trophies as evidence.

And McLeish may claim another, a third, on Saturday when he takes his team to Hampden for the Tennent's Scottish Cup Final and again his ears will be assaulted by the deafening praise which rang all around him.

There were 49,731 inside the stadium to celebrate Rangers' 50th championship and it was very, very special.

Rangers' players, quite rightly, milked every last drop of joy and emotion from the trophy celebration as Lorenzo Amoruso, who may have played his last game at Ibrox along with Arthur Numan, Claudio Caniggia and Michael Mols, removed his shirt to show off his washboard stomach.

McLeish had to make late, unexpected alterations because of injuries to Peter Lovenkrands and Stephen Hughes and although

conspiracy theories will abound now this title was all about nerve, courage, and an ability to go the distance and the way McLeish turned a dispirited squad around will be written into the club's folklore.

The din as Rangers walked from the tunnel was like nothing they had heard this season, probably even longer, and Dunfermline must have felt very lonely inside such a packed stadium, but in two minutes their worst nightmare began when they conceded the first goal.

Caniggia played a ball through to Mols, who turned as only he can and poked the ball into the net off a post.

Rangers' fans went crazy, but they were furious a minute later when Ronald de Boer missed an open goal, sending his header wide from only a few yards out, and it was an error which he and the fans would regret within eight minutes.

It was understandable that Dunfermline would need time to come to terms with the din and the tension, which could almost be touched, but played the ball through the midfield well in 11 minutes and Jason Dair belted forward in support. The ball was played back to him and he smacked it into the net from all of 22 yards.

McLeish was disgusted with his players, but his demeanour changed dramatically in 15 minutes when the ball, deflected into the path of Caniggia by a Fernando Ricksen tackle inside Dunfermline's box, was jabbed into the net beyond a stunned Stillie.

De Boer had to go to the sideline to have his left foot strapped up but Dunfermline didn't do much with their superior numbers and Rangers eventually made their way back downfield with Amoruso of all players chasing a lost cause along Dunfermline's bye-line.

The big defender caught the ball before it went over and although he could have played a pass back to Numan he decided to put in a low cross which Dunfermline didn't expect. Shota Arveladze did and he dipped to head into the left-hand corner of Stillie's net.

Dunfermline had Stevie Crawford lying deep and he was enjoying the time and space granted in the midfield where only Barry Ferguson and Arteta were operating for Rangers, who couldn't get into a smooth flow in that area.

Their priority was to get as many players as possible forward to unnerve the opposition's defence. It was a risky strategy but they had little choice since Chris Sutton was taking care of business for Celtic at Rugby Park.

McLeish kept Caniggia indoors at

So you can get on with the job

Wickes

SLICK

Pictures: CRAIG HALKETT and RICHARD PARKER

ART OF THE PENALTY KICK: Spanish kid Mikel Arteta clinches the title for Rangers as he strokes in a last-minute spot-kick for No.6 and celebrates at the end with Claudio Caniggia, inset

half-time and sent Neil McCann out to play and within seconds the little winger had cut the ball back for de Boer to have a go, but he didn't even connect and another excellent chance had gone.

However, the Dutchman would get it right in time to help his team through in the second half.

David Grondin didn't come back out and his place was taken by Gary Dempsey but before he could make any impression Scott Wilson had hacked Mols down, presenting Rangers with a free-kick 25 yards out. Amoruso took charge and curled the ball over the wall but Stillie held easily.

He didn't have to bother coming from his line even though Craig

Moore's chip forward found de Boer because the Dutchman squirted his shot wide again then, in 57 minutes, an Arveladze shot appeared to hit Chris McGroarty on an arm.

The referee was unsighted but gave Rangers a free-kick nine yards from goal after deciding Stillie had picked up Gus MacPherson's passback.

The Pars were enraged because the ball had actually come off de Boer, but MacPherson was booked for complaining too much and when order was restored Amoruso smacked the ball over the bar.

Rangers won a corner on their left and before it was taken Mols went off with Steven Thompson going on in the hope of attacking the corner

but it was cleared, allowing Dunfermline to surge away again.

They sped to the other end and Stefan Klos had to make a terrific save from Craig Brewster but immediately Rangers clattered to the opposite end, winning a corner taken by McCann on the left.

This time de Boer timed everything – his run, jump and header – to perfection and Stillie was beaten. Rangers, with 64 minutes gone, were back on top of the league by one goal of a difference and two minutes later Thompson bundled in a fifth goal.

The Ibrox faithful were ecstatic and Thompson almost gave them another goal but his header bounced only a foot wide and then it became

clear one more was required because Stilian Petrov had scored.

As the game rushed into time added on McCann went for the ball with Stillie, who held his face and got the foul, but in the second minute of the extra three McCann was brought down and won a penalty.

Players and fans alike looked away as Arteta prepared himself, de Boer turned to McLeish, the pair of them standing in total silence, and then they burst back into life as the corwd roared.

Arteta sent Stillie the wrong way and once more Ibrox was rocking with wild, delirious celebration.

MAN OF THE MATCH
Craig Moore (Rangers)

RANGERS v DUNFERMLINE		
56%	POSSESSION	44%
6	GOALS	1
12	SHOTS ON TARGET (INC GOALS)	3
9	SHOTS OFF TARGET	2
6	BLOCKED SHOTS	3
14	CORNERS	0
12	FOULS CONCEDED	17
5	OFFSIDES	0
1	YELLOW CARDS	2
0	RED CARDS	0

STATS SUPPLIED BY OPTA

YOU COULDN'T

Amo heads Gers to the treble with finish fit for Hollywood

IT had to be Lorenzo – Hollywood script writers simply couldn't have come up with a better ending.

You couldn't have wished for a more dramatic character to grab the goal that sealed the treble for Rangers – or a better way for the limelight-loving Italian to sign off his Ibrox career.

With the fans' favourite looking destined to leave the club this summer it was the perfect way to bring down the curtain on a turbulent six-year spell.

His 65th-minute header was the only thing between the champions and gutsy Dundee who gave everything and came away with nothing but pain and pride.

As the whistle blew on the seventh treble in the club's history big Amo slumped to his knees in tears.

It's no surprise he got the biggest cheer of the day when he predictably stayed at the back of the line to lift the cup last.

We'll know in the next few weeks if it's also the end of the line for his time in Scotland. But yesterday was just about enjoying the victory ground out from a disjointed performance by a tired Rangers.

Of course, Dundee deserve a large chunk of praise for not letting the favourites take command of the Dark Blues first cup final appearance in 39 years.

Determined

Boss Jim Duffy wrestled with a pre-match dilemma. Should he go against the principles his entertaining side stood for all season and try to contain Rangers?

Or stick to his guns and send his men into the biggest game of their young lives with the stirring message to go for it?

Thankfully Duff is not the sort of man to go back on what he believes and his selection gave an uplifting indication Dundee were determined not to let their big chance pass.

With only suspended Lee Wilkie missing from his usual arsenal he played all his aces in a bid to bring the cup back to Dens Park for the first time in 93 years.

Dundee's cause was boosted when it emerged Gers would be without Mikel Arteta who had picked up a calf injury in training.

With Stephen Hughes also crocked, Alex McLeish's options were limited so he was forced to ask centre half Bob Malcolm to step forward into unfamiliar territory.

Far more comfortable in the midfield engine room was Dundee's impressive Gavin Rae who played a major role as his side almost got off to a flying start as early as the fourth minute.

The Scotland star did well to dash past Malcolm into the box but his shot rebounded off Amoruso only as far as Barry Smith on the edge of the box.

The Dens skipper has only scored three goals in eight years at Dens but he looked like a seasoned striker as he let rip first time – only to see the ball crash off a post.

Smith was criticised for not celebrating a goal against former side Celtic but had this one gone in there's no doubt he would have milked it for all it was worth.

The Taysiders gave Duffy the

HEADING FOR A TREBLE: Hampden hero Lorenzo Amoruso soars above the Dundee defence to nod home the Tennent's Scottish Cup winner yesterday then starts the celebrations with Rangers team-mates Fernando Ricksen, Steven Thompson, Bob Malcolm and Craig Moore

DUNDEE 0
RANGERS 1

Euan **McLEAN** reports

positive start he wanted and they carved another good chance five minutes later when Mark Burchill's lovely weighted ball sent Steve Lovell through.

He was blocked by the alert Stefan Klos diving at his feet but the underdogs were enjoying the best of the game.

Yet they almost found themselves harshly behind in 14 minutes after conceding a controversial free-kick. Lovell looked to have clearly taken the ball when he slid in on Fernando Ricksen on the right of Dundee's box.

Referee Kenny Clark had other ideas though, judging it a reckless two-footed lunge and danger came from the free-kick.

Ricksen whipped the ball in and Michael Mols rose above the rest only to see his header shudder the bar before Rae cleared.

It sparked a rise in pace from the Ibrox players who began to impose themselves more.

As always, the key men were Barry Ferguson and Ronald de Boer who pulled the strings and the pair combined in 28 minutes to

produce their side's best chance so far. Fergie's ball forward found the classy Dutchman with his back to Zurab Khizanishvili and he sweetly turned the Georgian – expected to become a Ranger in the summer – and bounded towards goal.

De Boer showed great strength to hold off the backtracking stopper before clipping a good effort that crept inches wide.

This was not proving to be the cakewalk the bookies, offering crazy odds of 10-1 against Dundee, predicted as the underdogs again drove forward promisingly.

They won a corner and there was anarchy in the Gers box as hordes

of bodies tried to latch on to the loose ball. Craig Moore had to throw himself in front of Khizanishvili's shot but it cannoned only as far as Rae whose 25-yard drive screamed not far wide.

Shota Arveladze earned the first booking two minutes from the break for a late lunge on Rae.

The champions needed some fresh inspiration yet no-one expected the half-time change McLeish made, switching Mols for full-back Mo Ross.

It allowed Ricksen to push forward into right midfield, an area Rangers struggled woefully to exploit. It was clearly an attempt to take command of the middle of

the park as the full scale of the creative Arteta's absence became clear. But it didn't take long for frustrated Eck to decide another switch was needed as Steven Thompson replaced Arveladze.

Still the chances were happening at the other end.

Lovell cut into the heart of the Ibrox side on a swift counter attack, surging 40 yards and sucking in the rearguard before squaring to Fabien Caballero.

In space inside the box, it was the chance the Argentine had been waiting for – but he hesitated and was crowded out.

Moore copped a booking for a cynical 58th-minute foul on

SCOTTISH CUP SCOTTISH CUP SCOTTISH CUP **SCOTTISH CUP** ■

MAKE IT UP

Eck

MAC MY DAY: Rangers winger Neil McCann was drafted in for the injured Peter Lovenkrands and grabbed his chance with both hands, giving young Dundee defender Dave MacKay a torrid time, above and below, and setting up the winner for Lorenzo Amoruso who showed his appreciation, right

● FROM BACK PAGE

he had already used his full quota. McLeish said: "I told Andy Watson to get Stevie McLean warmed up because I wanted to put him on.

"But Andy said 'you've used your three subs already' and I could only ask him when. He had to talk me through them."

The Gers gaffer put his temporary amnesia down to mental fatigue – but it was the physical tiredness of his players that most worried McLeish.

After seeing out the closest title run-in for years he feared his stars would not be able to raise themselves one last time.

The Ibrox boss admitted there were countless times during the 90 minutes when he thought Gers would fall at the final hurdle.

But a rallying call at half-time helped raise his side one last time to close the deal on the seventh domestic clean sweep in the club's 130-year history.

McLeish said: "I was worried the players would be unable to go back to the highs of last weekend.

"They were tired and lacked spark and Dundee were excellent – so there were many times when I thought it wasn't going to be our day.

"In the dressing-room at half-time I tried to raise them. It was the usual cliched stuff but there were some rousing Braveheart shouts just before we went back out.

"We showed great steel and resilience to see it through and make it over that last hurdle."

Now McLeish will take a day's rest to enjoy the moment before turning his attention to next season.

Dutchman Arthur Numan is leaving and there is growing speculation that Amoruso, Claudio Caniggia and Michael Mols will also go this summer.

Quality

But Eck insists none of the players' futures is decided. He will hold a crunch budget meeting with chairman John McClelland later this week.

The outcome will decide the Ibrox future of yesterday's goal hero Amo. McLeish added: "Arthur's gone out at the top but the situation with Lorenzo and the rest is not cut and dried.

"I can't talk about contracts until I have discussed finances with the chairman. We face a Champions League qualifier and to get to the next stage we must replace the quality that leaves this summer.

"As for Lorenzo, it was as if the script was written for him. I had a feeling he would pop up with a goal after all the speculation. If he leaves he has signed off in great style."

Meanwhile, gutted Dundee boss had a go at ref Kenny Clark for awarding the free-kick that led to Amoruso's 66th-minute winner.

The Dens gaffer had earlier been incensed by a soft free-kick in the first half that had resulted in Michael Mols hitting the bar in the first half.

But despite his disappointment at the whistler's crucial decision, Duff praised his players for giving their all.

He said: "Rangers had two chances to score from free-kicks and neither was merited.

"For the one that led to the goal, Steven Thompson had kicked the ball out and then Zurab Khizanishvili ran across him after it had gone out of play. Things like that happen in games but it was soft.

"However, Rangers have had a magnificent season. Congratulations to them but it has also been a good year for us. We have raised the standard at Dundee and the stature of the club so our challenge for next season is to build on that.

"I can't criticise my boys. It was an even contest and at no time did I feel we were under pressure."

POSTER POWER

HERE'S your chance to get a glossy A3-sized poster replica of the centre spread of our cup final tribute to treble winners Rangers.

It's a must have and to get a copy of this prized memento all you have to do is call our hotline on 0906 971 0228. Calls cost £1 per minute and should last no longer than two minutes. Postage and packaging included.

Burchill and was treading on thin ice again when he fouled Giorgi Nemsadze soon after.

This was shaping up nicely for Duffy but just as he prepared to go for the throat by sending on the speedy Nacho Novo his plans were thrown into turmoil by Amoruso in 66 minutes.

Neil McCann swung in a free-kick from the right and Amo charged in to power his header into the top left corner.

Simple, but devastating for Dundee who had grafted and crafted.

There were even a few lumps in the Gers fans' throats three minutes later when Arthur Numan

took his final bow before leaving this summer. The Dutchman marched off to a hero's reception, to be replaced by Kevin Muscat.

Novo came on soon after and should have grabbed an equaliser with 15 minutes left when he just failed to latch on to a Jonay Hernandez cross in front of goal.

Dundee went for it now and Duffy swapped defender for striker in 78 minutes when Steven Milne went on for Dave MacKay.

Novo had another great chance as the clocked ticked into the last 10, working a neat one-two with Rae. But again he lacked composure at the crucial moment.

It was another painful example

that it was slipping away from Dundee as Duffy played his final card, giving Rae a well-earned rest and introducing Garry Brady.

The frustration took its toll on Novo who earned a yellow card for dissent and you could understand the pain behind his tantrum.

McCann was also booked for flooring Khizanishvili, adding physical pain to the mental torture.

It was a brave fight that in the end brought only heartache for Dundee who can head off on holiday with their heads high.

Where Amo's heading is unclear but wherever it is he'll always have a special place in the hearts of the Rangers legions.

Match Stats		opta
	DUNDEE	RANGERS
POSSESSION %	38%	62%
GOALS	0	1
SHOTS ON TARGET (inc goals)	2	3
SHOTS OFF TARGET	10	5
BLOCKED SHOTS	2	3
CORNERS	3	5
FOULS	15	21
OFFSIDES	0	1
YELLOW CARDS	1	3
RED CARDS	0	0

BLOWN AWAY

Man BY Man

Compiled by Neil Cameron

RANGERS

Ronald Waterreus 7
He was helpless at the goal but didn't have much to do for rest of game. Again excellent with his distribution – the keeper is a better footballer than some of his team-mates.

Maurice Ross 8
Dream start when he scored a great goal and won the corner which lead to the second. Full of confidence after that and always wanted the ball.

Sotirios Kyrgiakos 7
Up and down day for the big Greek. The good parts came with his two goals and when he won his tackles on the ground. But he lost Partridge at Well's counter and then could've been sent off for a stupid push on Craigan.

Bob Malcolm 7
In for the injured Marvin Andrews and did OK. Gave his all and McDonald looked sick of the sight of him by the end. Like every Rangers defender, was suspect at set-pieces in the first half.

Michael Ball 6
Made one great clearance early on that would have settled his nerves. Was beaten a few times for pace but had a steady enough afternoon.

Thomas Buffel 8
The Belgian is great on the ball and his pass for Ross at the opening goal was perfect. There are still some questions marks over him but this was one of his best games in a Rangers jersey.

Barry Ferguson 8
Seemed to have all the time in the world whenever he had possession of the ball. Makes you wonder what those fans who didn't want him back now think.

Fernando Ricksen 7
A free-kick the great Coop would have been proud of. His season just keeps getting better and while this wasn't his greatest game, his brilliant goal killed off Motherwell. Player of the Year?

Gregory Vignal 7
The Frenchman is a strange one. His ball for Novo's goal was perfection but some of his other passes were questionable to say the least.

Dado Prso 7
Has a lovely touch for a big man and while he will never be a natural goalscorer, the Croat is superb at bringing his team-mates into play.

Nacho Novo 7
Should've buried his chance just before half-time when his wee legs couldn't quite stretch to knock the ball over the line. Got on the scoresheet though.

Subs:
A Rae – His 12 minutes was probably the best of his life, 3. **Thompson** – Got a late run-out and looked pretty sharp, 3.

HIGH FIVE: Ricksen takes to the air after his goal, right, in Rangers' five-star show

L+CIS CUP FINAL+CIS CUP FINAL+CIS CUP

LIKE CONFETTI

Motherwell's dream in tatters after Rangers let rip in ticker-tape show

Man BY Man

Compiled by Neil Cameron

THE blue and white confetti which continued to dance all round Hampden in the evening breeze long after the players had left the scene told the story of a CIS Cup Final which was over almost before it had started.

As Rangers climbed the Hampden stairs to collect the first silverware of the season Motherwell's ruined dream lay somewhere under all the litter.

A Sunday afternoon which held immense promise closed in abject despair for the Lanarkshire side and all their supporters, who had actually provided most of the colour in the immediate build-up. But within eight minutes they were forced to confront the horror of impending defeat.

Maurice Ross and Sotirios Kyrgiakos had scored and although David Pattridge's terrific header closed the gap, Rangers captain Fernando Ricksen belted in a free-kick to settle the affair before the interval.

The Ibrox side added two more goals in the second period but they could have scored a few more against Motherwell, who lost their discipline as the Final was played out.

One wonders what the Ibrox and Fir Park legend Davie Cooper would have made of it all. Would he have managed a smile, or would the margin of Rangers' victory have caused him pain?

He'd certainly have had a wry smile at Gregory Vignal wearing a blue shirt with his former number on it. It said 11 but there the similarities between the two started and also ended.

However, Cooper might have had a few kind words for Motherwell's keeper Gordon Marshall, who will be 41 next month. Unfortunately for Motherwell and himself he looked every day of his age yesterday.

Criticism

His thought process was slow as was his body and last night would have been a sleepless one for the veteran, who has now been on the losing side in three league cup finals with three different sides, Celtic and Kilmarnock the two others. It was difficult to see through the crowded scenes at the end but Marshall might not even have made the walk up to the centre of the main stand to collect his runners-up medal.

Who needs a hat-trick of those anyway, but his manager Terry Butcher won't single the old-timer out for criticism because there were too many others who lost concentration at crucial moments when Rangers clicked into forward gear. They chose this, the most important day they've had for a long time, to get it wrong and Alex McLeish's men took full advantage.

McLeish didn't have Marvin Andrews, who failed to recover from his knee injury, at the back but it didn't matter. His stand-in, Bob Malcolm, wasn't troubled greatly and, in fact, his central defensive partner, Kyrgiakos, had a wonderful time bagging a second-half goal to go with his first.

This was the first time these sides had met in the final of this tournament and it was thought memories of Cooper might have formed some kind of bond between the two sets of fans. No chance. Rangers' fans wasted no time in belting out the same old offensive rubbish and were up to their knees in it within minutes.

It was almost as though they were trying to send out a defiant message to their club's owner David Murray, who was bold enough to tell the bigots among Rangers' following

By James Traynor

that they weren't welcome. Unfortunately for him and every other decent citizen they refuse to go away and it will be some time before we are all finally rid of these utterly horrible morons.

We were saved more of the same because of Rangers' lightning start to the match, winning a corner in the very first minute. Kyrgiakos and Ricksen combined but Marshall was able to gather the ball in easily and comfortably but that was not a sign of things to come.

Ross made good ground down Rangers' right in four minutes and fed the ball in to Thomas Buffel, who saw the defender continue his run, but this time veering inside. Buffel threaded the ball through to Ross who looked up and saw Marshall almost right in front of him.

Ross managed to supress his surprise and lobbed the keeper. Simple and as awful as that but worse was to come four minutes

PLAYING HIS PART: David Partridge scores a cracking header but it is the only bright spot for Motherwell

Rangers	5	Motherwell 1
Ross 4		Partridge 13
Kyrgiakos 8, 86		HT: 3-1
Ricksen 32 Novo 48		Att: 50,182

later when Ross again barrelled down the right this time winning a corner.

Vignal curled the ball in and tempted Phil O'Donnell to stretch too far to head the ball and tee it up for Kyrgiakos. He nodded his approval and Rangers were two ahead.

Kyrgiakos was in the mood and he even played keepy-uppy for a moment deep inside his own territory but referee Mike McCurry was told by assistant Keith Sorbie that the Greek had tugged Kevin McBride's jersey and the foul was given.

The defender looked bemused and may still have been wondering why when Partridge escaped him to bullet in a header from Stevie Hammell's free-kick.

Suddenly we thought we had a final to savour but Stephen Craigan hacked at Buffel giving away a foul only yards outside his own box in 32 minutes. He was booked but that wasn't the worst of the punishment.

Ricksen took the free-kick and curled the ball low into Marshall's right-hand corner but the big keeper was painfully slow getting across.

Nacho Novo should have scored five minutes later but failed to connect with Dado Prso's header from a Vignal free-kick but three minutes into the second half the little Spaniard made amends.

Prso's flick to Vignal was sublime and the midfield player then sent Novo clear. Again Marshall came way off his line and again he was lobbed.

Motherwell made a double switch in 64 minutes, sending David Clarkson on for Richie Foran and Marc Fitzpatrick for Jim Paterson, but little changed.

They claimed for a penalty in 70 minutes when Craigan collapsed in Rangers' box but McCurry didn't see the shoving match between the Motherwell defender and Kyrgiakos which was just as well. Had he witnessed this piece of nonsense he might have given them lines as a punishment.

Rangers sent Alex Rae on for Vignal in 78 minutes and then Novo made way for Stevie Thompson, with Paul Quinn taking over from McBride, but Motherwell were done. They knew they had lost this final and four minutes from time Kyrgiakos got No.5.

He spun away from his markers, rose unchallenged and sent a powerful header zooming into poor Marshall's net. His confidence was as shredded as the blue and white paper that the giant wind machines blasted up into the air as Rangers began their celebrations.

MAN OF THE MATCH
Dado Prso (Rangers)

CHEERS AND TEARS AS RANGERS

Paradise lost at Fir Park

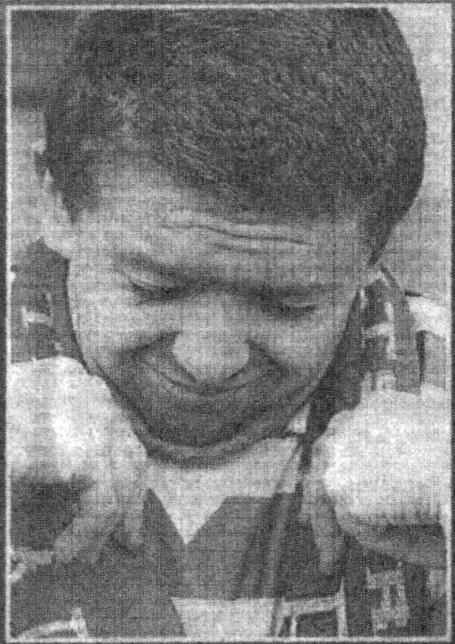

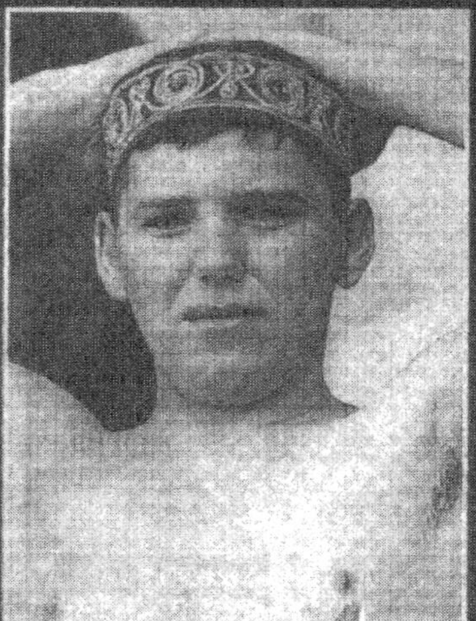

SIMPLY

DIVINE INTERVENTION: Marvin Andrews is mobbed as his pastor drives him away from Easter Road

Marvin thanks the Lord for title triumph

RANGERS fans celebrated a title miracle last night – and Marvin Andrews went to his church to give thanks.

While his mates headed to Ibrox for a party after their last-gasp triumph over Celtic, the stopper was on his way to the Zion Praise Centre at Kirkcaldy.

It was a fitting choice for the man who told the fans to "believe" as the SPL's most incredible title race came to a stunning climax.

Marvin's pastor, the Reverend Joe Nwokoye, drove him to the church after Rangers won 1-0 at Hibs' Easter Road. Hundreds of fans mobbed their car.

Joe said: "Marvin was meant to go straight to Ibrox but he told them, 'First, I'm going to church.'

"God is everything to Marvin. He believes God gave Rangers the title – he didn't doubt it.

"He told the manager, players and fans, 'I believe.'

"When we left Easter Road it was unbelievable. The moment the fans saw Marvin, they went wild.

"All the fans were singing, 'We believe, we believe.'

Three fans climbed on to the roof.

"The police had to help us

Exclusive
By Kevin Turner
k.turner@dailyrecord.co.uk

get out." Marvin, who believes God helped him play on with a serious knee injury, preached at church before heading to Ibrox.

Parties went on across Scotland as Gers fans relived a day's action.

They needed a staggering turn-around to become champions. All they could do was cling to a banner reading: "Keep Believing."

Celtic had to win at Motherwell to retain the title and were 1-0 up with less than three minutes to go.

Then striker Scott McDonald, a boyhood Celtic fan, hooked home the equaliser.

At Easter Road, Rangers fans listening in on radios went crazy. Seconds later, McDonald scored again.

When Celtic's time ran out, all hell broke loose in the Rangers end. And fans shared the glory in packed pubs.

At Glasgow's Loudon Tavern, Rangers-daft Jamie Rennie, 20,

IT'S A MIRACLE: Andrews

said: "It was unbelievable. People came here prepared to end the season empty-handed."

Celtic supporters' shock and despair ran just as deep. Fans at Motherwell's ground wept as thousands more spilled out of pubs in a daze.

RECORD VIEW: Page 8

RIOTS ERUPT IN ULSTER

RIOTS broke out in Belfast following the Rangers victory.

Around 200 rival supporters clashed on the streets of the Ardoyne area.

Police using water canons were pelted with stones, bottles and other missiles.

Eighteen officers were hurt and community leaders appealed for calm.

There were also clashes in other sectarian flashpoint areas of north Belfast.

The riots were brought under control by 6.30pm.

CLINCH LEAGUE IN THREE MINUTES OF DRAMA

UNBELIEVABLE

DANCING FOR JOY: Rangers stars at Ibrox last night, main pic. Above, Alex McLeish arrives to take the fans' applause, left. Above left, Gers fans at Easter Road keep the faith

THE BOYD

United Kris their dream goo

HOW desperately cruel. But wait. How wonderfully sweet.

Dundee United lost the CIS Cup Final in such heartbreaking circumstances, yet at the same time Rangers won their first piece of silverware since 2005 in the most incredible and dramatic fashion.

They won the championship in 2005 but before that, in the February, they had won this same CIS trophy. Is history about to repeat itself?

Who knows? But what is certain is the remarkable resilience and determination of this side Walter Smith has cobbled together. They simply do not know when they are beaten.

It was this refusal to give up that wrenched the fingers of Dundee United off the Cup even though they had been ahead twice and were in front in one of those stomach-churning tests of skill and courage, the penalty shoot-out.

There were times when Rangers looked as if they had squandered their chance to claim the season's first prize but then they had Kris Boyd.

He scored both Rangers' goals and then hit the winning penalty in the shoot-out. A hat-trick of sorts yet he didn't even start the game.

But boy did he finish it to leave United's courageous players and their manager struggling to comprehend what had just happened to them. And Eddie Thompson, their owner?

Fate has already dealt him a miserable hand as he fights cancer but yesterday this astonishingly brave man was forced to suffer some more.

Yet, when Noel Hunt put United in front in a first half they dominated, Thompson and 17,000 United fans started to believe.

Even when Boyd – a substitute for Sasa Papac as Rangers changed shape and reached out for the trophy – equalised, United's fans never stopped believing.

Neither did Mark de Vries, who scored early in the first period of extra time. Thompson pumped the air. Levein stood, arms aloft. He must have felt this was to be their day.

After all, they were all doing it for Eddie. This was for the man who has given the Tannadice club so much hope again and because of his desperate circumstances surely life was going to be more generous.

But Boyd hadn't read the script. His goals, one five minutes from the end of regulation time and the other seven from the end of extra time, dragged Rangers back into the game. He gave them fresh belief when they were running on empty.

They forget the searing pains in their muscles and their punishing schedule. They dug deep and came up with the goods.

Allan McGregor excelled in the shoot-out, saving two, then it was left to Boyd.

Willo Flood, who was absolutely superb, scored the first penalty and when Jean-Claude Darcheville – who gave Rangers greater threat when he took over from Brahim Hemdani at half-time – smacked his kick off the bar, United fans behind the goal chosen for the shoot-out could barely believe it.

Walter Smith couldn't look. Ally McCoist, Kenny McDowall, Jim Stewart and the rest of the backroom staff slumped to their knees but kept their arms linked.

Craig Conway's penalty hit McGregor's left-hand post, then Steven Whittaker's kick made the net off the same post.

Big de Vries scored and then Steve Davis beat United's keeper, Lukasz Zaluska, before David Robertson stepped forward. McGregor saved and then it was down to Lee McCulloch to put Rangers ahead in the shoot-out. Zaluska saved.

Four penalties each and only two goals each. Lee Wilkie marched to the spot, looked at the ball then McGregor and made his run. The Rangers keeper saved again and when Boyd emerged from the pack to take Rangers' fifth penalty you knew. You just knew.

He scored. The Rangers end erupted. United's players and fans broke down.

Levein and Thompson had been locked

1-0

1-1

PLAYING FOR THE GERS-EY: Noel Hunt bags the opener, above left, Kris Boyd le

DUNDEE UNITED	2
RANGERS	**2**

AET, 90mins: 1-1, Rangers win 3-2 on penalties

JAMES TRAYNOR REPORTS FROM HAMPDEN

in an embrace just before the kick-off but this was to be an afternoon that would tear at their belief and faith.

United left Darren Dods on the bench which meant Garry Kenneth would partner Wilkie at the heart of the defence, the manager believing Kenneth would use the ball better than Dods, who was on the bench.

But before his skills of possession could be tested Chris Burke cut in from Rangers' left and had challenged Wilkie twice. The first time the Rangers player felt he should have had a foul and the second he got one.

Both times McCulloch had taken up position on the edge of United's box hoping to get on the end of a delivery and repay Smith for giving him the nod over Boyd and Darcheville.

The first real chance came at the other end, though, when Flood's dangerous cross from the right curled in between McGregor and Carlos Cuellar, who was facing his own goal. Lurking behind him was de Vries but the defender stayed calm and managed to swipe the ball clear.

Cuellar had another terrific match and held Rangers together at the back when they were losing it in midfield. United

settled quickly but Kirk Broadfoot belted in a low cross from the right that McCulloch moved to collect. Then, at the last moment, he stepped over the ball and Ferguson was in. The Rangers captain made the sweetest of connections and Zaluska had to make a good save.

Suddenly Rangers had stepped up their level of play and United were beginning to creak at the back where, in 25 minutes, Kenneth had to leap to clear a cross from Burke, who had been sent clear on the left by a terrific pass from David Weir.

United forced their way back into the game, their midfield running with greater energy and playing better passes, and when McGregor failed to grasp a high ball the alarm bells should have been ringing in Rangers' technical area.

But before anyone there could issue instructions Hunt pounced in 34 minutes.

He tried a shot from the edge of the box and McGregor could only fist the ball back out and United swept forward. The ball was played across the box and Hunt was there bustling through and prodding the ball into the net with a few Rangers players trying in vain to get to him in time.

McGregor and Papac combined to present United with another chance a minute from the break. The ball bounced off Papac's knee as his keeper came to gather it and ran through towards goal. It was cleared off the line and Rangers were relieved to get indoors without having fallen further behind.

Hemdani was kept indoors and Darcheville started the second half up front. Also, Burke was switched over to the right wing hoping to make better progress against Christian Kalvenes than he did against Mihael Kovacevik but the truth is

CUP WINNERS

DONE GOOD

dbye as supersub fails to read the script

vels, above right, Mark de Vries puts United back in front, below left, but Boyd strikes again and plays to the crowd after hitting the winning penalty

Burke was ineffective. If only he could be as flamboyant as his hairstyle.

Darcheville's threat was demonstrated almost immediately when he knocked the ball beyond Kenneth and then left him standing. However, the burly striker's cutback was poor. Ferguson's wasn't a minute later but United managed to deal with the danger and moved downfield again.

They drove right into Rangers' box and Cuellar had to strong arm Kalvenes off the ball. United's fans and manager screamed for a penalty but referee Kenny Clark looked and then shook his head. It did look like a penalty even though Kalvenes didn't make much of the challenge.

You'd have thought then that Kalvenes would have been thanked by Rangers' players but Broadfoot was booked for a foul on the defender.

When Rangers took off Papac to get Boyd on Christian Dailly moved to right-back. McCulloch edged to the left of the midfield and got himself booked for taking the legs away from Flood.

But at least Rangers were fighting now and forcing United deeper and deeper. Hunt was hobbling and had to leave the pitch with, Conway taking over, and Rangers had to be wary of his pace as they pushed in the last 12 minutes to equalise.

Darcheville almost secured it eight minutes from time but Zaluska made a wonderful save. Rangers, though, kept coming and Boyd took full advantage of Kerr's shocking passback. The ball rolled perfectly into the striker's path and he did what he usually does in that situation.

Extra time it was and Kalvenes was booked for tripping Burke but as soon as the ball started rolling again Ferguson was dispossessed by Flood and United surged

down the pitch. Conway galloped on the left, turned the ball into Prince Buaben, he drew Weir forward and then slipped a pass to de Vries.

He skipped around Broadfoot and buried the ball in McGregor's net.

United took off Buaben and sent on David Robertson and all they had to do was hold out for a memorable triumph that would have meant so much to so many people but one in particular. However, Boyd was waiting to strike in 112 minutes.

It looked as though Rangers had ruined a chance to score when Zaluska slapped at the ball but it fell to Davis and his chip to the far post was met by Boyd.

The ball flew into the net and again United were undone.

Burke was taken off a few minutes later and Steven Whittaker went on with penalties and defeat for United looming.

KEY MOMENTS

20mins The first real chance of the game falls to Barry Ferguson after Kirk Broadfoot's cross is cleverly left by Lee McCulloch. Ferguson turns a half-volley towards goal, but Lukasz Zaluska makes a strong block.

34mins GOAL – DUNDEE UTD 1, RANGERS 0. Noel Hunt's thumping drive is beaten away by Allan McGregor but when Prince Buaben's subsequent cross is neatly flicked on by Mark de Vries, the Irishman steers a close-range shot past McGregor. The ball gets stuck against a post but Hunt wins a duel with Steve Davis to score.

45mins Rangers survive a real scare when a header from de Vries is carelessly knocked back towards goal by Sasa Papac but Carlos Cuellar is well placed on the line to clear the danger.

53mins Christian Kalvenes surges into the Rangers box and is met by Cuellar. The Norwegian gets a fortunate break of the ball only to be shoved to the ground by Cuellar, who is extremely fortunate not to concede a penalty.

59mins Substitute Jean-Claude Darcheville embarks on a surging run but sees his low shot from an acute angle brilliantly saved by Zaluska.

77mins Rangers think they have scored an equaliser

NOEL DANGER: Hunt celebrates in style when Darcheville heads in after a quick free-kick from Ferguson. But the delirium among their support is short-lived as although the ball ends up in the net referee Kenny Clark had not restarted play yet.

83mins Darcheville shows great technique to turn and shoot but his effort is brilliantly saved by Zaluska.

84mins GOAL – DUNDEE UTD 1, RANGERS 1. Mark Kerr's abysmal attempted pass back to Zaluska is pounced on by Kris Boyd who finishes in clinical fashion.

95mins GOAL – DUNDEE UTD 2, RANGERS 1. De Vries skips past Gers defender Broadfoot with ease and fires a superb shot past McGregor.

109mins Boyd takes a touch to steady himself in the penalty area before hooking a volley over as Rangers press to restore parity.

113mins GOAL – DUNDEE UTD 2, RANGERS 2. There is no mistake from Boyd this time as the prolific striker heads in from close range after connecting with a clipped Davis cross.

120mins Rangers win a penalty shoot-out 3-2. McGregor saves United's last two from Lee Wilkie and David Robertson, before Boyd strikes the winner.

UEFA CUP JOY NIGHT

MAN BY MAN

Compiled by CRAIG SWAN

FIORENTINA

Sebastien Frey   6
French international had little to do in the first game at Ibrox and that didn't change for the first 45 minutes here. Just a spectator after the break too. Saved from Ferguson in the shoot-out.

Martin Jorgensen   7
Right-back wanted to get forward but Whittaker managed to keep him at bay for long spells. More of an influence after the interval, though, and kept driving on.

Tomas Ujfalusi   8
Skipper was the dominant rock from which Fiorentina wanted to build and covered around the back of Gamberini. Never flustered for most of the game and almost scored a stunner.

Alessandro Gamberini   6
Weaker of the central-defensive pair but managed to use his pace to bail himself out on a couple of occasions. Wobbly but got through.

Massimo Gobbi   8
Restored in the left-back slot and signalled his adventurous intentions with a surging early run into the Rangers box. Never stopped charging up and down the flank.

Fabio Liverani   7
Stepped back into midfield at the expense of Kuzmanovic and orchestrated his team from the engine room. Missed crucial penalty in the shoot-out.

Marco Donadel   3
Got himself involved in a tussle with Thomson and was right up for the battle before being forced to limp off in the first period.

Ricardo Montolivo   6
Talented playmaker is smooth and skilful on the ball but too much good work wasn't done in danger areas. Not enough of an influence in a crucial role.

Mario Alberto Santana   5
Worked Papac at every opportunity and was a threat. Too often, however, his final ball was lacking and, despite total effort, that's what counts.

Giampaolo Pazzini   6
Central striker in the flexible front three found Weir and Cuellar tough cookies. Flashed a decent half-chance wide after the break and his frustration grew as the game wore on.

Adrian Mutu   7
Fiorentina's star man started from the left but wandered around free to try to cause bother. Missed a good headed chance, went close with two free-kicks and had a drive blocked in the box.

Substitutes:

Zdravko Kuzmanovic   5
Got a shout from the bench in the first half when Donadel hobbled out of the fray and passed ball well enough.

Christian Vieri   3
Came on for Pazzini to add power to the attack. Should have scored with first touch and blasted over in penalty shoot-out.

Franco Semioli   2
On at the start of extra time but had little impact on proceedings.

Subs not used: Avramov, Dainelli, Osvaldo, Pasqual.

MR COOL: Novo keeps the head and sends Sebastien Frey the wrong way to seal a UEFA Cup Final slot and start the party for Gers' travelling supporters

TINA CHURNER ENDS IN GLORY

Walt aces edge it in spot-kick nerve-shredder

THEY defied everything. Fiorentina's best shots, a raucous, passionate 40,000 crowd, the heat, exhaustion, the dismissal of Daniel Cousin and also gravity to remain upright.

Rangers survived their most punishing night to reach a European final for the first time in 36 years. And it might take that long again for any of us to understand fully how they did it.

They had played 120 minutes of football but had barely created a decent chance. They were keeping it all for the penalty shootout.

For the third time this season Walter Smith's side triumphed from the spot. They probably knew they shouldn't have got that far in the Artemio Franchi Stadium but they did hold their nerve longer than their rivals.

The Serie A side did almost all of the attacking but were hopeless in front of goal and another astounding performance from those twin defensive pillars, David Weir and the superb Carlos Cuellar, kept Rangers in it.

Fiorentina will never understand why they aren't going to the UEFA Cup Final in Manchester on May 14 but that's their problem. Smith's concern is how to keep his players upright. They gave their all even if they were far from pleasing on the eye but they are in the final where they'll go up against their old boss, Dick Advocaat. The Little General's Zenit St Petersburg thrashed Bayern Munich earlier in the day and now Smith will pit his wits against the Dutchman.

It's Scotland v Russia again just as it was in 1972 when Rangers beat Moscow Dynamo for the European Cup Winners Cup.

Could that be an omen? With this Rangers team anything is possible. They simply refuse to admit defeat and time after time last night they stood firm against a Fiorentina side given the benefit of every doubt by a woeful Belgian referee.

Even when Barry Ferguson missed the first penalty, they refused to buckle. If it comes down to courage and determination in the final, Smith's side just might have their finest triumph yet.

The manager went round his leg-weary troops before the shootout and shook hands with each one of them. It had come down to a test of nerve and the captain went first.

He tried to fire it into Sebastien Frey's top right-hand corner but the huge keeper flung himself into the air and slapped the ball away. Ferguson trudged back to the centre circle looking a broken man.

Zdravko Kuzmanovic was first for Fiorentina and scored. Steven Whittaker did the same and then Riccardo Montolivo sent Neil Alexander the wrong way.

Moscow and that final looked an awful long way off but Sasa Papac scored and then it was the turn of Fabio Liverani. Alexander sprang to his left and saved.

Brahim Hemdani walked up and sent Frey the wrong way, so Christian Vieri was next. He ballooned his shot over the bar and then it was down to Nacho Novo.

The little Spaniard took his time placing the ball on the spot and then blasted Rangers into the final.

It was unbelievable. It was incredible. It was so very unfair on Fiorentina – but did Rangers care? Did they Hell.

Pursued by the entire backroom staff, the players sprinted away to their 4000 fans squeezed into a corner of the stadium. The dull, boring style they had used to get beyond Fiorentina was forgotten. Rangers had won. They were in the final.

They had been in a bit of a state at times as they hurled themselves in front of shots and passes but at the end they were in a state of delirium.

It had all been very civilised at the start. About 90 minutes before kick-off Smith arrived with his players to have a stroll on the turf and the Fiorentina fans gave them a loud round of applause.

Well, Florence is an extremely civilised, cultured city and you would have thought Rangers might return the gesture.

But they went to their own supporters and applauded them instead. You can take the boys out of Glasgow but you can't take Glasgow out of...well, you know how it goes.

Still, it wasn't personal, it was business and, besides, if the locals felt snubbed they didn't seem to care because when the ball started rolling they went wild. They pumped up the volume for their own heroes, the

FIORENTINA	0
RANGERS	0

By James Traynor   *aet: Rangers win 4-2 on penalties*

PICTURES: ROB CASEY

UEFA CUP JOY NIGHT

KNEESY DOES IT: Joy for Novo after scoring winning penalty, main pic, and Alexander keeps one out, above

MAN BY MAN

Compiled by CRAIG SWAN

RANGERS

Neil Alexander   **8**
Confident first claim of Liverani's cross but flapped at the next from Gobbi. Managed to grab vicious Mutu free-kick at second attempt and produced vital save from Liverani in penalty shoot-out.

Kirk Broadfoot   **6**
Had the job of dealing with Mutu but the Romanian's keenness to drift infield gave him a breather. Distribution not great at times but worked hard.

Carlos Cuellar   **9**
Some terrific interventions and tackles proved his worth to Smith within the crucial opening period. Totally at home in the environment and made another vital contribution.

David Weir   **8**
Patched-up veteran recovered to take his usual spot at centre-half and used all of his know-how to get into the right areas at the right times. A magnet for cross balls.

Sasa Papac   **7**
Bosnian had to be at his sharpest to keep an eye on the raiding Santana and covered inside with diligence. Had one or two scares but did fine.

Steven Davis   **6**
Northern Irishman ran himself into the ground but most of his work was covering space and tracking back. Never stopped for his manager and a real workhorse.

Brahim Hemdani   **6**
European expert was happy to take a role in front of Weir and Cuellar. Also shuffled across to help the full-backs but was hustled into one or two rare errors.

Barry Ferguson   **6**
Rangers captain tried to go on and assist Darcheville but found himself in no man's land at times as striker couldn't hold it up. Worked really hard but missed from the spot.

Kevin Thomson   **8**
Intelligently made angles for team-mates and gave them options. Booked for a cynical trip on Santana but passed the ball long and short with real aplomb, especially first half.

Steven Whittaker   **6**
Operated down the left of midfield and tried to push on and occupy Jorgensen. Did not venture forward often until late effort saved by Frey.

Jean-C Darcheville   **5**
Given the usual shift up front alone and tried to play on the shoulder of weak-link Gamberini. Struggled to hold the ball up and no scoring chances before being hooked.

Substitutes:

Daniel Cousin   **2**
Brought on after 65 minutes. Came close with deflected shot in extra time before stupidly getting himself sent off.

Nacho Novo   **7**
Took the place of Davis with nine minutes of normal time remaining and buzzed around. Hero at the end with coolly-taken winning penalty.

Subs not used: G Smith, Buffel, Boyd, Dailly, Faye.

Referee: F De Bleeckere (Belgium).

Viola. And so once again in a marathon season Rangers players faced a test of their courage, skills, and belief.

As they slapped palms together, encouraging one another, they were well aware beaten semi-finalists are never remembered.

Smith went with Jean-Claude Darcheville as the lone front runner rather then Cousin, who was on the bench. Ferguson operated just behind the striker with Whittaker also pushing up on the left.

Steven Davis was trying to get up on the right flank but Fiorentina, as expected, were doing most of the attacking at the start. However, through the tenacity of Darcheville, the SPL side won a corner but Davis couldn't deliver a telling ball.

Rangers knew they had to keep the ball for as long possible when they had it but too many passes weren't finding their intended targets, giving Fiorentina easy possession. Even so, they were finding it difficult to get through a Rangers defence in which Cuellar and Weir looked solid.

Liverani tried a shot from distance, then Giampaolo Pazzini and Montolivo did the same but Alexander remained untroubled. However, the keeper fumbled the ball when he tried to cut out a Massimo Gobbi cross from the left and the Italians failed to make the most of the error.

Kevin Thomson nudged Mario Santana off the ball and referee Frank De Bleeckere decided the Rangers man deserved a yellow card for persistent fouling.

Minutes later Rangers' defence was all over the place and in a panic, with Papac booting the ball almost out of his own keeper's hands.

Ferguson, who had barely featured in the first half, combined with Darcheville to create an opening but the final pass through to the skipper found him just offside.

Fiorentina were forced to make a change a minute before half-time, Marco Donadel limping off and Kuzmanovic taking over.

The second half followed a pretty similar pattern.

Martin Jorgensen thumped a 25-yard shot way over Alexander's bar and then Adrian Mutu, who had turned away from Kirk Broadfoot, sent his cross over the top.

More would have to come from skipper Ferguson, Davis, Whittaker and Thomson to bring Darcheville into play but Fiorentina did come close when Mutu released Pazzini and his shot on the turn flashed a yard wide.

The traffic was one way and Rangers were creaking at the back. A better side than Fiorentina would have done some damage but time was slipping away from them.

The Italian fans were doing their best to drive their heroes on but woeful finishing was keeping Rangers in the match.

In 66 minutes, Smith made his first change. Darcheville was withdrawn and Cousin took over but before he cold get his first touch Fiorentina had a free-kick deep in Rangers' half after Cuellar had brought down Pazzini. Again the ball was cleared.

Within seconds Alexander and his defence were having to deal with yet another corner. They did but Fiorentina just kept coming and Weir was booked for a foul on Pazzini. The free-kick was 30 yards out but Mutu went for goal and Alexander, perhaps caught by surprise, spilled the ball.

Pazzini was in but the keeper recovered and gathered the loose ball.

Cousin was booked even though it seemed as though Tomas Ujfalusi had barged into him.

Davis nipped in and took the ball after Ujfalusi had lost possession in his own box but the midfield player's attempt at goal was dreadful. Rangers' first real chance and it was squandered.

Pazzini was taken off and Vieri sent on to get on the end of a Liverani free-kick. He did but fell over the ball and Rangers, who replaced Davis with Novo, breathed again.

Extra time was looming but a goal now, for either side, would settle the issue.

Whittaker almost did the trick with a shot that Frey had to beat away.

With one or two Rangers players looking exhausted, the semi lurched into overtime.

Thomson chested the ball into the path of Montolivo, who sent Vieri clear, but the big striker's angled shot crept a foot wide. Kuzmanovic then headed just wide as extra time started the way regulation time had ended.

Cousin's glanced header gave Rangers fans hope. Then the same player's shot took a deflection and the ball looped over.

But after 110 minutes Cousin was sent off after a clash with Liverani, who staggered away as if the Rangers player had butted him. Cousin was silly to go face to face but the action hardly merited a second yellow.

In the end, though, it all came down to those penalties and here at least the Ibrox side had the edge on the Italians.

Rangers' bandwagon just keeps rolling along and it would be no surprise if they now asked for the season to be extended until July to give them a crack at the Open and Wimbledon as well.

GERS DREAM IS OVER....

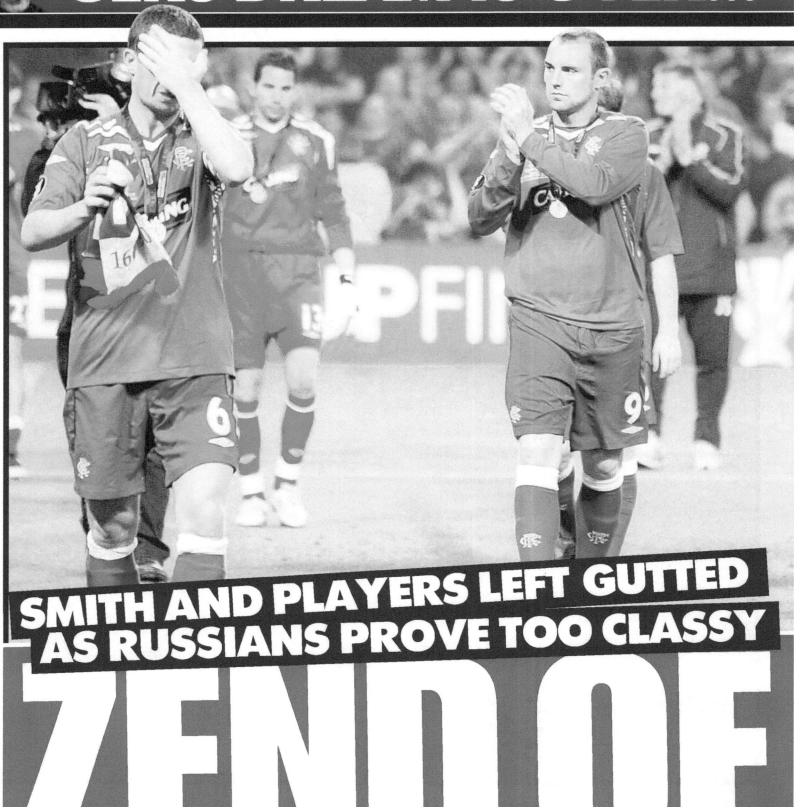

SMITH AND PLAYERS LEFT GUTTED AS RUSSIANS PROVE TOO CLASSY

ZEND OF

WALTER SMITH and his players stood side by side with shoulders sagging, just staring at the turf. They were silent, perhaps fighting to hold back tears.

It was not supposed to be this way. This was supposed to be the night Rangers became heroes.

They went to the City of Manchester Stadium believing they could join the Ibrox legends and the banners draped around this splendid arena urged them to do exactly that.

The scene was set perfectly. The sun was still beating down when the game kicked off. The pitch was perfect and the fans were in full voice.

Scottish legend Denis Law placed the UEFA Cup on a pedestal before kick-off and we hoped another Scot would pick it up at the end.

Had Smith been able to get the trophy it would have been a spectacular conclusion to one of the longest ever European campaigns. And make no mistake – he wanted it.

The Rangers manager never gives too much away but he had a burning desire to be a winner in Europe and wanted it also for players who have served him so well this season.

His team had been miserly in defence throughout the UEFA Cup campaign and started off the same way last night but after 72 minutes they finally cracked.

Igor Denisov pounced and although Smith changed style completely, putting three up front in a desperate attempt to get themselves back in touch with the glory they had craved, Rangers couldn't find a way through and Zenit won their first European trophy.

Konstatin Zyrianov made it 2-0 in the second minute of time added on and the dream was over.

Blunt

Rangers were left exhausted and forlorn. The 30,000 of their fans who had taken up most of the 40,000-capacity stadium and the 175,000 or so in Manchester city centre were also in the depths of despair.

Perhaps it was just as well the giant screens in the city centre failed to work because this was painful. Many had believed this would be Rangers' night but while the defensive strategy was solid enough for much of the night, the cutting edge was rather blunt.

Dick Advocaat's side deserved victory because they were slicker and more mobile. They were more intelligent as well and the UEFA Cup belonged to them.

But Manchester had belonged to Rangers. Their fans were everywhere and if there is to be a next time for them then hopefully there will be a few more Scottish flags on display.

This was a Scottish club against one from Russia but you would never have known it. There were many Union Jacks fluttering in the breeze but thankfully the odd banner harking back to darker ancient times was taken down long before the start of play.

All day the last of Rangers' fans had been arriving and how Manchester managed to squeeze them all in defied belief.

They were everywhere. On every street, every piece of grass and packed into every bar and fan zone. Inside the ground they dwarfed the Russian side's support.

It was an unbelievable surge of people. Rangers were on the move but by the end of the night their players were left standing, thinking of what might have been.

Like Celtic in 2003, they just couldn't reach out and grab that trophy. They gave what they had in their 19th European match of the season but it wasn't enough.

The Prime Minister, Gordon Brown, had called Smith in the afternoon to wish him luck but that didn't help either. And so

ZENIT ST PETERSBURG	2
RANGERS	0

By James Traynor *from The City of Manchester Stadium*

Smith and his players had to accept second best. They didn't become legends but Zenit gave them great respect by forming a guard of honour at the end as the Ibrox players collected the runners-up medals.

These players might never have a better opportunity to join the immortals. They went home broken men and Smith will have to pick them up if they hope to claim the SPL title. It won't be easy. Some of the players were distraught as they left the pitch last night. Some might never recover.

Those chosen to start had an enormous responsibility and it was an emotional assistant manager Ally McCoist who said before kick-off it had been heartbreaking to leave the likes of Nacho Novo on the bench. But Rangers had come to win and couldn't think of any individual's feelings.

The Ibrox side had taken part in more European matches than anyone else to get to this final hurdle.

They could see the trophy at the mouth of the tunnel but knew they had to win their own battles to lay hands on it.

Apart from the masses, who had swamped Manchester from Australia, USA, Europe, the Middle East, Timbuktu, Brigadoon and other far-flung, strange places like Airdrie just to be there and soak in the atmosphere, many more were tuning in even in the most remote corners.

Those squinting at flickering TV screens and straining ears to cut through static to hear commentary on radios would have winced after three minutes when Anatoliy Tymoschuk was allowed to run clear after a Brahim Hemdani error.

Fortunately, the Zenit captain's shot found only the side netting but Rangers' ploy of flooding the midfield to deny their opponents space – Hemdani and Kevin Thomson were sitting deep – wasn't really working, although Rangers did clatter downfield with Jean-Claude Darcheville trying to cut the ball across the face of goal.

Zenit managed to clear but Rangers fans were encouraged and belting out their backing. The stadium shook as they bounced up and down in support.

Zenit, though, had terrific movement, especially up front where they had Viktor Fayzulin, Fatih Tekke, and Andrei Arshavin inter-changing at pace.

When Rangers had good possession in midfield they were unable to make further progress because there was very little movement up front.

Aleksandr Anyukov pounced when Hemdani again lost control, hitting a long-range shot that Neil Alexander grabbed at the second attempt.

Five minutes from the break, Rangers had to send a posse after Tekke who was only stopped inside Alexander's box by Thomson. His tackle was perfectly timed and it had to be.

Two minutes later, Roman Shirokov

PICTURES: CRAIG HALKETT AND ROB CASEY

GERS DREAM IS OVER...

TEARIO: Rangers players and manager Walter Smith acknowledge the hoardes of fans as their UEFA Cup bid ends in agony and, below, Anatoliy Tymoschuk shows off the trophy

THE ROAD

fouled Darcheville 20 yards out and Rangers had a free-kick.

Thomson couldn't get his shot through the Zenit wall but the SPL side made it to the interval with their hopes intact even though Kirk Broadfoot's right arm had blocked a cross.

The Swedish referee was kind to Rangers and their fans breathed again.

Darcheville had to change footwear a few minutes into the second half and the first time he got the ball it looked as though he had tied on his dancing shoes. He tried to soft-shoe shuffle his way through the defence but was always out of step and eventually found himself crowded out.

Rangers piled into the box in 54 minutes and might have had a penalty when the ball appeared to strike an arm of Denisov.

However, the referee shook his head and was probably correct, although Rangers

kept charging in and eventually Shirokov cleared off his own line.

Rangers were frustrating Zenit, just as they had done to many teams throughout this long season. Could they do it again and squeeze one more victory?

Steven Whittaker cut in from the left, dragging the ball beyond lunging tackles but his shot was deflected for a corner.

Arshavin got through at the other end when a long clearance caught Whittaker out of position and Alexander, for some bizarre reason, raced 35 yards from his line. Arshavin went around the keeper but was forced wide and when he tried to chip into the net Sasa Papac was back to head clear from the goal line.

It was a let off but Rangers shook off the fright and settled back in to their defensive style.

Rangers sent all their substitutes to

warm up in 71 minutes but Zenit finally opened up Smith's defence 60 seconds later.

Broadfoot and Carlos Cuellar were caught out as Arshavin sent Denisov through the middle and he had little trouble in flicking the ball past Alexander.

The scorer wheeled away to celebrate pursued by his team-mates while Rangers looked around in dismay. They were still in disarray a few minutes later when Zyrianov hit a shot that clipped a post.

Rangers had to change and Papac was taken off so Novo could get on. Whittaker dropped back to left-back with Novo pushing forward on Darcheville's left.

Hemdani went off in 79 minutes and Lee McCulloch, injured in the last Old Firm match, took over through the middle with Darcheville edging out to the right of a three-man forward line. Whittaker was

taken off with only four minutes left and Kris Boyd galloped on.

Could the under-used striker emerge as the hero who was so badly needed now with time running away from Rangers as fast as some of the Zenit players had done?

Three minutes of stoppage time were added and at the end of the first one Novo ballooned a shot from close range over the bar.

He had been put off by McCulloch but even so Novo knew he should have done better.

It was Rangers' last chance to grab a goal.

It was also their last chance to be heroes because Zyrianov planted the ball in Alexander's net with a minute left.

It was all over.

Rangers' players were distraught. It was such a sad and tearful end to what had been a marathon European campaign.

THE KING OF

Deadly Kris sinks brave Queens by netting 2nd cup double

KRIS BOYD was the Hampden hero yet again for Rangers as his glory double made it 25 goals in a season where he's struggled to even get a regular game.

The striker opened the scoring in 33 minutes and Gers were cruising when DaMarcus Beasley made it two before the interval.

Yet Queens staged a stunning fightback to claw level through Steve Tosh and Jim Thomson.

But Boyd popped up to head the winner in 72 minutes and prove beyond doubt he is the most prolific hitman at the club – in only his 24th start from Gers' 68 games this term.

For all his goals Boyd will never be an automatic choice and that's why yesterday's winner could be his last in light blue.

English teams are sniffing and it is certain Walter Smith will have to decide

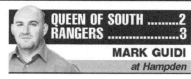

QUEEN OF SOUTH 2
RANGERS 3

MARK GUIDI
at Hampden

whether to accept bids of around £2million.

Boyd's heroics helped Rangers smile again after the disappointment of the past 10 days. However, they had to endure several scary moments.

There wasn't enough passion and aggression being shown early on for Ally McCoist's liking. In seven minutes the Ibrox No.2 raced to the touchline to give his lethargic looking players a rollicking.

It took a while for the response but Beasley should have scored in 26 minutes only to fire wide from just inside the box.

Boyd then had a free header from eight yards but also failed to trouble keeper Jamie MacDonald. Despite having no one in top form Rangers were now in total control and putting the Queens defence under serious pressure.

The SPL side opened the scoring just after the half hour.

They won a free-kick 25 yards out when Ryan McCann fouled Beasley, Barry Ferguson tapped the ball to Boyd who rattled it through the legs of the charging Bob Harris and into MacDonald's top left-hand corner. Unstoppable.

The lead was doubled two minutes before the break and Queens looked doomed. They couldn't clear a corner and the ball broke to Beasley after

HAMPDEN

Boyd

●FROM BACK PAGE

clearly worn thin. Even his second cup final brace of the season – he also netted two against Dundee United in the CIS Cup – couldn't hide the 24-year-old's frustration.

The striker openly admitted he's going to mull over his future and that could lead to clubs chasing him.

The former Kilmarnock man opened the scoring before DaMarcus Beasley added a second to put Gers on what looked like easy street.

But Steve Tosh and Jim Thomson scored early in the second half to stun the Ibrox men and level the match before Boyd headed the winner.

Afterwards the Gers hero said: "I'm delighted to get the goals and hopefully I've shown the gaffer what I can do. But over the summer I'm going to have a long think about things and we'll take it from there.

"In terms of the two cup finals it has been a good season for me but I'd like to have played more. It gets to you so I have to think about it.

"Will I be speaking to the manager about it? No. I'll go and think about what's best for me. I've had criticism of my game for years but it doesn't bother me as long as I keep putting the ball in the net.

Forfeit

"You win a game by scoring goals and that's always what I aim to do.

"It's the manager's decision, there's nothing much else I can do. If you lose the self belief then you have problems but I know I can score goals."

The Rangers players mocked Boyd in the celebrations for his winner after he sported a tache as a forfeit in a bet with team-mate McCulloch.

But there was a serious side to Gers' victory as they ended the season on a high after blowing the UEFA Cup and SPL. However, Boyd – a doubt for Scotland's friendly in Prague this week with a hamstring injury – says the win didn't make up for that.

He said: "We were disappointed after losing the league on Thursday and it was hard to take.

"We had to raise ourselves for the Cup Final and we did that.

"But it doesn't make up for losing the UEFA Cup and SPL.

"We were disappointed to lose both those trophies but before the game we wanted to win the Scottish Cup and we've done that.

"After the way the game went on Thursday I thought I might have had a chance of starting but I didn't know until Saturday morning.

"Once the gaffer read out the team I was delighted. We made hard work of it but got there in the end.

"The Scottish Cup final is more prestigious than the League Cup so I'm delighted to get the goals."

SCOTLAND WILL HOST MINI-LIGA

SEVILLE are set to become the second Spanish side to head to Scotland for pre-season training by joining Barcelona at St Andrews.

And the La Liga cracks are desperate to set up a glamour friendly against one of the Old Firm as part of their preparations.

Seville coach Manuel Jiminez is heading to St Andrews to check out facilities and negotiate friendlies.

Barca trained in the east coast resort town last year and are returning this summer before playing Hibs and Dundee United.

Seville want to play at least three matches on their mini-tour and are looking at the possibility of a friendly against Rangers or Celtic.

The Spanish side won the UEFA Cup at Hampden last year and Jiminez said: "We have an excellent rapport with the Scottish people and it's almost certain we will go there for pre-season but I want to see the facilities myself."

Glory at the double: Prolific Kris Boyd slams an unstoppable opener past Jamie MacDonald (main pic), DaMarcus Beasley slots No.2 (above) and Boyd kills off Queens' brave comeback by heading the winner (below) to land Gers second cup of the season

team-mates Thomson and McCann collided. The American then kept his shot low to place it past MacDonald from eight yards.

Beasley was delighted with his first goal since a long injury lay-off but MacDonald should have saved it.

Queens tried to hit back yet when they gained possession and tried to get at Rangers, Sean O'Connor looked isolated.

The striker's team-mates rarely got close enough in support and simple passes also went astray.

That was to change in the 50th minute however. O'Connor tore into the box and left hesitant Carlos Cuellar trailing before

cutting back to the onrushing Tosh who used his crown jewels to force the ball past Neil Alexander from close range. It was well worked and credit to O'Connor.

Just two minutes later Queens sensationally levelled as Harris swung a free-kick to the back post where towering Thomson outjumped Lee McCulloch and Cuellar to power home a seven-yard header.

The final had burst into life and Gordon Chisholm's marauding men looked likely to get another.

But it was Gers who regained control in 72 minutes with what proved the winner. Beasley's corner hung in the air

and Boyd got above Harris to bullet a header from five yards beyond MacDonald who got a touch but couldn't tip it over.

With five minutes left 16-year-old John Fleck came on for Jean-Claude Darcheville to become the youngest ever player to appear in a Scottish Cup Final.

The teenager was given a terrific reception from the Rangers fans.

That same welcome will not be afforded to Kenny Miller should Gers pursue their interest in the striker.

Once again the Ibrox fans made their feelings clear by chanting "You can stick Kenny Miller up your a****". Fleck had

a chance to score a minute from time after being set up by Ferguson but his shot was blocked.

The skipper should have been more selfish though and finished it himself.

But it was irrelevant as Rangers held on to claim the domestic cup double. Despite their SPL and Euro agony they can still celebrate a season far more successful than the previous two.

Chisholm and his players also come away with great credit for contributing to an entertaining game on a fine surface.

They now have the UEFA Cup to look forward to but will also want to make an impact in the First Division promotion race.

A GUT ABOVE

Gers show they've got stomach for fight in title romp

DOUBTS and suspicions about Rangers' desire and ability had dogged Walter Smith's players from the first kick of the campaign but at the end of a long, gruelling season the doubts were banished.

On the final day Walter Smith's players were faced with their moment of truth.

Did they have the nerve, the courage, the skills to reach out and wrench the title from Celtic's grasp and prevent their ancient rivals from winning four in a row?

The stakes were high. Pride, bragging rights, money and ultimately jobs were on the line and only the bravest would cope.

Dundee United had caused Rangers problems throughout the season but Smith finally found his players are indeed made of the right stuff.

This time, when there was no further room for error, Rangers did not even blink. They didn't flinch. Their inhibitions were kicked off and they kicked on towards the title in style, winning it by four points.

Kyle Lafferty, Pedro Mendes, and Kris

DUNDEE UTD	0
RANGERS	**3**

JAMES TRAYNOR REPORTS

Boyd struck the three goals which did more, much more than secure the Scottish game's most prized trophy. Their goals and this team's grit and boldness all add up to £10million.

Possibly as much as £12m because as Scotland's champions Rangers will now be granted automatic entry into the money-spinning Champions League.

But yesterday's triumph, which had seemed highly unlikely back in December when Celtic won 1-0 at Ibrox to open up a seven-point gap, wasn't about money.

Smith simply wanted this more than anything. He needed it. And probably more than ever before Rangers needed it.

This was Smith's third domestic trophy since he returned to save the club in January 2006 and if Rangers win the Scottish Cup on Saturday he'll have delivered four of the six available to him. And remember, he also led them to a UEFA Cup Final. Yet some

Rangers fans have been calling for his head. But when the helicopter carrying the trophy presentation party appeared in the sky over Tannadice 20 minutes before the end it was also clear just how badly Rangers' hordes wanted this triumph.

A number of them had lapsed into their old ways, releasing some of the bile which has besmirched their club, but at the end they were in raptures along with their team.

Just as they had done every time the ball landed in United's net the occupants in the dugout erupted.

Barry Ferguson, who was left out again, led the surges and he was the first to applaud the fans. He also threw his jersey to them, perhaps signaling this is the end for him.

With Celtic failing to beat Hearts the afternoon belonged to Rangers. So, too, once again did Tannadice even though the match was weighted with history for United who were founded 100 years ago to the day.

They, too, had Europe on their minds. They had to get at least a draw to clinch a Europa League place but with Aberdeen winning 2-1 against Hibs that meant United lost again. The Dons are in Europe

but Tannadice and the title belonged to Rangers who clinched the trophy on this ground for the fourth time.

Smith opted for the same line-up as last week which meant Ferguson had to kick his heels on the sidelines but he was on his feet with every other Rangers fan when Steve Davis ran on to a superb Sasa Papac diagonal pass which landed deep on the right. Davis wriggled free and cut the ball across the face of United's goal for Boyd.

The blue sections rose as Boyd moved but he stepped over the ball presumably hoping Kenny Miller would apply the touch. He didn't and a terrific early opportunity was lost.

However, they were all 10 feet off the ground in five minutes when Davis stuck the ball to Boyd and he squared for Lafferty. The big fellow slid in and the ball ended up behind Celtic-bound Lukasz Zaluska and in the back of his net.

With one touch the rogue of a week ago and the cause of acute Rangers embarrassment suddenly became a hero. He stood up properly for his team this time and the main stand rocked as Rangers' hordes went wild with delight. Lee Wilkie was wild, too, but it

was with anger after he'd been pulled up for a foul on Miller. The United skipper was booked and Rangers continued to force the pace with Boyd moving with greater purpose and speed than ever before.

He looked in the mood while United appeared stunned. But they quickly came to terms with their setback and started to get forward creating a chance for David Robertson but his header didn't trouble Neil Alexander.

Even so, United were enjoying a lot of possession and were emerging as the more composed of the two sides. Their full-backs were getting forward and in 20 minutes David Goodwillie won an aerial challenge with David Weir, who required treatment, before barging into the box.

He beat Madjid Bougherra but the sliding Papac blocked the shot, although it was obvious the strength of Goodwillie was unnerving Rangers' defenders.

Paul Caddis, on loan from Celtic, was also causing problems but Rangers thought they had scored a second in 31 minutes when Lafferty bundled the ball over the line. The referee, Dougie McDonald, agreed

1-0

2-0

3-0

KYLES BETTER: Lafferty celebrates, main pic, after firing Gers in front, top, and further strikes by Mendes and Boyd seal win that has goal heroes on a high, below

with the linesman and gave offside but Rangers were forcing their way back into the match with Boyd still working hard and won their first corner in 35 minutes.

Mendes curled the ball in but Zaluska grabbed it, although he was nowhere three minutes later when Papac sent another terrific ball in from the left. Boyd killed it, twisted, turned and spun until he found daylight and then fired for goal.

The ball was netbound until miraculously Mihael Kovacevic stretched his long frame to its limits and headed clear. It was a fantastic piece of defending and after Mendes' corner had been tidied up United were back at the opposite end where Goodwillie again was winning his tussles.

Darren Dods won his battle with Maurice Edu but the challenge was illegal, although United's players didn't think so and Prince Buaben was booked for dissent. Worse was to follow and just as McDonald checked his watch to signal half time, Mendes struck.

United failed to clear the ball properly and it fell to the Portuguese player 20 yards out. He drilled a low shot into the net and again

Rangers' fans were ecstatic and remained that way throughout the interval.

Rangers were two up against Hearts in March and were pulled back but surely this time and with so much at stake on this final day they wouldn't be pegged back by United even though they could see their own European dream crumbling.

It fell apart in 51 minutes when Boyd claimed just reward for his endeavours. Mendes pushed a pass through to Steven Whittaker on the right and he slid a perfect delivery into the middle for Boyd. He slammed the ball into the net, wheeled away and was swamped by his mates.

United took off David Robertson and sent on Francisco Sandaza while Garry Kenneth took over from the injured Wilkie but this game, with 35 minutes to play, was over.

The helicopter was on its way and wouldn't be changing direction now. Rangers knew they were champions and so too did Celtic who were toiling to break down Hearts in Glasgow yet, at the same time the Parkhead club's fans were trying to cope with broken Hearts.

United made their third switch in 64

minutes, taking off Craig Conway for Danny Swanson, and a couple of minutes later Rangers took off Boyd to get Nacho Novo on the pitch. Then with just fewer than 20 minutes remaining Ferguson was allowed to play his part, perhaps for the last time when he took the place of Miller.

Weir was booked for a foul and then Lafferty made way for Lee McCulloch as the chopper hovered directly over Tannadice sending Rangers' fans into a frenzy.

Ten minutes from time United manager Craig Levein walked over to Rangers' dug-out and offered his congratulations to Walter Smith, Ally McCoist, who was fighting back tears of joy, and Kenny McDowall.

Smith was brought back to restore pride and coincidentally enough he started the fightback with a 5-0 win against United.

Rangers were 17 points behind Celtic when he returned to Ibrox and yesterday and the job was completed when he sent Rangers out to beat United and reclaim top spot.

MAN OF THE MATCH
Kris Boyd (Rangers)
Magic Moment: Lafferty's early goal proved Rangers were up for the fight.

MAN BY MAN

By Gordon Parks & Gary Ralston

DUNDEE UTD

Lukasz Zaluska 6
The Celtic-bound Pole could do little about any of the three that beat him.

Paul Caddis 6
Pushed forward and caused moments of panic by getting the better of Papac.

Mihael Kovacevic 6
Goal-line headed clearance to deny Boyd but lost Lafferty at crucial opener.

Lee Wilkie 5
Booked for dissent. Far too casual in possession before being replaced.

Darren Dods 5
Fortunate to escape punishment for a late lunge on Edu. Not at the races.

Paul Dixon 5
Picked out his passes but never comfortable with defensive duties.

David Robertson 5
Tame early header and tried to link midfield with attack well until replaced.

Morgaro Gomis 7
As strong on the ball as he is subtle with it. Dominated Edu in midfield for spells.

Prince Buaben 6
Couldn't be faulted for graft but could have closed Mendes down at his goal.

Craig Conway 5
Didn't do enough in last third as he let Whittaker off the hook. Subdued.

David Goodwillie 6
Held the ball up well but too often muscled out.

Subs: Francisco Sandaza – couldn't trigger a comeback, 4, Garry Kenneth – allowed Novo to run off his shoulder, 4. Danny Swanson – little impact, 3.

RANGERS

Neil Alexander 6
Plucking swerving corner from under bar was just about all he had to do.

Steven Whittaker 8
Linked well with Davis going forward and quelled danger down his wing.

David Weir 7
Read game superbly, rarely exposed and organised a tight defensive unit.

Madjid Bougherra 8
United could have thrown the kitchen sink at Rangers and it would still have bounced off his chest.

Sasa Papac 8
Great first-half block, defensively diligent and a final-third danger.

Maurice Edu 8
Mopped up almost everything in middle of park as Mendes reaped reward.

Pedro Mendes 8
A front-foot performance of power, capped with dream goal.

Steven Davis 9
Lively, nimble and always looked capable of threading a crucial pass.

Kyle Lafferty 7
Vital opener capped hard working rather than heroic display.

Kris Boyd 9
Wasted a terrific first-half chance and bust a gut for his team.

Kenny Miller 7
Didn't give United defence moment's peace with workaholic display.

Subs: Nacho Novo – on to make a nuisance of himself late on, 3. Barry Ferguson – if this is Gers swansong, went out on ultimate high, 3. Lee McCulloch – given last 10 minutes, 2.

SCOTTISH CUP

GERS STRIKE

He's a volley good fellow: Jubilant Rangers stars swamp Novo after his wonder winner

Novo's glory goal snatches win that was cruel to Bairns

IT was a goal fit to win any final. But a performance that would normally end in defeat.

Rangers can consider themselves lucky to have left Hampden clutching the Homecoming Scottish Cup.

They were poor, they were tired – but they were not punished.

Had Falkirk been more incisive in the Gers penalty box they would have won this trophy for the first time since 1957.

But Walter Smith's men were victorious thanks to Nacho Novo's blistering strike right at the start

| RANGERS | ....1 |
| FALKIRK | ....0 |

MARK GUIDI
at Hampden

of the second half. John Hughes threw on three attackers in the final minutes in a desperate search for an equaliser but it was not to be.

The Bairns seemed panic stricken every time they got a glimpse of goal. Their passing and movement was better than their opponents but not their finishing.

Falkirk knew they had to avoid losing an early goal and were

never in any danger. In fact they came closest to opening the scoring a couple of times through Neil McCann.

In 14 minutes Madjid Bougherra backed off former Ibrox star at the edge of the box and he unleashed a shot that skimmed the top of Neil Alexander's bar.

Poor

Seven minutes later McCann squandered a glorious chance. **Darren Barr's cross from the right was missed by Bougherra and dropped in the winger's path.**

He caught the ball on the volley with his right foot but from

12 yards sclaffed it a yard past Alexander's left-hand post.

He should have scored.

With an extra man in midfield Falkirk had most of the ball although it was made easy for them by Kyle Lafferty and Steve Davis often wasting possession.

Scott Arfield and Kevin McBride played well for the underdogs in the central area and McCann loved his roving role.

But Falkirk failed to work Alexander often enough. They were poor in the final third.

Ally McCoist was far from happy with his players and Barry Ferguson and Lee McCulloch

SCOTTISH CUP

IT LUCKY

NOVO

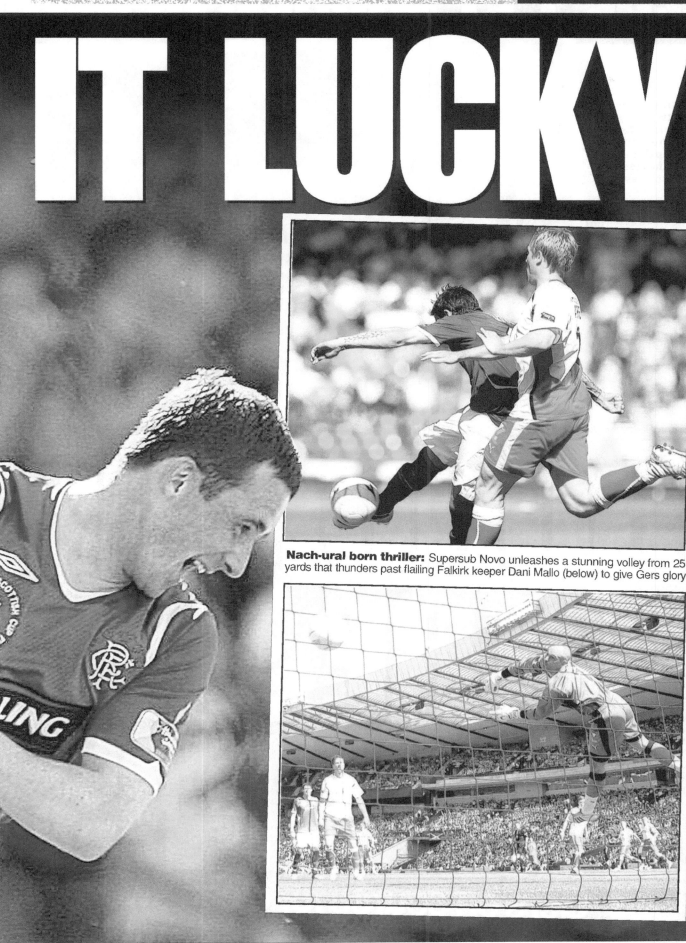

Nach-ural born thriller: Supersub Novo unleashes a stunning volley from 25 yards that thunders past flailing Falkirk keeper Dani Mallo (below) to give Gers glory

Falkirk side but the result is all that matters."

And it mattered just as much to Double-winning skipper Weir.

The 39-year-old filled the void left by Ferguson's boozy antics on Scotland duty – and has now told Smith he's ready to do it all again at 40.

Weir has hedged his bets on his Gers future for the last month, insisting the decision was not his to make.

But after lifting the cup he said: "It's a great feeling. It's a big achievement for the team to get the Double and I'm very proud.

"And yes, I want to stay. If the manager wants me I'd love to stay. I'm sure we will sit down and discuss that but if that's not the case then I would understand.

"I'm enjoying it and feel fine. I love playing football so intend to carry on as long as I can.

"When you're at Rangers you have to be winning trophies or you won't be here for long."

However, Weir admitted they came perilously close to winning nothing yesterday.

He said: "Falkirk were the better team – simple as that. First half especially they were very good then Nacho scored a great goal and changed the game.

"Falkirk put a lot in to the match, played really well and probably deserved more."

They walked out with nothing but pride though.

Smith, on the other hand, added yet another piece of silverware to an already legendary haul. And despite fierce criticism of his stewardship from the stands

●FROM BACK PAGE

this year, Weir angrily rejected the idea that his gaffer was anything other than one of the greatest in the club's history.

He said: "You can't question what Walter has done here. He's been back two-and-a-half years and last season was close to being the best in Rangers' history.

"Tiredness beat us last year, albeit Celtic were a very good team too.

"To turn that disappointment round and win the Double is unbelievable.

"I'm not sure exactly what Walter's record is but he's won something like eight out of 10 championships in his years with Rangers.

Reaction

"If that's not one of the best in history I'd be amazed."

Smith and assistant Ally McCoist had their work cut out yesterday. However, a crucial change forced on them at half-time turned the tide.

Kris Boyd was hooked, apparently due to dehydration, and his replacement won the game in an instant.

Weir said: "There was a reaction but not shouting and bawling at half-time.

"We rearranged the team, the gaffer and Ally changed it round to counter them and suit us a little bit better.

"We took Boydy off, stuck Nacho on and he scored the goal after 30 seconds.

"I'm sure he wasn't envisaging that when he changed it but Nacho scored a great goal against Dundee United with his left foot and the timing of this one was so important."

WALTER

Madjid Bougherra and Steve Davis. The Gers manager sees the central defender and wide midfielder as a major part of his plans.

But if he is told they have to be put up for sale it is believed he will seriously consider standing down.

Smith is happy to have the nucleus of a team in place but feels he needs three quality signings to help retain the title and make a decent attempt at the Champions League.

He would like to bring in a central defender, left-sided midfielder and centre

●FROM BACK PAGE

forward. The manager also wants to keep veteran stopper Davie Weir for another year.

Smith is keen to remain in charge and hopes Murray will give him the assurances he wants this week.

But he will not risk going in to next season with a squad no stronger than the one he has worked with this campaign.

If Murray delivers bad news Walter will stand down and that is likely to lead to his assistant Ally McCoist taking over as manager.

STRACH

say goodbye to players and staff. He will do that today and also receive a warm reception from a crowd expected to top 40,000.

Neil Lennon will now take charge of the Celtic team and the coach may learn this week who the new gaffer will be.

It's understood West Brom boss Tony Mowbray and Dundee United gaffer Craig Levein top the short list.

Mowbray has a compensation clause in his deal that would require Celts to pay more than £1.25million.

If they feel he is the right candidate they will shell out

●FROM BACK PAGE

and allow him to bring in his own backroom staff.

Levein's track record has also impressed the Celtic board and he is seriously in the frame. They will be joined by two more names and it seems all will four be interviewed by Hoops chiefs.

Roy Keane has not been ruled out and Alan Curbishley has also been considered.

That list, however, will not include the likes of Croatia manager Slaven Bilic, West Ham coach Steve Clarke, Frank Rijkaard or Swansea's Roberto Martinez.

---

never got going in midfield. He gave the sluggish duo pelters while Gers' defence also sat far too deep.

Steven Whittaker was booked for chopping down Tam Scobbie after the Falkirk defender had nutmegged him.

Jackie McNamara was next to have his name taken for a tug on Lafferty's shirt as the first half fizzled out.

Smith clearly was not content and made a change at the interval hooking Kris Boyd for Novo – and the switch paid off instantly.

The Spaniard collected a Sasa Papac throw-in out on the left then sent a sensational right-foot volley dipping over Dani Mallo and into the net from 25 yards.

Without taking anything away from the quality of the goal, the keeper – three yards off his line – could have saved it. He did not get his feet moving quickly enough.

Troubled

Gers looked much more comfortable now and moved Davis in beside Ferguson and McCulloch for a three-man central midfield.

But, like Falkirk, they never troubled the keeper. Hughes made a triple change in 74 minutes – Michael Higdon, Carl Finnigan and Mark Stewart on for Kevin

McBride, Paddy Cregg and McCann. Finnigan put the ball in the net 60 seconds later although, it was correctly ruled offside.

With legs tiring in the soaring heat, gaps appeared all over the pitch and Novo missed a good chance nine minutes from time after fine play from Kenny Miller.

That was Miller's last involvement as he made way for Steven Naismith while Christian Dailly came on for Lafferty. Dailly's first act was to cop a booking within 20 seconds for a lunge on Gerard Aafjes.

Bairns came agonisingly close in the dying stages when Stevie

Lovell hit a post from 10 yards following a goalmouth scramble.

That was the best of it for Hughes and his players as Rangers completed the Double to finish off a season they can be proud of.

The spotlight will now turn on Ferguson, Boyd and skipper Davie Weir. Have they played their last games for the club?

And what of Smith, Gers' most successful manager? During the celebrations he took his granddaughter Jessica on to the pitch to share special moments in the Hampden sunshine.

It may well be his last game in charge. What an act to follow.

The **co-operative** insurance cup

RANGERS 1 ST MIRREN 0: RED

FUY: Thomson and Jack Ross

SMITH: REF WON US CUP

From Back Page

to cling on for dear life against St Mirren before Kenny Miller grabbed the only goal of the game six minutes from time.

Smith admitted Thomson had done his side a favour with the decisions that sparked a lethargic Rangers back to life – and had his players simmering with feelings injustice.

The boss said: "St Mirren were the better side until, strangely, the first ordering off. Once we went down to 10 men we managed to pick ourselves up and had by far our best spell of the game immediately after Kevin Thomson's ordering off.

"Once we went down to nine men I still thought it would be an unlikely circumstance that we were going to win it. But we managed to do so and everybody is delighted.

"I said to the lads at half time we had not acquitted ourselves well in the first half. You could see the lift that getting themselves into a final had on St Mirren. They had an extra edge to their game we didn't have until we faced the orderings off."

Wary

But despite admitting the red cards brought out the best in his group, Smith believes Thomson should not have been sent packing for a lunge on Steven Thomson.

He said: "The first ordering off, in the context of the tackles which went before, was maybe a bit soft. But that's the referee's opinion. By the letter of the law these days if he deems the second one a goalscoring opportunity – and it's difficult to say it wasn't – he is correct in the decision he made.

"Thomson saw a wee bit of red mist. But, equally, John Potter's foul on him moments earlier was a bad one too.

"In the end the biggest thing for me was our performance which wasn't really good enough until we were up against it a bit."

Rangers now head into a Scottish Cup quarter-final replay with Dundee United on Wednesday looking to take another massive step towards a domestic clean sweep.

But Smith is wary of treble talk. He said: "I think it's a dangerous thing to consider that. I still think there's a lot of football to be played this season."

However, the boss was heartened by the resilience of his squad. He said: "They have a superb attitude – never say die! They have that and maybe because we haven't been able to buy a player for a couple of years now, that spirit is there."

THIS story becomes more astonishing with every jaw-dropping twist. The most improbable treble of all time just got a huge step closer. And typically, it came in the most extraordinary of circumstances.

Rangers could not simply just turn up and win yesterday's Co-operative Insurance Cup Final. No, they had to do it the hard way. In fact, they chose a route that seemed very nigh impossible and in doing so they broke the heart of all of Paisley.

St Mirren had come here to make a real match of this final – the club's first since that glory day in May 1987. Gus MacPherson's side gave it everything and for long, long spells were the better of these two sides.

It was not until Rangers started losing players and finding a sense of injustice that they finally seized control. First Kevin Thomson was dismissed for a bad-tempered lunge on St Mirren's Steven Thomson by a third Thomson, ref Craig.

Then youngster Danny Wilson was red-carded also, leaving Rangers down to nine men for the final 20 minutes.

All St Mirren had to do was reach out and grab their moment in history. But as they piled forward in search of a winning goal they were floored by the counter punch to end them all.

A quite sublime Kenny Miller header in 84 minutes completed this smash-and-grab act and sent the Rangers end of the National Stadium into a state of all-out, blood-pumping euphoria.

As Rangers erupted, St Mirren caved in. This one moment had ripped out their insides and scattered them over the Hampden surface.

Fright

It really was a remarkable, unforgettable occasion and one that sums up the resilience of a Rangers side that continues to hunt down a domestic clean sweep like a pack of starving hounds.

And yet they didn't have to make a meal of securing the first silverware of the season. The opening exchanges – that were played out almost entirely inside the Rangers half – proved St Mirren's players had not been struck down by stage fright.

It was Rangers who looked more than a little unsettled by the rampant manner in which their opponents had opened up.

This was perfectly illustrated in four minutes when Ibrox skipper Davie Weir dribbled out from the back and, tentatively, attempted to round Billy Mehmet.

Weir stubbed a toe, stumbled and then looked on as Mehmet clattered off towards goal. The striker was prevented from a clear strike on target by Danny Wilson who made a timely block and, as the ball spun high across the six-yard box, Sasa Papac got up to head behind for a corner.

Rangers began to look increasingly ragged as St Mirren continued to throw bodies forward in decent numbers. They hustled and harried in little black-and-white striped packs, taking it in turns to harass the opposition into giving up the ball.

It wasn't particularly pretty and nor did

WHAT A BUNCH OF TREBLE MAKERS

Gers on course for clean sweep

| RANGERS | 1 | ST MIRREN | 0 |

KEITH JACKSON REPORTS FROM HAMPDEN

it harvest a whole crop of goalscoring chances, but it was impressively high tempo stuff and, more importantly, it was rattling the cages of a Rangers side that seemed not to know how best to respond.

Kevin Thomson had an idea though. He hurled himself into some trademark industrial-strength tackles and also set off on a surging run, bullishly brushing aside St Mirren's midfielders one by one on his way across the halfway line before being chopped down.

Nacho Novo also tried to get his side moving forward but all too often with little or no support from his team-mates, especially the sluggish front pairing of Kris Boyd and Miller. In fact, Rangers managed just a single shot on target in the first half – Steven Whittaker's rather feeble effort from distance that was comfortably grasped by St Mirren keeper Paul Gallacher.

It was not so comfortable at the other end where Michael Higdon and Mehmet were causing all manner of problems. The chance of the half came in 39 minutes when Higdon bulldozed his way through a timid-looking Weir challenge and from the byeline picked out Thomson with a perfect cutback.

Thomson looked a certain scorer as he tugged on the trigger but somehow Neil Alexander jabbed out a boot to make a truly extraordinary reflex save. The keeper rolled into the back of his net but the ball was redirected to safety.

Alexander was hurling himself through the air again moments later when David Barron let rip from 25 yards with a dipping drive but it clipped the top of the bar on its way over and Rangers looked relieved to get inside without suffering serious damage.

Relieved that is, until they found their manager inside waiting for them with a face like thunder. Smith had stormed down the stairs from his seat in the main stand on the last blast of Thomson's whistle. He had much to sort out.

Virus victim Steve Davis – who had barely been noticed – was kept inside. Maurice Edu was told to get stripped and Lee McCulloch was given a new set of orders – to provide

& SILVER FOR WALTER

CUP FOR IT: Kenny Miller leaps the advertising boards to start the celebrations after his header, inset, wins the trophy for the Ibrox side

HOTLINE

ANTHONY HAGGERETY TAKES YOUR CALLS

IT WAS Miller time at Hampden as nine-man Rangers scooped the Co-Operative Insurance Cup against St Mirren.

The first leg of a potential domestic Treble was secured thanks to Kenny Miller's late winner.

However, referee Craig Thomson took centre stage with his controversial decisions to send off Rangers duo Kevin Thomson and Danny Wilson.

First up was regular caller **Alan McGaw, Grangemouth,** who said: "Well done to Rangers and Walter Smith whose substitution of Kris Boyd for Steven Naismith was a masterstroke.

"If St Mirren cannot beat Rangers with nine men they do not deserve to win the Cup."

Chic Craig, Barrhead, said: "The Co-Operative Insurance Cup Final started with 11 men versus 11. It then became 12 against 11 and degenerated into 12 v nine.

"Rangers were magnificent and refused to lie down but the refereeing performance was a disgrace."

Gordon Blackwell, Glasgow, said: "Congratulations to Rangers on winning a trophy despite such adversity.

"Gus MacPherson should be ashamed of himself for his part in Thomson's sending off.

"I hope this match puts to bed all talk of refereeing conspiracy theories."

Evelyn Flannery, Glasgow, said: "When Thomson was sent off the referee automatically became the nasty man in black and the Rangers fans subjected him to dogs' abuse.

"I thought it was supposed to only be the Celtic supporters who were paranoid?"

Ian Semple, Kilwinning, said: "Despite the ref's best attempts Rangers triumphed in the end.

"What fighting spirit, guts and determination were shown by Smith's Light Blues – and both sending offs were a joke."

Buddies fan **James Reid, Paisley,** said: "St Mirren will never have a better chance of winning a trophy against one of the Old Firm in Glasgow. Against nine men we should never

QUOTE OF THE DAY

'If St Mirren cannot beat a Rangers side that's down to nine men then they don't deserve to win the Cup'

have lost and to get beat with a three on two break is absolutely criminal.

"MacPherson really has taken St Mirren as far as he can. The chance was there to become legends and Gus blew it because of his inexperience at that level and not knowing how to handle the pressure.

"The players got over-excited at the thought of lifting the silverware and forgot they had to score to win the game.

"It's a terrible result and I now fear for the Saints for the rest of the season."

Thomas Campbell, Rutherglen, said: "The Co-op Cup Final apart, the reason Rangers have not had the credit they deserve this season is because nearly every SPL club have been the victims of rough justice against them.

"Celtic, Hearts, St Mirren, Motherwell and Hamilton have all fallen foul of refereeing decisions when facing Rangers and it has happened too often to be just a coincidence."

Gers fan Stewart **Douglas, Bishopbriggs,** could not resist having a wee pop at the Hoops.

He said: "Celtic have won their last three matches and we have not heard the four Ms for the past couple of weeks – Mogga's Monday morning moans.

"It's a shame as I was quite enjoying them."

Colin Wilkie, Barmulloch, said: "I suppose you will not hear many of the paranoia brigade given the fact Celtic got a dodgy penalty against St Johnstone and won the match."

Finally **Mark Ferguson, Glasgow,** rang in to have a go at *Record Sport* columnist Jim McLean.

Mark said: "As a Dundee United fan I am getting tired of reading how much McLean regrets turning down the Rangers job 25 years ago.

"Get over it Jim or risk losing the respect of all United supporters."

Some people have no respect. Exactly how many titles have United won since McLean quit Tannadice? None. Although it could be worse Mark, you could support St Mirren. Ouch!

Call Hugh Keevins today from 10AM till 12 noon on: 0141 309 3306 or email us: hotline@dailyrecord.co.uk

Weir and Wilson with badly-needed help. McCulloch slotted in to a three-man defence as Smith shaped up with a 3-4-1-2. But not for long.

Very soon another reshuffle would be called for after Thomson was dismissed for an angry lunge at his St Mirren namesake. But it was the third Thomson, ref Craig, who was in most danger of losing the place.

Had he spotted John Potter's rugby tackle on Thomson moments earlier this whole flashpoint could have been avoided.

But the whistler and his assistants all missed it and suddenly tempers boiled over. Miller had Potter by the throat but the officials missed that also as the ball found its way to Steven Thomson, with Kevin in hot pursuit.

The Rangers man launched himself into a tackle but did not get any of the ball. Instead

he left Thomson in a crumpled heap. And, perhaps fearing he was losing all control, ref Thomson whipped out a straight red.

St Mirren continued to cause problems at the other end and when the exhausted Mehmet made way for Craig Dargo, the final was about to take another dramatic twist.

Wilson misjudged a through ball and let Dargo get a run on him. The youngster tugged on the sleeve of his man, sending him sprawling on the edge of the box – and Rangers were down to NINE.

And just when it seemed as if they could do little more than attempt to hang on and take it to penalties Rangers conjured something quite astonishing to win it.

Weir got it started when he strode out from the back to intercept a stray pass then send sub Steven Naismith – who had just replaced Boyd – darting down the right. Naismith

looked up to see Miller and Novo screaming for the cross and conjured the perfect supply.

Miller got up to meet it with a textbook header, jack-knifing in the air and planting the ball in the bottom right-hand corner.

It was one of those special Hampden moments. The kind of goal that seems to be scored in slow motion.

Then Miller was off, veins bulging as he leapt the advertising boards in wild-eyed celebration. He was booked for his bother. But he had floored Saints and secured the first leg of what might be the most improbable treble of all time.

RANGERS: CHAMPION

CHAMPIONS AGAIN 53

WHAT is it they say? He who Laffs last Laffs loudest? Well, if ever the theory was proven beyond doubt then surely it was yesterday at Easter Road.

For the second successive season, Scottish football's favourite fall-guy stole centre stage on title day. Yep, love him, or loathe him, there is no denying that Kyle Lafferty has a sense of occasion.

Less than a year on from his final-day heroics at Tannadice, not only did he choose this day at the end of a marathon season to turn in his best performance in a Rangers shirt but he also scored the winning goal, conjuring up a strike of outrageous quality to drag his team over the finishing line.

Of course, he had his moments of eccentricity also. For example, there was one magnificently-woeful second-half shot which was sliced so badly it disappeared into the wasteground where the old East Stand used to sit. Then there was body popping, which requires a great deal of working on.

But, even so, this was Lafferty's day as he showed more than a glimpse of why Walter Smith paid over £3million to land him in the first place.

You never know. There might just be a player in there trying to get out. He has been well hidden but yesterday he stepped back out into the open and his contribution – as the man preferred to Kris Boyd – will be remembered for some time to come.

Rangers arrived at the ground at lunchtime, still hoping the title might be won before their warm-up.

With Madjid Bougherra limping back to the sidelines with his latest injury, Smith might even have been hoping against hope for some welcome news from Tayside but, as his players were going about their final stretches, word came through of Robbie Keane's late settler for Celtic. His players would have to do this one for themselves.

Designed

Lee McCulloch was dispatched to fill in at centre half with Maurice Edu handed a starting place in the centre of midfield.

But Smith was not the only one tinkering as Hibs boss John Hughes was also making adjustments. It was left to Anthony Stokes to plough a lone furrow up top with back-up from the flanks – Derek Riordan coming in from the left and David Wotherspoon from the right.

This system was designed not only to provide Stokes with support but also to outnumber Rangers in midfield whenever the would-be champions were in possession.

It worked for the first 10 minutes or so as Smith's players struggled to find any kind of rhythm. In fact they were sluggish and flat and spent a great deal of these opening exchanges deep inside their own territory.

And yet the first glimpses of goal arrived at the other end and both fell to the feet of Kenny Miller. The striker diverted the first over the top from close in after David Weir had headed a Kevin Thomson corner towards goal. Then, three minutes later he raced on to a Lafferty flick but, under pressure, looped a shot over Graeme Smith's bar.

It has to be said, Lafferty had started the game looking bright and busy but even so what the big man came up with next really was of startling quality.

With 17 minutes on the clock he burst through the Hibs defence on to Miller's cleverly-cushioned pass. There was still a lot of work to be done as Chris Hogg was in close pursuit but Lafferty showed pace and power to muscle his way through and produce a finish of stunning quality, lashing a left-foot shot across Smith and in at the keeper's left-hand post.

It was a sublime piece of play from Lafferty who celebrated with his ridiculous

TITLE CLINCHER: Kyle Lafferty shrugs off Chris Hogg to fire in the winner

HIBS	0
RANGERS	1

By Keith Jackson at Easter Road

self-styled Lager-bot routine as Rangers began to sense the start of the end.

In fact, they came forward from that point in little droves of blue looking to finish Hibs off before the break. One superb Miller pass put Steve Davis and Thomson away in 24 minutes but the midfield pair seemed to get in something of a muddle and the move ended with Davis attempting to be too clever with a set-up inside the box.

Thomson was forced to lunge for it and ended up clattering into keeper Smith who had raced out bravely from his line. The Rangers man was booked for the foul by ref Willie Collum, which even the Hibs No.1 seemed to suggest was harsh.

At the other end Allan McGregor was getting through the game without the need to dirty his new all-white outfit although he did have to react smartly to keep out one

swerving long-range effort from Riordan. Then, five minutes before the break, Hibs went close again when Paul Hanlon headed a foot wide of McGregor's right-hand post.

These scares convinced Ibrox boss Smith to reshuffle at the break. Lafferty was shifted to the left flank, Stevie Naismith crossed over to the right and Davis was repositioned in an advanced role, behind Miller but in front of Edu and Thomson.

Smashed

It was the Northern Ireland midfielder's job to pick holes in the Hibs' defence which had also been rejigged at the break with Steven Thicot replacing Hogg.

Hughes made a further change when he replaced Patrick Cregg with Colin Nish 10

'This was Lafferty's day as he finally showed why Walter Smith

S SEASON 2009/2010

Clydesdale Bank *PREMIER LEAGUE*

KYLE HIGH CLUB

Gers star has the last Laff as he sews up title

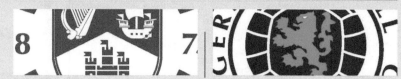

MATCH STATS

HIBS 8		RANGERS 7
52	**POSSESSION**	48
5	**SHOTS ON**	5
6	**SHOTS OFF**	8
11	**FOULS**	15
6	**CORNERS**	5
1	**BOOKINGS**	2

HIBS

Graeme Smith 7
Helpless with Rangers' goal but was otherwise commanding and alert.

Darren McCormack 6
Fine defensively but Hibs needed more from him in an attacking sense.

Chris Hogg 5
Read game well in front of him but should have been stronger for Gers goal as Lafferty brushed him off.

Paul Hanlon 6
While Miller's runs were a menace on the counter, he staked his territory confidently enough.

Ian Murray 6
Kept his side of the pitch well enough protected.

Kevin McBride 7
Worked hard to establish his midfield foothold in the game.

Patrick Cregg 6
Found himself neutered in the middle of the park by Thomson and Edu – then by Davis when moved into the middle.

David Wotherspoon 6
One second half move apart, too keen to sit off and wait for things to happen.

John Rankin 6
Made some decent runs beyond strikers but not on ball often enough.

Anthony Stokes 6
Movement decent enough but forced to scrap on meagre rations. Booked.â

Derek Riordan 6
Second-half volley apart, cutting edge missing for once.

Subs: Steven Thicot – slotted into centre of defence, 5. Colin Nish – chances few and far between, 4. Benji – lively contribution, 4.

RANGERS

Allan McGregor 7
Had to look lively when Riordan surprised him with swerving hit then brilliant save denied the striker again.

Steven Whittaker 5
Found it difficult to cope with Murray and Riordan's raids down left flank and gave away needless fouls. Lucky not to concede penalty.

Lee McCulloch 7
Dominant in the air and swept up really well behind Weir.

David Weir 7
Had work cut out with Stokes then Nish but never let either in behind him.

Sasa Papac 6
Wasted good chance in first half to make it 2-0. Booked.

Steven Davis 7
Far more effective in central midfield but drifted in to good effect. Just couldn't produce a killer ball.

Maurice Edu 6
Solid and industrious. But offers little creativity beyond halfway line.

Kevin Thomson 8
Terrific display. Broke up home side's attacks and passed it well. Booked.

Steven Naismith 6
Struggled against McCormack in first half but improved after the break.

Kenny Miller 7
Led the line really well. Brilliant pass for Gers' goal.

Kyle Lafferty 8
Best game yet in a Rangers jersey. Looked hungry and stunning finish.

Subs: Nacho Novo – added energy up front but couldn't repeat title-winning goal of 2005 on same ground, 2.

THE MANAGERS

John Hughes 7
Played Stokes up top on his own but he was too isolated in first half. Threw Nish on and he caused Gers more problems. Missed Liam Miller in middle of park.

Walter Smith 9
Left out top scorer Kris Boyd to give Lafferty a chance in favoured position up front and it paid off big time. Squeezed every ounce of energy out of his team.

THE MAN IN BLACK

Willie Collum: Thomson's booking looked harsh. Had to make two big decisions in second half. Could easily have given penalty after Whittaker's clumsy tackle on Riordan but was right to rule out Nish goal for a push on McCulloch. 6

MAN OF THE MATCH

Kyle Lafferty (Rangers)

minutes in, with his side pushing hard for an equaliser.

Moments earlier Wotherspoon had smashed an effort over the top after superb set-up work from John Rankin. For the first time Rangers, despite the sterling efforts of Thomson in midfield, were looking tired and more than a little vulnerable.

Smith responded by reverting to his original 4-4-2, with Lafferty and Miller up top. It was now all about getting over that finishing line – the best way they knew how.

Thomson chased and harried for every ball but Hibs kept coming forward and there were moments when it seemed they might keep this flag race alive a bit longer. In fact,

it was desperate towards the end. McGregor made one terrific save at his left to claw out a Riordan drive and Hibs had a penalty appeal turned down when the same player tumbled a little too easily under the challenge of Steven Whittaker.

Then, six minutes from time, Nish crashed the ball into the back of McGregor's net but was penalised for pushing McCulloch to the ground to the fury of the home support who were willing their side to ruin the title party.

But finally, Rangers made it home. And Lafferty had never felt so welcome.

BLUE HEAVEN: Lafferty celebrates his winner

paid out over £3million for him'

CO-OP CUP FINAL SPECIAL... CO-OP CUP

Teddy Bears picnic as two shots off the post give Gers the trophy

IF YOU GO DOWN TO THE WOODS TODAY....

THERE were cup final heroes all over Hampden yesterday. And yet it was a lump of wood that won it for Rangers.

No, not Nikica Jelavic, the man who hit the decisive goal of a lung-bursting, nail-chewing, stomach-churning half hour of extra time. The Croat was excellent.

But even so he needed the help of an incredibly obliging white post to get the job done. The exact same part of the exact same post, in fact, that kissed the first-half shot from Steven Davis which had given Rangers first blood earlier on in this enthralling slugfest for the season's first piece of silver.

But it was even kinder to Jelavic. It didn't just help his shot on its way, it actually managed to apply the backspin which carried it home. This piece of wood has missed its vocation. It ought to have been a snooker cue.

And it can think itself fortunate not to have been snapped into kindling by Celtic's giant lumberjack of a goalkeeper, Fraser Forster.

The post colluded with Rangers twice to shatter Forster's and Celtic's dreams on a day which was meant to belong to them. They had travelled across the city to the south side convinced they were about to witness a crowning moment in the career of their fledgling boss Neil Lennon.

Instead, Lennon watched this most painful of defeats from a seat in the main stand before heading downstairs to console his players in their dressing room. Outside, meanwhile, Rangers boss Walter Smith was leading the celebrations – punching the air with raw delight as he lifted the 20th trophy of his two stints in charge at Ibrox.

Triumph

Smith is well practised in lifting these things but there seemed to be some extra emotion about the way in which he lapped this latest one up. Perhaps that was because yesterday's triumph ensures he will not be going out at the end of the season empty-handed. Or perhaps it was just because he enjoys beating Celtic.

Either way, Smith left Hampden a hero again yesterday and in all his unbridled joy he should have taken that post with him. Or at least given it a medal.

It really was an afternoon of exceptional drama and it should be said both sides deserve credit for making this final a showcase event – despite all the navel-gazing and brow-beating which went on after their last coming together.

They went at each other from start to finish and it made for truly tremendous viewing. Smith's hand may have been forced a little by injuries but he opted to be bolder than expected. And it worked.

Rangers started brightly, as if the shackles had been taken off. Youngster Gregg Wylde looked high on energy and confidence down the left and Jelavic too seemed in determined mood.

The Croat almost got the game off to a flier early on when he ghosted on to a hanging cross from Sasa Papac and tried a spectacular volley. It would have been a Hollywood finish but Jelavic fluffed his line and his effort sliced off the outside of his boot before flying high and wide.

Still, this was a signal of Rangers' intent. Celtic's front two were isolated

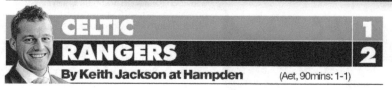

| CELTIC | 1 |
| RANGERS | 2 |

By Keith Jackson at Hampden   (Aet, 90mins: 1-1)

and when the ball did reach Gary Hooper or Georgios Samaras they found David Weir and Madjid Bougherra in top form.

They did have a penalty claim after 15 minutes when Mark Wilson tumbled over Papac's leg but ref Craig Thomson waved away the claims. More of this later.

But for now Lennon's players were starting to settle and skipper Scott Brown nearly put them in front when he surged into the box to meet a Commons cross only for his header to bullet wide.

But Rangers were still carrying a threat of their own and, in 23 minutes, they made the breakthrough.

There didn't seem much danger as Charlie Mulgrew got his head on a hopeful, high probe but the ball dropped

into the path of Steve Davis who chose to drive forward.

He made it to the edge of the D and then let fly with a precision shot which beat Forster's huge wingspan and went in off the inside of his left-hand post.

This could have ruffled Celtic who knew they were in a fight now. But they needed just seven minutes to get back on terms when Emilio Izaguirre's cross spun up off Kyle Lafferty and into the six-yard box. Samaras reacted first, soaring above Bougherra to flick it on and, at his back, Ledley followed in to head home.

This final was now on fire. But the blaze threatened to rage out of control moments later when Jelavic looked to

have been fouled by Thomas Rogne inside Celtic's box.

Again, ref Thomson was ideally positioned and he did at least appear to point to the spot. If he did then in a second he had a complete change of heart and booked Jelavic for diving.

Although TV replays showed one of Rogne's studs may have brushed across the striker's knee, the ref's on-the-spot reassessment was on the money again.

Rangers were back on the front foot before the break but Bougherra missed the target with a free header and then Lafferty failed to hit the target after rising above Izaguirre at the back post.

At the start of the second half Steven

FINAL SPECIAL... CO-OP CUP FINAL

WOOD YOU BELIEVE IT: Nikica Jelavic, main, wheels away after his winner goes in off the post, shown in sequence above, while Steven Davis fires home the opener, below

WE CAN NIK THE CROWN

From Back Page

savoured by Smith. His team had been doubted, he had been doubted but he and his players dragged themselves through a 120-minute marathon and refused to let go of their League Cup.

This was Rangers' 27th League Cup Final win and Smith loved it.

But he wasn't happy with referee Craig Thomson, who twice denied Rangers' appeals for penalties.

The first, in 31 minutes, was the more controversial. Thomas Rogne challenged Nikica Jelavic in the box, the Croat went down and Thomson pointed to the spot.

But surrounded by Celtic players he changed his mind and booked Jelavic for diving. Smith couldn't believe it and was still baffled an hour after the end and questioned if Rangers would have had the same benefit if the incident had happened in their box.

He said: "It's dangerous for a referee to do that. If it had happened in the other box ... I don't know.

"I've said before Celtic mounted a campaign at the start of the season but if you are good enough you'll win despite a refereeing decision. Today we've won and I am delighted.

"I felt aggrieved Jelavic was booked because the referee's first reaction was he'd been fouled. The referee gave the penalty and then didn't.

"But he must have thought there was something in it to give it in the first place. I don't know why he changed his mind but that's what he told the players.

Praise

"We went on to win and you could say everything is fine. Nonetheless it matters. But I hope both teams get a bit of praise for what they've done."

Smith was referring to the appeals for calm before the Final. The First Minister, police and religious leaders had all chipped in but the Final, while tough and uncompromising, was a thriller for all the right reasons.

Smith said: "It was a terrific game. We deserved to win and I can't say if Kyle Bartley being injured worked in our favour in the way we had to set up.

"Steven Davis was by far the man of the match but we had a lot of good players. We have a really good group of boys who even though some have come in halfway through the season still know what is required.

"Our players have given everything for the club and I didn't see that they'd anything to prove. Now they just have to keep winning but today was testimony to their desire to win.

"I never use what anyone says about us as motivation because motivation has to come from yourselves. You need to have the desire to go out and win.

"You could see that in them today and this, I must admit, was a nice one to win.

"I know I'm leaving and while I didn't want to go without another trophy the most important thing is the club, the team won.

"But will it help us in the remainder of the season? It might but we could still be badly affected by injuries.

"Steven Whittaker played in his eighth position so far this season. And Maurice Edu finished today at full-back.

"We're here to win. That's what we did and it feels nice."

Whittaker's rasping effort forced Forster into a save as Rangers' forward momentum continued to grow.

But Celtic came close too when Papac attempted to cut out a Commons cross and nearly misfired into his own net. The Bosnian was then booked for a body check on Izaguirre. If this was an easy call for ref Thomson then his next big decision was anything but.

Another penalty claim for Rangers – another dismissive shrug of the shoulders. But this time, the evidence on camera did not fully support the ref's decision.

Rather than being hit by the ball at close range, Wilson appeared to throw up his arm to block Maurice Edu's effort.

This one could easily have been given and Smith, who screamed for it, clearly felt it ought to have been.

But if Celtic's luck was in Brown's was not as soon after he limped off to have place taken by Ki Sung Yueng. Yet Brown was not alone. Rogne hobbled off, replaced by Glenn Loovens then, when Bougherra's hamstring packed in, midfielder Kyle Hutton took the defender's place. Whittaker moved from right-back to centre-half and Edu went to right-back.

But still, the deadlock continued as Hooper, who hadn't had a sniff at goal all day, fired a half chance over the top. Celtic were coming on stronger the longer the game went on and Ledley forced

Alexander into a late goal-line save from a snap shot following a corner.

This was the last big chance of the 90 minutes. Extra time, and a post, would be required to separate these city sluggers.

Before it had begun, though, Smith sent for sub Vladimir Weiss who was to play a superb cameo role. It was his quick-thinking which sent Jelavic away with a smartly-taken free-kick.

Mulgrew attempted to keep up but couldn't outmuscle his man and the Croat slipped a shot wide of Forster and in off that very special lump of wood.

There was still time for Izaguirre to see red for a last-man foul on Weiss to complete Celtic's misery.

RANGERS: CHAMPIONS 2011

00:45

05:00

07:00

49:00

Kyle's 45-second goal sets up 3 in a row for rampant Rangers

LAFFA

HELICOPTER Sunday. That's what they dubbed it. But Rangers ripped through Kilmarnock yesterday to make a mockery of the expected nerve-tingling last day scenario.

Three goals inside the opening seven minutes, another two at the top of the second half and the 10th title of Walter Smith's 12 years in charge was secured.

It was as if these players simply could not even contemplate allowing their manager to walk away without one last heroic triumph and so they went to work at Rugby Park as if their very lives depended upon the outcome.

In the crowning moment of a magnificent championship defence, Smith's Rangers were awesome. They unleashed hell on the home side before sending Smith and his followers soaring towards the heavens with one last breath-taking performance for the boss.

Kyle Lafferty, whose devastating end-of-season form may finally have justified Smith's £3.5million punt on him, bagged a sensational hat-trick. Nikica Jelavic, whose £4m fee always did look like money well spent, netted his 19th of the season and the outstanding Steven Naismith grabbed one too to cap another immense individual display.

Together this three-pronged attack had, over the closing weeks of the campaign, blasted a path towards this triumph. Yesterday they finished off the job in crushing and emphatic style, backed up as ever by the skills of their chief supply man Steve Davis.

But although some of these players have excelled themselves during the run-in, it was the man in charge who led them here to this third successive SPL crown.

Smith has single-handedly saved Rangers from the clutches of disaster during this his second spell in charge.

But yesterday he may even have surpassed his own expectations as he took charge for the last time to clinch the most unlikely title of them all. It was an astonishing way to end a season of extremes.

Pulse

And to think, at first it didn't even feel much like the last day of the campaign. Kilmarnock was wrapped in a blanket of thick grey morning cloud and an icy drizzle came swirling into the ground from every opening as bleary-eyed supporters filed in through the gates.

Maybe it was the early start. Or it could have been down to the soaring levels of high anxiety.

But whatever the reason, there was a nervous hush around the place for a long while as the teams went about their final preparations.

And yet, although it took a while for them to get warmed up, by kick-off time Rugby Park had developed its own pulse. The old place was positively throbbing with noise and crackling with a sense of anticipation which was cascading down to pitch level from the stands.

It was into this bedlam that Rangers emerged. And they gorged on it until they too had become super-charged. By the first blast of the whistle they had become an invincible force.

And what happened next was nothing short of astonishing.

Six minutes and 15 seconds later they were 3-0 up and all around the ground Killie supporters – who were agitated at sharing their own sections with so many unfamiliar faces in the first place – were streaming towards the exits, leaving the infiltrators to it.

It may have been one of the quickest walk-outs of all time but there was no point in hanging around, their team had already been smashed into submission.

Rangers roared into action with an opener inside the first 45 seconds after a magnificent piece of quick thinking from Davis. He launched himself into a diving

KILMARNOCK	1
RANGERS	5

By Keith Jackson at Rugby Park

header to send Lafferty into a foot race with Manuel Pascali – one that the Italian was never in danger of winning.

Lafferty's long legs gobbled up the ground to get him there first and then, 18 yards from goal, he stretched out his left to cushion a perfect lob over Cammy Bell.

As it dropped down under the keeper's crossbar and into the back of his net, Rangers had lift-off. Very soon they had disappeared completely out of sight and somewhere into orbit.

Four minutes later it was 2-0 and once

again the speed of Rangers' thinking was what took Kilmarnock's defences apart.

This time they broke from the edge of their own box after Davis had made a tidy interception and shuttled the ball back towards Sasa Papac.

The Bosnian moved it instantly on to Naismith who looked up to spot Gregg Wylde scorching off down the left flank and picked the youngster out with a magnificent first time pass.

Wylde kept motoring until he was level with the 18-yard box and Naismith was

catching up. The winger slipped the ball inside and Naismith took one touch with his right boot before smashing the laces of his left through it to send a shot ripping into the bottom left corner of Bell's net.

If Kilmarnock players and fans were shell-shocked by this lightning blitz then, even before they had time to recover or even catch a breath, they were floored by a third crushing blow.

This time the full might of Jelavic came thundering at them down the Rangers right and, with Bell's back four in a state of disarray, the Croat was able to measure the perfect low cross and slide it into Lafferty's path.

Again the finish, this time with an instep, was so cool and clinical is was if the occasionally hot-headed hitman had ice pumping through his veins. Six

minutes and 15 seconds – helicopter Sunday was over.

Neil Doncaster could have set off from base camp there and then, carrying the trophy on foot, and still got there on time for the presentation without having a shell out a fortune on fuel for his chopper.

Certainly, as a contest, this game was going nowhere now. The rest of the first half was all rather meaningless.

Mehdi Taouil – filling in for Alexei Eremenko in the playmaker role – fired a decent drive over the top and James Dayton forced a typically strong-handed save from Allan McGregor but this was token resistance from Killie. In truth, they were bracing themselves for a second flurry of hammer blows.

Tim Clancy managed to snuff one out with a brilliant saving tackle to deny

RAN... CHAMPIONS 2011

57:00

MINUTE

RAPID FIRE: Lafferty, main pic, got the party started early as Rangers hit Killie for five, to the delight of Bain and Smith, below left, and McGregor, below

KILMARNOCK

⭐ **STARMAN**

James Dayton	**6**

Went close in first half and scored from free-kick.

Cammy Bell	**5**

Had to pick ball out net three times in first six minutes.

Tim Clancy	**5**

Dragged all over place and completely over-run.

Garry Hay	**5**

Penned back for long spells and struggled to get going.

James Fowler	**6**

Pace helped him against Wylde but it was a lost cause.

Liam Kelly	**5**

No shortage of effort but he was chasing shadows.

Manuel Pascali	**5**

Caught out inside a minute and repeatedly exposed.

Craig Bryson	**6**

Attempted to get foot on ball but always closed down.

Willy Aubameyang	**5**

Starved of any decent service he really struggled.

Mehdi Taouil	**5**

Playmaker failed to make impact on final appearance.

David Silva	**5**

Had one long-range effort and that was it.

Subs: Mo Sissoko – he replaced Silva after the break but was really up against it as a dominant Rangers coasted through the game, 4. Gary Fisher – did little after his arrival apart from pick up a booking for a poor challenge on Bougherra, 2.

RANGERS

⭐ **STARMAN**

Kyle Lafferty	**9**

Northern Irishman helped himself to three stunners.

Allan McGregor	**7**

Made tremendous first-half stops to deny both Dayton and Bryson. Beaten by deflection.

Steven Whittaker	**7**

Rangers' "Mr Versatility" rampaged down right flank.

Sasa Papac	**7**

Solid display on what looks like his farewell appearance.

Davie Weir	**7**

The 41-year-old continues to turn the clock back.

Madjid Bougherra	**7**

Steady, strong and a few swashbuckling runs.

Maurice Edu	**7**

Did the dirty work in the midfield engine room.

Gregg Wylde	**7**

Scorching pace caused problems for Killie's defence.

Steven Davis	**8**

Ran the show with effortless ease in midfield.

Steven Naismith	**8**

Found target early on then set up Lafferty's third.

Nikica Jelavic	**7**

Led the line brilliantly and crashed home a free-kick.

Subs: Lee McCulloch – return from injury saw the veteran get the last 20 minutes, 3. El Hadj Diouf – on-loan Blackburn attacker was thrown on with 10 minutes to go, 2. David Healy – on for celebrations, 2.

MEN WHO MATTER

KENNY SHIELS	**WALTER SMITH**
HAMSTRUNG by injuries and suspensions his patched-up Kilmarnock team were completely steamrollered during an incredible opening period from Gers. **5**	KEPT faith with the same starting line-up that has served him so well during title run-in and he was amply rewarded. Masterminded 10 titles in two spells at Ibrox. **9**

VERDICT

A THREE-GOAL blitz inside seven minutes eased any nerves and ensured the title would be heading back to Ibrox for the third year on the spin. Gers simply obliterated Kilmarnock on their own turf.

■ MAN IN BLACK

CRAIG THOMSON has been at the centre of so much controversy this season but the whistler was virtually anonymous during Rangers' title party. **6**

Naismith after Davis and Whittaker had come tearing down the Rangers right.

Then, five minutes before the break, Davis cut in from the other side to smack a shot off the base of Bell's left-hand post.

But Rangers refuelled and reloaded at the break and they returned to finish off the job.

Lafferty ought to have bagged his hat-trick when he was superbly played in by Whittaker but even though he misfired, Kilmarnock's defences were being burst open again.

Less than a minute later, after the frazzled Pascali had brought Jelavic down on the edge of his own box, it was 4-0. Jelavic picked himself up, placed the ball and then lashed it into the gap inside Bell's left-hand post. It was an awesome example of the Croat's class and it thudded on to Kilmarnock's jaw with maximum impact.

As the knees buckled again, they found themselves under all out attack.

And in less than a minute Lafferty had piled through them to complete his own personal treble, albeit with the aid of a fortuitous flick off his heel which allowed him to take in Naismith's pass and round Clancy all in one movement.

But Lafferty then stayed composed enough to slot a low shot under the by now utterly bedraggled Bell.

He was beaten again soon after by Naismith but this time a linesman's flag came to his rescue.

Bell then pulled off a fine save to keep out a thumping volley from Davie Weir of all people, as Rangers swarmed all over the poor man's box. There was some respite in 65 minutes when Dayton's free-kick clipped the Rangers wall and deflected in off McGregor's left-hand post to make it 5-1 but Rangers were in rampant, relentless mood.

And they almost crowned their glory day with a goal of Harlem Globetrotting quality when, after linking up with Davis and Jelavic as the trio threaded their way in from the right flank, Naismith whacked a shot off the face of Bell's bar.

Now that one really would have slammed the tin lid down on title day. But it didn't matter. Smith's final triumph was spectacular enough already.

email ✉ reporters@sundaymail.co.uk

Rangers 1 Berwick 0

Coisty

Rob Fairburn
Ibrox Stadium

FEELING CHAMPION Aird nods the winner (above right) then celebrates before joining his team-mates for a party as they show off the trophy (right)

■ **FROM BACK PAGE**

Young of the Beeb were asked to leave Ibrox yesterday ahead of the 1-0 win over Berwick as Gers lifted the Third Division trophy.

But McCoist refused to blow a fuse over the document, saying: "I believe the person who drew up the dossier was an electrician.

"If so I am heading straight home to do a thesis on electrical engineering.

"I'll hand it to you on Monday morning on the way forward for electrical engineering.

"If the gentleman who wrote it can promise Cruyff and Rijkaard, I will drive over there, bring them back and they can sit in my office.

"I would certainly move sideways for those two."

Asked about the criticism of his performance at Rangers, McCoist replied: "It gets weary for a split second but then the gallows humour kicks in.

"It has kept us going for the last two years.

"I would hate you to think I am being flippant.

"When you have good people round you and working with you, that is the most important thing. I just want the chance to prove I am the man for Rangers."

Gers partied with their prize after yesterday's victory over Berwick and McCoist is already planning for next season.

But he told fans there will be no big-name additions to his squad with the club under a transfer embargo until September.

He said: "I don't think there will be massive amounts of change for next season.

"We are bringing in free transfers and they are free transfers for a reason. We can't register them until September 1. We are not going to get the best youngsters – the 22, 23 or 24-year-olds.

"That is not going to happen because they cost a lot of money.

"We are going to have to get a group of players who can get us out of the next division. Hopefully with one or two better performances."

But McCoist did some big thinking of his own as he claimed Gers should be modelled along the lines of Bayern Munich.

He said: "The club I look at and respect – probably more than any other – is Bayern.

"The way they model themselves is wonderful and I would love us to get a similar model. By that I mean a spine of people within Rangers who feel for the club.

"I'm not necessarily saying all business people should have blue blood. But it's healthy if you have the likes of John Greig, Sandy Jardine, Walter Smith and people like that who the fans can relate to and have confidence in."

Jardine, who is battling against cancer, sent McCoist a text message last night urging him to enjoy the title party.

And the Ibrox manager said: "That gesture just sums the man up."

Rangers kid Fraser Aird claimed beating Berwick felt like a Champions League night after his winner sparked a party in front of an Ibrox full house.

Gers fans turned out in force to watch their heroes be presented with the Third Division trophy at the end of a rollercoaster campaign.

And Aird's 32nd-minute header made sure Ally McCoist's men finished the season on a winning note.

The Wee Rangers also had something to celebrate as the defeat wasn't enough to rob them of a play-off spot.

It all made for a cracking atmosphere and Aird was thrilled to mark the occasion with his first Ibrox goal.

The 18-year-old winger said: "It was a brilliant experience for the boys playing in front of a sell-out crowd.

"It felt like a Champions League night out there. Scoring my first goal at Ibrox meant so much to me. To do it in such a big game meant even more.

"My job is to get in from the back post when crosses come into the box.

"That's all I did so I just had to dive and get my head on the end of it."

Aird was born in Canada and the youngster was thrilled to give his family something to cheer as they ate their breakfast in Toronto.

He said: "I have family here but others back home were watching on TV.

"They go to the Toronto No.1 Supporters Club and put on a big breakfast to watch the game. There are quite a number of folk over there watching me.

"Winning is a big weight lifted off our shoulders. We won the league a couple of weeks ago but to finally get the trophy and our medals means a lot.

"It's the first championship for a lot of the lads in the squad but hopefully there are a lot more to come."

The winger has been one of several kids thrown in by boss McCoist this season but Aird would welcome more competition for places next term.

He said: "Hopefully the gaffer does bring in older boys. It was the experienced lads who took us over the line this season.

"Guys such as Lee McCulloch and Neil Alexander have done it before.

"We want to win the championship next year so it would be good if he brought guys in while keeping the balance with youth. It has been a long journey. For us boys to get a chance has been brilliant.

"I don't think any of us would have thought at the start of the season that this would happen to us.

"But we have to take this with us and move on now."

The match itself won't live long in the memory as the teams struggled for form in difficult conditions.

Apart from the swirling wind, both sets of players had to wade through the toilet rolls and balloons thrown on the pitch before the game.

David Templeton was lively from the start and was hauled down on the edge of the box after a great piece of skill.

But the former Hearts star fired the free-kick wildly over.

The deciding goal came when Kyle Hutton drifted over to the left and swung in a cross that was guided into the far corner

Third Division

WALKING ON AIRD

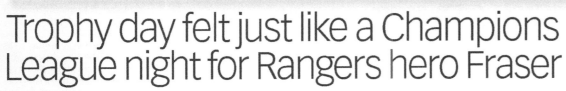

Trophy day felt just like a Champions League night for Rangers hero Fraser

by winger Aird. Everyone could have gone home happily after that – especially Berwick who needed to avoid an eight-goal swing with play-off rivals Elgin entertaining East Stirling.

Andy Mitchell's 30-yarder had Berwick keeper Marc McCallum scrambling across goal as it slipped narrowly wide.

The minnows then had a reasonable shout for a penalty when Damian Gielty was clipped by Ian Black as he burst into the box.

There were other opportunities for the Shielfield men with Scott Dalziel seeing his header saved by Alexander.

And Berwick midfielder Steven Notman – who celebrated becoming a dad in midweek – had a couple of long-range efforts which were not far off the mark.

But Rangers had plenty of chances to kill the game off and youngster Lewis Macleod weaved his way into the box before firing inches wide.

Sub Kane Hemmings also poked the ball over from close range and in the dying minutes there was a chance for skipper Lee McCulloch to get on the scoresheet. Hutton's shot was blocked by McCallum and McCulloch latched on to the rebound. He managed to get round the keeper but Andy McLean was back to cover and blocked his shot.

It was party time for both camps at full time and Berwick took the salute from their loyal fans as they celebrated clinching a play-off spot with six goals to spare over Elgin.

McCulloch then received the Third Division trophy before McCoist took the microphone and delivered the words the Ibrox faithful wanted to hear.

He told them how he had received a good luck text the previous night from club legend Sandy Jardine then praised the fans by saying: "You guys have shown a support without which this club would never have survived.

"The lifeline of our great football club is every one of you in this stadium.

"With your support along the way we will get back to where we belong."

The Ibrox boss accepted there had been stutters along the way but pointed out his side won the title by 24 points when they had started pre-season with just six players and were still waiting for a licence to play on the eve of the campaign.

He added: "That is stage one complete for the club now."

McCoist then told the punters they will be ready for stage two and vowed to bring players in after the club's transfer embargo was lifted in September.

Yesterday's attendance of 50,048 was a Third Division record and McCoist added to roars from the Ibrox legions: "We are the only club who can do that. We are the people."

SILVER LINING McCulloch lifts the trophy (from top) before Hemmings, Naismith, Little, Aird, Templeton and Hutton get their hands on it

Rangers 3 Stranraer 0

Lee: No need to bring in players

■ Gordon Parks

Lee McCulloch insists Rangers don't need a squad revamp to win the Championship title.

After lifting the League One trophy yesterday, the skipper swore the current squad is strong enough to reach the top flight.

McCulloch is adamant they will build on their success even with the same faces in place next season.

He said: "We will be a better team again and I believe we can win the title with the players we have.

"I'm only talking for the dressing room but we'd be confident of winning the title and going back to the top flight where we belong.

"We must be confident. We have taken 101 points and scored more than 100 goals and know next season we will be in a more competitive league.

"With the new players

PRIDE Lee McCulloch

getting through their first season along with the young boys who have progressed, it's been a massive plus."

McCulloch said the players were fired up to beat Stranraer and dedicate the win to the memory of Sandy Jardine. He said: "It was a day of mixed emotions and a great turnout by the fans.

"Getting the win and dedicating it to Sandy was brilliant and the dressing room is happy about that.

"It's been a bit of a wait but when you lift a trophy in front of a full house at Ibrox, it doesn't feel any better than that.

"But it has also been sad. The players spoke before the game about going out and getting a win because that is what Sandy would have wanted.

"What a man he was. He will be sorely missed around Ibrox and at Murray Park."

WE'RE TWO GOOD Arnold Peralta (left) beams after hitting his first Rangers goal before Dean Shiels celebrates strike No.3

Gers turn their title party into touching tribute to Sandy

A DAY 2 TREASURE

BIG DADDY Ally McCoist gives son Arran a lift as the title party begins

Trophy day started with tears of sorrow as Ibrox grieved the loss of Sandy Jardine.

An afternoon of remembrance and tribute was fittingly marked with a Rangers victory to honour a legend's memory.

Strikes from Fraser Aird, Arnold Peralta and Dean Shiels also propelled Ally McCoist's side through the 100-point barrier for the season.

But as is often the case with this club in recent times, most of the attention focused on events off the pitch.

This time though it was about dignified respect rather than protest amid the financial mayhem.

The big screens beamed a short montage of clips from the

Gordon Parks
Ibrox

life and times of a club legend to the tune of Simply the Best in a poignant prelude to an afternoon originally dedicated to the delivery of the League One trophy.

But celebrations temporarily took a back seat as club and fans remembered a player who typified the traditions and values of this institution.

Rangers players filtered out of the tunnel in a dignified tribute to the man who lost his battle with cancer on Thursday, all wearing Jardine's No.2 on their shorts.

As the stadium hushed for a minute's silence, it was clear this was a day to put boardroom affairs to one side in favour of muted respect and reflection.

Quiet gave way to rapturous applause which boomed across the stadium in the second minute in another fitting show of the affection with which Jardine is held among fans.

The opening was slick and sharp from the hosts and Steven Smith's drilled cross was met by the head of Jon Daly but David Mitchell parried the effort to safety.

Seconds later the Stranraer keeper rushed out to block Dean Shiels' shot.

Rangers were determined their coronation wouldn't fall flat and Law rifled the ball inches wide as the Stranraer backline began to creak.

Stranraer's last visit to Ibrox on Boxing Day brought a last-minute goal to earn a point but uncertain,

turgid and uninspiring displays look to be a thing of the past for McCoist's men.

Aird's corner in 21 minutes was half cleared by David McGregor and Law thundered a shot over the top from the edge of the box.

A Daly attempt was deflected off Scott Robertson and clipped the bar on its way for a corner but for all of their possession, Rangers were misfiring when it mattered most and another Smith cross found its way to Arnold Peralta but his wild effort from 18 yards sailed over.

The football at least provided a distraction from a turbulent few days for the club with the death of a legend and the fall-out from chief executive Graham Wallace's 120-day review but there was little appetite for protest.

Even a mild-mannered rendition

League One

WE ONE THE LEAGUE Rangers players kick off an Ibrox party after collecting the League One trophy

STRIKE ONE Aird rifles in the opener (top) before legends Johnny Hubbard and Bobby Brown bring out the league trophy

of Sack the Board from the Govan Stand failed to gather momentum.

The mood among the support lightened eight minutes from the break when Rangers at last found a cutting edge.

Aird took a pass from Law before dropping a shoulder which left Robertson bewildered and provided time to explode a shot past Mitchell from 20-yards.

But there almost a twist before half-time when a corner from the right found Frank McKeown unmarked at the back post but the defender failed to hit the target when he should have.

It was a warning which should have been heeded after Stranraer's previous trip to Glasgow.

Bilel Mohsni surged forward in 56 minutes and his shot was well held by Mitchell as Rangers fought to extend their lead. And they didn't

have long to wait as Peralta hit his first goal for the club.

Aird burst through the middle then released the Honduran on the right and he strode into the box and slipped a shot under Mitchell.

Aird went agonisingly close with a 30-yard effort which flew inches wide before Rangers hit their third.

The much improved Smith arched a cross in from the left which found Shiels whose header was parried by Mitchell and the Northern Irishman followed up to stab home from close range.

Kyle Hutton rattled the bar with a shot before the end as Gers cruised towards the final whistle and the trophy presentation.

Then it was on with the party, but amid the joy, thoughts were still wandering towards Sandy Jardine.

East Fife 1
Brechin City 2

Dougie Anderson rued the Fifers' lack of class as they failed to nail the play-off spot at the basement.

The Methil men now face Ayr in their bid to beat the drop with bottom side Arbroath a point behind.

Andy Jackson and Alan Trouten struck to wrap up the win for City before Pat Clarke replied late on.

Coach Anderson said: "We lacked a bit of quality and need to go again."

Stenh'muir 1
Airdrie 2

Boss Scott Booth admitted Stenny blew the chance to shape their own play-off fate with this defeat.

Scott Stewart and Craig Barr netted for Airdie and Sean Dickson hit back.

Stenny must now win at Brechin on the final day and hope East Fife beat Ayr to finish in the top four.

Booth said: "We had an opportunity to keep it in our hands but are relying on other results now."

TOP GEGG Pars ace Andy Geggan celebrates his winner

I'M SHEER WE'LL GET TO STAY UP

Arbroath ....1 Dunf'line 2   ■ Ewan Smith

Paul Sheerin insists Arbroath can outgun fellow strugglers East Fife on the final day to avoid automatic relegation.

The Red Lichties travel to Airdrie next weekend knowing they must win and hope East Fife slip up at Ayr to sneak ninth spot.

And while Arbroath are a point behind the Fifers – after Andy Geggan's late winner cancelled out defender Michael Travis' equaliser following Pars ace Ryan Thomson's opener – Gayfield Park gaffer Sheerin is adamant the momentum is with his side.

He said: "We're disappointed to lose but we are still in it. I wanted to take it to the last day and ask questions of East Fife. They are a team who are struggling to score goals and we're not."

The visitors took the lead when Stephen Husband's 25-yard strike was spilled by keeper Scott Morrison into the path of Thomson who flicked into an empty net.

But within seven minutes of the re-start the Angus side got the leveller.

Bobby Linn's corner was met at the front post by Travis who bulleted home a header.

However, Geggan won it by squeezing home a Danny Grainger cross.

Pars boss Jim Jefferies said: "My players showed why they should be in my plans for the play-offs."

Loons have all to play-off for

Forfar Ath 4
Ayr Utd 2

Forfar kept their play-off hopes alive by seeing off promotion rivals Ayr.

Dale Hilson netted two, with Jamie McCluskey and Omar Kader also on target. Ayr replied with a Michael Moffat penalty and Brian Gilmour goal.

Forfar assistant Ian Campbell said: "It was a great performance." Ayr boss Mark Roberts said: "We were a shambles."

PETROFAC CUP GERS FINALLY END

HITTING THE MARK Warburton celebrates his first cup success at Gers

THE only thing on display at Hampden yesterday laying claims to be evergreen was Rangers striker Kenny Miller.

The former Scotland star rolled back the years as the national stadium bosses, disgracefully, were forced to roll back the dreadful playing surface for the second time in little more than a month.

The red, white and blue confetti hadn't even been swept from the threadbare, patchy pitch as the Light Blues celebrated their Petrofac Cup Final success before the tractors were moving in again.

An own goal from Ally Gilchrist and a stunning volley from James Tavernier, both in the first half and both inspired by Miller, helped ease Rangers to their second trophy of the season.

Andy Halliday's late penalty underlined the gap in standards between the sides before Miller, fittingly, slotted home the fourth in the last minute of the match.

Hampden bosses have been forced into the desperate pitch move ahead of next weekend's Scottish Cup semi-finals in a bid to give the showpiece fixtures the high-class horticulture they deserve.

Replacing a playing surface and hoping it beds in after only five days represents a bigger gamble than lumping your hard earned on the Blue Toon to win yesterday at 8-1 as the quality between both squads told.

The pitch at the national stadium has now been laid more times than Charlie Sheen – a legacy, in part, of a controversial 20-year lease negotiated in 1999 with Queen's Park by those with a foot in both camps that allowed the amateurs the right to play every week on the hallowed turf.

Now? Scottish football's neutral acre is more cursed than clipped.

And it remains to be seen if the SPFL will be in a rush to pay the bill for hiring the old ground as the quality of the rush job on the playing surface before last month's League Cup Final is called into question.

Let's face it, who'd pay top whack for the honeymoon suite when rusty springs are poking through the mattress of the divan?

Rangers boss Mark Warburton remains in the first flushes of love with his club's support, who celebrated the winning of this modest trinket as if was one of the game's major prizes.

However, these fans have been through such wretched times these last five years few would deny them their moment in the spring sunshine.

This was another step in the right direction – and their first win in the competition in four previous attempts.

Barring a disaster, for Rangers it was

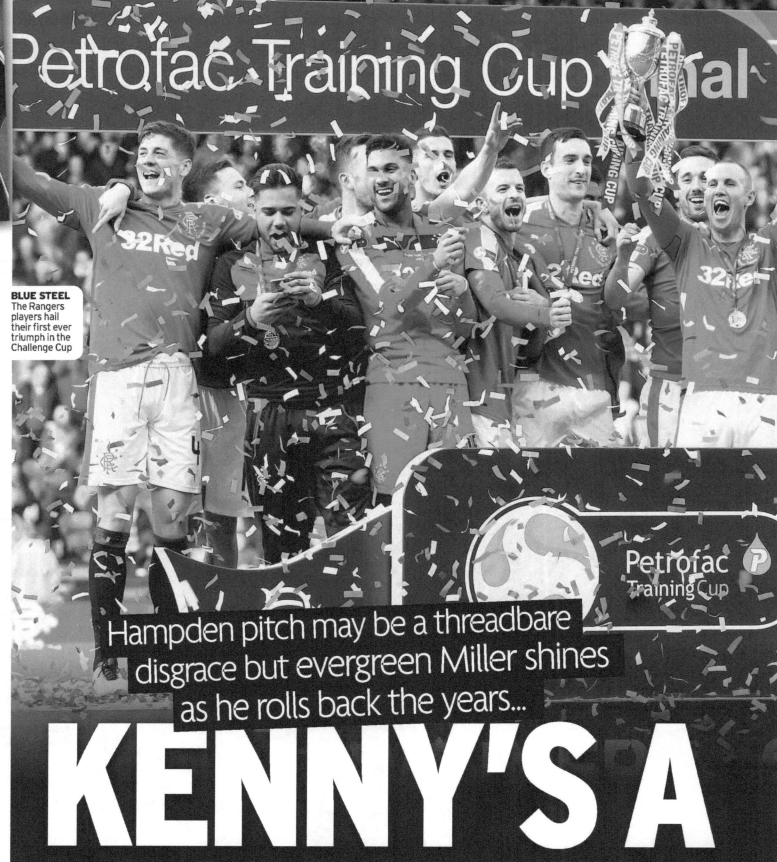

BLUE STEEL The Rangers players hail their first ever triumph in the Challenge Cup

Hampden pitch may be a threadbare disgrace but evergreen Miller shines as he rolls back the years...

KENNY'S A

►► RANGERS..4 PETERHEAD..0

GARY RALSTON AT HAMPDEN

always destined be a dress rehearsal for Sunday's Old Firm clash and they are now free to concentrate on Celtic, even if the sight of Harry Forrester limping off midway through the second half caused concern.

He was replaced by Billy King and, with one eye already on facing down the Scottish champions, Lee Wallace was also taken off and replaced by Michael O'Halloran as Rangers eased their way through the second half.

In truth, it was all very low key until

another late flourish, with much of the second half being played on the Ibrox men's terms, at training ground pace, as they preserved their energy for their next visit to Mount Florida, which will be slightly more raucous.

Peterhead worked hard to avoid the ignominy of a five or six-goal defeat that wouldn't have needed a translation from Gaelic on BBC Alba to be described as a drubbing in front of a crowd of 48,133.

For their part, Rangers did what they

had to do without ever scaling the heights they have shown at times this season en route to the Championship and their place in the last four of the Scottish Cup.

Miller ensured their nerves were settled as early as the 17th minute when he burst clear into the box down the left-hand side and delivered a wicked, low cross that was turned past keeper Graeme Smith by Blue Toon defender Gilchrist at the front post.

Until then Jim McInally's side had been compact and competitive but in their desire to squeeze space in the middle of the park they left gaps in behind, which Rangers exploited.

The only surprise was it took

Warburton's side until five minutes before half-time to add to their lead.

Although it was a goal well worth the wait as Rangers again made hay down the left-hand side.

This time Wallace's cross broke to Barrie McKay, who fed the ball back to Miller, who thought of shooting before hooking the ball over his shoulder to Tavernier.

The full-back didn't hesitate as he thundered a glorious first-time volley high past the helpless Smith from 25 yards.

Peterhead had neither the confidence nor know-how to persistently trouble the Rangers defence, although Jason Holt was alert

►► **Replacing a playing surface and hoping it beds in after five days is a bigger gamble**

DROUGHT AS THEY EASE TO TROPHY

Petrofac Training Cup

>> 1-0

ON ALL FOURS Gilchrist lies dejected, Tavernier nets and Halliday fires a penalty

>> 2-0

>> 3-0

GRASS ACT

>> 4-0

RUN OF MILL Kenny Miller caps off a top display with the fourth

to block a goalbound header from Scott Ross on the line three minutes before half-time before Tavernier cleared the danger.

Sub Nicky Riley also fired into the side net after an hour – the small knot of around 1500 Blue Toon fans saw the billowing of the net and thought he had scored but their cheers were in vain.

Sadly for the Balmoor bridgade it would be the last time in the game they would become so animated as Rangers worked through the gears and underlined their superiority with two late goals.

Holt's mazy run into the box in 85 minutes ended with him being upended by Steven Noble and the penalty award

was inevitable, with Halliday slotting the spot-kick confidently inside Smith's right-hand post.

Halliday had earlier missed a header from point-blank range and Smith also denied him with a brilliant block, with the former Ibrox keeper also keeping out a header from Miller.

However, the Gers striker would not be denied and was well placed at the back post to slot home the fourth in 89 minutes after a cross from O'Halloran had been put into his path by Halliday.

It left only a lap of honour for the Rangers players to undertake as they walked around the pitch to the sounds of Penny Arcade but the biggest gamble on this wretched grass is about to come.

than tipping Peterhead to win yesterday

man by man

RANGERS

WES FODERINGHAM   7
Defence in front of him gave him a couple of headaches but nothing too stressful.

ROB KIERNAN   6
Had a pretty comfortable afternoon but did suffer from the odd lapse in concentration.

DANNY WILSON   6
Strolled through the game and didn't give Rory McAllister much of a sniff.

LEE WALLACE   7
Wasn't charging up the park quite as much as usual and was disciplined at the back before being rested.

DOMINIC BALL   7
Shielded his back four and didn't muck about with the ball in a tight midfield area.

ANDY HALLIDAY   7
Produced a couple of impressive bursts into the box and deserved his goal from the spot.

JASON HOLT   7
Buzzed around just off the front and made a great drive into the box to win the penalty.

HARRY FORRESTER   7
Trickery and pace caused problems in the first half but taken off with a view to Sunday.

BARRIE MCKAY   7
Surface hardly ideal for his game but held the ball up neatly and brought others into play.

KENNY MILLER   7
Did the damage to earn the opening goal and was always a threat in the penalty area.

SUBSTITUTES

MICHAEL O'HALLORAN   5
His pace was a boost as game became stretched.

BILLY KING   5
Was always keen to get on the ball.

DEAN SHIELS   5
Looked determined to make an impression.

star man

JAMES TAVERNIER   8
The Rangers defender was at his rampaging best and scored a wonder goal that would not have been out of place on any stage.

PETERHEAD

GRAEME SMITH   7
Made a terrific save in the first half and had no chance with any of the goals.

SCOTT ROSS   7
Had his hands full but never gave his opponents any peace on the ball.

ALLY GILCHRIST   6
Horror own goal but recovered to put in an impressive shift to keep Rangers at bay.

RYAN STRACHAN   4
Was up against it early on before his day was ruined by a first-half injury.

STEVEN NOBLE   7
Ran himself into the ground in the middle and constantly chased down his opponents.

SIMON FERRY   6
Always looked to be positive with the ball but could have done with more service.

JAMIE REDMAN   6
Bust a gut to keep his side in the game and was eventually replaced.

JORDON BROWN   6
More involved after the break and found some decent areas in and around the box.

SHANE SUTHERLAND   6
Tried to get up to support the front man and dug in deep when needed.

RORY MCALLISTER   6
Posed a threat whenever he got in the box but was limited to just a couple of half chances.

SUBSTITUTES

JAMIE STEVENSON   6
Slotted in and looked solid throughout.

NICKY REILLY   5
Came close when he hit side netting.

LEIGHTON MCINTOSH   5
Added energy to his side late on.

star man

KEVIN DZIERZAWSKI   7
The young American put in a solid performance in the middle of the park as he pressed and challenged for every ball.

email ✉ reporters@sundaymail.co.uk

Rangers 1 Alloa 1

GIVING

He might only have played a tiny part in Rangers' celebrations.

But it was fitting that the club's biggest legend, John Greig, dished out their Championship medals.

The man voted "greatest ever Ranger" by supporters has been absent from Ibrox for the majority of the past four years.

In the dark days of administration, liquidation and bottom-tier football, Greig was treated shamefully.

But after being brought back by new owner Dave King earlier this season, he was on the podium yesterday as Mark Warburton's side picked up the league trophy.

And Greig's return, met with a rousing reception, was symbolic of the club being back where they belong in the country's top league.

This was their last home game of a tumultuous journey to the Premiership and it was only right that Greig was involved.

Iconic figures such as

Greig back in his rightful place

Scott McDermott

Walter Smith and Brian Laudrup were also in attendance but there was no sign of ex-boss Ally McCoist.

Irrespective of his talents as a gaffer and his failure to get Gers out of this division last year, McCoist's efforts shouldn't be forgotten.

And King should ensure he's also welcomed back next term.

Skipper Lee Wallace lifted the trophy in front of a packed stadium after a rather flat draw with Alloa.

Amidst the fireworks and confetti, in typical Greig fashion he slipped off into the background and allowed Warburton to take the plaudits.

But his presence on the pitch wasn't lost on defender Danny Wilson who hailed the influence he has at the club.

The centre-back said: "It was fitting that John was here to give us our medals.

"He's always about the place and giving us pelters! But I'm delighted he was here.

"When I was a kid here, John was always around at Murray Park and Ibrox. He's not there so much now.

"But he was always a great help and an inspiring figure for the young boys to look up to.

"It was nice to have that kind of experienced and successful figure to put his arm around me and tell me what I did or didn't need to do.

"So it is great that he is now back at the club."

Alloa didn't exactly spoil Rangers' party – but they certainly put a dampener on the title celebrations.

After losing at Hibs in midweek, Warburton's side produced another slack display.

Just a week after beating Celtic at Hampden and off the back of their Championship and Petrofac Cup success, it was maybe to be expected.

But Wilson knows Gers will have to stay mentally attuned if they're to cap a dream season by beating the Hibees on May 21 to lift the Scottish Cup.

He said: "That was nowhere near where we've been all

Jack hails his party poopers

Proud Alloa gaffer Jack Ross heaped praise on his part-time players for putting a dampener on Rangers' title party.

A crowd of over 50,000 packed Ibrox but the relegated Wasps defended brilliantly to hold out for a deserved 1-1 draw.

Ross said: "The players knew that if they didn't produce a performance full of energy and commitment it could be a long and very difficult afternoon.

"Although they're part-time, the players here have a huge amount of professional pride.

"I don't think we got carved open too many times which was to our credit."

HIGH PRIZE Gers lift trophy (right) and party (from top left) as Greig (below left) dishes out medals

LEGEND

as Gers land trophy

season. And it put a wee dampener on the day. Last Sunday was such a high but a defeat and a draw since then has put us on a bit of a downer.

"We need to stay mentally focused for the cup final. But if you can't motivate yourself for that game, you're not worth your salt as a footballer.

"We HAVE to win it. That will be enough motivation for us."

Motivation looked a problem against the Wasps though.

The highlight yesterday was James Tavernier breaking a record held by Greig and the late Sandy Jardine for goals scored by a Rangers defender in a season.

The Englishman's 15th of a terrific campaign cancelled out Michael Duffy's early opener but Gers failed to build on

Tavernier's header and the game itself was a curious affair.

"You sensed that for the Ibrox punters, the 90 minutes was just getting in the way of a lap of honour.

But credit to Jack Ross' relegated side. Sure, they were pinned back for long spells and their midfielders chased shadows all afternoon.

But they defended brilliantly and former Gers keeper Scott Gallacher was in fine form.

When they got a chance – a solitary opportunity after eight minutes – they took it.

Andy Halliday's woeful back pass allowed on-loan Celtic kid Duffy in on goal and he tucked it away superbly.

It was a backs-to-the-wall job after that and they were helped by Warburton's men being far from their best.

It looked like Rangers would find their

equaliser from the spot. But Halliday's afternoon got worse when he fired wide after Barrie McKay had been upended by Kyle McAusland.

The midfielder, who has been one of Warburton's top performers, made amends just before the break when his cross found Tavernier who nodded home from close range at the back post.

That should have been the catalyst for the home side to rack up more in the second half.

But while Alloa defended stoutly there was a unusual lethargy about Rangers.

And that will worry their manager just four weeks before that Scottish Cup Final.

This end-of-season stroll is reminiscent of 1994 when Walter Smith's all-conquering Rangers team were going for a 'double Treble'.

With the title wrapped up long before the Scottish Cup Final, they ended up losing 1-0 to Dundee United at Hampden.

It's a warning to Warburton's class of 2016 but no one can argue they aren't worthy champions.

Champs won't be slackers

From **Back Page**

simply can't happen as they prepare to meet Hibs at Hampden on May 21 with a Europa League spot at stake. Warburton said: "It's important to get it right.

"We'll give the players four days off after the final league game. Any longer is dangerous as they get into holiday mode.

"Then we'll get them back in and try to keep them sharp. The week up to the final will be the same as always and it's important to finish the season on a high.

"Hopefully we will deliver a performance at Hampden because there's European football at stake too. That's a big thing for the club so we'll go all out to win that trophy.

"We wanted to avoid being flat after last week but we highlighted it as a possibility.

"The players had their own inquest at half-time today. It wasn't good enough and captain Lee Wallace spoke tremendously well about falling below standards.

"The fact the players are arguing among themselves speaks volumes and bodes well for the future. They know they have to deliver the highest of standards. But after winning the league, the Petrofac and last Sunday, maybe it's a natural reaction.

"We need to pick it up pretty quickly – but we will."

Warburton was thrilled to clutch the trophy and that Ibrox legend John Greig handed out the medals. He said: "It was good that the players got their rewards.

"When you get them, you have to enjoy it. It's great for the fans too. It means we're back in the top flight and we've got to savour that.

"It was special to have John out there, because of his status within the club."

I'm hungrier than ever after losing Queens crown

James Fowler insists his shock Queen of the South exit has only made him hungrier for success.

The 35-year-old was relieved of his duties last week, despite keeping the Palmerston club safe in the Championship.

Fowler is convinced he's a better manager for the experience and is eager to get back in the game as soon as possible.

He left despite enjoying a good relationship with Queens chairman Billy Hewitson and the board.

MailSport understands the decision to part company was made after discussions regarding next season's budget and expectations.

Fowler expressed his gratitude to Hewitson for handing him his first managerial role – and believes he has left the club in a healthy state.

The former Kilmarnock midfielder reduced the age of the squad, improved their scouting and analysis network and had the club challenging for a play-off spot.

And he's adamant kids such as Jake Pickard and Jordan Marshall will be huge assets in the future.

Now Fowler is ready to enhance his own growing reputation elsewhere.

He told *MailSport*: "I'm as hungry and ambitious as ever. The last two years haven't even scratched the surface in terms of my education as a manager.

"When I reflect, I might think I should have done a few things differently.

"But I tried to play an attractive style of football. Look at the success Rangers have had this season.

"I've had messages and calls from managers complimenting the way we tried to play.

"I'd like to get back in as soon as possible. I've had positive messages from people in the game, which gives me encouragement

Scott McDermott
EXCLUSIVE

for the future.

"It has made me more determined to get back in at the right club, with the right ambitions."

After a terrific first season, Fowler found it tougher this term after losing key men Gavin Reilly, Mark Durnan, Kevin Holt, Ian McShane and Danny Carmichael.

Despite wholesale changes, he introduced talented kids as well as keeping the club competitive in the league.

He said: "This was always going to be a transitional season.

"It takes time to bed everyone in after losing so many players.

"But half of the squad was 21 or under.

"That was the profile of player we tried to bring in.

"So I feel I've left the club in a good position, with good foundations.

"Lewis Kidd is a year more experienced.

"Marshall will pick up Player of the Year awards at 18 this season.

"He has been a standout and Pickard, another 18-year-old, has also played 24 games.

"We were building for the future but at the same time juggling it to try and get consistent results.

"It's disappointing not to see the job through."

Assistant Gavin Skelton has taken charge with Jim Thomson until the end of the season with Queens winning 3-1 against Livingston yesterday.

And Fowler said: "I'll always be grateful for the chance Queens gave me.

"Now I hope Gavin is given the chance to continue the rebuild we started. I wish the club every success."

TEAMS

Rangers –

Foderingham	6
Tavernier	7
Kiernan	6
Wilson	6
Wallace	6
Halliday	5
King	6
Zelalem	6
Holt	6
McKay	7
Clark	5

Subs: Burt 2, Shiels 3, Miller 3

Alloa –

Gallacher	8
McAusland	7
Hill	7
Hamilton	8
Marr	7
Duffy	7
Caddis	5
Flannigan	6
Hetherington	6
Holmes	5
Megginson	6

Subs: Layne 2, Ferns 2, McManus 3.

StatZone

Rangers		Alloa
	75 ⚽ **25**	

Analysis

Rangers		Alloa
10	Shots on	2
16	Shots off	2
14	Corners	0
7	Fouls	8
0	Bookings	3

★Ref watch

CRAIG CHARLESTON got penalty spot on and his bookings right. 7/10.

★ Man of the match

SCOTT GALLAGHER pulled off a string of good saves against his former club.

HIBS FALTER AS BAIRNS SNATCH POINT AT RAITH

SEE PAGE 73

GERRARD AT RANGERS

GREAT MOVE Souness

Gerrard will bring Ibrox spark back says Souey

BY ALAN MARSHALL

IBROX legend Graeme Souness last night backed Steven Gerrard to "electrify" Rangers.

Gerrard is following in the footsteps of Souness who became Gers boss in 1986 after achieving iconic status as a Liverpool player.

And the former Scotland skipper is thrilled at Gerrard's arrival on a four-year deal although he admits the 37-year-old has his work cut out in his first managerial role.

Souness said: "I'm delighted because I'm a Rangers supporter and he'll electrify the situation up there. We need something.

"I wish him luck. It's not going to be easy but he's joining a great club.

"He's a lucky man, as I was, to have worked for both Liverpool and Rangers - two institutions. You realise what passion there is in Glasgow, it's a very special place to work."

Gerrard's managerial experience extends only to this season as boss of Liverpool's Under-18s.

Souness added: "He'll learn from his mistakes and that's how it should be.

"He has been a top player for a long time but I'm not sure how much that will help him in management.

"It is such a different job. The responsibilities you feel as manager are enormous."

BY GARY RALSTON

THE big hoose stayed opened - and almost 8000 fans flooded into Ibrox yesterday to welcome Steven Gerrard as the new Rangers boss.

Ian Durrant lost his song in the process as the Light Blues legions hailed their new blue and white dynamite to the tune they used to dedicate to their former midfield marvel.

They left with beaming smiles an hour after flooding in as Gerrard vowed entering the ground with a spring in their step will soon be commonplace.

For much of the season Rangers fans have trudged out as Pedro Caixinha and then Graeme Murty oversaw the club's worst league record at home in more than a century.

There are challenges ahead, as Gerrard was quick to acknowledge, but there was a deliberate refusal to linger on the domestic dominance Celtic have enjoyed over the last seven seasons.

Gerrard underlined his priorities like a general rallying his troops as he focused on repairing the damage to fortress Ibrox.

He said: "Where I sit right now it's not the right time and place for me to talk about Celtic. There will be plenty of time for that when we move forward and start the challenge of the new season.

"My priority is Rangers and this house. I need to get this house in order. I need to produce a team and squad capable of winning games.

"I want supporters to skip into this place to watch and be proud and to see we can take the team and club forward and make it competitive.

"The supporters are THE main thing here, not just one of the main things. My relationship with

WELCOME PARTY Gerrard is greeted by an adoring public at his Ibrox bow yesterday

> "
> The fans are THE main thing here and a big reason I've come
>
> STEVEN GERRARD

CHEER WE GO New Rangers boss Gerrard salutes the fans

those supporters, if I can get them with me, if I can create a team they are proud of, that they look forward to coming here to watch – then we'll be in a good place.

"The supporters were a big reason I wanted to come here and be a leader for them. Their loyalty and how they've stuck by this club are values I believe in.

"I can't wait to be out there leading this team in front of them. That's my priority, not what Celtic have been doing. For us to come out on top we need to sort Rangers out first."

Gerrard has been coach of Liverpool's Under-18s for only a season and has no top-flight management experience. But if prior knowledge was a prerequisite for any new adventure they would never have put a man on the moon.

For every Kenny Dalglish and Graeme Souness there's a John Barnes but the former England captain doesn't doubt his ability to succeed. Gerrard said: "Inexperience is not an issue for me. It seems to be an issue for other people but I can't control that.

"I have been around a big club for a long time, I've been around big matches, I've watched big managers perform and I've worked under big managers.

"I can't do anything about having no experience where I sit right now. There's only one way to get experience and that is to believe in yourself that you have the right

HOME REPAIR JOB

Rangers first

...I'll worry about Celts later says boss Stevie

LET'S GO SAYS NEW GAFFER

From Back Page

next month. He will be joined by former Scotland skipper Gary McAllister and Rangers fans have already rallied behind their new management team after almost 8000 turned up to form a welcoming committee on Edmiston Drive.

Commitments with Liverpool, where he is academy coach, and pundit duties with BT Sport will prevent Gerrard taking in today's match against Kilmarnock at Ibrox.

But he has promised his new support the good times will roll again as he swatted aside fears around his lack of experience in top-flight football management.

Asked for a message to his new supporters, Gerrard said: "Let's go – I'm looking forward to the fun we can have together.

"I have confidence in myself and my ability.

"I have weighed the gamble up and the risk and I have confidence that I can deliver for these supporters.

"The only thing that matters to me is if I think I can do a good job as the manager of Glasgow Rangers. In my mind, it's yes.

"My parents brought me up to always front a challenge. Go and front it up and give it your best shot. That's exactly what I'm going to do here.

"Pressure's not a bad thing. I played under pressure, I have lived under pressure since I left school. In football if you are working under pressure you are in a good place.

"I know, as Rangers manager, there will be a lot of scrutiny but that's what I love about the game. Bring it on. I'm up for the challenge and I will do my best."

Rangers chairman Dave King has offered Gerrard reassurances of the budget

STEVIE SCOOP How we broke the news of Gerrard's arrival yesterday

available to him from June 1 as he bids to mount a more credible title challenge to Celtic than previous bosses Mark Warburton and Pedro Caixinha.

Gerrard said: "There was a lot of positivity around the club's ambition, which matches mine. I have a confidence I can deliver and I'm very excited about it."

McAllister started his career at Motherwell and has long had a soft spot for Rangers.

It's understood Anfield coach Michael Beale will also join Gerrard at Ibrox.

Beale has coached at the Liverpool Academy and also worked with the Brazilian outfit Sao Paulo.

And it's understood Gerrard will raid the Reds for 18-year-old Welsh forward Ben Woodman and 21-year-old Welsh midfielder Harry Wilson.

Gerrard said: "Mark Allen (Rangers' director of football) and I have had a couple of brief chats but it is early days in terms of the recruitment process. In the coming weeks and months we will certainly be having lots of discussions in trying to help the current squad capable of competing."

» GERS CHIEF: I'LL HAND OVER KING-SIZED KITTY

SEE PAGES 64&65

---

characteristics to take the challenge head on.

"One day I'll be experienced and I have confidence this journey will help me.

"A huge opportunity presented itself. I'm very aware of Rangers and the size of the club. I have watched them from afar for many years and been lucky enough to come up and sample some of the Old Firm games.

"I'm a human being so I'm going to make mistakes. I've made plenty in my playing career and this season as a

coach. But I see mistakes as opportunities to grow and learn. I believe in the staff I'm bringing with me.

"I'm not perfect but will put people around me to support me, to complement where I need help and guidance. As a team we will park the egos up and front it together."

His football skills have made Gerrard a wealthy man and his punditry work with BT Sport pays enough to top up a pension that won't exactly be at the level of the minimum state provision. He

could have sat comfortably on Merseyside, played golf and watched games at the Parc des Princes and Bernabeu from the comfort of a TV studio rather than swapping Madrid and Paris for Motherwell and Pittodrie.

Gerrard added: "From when I first signed as a professional at Liverpool I've competed for three important points, that's been the buzz.

"Since my playing days ended I've really missed it.

"I've been around some talented players at the

Liverpool academy and enjoyed it and I've done a lot of learning in the last 12 months. But I always knew one day I wanted to compete for three important points.

"I wanted to feel that pressure, the buzz again of coming in on a Monday morning to prepare for the game on a Saturday. That's what I loved most about my life when I was a player.

"I've learned an awful lot from world-class managers and I've worked around other top coaches as well."

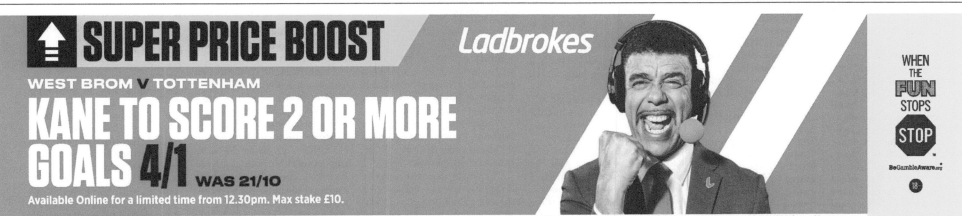

email ✉ reporters@sundaymail.co.uk

BIG MATCH SPECIAL

PARTY players celebrate with fans outside

'Millimetres' from crown

Alfredo Morelos even continued the party from a window ledge at Ibrox as the Colombian striker cracked open a beer in anticipation of an imminent title win.

Gerrard admits it's now difficult to contain his excitement, with the gaffer on the verge of securing legendary status at the club.

He said: "We're now millimetres from being champions but we'll try to stay humble.

"It's tough because we're so close and it's been a long journey over the three years.

"There have been highs and lows but I've just walked into a happy dressing-room because we're so close now.

"When I turned up at the stadium it was emotional. You could see on the fans' faces what it meant.

"How are my emotions now?

"Bubbling. I'm really happy and proud.

"At the same time I want to stay controlled because it's not confirmed as of yet.

"But everyone knows it's 99.99 per cent done.

"Because of what's going on in the world right now, it's difficult to get carried away and celebrate for real.

"I'm trying to keep a lid on things."

That will be especially hard for the fans who broke Covid lockdown rules to gather at Ibrox and salute their heroes.

Gerrard's car was mobbed by fans on his way to the ground with flares and fireworks going off around him.

He says he's well aware of people's safety being the top priority.

But at the same time, he refused to condemn diehards who have been through the most turbulent period in the club's history. Gerrard

FROM BACK PAGE

said: "I've got to get my words right here because we are still involved in a pandemic.

"So it's important that fans try to stay safe. That's the priority.

"But at the same time, if you've got anything inside your heart, you understand what the fans have been through.

"It's my job to try and control that and safety is paramount.

"But it's tough as it has been an emotional three years for me.

"The fans have been here much longer than that, they've been through a lot in 10 years. So you can certainly understand it.

"We heard rumours about how it could be when we turned up. That can take you to an emotional place.

"Some of my new players haven't seen the supporters yet so it was a big eye-opener.

"But I had a good idea what it would be like. The day I turned up here on May 4, 2018, I didn't expect 8000 fans.

"So I had an idea that once we got that first big success what the reaction would be like."

The league flag could be sealed tomorrow if Celtic fail to beat Dundee United.

Gerrard revealed he and his players will have lunch together while the action unfolds on Tayside.

He said: "We'll come in for a recovery session and have lunch.

"I'm sure the game will be on. We'll see what happens.

"But the priority is getting ready for Thursday night against Slavia Prague in the Europa League. That's going to be a tough game, probably the most difficult so far."

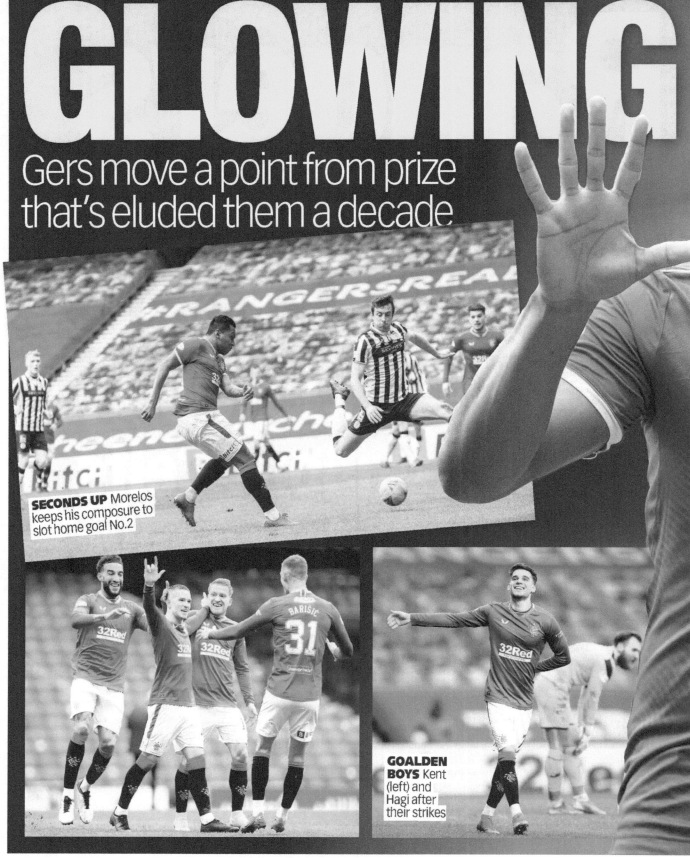

SECONDS UP Morelos keeps his composure to slot home goal No.2

GOALDEN BOYS Kent (left) and Hagi after their strikes

GLOWING
Gers move a point from prize that's eluded them a decade

Get the Champagne uncorked. Get the red, white and blue ribbons on the trophy.

RANGERS	3
ST MIRREN	0

SCOTT McDERMOTT AT IBROX

Steven Gerrard can even get that painter and decorator in at Auchenhowie now.

Because all of those 54s CAN now finally come off the walls at Rangers' training ground and be replaced by 55s.

Officially, his team might still be a point away from clinching the Scottish Premiership title.

But unofficially, it's done.

The Rangers players know it, Gerrard knows it – and the fans, who have craved this moment for a decade, certainly know it.

The Ibrox club can now afford to lose every one of the six games

they've got left and still win the crown on goal difference.

But that won't happen. And yesterday's win over St Mirren sealed it – irrespective of what happens at Tannadice today when Celtic face Dundee United.

Whether it's clinched on Tayside without kicking a ball or at Parkhead under their own steam in a fortnight, it's over.

Gerrard's side thoroughly deserve the acclaim that's coming their way. Goals from Ryan Kent, Alfredo Morelos and Ianis Hagi

secured yet another three points against the Buddies that kept Gers unbeaten in the league.

Gerrard said: "The performance was strong, really mature.

"It epitomised our season because we have played with maturity and control throughout.

"On a monumental day for the club, this is probably the most important three points we have delivered. It's another clean sheet and we could have won by more. Our goals were outstanding."

Outside before kick-off, the fans

started the party early. Thousands gathered to welcome their heroes with Gerrard's car getting its own guard of honour into the stadium.

The manager said: "It was vital we connected with what was going on outside, respected it, but at the same time didn't forget the game plan or what we had to do to get the three points."

St Mirren are the only side to defeat Rangers domestically so far this season in the League Cup.

But Jim Goodwin's men, who tried to get after the home side, could do little to stop them.

Gerrard made one change from the team who beat Livingston – recalling Hagi in place of Scott Arfield, with the Romanian's creativity required to break down the stubborn Saints. Goodwin's

SCOTTISH PREMIERSHIP

FOR 55

ALL THE FIVES Alf celebrates after taking Rangers to verge of 55

DRUM ROLL PLEASE fans outside Ibrox could sense the big occasion

32Red STAY IN CONTROL

⚽ THE STATS

■ TEAMS

RANGERS: McGregor 7, Patterson 7, Goldson 8, Helander 7 (Balogun 3), Barisic 7, Davis 7 (Arfield 3), Kamara 7, Aribo 7. Hagi 8 (Wright 3), Morelos 8 (Defoe 3), Kent 8 (Stewart 1).
ST MIRREN: Alnwick 7, Fraser 6, McCarthy 6, Shaughnessy 6, Tait 7, Connolly 5 (MacPherson 3), Doyle-Hayes 6, Erhahon 6 (Reid 1), McGrath 5 (Flynn 3), Durmus 5 (McAllister 4), Quaner 5 (Obika 4).
REFEREE: Steven McLean 6.

■ ANALYSIS

RANGERS		ST MIRREN
68	POSSESSION	32
7	SHOTS ON	1
3	SHOTS OFF	4
7	CORNERS	6
12	FOULS	10
1	BOOKINGS	2
0	REDCARDS	0

■ MAN OF THE MATCH

Rangers' front three grabbed the goals and headlines but **CONNOR GOLDSON** is the beating heart of this side. Rock solid at the back, the stand-in skipper shouted, cajoled and set the standard throughout.

We'd no answer to Gers

■ Scott McDermott

Jim Goodwin admits St Mirren couldn't live with red-hot Rangers at Ibrox.

The Buddies gaffer refused to criticise his team after their defeat to the champions-elect.

Goals from Ryan Kent, Alfredo Morelos and Ianis Hagi sealed the win for Steven Gerrard's men, who are now just a point from the Premiership title.

Goodwin believes Gers are worthy champs.

The Saints boss said: "Rangers were excellent. We couldn't handle their rotation in forward areas.

"They seemed to have time and space. It wasn't a lack of effort from us – sometimes you have to say the other team were better.

"We'd hoped they would have an off day but we knew they wouldn't with what was at stake.

"Rangers deserve all the pats on the back they've

GOODWIN outclassed

had." Goodwin's team had to walk through hundreds of Rangers supporters who'd gathered outside Ibrox before kick-off.

Even though they were breaching Covid-19 regulations, the Saints boss had no complaints about their behaviour.

He said: "It didn't have any impact on us. Yes, they shouldn't be there but can you blame them?

"It was all in good humour, no malice. I walked through about 100 of them and it was fine.

"They generated a good atmosphere and Rangers didn't let them down."

One positive for Saints was a late debut for 16-year-old Dylan Reid, who became Premiership's youngest ever player.

He said: "I was delighted to give Dylan a chance. He's still a baby physically but technically very good.

"We're just delighted that he's one of ours and we're looking forward to seeing him develop in years to come."

---

men were willing to press high at certain trigger points.

But when Rangers got into their half, Saints squeezed space between the lines. That's when you need genuine quality to make a difference and in the likes of Kent, Hagi and Joe Aribo, Gerrard has that in abundance.

Kent collected a Connor Goldson pass 20 yards out, chopped on to his left-foot and fizzed a stunner past Jak Alnwick.

It got Gerrard – who was serving a dugout ban – off his seat in the director's box and the singing punters outside into full voice.

It was the start Rangers must have prayed for as they looked to get the job done early.

And it was complete two minutes later when Morelos made

it 2-0. This time it was Glen Kamara producing a sublime pass down the side of St Mirren skipper Joe Shaughnessy and the Colombian fired back across Alnwick to score.

That put the game to bed, even if Buddies winger Dylan Connolly had a chance after a slackness from Hagi but slid his effort wide.

But it was curtains for Goodwin's team within seconds of the second-half restart.

Kent got down the left far too easily and his cross found Hagi at the back post. He was able to take a touch to compose himself before giving Alnwick the eyes and slotting into the near corner.

The champions elect were now in cruise control.

They could afford to relax with a three-goal cushion. But that's

not their style. When Connolly tested Filip Helander on the right, Kent sprinted 50 yards to help the Swede snuff out any danger.

That just about summed up the mentality Gerrard has instilled.

At the other end, the winger cut infield to unleash another piledriver that was saved by the scrambling keeper's legs.

The manager could afford the luxury of taking off Helander and Steven Davis for a rest before Thursday night's Europa League tie against Slavia Prague.

Later, Hagi, Morelos and Kent were also wrapped in cotton wool ahead of the trip to the Czech Republic.

Saints kept going, to their credit, and forced Allan

PARTY PLAN Tavernier and Patterson at end

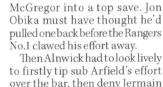

McGregor into a top save. Jon Obika must have thought he'd pulled one back before the Rangers No.1 clawed his effort away.

Then Alnwick had to look lively to firstly tip sub Arfield's effort over the bar, then deny Jermain Defoe a certain goal with a brilliant point-blank save.

Rangers were still pressing for a fourth and the fans were still singing outside.

At full-time, the players went to that corner of the ground to celebrate with them.

And with Gerrard's side on the verge of achieving something special, that's the only real shame – that those supporters can't get into the stadium to see history.

THE CHAMPIONS

KING: STEVIE WON'T WALK

FROM BACK PAGE

signed a new deal at Ibrox two years ago tying him down until 2024 – is going nowhere.

He said: "Steven extended his contract with Rangers knowingly and willingly to achieve what he wants to achieve.

"And he's got a lot to achieve at this club before he moves on.

"**Winning this title has been fantastic but we all know how quickly the few weeks will go past and it'll be defending the title.**

"Steven, in terms of his personal motivation and growth, is really looking forward to defending the title and establishing Rangers as being, not a one-season wonder but as the top team in Scotland."

After tying up the title with six games to go, Rangers still have designs on success in Europe and the Scottish Cup.

And it's the prospect of regular continental football King reckons that will appeal most to Gerrard, who led Liverpool to Champions League glory as captain 16 years ago.

On the Essential Scottish Football Podcast, he said: "Why would he leave Rangers? You know we can get into Champions League, we're playing European football, he's loving winning trophies.

"Why would he leave that and go to manage a Championship side, bottom-end Premier League side?

"I also don't think he's the type of person who enters into a contract to extend with Rangers as he did and

GOING NOWHERE Gerrard

he'll walk away from that contract. It's just not the man as I know him to be."

Gerrard, speaking after Saturday's win over St Mirren, indicated he's in it for the long haul. He told Rangers TV: "I want more,

"I'm hungry for more and I hope my players share that. If they do, it's exciting times to be a Rangers fan.

"Since I was a young lad I just want success and I want to win. I want to win football matches and I want to have moments like that in the dressing room. That's what it is all about.

"It's been an emotional day, arriving here and seeing the scenes. It was an incredible feeling. This club have been to hell and back over the past 10 years.

"I've only been part of it for three but I can certainly relate. I've got that feeling and that affection with the fans – and I know what they've been through.

"The star is the team. There is no ego in the team. There's a lot of fearless young players and some real calm heads. We've got the balance spot-on.

"That doesn't mean we're set. We need to keep moving it forwards and improve things and we will."

Celtic reaction a 'surprise'

DAVE KING admits he's been shocked to see Peter Lawwell and Neil Lennon "hounded out" of Celtic after the implosion of their 10-in-a-row hopes.

The former Rangers chairman, still majority shareholder, famously said the Parkhead club would "fold like a pack of cards" if Steven Gerrard could deliver a title to Ibrox.

But before that title was secured Celtic had axed Lennon – manager for five of the nine in a row – while chief executive Lawwell announced he'd leave at the end of the season.

King said: "It's no disgrace

BY FRASER WILSON

to any team to come second to this Rangers team.

"For what Lawwell and Lennon have done for the club in terms of success, OK you could say the competition wasn't great but they still beat what was in front of them.

"They were completely dominant in Scotland, set records and I'd have thought they'd have been given another chance to come back stronger next season.

"I was a little surprised they were effectively hounded out the club given the success they've given supporters the last decade."

SCOTT IT Arfield's on a high as the title win finally sinks in

WHEN Dave King returned to Rangers to seize control with his Three Bears consortium six years ago, he wondered if the Ibrox club would EVER be back at the top of the pile.

That's why the former chairman is adamant when he insists the title delivered by Steven Gerrard and his players over the past eight months is by far the most important in Rangers' 149-year history.

That's a hefty statement indeed.

But King, who never shied from making bullish claims when in charge at Ibrox – none more so than predicting Celtic would "fold like a pack of cards" if Rangers could win just one title under the ex-Liverpool captain – couldn't be clearer.

The boyhood Light Blues

BY FRASER WILSON

fan watched his side conquer Europe in the 70s, romp to a nine-in-a-row championship charge in the 80s and 90s, and was in a first term on the board as they enjoyed domestic success in the noughties, leading to a 54th championship in 2011.

But after plunging into administration and then slumming it in the bottom division a few months later, the Ibrox side's quest for 55 has been anything but plain sailing.

Such was the state of the club and its infrastructure after years of mismanagement following the financial turmoil of 2012 that King admits there was a genuine possibility when he took over, along with Douglas Park, George Letham and George Taylor, that Rangers might never have recovered from it.

So after watching his boyhood heroes end a decade-long wait to claim the Scottish football

crown, the South Africa-based businessman was understandably elated by the feat.

He said: "It's No.55, so you would think it's one of many and it kind of gets lost in that.

"**But this to me is by far the most important title Rangers have ever won.**"

Speaking to the Essential Scottish Football Podcast, the 65-year-old explained exactly why.

He said: "I was a kid growing up in Glasgow when Celtic were doing their nine in a row and Celtic had this invincible team.

"And when they're going six, seven, eight, it seems like you can't understand where the next title will come from at that point in time.

"But you know somehow it will turn around and Rangers will get back there.

"And the same with when Rangers were doing nine in a row, I was on the other side of that.

"I was on the board already

CROWNING GLORY

DAVE KING TITLE 55 IS SIMPLY THE BEST

Gers saviour insists this crown tops all others

BEST BAR NONE Gers stars savour title success

TAV THAT skipper's joy

There will be no Tav measures

BY **KEITH JACKSON**

JAMES TAVERNIER has warned the rest of the Scottish game that relentless Rangers won't ease up now the title has been secured.

Tavernier was leading the celebrations at the club's Auchenhowie HQ after Celtic's slip at Tannadice secured the Ibrox club a first top-flight crown in 10 years.

The skipper insisted Rangers will now target more domestic silverware from the Scottish Cup and Europa League last-16 glory against Slavia Prague.

He told Rangers TV: "We've got to soak up today and really enjoy this moment but we've still got some really important games, one on Thursday.

"We've got two legs to try to get into the next round and we've got possibilities of doing that if we apply ourselves right.

"Then also we have a cup to play in.

"We are not going to take the foot off the gas because we have won it now. We want to finish this season off strong and really put down a marker."

Tavernier has often been made the fall guy as Rangers struggled to compete against Celtic.

He said: "All the criticism I received over five years... but people stuck by me, my family stuck by me and it's really helped us push.

"When I first came here, I wanted to put the club where it belonged. We've finally brought 55 home."

Rangers chairman Douglas Park told Rangers TV: "Absolutely unbelievable. We've achieved 55.

"I couldn't be more happy for the club, the supporters and everyone.

"It's been a hard, hard road but we want this to be the start of many."

---

and that team looked like it would go on to 10, 11, 12 and it didn't happen.

"But there was still a sense that it would shift and Rangers might dominate, Celtic might dominate, other clubs might come in from time to time.

"But this one was different. When I got involved with the club again, it wasn't a normal situation where we were waiting for some change in fortune.

"The club was just in such bad shape that there was a genuine possibility at that time of the club never having recovered.

"So if I look at it in that context, then certainly in getting back and saying we have recovered, we are back, we are strong, emotionally and intellectually I consider this to be, by far, the most important title the club have ever won."

Gerrard's appointment in May 2018 undoubtedly proved the turning point from a footballing perspective. It may have taken three years but the Anfield legend, in his first senior management job, has built a team that has swept aside anything in its way this term.

They demolished Celtic's bid for a historic 10 in a row and wrapped up the title with six games to spare.

Employing the untested Gerrard was a bold move by King, a gamble after the failed Pedro Caixinha experiment.

Rangers had to get it right if they were to stop the Celtic juggernaut.

King insists Gerrard has delivered on his timescale while the club have the infrastructure in place to go on and lead Scottish football once again.

He said: "When I re-engaged with the club, we failed to get out of the Championship that season so were relegated to another season in the Championship.

"On the best basis we were looking at that time to four to five years. Four to five years in terms of getting the team out of the Championship was priority No.1, then building the club to get back into Europe.

"And doing that in parallel with all the infrastructure demands that we had as well meant the money could not all go into the football team.

"At best I think it could have been one season earlier.

"I think that we did have a misstep on the footballing side with the changes in managers, with Mark (Warburton) going out, with Pedro coming in and then, ultimately, moving on to Steven.

"I think that we missed maybe a year in terms of football development.

"Bringing in Steven probably accelerated things a bit because he has pretty much delivered on his timetable.

"When I initially spoke to Steven, we both agreed that turning the footballing side around

> "
> **Steven has pretty well delivered on his timetable for the club**
>
> **DAVE KING** HAILS THE EFFECT OF GERRARD

BEAR UP King is elated at title win

– assuming that financial resources were available to him – we were maybe looking at four transfer windows. It couldn't be a big bang approach because that wouldn't work and it doesn't work in footballing terms."

King will sell his 20 per cent stake to supporters group Club 1872 over the next three years.

And he said: "I think my main achievement would be winning the title.

"But winning the title on the basis where the resources to achieve that were equally balanced with a need to restore the club to be fit for purpose.

"We've got an infrastructure in place. We've got a scouting system, we've got a management team, we've got sports science.

"Rangers are now back to being a leading club in how we go about running the football business."

BIG MATCH SPECIAL

GRANITE&

Gers finish title run as they started by dumping Dons

GOAL BAND Roofe (top), Lewis own goal (centre) and Defoe (above) make it a stroll

Gerrard hails his champs

FROM BACK PAGE

of Aberdeen capped an incredible season for Gers who finished the campaign on 102 points, 25 clear of Celtic.

The Light Blues racked up 32 wins and 26 clean sheets along the way.

A Kemar Roofe double, a Jermain Defoe strike and Joe Lewis' OG topped off the season.

Gerrard said: "Some of the numbers the players have posted this season have been so impressive.

"But when the dust settles we'll hit reset to go again. The stats will probably go against us because they will add pressure.

"The expectation will go up but that's what happens at this club.

"It's special for all of us because we all worked ever so hard for it.

"The players deserve

ROOFE double joy

all the plaudits, they just needed the guidance.

"To go unbeaten, I think it's happened four times but only twice in a 38-game season.

"The other two were 18-game leagues.

"Listen it's a special achievement. It's very rare. The consistency levels have been superb.

"It feels really good and I want more of it. I'm as hungry as anyone.

"It's in my DNA to go on and fight for more. That's what I've tried to instil in my players since day one.

"This is right up there in my career because I love winning.

"I've had some really interesting meetings with the board and they're with me. They'll back me.

"Can I keep these players together? Well, let me flip the question. If anyone wants to take them away from me, they best bring an army with them."

It started 286 days ago in the Granite City.

Yesterday it ended with solid silver for Rangers.

After a decade of unbearable pain and despair, the red, white and blue ribbons were finally back on the Scottish Premiership trophy.

The campaign began with a 1-0 victory over Aberdeen back in August.

Another win over the Dons at Ibrox sealed an invincible league season for Steven Gerrard's men, who racked up 102 points.

Exactly 10 years on from their last title success at Rugby Park, players, staff and supporters across the city celebrated 55.

Plenty has happened to Rangers in between. No club in

RANGERS.........................4
ABERDEEN.........................0

SCOTT McDERMOTT REPORTS

Europe has experienced the level of turmoil which engulfed Ibrox for far too long.

There was administration and liquidation. The journey from the Third Division back to the top.

There were the charlatans who attempted to rip the heart and soul out of the club.

And there was a glut of players and managers who failed to deliver what was required on the pitch.

That all changed this season under Gerrard.

Rangers have amassed 32 wins

– 19 straight at Ibrox – and 26 clean sheets but this league triumph was never in doubt for most of the campaign.

Yesterday it culminated in Gers skipper James Tavernier, who has been through the mill himself at the club, holding aloft that elusive silverware.

Of course, they wanted to finish on a high, especially given the welcome they received from fans on their way into Edmiston Drive.

Under Gerrard, they've never lost a league game on a Saturday

and Stephen Glass' men gave the champions a goal of a start after just five minutes.

Tavernier's cross took a deflection off young Jack MacKenzie but Dons captain Joe Lewis – back in the side after injury – showed his rustiness by pawing the ball into his net for an own goal.

Luck is something Rangers haven't had to rely on but they got an early slice of it here.

The points and the Invincibles tag were secured before half-time. Ryan Kent kept up his stunning form with a terrific touch and control on the left flank.

The winger drove into the box before cutting a pass back to Kemar Roofe who had darted to

the near post. His stabbed effort at goal took another little nick of the unfortunate MacKenzie but this was no own goal as Roofe celebrated his 17th of the season.

The title parties across the country could really get started in earnest now.

Aberdeen had to be careful not to become victims of a final-day massacre in Govan.

Glass wants to change the Dons' style, getting them to build more from the back.

But if this Rangers team is at it and you show any sign of slackness, you'll be ruthlessly punished by the likes of Kent, Roofe and others.

At the break, Glass tried to shake things up by throwing on striker Fraser Hornby in place of

SCOTTISH PREMIERSHIP

SILVER

SUPER GROUP jubilant Rangers squad savour the moment as they finally get their hands on Premiership trophy after 10-year wait for club to return to summit

EMOTIONAL Tavernier with the league trophy

Tav dedicates league title to loyal support

■ **Scott McDermott**

Emotional James Tavernier was ecstatic after finally getting his hands on the Premiership trophy yesterday.

But the Ibrox skipper insists the invincible title triumph is for the fans who've stood by Rangers after 10 years of agony.

Tav held the trophy aloft after yesterday's 4-0 victory over Aberdeen, which was achieved thanks to Kemar Roofe's double, a Jermain Defoe strike and Joe Lewis' OG.

The 29-year-old has suffered setbacks along the way since arriving at the club back in 2015.

At times he was heavily criticised when Rangers were trailing behind Old Firm rivals Celtic.

But Steven Gerrard's appointment as gaffer has taken the full-back's game to a new level.

And he has finished this term as the team's top scorer with 19 goals.

He was speechless at the celebrations but hailed the club's support for their backing.

Tavernier said: "I'm lost for words. This is what it's all about, all the hard work we've put in.

"We've been so relentless for the whole season and you know what? This is for the fans.

"And it's for this amazing football club that I grow to love more with every passing day.

"But it's mainly for the fans around the world.

"It has been a hell of a journey with its ups and downs. I've always wanted to get my hands on the trophy and to do it

as captain – I don't know what to say.

"I'm so proud of what the boys have done this season. It's been a tough time but we've dug our heels in and the fans have stuck by us.

"This is a taste of more to come now."

Gerrard's side went through the full league campaign unbeaten, winning every one of their 19 games at Ibrox and losing just 13 goals at the back.

Tavernier says it was a collective effort that will be remembered for a long time. He said: "To go unbeaten in the league is unbelievable.

"We worked hard in pre-season and we've been relentless since.

"Everyone works so hard for the team, even the subs. Look at the impact Jermain had against Aberdeen.

"This is a legacy at the club now, which all the boys have achieved.

"How did I bounce back from the setbacks? I think that's just me as a person. I want to win things.

"My family has been extremely close and supportive. The gaffer has supported us during the times that we've had and been a massive help to us.

"And I've a great group around me, the senior players – Greegsy, Davo and Connor. They help make my job easier. We all push each other along.

"We knew this day was coming but now we've had a taste, we've want more."

Callum Hendry. Hornby has yet to score for Aberdeen since arriving on loan and he kept up that record by missing a sitter from a Ryan Hedges cross.

Woefully short of confidence, he failed to convert and the lowest-scoring side in Scotland this year – with just nine goals to their name – remained 2-0 down.

The Dons were more positive in the second half, engaging Rangers further up the pitch.

It left you wondering why they hadn't adopted a similar policy from the start.

Aberdeen fully deserved to pull a goal back for their bright second-half response.

Lewis Ferguson simply had to score when Hornby picked him out but facing an open goal

he contrived to crash his shot against the bar.

Allan McGregor then denied Hedges with his feet and boy did Glass' boys pay the harshest price for their profligacy.

Right on the hour mark Rangers, who had barely been out their own half since the interval, killed the game off in utterly ruthless fashion.

Tommie Hoban gifted them possession with a poor pass, Ianis Hagi pounced to tee up Roofe and the striker calmly slotted past Lewis for 3-0.

Near the end, Jermaine Defoe – as he has done so often this season – had the final word with a fourth.

More slackness from the Dons allowed Greg Stewart to pick him

out and the Englishman buried a finish to put the icing on Rangers' celebration cake.

That was curtains for Aberdeen and it was now all about that trophy presentation.

In the end, Rangers finished 25 points clear of closest rivals Celtic at the top of the Premiership table.

Tavernier followed legendary captains John Greig, Terry Butcher, Richard Gough, Barry Ferguson and Lorenzo Amoruso by holding that silver trophy aloft.

When Gerrard arrived as manager three years ago, everyone knew he had the raw materials to become one of the club's iconic gaffers.

Yesterday finally cemented his place alongside them.

⚽ THE STATS

■ TEAMS

RANGERS: McGregor 7, Tavernier 7, Goldson 6, Simpson 6, Aribo 7 (Itten 80, 2), Davis 8, Kamara 7, Hagi 7 (Arfield 62, 4), Roofe 8 (Stewart 69, 4), Morelos 6 (Defoe 62, 4), Kent 8 (Wright 69, 3).

ABERDEEN: Lewis 5, McLennan 6, Hoban 6, Considine 6, MacKenzie 6, Hedges 8 (Ramsay 89 ,1), McGeouch 6, Ferguson 6, Hayes 6 (McGinn 75, 2), Kamberi 4 (Campbell 46, 5), Hendry 4 (Hornby 46, 4).

■ ANALYSIS

RANGERS		ABERDEEN
55	POSSESSION	45
4	SHOTS ON	4
5	SHOTS OFF	7
6	CORNERS	3
10	FOULS	5
1	BOOKINGS	0
0	RED CARDS	0

■ MAN OF THE MATCH

STEVEN DAVIS The likes of Roofe, Kent and Tavernier grab more headlines with assists and goals but the veteran once again made Rangers tick.

Mail Sport

SUNDAY, MAY 16, 2021

LAST WAVE
Scott's farewell

A PARTING SHOT

Scott Brown signed off as a Celtic legend yesterday – with a pop at Rangers on his way out.

The outgoing Hoops skipper called time on 14 trophy-laden years at Parkhead in a 0-0 draw at first club Hibs and told his Ibrox foes that he departs as a **PROPER** Invincible.

Brown failed to achieve a

■ **Michael Gannon**

fairytale finish this season as Gers ended the Hoops 10-in-a-row bid by claiming the Premiership title without suffering a single defeat.

But Aberdeen-bound Brown was part of the Celtic side which completed

PAGE 66

| P38 | W32 | D6 | L0 | GF92 | GA13 | GD79 | PTS102 |

INVINCIBLE 55

PREMIERSHIP CHAMPIONS 2020/21

CAN'T BEAT THIS FEELING
Gers stars lift trophy

Gerrard's joy as he targets more glory

Rangers boss Steven Gerrard hailed his invincible champions as they lifted the club's 55th title.

And after the unbeaten run Gerrard (right) warned

■ **Scott McDermott**

any suitors they'll need an ARMY to prise his stars from Ibrox.

Yesterday's 4-0 rout

PAGE 70

FREE INSIDE: 8-PAGE TRIBUTE TO THE KINGS OF SCOTLAND